The Crowell College Reader

Sheridan Baker
David B. Hamilton

University of Michigan

Thomas Y. Crowell Company
New York   Established 1834

Library of Congress Cataloging in Publication Data

Baker, Sheridan Warner, 1918-   comp.
    The Crowell college reader.

    1. College readers.   I. Hamilton, David B.,
joint comp.   II. Title.
PE1122.B33   808'.04275   74-844
ISBN 0-690-00170-3

Design by W. P. Ellis

Cover photograph by Frank Dunand

Manufactured in the United States of America

ACKNOWLEDGMENTS

A. Alvarez, "Sylvia Plath: A Memoir,"
    in *The Savage God: A Study of
    Suicide*. Copyright © 1971 by A.
    Alvarez. Reprinted by permission of
    Random House, Inc. and Robert
    Lantz-Candida Donadio Literary
    Agency, Inc.
James Baldwin, "Fifth Avenue Uptown:
    A Letter from Harlem," in *Nobody
    Knows My Name* (New York: Dial
    Press, 1961). Copyright © 1960 by
    James Baldwin. Originally published
    in *Esquire*. Reprinted by permission
    of The Dial Press.
John Bardach, "Rivers and History," in
    Downstream. Copyright © 1964 by
    John Bardach. Reprinted by
    permission of Harper & Row,
    Publishers, Inc.
Roland Barthes, "Authors and Writers,"
    in *Critical Essays*, trans. Richard
    Howard (Evanston, Ill.:
    Northwestern University Press,
    1972), pp. 143–150. First published

in *New American Review*. Reprinted
    by permission of Northwestern
    University Press.
Gordon E. Bigelow, "A Primer of
    Existentialism," *College English*
    (December 1961). Copyright ©
    1961 by the National Council of
    Teachers of English. Reprinted by
    permission of the publisher and the
    author.
Gwendolyn Brooks, "Of De Witt Williams
    on His Way to Lincoln Cemetery,"
    in *The World of Gwendolyn Brooks*
    (New York: Harper & Row, 1971).
    Copyright 1945 by Gwendolyn
    Brooks Blakely. Reprinted by
    permission of Harper & Row,
    Publishers, Inc.
———, "We Real Cool," in *The World of
    Gwendolyn Brooks* (New York:
    Harper & Row, 1971). Copyright ©
    1959 by Gwendolyn Brooks.
    Reprinted by permission of Harper
    & Row, Publishers, Inc.

C. P. Cavafy, "Expecting the Barbarians," in *The Complete Poems of Cavafy,* trans. Rae Dalven. Copyright 1949 by Rae Dalven. Reprinted by permission of Harcourt Brace Jovanovich, Inc.

Noam Chomsky, from "The Case Against B. F. Skinner," in *For Reasons of State* (New York: Random House, Pantheon Books, 1973). Copyright © 1971 by Noam Chomsky. Reprinted by permission of Pantheon Books, a Division of Random House, Inc.

Robert Coles, "Two Languages, One Soul," *American Poetry Review* (May/June 1973), pp. 3–5. Reprinted by permission of the author.

Charles Horton Cooley, "Books and Persons," "Character," and "Strategy of the Youth Movement," in *Life and the Student* (New York: Knopf, 1931). Reprinted by permission of Mary E. Cooley.

Countee Cullen, "A Brown Girl Dead," "Incident," and "Heritage," in *On These I Stand* (New York: Harper & Row, 1947). Copyright 1925 by Harper & Row, Publishers, Inc.; renewed 1953 by Ida M. Cullen. Reprinted by permission of Harper & Row, Publishers, Inc.

——, "Advice to a Beauty," in *On These I Stand* (New York: Harper & Row, 1947). Copyright 1927 by Harper & Row, Publishers, Inc.; renewed 1955 by Ida M. Cullen. Reprinted by permission of Harper & Row, Publishers, Inc.

Roald Dahl, "Taste," in *Someone Like You* (New York: Knopf, 1953). Copyright 1951 by Roald Dahl. Originally appeared in *The New Yorker.* Reprinted by permission of Alfred A. Knopf, Inc.

Jaime De Angulo, from "Indians in Overalls," *Hudson Review* 3, no. 3 (Autumn 1950). Copyright 1950 by The Hudson Review, Inc. Reprinted by permission of the publisher.

Babette Deutsch, "The Dispassionate Shepherdess," in *The Collected Poems of Babette Deutsch* (New York: Doubleday, 1969). Copyright © 1969 by Babette Deutsch. Reprinted by permission of the author.

Albert Einstein, "Johannes Kepler," in *Ideas and Opinions* (New York: Crown Publishers, 1954), p. 262. Reprinted by permission of the Estate of Albert Einstein.

Ralph Ellison, "Hidden Name and Complex Fate," in *Shadow and Act.* Copyright © 1964 by Ralph Ellison. Reprinted by permission of Random House, Inc.

Nora Ephron, "A Few Words About Breasts: Shaping Up Absurd," *Esquire* (May 1972). Copyright © 1972 by Nora Ephron. First published in *Esquire Magazine.* Reprinted by permission of the author and International Famous Agency.

William Faulkner, "Impressions of Japan," in *Essays, Speechs and Public Letters,* ed. James B. Meriwether (New York: Random House, 1965). Copyright © 1958 by William Faulkner. Reprinted by permission of Random House, Inc.

——, "Nobel Prize Acceptance Speech," in *Essays, Speechs and Public Letters,* ed. James B. Meriwether (New York: Random House, 1965). Copyright © 1965 by Random House, Inc. Reprinted by permission of the publisher.

Irving Feldman, "As Fast as you Can," in *Lost Originals* (New York: Holt, Rinehart and Winston, 1972). Copyright © 1965, 1966, 1967, 1971, 1972 by Irving Feldman. Reprinted by permission of Holt, Rinehart and Winston, Inc.

F. Scott Fitzgerald, from "The Notebooks," in *The Crack-Up.* Copyright 1936 by Esquire, Inc., copyright 1945 by New Directions Publishing Corporation. Reprinted by permission of New Directions Publishing Corporation.

John L. Foster, "On Translating Hieroglyphic Love Songs," *Chicago Review* 23, no. 2 (Autumn 1971). Reprinted by permission of the publisher.

Robert Frost, "Birches," in *The Poetry of Robert Frost,* ed. Edward Connery Lathem (New York: Holt, Rinehart and Winston, 1969). Copyright 1916, © 1969 by Holt, Rinehart and Winston, Inc. Copyright 1944 by Robert Frost. Reprinted by permission of Holt, Rinehart and Winston, Inc.

John Graves, *Goodbye to a River* (New York: Knopf, 1960), pp. 28–29. Copyright © 1959 by Curtis Publishing Company. Copyright © 1960 by John Graves. Reprinted by permission of Alfred A. Knopf, Inc.

Francine du Plessix Gray, "On Safari," *New York Review of Books* (June 28, 1973). Copyright © 1973 by Nyrev, Inc. Reprinted by permission of *The New York Review of Books*.

Germaine Greer, "The Stereotype," in *The Female Eunuch* (New York: McGraw-Hill, 1971), pp. 47–55. Copyright © 1970, 1971 by Germaine Greer. Reprinted by permission of McGraw-Hill Book Company and Granada Publishing Ltd.

Martin Halpern, "To His Coy Mistress," *Beloit Poetry Journal* 4 (Summer 1954). Reprinted by permission of the publisher.

Joe Hill, "My Last Will," in *Rebel Voices: An I.W.W. Anthology*, ed., Joyce L. Kornbluh (Ann Arbor: University of Michigan Press, 1964). Reprinted by permission of The Industrial Workers of the World, 752 West Webster Ave., Chicago, Illinois 60614.

Richard Hofstadter, from "Democracy and Anti-Intellectualism in America," in *Michigan Alumnus Quarterly Review* (August 8, 1953). Reprinted by permission of The Michigan Quarterly Review.

Langston Hughes, "The Negro Speaks of Rivers," and "I, Too," in *Selected Poems* (New York: Knopf, 1959). Copyright 1926 by Alfred A. Knopf, Inc. and renewed 1954 by Langston Hughes. Reprinted by permission of the publisher.

R. Prawer Jhabvala, "Open City—Letter from Delhi," *Encounter* (May 1964). Copyright © 1964 by Encounter Ltd. Reprinted by permission of Russell & Volkening, Inc., as agents for the author.

Alan S. Katz, "The Use of Drugs in America: Toward a Better Understanding of Passivity," *Boston University Journal* 19, no. 2 (Spring 1971). Reprinted by permission of the Editors, *Boston University Journal*.

Lysander Kemp, "The Coy Mistress Replies," *Beloit Poetry Journal* 5 (Winter 1954–55). Reprinted by permission of the publisher.

X. J. Kennedy, "Little Elegy," in *Nude Descending a Staircase*. Copyright © 1969 by X. J. Kennedy; originally appeared in *The New Yorker*. Reprinted by permission of Doubleday & Co., Inc.

Herbert Kohl, "Children Writing: The Story of an Experiment," *New York Review of Books* (November 17, 1966). Copyright © 1966 by Herbert Kohl. Reprinted by permission of Robert Lescher, Literary Agency.

C. Day Lewis, "Two Songs," in *Selected Poems* (New York: Harper & Row, 1967). Copyright © 1967 by C. Day Lewis. Reprinted by permission of Harper & Row, Publishers, Inc. and A. D. Peters and Company.

Ross Macdonald, *Sleeping Beauty* (New York: Knopf, 1973), pp. 103–107. Copyright © 1973 by Ross Macdonald. Reprinted by permission of Alfred A. Knopf, Inc.

James Alan McPherson, "Of Cabbages and Kings," in *Hue and Cry* (Boston: Little, Brown, 1969). Copyright © 1968, 1969 by James Alan McPherson. Reprinted by permission of Little, Brown and Co. in association with The Atlantic Monthly Press.

William Maxwell, "Virginia Stephen/Virginia Woolf," *New Yorker* (February 3, 1973). Copyright © 1973 by The New Yorker Magazine, Inc. Reprinted by permission.

Norman E. Nelson, "Science and the Irresponsible Imagination," *Yale Review* (Autumn 1953). Copyright 1953 by Yale University Press. Reprinted by permission.

H. V. S. Ogden, "The Uses of History," *Michigan Quarterly Review* 8 (winter 1969). Copyright © 1969 by The University of Michigan. Reprinted by permission of The Michigan Quarterly Review.

George Oppén, "Ozymandias," in *The Materials*. Copyright © 1962 by George Oppen. Reprinted by permission of New Directions Publishing Corporation and San Francisco Review.

George Orwell, "Politics and the English Language," in *Shooting an Elephant and Other Essays*. Copyright 1945, 1946, 1949, 1950 by Sonia Brownell

Orwell. Reprinted by permission of Harcourt Brace Jovanovich, Inc., Mrs. Sonia Brownell Orwell, and Secker & Warburg.

Ron Padgett, "Birches," in *Great Balls of Fire* (New York: Holt, Rinehart and Winston, 1969). Copyright © 1965, 1967, 1968, 1969 by Ron Padgett. Reprinted by permission of Holt, Rinehart and Winston, Inc.

Donald Culross Peattie, "June Third," in *Almanac for Moderns*. Copyright 1935, renewed 1963, by Donald Culross Peattie. Reprinted by permission of G. P. Putnam's Sons.

George Plimpton, "Everyone Can't Be First String," *Sports Illustrated* (December 18, 1972). Copyright © 1973 by George Plimpton. Reprinted by permission of Russell & Volkening, Inc., 551 5th Ave., N.Y., N.Y. 10017, as agents for the author.

Katherine Anne Porter, "Paris: A Little Incident in the Rue de l'Odéon," *Ladies Home Journal* (August 1964). Copyright © 1964 by Katherine Anne Porter. Reprinted by permission of Cyrilly Abels, Literary Agent.

Ezra Pound, "A Virginal," in *Personae*. Copyright 1926 by Ezra Pound. Reprinted by permission of New Directions Publishing Corporation.

Theodore Roethke, "Cuttings" and "Cuttings" (later), in *The Collected Poems of Theodore Roethke*. Copyright 1948 by Theodore Roethke. Reprinted by permission of Doubleday & Company, Inc.

——, "I Knew a Woman," in *The Collected Poems of Theodore Roethke*. Copyright 1954 by Theodore Roethke. Reprinted by permission of Doubleday & Company, Inc.

Murray Ross, "Football Red and Baseball Green," *Chicago Review* 22, nos. 2–3 (January-February 1971). Reprinted by permission of the publisher.

Allan Seager, "Roethke's Birthplace," in *The Glass House: The Life of Theodore Roethke* (New York: McGraw-Hill, 1968), pp. 1–8. Copyright © 1968 by Allan Seager. Reprinted by permission of McGraw-Hill Book Company.

Anne Sexton, "Snow White and the Seven Dwarfs," in *Transformations* (Boston: Houghton Mifflin, 1972). Copyright © 1972 by Anne Sexton.

Reprinted by permission of Houghton Mifflin Company.

Louis Simpson, "Birch," in *At The End of the Open Road* (Middletown, Conn.: Wesleyan University Press, 1963). Copyright © 1963 by Louis Simpson. Reprinted by permission of Wesleyan University Press.

Alexander Solzhenitsyn, *The Nobel Lecture,* trans. from the Russian by F. D. Reeve (New York: Farrar, Straus & Giroux, 1972), pp. 3–34. Copyright © 1972 by the Nobel Foundation, English translation copyright © 1972 by Farrar, Straus & Giroux, Inc. Reprinted by permission of Farrar, Straus & Giroux, Inc.

George Steiner, "A Supplement to the Oxford English Dictionary," *New York Times Book Review* (November 26, 1972). Copyright © 1972 by The New York Times Company. Reprinted by permission.

Charles D. Stewart, "A Pilfering by Poe," *Atlantic Monthly* (December 1958). Copyright © 1958 by The Atlantic Monthly Company, Boston, Mass. Reprinted by permission.

Sam Toperoff, "Cassius," *New American Review* 10 (1970), 90–98. Copyright © 1970 by Sam Toperoff. Reprinted by permission of the author.

Diana Trilling, "The Death of Marilyn Monroe," in *Claremont Essays* (New York: Harcourt Brace Jovanovich, 1964). Copyright © 1963 by Diana Trilling. Reprinted by permission of Harcourt Brace Jovanovich, Inc.

John Updike, "To An Usherette," in *The Carpentered Hen and Other Tame Creatures* (New York: Harper & Row, 1958). Copyright © 1955 by John Updike. Originally appeared in *The New Yorker* and reprinted by permission of Harper & Row, Publishers, Inc.

Mona Van Duyn, "A Garland for Christopher Smart," *Poetry* 104 (April 1964). Copyright © 1964 by The Modern Poetry Association. Reprinted by permission of the Editor of *Poetry* and Mona Van Duyn.

Stanley Vestal, "The Man Who Killed Custer," in *Sitting Bull: Champion of the Sioux*. New edition copyright © 1957 by the University of Oklahoma Press. Reprinted by permission.

Esther Wagner, "Beat Down Frigid

Rome," *Atlantic Monthly* (April 1968). Copyright © 1958 by The Atlantic Monthly Company, Boston, Mass. Reprinted by permission of the publisher and Esther Wagner.

James Wellard, "The Lost Cities," in *The Great Sahara* (London: Hutchinson Publishing Group, 1964), pp. 84–93. Reprinted by permission of Curtis Brown Ltd. on behalf of the author.

E. B. White, *One Man's Meat* (New York: Harper & Row, 1944), pp. 232–234 ["Spring"]. Copyright 1941 by E. B. White. Reprinted by permission of Harper & Row, Publishers, Inc.

——, "The Dream of the American Male," in *The Second Tree from the Corner* (New York: Harper & Row, 1954). Copyright 1941 by E. B. White. Originally appeared in *The New Yorker* and reprinted by permission of Harper & Row, Publishers, Inc.

Tom Wolfe, "The Birth of the New Journalism," *New York* 5, no. 7 (February 14, 1972). Copyright © 1972 by Tom Wolfe. First published in *New York*. Reprinted by permission of the author and International Famous Agency.

Virginia Woolf, "The New Dress," in *A Haunted House and Other Stories* (New York: Harcourt Brace Jovanovich, 1944). Copyright 1944, 1972 by Harcourt Brace Jovanovich, Inc. Reprinted by permission of Harcourt Brace Jovanovich, Inc., the Author's Literary Estate, and The Hogarth Press.

Sir Leonard Woolley, "The Flood," in *Myth or Legend,* ed. G. E. Daniel et al. (New York: G. P. Putnam's Sons, 1968). Reprinted by permission of G. Bell & Sons, Ltd., London.

William Butler Yeats, "Whence Had They Come," in *Collected Poems* (New York: Macmillan, 1956). Copyright 1934 by Macmillan Publishing Co., Inc., renewed 1962 by Bertha Georgia Yeats. Reprinted by permission of Macmillan Publishing Co., Inc. (N.Y.), M. B. Yeats, and the Macmillan Co. of Canada.

Philip Young, "The Mother of Us All: Pocahontas Reconsidered," in *Three Bags Full* (New York: Harcourt Brace Jovanovich, 1972). Copyright © 1962 by Philip Young. First published in *Kenyon Review*. Reprinted by permission of Harcourt Brace Jovanovich, Inc.

Preface

This book is a reader for writers, for people, that is, for all of us, since we discover our thoughts fully—we *realize* them—only by writing them out, and only as people. We see what we see, know what we know, only as ourselves, as identifiable human beings. We may disguise ourselves as a committee, in a monotone of print, but, if we do, we hide not only ourselves but our thoughts as well. Only as persons can we make our thoughts live for the reader as they live for us. So this book of readings for expository writing begins with the writer's voice, to encourage the student to find his or her written voice by attending to the ones of lively people and responding to their ideas. Then, alerted, the student follows the major rhetorical modes from description up to argumentation, illustrated on opportunity from poetry and fiction, too, for the liveliest variety.

The student will see unity in this variety. To see an argumentative pattern in both a brief poem and an extended essay, for instance, is to see that pattern clearly for the first time—and to enjoy both more. To see that each piece of writing, however different, coheres around one central idea, one organizing nucleus, is another discovery of highest value. This is in fact this book's own organizing idea, as we move through the major varieties of writing, persistently asking the student to discover and state the central idea so that he may learn to gather meanings into one sharp sentence, and to skewer his thoughts with one sharp meaning as he writes, in turn.

The writer may not state his meaning, but he makes us see it nevertheless. The major varieties of writing—description, narration, exposition, argumentation—are all modes of seeing, or indeed, modes of saying as seeing. "How can I know what I think till I see what I say?" writes W. H. Auden, in explaining how poetry is a "game of knowledge, a bringing to consciousness, by naming them, of emotions and their hidden relationships." All writing, as we have already suggested, bears out Auden's observations, bringing to consciousness, by naming them, not only our emotions and their hidden relationships but all our wordless visual pictures and all our pictureless ideas as well. Writing is seeing, or seeing anew, and in a more enduring way. In a sense, then, and to repeat: we do not see the woods and the trees, nor the valid and the invalid, until we conceptualize them in words, telling one from the other.

After establishing the writer's voice, then, we move to Description, where the writer most immediately gets his sights straight, pointing to the telling details. He may not state his central point, if he is sure his etching has stamped its implications clearly. So it is with Narration, the next major mode, which is Description stretched through time. And here, when narration extends all the way to art, to the complete short story, the writer would rather lose his voice altogether than state the meaning his narrative acts out and implies. The inherent strength of Description and Narration is implication.

The inherent strength of Exposition and Argument is statement. Both use Description and Narration to illustrate their ideas. In fact, as the selections throughout this book show, no piece of writing is purely one thing nor another, nor would we want it so: each borrows from the others as much as it needs to carry its point, to bring itself home. In a sense, Exposition is the narrative description of ideas, and Argument subsumes all in the highest reaches of reason, where we see what is what at last.

This book takes the student from the simple to the complex, from the palpable and colorful details of things up to the heights of clearer vision, encouraging him to cultivate his personal voice and views on the way, and to seek in each experience, in what he reads and what he sees around him, as the one reflects the other, the central idea behind it all. The book offers a wide variety from which to select, and a number of thematic lines, as the Thematic Table of Contents (page 571) shows, which the teacher may follow in larger or smaller units of work through the semester. Each set of introductions and "Suggestions for Writing" offers both particular and thematic possibilities. We have added biographical notes to help the student place each author as a person, seeking the human detail where it was forthcoming, varying the length as interest or necessity demanded.

Sheridan Baker
David B. Hamilton

Contents

III.

Narration:
The Element of Story in Essays

99

IV.

Exposition:
Comparison and Contrast

147

V.

Exposition:
Cause and Effect

189

VI.

Exposition:
Problem and Solution

249

VII.

Style:
Tone and Figurative Language

293

VIII.

Toward Argument:
Induction and Deduction

329

IX.

Growing Argumentative:
Definitions, or Pinning Distinctions Down
401

X.

Growing Argumentative:
Analysis and Responsible Speculation
437

XI.

Argument:
The Shape of Thesis and Evidence
469

XII.

Varieties of Argument
533

I. The Writer's Voice

WITH ALMOST EVERYTHING WE READ, we want very much to know whether, in Charles Cooley's phrase, anyone is really "at home." What kind of person is writing, and why should we listen to her or to him? Are not most books unsatisfying, Cooley continues, because of a "lack of character, of reality"? In such books, he seems to imply, we hear no "writer's voice," can sense no real personality. For someone human must be there—someone whose fate is linked to ours if we are to grant him our attention. But though a voice requires "color," as we sometimes say, if it is to come through as a human voice convincingly, we are not apt to listen long to someone who is just showing off. You may assess this very real and endlessly complex problem as you read the varied selections of this first section.

Greer and White not only convey their own voices, but write of character in another sense. They describe general attitudes toward the "feminine." The first five poets amplify this theme, and the first four of them share an image. Do all these voices come through distinctively? Does the phrasing of poetry complicate the question of "voice"?

You can also compare the voices of Baldwin and Wolfe, writing of New York from different ends of town, and with different commitments. How would you describe them—aloof? agitated? excited? serene? Do their subjects correlate well with the voices we hear? Sitting Bull's speech is a special case. Formal and hortatory, it is a call to action. What better test of a voice can you conceive than to ask whether to assent and follow it? Wolfe and Baldwin also seek assent. Might you grant it more readily to either of them?

1. Life and the Student

CHARLES HORTON COOLEY

Cooley (1864–1929) was Professor of Sociology at the University of Michigan. His books, including *Human Nature and the Social Order, Heredity or Environment*, and *Genius, Fame and the Comparison of Races*, were written around the turn of the century as sociology was just taking shape as a discipline. The first of those books went through several editions and became a standard text. *Life and the Student*, from which these reflections are taken, appeared in 1927.

Books and Persons

AN INTELLIGENT READER goes slowly when he feels that each word has its peculiar and essential force. He watches the author. We *want* to make out personality, and if there is the least trace of it imagination is excited and puts forth guesses, we become clairvoyant. We want the author himself, as an explanation, a guaranty, a vehicle for the thought. And we find him in his choice of words, in the movement of his sentences, in the attitudes and habits of feeling implicit in what he says, in a hundred signs not less telling, to the sensitive reader, than the visible and audible man.

I know one who can keep children laughing with only a droll look now and then, and so there are authors who keep you amused and expectant of humor though they but rarely deliver it. We act on others not so much by what we explicitly do as by inciting their imaginations to work in a certain direction.

IF a man writes thoughtfully he will not fail to impart his spirit, however slight the matter may seem. From Gissing's * sketches of travel By the Ionian Sea I get a deep and moving sense of his personality: just how and where it is conveyed would be hard to say. Like everything he wrote it is interfused with a fine kind of pride.

* George Gissing (1827–1903), English novelist.

I LOVE good books of travel, with a real atmosphere of strange places, but I find very few of them. I go to the library to find a book on Italy, and try one after another without satisfaction. The trouble is, in general, that there is nobody at home. The writer forsook himself when he wrote, he was not heartily in it, the works are perfunctory, not containing any full stream of spirit to float you away into new regions of life, thin, colorless, hardly existent.

IF I think of certain academic men and ask whether they would be interesting in literature, I see that they would not. They are too anxious about being something else than simply men, not firmly enough poised. They see themselves in the light of some phase of opinion, as literary or scientific. A solid carpenter is better, he seems more human, less institutional.

I FIND Henry James's early letters from Europe less interesting than Mr. Dreiser's * rather crude book A Traveler at Forty. There is no stark personality in them; it is impersonal culture and craftsmanship; he is lost in his art.

A CHOICE spirit defines itself in great part by what it avoids—the trite, the superfluous, the insincere, the immoderate—and may hold our attention more by this than by positive matter. The harm of a needless word is not so much in wasting the reader's attention as in impairing his confidence in the writer.

How grateful are limits! In a tale of Jane Austen you may be sure there are no social problems, no intellectual puzzles, no harrowing emotion. It is all well within your reach, clearly imagined, spirited, witty, exquisite of its kind. Second-rateness consists largely in slopping over, in not drawing a firm line around your picture, in doing poorly what you ought not to do at all.

HENRY JAMES is one of the authors that I can read with delight over and over again. He has a whole-hearted joy in his work and exhales a joyous though much rarefied atmosphere, wherein, if you can breathe it, you may recreate your mind with exploration of a subtile and enticing world. In his earlier books he has also a light ingratiating humor and a caressing flow of speech. That his range is limited, that there is no passion in him except the passion for literature, is perhaps an added charm; he invites you into an enclosed garden where nothing lives but literary grace and psychological intelligence.

I READ the French moralists—de la Rochefoucauld, La Bruyère, Pascal

* Theodore Dreiser (1871–1945), American novelist.

—not so much for the value of their ideas, however great that may be, as because I like the company of men who are interested in such ideas.

Character

WHAT is it that makes most books unsatisfying? Is it not lack of character, of reality? A certain opportunism, aiming at the market rather than at truth? The writers seem too much applicants for favor. They offer, for the most part, not solid individual contributions but voices in a chorus, each taking the key from the rest but striving to be a little louder or clearer or sharper or in some way consciously distinct, so as to be sure of being heard. What we want, apparently, is to hear voices that are *un*consciously distinct, not anxious about being heard, speaking from a quiet background of normal life and expressing without strain a natural and interesting self.

COMPOSURE is communicated by the gesture of a book, a way about it that makes one feel that the writer is in no hurry, is not trying too hard and enjoys his paragraph as he makes it. We wish him to create a world of his own, joyous and serene, and then make it our world. He must be bold and unique for us, because we are to enter into him. He should live the most satisfying life he can, so that we may see how it is done. Apology is as distasteful as it would be in an actor, it destroys our illusion.

ONE must be in quiet and secure possession of some sort of a homestead in order to be worth while in literature.

TWO CHARACTERS OF WOMEN

2. The Stereotype

GERMAINE GREER

Germaine Greer (1939–   ), an Australian who trained as a Shakespeare scholar at Cambridge University, published

5

The Female Eunuch in 1971, thus establishing herself as one of the major speakers for the women's movement.

In that mysterious dimension where the body meets the soul the stereotype is born and has her being. She is more body than soul, more soul than mind. To her belongs all that is beautiful, even the very word beauty itself. All that exists, exists to beautify her. The sun shines only to burnish her skin and gild her hair; the wind blows only to whip up the color in her cheeks; the sea strives to bathe her; flowers die gladly so that her skin may luxuriate in their essence. She is the crown of creation, the masterpiece. The depths of the sea are ransacked for pearl and coral to deck her; the bowels of the earth are laid open that she might wear gold, sapphires, diamonds and rubies. Baby seals are battered with staves, unborn lambs ripped from their mothers' wombs, millions of moles, muskrats, squirrels, minks, ermines, foxes, beavers, chinchillas, ocelots, lynxes, and other small and lovely creatures die untimely deaths that she might have furs. Egrets, ostriches and peacocks, butterflies and beetles yield her their plumage. Men risk their lives hunting leopards for her coats, and crocodiles for her handbags and shoes. Millions of silkworms offer her their yellow labors; even the seamstresses roll seams and whip lace by hand, so that she might be clad in the best that money can buy.

The men of our civilization have stripped themselves of the fineries of the earth so that they might work more freely to plunder the universe for treasures to deck my lady in. New raw materials, new processes, new machines are all brought into her service. My lady must therefore be the chief spender as well as the chief symbol of spending ability and monetary success. While her mate toils in his factory, she totters about the smartest streets and plushiest hotels with his fortune upon her back and bosom, fingers and wrists, continuing that essential expenditure in his house which is her frame and her setting, enjoying that silken idleness which is the necessary condition of maintaining her mate's prestige and her qualification to demonstrate it. Once upon a time only the aristocratic lady could lay claim to the title of crown of creation: only her hands were white enough, her feet tiny enough, her waist narrow enough, her hair long and golden enough; but every well-to-do burgher's wife set herself up to ape my lady and to follow fashion, until my lady was forced to set herself out like a gilded doll overlaid with monstrous rubies and pearls like pigeon's eggs. Nowadays the Queen of England still considers it part of her royal female role to sport as much of the family jewelry as she can manage at any one time on all public occasions, although the male monarchs have escaped such showcase duty, which devolves exclusively upon their wives.

At the same time as woman was becoming the showcase for wealth and caste, while men were slipping into relative anonymity and "handsome is as handsome does," she was emerging as the central emblem of western art. For the Greeks the male and female body had beauty of a human, not necessarily a sexual, kind; indeed they may have marginally favored the young male form as the most powerful and perfectly proportioned. Likewise the Romans showed no bias towards the depiction of femininity in their predominantly monumental art. In the Renaissance the female form began to predominate, not only as the mother in the predominant emblem of *madonna col bambino,* but as an aesthetic study in herself. At first naked female forms took their chances in crowd scenes or diptychs of Adam and Eve, but gradually Venus claims ascendancy, Mary Magdalene ceases to be wizened and emaciated, and becomes nubile and ecstatic, portraits of anonymous young women, chosen only for their prettiness, begin to appear, are gradually disrobed, and renamed Flora or Primavera. Painters begin to paint their own wives and mistresses and royal consorts as voluptuous beauties, divesting them of their clothes if desirable, but not of their jewelry. Susanna keeps her bracelets on in the bath, and Hélène Fourment keeps ahold of her fur as well!

What happened to women in painting happened to her in poetry as well. Her beauty was celebrated in terms of the riches which clustered around her: her hair was gold wires, her brow ivory, her lips ruby, her teeth gates of pearl, her breasts alabaster veined with lapis lazuli, her eyes as black as jet. The fragility of her loveliness was emphasized by the inevitable comparisons with the rose, and she was urged to employ her beauty in love-making before it withered on the stem. She was for consumption; other sorts of imagery spoke of her in terms of cherries and cream, lips as sweet as honey and skin white as milk, breasts like cream uncrudded, hard as apples. Some celebrations yearned over her finery as well, her lawn more transparent than morning mist, her lace as delicate as gossamer, the baubles that she toyed with and the favors that she gave. Even now we find the thriller hero describing his classy dames' elegant suits, cheeky hats, well-chosen accessories and footwear; the imagery no longer dwells on jewels and flowers but the consumer emphasis is the same. The mousy secretary blossoms into the feminine stereotype when she reddens her lips, lets down her hair, and puts on something frilly.

Nowadays women are not expected, unless they are Paola di Liegi or Jackie Onassis, and then only on gala occasions, to appear with a king's ransom deployed upon their bodies, but they are required to look expensive, fashionable, well-groomed, and not to be seen in the same dress twice. If the duty of the few may have become less onerous, it has also become the duty of the many. The stereotype marshals an army of servants. She is supplied with cosmetics, underwear, foundation garments, stockings, wigs, postiches and hairdressing as well as her outer garments, her jewels and furs. The effect is to be built up layer by layer, and it is expensive. Splendor has given way to fit, line and cut. The spirit of competition must be kept up, as more and more women struggle towards the top drawer, so that the fashion industry can rely upon an expanding market. Poorer women fake it, ape it, pick up on the fashions a season too late, use crude effects, mistaking the line, the sheen, the gloss of the high-class article for a garish simulacrum. The business is so complex that it must be handled by an expert. The paragons of the stereotype must be dressed, coifed and painted by the experts and the style-setters, although they may be encouraged to give heart to the housewives studying their lives in pulp magazines by claiming a lifelong fidelity to their own hair and soap and water. The boast is more usually discouraging than otherwise, unfortunately.

As long as she is young and personable, every woman may cherish the dream that she may leap up the social ladder and dim the sheen of luxury by sheer natural loveliness; the few examples of such a feat are kept before the eye of the public. Fired with hope, optimism and ambition, young women study the latest forms of the stereotype, set out in *Vogue, Nova, Queen* and other glossies, where the mannequins stare from among the advertisements for fabulous real estate, furs and jewels. Nowadays the uniformity of the year's fashions is severely affected by the emergence of the pert female designers who direct their appeal to the working girl, emphasizing variety, comfort, and simple, striking effects. There is no longer a single face of the year: even Twiggy has had to withdraw into marketing and rationed personal appearances, while the Shrimp works mostly in New York. Nevertheless the stereotype is still supreme. She has simply allowed herself a little more variation.

The stereotype is the Eternal Feminine. She is the Sexual Object sought by all men, and by all women. She is of neither sex, for she has herself no sex at all. Her value is solely attested by the demand she excites in others. All she must contribute is her existence. She need achieve nothing, for she is the reward of achievement. She need never give positive evidence of her moral character because virtue is assumed from her loveliness, and her passivity. If any man who has no right to her be found with her she will not be punished, for she is morally neuter. The matter is solely one of male rivalry. Innocently she may drive men to madness and war. The more trouble she can cause, the more her stocks go up, for possession of her means more the more demand she excites. Nobody wants a girl whose beauty is imperceptible to all but him; and so men welcome the stereotype because it directs their taste into the most commonly recognized areas of value, although they may protest because some aspects of it do not tally with their fetishes. There is scope in the stereotype's variety for most fetishes. The leg man may follow miniskirts, the tit man can encourage see-through blouses and plunging necklines, although the man who likes fat women may feel constrained to enjoy them in secret. There are stringent limits to the variations on the stereotype, for nothing must interfere with her function as sex object. She may wear leather, as long as she cannot actually handle a motorbike: she may wear rubber, but it ought not to indicate that she is an expert diver or waterskier. If she wears athletic clothes the purpose is to underline her unathleticism. She may sit astride a horse, looking soft and curvy, but she must not crouch over its neck with her rump in the air.

Because she is the emblem of spending ability and the chief spender, she is also the most effective seller of this world's goods. Every survey ever held has shown that the image of an attractive woman is the most effective advertising gimmick. She may sit astride the mudguard of a new car, or step into it ablaze with jewels; she may lie at a man's feet stroking his new socks; she may hold the petrol pump in a challenging pose, or dance through woodland glades in slow motion in all the glory of a new shampoo; whatever she does her image sells. The gynolatry of our civilization is written large upon its face, upon hoardings, cinema screens, television, newspapers, magazines, tins, packets, cartons, bottles, all consecrated to the reigning deity, the female fetish. Her dominion must not be thought to entail the rule of women, for she is not a woman. Her glossy lips and mat complexion, her unfocused eyes and flawless fingers, her extraordinary hair all floating and shining, curling and gleaming, reveal the inhuman triumph of cosmetics, lighting, focusing and printing, cropping and composition. She sleeps unruffled, her lips red and juicy and closed, her eyes as crisp and black as if new painted, and her false lashes immaculately curled. Even when she washes her face with a new and creamier toilet soap her expression is as tranquil and vacant and her paint as flawless as ever. If ever she should appear tousled and troubled, her features are miraculously smoothed to their proper veneer by a new washing powder or a bouillon cube. For she is a doll: weeping, pouting or smiling, running or reclining, she is a doll. She is an idol. formed of the concatenation of lines and masses, signifying the lineaments of satisfied impotence.

Her essential quality is castratedness. She absolutely must be young, her body hairless, her flesh buoyant, and *she must not have a sexual organ.* No musculature must distort the smoothness of the lines of her body, although she may be painfully slender or warmly cuddly. Her expression must betray no hint of humor, curiosity or intelligence, although it may signify hauteur to an extent that is actually absurd, or smoldering lust, very feebly signified by drooping eyes and a sullen mouth (for the stereotype's lust equals irrational submission), or, most commonly, vivacity and idiot happiness. Seeing that the world despoils itself for this creature's benefit, she must be happy; the entire structure would topple if she were not. So the image of woman appears plastered on every surface imaginable, smiling interminably. An apple pie evokes a glance of tender beatitude, a washing machine causes hilarity, a cheap box of chocolates brings forth meltingly joyous gratitude, a Coke is the cause of a rictus of unutterable brilliance, even a new stick-on bandage is saluted by a smirk of satisfaction. A real woman licks her lips and opens her mouth and flashes her teeth when photographers appear: *she* must arrive at the premiere of her husband's film in a paroxysm of delight, or his success might be murmured about. The occupational hazard of being a Playboy Bunny is the aching facial muscles brought on by the obligatory smiles.

So what is the beef? Maybe I couldn't make it. Maybe I don't have a pretty smile, good teeth, nice tits, long legs, a cheeky arse, a sexy voice. Maybe I don't know how to handle men and increase my market value, so that the rewards due to the feminine will accrue to me. Then again, maybe I'm sick of the masquerade. I'm sick of pretending eternal youth. I'm sick of belying my own intelligence, my own will, my own sex. I'm sick of peering at the world through false eyelashes, so everything I see is mixed with a shadow of bought hairs; I'm sick of weighting my head with a dead mane, unable to move my neck freely, terrified of rain, of wind, of dancing too vigorously in case I sweat into my lacquered curls. I'm sick of the Powder Room. I'm sick of pretending that some fatuous male's self-important pronouncements are the objects of my undivided attention, I'm sick of going to films and plays when someone else wants to, and sick of having no opinions of my own about either. I'm sick of being a transvestite. I refuse to be a female impersonator. I am a woman, not a castrate. . . .

3. The Dream of the American Male

E. B. WHITE

White (1899–   ) is well known for his children's books, *Charlotte's Web, Stuart Little,* and *The Trumpet of the Swan.* For years he has been a staff writer for *The New Yorker.* He collaborated with James Thurber on *Is Sex Necessary?* (1929). His edition of William Strunk, Jr.'s *The*

Elements of Style has been a best-selling text. White's essays and other prose pieces have been collected under the titles *One Man's Meat* (1944), *The Second Tree from the Corner* (1954), and *The Points of My Compass* (1962). His verse collections are *The Lady Is Cold* (1929) and *The Fox of Peapack* (1938).

DOROTHY LAMOUR is the girl above all others desired by the men in Army camps. This fact was turned up by *Life* in a routine study of the unlimited national emergency.* It is a fact which illuminates the war, the national dream, and our common unfulfillment. If you know what a soldier wants, you know what Man wants, for a soldier is young, sexually vigorous, and is caught in a line of work which leads toward a distant and tragic conclusion. He personifies Man. His dream of a woman can be said to be Everyman's dream of a woman. In desiring Lamour, obviously his longing is for a female creature encountered under primitive conditions and in a setting of great natural beauty and mystery. He does not want this woman to make any sudden or nervous movement. She should be in a glade, a swale, a grove, or a pool below a waterfall. This is the setting in which every American youth first encountered Miss Lamour. They were in a forest; she had walked slowly out of the pool and stood dripping in the ferns.

The dream of the American male is for a female who has an essential languor which is not laziness, who is unaccompanied except by himself, and who does not let him down. He desires a beautiful, but comprehensible, creature who does not destroy a perfect situation by forming a complete sentence. She is compounded of moonlight and shadows, and has a slightly husky voice, which she uses only in song or in an attempt to pick up a word or two that he teaches her. Her body, if concealed at all, is concealed by a water lily, a frond, a fern, a bit of moss, or by a sarong—which is a simple garment carrying the implicit promise that it will not long stay in place. For millions of years men everywhere have longed for Dorothy Lamour. Now, in the final complexity of an age which has reached its highest expression in the instrument panel of a long-range bomber, it is a good idea to remember that Man's most persistent dream is of a forest pool and a girl coming out of it unashamed, walking toward him with a wavy motion, childlike in her wonder, a girl exquisitely untroubled, as quiet and accommodating and beautiful as a young green tree. That's all he really wants. He sometimes wonders how this other stuff got in—the instrument panel, the night sky, the full load, the moment of exultation over the blackened city below. . . .

* The official phrase describing America's mobilization just prior to active entry into World War II.

4. Birch

LOUIS SIMPSON

Simpson (1923–   ) was born in Jamaica. He served with the American infantry in World War II. His several volumes of poems include *At the End of the Open Road,* which won the Pulitzer Prize for 1964 and *Adventures of the Letter I* (1971). He has written a novel, *Riverside Drive* (1962), a critical study of James Hogg, and an autobiography, *North of Jamaica* (1972).

Birch tree, you remind me
Of a room filled with breathing,
The sway and whisper of love.

She slips off her shoes;
Unzips her skirt; arms raised,
Unclasps an earring, and the other.

Just so the sallow trunk
Divides, and the branches
Are pale and smooth.

5. Birches

RON PADGETT

Padgett (1942–   ) is the author of *Great Balls of Fire* (1969), a collection of poems. He identifies with the "New

York school" of poets and contributes occasionally
to the *Paris Review.*

When I see birches
I think of nothing
But when I see a girl
Throw away her hair and brains
I think of birches and I see them
One could do worse than see birches

---

6. Birches

ROBERT FROST

When Robert Frost (1875–1963) died, he had read for John
Kennedy's inauguration, traveled to Israel and Russia as
the guest of their governments, and was the unchallenged
dean of American poetry. Few fine poets in modern
times have been as widely read as he. He kept at poetry all
his life, beginning to publish rather late, when he was
nearing forty; and he won nearly all its prizes, including
four Pulitzer Prizes and the Bollingen Prize in 1963.

When I see birches bend to left and right
Across the lines of straighter darker trees,
I like to think some boy's been swinging them.
But swinging doesn't bend them down to stay
As ice storms do. Often you must have seen them
Loaded with ice a sunny winter morning
After a rain. They click upon themselves
As the breeze rises, and turn many-colored
As the stir cracks and crazes their enamel.
Soon the sun's warmth makes them shed crystal shells
Shattering and avalanching on the snow crust—
Such heaps of broken glass to sweep away
You'd think the inner dome of heaven had fallen.
They are dragged to the withered bracken by the load,
And they seem not to break; though once they are bowed

So low for long, they never right themselves:
You may see their trunks arching in the woods
Years afterwards, trailing their leaves on the ground
Like girls on hands and knees that throw their hair
Before them over their heads to dry in the sun.
But I was going to say when Truth broke in
With all her matter of fact about the ice storm,
I should prefer to have some boy bend them
As he went out and in to fetch the cows—
Some boy too far from town to learn baseball,
Whose only play was what he found himself,
Summer or winter, and could play alone.

One by one he subdued his father's trees
By riding them down over and over again
Until he took the stiffness out of them,
And not one but hung limp, not one was left
For him to conquer. He learned all there was
To learn about not launching out too soon
And so not carrying the tree away
Clear to the ground. He always kept his poise
To the top branches, climbing carefully
With the same pains you use to fill a cup
Up to the brim, and even above the brim.
Then he flung outward, feet first, with a swish,
Kicking his way down through the air to the ground.
So was I once myself a swinger of birches.
And so I dream of going back to be.
It's when I'm weary of considerations,
And life is too much like a pathless wood
Where your face burns and tickles with the cobwebs
Broken across it, and one eye is weeping
From a twig's having lashed across it open.
I'd like to get away from earth awhile
And then come back to it and begin over.
May no fate willfully misunderstand me
And half grant what I wish and snatch me away
Not to return. Earth's the right place for love:
I don't know where it's likely to go better.
I'd like to go by climbing a birch tree,
And climb black branches up a snow-white trunk
Toward heaven, till the tree could bear no more,
But dipped its top and set me down again.
That would be good both going and coming back.
One could do worse than be a swinger of birches.

7. A Virginal

EZRA POUND

Between his birth in Idaho and his death in Venice, Ezra
Pound (1885–1972) was one of the most influential and
individual poets, and certainly the most controversial one,
of the English-speaking world. Nearly all the poets of this
century are in some way connected to him. Yeats, Joyce,
Eliot, and Frost were each directly assisted by Pound at
crucial points in their careers. His long poem, *Cantos,*
remains a challenge to our century. In 1943, he was
indicted for treason; he had delivered broadcasts from Italy
that favored the policies of Mussolini. He was awarded
the Bollingen Prize for 1949; the debate over that award,
and over Pound generally, has yet to subside.

No, no! Go from me. I have left her lately.
I will not spoil my sheath with lesser brightness,
For my surrounding air hath a new lightness;
Slight are her arms, yet they have bound me straitly
And left me cloaked as with a gauze of aether;
As with sweet leaves; as with subtle clearness.
Oh, I have picked up magic in her nearness
To sheathe me half in half the things that sheathe her.
No, no! Go from me. I have still the flavour,
Soft as spring wind that's come from birchen bowers.
Green come the shoots, aye April in the branches,
As winter's wound with her sleight hand she staunches,
Hath of the trees a likeness to the savour:
As white their bark, so white this lady's hours.

8. Advice to a Beauty
A Brown Girl Dead

COUNTEE CULLEN

Cullen (1930–1946), born in Missouri, joined Langston Hughes in the Harlem Renaissance of the 1920's, contributing a touch of Harvard, where he studied the writing of poetry under Robert Hillyer. He followed his first book of poems, *Color*, 1925, with three more by 1930. He wrote a novel, a musical (in collaboration), and a classical play, *The Medea.*

Advice to a Beauty

(To Sydonia)

Of all things, lady, be not proud;
Inter not beauty in that shroud
Wherein the living waste, the dead,
Unwept and unrememberéd,
Decay. Beauty beats so frail a wing;
Suffer men to gaze, poets to sing
How radiant you are, compare
And favor you to that most rare
Bird of delight: a lovely face
Matched with an equal inner grace.
Sweet bird, beware the Fowler, Pride;
His knots once neatly crossed and tied,
The prey is caged and walled about
With no way in and no way out.

A Brown Girl Dead

With two white roses on her breasts,
   White candles at head and feet,
Dark Madonna of the grave she rests;
   Lord Death has found her sweet.

Her mother pawned her wedding ring
    To lay her out in white;
She'd be so proud she'd dance and sing
    To see herself tonight.

---

9. Fifth Avenue Uptown: A Letter from Harlem

JAMES BALDWIN

Baldwin (1924–   ), born in poverty in Harlem, tyranized by his stepfather and overworked as a babysitter by his mother, began writing in the Frederick Douglass Junior High School in Harlem, where Countee Cullen was one of his teachers. After high school, he experienced a religious conversion at Mother Horn's Church and preached for three years to a growing congregation. World War II brought work in a defense plant and an eventual move to Greenwich Village, where Richard Wright encouraged him, and got him his first of several fellowships and awards, including a Guggenheim. But he bought a one-way ticket to France in 1948, intending never to return. His first novel, *Go Tell It on the Mountain,* appeared in 1953. After a decade of living around Europe, he returned to the United States, where he now spends most of his time. His essays in his collections *Notes on a Native Son* (1955), *Nobody Knows My Name* (1960), and *The Fire Next Time* (1963) have become classic statements of racial injustice. His *A Rap on Race* (1971) is a series of conversations, from tapes, with Margaret Mead.

THERE IS A HOUSING PROJECT standing now where the house in which we grew up once stood, and one of those stunted city trees is snarling where our doorway used to be. This is on the rehabilitated side of the avenue. The other side of the avenue —for progress takes time—has not been rehabilitated yet and it looks exactly as it looked in the days when we sat with our noses pressed against the windowpane, longing to be allowed to go "across the street." The grocery store which gave us credit is still there, and there can be no doubt that it is still giving credit. The people in the project certainly need it—far more, indeed, than they ever needed the project. The last time I passed by, the Jewish proprietor was still standing among his shelves, looking sadder and heavier but scarcely any older. Farther down the block stands the shoe-repair store in which our shoes were repaired until reparation became impossible and in which, then, we bought all our "new" ones. The Negro proprietor is still in the window, head down, working at the leather.

These two, I imagine, could tell a long tale if they would (perhaps they would be glad to if they could), having watched so many, for so long, struggling in the fishhooks, the barbed wire, of this avenue.

The avenue is elsewhere the renowned and elegant Fifth. The area I am describing, which, in today's gang parlance, would be called "the turf," is bounded by Lenox Avenue on the west, the Harlem River on the east, 135th Street on the north, and 130th Street on the south. We never lived beyond these boundaries; this is where we grew up. Walking along 145th Street—for example—familiar as it is, and similar, does not have the same impact because I do not know any of the people on the block. But when I turn east on 131st Street and Lenox Avenue, there is first a soda-pop joint, then a shoeshine "parlor," then a grocery store, then a dry cleaners', then the houses. All along the street there are people who watched me grow up, people who grew up with me, people I watched grow up along with my brothers and sisters; and, sometimes in my arms, sometimes underfoot, sometimes at my shoulder —or on it—their children, a riot, a forest of children, who include my nieces and nephews.

When we reach the end of this long block, we find ourselves on wide, filthy, hostile Fifth Avenue, facing that project which hangs over the avenue like a monument to the folly, and the cowardice, of good intentions. All along the block, for anyone who knows it, are immense human gaps, like craters. These gaps are not created merely by those who have moved away, inevitably into some other ghetto; or by those who have risen, almost always into a greater capacity for self-loathing and self-delusion; or yet by those who, by whatever means—World War II, the Korean war, a policeman's gun or billy, a gang war, a brawl, madness, an overdose of heroin, or, simply, unnatural exhaustion—are dead. I am talking about those who are left, and I am talking principally about the young. What are they doing? Well, some, a minority, are fanatical churchgoers, members of the more extreme of the Holy Roller sects. Many, many more are "moslems," by affiliation or sympathy, that is to say that they are united by nothing more—and nothing less—than a hatred of the white world and all its works. They are pres-

18

ent, for example, at every Buy Black street-corner meeting—meetings in which the speaker urges his hearers to cease trading with white men and establish a separate economy. Neither the speaker nor his hearers can possibly do this, of course, since Negroes do not own General Motors or RCA or the A & P, nor, indeed, do they own more than a wholly insufficient fraction of anything else in Harlem (those who *do* own anything are more interested in their profits than in their fellows). But these meetings nevertheless keep alive in the participators a certain pride of bitterness without which, however futile this bitterness may be, they could scarcely remain alive at all. Many have given up. They stay home and watch the TV screen, living on the earnings of their parents, cousins, brothers, or uncles, and only leave the house to go to the movies or to the nearest bar. "How're you making it?" one may ask, running into them along the block, or in the bar. "Oh, I'm TV-ing it"; with the saddest, sweetest, most shamefaced of smiles, and from a great distance. This distance one is compelled to respect; anyone who has traveled so far will not easily be dragged again into the world. There are further retreats, of course, than the TV screen or the bar. There are those who are simply sitting on their stoops, "stoned," animated for a moment only, and hideously, by the approach of someone who may lend them the money for a "fix." Or by the approach of someone from whom they can purchase it, one of the shrewd ones, on the way to prison or just coming out.

And the others, who have avoided all of these deaths, get up in the morning and go downtown to meet "the man." They work in the white man's world all day and come home in the evening to this fetid block. They struggle to instill in their children some private sense of honor or dignity which will help the child to survive. This means, of course, that they must struggle, stolidly, incessantly, to keep this sense alive in themselves, in spite of the insults, the indifference, and the cruelty they are certain to encounter in their working day. They patiently browbeat the landlord into fixing the heat, the plaster, the plumbing; this demands prodigious patience; nor is patience usually enough. In trying to make their hovels habitable, they are perpetually throwing good money after bad. Such frustration, so long endured, is driving many strong, admirable men and women whose only crime is color to the very gates of paranoia.

One remembers them from another time—playing handball in the playground, going to church, wondering if they were going to be promoted at school. One remembers them going off to war—gladly, to escape this block. One remembers their return. Perhaps one remembers their wedding day. And one sees where the girl is now—vainly looking for salvation from some other embittered, trussed, and struggling boy —and sees the all-but-abandoned children in the streets.

Now I am perfectly aware that there are other slums in which white men are fighting for their lives, and mainly losing. I know that blood is also flowing through those streets and that the human damage there is incalculable. Peeple are continually pointing out to me the wretchedness of white people in order to console me for the wretchedness of blacks. But an itemized account of the American failure does not console me and it should not console anyone else. That hundreds of thousands of white people are living, in effect, no better than the "niggers" is not a fact to be regarded with complacency. The social and moral bankruptcy suggested by this fact is of the bitterest, most terrifying kind.

The people, however, who believe that this democratic anguish has some consoling value are always pointing out that So-and-So, white, and So-and-So, black, rose from the slums into the big time. The existence—the public existence—of, say, Frank Sinatra and Sammy Davis, Jr., proves to them that America is still the land of opportunity and that inequalities vanish before the determined will. It proves nothing of the sort. The determined will is rare—at the moment, in this country, it is unspeakably rare—and the inequalities suffered by the many are in no way justified by the rise of a few. A few have always risen—in every country, every era, and in the teeth of regimes which can by no stretch of the imagination be thought of as free. Not all of these people, it is worth remembering, left the world better than they found it. The determined will is rare, but it is not invariably benevolent. Furthermore, the American equation of success with the big time reveals an awful disrespect for human life and human achievement. This equation has placed our cities among the most dangerous in the world and has placed our youth among the most empty and most bewildered. The situation of our youth is not mysterious. Children have never been very good at listening to their elders, but they have never failed to imitate them. They must, they have no other models. That is exactly what our children are doing. They are imitating our immorality, our disrespect for the pain of others.

All other slum dwellers, when the bank account permits it, can move out of the slum and vanish altogether from the eye of persecution. No Negro in this country has ever made that much money and it will be a long time before any Negro does. The Negroes in Harlem, who have no money, spend what they have on such gimcracks as they are sold. These include "wider" TV screens, more "faithful" hi-fi sets, more "powerful" cars, all of which, of course, are obsolete long before they are paid for. Anyone who has ever struggled with poverty knows how extremely expensive it is to be poor; and if one is a member of a captive population, economically speaking, one's feet have simply been placed on the treadmill forever. One is victimized, economically, in a thousand ways—rent, for example, or car insurance. Go shopping one day in Harlem—for anything—and compare Harlem prices and quality with those downtown.

The people who have managed to get off this block have only got as far as a more respectable ghetto. This respectable ghetto does not even have the advantages of the disreputable one—friends, neighbors, a familiar church, and friendly tradesmen; and it is not, moreover, in the nature of any ghetto to remain respectable long. Every Sunday, people who have left the block take the lonely ride back, dragging their increasingly discontented children with them. They spend the day talking, not always with words, about the trouble they've seen and the trouble—one must watch their eyes as they watch their children—they are only too likely to see. For children do not like ghettos. It takes them nearly no time to discover exactly why they are there.

The projects in Harlem are hated. They are hated almost as much as policemen, and this is saying a great deal. And they are hated for the same reason: both reveal, unbearably, the real attitude of the white world, no matter how many liberal speeches are made, no matter how many lofty editorials are written, no matter how many civil-rights commissions are set up.

The projects are hideous, of course, there being a law, apparently respected throughout the world, that popular housing shall be as cheerless as a prison. They are lumped all over Harlem, colorless, bleak, high, and revolting. The wide windows look out on Harlem's invincible and indescribable squalor: the Park Avenue railroad tracks, around which, about forty years ago, the present dark community began; the unrehabilitated houses, bowed down, it would seem, under the great weight of frustration and bitterness they contain; the dark, the ominous schoolhouses from which the child may emerge maimed, blinded, hooked, or enraged for life; and the churches, churches, block upon block of churches, niched in the walls like cannon in the walls of a fortress. Even if the administration of the projects were not so insanely humiliating (for example: one must report raises in salary to the management, which will then eat up the profit by raising one's rent; the management has the right to know who is staying in your apartment; the management can ask you to leave, at their discretion), the projects would still be hated because they are an insult to the meanest intelligence.

Harlem got its first private project, Riverton *—which is now, nat-

* The inhabitants of Riverton were much embittered by this description; they have, apparently, forgotten how their project came into being; and have repeatedly informed me that I cannot possibly be referring to Riverton, but to another housing project which is directly across the street. It is quite clear, I think, that I have no interest in accusing any individuals or families of the depredations herein described: but neither can I deny the evidence of my own eyes. Nor do I blame anyone in Harlem for making the best of a dreadful bargain. But anyone who lives in Harlem and

urally, a slum—about twelve years ago because at that time Negroes were not allowed to live in Stuyvesant Town. Harlem watched Riverton go up, therefore, in the most violent bitterness of spirit, and hated it long before the builders arrived. They began hating it at about the time people began moving out of their condemned houses to make room for this additional proof of how thoroughly the white world despised them. And they had scarcely moved in, naturally, before they began smashing windows, defacing walls, urinating in the elevators, and fornicating in the playgrounds. Liberals, both white and black, were appalled at the spectacle. I was appalled by the liberal innocence—or cynicism, which comes out in practice as much the same thing. Other people were delighted to be able to point to proof positive that nothing could be done to better the lot of the colored people. They were, and are, right in one respect: that nothing can be done as long as they are treated like colored people. The people in Harlem know they are living there because white people do not think they are good enough to live anywhere else. No amount of "improvement" can sweeten this fact. Whatever money is now being earmarked to improve this, or any other ghetto, might as well be burnt. A ghetto can be improved in one way only: out of existence.

Similarly, the only way to police a ghetto is to be oppressive. None of the Police Commissioner's men, even with the best will in the world, have any way of understanding the lives led by the people they swagger about in twos and threes controlling. Their very presence is an insult, and it would be, even if they spent their entire day feeding gumdrops to children. They represent the force of the white world, and that world's real intentions are, simply, for that world's criminal profit and ease, to keep the black man corraled up here, in his place. The badge, the gun in the holster, and the swinging club make vivid what will happen should his rebellion become overt. Rare, indeed, is the Harlem citizen, from the most circumspect church member to the most shiftless adolescent, who does not have a long tale to tell of police incompetence, injustice, or brutality. I myself have witnessed and endured it more than once. The businessmen and racketeers also have a story. And so do the prostitutes. (And this is not, perhaps, the place to discuss Harlem's very complex attitude toward black policemen, nor the reasons, according to Harlem, that they are nearly all downtown.)

It is hard, on the other hand, to blame the policeman, blank, good-natured, thoughtless, and insuperably innocent, for being such a perfect representative of the people he serves. He, too, believes in good intentions and is astounded and offended when they are not taken for

imagines that he has not struck this bargain, or that what he takes to be his status (in whose eyes?) protects him against the common pain, demoralization, and danger, is simply self-deluded.

the deed. He has never, himself, done anything for which to be hated —which of us has?—and yet he is facing, daily and nightly, people who would gladly see him dead, and he knows it. There is no way for him not to know it: there are few things under heaven more unnerving than the silent, accumulating contempt and hatred of a people. He moves through Harlem, therefore, like an occupying soldier in a bitterly hostile country; which is precisely what, and where, he is, and is the reason he walks in twos and threes. And he is not the only one who knows why he is always in company: the people who are watching him know why, too. Any street meeting, sacred or secular, which he and his colleagues uneasily cover has as its explicit or implicit burden the cruelty and injustice of the white domination. And these days, of course, in terms increasingly vivid and jubilant, it speaks of the end of that domination. The white policeman standing on a Harlem street corner finds himself at the very center of the revolution now occurring in the world. He is not prepared for it—naturally, nobody is—and, what is possibly much more to the point, he is exposed, as few white people are, to the anguish of the black people around him. Even if he is gifted with the merest mustard grain of imagination, something must seep in. He cannot avoid observing that some of the children, in spite of their color, remind him of children he has known and loved, perhaps even of his own children. He knows that he certainly does not want *his* children living this way. He can retreat from his uneasiness in only one direction: into a callousness which very shortly becomes second nature. He becomes more callous, the population becomes more hostile, the situation grows more tense, and the police force is increased. One day, to everyone's astonishment, someone drops a match in the powder keg and everything blows up. Before the dust has settled or the blood congealed, editorials, speeches, and civil-rights commissions are loud in the land, demanding to know what happened. What happened is that Negroes want to be treated like men.

Negroes want to be treated like men: a perfectly straightforward statement, containing only seven words. Peoples who have mastered Kant, Hegel, Shakespeare, Marx, Freud, and the Bible find this statement utterly impenetrable. The idea seems to threaten profound, barely conscious assumptions. A kind of panic paralyzes their features, as though they found themselves trapped on the edge of a steep place. I once tried to describe to a very well-known American intellectual the conditions among Negroes in the South. My recital disturbed him and made him indignant; and he asked me in perfect innocence, "Why don't all the Negroes in the South move North?" I tried to explain what *has* happened, unfailingly, whenever a significant body of Negroes move North. They do not escape Jim Crow: they merely encounter another, not-less-deadly variety. They do not move to Chicago, they move to the South Side; they do not move to New York, they move to Harlem. The pressure within the ghetto causes the ghetto walls to expand, and this expansion is always violent. White people hold the line as long as they can, and in as many ways as they can, from verbal intimidation to physical violence. But inevitably the border which has divided the ghetto from the rest of the world falls into the hands of the ghetto. The white people fall back bitterly before the black horde; the landlords make a tidy profit by raising the rent, chopping up the rooms, and all but dispensing with the upkeep; and what has once been a neighborhood turns into a "turf." This is precisely what happened when the Puerto Ricans arrived in their thousands—and the bitterness thus caused is, as I write, being fought out all up and down those streets.

Northerners indulge in an extremely dangerous luxury. They seem to feel that because they fought on the right side during the Civil War, and won, they have earned the right merely to deplore what is going on in the South, without taking any responsibility for it; and that they can ignore what is happening in Northern cities because what is happening in Little Rock or Birmingham is worse. Well, in the first place, it is not possible for anyone who has not endured both to know which is "worse." I know Negroes who prefer the South and white Southerners, because "At least there, you haven't got to play any guessing games!" The guessing games referred to have driven more than one Negro into the narcotics ward, the madhouse, or the river. I know another Negro, a man very dear to me, who says, with conviction and with truth, "The spirit of the South is the spirit of America." He was born in the North and did his military training in the South. He did not, as far as I can gather, find the South "worse"; he found it, if anything, all too familiar. In the second place, though, even if Birmingham is worse, no doubt Johannesburg, South Africa, beats it by several miles, and Buchenwald was one of the worst things that ever happened in the entire history of the world. The world has never lacked for horrifying examples; but I do not believe that these examples are meant to be used as justification for our own crimes. This perpetual justification empties the heart of all human feeling. The emptier our hearts become, the greater will be our crimes. Thirdly, the South is not merely an embarrassingly backward region, but a part of this country, and what happens there concerns every one of us.

As far as the color problem is concerned, there is but one great difference between the Southern white and the Northerner: the Southerner remembers, historically and in his own psyche, a kind of Eden in which he loved black people and they loved him. Historically, the flaming sword laid across this Eden is the Civil War. Personally, it is the Southerner's sexual coming of age, when, without any warning, unbreakable taboos are set up between himself and his past. Everything, thereafter, is permitted him except the love he remembers and has never ceased to need. The resulting, indescribable torment affects every Southern mind and is the basis of the Southern hysteria.

None of this is true for the Northerner. Negroes represent nothing to him personally, except, perhaps, the dangers of carnality. He never sees Negroes. Southerners see them all the time. Northerners never think about them whereas Southerners are never really thinking of anything else. Negroes are, therefore, ignored in the North and are under surveillance in the South, and suffer hideously in both places. Neither the Southerner nor the Northerner is able to look on the Negro simply as a man. It seems to be indispensable to the national self-esteem that the Negro be considered either as a kind of ward (in which case we are told how many Negroes, comparatively, bought Cadillacs last year and how few, comparatively, were lynched), or as a victim (in which case we are promised that he will never vote in our assemblies or go to school with our kids). They are two sides of the same coin and the South will not change—*cannot* change—until the North changes. The country will not change until it reexamines itself and discovers what it really means by freedom. In the meantime, generations keep being born, bitterness is increased by incompetence, pride, and folly, and the world shrinks around us.

It is a terrible, an inexorable, law that one cannot deny the humanity of another without diminishing one's own: in the face of one's victim, one sees oneself. Walk through the streets of Harlem and see what we, this nation, have become.

10. We Real Cool

GWENDOLYN BROOKS

Gwendolyn Brooks (Mrs. Henry L. Blakely) was born in Topeka, Kansas, in 1917. She has taught at Columbia College, Chicago (her alma mater), Northwestern, and Illinois State College. In 1945, *Mademoiselle* magazine named her among the Ten Women of the Year. In 1950, she won the Pulitzer Prize for poetry. In 1969, the state of Illinois named her its Poet Laureate. She has published seven volumes of poetry, fiction for children, and a novel, *Maud Martha* (1953).

The Pool Players.
Seven at the Golden Shovel.

We real cool. We   Sing sin. We
Left school. We   Thin gin. We

Lurk late. We   Jazz June. We
Strike straight. We   Die soon.

11. The Birth of "The New Journalism"

TOM WOLFE

Wolfe took a Ph.D. in American Studies at Yale before turning to journalism. His books, each an example of the "new journalism" he writes about here, include *The Kandy-Kolored Tangerine-Flake Streamline Baby* (1965), *The Pump House Gang* (1968), *The Electric Kool-Aid Acid Test* (1968), and *Radical Chic and Mau-Mauing the Flak Catchers* (1970).

I. The Feature Game

I DOUBT IF MANY of the aces I will be extolling in this story went into journalism with the faintest notion of creating a "new" journalism, a "higher" journalism, or even a mildly improved variety. I know they never dreamed that anything they were going to write for newspapers or magazines would wreak such evil havoc in the literary world . . . causing panic, dethroning the novel as the number one literary genre, starting the first new direction in American literature in half a century . . . Nevertheless, that is what' has happened. Bellow, Barth, Updike—even the best of the lot, Philip Roth—the novelists are all out there ransacking the literary histories and sweating it out, wondering where they now stand. Damn it all, Saul, the *Huns* have arrived . . .

God knows I didn't have anything new in mind, much less anything literary, when I took my first newspaper job. I had a fierce and unnatural craving for something else entirely. Chicago, 1928, that was the general idea . . . Drunken reporters out on the ledge of the *News* peeing into the Chicago River at dawn . . . Nights down at the saloon listening to "Back of the Stockyards" being sung by a baritone who was only a lonely blind bulldyke with lumps of milk glass for eyes . . . Nights down at the detective bureau—it was always nighttime in my daydreams of the newspaper life. Reporters didn't work during the day. I wanted the whole movie, nothing left out . . .

I was aware of what had reduced me to this Student Prince Maudlin state of mind. All the same, I couldn't help it. I had just spent five years in graduate school, a statement that may mean nothing to people who never served such a stretch; it is the explanation, nonetheless. I'm not sure I can give you the remotest idea of what graduate school is like. Nobody ever has. Millions of Americans now go to graduate schools, but just say the phrase—"graduate school"—and what picture leaps into the brain? No picture, not even a blur. Half the people I knew in graduate school were going to write a novel about it. I thought about it myself. No one ever wrote such a book, as far as I know. Everyone used to sniff the air. How morbid! How poisonous! Nothing else like it in the world! But the subject always defeated them. It defied literary exploitation. Such a novel would be a study of frustration, but a form of frustration so exquisite, so ineffable, nobody could describe it. Try to imagine the worst part of the worst Antonioni movie you ever saw, or reading *Mr. Sammler's Planet* at one sitting, or just reading it, or being locked inside a Seaboard Railroad roomette, sixteen miles from Gainesville, Florida, heading north on the Miami-to-New York run, with no water and the radiator turning red in an amok psychotic overboil, and George McGovern sitting beside you telling you his philosophy of government. That will give you the general atmosphere.

In any case, by the time I received my doctorate in American studies in 1957 I was in the twisted grip of a disease of our times in which the sufferer experiences an overwhelming urge to join the "real world." So I started working for newspapers. In 1962, after a cup of coffee here and there, I arrived at the *New York Herald Tribune* . . . This must be the place! . . . I looked out across the city room of the *Herald Tribune*, 100 moldering yards south of Times Square, with a feeling of amazed bohemian bliss . . . Either this is the real world, Tom, or there is no real world . . . The place looked like the receiving bin at the Good Will . . . a promiscuous heap of junk . . . Wreckage and exhaustion everywhere . . . If somebody such as the city editor had a swivel chair, the universal joint would be broken, so that every time he got up, the seat would keel over as if stricken by a lateral stroke. All the intestines of the building were left showing in diverticulitic loops and lines—electrical conduits, water pipes, steam pipes, effluvium ducts, sprinkler systems, all of it dangling and grunting from the ceiling, the walls, the columns. The whole mess, from top to bottom, was painted over in an industrial sludge, Lead Gray, Subway Green, or that unbelievable dead red, that grim distemper of pigment and filth, that they paint the floor with in the tool and die works. On the ceiling were scalding banks of fluorescent lights, turning the atmosphere radium blue and burning bald spots in the crowns of the copy readers, who never moved. It was one big pie factory . . . A Landlord's Dream . . . There were no interior walls. The corporate hierarchy was not marked off into office spaces. The managing editor worked in a space that was as miserable and scabid as the lowest reporter's. Most newspapers were like that. This setup was instituted decades ago for practical reasons. But it was kept alive by a curious fact. On newspapers very few editorial employees at the bottom—namely, the reporters—had any ambition whatsoever to move up, to become city editors, managing editors, editors-in-chief, or any of the rest of it. Editors felt no threat from below. They needed no walls. Reporters didn't want much . . . merely to be *stars!* and of such minute wattage at that!

That was one thing they never wrote about in books on journalism or those comradely blind-bulldagger boots-upon-the-brass-rail swill-bar speakeasy memoirs about newspaper days and children of the century . . . namely, the little curlicues of newspaper status competition . . . For example, at the desk behind mine in the *Herald Tribune* city room sat Charles Portis. Portis was the original laconic cutup. At one point he was asked onto a kind of *Meet the Press* show with Malcolm X, and Malcolm X made the mistake of giving the reporters a little lecture before they went on about how he didn't want to hear anybody calling him "Malcolm," because he was not a dining-car waiter—his name happened to be "Malcolm X." By the end of the show Malcolm X was furious. He was climbing the goddamned acoustical tiles. The original laconic cutup, Portis, had invariably and continually addressed him as "Mr. X" . . . "Now, Mr. X, let me ask you this . . ." Anyway, Portis had the desk behind mine. Down in a bullpen at the far end of the room was Jimmy Breslin. Over to one side sat Dick Schaap. We were all engaged in a form of newspaper competition that I have never known anybody to even talk about in public. Yet Schaap had quit as city editor of the *New York Herald Tribune*, which was one of the legendary jobs in journalism—moved *down* the organizational chart, in other words—just to get in this secret game.

Everybody knows about one form of competition among newspaper reporters, the so-called *scoop* competition. Scoop reporters competed with their counterparts on other newspapers, or wire services, to see who could get a story first and write it fastest; the bigger the story—i.e., the more it had to do with matters of power or catastrophe—the better. In short, they were concerned with the main business of the newspaper. But there was this other lot of reporters as well . . . They tended to be what is known as "feature writers." What they had in common was that they all regarded the newspaper as a motel you checked into overnight on the road to the final triumph. The idea was to get a job on a newspaper, keep body and soul together, pay the rent, get to know "the world," accumulate "experience," perhaps work some of the fat off your style—then, at some point, quit cold, say goodbye to journalism, move into a shack somewhere, work night and day for six months, and light up the sky with the final triumph. The final triumph was known as The Novel.

That was Someday, you understand . . . Meanwhile, these dream-boaters were in there banging away, in every place in America that had a newspaper, competing for a tiny crown the rest of the world wasn't even aware of: Best Feature Writer in Town. The "feature" was the newspaper term for a story that fell outside the category of hard news. It included everything from "'brights," chuckly little items, often from the police beat . . . There was this out-of-towner who checked into a hotel in San Francisco last night, bent upon suicide, and he threw himself out of his fifth-story window—and fell nine feet and sprained his ankle. What he didn't know was—the hotel was on a steep hill! . . . to "human interest stories," long and often hideously sentimental accounts of hitherto unknown souls beset by tragedy or unusual hobbies within the sheet's circulation area . . . In any case, feature stories gave a man a certain amount of room in which to write.

Unlike the scoop reporters, the feature writers did not openly acknowledge the existence of their competition, not even to one another. Nor was there any sort of scorecard. And yet everyone in the game knew precisely what was going on and went through the most mortifying sieges of envy, even resentment, or else surges of euphoria, depending on how the game was going. No one would ever admit to such a thing, and yet all felt it, almost daily. The feature writers' arena differed from the scoop reporters' in another way. Your competition was not necessarily working for another publication. You were just as likely to be competing with people on your own paper, which meant you were even less likely to talk about it.

So here was half the feature competition in New York, right in the same city room with me, because the *Herald Tribune* was like the main Tijuana bullring for feature writers . . . Portis, Breslin, Schaap . . . Schaap and Breslin had columns, which gave them more freedom, but I figured I could take the both of them. You had to be brave. Over at the *Times* there was Gay Talese and Robert Lipsyte. At the *Daily News* there was Michael Mok. (There were other contenders, too, on all the newspapers, including the *Herald Tribune*. I am only mentioning those I remember most clearly.) Mok I had been up against before, when I worked on the *Washington Post* and he worked on the *Washington Star*. Mok was tough competition, because, for one thing, he was willing to risk his hide on a feature story with the same wild courage he later showed in covering Vietnam and the Arab-Israel war for *Life*. Mok would do . . . eerie things. For example, the *News* sends Mok and a photographer out to do a feature on a fat man who is trying to lose weight by marooning himself on a sailboat anchored out in Long Island Sound ("I'm one of those guys, I walk past a delicatessen and breathe deep, and I gain ten pounds"). The motorboat they hire conks out about a mile from the fat man's sloop, with only four or five hours to go before the deadline. This is March, but Mok dives in and starts swimming. The water is about 42 degrees. He swims until he's half dead, and the fat man has to fish him out with an oar. So Mok gets the story. He makes the deadline. There are pictures in the *News* of Mok swimming furiously through Long Island Sound in order to retrieve this great blob's diet saga for two million readers. If, instead, he had drowned, if he had ended up down with the oysters in the hepatitic muck of the Sound, nobody would have put up a plaque for him. Editors save their tears for war correspondents. As for feature writers—the less said, the better. (Just the other day I saw one of the *New York Times*'s grand panjandrums react with amazement to superlative praise for one of his paper's most popular writers, Israel Shenker, as follows: "But he's a *feature* writer!") No, if Mok had bought the oyster farm that afternoon, he wouldn't even have rated the quietest award in journalism, which is 30 seconds of silence at the Overseas Press Club dinner. Nevertheless, he dove into Long Island Sound in March! Such was the raging competition within our odd and tiny grotto!

At the same time everybody in the game had terrible dark moments during which he lost heart and told himself: "You're only kidding yourself, boy. This is just one more of your devious ways of postponing the decision to put it *all* on the line . . . and go into the shack . . . and write your novel." Your Novel! At this late date—partly due to the New Journalism itself—it is hard to explain what an American dream the idea of writing a novel was in the 1940s, the 1950s, and right into the early 1960s. The Novel was no mere literary form. It was a psychological phenomenon. It was a cortical fever. It belonged in the glossary to *A General Introduction to Psychoanalysis*, somewhere between Narcissism and Obsessional Neuroses. In 1969 Seymour Krim wrote a strange confession for *Playboy* that began: "I was literally made, shaped, whetted and given a world with a purpose by the American realistic novel of the mid- to late-1930s. From the age of fourteen to seventeen, I gorged myself with the works of Thomas Wolfe (beginning with *Of Time and the River*, catching up with *Angel* and then keeping pace till Big Tom's stunning end), Ernest Hemingway, William Faulkner, James T. Farrell, John Steinbeck, John O'Hara, James Cain, Richard Wright, John Dos Passos, Erskine Caldwell, Jerome Weidman, and William Saroyan, and knew in my pumping heart that I wanted to be such a novelist." The piece turned into a confession because first Krim admitted that the idea of being a novelist had been the overwhelming passion of his life, his spiritual calling, in fact, the Pacemaker that kept his ego ticking through all the miserable humiliations of his young manhood—then he faced up to the fact that he was now in his forties and had never written a novel and more than likely never would. Personally I was fascinated by the article, but why *Playboy* was running it, I didn't know, unless it was the magazine's monthly 10 cc. of literary penicillin . . . to hold down the gonococci and the spirochetes . . . I couldn't imagine anyone other than writers being interested in Krim's Complex. That, however, was where I was wrong.

After thinking it over, I realized that writers comprise but a fraction of the Americans who have experienced Krim's peculiar obsession. Not so long ago, I am willing to wager, half the people who went to work for publishing houses did so with the belief that their real destiny was to be novelists. Among people on what they call the creative side of advertising, those who actually dream up the ads, the percentage must have reached 90 per cent. In 1955, in *The Exurbanites*, the late A. C. Spectorsky depicted the well-paid Madison Avenue advertising genius as being a man who wouldn't read a novel without checking out the dust jacket blurb and the picture of the author on the back . . . and if that ego-flushed little bastard with the unbuttoned shirt and the wind rushing through his locks was younger than he was, he couldn't bear to open the goddamn book. Such was the grip of the damnable Novel. Likewise among people in television, public relations, the movies, on the English faculties of colleges and high schools, among framing shop clerks, convicts, unmarried sons living with Mom . . . a whole swarm of fantasizers out there steaming and proliferating in the ego mulches of America . . .

The Novel seemed like one of the last of those superstrokes, like finding gold or striking oil, through which an American could, overnight, in a flash, utterly transform his destiny. There were plenty of examples to feed the fantasy. In the 1930s all the novelists had seemed to be people who came blazing up into stardom from out of total obscurity. That seemed to be the nature of the beast. The biographical notes on the dust jackets of the novels were terrific. The author, you would be assured, was previously employed as a hod carrier (Steinbeck), a truck dispatcher (Cain), a bellboy (Wright), a Western Union boy (Saroyan), a dishwasher in a Greek restaurant in New York (Faulkner), a truck driver, logger, berry picker, spindle cleaner, crop duster, pilot . . . There was no end to it . . . Some novelists had whole strings of these credentials . . . That way you knew you were getting the real goods . . .

By the 1950s The Novel had become a nationwide tournament. There was a magical assumption that the end of World War II in 1945 was the dawn of a new golden age of the American Novel, like the Hemingway-Dos Passos-Fitzgerald era after World War I. There was even a kind of Olympian club where the new golden boys met face-to-face every Sunday afternoon in New York, namely, the White Horse Tavern on Hudson Street . . . Ah! There's Jones! There's Mailer! There's Styron! There's Baldwin! There's Willingham! In the flesh—right here in this room! The scene was strictly for novelists, people who were writing novels, and people who were paying court to The Novel. There was no room for a journalist unless he was there in the role of would-be novelist or simple courtier of the great. There was no such thing as a *literary* journalist working for popular magazines or newspapers. If a journalist aspired to literary status—then he had better have the sense and the courage to quit the popular press and try to get into the big league.

As for our little league of feature writers—two of the contestants, Portis and Breslin, actually went on to live out the fantasy. They wrote their novels. Portis did it in a way that was so much like the way it happens in the dream, it was unbelievable. One day he suddenly quit as London correspondent for the *Herald Tribune*. That was generally regarded as a very choice job in the newspaper business. Portis quit cold one day; just like that, without a warning. He returned to the United States and moved into a fishing shack in Arkansas. In six months he wrote a beautiful little novel called *Norwood*. Then he wrote *True Grit*, which was a best seller. The reviews were terrific . . . He sold both books to the movies . . . He made a fortune . . . A *fishing* shack! In *Arkansas!* It was too goddamned perfect to be true, and yet there it was. Which is to say that the old dream, The Novel, has never died.

And yet in the early 1960s a curious new notion, just hot enough to inflame the ego, had begun to intrude into the tiny confines of the feature statusphere. It was in the nature of a discovery. This discovery, modest at first, humble, in fact, deferential, you might say, was that it just might be possible to write journalism that would . . . read like a novel. *Like* a novel, if you get the picture. This was the sincerest form of homage to The Novel and to those greats, the novelists, of course. Not even the journalists who pioneered in this direction doubted for a moment that the novelist was the reigning literary artist, now and forever. All they were asking for was the privilege of dressing up like him . . . until the day when they themselves would work up their nerve and go into the shack and try it for real . . . They were dreamers, all right, but one thing they never dreamed of. They never dreamed of the approaching irony. They never guessed for a minute that the work they would do over the next ten years, as journalists, would wipe out the novel as literature's main event.

II. Like a Novel

What inna namea Christ is this—in the fall of 1962 I happened to pick up a copy of *Esquire* and read a story called "Joe Louis: the King as a Middle-aged Man." The piece didn't open like an ordinary magazine article at all. It opened with the tone and mood of a short story, with a rather intimate scene; or intimate by the standards of magazine journalism in 1962, in any case:

" 'Hi, sweetheart!' Joe Louis called to his wife, spotting her waiting for him at the Los Angeles airport.

"She smiled, walked toward him, and was about to stretch up on her toes and kiss him—but suddenly stopped.

" 'Joe,' she said, 'where's your tie?'

" 'Aw, sweetie,' he said, shrugging, 'I stayed out all night in New York and didn't have time—'

" 'All *night!*' she cut in. 'When you're out here all you do is sleep, sleep, sleep.'

" 'Sweetie,' Joe Louis said, with a tired grin, 'I'm an ole man.'

" 'Yes,' she agreed, 'but when you go to New York you try to be young again.' "

The story featured several scenes like that, showing the private life of a sports hero growing older, balder, sadder. It wound up with a scene in the home of Louis's second wife, Rose Morgan. In this scene Rose Morgan is showing a film of the first Joe Louis-Billy Conn fight to a roomful of people, including her present husband.

"Rose seemed excited at seeing Joe at the top of his form, and every time a Louis punch would jolt Conn, she'd go, 'Mummm' (sock). 'Mummm' (sock). 'Mummm.'

"Billy Conn was impressive through the middle rounds, but as the screen flashed Round 13, somebody said, 'Here's where Conn's gonna make his mistake; he's gonna try to slug it out with Joe Louis.' Rose's husband remained silent, sipping his Scotch.

"When the Louis combinations began to land, Rose went, 'Mummmmm, 'mummmmm,' and then the pale body of Conn began to collapse against the canvas.

"Billy Conn slowly began to rise. The referee counted over him. Conn had one leg up, then two, then was standing—but the referee forced him back. It was too late.

"—and then, for the first time, from the back of the room, from out of the downy billows of the sofa, comes the voice of the present husband—*this Joe Louis crap again*—

" 'I thought Conn got up in time,' he said, 'but that referee wouldn't let him go on.'

"Rose Morgan said nothing—just swallowed the rest of her drink."

What the hell is going on? With a little reworking the whole article could have read like a short story. The passages in between the scenes, the expository passages, were conventional 1950s-style magazine journalism, but they could have been easily recast. The piece could have been turned into a non-fiction short story with very little effort. The really unique thing about it, however, was the reporting. This I frankly couldn't comprehend at first. I really didn't understand how anyone could manage to do reporting on things like the personal by-play between a man and his fourth wife at an airport and then follow it up with that amazing cakewalk down Memory Lane in his second wife's living room. My instinctive, defensive reaction was that the man had piped it, as the saying went . . . winged it, made up the dialogue . . . Christ, maybe he made up whole scenes, the unscrupulous geek . . . The funny thing was, that was precisely the reaction that countless journalists and literary intellectuals would have over the next nine years as the New Journalism picked up momentum. *The bastards are making it up!* (I'm telling you, Ump, that's a *spitball* he's throwing . . .) Really stylish reporting was something no one knew how to deal with, since no one was used to thinking of reporting as having an *esthetic* dimension.

At the time I hardly ever read magazines like *Esquire*. I wouldn't have read the Joe Louis piece except that it was by Gay Talese. After all, Talese was a reporter for the *Times*. He was a player in my own feature game. What he had written for *Esquire* was so much better than what he was doing (or was allowed to do) for the *Times*, I had to check out what was going on.

Not long after that Jimmy Breslin started writing an extraordinary local column for my own paper, the *Herald Tribune*. Breslin came to the *Herald Tribune* in 1963 from out of nowhere, which is to say he had written a hundred or so articles for magazines like *True, Life,* and *Sports Illustrated.* Naturally he was virtually unknown. At that time knocking your brains out as a free-lance writer for popular magazines was a guaranteed way to stay anonymous.* Breslin caught the attention of the *Herald Tribune*'s publisher, Jock Whitney, through his book about the New York Mets called *Can't Anybody Here Play This Game?*

---

* Richard Gehman once told me about running into Abe Rosenthal (now managing editor of the *New York Times*) shortly after Rosenthal had won the Pulitzer Prize for his coverage of the Polish rebellion of 1960. Gehman congratulated him profusely, whereupon Rosenthal, by way of being polite, asked Gehman if he were still writing for magazines. Gehman stared at him. He was dumbfounded. "Still writing?" At that moment he had sixteen articles on newsstands, in magazines ranging from men's adventures to the *Atlantic Monthly*.

The *Herald Tribune* hired Breslin to do a "bright" local column to help offset some of the heavy lumber on the editorial page, paralyzing snoremongers like Walter Lippmann and Joseph Alsop. Newspaper columns had become a classic illustration of the theory that organizations tend to promote people up to their levels of incompetence. The usual practice was to give a man a column as a reward for outstanding service as a reporter. That way they could lose a good reporter and gain a bad writer. The archetypical newspaper columnist was Lippmann. For 35 years Lippmann seemed to do nothing more than ingest the *Times* every morning, turn it over in his ponderous cud for a few days, and then methodically egest it in the form of a drop of mush on the foreheads of several hundred thousand readers of other newspapers in the days thereafter. The only form of reporting that I remember Lippmann going for was the occasional red-carpet visit to a head of state, during which he had the opportunity of sitting on braided chairs in wainscotted offices and swallowing the exalted one's official lies in person instead of reading them in the *Times*. I don't mean to single out Lippmann, however. He was only doing what was expected of him . . .

In any case, Breslin made a revolutionary discovery. He made the discovery that it was feasible for a columnist to leave the building, go outside and do reporting on his own, actual legwork. Breslin would go up to the city editor and ask what stories and assignments were coming up, choose one, go out, leave the building, cover the story as a reporter, and write about it in his column. If the story were big enough, his column would start on page one instead of inside. As obvious as this system may sound, it was unheard of among newspaper columnists, whether local or national. If possible, local columnists are even more pathetic. They usually start out full of juice, sounding like terrific boulevardiers and raconteurs, retailing in print all the marvelous *mots* and anecdotes they have been dribbling away over lunch for the past few years. After eight or ten weeks, however, they start to dry up. You can see the poor bastards floundering and gasping. They're dying of thirst. They're out of material. They start writing about funny things that happened around the house the other day, homey one-liners that the Better Half or the Avon lady got off, or some fascinating book or article that started them thinking, or else something they saw on the TV. Thank God for the TV! Without television shows to cannibalize, half of these people would be lost, utterly catatonic. Pretty soon you can almost see it, the tubercular blue of the 23-inch screen, radiating from their prose. Anytime you see a columnist trying to squeeze material out of his house, articles, books, or the television set, you've got a starving soul on your hands . . . You should send him a basket . . .

But Breslin worked like a Turk. He would be out all day covering a story, come back in at 4 p.m. or so and sit down at a desk in the middle of the city room. It was quite a show. He was a good-looking Irishman with a lot of black hair and a great wrestler's gut. When he sat down at his typewriter he hunched himself over into a shape like a bowling ball. He would start drinking coffee and smoking cigarettes until vapor started drifting off his body. He looked like a bowling ball fueled with liquid oxygen. Thus fired up, he would start typing. I've never seen a man who could write so well against a daily deadline. I particularly remember one story he wrote about the sentencing, on a charge of extortion, of a Teamster boss named Anthony Provenzano. Early in the story Breslin set up the image of the sun coming through the moldering old windows of the Federal courthouse and exploding off Provenzano's diamond pinky ring:

"It did not seem like a bad morning at all. The boss, Tony Provenzano, who is one of the biggest men in the Teamsters Union, walked up and down the corridor outside of this Federal courtroom in Newark and he had a little smile on his face and he kept flicking a white cigarette holder around.

"'Today is the kind of a day for fishing,' Tony was saying. 'We ought to go out and get some fluke.'

"Then he spread his legs a little and went at this big guy named Jack, who had on a gray suit. Tony stuck out his left hand so he could throw a hook at this guy Jack. The big diamond ring on Tony's pinky flashed in the light coming through the tall windows of the corridor. Then Tony shifted and hit Jack with a right hand on the shoulder.

"'Always the shoulder,' one of the guys in the corridor laughed. 'Tony is always banging Jack on the shoulder.'"

The story went on in that vein with Provenzano's Jersey courtiers circling around him and fawning, while the sun explodes off his pinky ring. Inside the courtroom itself, however, Provenzano starts getting his. The judge starts lecturing him, and the sweat starts breaking out on Provenzano's upper lip. Then the judge sentences him to seven years, and Provenzano starts twisting his pinky ring finger with his right hand. Then Breslin wraps it up with a scene in a cafeteria where the young prosecutor who worked the case is eating fried scallops and fruit salad off a tray.

"Nothing on his hand flashed. The guy who sunk Tony Pro doesn't even have a diamond ring on his pinky."

Well—all right! Say what you will! There it was, a short story, complete with symbolism, in fact, and yet true-life, as they say, about something that happened today, and you could pick it up on the newsstand by 11 tonight for a dime . . .

Breslin's work stirred up a certain vague resentment among both journalists and literati during the first year or two of his column—vague, because they never fully understood what he was doing . . .

only that in some vile Low Rent way the man's output was *literary*. Among literary intellectuals you would hear Breslin referred to as "a cop who writes" or "Runyon on welfare." These weren't even intelligent insults, however, because they dealt with Breslin's attitude, which seemed to be that of the cab-driver with his cap tilted over one eye. A crucial part of Breslin's work they didn't seem to be conscious of at all: namely, the reporting he did. Breslin made it a practice to arrive on the scene long before the main event in order to gather the off-camera material, the byplay in the make-up room, that would enable him to create character. It was part of his *modus operandi* to gather "novelistic" details, the rings, the perspiration, the jabs on the shoulder, and he did it more skillfully than most novelists.

Literary people were oblivious to this side of the New Journalism, because it is one of the unconscious assumptions of modern criticism that the raw material is simply "there." It is the "given." The idea is: Given such-and-such a body of material, what has the artist done with it? The crucial part that reporting plays in all story-telling, whether in novels, films, or non-fiction, is something that is not so much ignored as simply not comprehended. The modern notion of art is an essentially religious or magical one in which the artist is viewed as a holy beast who in some way, big or small, receives flashes from the godhead, which is known as creativity. The material is merely his clay, his palette . . . Even the obvious relationship between reporting and the major novels—one has only to think of Balzac, Dickens, Gogol, Tolstoy, Dostoyevsky and, in fact, Joyce—is something that literary historians deal with only in a biographical sense. It took the New Journalism to bring this strange matter of reporting into the foreground.

But these were all matters that came up later. I don't remember a soul talking about them at the time. I certainly didn't. In the spring of 1963 I made my own entry into this new arena, although without meaning to. I have already described (in the introduction to *The Kandy-Kolored Tangerine-Flake Streamline Baby*) the odd circumstances under which I happened to write my first magazine article—"There Goes (Varoom! Varoom!) That Kandy-Kolored (Thphhhhhh!) Tangerine-Flake Streamline Baby (Rahghhh!) Around the Bend (Brummmm mmmmmmmmmmmmmm) . . . . . ."—in the form of what I thought was merely a memorandum to the managing editor of *Esquire*. This article was by no means like a short story, despite the use of scenes and dialogue. I wasn't thinking about that at all. It is hard to say what it was like. It was a garage sale, that piece . . . vignettes, odds and ends of scholarship, bits of memories, short bursts of sociology, apostrophes, epithets, moans, cackles, anything that came into my head, much of it thrown together in a rough and awkward way. Its virtue was precisely in showing me the possibility of there being something "new" in journalism. What interested me was not simply the discovery that it was possible to write accurate non-fiction with techniques usually associated with novels and short stories. It was that—plus. It was the discovery that it was possible in non-fiction, in journalism, to use any literary device, from the traditional dialogisms of the essay to stream-of-consciousness, and to use many different kinds simultaneously, or within a relatively short space . . . to excite the reader both intellectually and emotionally. I am not laying all those gladiolas on that rather curious first article of mine, you understand. I'm only talking about what it suggested to me.

I soon had the chance to explore every possibility I could think of. The *Herald Tribune* assigned me split duties, like a utility infielder's. Two days a week I was supposed to work for the city desk as a general assignment reporter, as usual. The other three days I was supposed to turn out a weekly piece of about 1,500 words for the *Herald Tribune*'s new Sunday supplement, which was called *New York*. At the same time, following the success of "There Goes (Varoom! Varoom!) That Kandy-Kolored (Thphhhhhh!) Tangerine-Flake Streamline Baby (Rahghhh!) Around the Bend (Brummmmmmmmmmmmmmm) . . . ."—I was also cranking out stories for *Esquire*. This setup was crazy enough to begin with. I can remember flying to Las Vegas on my two regular days off from the *Herald Tribune* to do a story for *Esquire*—"Las Vegas! ! ! !"—and winding up sitting on the edge of a white satin bed in a Hog-Stomping Baroque suite in a hotel on the Strip—in the decor known as Hog-Stomping Baroque there are 400-pound cut-glass chandeliers in the bathrooms—and picking up the phone and dictating to the stenographic battery of the *Trib* city desk the last third of a story on demolition derbies in Long Island for *New York*—"Clean Fun at River-head"—hoping to finish in time to meet a psychiatrist in a black silk mohair suit with brass buttons and a shawl collar, no lapels, one of the only two psychiatrists in Las Vegas County at that time, to take me to see the casualties of the Strip in the state mental ward out Charleston Boulevard. What made it crazier was that the piece about the demolition derbies was the last one I wrote that came anywhere close to being 1,500 words. After that they started climbing to 3,000, 4,000, 5,000, 6,000 words. Like Pascal, I was sorry, but I didn't have time to write short ones. In nine months in the latter part of 1963 and first half of 1964 I wrote three more long pieces for *Esquire* and twenty for *New York*. All of this was in addition to what I was writing as a reporter for the *Herald Tribune* city desk two days a week. The idea of a day off lost all meaning. I can remember being furious on Monday, November 25, 1963, because there were people I desperately needed to talk to, for some story or other, and I couldn't reach them because all the offices in New York seemed to be closed, every one. It was the day of President Kennedy's funeral. I remember staring at the television set . . . morosely, but for all the wrong reasons.

Yet in terms of experimenting in non-fiction, the way I worked at that point couldn't have been more ideal. I was writing mostly for *New York*, which, as I say, was a Sunday supplement. At that time, 1963 and 1964, Sunday supplements were close to being the lowest form of periodical. Their status was well below that of the ordinary daily newspaper, and only slightly above that of the morbidity press, sheets like the *National Enquirer* in its "I Left My Babies in the Deep Freeze" period. As a result, Sunday supplements had no traditions, no pretensions, no promises to live up to, not even any rules to speak of. They were brain candy, that was all. Readers felt no guilt whatsoever about laying them aside, throwing them away or not looking at them at all. I never felt the slightest hesitation about trying any device that might conceivably grab the reader a few seconds longer. I tried to yell right in his ear: *Stick around!* . . . Sunday supplements were no place for diffident souls. That was how I started playing around with the device of point-of-view.

For example, I once did a story about the girls in jail at the Women's House of Detention in Greenwich Village at Greenwich Avenue and the Avenue of the Americas, an intersection known as Nut Heaven. The girls used to yell down to boys on the street, to all the nice free funky Village groovies they saw walking around down there. They would yell every male first name they could think of— "Bob!" "Bill!" "Joe!" "Jack!" "Jimmy!" "Willie!" "Benny!"—until they hit the right name, and some poor fool would stop and look up and answer. Then they would suggest a lot of quaint anatomical impossibilities for the kid to perform on himself and start laughing like maniacs. I was there one night when they caught a boy who looked 21 named Harry. So I started the story with the girls yelling at him:

" 'Hai-ai-ai-ai-ai-ai-ai-ai-ai-ai-ai-ai-ai-ai-ai-ai-ai-ai-ai-ai-ai-ai-ai-ai-ai-ai-ai-ai-ai-ai-ai-ai-ai-ai-ai-ai-ai-ai-ai-ai-ai-ai-ai-ai-ai-ai-ai-ai-ai-ai-ai- ai-ai-ai-ai-aireeeeeeeeeeeeeeeeeeeee!' "

I looked at that. I liked it. I decided I would enjoy yelling at the little bastard myself. So I started lambasting him, too, in the next sentence:

"O, dear Sweet Harry, with your French gangster-movie bangs, your Ski Shop turtleneck sweater and your Army-Navy Store blue denim shirt over it, with your Bloomsbury corduroy pants you saw in the *Manchester Guardian* airmail edition and sent away for and your sly intellectual pigeon-toed libido roaming in Greenwich Village—that siren call really for you?"

Then I let the girls have another go at it:

" 'Hai-ai-ai-ai-ai-ai-ai-ai-ai-ai-ai-ai-ai-aireeeeeeeeeee!' "

Then I started in again, and so on. There was nothing subtle about such a device, which might be called the Hectoring Narrator. Quite the opposite. That was precisely why I liked it. I liked the idea of starting off a story by letting the reader, via the narrator, talk to the characters, hector them, insult them, prod them with irony or condescension, or whatever. Why should the reader be expected to just lie flat and let these people come tromping through as if his mind were a subway turnstile? But I was democratic about it, I was. Sometimes I would put myself into the story and make sport of me. I would be "the man in the brown Borsalino hat," a large fuzzy Italian fedora I wore at the time, or "the man in the Big Lunch tie." I would write about myself in the third person, usually as a puzzled onlooker or someone who was in the way, which was often the case. Once I even began a story about a vice I was also prone to, tailor-made clothes, as if someone else were the hectoring narrator . . . treating *me* in a flippant manner: "Real buttonholes. That's it! A man can take his thumb and forefinger and unbutton his sleeve at the wrist because this kind of suit has real buttonholes there. Tom, boy, it's terrible. Once you know about it, you start seeing it. All the time!" . . . and so on . . . anything to avoid coming on like the usual non-fiction narrator, with a hush in my voice, like a radio announcer at a tennis match.

The voice of the narrator, in fact, was one of the great problems in non-fiction writing. Most non-fiction writers, without knowing it, wrote in a century-old British tradition in which it was understood that the narrator shall assume a calm, cultivated and, in fact, genteel voice. The idea was that the narrator's own voice should be like the off-white or putty-colored walls that Syrie Maugham popularized in interior decoration . . . a "neutral background" against which bits of color would stand out. *Understatement* was the thing. You can't imagine what a positive word "understatement" was among both journalists and literati ten years ago. There is something to be said for the notion, of course, but the trouble was that by the early 1960s understatement had become an absolute pall. Readers were bored to tears without understanding why. When they came upon that pale beige tone, it began to signal to them, unconsciously, that a well-known bore was here again, "the journalist," a pedestrian mind, a phlegmatic spirit, a faded personality, and there was no way to get rid of the pallid little troll, short of ceasing to read. This had nothing to do with objectivity and subjectivity or taking a stand or "commitment"—it was a matter of personality, energy, drive, bravura . . . style, in a word . . . The standard non-fiction writer's voice was like the standard announcer's voice . . . a drag, a droning . . .

To avoid this I would try anything. For example, I wrote a story about Junior Johnson, a stock car racer from Ingle Hollow, North Carolina, who had learned to drive by running moonshine whiskey to

Charlotte and other distribution points. "There ain't no harder work in the world than making whiskey," Junior would say. "I don't know of any other business that compels you to get up at all times of night and go outdoors in the snow and everything else and work. H'it's the hardest way in the world to make a living, and I don't think anybody'd do it unless they had to." Now, as long as Junior Johnson was explaining the corn liquor industry, there was no problem, because (a) dialogue tends to be naturally attractive, or involving, to the reader; and (b) Johnson's Ingle Hollow lingo was unusual. But then I had to take over the explanation myself, in order to compress into a few paragraphs information that had come from several interviews. So . . . I decided I would rather talk in Ingle Hollow accents myself, since that seemed to go over all right. There is no law that says the narrator has to speak in beige or even New York journalese. So I picked up the explanation myself, as follows: "Working mash wouldn't wait for a man. It started coming to a head when it got ready to and a man had to be there to take it off, out there in the woods, in the brush, in the brambles, in the muck, in the snow. Wouldn't it have been something if you could have just set it all up inside a good old shed with a corrugated metal roof and order those parts like you want them and not have to smuggle all that copper and all that sugar and all that everything out here in the woods and be a coppersmith and a plumber and a cooper and a carpenter and a pack horse and every other goddamned thing God ever saw in the world, all at once.

"And live decent hours—Junior and his brothers, about two o'clock in the morning they'd head out to the stash, the place where the liquor was hidden after it was made . . ."

I was feigning the tones of an Ingle Hollow moonshiner, in order to create the illusion of seeing the action through the eyes of someone who was actually on the scene and involved in it, rather than a beige narrator. I began to think of this device as the *downstage voice*, as if characters downstage from the protagonist himself were talking.

I would do the same thing with descriptions. Rather than just come on as the broadcaster describing the big parade, I would shift as quickly as possible into the eye sockets, as it were, of the people in the story. Often I would shift the point of view in the middle of a paragraph or even a sentence. I began a story on Baby Jane Holzer, entitled "The Girl of the Year," as follows:

"Bangs manes bouffant beehives Beatle caps butter faces brush-on lashes decal eyes puffy sweaters French thrust bras flailing leather blue jeans stretch pants stretch jeans honeydew bottoms eclair shanks elf boots ballerinas Knight slippers, hundreds of them, these flaming little buds, bobbing and screaming, rocketing around inside the Academy of Music Theater underneath that vast old moldering cherub dome up there—aren't they super-marvelous!

" 'Aren't they super-marvelous!' says Baby Jane, and then: 'Hi, Isabel! Isabel! You want to sit backstage—with the Stones!'

"The show hasn't even started yet, the Rolling Stones aren't even on the stage, the place is full of a great shabby moldering dimness, and these flaming little buds.

"Girls are reeling this way and that way in the aisle and through their huge black decal eyes, sagging with Tiger Tongue Lick Me brush-on eyelashes and black appliqués, sagging like display-window Christmas trees, they keep staring at—her—Baby Jane—on the aisle."

As you see, the opening paragraph is a rush of Groovy clothes ending with the phrase "—aren't they super-marvelous!" With this phrase I shifted into the point-of-view of Baby Jane, looking through her eyes at the young girls, "the flaming little buds," who are running around the theater. The description continues through Jane's eyes until the phrase "they keep staring at—her—Baby Jane," whereupon the point-of-view shifts to the young girls, and the reader is suddenly looking through *their* eyes at Baby Jane: "What the hell is this? She is gorgeous in the most outrageous way. Her hair rises up from her head in a huge hairy corona, a huge tan mane around a narrow face and two eyes opened—swock!—like umbrellas, with all that hair flowing down over a coat made of . . . *zebra!* Those motherless stripes! Oh, damn! Here she is with her friends, looking like some kind of queen bee for all flaming little buds everywhere."

In fact, three points-of-view are used in that rather short passage, the point-of-view of the subject (Baby Jane), the point-of-view of the people watching her (the "flaming little buds"), and my own. I switched back and forth between points-of-view continually, and often abruptly, in many articles I wrote in 1963, 1964, and 1965. Eventually a reviewer called me a "chameleon" who instantly took on the coloration of whomever he was writing about. He meant it negatively. I took it as a great compliment. A chameleon . . . but precisely!

Sometimes I used point-of-view in the Jamesian sense in which fiction writers understand it, entering directly into the mind of a character, experiencing the world through his central nervous system throughout a given scene. Writing about Phil Spector ("The First Tycoon of Teen"), I began the article not only inside his mind but with a virtual stream of consciousness. One of the news magazines apparently regarded my Spector story as an improbable feat, because they interviewed him and asked him if he didn't think this passage was merely a fiction that appropriated his name. Spector said that, in fact, he found it quite accurate. This should have come as no surprise, since every detail in the passage was taken from a long interview with Spector about exactly how he had felt at the time:

"All these raindrops are *high* or something. They don't roll down the window, they come straight back, toward the tail, wobbling, like all those Mr. Cool snowheads walking on mattresses. The plane is taxiing out toward the runway to take off, and this stupid infarcted water wobbles, sideways, across the window. Phil Spector, 23 years old, the rock and roll magnate, producer of Phillies Records, America's first teen-age tycoon, watches . . . this watery pathology . . . it is *sick, fatal.* He tightens his seat belt over his bowels . . . A hum rises inside the plane, a shot of air comes shooting through the vent over some-body's seat, some ass turns on a cone of light, there is a sign stuck out by the runway, a mad, cryptic, insane instruction to the pilot— Runway 4, Are Cylinder Laps Mainside DOWN?—and beyond, dis-oriented crop rows of sulphur blue lights, like the lights on top of a New Jersey toothpaste factory, only spreading on and on in sulphur blue rows over Los Angeles County. It is . . . disoriented. Schizoid raindrops. The plane breaks in two on takeoff and everybody in the front half comes rushing toward Phil Spector in a gush of bodies in a thick orange—*napalm!* No, it happens aloft; there is a long rip in the side of the plane, it just rips, he can see the top ripping, folding back in sick curds, like a sick Dali egg, and Phil Spector goes sailing through the rip, dark, freezing. And the engine, it is *reedy—*

"Miss!"

"A stewardess is walking to the back to buckle herself in for the takeoff. The plane is moving, the jets are revving. Under a Lifebuoy blue skirt, her fireproof legs are clicking out of her Pinki-Kinki-Panti Fantasy—"

I had the feeling, rightly or wrongly, that I was doing things no one had ever done before in journalism. I used to try to imagine the feeling readers must have had upon finding all this carrying on and cutting up in a Sunday supplement. I liked that idea. I had no sense of being a part of any normal journalistic or literary environment. Later I read the English critic John Bayley's yearnings for an age when writers had Pushkin's sense of "looking at all things afresh," as if for the first time, without the constant intimidation of being aware of what other writers have already done. In the mid-1960s that was exactly the feeling I had.

I'm sure that others who were experimenting with magazine ar-ticles, such as Talese, began to feel the same way. We were moving beyond the conventional limits of journalism, but not merely in terms of technique. The kind of reporting we were doing struck us as far more ambitious, too. It was more intense, more detailed, and certainly more time-consuming than anything that newspaper or magazine re-porters, including investigative reporters, were accustomed to. We de-veloped the habit of staying with the people we were writing about for days at a time, weeks in some cases. We had to gather all the material the conventional journalist was after—and then keep going. It seemed all-important to *be there* when dramatic scenes took place, to get the dialogue, the gestures, the facial expressions, the details of the environment. The idea was to give the full objective description, plus something that readers had always had to go to novels and short stories for: namely, the subjective or emotional life of the characters. That was why it was so ironic when both the journalistic and literary old guards began to attack this new journalism as "impressionistic." The most important things we attempted in terms of technique depended upon a depth of information that had never been demanded in newspaper work. Only through the most searching forms of reporting was it possible, in non-fiction, to use whole scenes, extended dialogue, point-of-view, and interior monologue. Eventually I, and others, would be accused of "entering people's minds" . . . But exactly! I figured that was one more doorbell a reporter had to push.

Most of the people who eventually wrote about my style, however, tended to concentrate on certain mannerisms, the lavish use of dots, dashes, exclamation points, italics, and occasionally punctuation that never existed before :::::::::: and of interjections, shouts, nonsense words, onomatopoeia, mimesis, pleonasms, the continual use of the historical present, and so on. This was natural enough, because many of these devices stood out even before one had read a word. The typography actually *looked* different. Referring to my use of italics and exclamation points, one critic observed, with scorn, that my work looked like something out of Queen Victoria's childhood diary. Queen Victoria's childhood diaries are, in fact, quite readable; even charming. One has only to compare them with the miles of official prose she laid on the English people during the course of her Palmerston, Wellington, Gladstone reign to see the point I'm making. I found a great many pieces of punctuation and typography lying around dormant when I came along—and I must say I had a good time using them. I figured it was time someone violated what Orwell called "the Geneva conventions of the mind" . . . a protocol that had kept journalism and non-fiction generally (and novels) in such a tedious bind for so long. I found that things like exclamation points, italics, and abrupt shifts (dashes) and syncopations (dots) helped to give the illusion not only of a person talking but of a person thinking. I used to enjoy using dots where they would be least expected, not at the end of a sentence but in the middle, creating the effect . . . of a skipped beat. It seemed to me the mind reacted—*first!* . . . in dots, dashes, and exclamation points, then rationalized, drew up a brief, with periods.

I soon found that people loved to parody my style. By 1966 the parodies began to come in a rush. I must say I read them all. I suppose it's because at the heart of every parody there is a little gold ball of tribute (a notion that led to an amazing hassle in 1965, as we shall see). Even hostile parodies admit from the start that the target has a distinct voice.

It is not very often that one comes across a new style, period. And if a new style were created not via the novel, or the short story, or poetry, but via journalism—I suppose that would seem extraordinary. It was probably that idea—more than any specific devices, such as using scenes and dialogue in a "novelistic" fashion—that began to give me very grand ideas about a new journalism. As I saw it, if a new literary style could originate in journalism, then it stood to reason that journalism could aspire to more than mere emulation of those aging giants, the novelists.

In any case, a . . . New Journalism . . . was in the air. "In the air," as I say it; it was not something that anyone took note of in print at the time, so far as I can remember. I have no idea who coined the term the New Journalism or when it was coined. I have never even liked the term. Any movement, group, party, program, philosophy or theory that goes under a name with "new" in it is just begging for trouble, of course. But it is the term that eventually caught on. At the time, the mid-1960s, one was aware only that there was some sort of new *artistic* excitement in journalism.

I knew nothing about what history, if any, lay behind it. I was only aware of what certain writers were doing at *Esquire,* Thomas B. Morgan, Brock Brower, Terry Southern and, above all, Gay Talese . . . Even a couple of established novelists were in on it, Norman Mailer and James Baldwin, writing non-fiction for *Esquire* . . . and, of course, the writers on my own Sunday supplement, *New York,* chiefly Jimmy Breslin, but also Robert Christgau, Doon Arbus, Gail Sheehy, Tom Gallagher, Robert Benton and David Newman. Magazine writers were also beginning to provide the only portraits of the bizarre new styles of life that were cropping up in the 1960s (novelists were strangely shy about dealing with them, as it developed). I was turning out articles as fast as I could write and checking out all these people to see what new spins they had come up with. I was completely wrapped up in . . . this new thing that was in the air. It was a regular little league we had going.

But one thing never crossed my mind. I never had the slightest idea that what we were doing might have an impact on the literary world, or, in fact, on any sphere outside the small world of feature journalism. The first direct knowledge I had of the stir the New Journalism was creating in literary circles was when I read an article in the June, 1966, *Atlantic* by Dan Wakefield, entitled "The Personal Voice and the Impersonal Eye." The gist of this piece was that for the first time in anybody's memory, for the first time since the turn of the century when the occasional Nobel Prize was thrown to writers like

Theodor Mommsen, people in the literary world were beginning to talk about non-fiction as a serious artistic form. Wakefield attributed this remarkable change to two books: *In Cold Blood,* by Truman Capote, and *The Kandy-Kolored Tangerine-Flake Streamline Baby.*

But June, 1966, was actually pretty far down the line. The new form had already been paid a higher tribute, although I didn't comprehend that at the time. Namely, literary tribute in its cash forms: bitterness, envy, and resentment. This had all occurred during a curious interlude known as the *New Yorker* affair.

---

12. Incident

COUNTEE CULLEN

Once riding in Old Baltimore,
    Heart-filled, head-filled with glee,
I saw a Baltimorean
    Keep looking straight at me.

Now I was eight and very small,
    And he was no whit bigger,
And so I smiled, but he poked out
    His tongue and called me, "Nigger."

I saw the whole of Baltimore
    From May until December;
Of all the things that happened there
    That's all that I remember.

13. Sitting Bull Speaks

CHARLES A. EASTMAN
(Ohiyesa)

Sitting Bull (c. 1831–1890), the most famous chief of the Sioux, was killed by Indian police and U.S. soldiers on December 15, 1890, fourteen years after his people had defeated Custer at the Little Bighorn. During those intervening years, Sitting Bull had led his people to Canada; then as famine and disease stalked the Sioux, he had returned, surrendered, and settled at Standing Rock reservation. He consistently resisted the sale of tribal lands to the whites, and it was during the general unease surrounding the revival of the Ghost Dance religion in 1889–1890 that he was slain.

In 1866, the Sioux chiefs held council on the Powder River. They had granted white settlers rights of transit through Sioux territory on their way to Oregon. But then the Federal Government had built forts to protect the passing settlers. Sitting Bull delivered the following speech at this council, which decided to wipe out all the forts along the Oregon Trail in Sioux territory, beginning with Fort Phil Kearney, the farthest west. Crazy Horse led the attack, killing 80 men under Captain Fetterman, lured outside the fort, and then annihilating the fort. In 1867, the Federal Government evacuated the forts as part of an agreement with the Sioux chief Red Cloud.

Charles A. Eastman, who prepared the following translation, was a Sioux, named Ohiyesa.

BEHOLD, MY FRIENDS, the spring is come; the earth has gladly received the embraces of the sun, and we shall soon see the results of their love! Every seed is awakened, and all animal life. It is through this mysterious power that we too have our being, and we therefore yield to our neighbors, even to our animal neighbors, the same right as ourselves to inhabit this vast land.

Yet hear me, friends! we have now to deal with another people, small and feeble when our forefathers first met with them, but now great and overbearing. Strangely enough, they have a mind to till the soil, and the love of possessions is a disease in them. These people have made many rules that the rich may break, but the poor may not! They have a religion in which the poor worship, but the rich will not! They even take tithes of the poor and weak to support the rich and those who rule. They claim this mother of ours, the Earth, for their own use, and fence their neighbors away from her, and deface her with their buildings and their refuse. They compel her to produce out of season, and when sterile she is made to take medicine in order to produce again. All this is sacrilege.

This nation is like a spring freshet; it overruns its banks and destroys all who are in its path. We cannot dwell side by side. Only seven years ago we made a treaty by which we were assured that the buffalo country should be left to us forever. Now they threaten to take that from us also. My brothers, shall we submit? or shall we say to them: "First kill me, before you take possession of my fatherland!"

Suggestions for Writing

1. Write a commentary on one of the selections in this section. Use Cooley's remarks as a guide. Does the writer you discuss express a sense of character, of the reality of his or her voice?

2. Write an essay that is a variant on Greer or White. Is there a stereotype of the male, do you think, or a typical "dream of the American woman"?

3. How do you imagine the situations that gave rise to Brooks's poem "We real cool" or Cullen's "Incident"? Can you convey the setting, as you imagine it, for one of those poems?

4. Insofar as the set of poems by Simpson, Padgett, Frost, Pound, and Cullen are about seeing and knowing women, do those poets exemplify the ideas of White or Greer? Explain.

5. Write a short paper discussing the imagery of one of these poems, relating the choice of images to the tone of voice the poem conveys.

6. Compare the voices of Baldwin and Wolfe. Baldwin describes a "social and moral bankruptcy . . . of the bitterest, most terrifying kind." Does his tone reflect that bitterness? Would Wolfe's?

7. Write an account of your neighborhood as Baldwin does of his.

8. Write about some contemporary individual whom you and your audience would find interesting. Conceive of it as a feature story for a paper. Interview your subject if at all possible. Let Wolfe's style influence you if you find that possibility interesting.

II.
Description

Reports Through Space and Time

DESCRIPTION conveys the writer's subject, as his voice conveys himself. Description conveys the reality of the thing seen, enhanced by our sense that a real person is sharing this vision with us. His urgency to fill in the details of his impression convinces us of its significance. Description, of course, is interpretation, inevitably partial, even biased. Description, therefore, is a first step toward argument, for, again, this detailed urgency persuades us to accept his report.

In the first two selections, swift little sketches of related impressions flow in an almost directly sensory series. Toperoff's subject is Muhammad Ali; Faulkner's is Japan. Neither writer pins his subject down with thorough and exhausting descriptions. Both subjects are too complex for that. Toperoff cannot really know Ali any more than Faulkner can know Japan. Their rapid impressions attest to the complexity of their subjects, as well as to their subjects' freshness for them. For his subject, each writer sketches an array of attitudes or versions, which emanate from a center that eludes his grasp. Each writer suggests that center without pinning it down. Consider the tactfulness and wisdom of their strategy. You might also compare the implied argument that Delhi, however "open," is a city no outsider ever knows.

White and Fitzgerald sketch things differently. Each writer lingers over a single view—a day in spring, a street in St. Paul—and tries to pin it down. White amplifies a moment in Time. Fitzgerald details a tour through Space, as, in his imagination, he drives down a hometown street. Notice how Graves augments this special strategy, and Twain also, although his journey is more complex, ending in descriptive anecdote. Does his little story fit?

Time or Space also organizes the remaining three essays. Jhabvala lays Delhi geographically before us, showing us its spaces. Bardach and Seager follow changes through time. With Jhabvala, we sense forcefully again the writer's own voice. How would you describe her tone? What are her judgments as she describes the garden party and selects her details? What is her implied argumentative point? And Bardach's? And Hughes's? How much of their persuasiveness comes from their ability to describe? And, finally, watch Roethke root the tiny details of his poems and feelings in the loam of his father's greenhouse, making small matters tremendous.

14. Cassius

SAM TOPEROFF

Toperoff teaches at Hofstra University and was finishing, in 1973, his second novel, *Porcupine-Man*. *All the Advantages,* an autobiography, appeared in 1967.

I

A RICKETY SECOND-FLOOR GYM over the toughest poolroom in the colored section of Louisville. In the center of the quivering plywood floor is a boxing ring, its stanchions loose, its tattered ropes drooping sadly. A purple-colored man in black trunks, squat, with a shaved head and broad shoulders, hooks the heavy bag in his muscular left arm and throws thudding rights down and up the long bag. He grunts with each blow. A rangy man in sweat pants and shower clogs peppers the light bag, an achievement of coordination since the bag is no longer a true pear-shape. Two young boys skip rope in the corner; a tall and slender third boy, Cassius, throws darting combinations toward a lavender shadow in the streaked mirror.

A monkey-faced man—slits for eyes, big lobed ears—pulls the cord that rings a bell at three- and one-minute intervals. He is known only as "Greer," and he checks himself on an old wristwatch that has no wristband. The red second-hand sticks for three beats at the "five"; Greer reckons the extra seconds will help the fighters' wind.

Clang!

"Ready, you two?" Cassius leaves a shattering barrage in the mirror. The bald man throws a vicious final right-hand that lifts him off the ground. He moves to the ring. In the ring he places his fists on his chest and turns toward the far corner and the boy. Cassius' white basketball sneakers dance joyfully; his red plaid bathing suit is tight and climbing fast. And he is afraid.

"It could be murder," says Jake, a wizened brown man with no teeth.

"Kid cain't hit, an' his neck's too long," announces Greer. He checks his watch and pulls the cord.

The white sneakers dance forward. His leather gloves dart and slash. The bald man bends low at the waist under the misdirected barrage, hooks a left arm about the boy's waist, and smashes a right against the boy's temple which burns across the eyes and the bridge of the nose. Cassius starts to cry. Another right goes into his ribs. And Cassius falls to his knees.

Greer pulls the cord before the second hand comes off the "five."

II

"We'll be ready to go on the air in a few minutes," says the ex-shoe salesman, a smooth operator who has made interviewing sports figures on TV an adventure in provocation. He really considers his ability to ask outrageous questions a genuine talent. This will be the second of three interviews with Cassius. "Ready?"

The men are sitting on pale-blue plastic chairs that swivel easily. Cassius is excited, his eyes widen—circles within the larger facial circle within the roundness of the television lights. His face had been dusted, but rivulets of sweat are pushing down through the powder. A slight pomade sheen is on his hair. His body is full and lean at the same time. " 'Course ah'm ready."

"Thirty seconds." The red hand on the large wall clock sweeps upward.

Cassius sits with legs extended, heels locked into the thick blue carpet, toes pointed upward. He swivels back and forth in choppy arcs. "Now, how we gonna work this one? Am ah gonna bull-sheet you or are you gonna bull-sheet me?"

III

There is some criticism of Cassius in Rome in 1960. He is seen by some as an American, rather than as the eighteen-year-old boy who has sliced his way through the opposition in the Olympic boxing tournament as easy as watermelon. In his final three-round bout with Pietrzykowski, a solid Pole, some in the crowd accuse him of holding and hitting, but Cassius is too fast to be caught at it by the referee.

His speed soon confuses the Pole. Each round Cassius is quicker. He moves in, hits, grabs, hits, moves away. The Pole throws a desperate roundhouse right at nothing in particular. Cassius is back in—hit, grab, hit—and away again. In the third round the Pole is totally helpless. He looks stupidly to his corner for direction. Cassius stings and stings and stings—he is wonderful today.

Cassius is awarded the gold medal. He stands tall and proud to the national anthem. On his chest "U.S.A."

IV

Darkness pierced rhythmically by a flashing red light.

A police officer, his face not the predictable fat Southern sausage, but rather thin and pale and well-shaped, asks politely, "Can ah please see your license?" Nothing on his face looks to be evil; no mean curl to the lip, no cruelty in the dark eyes, none of that stuff.

Ali, dressed expensively in a dark suit of Thai silk, produces a license that has expired ten months earlier up in Kentucky. The flashlight scans the document. Ali looks coolly in the rear-view mirror. In the moist dark foliage that begins just beyond the shoulder of the road an insect riot is taking place.

"Registration."

There is none. Ali looks in the glove compartment, hoping to avoid a scene. The two men with him are each over thirty and have registrations for revolvers, but now they are unarmed. They may be brothers. Their similar eyes avert the policeman's face.

"The car is what you'd call borrowed. An' the registration jus' ain't here right now."

"You know I saw your last fight on the teevee, an' I just wants to say it don't matter a lick to me what you calls yourself, you're the goddamned best I ever have seen. An' I saw Joe Louis when he was in his prime."

"Ahmad," the champ says pleasantly. And one of the men produces an 8-by-10 glossy photograph of the champ throwing a jab, perfectly balanced and poised to follow the punch with a number of possible combinations.

V

Cassius was not yet a stylist when he met Joe Liebling, who was. Liebling saw the twenty-year-old professional work-out at the West Twenty-eighth Street Public Gym and Bath. "He can't take anyone out with one punch, but he can sting like a bee for ten rounds," was Liebling's preliminary report.

The garden is half-empty and papered with nonpayers to look good on the television. Sonny Banks is a 5-to-1 underdog from Detroit. Cassius has never seen him but has predicted in verse an easy victory. And bettors who have seen neither man have decided to believe him.

Banks hits Cassius with a rising left hook in the first round and dumps him. No slip. A clean knockdown. Cassius is up almost immediately but has to take a mandatory "eight" count from Ruby Goldstein, the referee. Cassius nods to his corner, which reassures the worried crowd.

He moves forward deliberately. He sticks, sticks, crosses, double shuffles, sticks, sticks. He is clearly out of trouble. Early in the fourth round, Goldstein stops the fight; Banks' face is a bloody mess.

The Poet comments on being knocked down:

> You got to be burned
> Before you can be learned.

VI

The students like him. Many of them had not liked him; others only thought that they should not. But now, with him standing there, true and tall and earnest and brown behind a rostrum with the school's crest—*Logos Vincit Omnia*—they like him in spite of themselves.

This is his first speech to white students, and he is very nervous. Repeatedly he flicks at an imaginary insect or a hair that appears to be near the corner of his left eye. He is not a clown. He is not a fool. They say that he is no longer champion of the world.

He will talk about Black Separatism. He does not smile or wave or bounce when he is introduced. Then the high-pitched, vibrant voice. They realize immediately that it has not been heard for a long time. Now, instead of the doggerel of victory, it pipes the testimony of a witness to the wonders of the great Elijah Muhammad. It is the testimony of a true believer, of a boy who has walked with Him and has talked with Him. His Catholic audience would rather hear how he felled the Big Bear.

He warms to his subject. His eyes become even more intense. He flicks at the corner of his left eye. "The lamb," he announces, "does not lie down with the wolf. He'd be a fool if he did. Some things was made to be kept separate. Even a child can see that. An' a black man would be a fool to trust a white man. He'd tear him up just like the wolf would to the lamb. In fact, he has been tearin' him up just like a wolf for four hundred years."

He pulls out a handkerchief and mops his brow. "Here come Mr. Castro and Mr. Khrushchev." The sentence is thrown like a jab-cross combination. " 'Hey, Mr. Castro, what's your nationality?'

" 'Ah'm a Cuban.'

" 'Hey there, Mr. Khrushchev, what's your nationality?'

" 'Ah'm a Russian.'

"An' Mr. DeGaulle, he's French. An' Mr. Nasser, he's Egyptian. Now here come Mr. George Lincoln Washington the Third. 'Hey there, Mr. Washington, now what's *your* nationality?'

" 'Why ah'm a NEE-GROW.' " The eyes become saucers. "Why, he ain't nothin'—he's a NEE-GROW. He ain't even a man; every real man has got a place that he can belong to."

VII

Hope, this time, is a Canadian—(nationality doesn't really matter where color is concerned)—very tough, and except for his whiteness a real ham-and-egger. But they say he fights like Marciano; they mean that he is white like Marciano.

Often it is hard to tell what is in Ali's mind. He sits on a stool in his corner; red welts mar his moist golden-brown body.

His trainer screams: "What the hell are you tryin' to pull, for Christ's sake?"

Ali had fought the first round of a championship fight and has not offered a punch. Furthermore, he has actually yielded up his body to the white onslaught, such as it was. It does not hurt as much as he had imagined.

Some people in a huge theater in New York, seeing the fuzzy outlines of the fighters, think they are seeing the beginning of a remarkable white upset. They had bet on "OO" and backed it up with State Lottery tickets. Certainly they do not know what is in Ali's mind.

"I hope you're satisfied. Whatever you're trying to prove. But I've seen times when . . ." The trainer fumbles with the water bottle. ". . . a guy like this gets off good and then begins to believe in himself.

"If you do it again this round, it may be too late. You may never be able to get started."

"Ah am started."

The buzzer rings. Ten seconds. They leave him. In his complex mind he considers alternatives, for only he knows his true worth. Only he knows what it will take to shut them up.

They have said that Cassius could not take a punch to the body.

He pushes in his mouth-piece. The seconds tick inexorably.

VIII

The statement to the press is read implacably by the Publicity Officer, Lt. Col. "Iron" Mike Pidgeon, a red-faced man recently returned from public relations duty in Saigon. The voice has only a trace of the twang that was forged in his child-years in Waycross, Georgia. His words: "During the administration of the oath, when the inductees were asked to take one step forward, Mr. Clay—or Mr. Ali, as he prefers to be called—refused, and at that moment he became liable to prosecution for violation of the Selective Service Act. That is all I can tell you gentlemen at this time. Thank you very much."

"Where is he now? Has he been placed under arrest?"

"I'm sorry. I can tell you nothing further at this time. I'm sure Mr. Clay will have his own statement to make to the press. I'd suggest you ask him any questions you may have when he makes his statement."

"Has he been formally charged with anything by the Army?"

"As I said, by refusing to step forward he has made himself liable to prosecution for violation of . . ."

"Where is he now?"

II. Description:
Reports Through Space and Time

"As I said . . ."

"This is Ted Bean, and I'm on the street behind the Federal Building speaking to some of the brand-new inductees who are out here waiting for the bus that will take them out to the airport, and from there to Fort Hood and Basic Training. And this young man was standing next to Muhammad Ali when the oath was administered. What's your name, son?"
"Otis Williams."
"Mr. Williams—our camera is up there—what did Cassius do when the oath was administered?"
"Nothin'."
"Did he refuse to salute?"
"There wasn't no salute. You just raise your hand."
"Did he refuse to do that?"
"Uh huh. An' he didn't step forward neither."
"What do you think of his actions?"
"What do you mean, what do I think?"
"I mean, do you approve of his actions?"
"It ain't up to me."
"Well—I guess I ought to call you *Private* Williams—good luck to you in your Army career."
Otis Williams remembers him standing serene and unspoiled in the auditorium. "Thanks."

IX

In 1909 Jack Johnson fights Stanislaus Kiecal, the middle-weight champion, a young man of Polish descent who calls himself Stanley Ketchel, the Michigan Assassin. A terrific hitter. Ketchel gives away thirty-five pounds. The two men hate each other. Johnson is carrying Ketchel so that he can hurt him. In the twelfth round a Ketchel punch puts Johnson down, but the black man is up immediately. He comes back flailing—a blow on the top of Ketchel's head knocks him out instantly.

In 1910 Jack Johnson beats Jim Jeffries into submission for the heavyweight championship of the world in fifteen rounds at Reno, Nevada; the result worries white America. A freak occurrence?

An uppity nigger whipped a white man. He fools around with white women, and he says some things about America that . . . Well, he just has to be taught the lesson. It was all there for Ali to see. On the stage of the Alvin Theatre on Fifty-second Street. *The Great White Hope.** What Johnson did and said and how they taught him. Ali had never before been to a "legitimate" theater; his seat is too small, his legs are cramped against the seat in front of him. It is hot. He

* A play by Howard Sackler, based on Jack Johnson's life.

perspires. They all know he is here; they can even see him from the balcony. He feels their eyes.

The black man who plays Johnson had shaved his head and managed to look like him and move like him in the ring—he must have studied films. Ali has heard of Jack Johnson the fighter. Now he sees the years of exile, the threat of imprisonment. The Ring Record Book says only: "Johnson remained abroad for several years."

When it is over he goes backstage and thanks the man who played Jack Johnson. He signs his name a few times and answers some questions from reporters. He says that he is sorry about what happened to Jack Johnson.

X

That night, in his bed, he dreams that he is fighting himself.

15. Impressions of Japan

WILLIAM FAULKNER

Faulkner (1897–1962) won the 1949 Nobel Prize (awarded 1950) for his Yoknapatawpha novels, then numbering eighteen. He was born in Albany, Mississippi, but soon moved to Oxford, Mississippi, where his father owned a livery stable and managed the business office of the University of Mississippi, and where Faulkner lived the rest of his life. After a ground-borne stint with the Canadian Flying Corps (letting people assume not only that he could fly but that he had flown with the Royal Air Force in France) and a short trial as bookstore clerk in New York, he returned to odd jobs in Oxford (where he was amiably known as "Count No Count"), reading much, and writing poetry. Sherwood Anderson suggested he write a novel, and helped him get *Soldier's Pay* (1926) into print. He struck his Yoknapatawpha vein with his third novel, *Sartoris* (1929).

THE ENGINES are long since throttled back; the overcast sinks slowly upward with no semblance whatever of speed until suddenly you see the aircraft's shadow scudding the cottony hillocks;

and now speed has returned again, aircraft and shadow now rushing toward one another as toward one mutual headlong destruction.

To break through the overcast and fling that shadow once more down, upon an island. It looks like land, like any other air-found landfall, yet you know it is an island, almost as if you saw both sea-bound flanks of it at the same instant, like a transparent slide; an island more miraculously found in the waste of water than Wake or Guam even, since here is a civilization, an ordered and ancient homogeny of the human race.

        ❀   ❀   ❀

It is visible and audible, spoken and written too: a communication between man and man because humans speak it; you hear and see them. But to this one western ear and eye it means nothing because it resembles nothing which that western eye remembers; there is nothing to measure it against, nothing for memory and habit to say, 'Why, this looks like the word for house or home or happiness'; not even just cryptic but acrostic too, as though the splashed symbols of the characters held not mere communication but something urgent and important beyond just information, promising toward some ultimate wisdom or knowledge containing the secret of man's salvation. But then no more, because there is nothing for western memory to measure it against: so not the mind to listen but only the ear to hear that chirrup and skitter of syllables like the cries of birds in the mouths of children, like music in the mouths of women and young girls.

        ❀   ❀   ❀

The faces: Van Gogh and Manet would have loved them: that of the pilgrim with staff and pack and dusty with walking, mounting the stairs toward the Temple in the early sunlight; the Temple lay-brother or perhaps servant, his gown tucked about his thighs, squatting in the gate of the compound before beginning, or perhaps having already set it into motion, the day; that of the old woman vending peanuts beneath the gate for tourists to feed the pigeons with: a face worn with living and remembering, as though not one life had been long enough but rather every separate breath had been needed to etch into it all those fine and myriad lines; a face durable and now even a comfort to her, as if it had by now blotted up whatever had ever ached or sorrowed behind it, leaving it free now of the anguishes and the griefs and the enduring: here is one anyway who never read Faulkner and neither knows nor cares why he came to Japan nor gives one single damn what he thinks of Ernest Hemingway.

        ❀   ❀   ❀

He is much too busy to have time to bother about whether he is happy or not, quite dirty, perhaps five years old, pastless and apparently immune even from parents, playing in the gutter with the stub of a cigarette.

❊   ❊   ❊

The bowl of mountains containing the lake is as full of hard rapid air as the mouth of a wind-tunnel; for some time now we have been thinking that maybe it is already too late to take a reef in the main-sail: yet there it is. It is only a skiff yet to the western eye it is as invincibly and irrevocably alien as a Chinese junk, driven by a battered U.S. made outboard engine and containing a woman in a kimono beneath an open paper parasol such as would have excited no comment in a sunny reach of the English Thames, as fragile and invulnerable in the center of that hard blue bowl of wind as a butterfly in the eye of a typhoon.

❊   ❊   ❊

The geisha's mass of blue-black lacquered hair encloses the painted face like a helmet, surmounts, crowns the slender body's ordered and ritual posturing like a grenadier's bearskin busby, too heavy in appearance for that slender throat to bear, the painted fixed expressionless face immobile and immune also above the studied posturing: yet behind that painted and lifeless mask is something quick and alive and elfin: or more than elfin: puckish: or more than puckish even: sardonic and quizzical, a gift for comedy, and more: for burlesque and caricature: for a sly and vicious revenge on the race of men.

❊   ❊   ❊

Kimono. It covers her from throat to ankles; with a gesture as feminine as the placing of a flower or as female as the cradling of a child, the hands themselves can be concealed into the sleeves until there remains one unbroken chalice-shape of modesty proclaiming her femininity where nudity would merely parade her mammalian femaleness. A modesty which flaunts its own immodestness like the crimson rose tossed by no more than one white flick of hand, from the balcony window—modesty, than which there is nothing more immodest and which therefore is a woman's dearest possession; she should defend it with her life.

❊   ❊   ❊

Loyalty. In her western clothes, blouse and skirt, she is merely one more dumpy and nondescript young woman though in kimono at the deft balanced rapid tripping glide she too comes into her own share of that national heritage of feminine magic. Though she has more than that; she partakes of her share of that other quality which women have in this land which was not given them by what they have on: loyalty, constancy, fidelity, not for, but at least one hopes not without, reward. She does not speak my language nor I hers, yet in two days she knows my countryman's habit of waking soon after first light so that each morning when I open my eyes a coffee tray is already on the balcony table; she knows I like a fresh room to breakfast in when I return from walking, and it is so: the room done for the day and the table set and the morning paper ready; she asks without words why I have no clothes to be laundered today, and without words asks permission to sew the buttons and darn the socks; she calls me wise man and teacher, who am neither, when speaking of me to others; she is proud to have me for her client and, I hope, pleased that I try to deserve that pride and match with courtesy that loyalty. There is a lot of loose loyalty in this land. Even a little of it is too valuable to be ignored. I would wish that all of it were deserved or at least appreciated as I have tried to do.

❖   ❖   ❖

This is the same rice paddy which I know back home in Arkansas and Mississippi and Louisiana, where it replaces now and then the cotton. This one is merely a little smaller and a little more fiercely cultivated, right up to the single row of beans which line the very edge of the irrigation canals, the work here done by hand where in my country machines do it since we have more machines than we have people; nature is the same: only the economy is different.

And the names are the same names too: Jonathan and Winesap and Delicious; the heavy August foliage is blue-gray with the same spray which we use. But there the resemblance ceases: every single apple enclosed in its twist of paper until that whole tree to this western eye becomes significant and festive and ceremonial like the symbolical tree of the western rite of Christmas. Only it is more significant here: where in the West there is one small often artificial tree to a family, wrested from the living dirt to be decked in ritual tinsel and then to die as though the tree were not the protagonist of a rite but the victim of a sacrifice, here not one tree to a family but every tree of all is dressed and decked to proclaim and salute older gods than Christ: Demeter and Ceres.

❖   ❖   ❖

Briefer and faster now, toward the journey's nearing end: goldenrod, as evocative of dust and autumn and hay fever as ever in Mississipppi, against a tall bamboo fence.

The scenery is beautiful but the faces are better still.

The swift supple narrow grace with which the young girl bows and in that same one flowing motion recovers, tougher through very tenderness than the rigid culture which bent her as is the willow bough itself to the hard gust which can never do more than sway it.

The tools they use evoke the ones Noah must have built his ark with, yet the framework of the house seems to rise and stand without nails in the fitted joints nor even the need for nails, as if here were a magic, an art in the simple building of man's habitations which our western ancestors seemed to have lost somewhere when they moved.

And always the water, the sound, the plash and drip of it, as if here were a people making constant oblation to water as some peoples do to what they call their luck.

So kind the people that with three words the guest can go any-where and live: Gohan: Sake: Arrigato. And one more word:

Tomorrow now the aircraft lightens, a moment more and the wheels will wrench free of the ground, already dragging its shadow back toward the overcast before the wheels are even tucked up, into the overcast and then through it, the land, the island gone now which memory will always know though eye no longer remembers. Sayonara.

[Press release by the United States Embassy in Tokyo, 1955; collected in Faulkner at Nagano, *ed. Robert A. Jelliffe, Tokyo, 1956, from which the text printed here has been taken, with corrections from an incomplete Faulkner typescript.]*

16. Spring

E. B. WHITE

THERE IS A STANZA in Robert Frost's poem "Two Tramps in Mud Time" which describes an April moment when air and sky have a vernal feeling, but suddenly a cloud crosses the path of the sun and a bitter little wind finds you out, and you're back in the middle of March. Everyone who has lived in the country knows that sort of moment—the promise of warmth, the raised hope, the ruthless rebuff.

There is another sort of day which needs celebrating in song—the day of days when spring at last holds up her face to be kissed, deliberate and unabashed. On that day no wind blows either in the hills or in the mind; no chill finds the bone. It is a day which can come only in a northern climate, where there has been a long background of frigidity, a long deficiency of sun.

We've just been through this magical moment—which was more than a moment and was a whole morning—and it lodges in memory like some old romance, with the same subtlety of tone, the same enrichment of the blood, and the enchantment and the mirth and the indescribable warmth. Even before breakfast I felt that the moment was at hand, for when I went out to the barn to investigate twins I let the kitchen door stay open, lazily, instead of closing it behind me. This was a sign. The lambs had nursed and the ewe was lying quiet. One lamb had settled itself on the mother's back and was a perfect miniature of the old one—they reminded me of a teapot we have, whose knob is a tiny replica of the pot itself. The barn seemed warmer and sweeter than usual, but it was early in the day, and the hint of springburst was still only a hint, a suggestion, a nudge. The full impact wasn't felt until the sun had climbed higher. Then came, one after another, the many small caresses which added up to the total embrace of warmth and life—a laziness and contentment in the behavior of animals and people, a tendency of man and dog to sit down somewhere in the sun. In the driveway, a deep rut which for the past week had held three or four inches of water and which had alternately frozen and thawed, showed clear indications of drying up. On the window ledge in the living room, the bare brown forsythia cuttings suddenly discovered the secret of yellow. The goose, instead of coming off her nest and joining her loud companions, settled down on her eleven eggs, pulled some feathers from her breast, and resigned herself to the twenty-eight-day grind. When I went back through the kitchen I noticed that the air that had come in was not like an invader but like a friend who had stopped by for a visit.

17. Crest Avenue, St. Paul

F. SCOTT FITZGERALD

Fitzgerald (1896–1940) went from St. Paul, Minnesota, to Princeton to Paris, wrote *The Great Gatsby* (1925), other stories and novels, and became almost a legendary character himself in the story of American literature.

AS THEY TURNED into Crest Avenue, the new cathedral, immense and unfinished in imitation of a cathedral left unfinished by accident in some little Flemish town, squatted just across the way like a plump white bulldog on its haunches. The ghost of four moonlit apostles looked down at them wanly from wall niches still littered with the white dusty trash of the builders. The cathedral inaugurated Crest Avenue. After it came the great brownstone mass built by R. R. Comerford, the flour king, followed by a half mile of pretentious stone houses built in the gloomy 90's. These were adorned with monstrous driveways and porte-cochères which had once echoed to the hoofs of good horses and with high circular windows that corseted the second stories.

The continuity of these mausoleums was broken by a small park, a triangle of grass where Nathan Hale stood ten feet tall, with his hands bound behind his back by stone cord, and stared over a great bluff at the slow Mississippi. Crest Avenue ran along the bluff, but neither faced it nor seemed aware of it, for all the houses fronted inward toward the street. Beyond the first half mile it became newer, essayed ventures in terraced lawns, in concoctions of stucco or in granite mansions which imitated through a variety of gradual refinements the marble contours of the Petit Trianon. The houses of this phase rushed by the roadster for a succession of minutes, then the way turned and the car was headed directly into the moonlight, which swept toward it like the lamp of some gigantic motorcycle far up the avenue.

Past the low Corinthian lines of the Christian Science Temple, past a block of dark frame horrors, a deserted row of grim red brick—an unfortunate experiment of the late 90's—then new houses again, bright blinding flowery lawns. These swept by, faded past, enjoying their moment of grandeur; then waiting there in the moonlight to be out-moded as had the frame, cupolaed mansions of lower down and the brownstone piles of older Crest Avenue in their turn.

The roofs lowered suddenly, the lots narrowed, the houses shrank up in size and shaded off into bungalows. These held the street for the last mile, to the bend in the river which terminated the prideful avenue at the statue of Chelsea Arbuthnot. Arbuthnot was the first governor—and almost the last of Anglo-Saxon blood.

All the way thus far Yanci had not spoken, absorbed still in the annoyance of the evening, yet soothed somehow by the fresh air of Northern November that rushed by them. She must take her fur coat out of storage next day, she thought.

"Where are we now?"

As they slowed down, Scott looked up curiously at the pompous stone figure, clear in the crisp moonlight, with one hand on a book and the forefinger of the other pointing, as though with reproachful symbolism, directly at some construction work going on in the street.

"This is the end of Crest Avenue," said Yanci, turning to him. "This is our show street."

"A museum of American architectural failures."

18. Open City:
Letter from Delhi

R. PRAWER JHABVALA

Ruth Prawer Jhabvala (1927–   ) has written several
novels, set usually in India. Her books include *Amrita*
(1956), *Esmond in India* (1958), *The Householder* (1960),
Get Ready for Battle (1962), and *A Backward Place* (1965).

ALL THROUGH THE WINTER there is a stream of foreign visitors.
They hold conferences and go shopping and admire Indian archi-
tecture, art, culture, food, tradition, and whatever else there is to
admire. They also, more or less each one of them, have an interview
with Mr. Nehru, whom they ask questions and to whom they tender
advice. They all seem to have this in common, that they feel a deep
personal concern for India's problems; they see that something is out
of joint and are eager, in a really nice, completely unselfish way, to
help set it right.

What is it about Delhi that makes almost everyone who comes
here so passionately interested in its affairs? It may be because everything seems so very open and accessible. Delhi is a capital and at a
certain level a very small and compact one, where inside information
is freely available and it is easy to be or to seem closely in touch. One
always knows everything long before and much better than the newspapers, for the place buzzes with stories of what really happened between the Defence Minister and the Chiefs of Staff and what one
Minister said to another at a cabinet meeting. Moreover, top people
are so excessively available that one gets an impression as if our Ministers are not only ready but also eager and waiting to give intimate
interviews to any foreign visitor who cares to seek them out. This is
very flattering for the foreign visitor, who probably does not operate
at this level back where he comes from; and he consequently begins to
feel himself intimately involved in local affairs and to develop a feeling
of almost personal responsibility towards them.

And it is not only political life that seems open and accessible. So
much goes on out in the streets that it is impossible to get away from
social, economic, religious, moral, cultural, linguistic, something for

everyone: and on all sides the clearest evidence of them is being offered, so that it is not at all difficult to gather proofs and statistics and talk with as much expertise as any expert. Our foreign visitors are for ever being led to believe that, one step more, and they will hold their own particular Indian problem in the hollow of their hand. Naturally they try and take that one step more, but when it comes out to be time and time again not the last after all, a certain restlessness sets in. It is always at this point that our visitors begin to find the interviews with Ministers no longer as satisfying as they once were and to start hankering after invitations to private homes, which alone will give them, so they now believe and persuasively tell us, "a true insight into the lives of the people."

BUT WHICH PEOPLE? Our foreign visitor's social conscience is tender and highly developed, and his first glances will be towards those miserable huts he sees wherever he drives in his taxi and the sight of which so appalled him when he first arrived. What sort of people live in them, what do they think about, how do they talk to one another, what do they eat, etc., etc.? If only it were possible to know! If only, imbued as one is with sympathy and understanding, one might be allowed access into those poor, dark, unknown lives! But it is not possible. No slum dweller is available to invite a foreign visitor to tea, and perhaps it is just as well, for even if there were no language difficulty, there would not really be much to talk about. There is not in the world's history any record of fruitful dialogue between those who have enough to eat and those who don't. Our foreign visitor turns away from the sight of those wretched hovels and feels sad. No longer quite as sad, perhaps, or as outraged as he felt when he first saw them—it never takes long to get used to other people's poverty—but the poor of Delhi will always be sure of his concern. He will often talk about them, and when he does so, he will make that special face we all make when we feel guilty about something (whether it is *apartheid*, political prisoners, or starving children) but are no longer sure that our feeling is still as deep as it ought to be.

BRANCHING OUT from India Gate (which we may take as the centre of everything that is best in official New Delhi) there are broad, tree-lined avenues. On these, each in its own spacious acre or two of land, stand large white houses, very dignified with their Palladian façades, their well-kept lawns rolling away in the front and their servants' quarters clustered together at the back. Let us pretend that we are a very lucky foreign visitor indeed, who has had an introduction to the master of one of these mansions. The temporary master, rather: for these houses, which were once the residences of British civil servants, have most of them been acquired by the government and are allotted to

Ministers and other high-ranking politicians, to senior officers of the armed forces and government servants in the upper echelons. As long as they hold their offices, they hold their houses, but once they are transferred or retired or—political life has its vicissitudes everywhere—sacked, it is good-bye to house and garden too, and they, like everyone else in an increasingly tight housing situation, have to scramble for whatever living space they can. But for the host of our lucky foreign visitor this evil day is not yet come, and he is still in radiant possession of the fruits of his promotion.

The invitation is for Sunday lunch, and since it is winter this is held in the garden. Everything is just perfect. The lawn has been well watered and is green, the roses and the chrysanthemums are in bloom, the winter sun is shining brilliantly, the sky is azure and delicately flecked with a few white puffs of cloud. Garden chairs and tables have been arranged on the lawn and dotted among them are striped umbrellas to guard one from the sun, which is mild and warm but tends to darken the complexion. Servants in white uniforms offer drinks from trays, beer, gin, rum, and whisky—all local Indian products and not too expensive—for the gentlemen, fruit juices for the ladies. Here is our host, an Additional Secretary to the Government of India, a man of weight, both literally and metaphorically, but looking completely relaxed and informal in baggy, out-of-date flannels, a yellow pullover, and a sports jacket. He smokes a pipe and speaks with an accent which shows that, though his schooling was Indian, his university days were spent at Oxford. The conversation is entirely in English: not only out of deference to the sprinkling of foreign guests—besides our visitor, there is also a Scandinavian expert on soil erosion, a Dutch journalist, and an enthusiastic American couple from the Ford Foundation—but also because English is the only language everyone has in common. As happens only in the top layers of Delhi society, this is an entirely non-communal gathering, consisting of Bengali-speaking Bengalis, Telugu- or Tamil- or Malayalam-speaking South Indians, Marathi- or Gujerati-speaking Bombaywallas, Urdu-speaking Muslims, etc., who are forced to (and perhaps rather like to?—they do it so well, with such ease and fluency) converse together in English both for their private and official purposes. With one or two exceptions—of whom more later—they are all high-ranking government servants, all talking in loud, confident voices, all widely-travelled, knowing, Westernised, and with modern wives.

Our foreign guest will probably not be surprised at these modern wives, but an Indian from a less advanced milieu well might be. Not only surprised, but indignant too: he might even, he frequently does, write letters to the newspapers about them. For these wives do not at all conform to the traditional pattern of Indian womanhood. They wear their hair short; they apply all sorts of modern make-up; their blouses are cut low. They have opinions and take a vigorous share in the conversation and allow men, who are neither brother, husband, or father to them, to talk to them familiarly and call them by their first names. Some of them smoke cigarettes; some can even be seen to eschew the fruit juices and help themselves unashamedly to the gin. The hostess, who is perhaps typical of all of them, is a tall, elegant, well-developed woman, with a voice almost as loud as her husband's. Her children are away at boarding-schools but all the same she keeps herself very busy. She has many outside interests which range from the cultural—she is secretary to a music, dance, and drama society—to her welfare work among destitute widows. She is an excellent hostess, a quality which is both inbred (she comes from a well-to-do family) and has been stimulated during her years as the wife of an important government officer who has many contacts to maintain. Her servants are superbly trained—how they glide over the smooth lawn! how so-licitously they bend over the guests!—her glass and cutlery imported and impeccable, the food, a judicious mixture of Eastern and Western cooking, beautifully prepared and served. Most of the Indian guests make for the Western dishes, the Western guests—who are just crazy about chapattis—for the Indian dishes. The birds are chirping in the trees, the guests eat and drink and chatter in their garden chairs. Everyone is happy. It is a lovely party.

THERE ARE TWO GUESTS who don't quite fit in. One of them is a prosperous businessman, dressed in too good a suit and wearing a ring or two too many. He has been invited because he has in the past shown a lot of hospitality to his host, with whom he has dealings over im-port licences or some such matter (his wife has also been invited but it was tacitly understood that she would not come). The other misfit is a poor relation of the host's, who wasn't invited at all but dropped in to pay his respects to his important cousin and was drawn into the lunch by mistake. Actually we are taking quite a bit of dramatic licence here because he would not have been drawn in at all: instead he would have begged and been permitted to take his leave the mo-ment the guests arrived. But we need him here, for our foreign visitor, ever eager to know all aspects of India, is going to strike up a con-versation with him. Both with him, and with the businessman. And so stimulating and friendly are these two conversations going to be that the businessman and the poor relation will both invite the foreigner to visit them in their homes. For they too are eager, on the one hand, to demonstrate their traditional Indian hospitality and, on the other, to make an interesting contact and learn what goes on in the great world of nylon and television beyond their shores.

SO IT HAPPENS that a day or two later the foreign visitor is sitting in a taxi on his way to the businessman's house. This is not in the area of spacious villas left behind by the British but further out, in a newly developed area which has been parcelled out and sold in plots to people who could afford to buy them. There are not many trees here; in fact, there aren't any, nor grass, nor anything green. Everything is still rather new and raw, still dusty, with a lot of scaffolding and building materials and makeshift huts to accommodate the building workers. But the finished houses are splendid. Our foreign visitor stands agape at the wonderful residence his second host has built for himself. No expense has been spared here, no decoration suggested by a vivid taste omitted. There are little Moorish balconies and Indian domes and squiggly lattice work and an air-conditioner in every window. Inside all is marble flooring and in the entrance hall there is a fountain lit up with green, yellow, and red bulbs. The curtains on the windows and in the door-ways are of silk, the vast sofa-suites are upholstered in velvet, the telephone is red, and huge vases are filled with plastic flowers.

There are rather more guests than the room can comfortably accommodate. Everybody—friends, relatives, acquaintances, business contacts—has been invited. The gentlemen sit on one side of a great circle of sofas and chairs, their wives on the other. The principal activity on the gentlemen's side is the drinking of Scotch whisky, which is fearfully expensive but which the host and his sons pour with a liberal hand. They will not endure an empty glass and there is much rallying and teasing as to the drinking capacity of each guest. This leads to a great deal of boisterous laughter and back-slapping, and the foreign guest, not wishing to seem out of anything, also smiles, though a little uncertainly for the banter is all in what he presumes is Hindustani (actually it is Punjabi). However, he too gets his share of attention as one after another of the guests comes up to engage him in courteous English conversation, which always starts off with the enquiry of how does he like India, leading on to an account of how much his interlocutor enjoyed the time he spent in foreign countries such as England, America, or Germany, and concluding with a barrage of eager questions as to the availability, in the foreigner's country of origin, and current price of transistor radios? tape-recorders? pop-up toasters?

From time to time the foreigner throws surreptitious glances at the ladies on the other side of the room. He notes that they do not seem to be enjoying themselves, though they are dressed up for enjoyment in their best silk saris with shiny satin blouses and flowers and a lot of oil in their hair and a great load of golden jewellery. Each holds a glass of pineapple juice in her hand and stares in front of her with patient eyes; there is no conversation. Their menfolk, who are having such a boisterous good time on their side of the room, don't seem to have the slightest difficulty in ignoring that silent other half; but the foreigner, brought up differently, feels a kind of social embarrassment

for these unhappy ladies and wonders whether there is no way of starting up a conversation with them. He soon finds there is not, for whenever by some mischance one of them encounters his glance, she looks
away in extreme confusion as if an indecent act had been committed.
He is sad, and begins to revise the estimate of the status of Indian
women he has so blithely formed at his former host's house. Perhaps
they are, after all, not as advanced as he had been led to believe.

HE HAS NO OPPORTUNITY to enlarge his findings at his third host's
house, for here he doesn't encounter any women at all. But then,
everything here is very different from both his previous places of entertainment. His third host, though his relative is an Additional Secretary, is himself only a minor employee in one of the Ministries, and
consequently the housing allotted to him is of a much humbler type.
It is also a very long way out. Our foreign visitor has long since left
behind India Gate and the tree-lined avenues and struck out into less
glamorous surroundings. He passes workshops and potteries and the
great gaunt shell of a building which was once started but, for lack
of funds, never finished. He travels through government housing colonies, all of which look alike, and also through much empty waste land
on which building work is going on to transform it into more government colonies.

His host's colony, when he finally reaches it, is like all the others:
row upon row of straight and narrow double-storeyed houses painted
yellow. There are many children, and a great deal of washing strung
up, but no trees and no grass and no parks, though there is a deserted
children's playground with a chute built of stone and a broken swing.
It takes him some time to find his host's house, for not only are the
rows of houses identical, they are also named and numbered in a very
mysterious fashion. *DIV 9/438* is not an easy address to locate—though,
did our foreign visitor but know it, it is a very revealing one. Like
all the identifications attached to government housing, it is an exactly
graded indication of rank, ensuring that once you know a man's
address, you also know what sort of post he holds, what salary he
draws, and whether he is entitled to a pension.

Our foreigner finds himself the only guest and in a tête-à-tête with
his host. The host's family seems to have been banished, though muffled
sounds can be heard from some adjacent room, and once there is a
feminine cough behind the door which makes the host nervously excuse
himself and return, looking even more nervous, after some urgent
whispering outside. Together with the family, all signs of family life
have been cleaned out of the room. Everything looks very scrubbed
and very bare. There is little furniture, just a couple of not too steady
cane-chairs for host and guest to sit on and a table covered with a clean
if somewhat faded tablecloth and a wall-cupboard, the contents of

which are hidden by a cotton curtain sagging from a string. A brightly coloured calendar of Rama and Sita (or is it Krishna and Radha?), presented with the compliments of a firm of sanitary contractors, hangs on the white-washed wall, and plaster figures of gods stand in little whitewashed niches.

A most sumptuous tea has been prepared for the lone guest: there are mounds of coloured sweetmeats and all sorts of fried things green with chili as well as, in deference to European taste, some thick slices of white bread thickly buttered. Two cups of very milky tea are brought in on a tin tray by a little servant boy about ten years old and wearing a torn shirt; he walks carefully, but nevertheless some of the tea slops over into the saucers. The host, in an agony of social unease, keeps cracking his finger-joints, and the guest eats more than he wants because there is so much and so much trouble has been taken. Conversation is very, very difficult.

If, however, the visitor is only patient enough, his host will begin to relax. The atmosphere changes and suddenly the host is talking— and not only talking but doing so with the greatest intimacy and urgency, like a man who has long waited for an oppportunity to un- burden himself. He freely mentions his salary and the difficulty of managing on it. He complains of rising prices and the cost of education; sadly dwells on the fact that children wear their shoes out very quickly and that they frequently, in spite of the high cost of medicines, fall sick. His house is a long way away from his office and because the buses are both irregular and overcrowded, he has had to take a loan and buy a bicycle, on which he cycles to and fro some twelve miles a day. His eldest daughter is fifteen—he himself is in his mid-thirties— and it is not long now before arrangements will have to be made for her marriage; and though of course the dowry system has been legally abolished (he smiles wryly at this), costly presents will have to be made to the bridegroom and his family and princely wedding enter- tainments provided for them and all their acquaintances. His sons will have to be put through colleges to get degrees to enable them to get good jobs in government service. He himself, of course, went to college and did his B.A. degree; he points to the framed scroll certifying this on the wall and falls into reminiscences of his student days when he played cricket and loved English literature. Suddenly he is reciting *The Lady of Shalott.*

BUT OUR FOREIGN VISITOR is not yet satisfied. He feels there is more, much more, that he has missed and for which no one will offer him an explanation. And perhaps he is right. The trouble with Delhi— and for Delhi one could say India—is that it appears to wear its heart on its sleeve and so incites everyone who comes to try and read it. Yet this openness is deceptive, and the place is actually extremely—

not secretive so much as reticent. One sees a lot in the street but it is all *appearance;* there is no way of finding out what it is all about except by living here for a long time and with patience. The foreigner may be invited into a home, he will be treated with great heartiness and a genuine hospitality, but he will be shown only what is fitting for him to see; what his host wants him to see, or thinks he would like to see. The rest has to be guesswork.

What chance has the short-term visitor of ever guessing that the Additional Secretary, in spite of his baggy flannels and his Oxford accent, still sometimes consults his family astrologer? Or that the repressed looking ladies he met at the businessman's house are strong-minded, vigorous women whose rule over their households is undisputed, who revel in fierce family fights and, in their lighter moments, are full of a gay, bawdy wit? And at this third host's house, where so much was said and so intimately—can he ever guess what went on in the adjacent room to which the family was banished, or what was whispered behind the door?

Reticence is not confined to private lives. A musical recital is a perfectly public occasion; anyone can buy a ticket and come in. The foreigner sits and listens to the music, he might even enjoy it for an hour or two; then he leaves for his next engagement and so do most of the other people in the front rows. This is the signal for the people in the cheaper seats at the back to throng forward, and for their friends, who couldn't afford to buy tickets, to wander in through various doors and sit wherever they can; and then the musician *really* starts to play.

19. Rivers and History

JOHN BARDACH

Bardach (1915–   ) is Director of the Marine Biological Station at the University of Hawaii. He has written *Aquaculture: The Farming and Husbandry of Freshwater and Marine Organisms; Downstream: A Natural History of the River* (1964); and, most recently, *Harvest of the Sea* (1968).

II. Description:
Reports Through Space and Time

FOR HUNDREDS OF MILLIONS OF YEARS animals had been coming to the streams and rivers of the world to drink, to bathe, to find their food, to set up breeding territories, or to build nests or dens. Here and there they had slightly modified the streamside by making a path down to the water, or the channel itself by the widening of a hippopotamus wallow or the building of a beaver dam. Then, somewhere between a million and five hundred thousand years ago, bands of a new kind of predator began to appear at the watering places of the grazers and browsers. These protohuman creatures walked on two legs; more vociferous than lions or leopards, they carried on their communal hunting with shouts and grunts that eventually became words; and they extended the power of their forelimbs by the use of clubs and spears.

A troop of these hunters might have had a territory comprising an entire river valley with its bluffs, lakes, and tributary streams. Like the animals they hunted, they would migrate frequently, following the river's course, but being less well adapted than many other animals to going without drinking for more than a few hours, they did not stray far from the water, and at first made no impact on the river itself or on the plants growing along its shores.

But several hundred thousand years later their descendants had developed a more sedentary way of life as a result of what was perhaps man's greatest cultural advance, the domestication of plants and of animals. Their communal life also had developed beyond mere cooperation in the hunt; the campsites by a clear spring, or on a solid hummock of land near the shellfish beds in an estuarine marsh, had become settled villages. The earliest agricultural settlements appear to have been those along tributaries of the upper Euphrates and Tigris rivers, and are now dated at around 7000 B.C.

The four valleys that were the center of the earliest civilizations —those of the Nile, the Indus, the twin rivers Euphrates and Tigris, and the Hwang Ho—are subject to heavy floods at regular times of the year, with rises of from fifteen to twenty feet at the crest of the flood. At some prehistoric period man took to building canals and dams, thus increasing the area of his croplands. In ancient Mesopotamia the earliest canal system put seven million acres under cultivation; the entire acreage of irrigated land in the American Southwest today is only about four times as large. The great river cultures became the granaries of the ancient world, supplying food not only to the inhabitants of the valleys but also to many others beyond them.

The kind of agriculture made possible by irrigation and the domestication of grain-bearing grasses—wheat, barley, and rice—was permanent and demanded a large-scale cooperation that led in turn to a closely knit social organization. Children, no longer the burden they had been to a band of hunters, became desirable as helpers. Thus the new settled life along the river, and perhaps a temporary food surplus, may have led to the first modest but permanent increase in population.

The cultivation of irrigated lands that tied man to the river valleys led invariably to the development of cities with their granaries, market places, administrative centers, and religious rites. In the city separate administrative and ruling classes arose, who were exempt from manual labor, and under whose direction the refinements of art and culture came into being. By degrees the rulers of cities extended their dominion over entire river valleys and watersheds, thus establishing the foundations of ancient empires whose influence was eventually to spread over still greater areas.

Irrigation and Water Power

To maintain a permanent system of irrigation along a river with seasonal high and low stages, the water had to be raised, at times over a dyke, at times to still higher ground. Among the several machines invented for this purpose were the primitive water wheels. A certain flow is necessary to turn a large paddlewheel with sufficient force to send the raised water trickling into a trough and thence into the fields. Where the flow is not sufficient, the wheel has to be powered by man or one of the animals he has domesticated.

Still more primitive devices for raising water probably consisted first of a bag of skin attached to a rope of plant fibers, and later of pottery vessels such as are described in early Babylonic writings. In ancient Babylonia the faster flow of the rivers as compared to those of Egypt, and the contours of the land, made possible an irrigation depending largely on the flow of gravity, whereas in the delta of the Nile large amounts of water had to be lifted from the slower-flowing arms of the river. To accomplish this the early Egyptians placed on the bank a pivot that supported a crossbeam with a water bucket at one end and a counterweight at the other that allowed the raising of the load with a minimum of effort. This lever arrangement, called a shadoof, is pictured on clay seals dating back to 2500 B.C., and is still in use today.

Another means of raising water is the treadmill, operated by stepping on a series of rotating pedals along the rim of a small wheel, to which is connected a larger one carrying a series of buckets or scoops. An adaptation of this same device, built on the bicycle principle, is still in use along the Mekong, where it existed long before bicycles had been introduced from Europe. Along the waterways of Cambodia and Vietnam a young peasant couple may often be seen treading away at the waterwheel in the shade of an isolated tree. The wheel drives a chain of upright plates resembling a caterpillar tread, which raises the water and sends it through a wooden gutter into a field ten feet above the level of the river. Although each plate moves only a small amount of water, the total effect is a steady flow.

Day after day the same couple will be at their job of irrigation for an hour or so in the morning and again in the cool of the evening. They chat with one another as they sit on their perches above the wheel, in evident enjoyment of the chore; after all, it removes them for a while from the presence of in-laws and children—a respite of privacy that must be welcome in this land of crowded households, the traditional warmth of Asian family affection notwithstanding.

Related to the simple machines that raise the water to irrigate the land are the water mills used for grinding grain or working metal, which are often cited as prime movers by historians of technology. The invention of every new prime mover—the steam engine is one example —has meant more available energy and another technological stride forward by mankind. But for the major part of his existence thus far *Homo sapiens* has been his own prime mover, dependent entirely upon the energy stored in his own muscles. The domestication of animals supplied a new source of tractive power, but it was not until less than three thousand years ago that man began to harness rapid streams for that most recurrent chore of every primitive household, the grinding of grain. The earliest mills were small, and their output of energy and hence of flour was low. They consisted of flat, circular millstones, connected by a vertical shaft with a horizontal paddlewheel that was turned by the current of the stream. This invention, simple as it was, must have given the early housewife not only relief from drudgery but a comparatively great amount of leisure. Having to grind or pound kernels by hand meant—as it still does in many parts of the world even now—that little if any flour could be stored, and that the work had to be done every day.

At about the time of Christ an unknown inventor revolutionized milling by adding to a paddlewheel on a horizontal shaft a set of gears that coupled it with the vertical shaft bearing the millstones. Thus the mill as it is known today—called the Vitruvian mill after the Roman historian who first described it—came into being. After millponds, dams, chutes, reservoirs, and aqueducts had been perfected in order to take full advantage of this development, the overshot wheel—as it is also called—was capable of generating as much as forty or even sixty horsepower. During the Middle Ages such mills sprang up in central and northern Europe and in China, where their development was favored by the relatively uniform rainfall more than it had been in the regions of intermittent rainfall which had been the first centers of civilization.

Gradually the size of reservoirs and dams increased, until finally, less than a hundred years ago, the hydraulic turbine for converting mechanical energy into electricity had been evolved, drawing for its mechanics on features both of the Vitruvian mill and of the more ancient horizontal paddlewheel. Since Edison's invention of the incandescent lamp, electricity has come to be taken so completely for granted in our own country that we are unable to function without it. In the hilly and mountainous regions of America, Europe, and the Soviet Union nearly all electric power is obtained from the driving force of water held behind dams. In most other parts of the world the power of rivers is still scarcely used, even though the potential amount is estimated to be many hundred times what is now being tapped. But although many millions still go to sleep when the sun has set, regardless of the hour, plans are being made to dam many tropical rivers, so that it may not be long before men in the remotest corners of the earth will be turning night into day simply by the flick of a switch.

Man travels farther and faster than any animal. Some of his mammalian relatives migrate long distances to follow a seasonal abundance of food; others avoid the rigors of winter by storing fat, lowering their temperature, and going into hibernation; but man is far less strictly governed by his external environment. Early man migrated on foot, as diverse remains from the stone age show, but when he began to domesticate animals his mobility on land was increased many times over; and as soon as his tool-making capacity had led to the invention of boats, the rivers began beckoning him to explore what lay around the next bend.

The first boats on the Nile were probably bundles of rushes tied together, on which a man rode between two sheaves that were the archetype of gunwales. On the twin rivers of Mesopotamia, where papyrus and other rushes were lacking, men buoyed themselves with inflated animal skins and kicked their way across the river. Later the skin floats were tied together to support rafts. Similar early devices for river navigation appeared in the arid Balkans and the American Southwest. A further step in the use of hides was to stretch them over a wooden scaffold like those of the Eskimo kayak and umiak (the larger boat in which women rode), which were in turn the forerunners of the modern canvas canoe. Where there were forests men hollowed out trees to produce dugout canoes—an idea possibly suggested by large pieces of bark such as may have supported hunters or warriors on the water. The various types of primitive boats that have sprung up independently all over the globe clearly indicate the close alliance of the earliest inventions to the nature of available materials.

The wooden boat was the easiest to enlarge and make seaworthy; therefore it grew in size and assumed many shapes. The invention of oars and sails notwithstanding, it was only the comparatively recent development of the steam engine and the steel hull that further enlarged the scope of boat-building, leading to the gigantic ocean liners of today. Traveling upstream was difficult and often slower than following the same route on horseback or even on foot. Furthermore, river travel was often just as seasonal as any animal migration because of winter ice and spring floods. Before the days of the railroad and the horseless carriage, men along the vast water network of the Mississippi anxiously awaited the coming of spring and the big ice push from the north. Moorings were reinforced, and the flat-bottomed floating palaces that hibernated in St. Louis were secured in their docks with thick iron chains. The ice push began usually in early March, when the floes would advance, slowly turning like huge millstones, and pushing over one another with a noise like the firing of distant cannon. In places they would be compressed between the arches of a bridge; some would be crushed, while others would circle more rapidly, to float out into the open stream again and vanish on their way toward the south. As the floes became smaller and smaller, changing in color from white to greenish grey, they would break, worn down by their long journey, to disappear completely by the time the first magnolia trees appeared along the shore. Up until late in the last century newspapers still carried announcements to prospective patrons that such a steamer as the *Great Republic* or the *Robert E. Lee* would begin its journey on such and such a day to Cairo, Vicksburg, and New Orleans, or upstream to Pittburgh or Cincinnati.

The Ohio, inasmuch as it drains an area greater than is drained by the Mississippi above the mouth of the Missouri, and lies in a zone of greater rainfall, carries nearly a quarter of all the waters that flow into the Gulf of Mexico. Its more or less westward course and its eminent navigability predestined *La Belle Rivière,* as it was originally called by the French, to become a historic highway for the white man's westward migration on the new continent. Nearly a hundred and fifty years were to pass after La Salle had first glimpsed the great river around 1670, before the valley it drained was settled by adventurous men from the east. The first travelers on the Ohio descended it in canoes and pirogues; then came barges, likewise traveling only downstream; but after Pittsburgh and other cities had been founded in the upper Ohio Valley, a craft was needed that could make the upstream journey. For this purpose the famous keelboats had running boards extending from end to end along their sides; on these the crew would walk slowly, carrying poles with which to push the boat upstream. At times, especially at high water, the shoreward crew would catch hold of the bushes or branches of trees on the river bank in order to pull the keelboat upstream—whence the word "bushwhack." Such keelboats did not exceed fifty feet in length and could thus ascend small rivers even up to some portages; in their own way they were as important in spreading people and goods as the steamers that followed them. In addition there were also the great barges that carried forty or fifty tons of freight and were manned by as many men, who helped to pull them upstream from the shores or who manned rows of oars to augment the force provided by the sails. Craft similar to all these were once found on all larger rivers; on some they make up the bulk of traffic even today.

A stretch of river more famous than any other for its incomparable scenery, its treacherously varied waters, and its dangers to navigation is the series of gorges along the Yangtze Kiang below Chunking in China. In the nearly vertical rock walls that contain the curves of the great river, towpaths have been hewn as high as five hundred feet above the level of low water. One junk can overtake a slower craft by raising its towline over that of the other; and although to facilitate this maneuver the ropes are attached to the mast instead of the bow, they may still become entangled. At such times the attempt to loosen them makes them vibrate from rock to rock, often sweeping past a group of coolies towing another boat and threatening to hurl them into the abyss below. The towpaths are lined with tablets and cairns, in lieu of tombs, commemorating just such misfortunes. The barges thus towed have no keel, but merely a pair of sideboards to enable them to sail upstream in the slower portions of the river, making good use of the summer monsoon as it sweeps upstream through the valley. Oars are used, and also stakes, as on the Ohio keelboats; and pilots directing the upstream journey are skilled at taking advantage of the counter-currents near the shore. Often, though, only towing will move the craft; then the entire crew is set ashore to man the long towrope braided from slit bamboo. Each coolie puts his shoulder into a kind of harness, so fashioned that he can slip out of it with ease. Even steamboats in the Yangtze gorges need a towing crew that may consist of hundreds of men, manning eight or more ropes.

Most rivers already had two-way traffic by the time recorded history began. At an even earlier time rivers gave direction to the spread of peoples; some, among them the Yangtze and the Hwang Ho of China, led the conquerors of new lands from the hearts of continents to the sea. Others directed migrations inland; one such, the Mackenzie, lying in a portion of the Canadian Arctic that was unglaciated through most of the last quarter of a million years, funneled toward the south the ancestors of certain tribes of American Indians after they had crossed the land bridge over the Bering Straits.

Now that man has explored and mapped nearly the entire globe, rivers have lost their importance as landmarks in the opening up of new regions. They are also less important as arteries of travel, although they still carry large amounts of freight. In places ground travel routes also still follow rivers—particularly in mountainous country, where the course of a stream is often the best one for a railroad or superhighway to follow. Nevertheless, even though such problems as that of upstream navigation have been solved, the relation between man and the moving water has become not less but more complex. Some of the problems yet unsolved are new and man-made; others are natural events as old as the rivers themselves. Of the latter, none is more awesome than the yearly rise and fall to which all rivers are subject, and which throughout human history has conferred benefit as well as disaster.

Floods

Without floods the development of human civilization in Egypt, in Mesopotamia, and in China could not have taken place. Though dams have long been built to control them, man also coped with floods by learning to live with them—as he still does in many parts of the tropics where the climate is warm and shelter can be quickly built. Of course, floods also occur in the temperate zone—the Ohio, the Tennessee, and the Missouri are only a few of America's flood-prone rivers—but in temperate areas, in part because housing there needs to be more permanent than in the tropics, and in part because industries and other valuable property are threatened by floods, Western man has developed intensive flood control measures. He has also coerced his rivers into regulated channels and has done as much as was in his power to prevent floods, rather than to roll with their punches as people in the tropics still do. An instance of the latter are the people of the valley of the Mekong, for whom rice and fish, the staples of diet in Southeast Asia, are both the legacy of the floods, and who continue to gear their lives to the yearly rise and fall of the river. At high water a layer of rich mud settles on the flooded land, and the use of fertilizer becomes superfluous. When the waters recede, the ground is ready either for seeding or for setting out young rice plants. In addition some water is retained by means of dykes and sluices.

When the water level falls it leaves behind, conveniently beached on dry land, the boat that needs repair, with ample time to repair it. In the following year, the river will rise again to set it afloat. At the same time it will inundate forests consisting of trees adapted to having their trunks submerged for part of the year. Here, during the dry season, the villager may gather firewood which he may float out on rafts when the river rises. At flood time wild animals congregate on higher ground and hunting becomes easier.

The final gift of the high water is to deliver a wealth of fish through the inundated forests and shrublands, where they grow big and fat. As a result the region of the lower Mekong was for decades the chief source of proteins for the dense populations of Vietnam and Java. Catching the fish is no problem; a fisherman only needs to build barrages to intercept them as they leave with the receding waters.

The fishermen's villages, which are built either on barges or on stilts, are the prototype of modern prefabricated housing. The walls and floors are sections of bamboo thatchwork, tied to upright supports which are sunk into the soft ground. At low water there is fishing only in the center of a lake that may be less than three feet deep, whereas in the fall, after the rains, the same lake will be twenty-five or more feet deep and twice its former area. The simplest way of dealing with these extremes is to move the whole village; in the new site it does not take long to have the houses ready again.

At all seasons the Mekong is alive with junks that carry vivid patchwork sails, and with little, gaily painted, flat-bottomed river steamers—their upper and lower decks full of sarong-clad travelers—as well as with fishermen's sampans operated by brown men in black tunics, each standing in the bow, patiently lifting and lowering and lifting again a large fork strung with thin black netting. In between the forks the jumping fish sparkle like jewels in the strong morning sun. Here and there the activity is interrupted by a long stretch of glassily calm, oily brown water, where there are neither boats nor people, and where the brown expanse is divided from the bone-dry blue sky above by a thin green strip of garden landscape, fringed at the horizon with the clustering tops of sugar palms.

The waters of the Mekong generally belong to the government, and exploitation rights are leased once a year to the highest bidder. A reserve of ready cash, the right connections, and some greasing of palms will permit an entrepreneur to lease many square miles of water for the placement of fish traps. Most big fishing operators sublease a part or all of their rights to smaller operators and make a handsome profit in so doing.

The fish are concentrated in the main channel when the water is low, awaiting the beginning of the rainy season and their spawning period. With the rising waters the young are carried over the vast inundated lands, where shallow temporary lakes and temporarily drowned forests become veritable hothouse cultures of protozoan, plankton, worm, and insect life. In the midst of this abundance the fish grow fast. When the waters recede and the fish are returning to the river, there is no creek or flowage of any kind that does not have a bamboo barrage with a catching cage at its downstream end. Out of the more than a thousand species of fish that live there, between eighty and a hundred kinds are marketed. Most of these are members of the minnow and catfish families, and some are so large that their tails drag in the mud between the pairs of men who carry them on poles strung through their gills.

Some of the Mekong's fishes have become adapted to staying behind in the lowlands even when the waters recede. Parts of the gills or mouth cavities have developed into lung-like structures, permitting the fish to breathe air. The same species have developed sturdy fins, enabling them to walk overland for miles from a drying water hole to a wetter one. (The first sight of a three-foot fish walking across the road on a moonlit night may cause the observer to review his living habits.) As the water of the river recedes farther, these fish bury themselves, finding the moist places that flood first and dry last, in which to estivate during the dry season.

The larger fishing sites are marked by clusters of houseboats and huts. At the river's edge there are drying platforms for salted fish, enveloped in the powerful smell emanating from the piles of fish offal. The site is dominated by traps and barricades whose buttresses and wings suggest those of a river fortress. High above the river a catwalk connects several platforms furnished with altars, flags, and banners, designed to reassure the spirits above and below the waters. The platforms are forbidden territory to women, since it is believed that a woman's presence there would ruin the fishing or have even worse consequences for the encampment—a superstition that gives the fishermen a chance to get away by themselves for a while.

When the downstream fish migration is at its peak the cages into which the fish are funneled may be lifted at regular intervals all around the clock. Those fish that are not kept alive to be sold fresh are treated on the spot by women who sit in long open sheds built over the water. Here they cut up the fish, letting the heads and entrails fall through the slats of the floor into the river below; the bodies are then split, placed in brine, and dried in the sun—a way of preserving fish that dates back to ancient Egypt.

Another method is to place the fish in vats with large amounts of salt, weight them down with stones, and leave them to ferment. After a few months the vats are tapped to yield a clear golden liquid of extraordinarily high nitrogen content. So nourishing is this *Tuk Trey* (a Cambodian name meaning "fish water"), that a French physician used it successfully as a substitute for milk in raising abandoned babies. The ancient Romans produced a similar liquid, equally salty, pungent, and tasty, which like *Tuk Trey* was used in soups or as a sauce for meat.

Undoubtedly the most pungent way of preserving the river's bounty—also of ancient origin and widespread throughout the Orient—is to turn fish into cheese. The recipe calls for certain thumb-long, short-lived fishes which occur by the billions. After these have been cleaned, cut, and mixed with salt, the mixture is left to rot in a vat. After six months—or for the best results even longer—the action of various bacteria will have turned it into a whitish paste, compounded of proteins and amino acids, and laced with calcium from the softened bones. The odor is very strong, but approached without prejudice and bearing in mind that Western cheese is of comparable origin, it can be delicious.

The people of Laos and Cambodia, and above all of Vietnam, are now becoming so numerous that they cannot continue in their age-old ways. Their leap from the past into the present involves stricter control of the river and the land around it. In the process they have burned large tracts of inundated forests that were once fish nurseries, and the ensuing erosion has led in turn to the rapid silting in of lakes and rivers, followed inevitably by a decline in the fishes of the region. The rise and fall of this and other tropical rivers will be further regulated, the land will be irrigated instead of being flooded naturally, and fifty years from now the Mekong may have dams and a navigable channel into Laos, with locks bypassing several rapids. The river will generate hydropower, and modern methods of agriculture will boost the rice harvest to several times its present volume. Although the people will still eat fish, most of these will be grown from selected stock in artificial ponds.

The Problem of Pollution

It is sometimes argued that the influence of man on his surroundings is merely one more biological force, differing only in degree from the instinctive habits of beavers or the tendency of sphagnum moss to fill a bog—or, conversely, that man is exerting a set of novel forces, no more comparable in kind than in degree with the processes of biological evolution. In any event, there can be no question of the rate at which man-made changes have occurred. Their dimensions are matters of historical record, with the changing rivers as prime witnesses.

The Ohio River is a classic case. Before 1800, travelers who made their way west told of wooded, vine-hung islands, and of forested hills coming down to the water's edge. In places there were high, steep banks dense with overhanging trees; in others the valley broadened into rich bottomland. The forest edge was studded with flowering bushes, fragrant with blossom in the spring, luscious with berries in the fall. Flocks of wild geese swarmed upon the water; turkeys and quail abounded on the shore, as did deer and other forest animals. A hunting party could easily bring in several hundred squirrels from one expedition, and kills of more than a thousand were reported. There were bears too, but they were wary even before the white man came. Flattened patches in the grass where they had rested and sunned themselves, and rotten logs torn to pieces in quest of ants, often indicated their presence. The forest trees were straight and high, and were of many different kinds.

A century and a half later, a description of the same area would have read as follows: The banks were littered with tin cans, with pieces of plaster in bizarre shapes, and with remnants of torn-down or left-over construction; here and there abandoned cars turned upside down lay rusting. Old gunny sacks hung limply on branches of brush remaining from the last high water, and bottles of all shapes were scattered up and down the shore. Even in July the elm trees along the shore road had lost most of their leaves, and the few that remained were yellow. The sun shone blurred through the smog that lay heavily over the valley. Where in days past a hunting party might have gone ashore to shoot squirrels, teen-agers from factory towns sat on the debris, aiming with slingshots at the many rats that scurried in and out of their hideaways among the garbage. Every now and then one was hit and fell into the river, adding its carcass to the already polluted waters of the Ohio.

The pollution of streams is not new. As soon as there were settlements in the river valleys, their wastes began to be emptied into the streams. The towns of the ancient Indus Valley civilization appear to have been provided with a kind of sewer system; yet from time to time these Indian towns appear to have been abandoned to escape the effects of pollution. The drains, it is now assumed, were storm sewers and did nothing to alleviate the accumulation of organic wastes in the rivers. Conditions did not improve through the ages. Imperial Rome and Elizabethan London were equally unsanitary places. And when the workshops of Europe before the industrial revolution were supplanted by the factories of the nineteenth century, the rivers continued to be used for the dumping of wastes as well as for an industrial water supply. It is no wonder that before the advent of the first sewage treatment plants late in the nineteenth century, the rivers near all large towns should have been foul-smelling and unsightly. The following verse, found on a boardroom table after a meeting of the Mersey and Irwell Joint River Committees in 1901, describes the situation in England at the turn of the century:

> If with a stick you stir well
> The poor old river Irwell
> Very sick of the amusement
> You will very soon become
> For fetid bubbles rise and burst
> But that is really not the worst
> For little birds can hop about
>   Dry-footed in the scum.

And at about the same time, a branch of the Des Plaines River near Chicago was reported to have become covered with a scum so thick that it could support the weight of a man.

Although the course of history leads in a straight line from the stone-age tanner who scraped his furs into a stream to the river-polluting tannery, oil refinery, or plating plant of the twentieth century, there is one important difference between the two. As recently as a century and a half ago, next to nothing was known of the consequences of pouring factory wastes into rivers. The factory owner of today no longer has this excuse. The nature of pollution is now understood, even though the problem itself is far from being solved.

20. The Negro Speaks of Rivers

LANGSTON HUGHES

Hughes (1902–1967) was the first prominent professional black writer. "The Negro Speaks of Rivers" (1921), his first publication, launched him into the beginnings of the Harlem Renaissance of the 1920's. He, like Cullen, was born in Missouri. After growing up in Detroit and Cleveland (where he began to write poetry), and some living in Mexico and Europe, he settled in Harlem for the rest of his life. His first book of poems was *The Weary Blues* (1926); his last, *The Panther and the Lash* (1967). He wrote two autobiographies, a play, a musical, and four volumes of shrewdly comic fiction concerning Jesse B. Semple, the universal black.

I've known rivers:
I've known rivers ancient as the world and
    older than the flow of human blood in human
    veins.

My soul has grown deep like the rivers.

I bathed in the Euphrates when dawns were
    young.
I built my hut near the Congo and it lulled me
    to sleep.

I looked upon the Nile and raised the pyramids
    above it.
I heard the singing of the Mississippi when Abe
    Lincoln went down to New Orleans, and I've

seen its muddy bosom turn all golden in the
sunset.

I've known rivers:
Ancient, dusky rivers.

My soul has grown deep like the rivers.

---

21. From *Goodbye to a River*

JOHN GRAVES

Graves (1920–   ) was Professor of English at Columbia
when he returned to the Brazos to float down that river
and write *Goodbye to a River* (1960). He has since
coauthored *Growing Up in Texas* (1971), and also
collaborated with Robert H. Boyle and T. H. Watkins on
The Water Hustlers (1972), a report on the development
of water resources in Texas, California, and New York.

T HE SILENT AIR of ruin is fragile.

Though the day was bleak and low still, moseying up the valley *
had cleansed my feeling about it, a little. Below the crossing's fast
water, bream were surface-feeding on midge nymphs or something else
too small to be seen. Anchoring with a rock, I cast a little Rio Grande
King to where the rippled water turned slick, but it wasn't little
enough. They ignored it for a dozen or so casts, and when one finally
took he was the size of a silver dollar with tail and fins, a goggle-eye.
To me, bream on a fly rod are as pretty fishing as a man can want,
but there are times when they aren't worth working for. I put the little
one back in the water, reeled in, and shoved on.

* Of the Brazos River.

84

Just around the bend there, the canoe balanced now and shooting smoothly along, I saw another cleanness. A bald eagle came flapping easily down the wind, passed within short shotgun range of me, and lit in a dead tree upstream. I put the glass on him and he sat there, spruce black and white, fierce-eyed enough for anyone's Great Seal. . . .

They practically do not exist any more in our part of the country. Those who study such matters believe that the whole nation, not counting Alaska, contains only a couple of thousand or so of them now. They don't adapt. They need big space and big time and big solitude for their living and their breeding, and not finding them, perish. . . .

Most people who feel at all about birds and animals seem to have a specialized affection for those species that adjust tidily to the proximity of man and man's mess. I lack it, mostly. A robin's nest in a pruned elm in one's garden is pleasant to watch, and English sparrows' squabbles and loves are worth laughing at if you haven't got anything better to laugh at, and gulls do circle with white grace about our coastal garbage dumps. But for me they lack the microcosmic poetry that some see in them. They lack the absoluteness of the spacious, disappearing breeds—of geese riding the autumn's southward thrust, of eagles, of grizzlies, of bison I never saw except in compounds . . . Of wolves . . . Of wild horses that have been hunted down in twenty years or so and have been converted into little heaps of dog dung on the nation's mowed lawns. And antelope, and elk grazing among the high aspens, an old bull always on guard . . .

I'm aware that the bald eagle eats carrion and has other unaesthetic habits, noted by good Benjamin Franklin. It doesn't affect the other feeling. Sheepmen shoot the goldens now with buckshot from airplanes, in the western country. We don't deserve eagles; they will go.

What hurt was knowing that when I was younger I would have shot this one. The gun lay by my foot, and an ancient itch had stirred my hand toward it as he passed. . . . For nothing, for pride of destruction that has marked us as a breed . . .

"Hell," the old-timers used to brag in front of the feed stores in Weatherford and Granbury, "I've done wore out three farms in my time. . . ."

Anyhow, he sat there on a barkless worm-runed branch, twisting his neck to set the full yellow glare of his eye upon me, and when my own neck was twisted around too totally for comfort, I waved him goodbye and took up the paddle again.

22. From *Life on the Mississippi*

MARK TWAIN

Mark Twain is the pseudonym of Samuel Langhorne
Clemens (1835–1910). He was born in Missouri, and was
an apprentice to a river boat pilot before becoming a writer.
Twain was a prolific writer; he traveled widely and became
very famous, especially as a humorist. *The Adventures
of Tom Sawyer* (1876) and of *Huckleberry Finn* (1884),
and *A Connecticut Yankee in King Arthur's Court* (1889)
are probably his best-known books, along with *Life on the
Mississippi* (1883), from which this selection comes.

A S I HAVE SAID, the big rise brought a new world under my
vision.* By the time the river was over its banks we had forsaken
our old paths and were hourly climbing over bars that had
stood ten feet out of water before; we were shaving stumpy shores,
like that at the foot of Madrid Bend, which I had always seen avoided
before; we were clattering through chutes like that of 82, where the
opening at the foot was an unbroken wall of timber till our nose was
almost at the very spot. Some of these chutes were utter solitudes.
The dense, untouched forest overhung both banks of the crooked little
crack, and one could believe that human creatures had never intruded
there before. The swinging grape-vines, the grassy nooks and vistas
glimpsed as we swept by, the flowering creepers waving their red
blossoms from the tops of dead trunks, and all the spendthrift richness
of the forest foliage, were wasted and thrown away there. The chutes
were lovely places to steer in; they were deep, except at the head; the
current was gentle; under the "points" the water was absolutely dead,
and the invisible banks so bluff that where the tender willow thickets
projected you could bury your boat's broadside in them as you tore
along, and then you seemed fairly to fly.

Behind other islands we found wretched little farms, and wretcheder
little log cabins; there were crazy rail fences sticking a foot or two

* Twain is observing the Mississippi as an apprentice pilot in 1857.

above the water, with one or two jeans-clad, chills-racked, yellow-faced male miserables roosting on the top rail, elbows on knees, jaws in hands, grinding tobacco and discharging the result at floating chips through crevices left by lost teeth; while the rest of the family and the few farm animals were huddled together in an empty wood-flat riding at her moorings close at hand. In this flatboat the family would have to cook and eat and sleep for a lesser or greater number of days (or possibly weeks), until the river should fall two or three feet and let them get back to their log cabins and their chills again—chills being a merciful provision of an all-wise Providence to enable them to take exercise without exertion. And this sort of watery camping out was a thing which these people were rather liable to be treated to a couple of times a year: by the December rise out of the Ohio, and the June rise out of the Mississippi. And yet these were kindly dispensations, for they at least enabled the poor things to rise from the dead now and then, and look upon life when a steamboat went by. They appreciated the blessing, too, for they spread their mouths and eyes wide open and made the most of these occasions. Now what *could* these banished creatures find to do to keep from dying of the blues during the low-water season!

Once, in one of these lovely island chutes, we found our course completely bridged by a great fallen tree. This will serve to show how narrow some of the chutes were. The passengers had an hour's recreation in a virgin wilderness, while the boat-hands chopped the bridge away; for there was no such thing as turning back, you comprehend.

From Cairo to Baton Rouge, when the river is over its banks, you have no particular trouble in the night; for the thousand-mile wall of dense forest that guards the two banks all the way is only gapped with a farm or woodyard opening at intervals, and so you can't "get out of the river" much easier than you could get out of a fenced lane; but from Baton Rouge to New Orleans it is a different matter. The river is more than a mile wide, and very deep—as much as two hundred feet, in places. Both banks, for a good deal over a hundred miles, are shorn of their timber and bordered by continuous sugar-plantations, with only here and there a scattering sapling or row of ornamental China trees. The timber is shorn off clear to the rear of the plantations, from two to four miles. When the first frost threatens to come, the planters snatch off their crops in a hurry. When they have finished grinding the cane, they form the refuse of the stalks (which they call *bagasse*) into great piles and set fire to them, though in other sugar countries the bagasse is used for fuel in the furnaces of the sugar-mills. Now the piles of damp bagasse burn slowly, and smoke like Satan's own kitchen.

An embankment ten or fifteen feet high guards both banks of the

Mississippi all the way down that lower end of the river, and this embankment is set back from the edge of the shore from ten to perhaps a hundred feet, according to circumstances; say thirty or forty feet, as a general thing. Fill that whole region with an impenetrable gloom of smoke from a hundred miles of burning bagasse piles, when the river is over the banks, and turn a steamboat loose along there at midnight and see how she will feel. And see how you will feel, too! You find yourself away out in the midst of a vague, dim sea that is shoreless, that fades out and loses itself in the murky distances; for you cannot discern the thin rib of embankment, and you are always imagining you see a straggling tree when you don't. The plantations themselves are transformed by the smoke, and look like a part of the sea. All through your watch you are tortured with the exquisite misery of uncertainty. You hope you are keeping in the river, but you do not know. All that you are sure about is that you are likely to be within six feet of the bank *and* destruction, when you think you are a good half-mile from shore. And you are sure, also, that if you chance suddenly to fetch up against the embankment and topple your chimneys overboard, you will have the small comfort of knowing that it is about what you were expecting to do. One of the great Vicksburg packets darted out into a sugar-plantation one night, at such a time, and had to stay there a week. But there was no novelty about it; it had often been done before.

I thought I had finished this chapter, but I wish to add a curious thing, while it is in my mind. It is only relevant in that it is connected with piloting. There used to be an excellent pilot on the river, a Mr. X, who was a somnambulist. It was said that if his mind was troubled about a bad piece of river, he was pretty sure to get up and walk in his sleep and do strange things. He was once fellow-pilot for a trip or two with George Ealer, on a great New Orleans passenger-packet. During a considerable part of the first trip George was uneasy, but got over it by and by, as X seemed content to stay in his bed when asleep. Late one night the boat was approaching Helena, Ark.; the water was low, and the crossing above the town in a very blind and tangled condition. X had seen the crossing since Ealer had, and as the night was particularly drizzly, sullen, and dark, Ealer was considering whether he had not better have X called to assist in running the place, when the door opened and X walked in. Now, on very dark nights, light is a deadly enemy to piloting; you are aware that if you stand in a lighted room, on such a night, you cannot see things in the street to any purpose; but if you put out the lights and stand in the gloom you can make out objects in the street pretty well. So, on very dark nights, pilots do not smoke; they allow no fire in the pilot-house stove, if there is a crack which can allow the least ray to escape; they order the furnaces to be curtained with huge tarpaulins and the skylights to be closely blinded. Then no light whatever issues from the boat. The undefinable shape that now entered the pilot-house had Mr. X's voice. This said:

"Let me take her, George; I've seen this place since you have, and it is so crooked that I reckon I can run it myself easier than I could tell you how to do it."

"It is kind of you, and I swear *I* am willing. I haven't got another drop of perspiration left in me. I have been spinning around and around the wheel like a squirrel. It is so dark I can't tell which way she is swinging till she is coming around like a whirligig."

So Ealer took a seat on the bench, panting and breathless. The black phantom assumed the wheel without saying anything, steadied the waltzing steamer with a turn or two, and then stood at ease, coaxing her a little to this side and then to that, as gently and as sweetly as if the time had been noonday. When Ealer observed this marvel of steering, he wished he had not confessed! He stared, and wondered, and finally said:

"Well. I thought I knew how to steer a steamboat, but that was another mistake of mine."

X said nothing, but went serenely on with his work. He rang for the leads; he rang to slow down the steam; he worked the boat carefully and neatly into invisible marks, then stood at the center of the wheel and peered blandly out into the blackness, fore and aft, to verify his position; as the leads shoaled more and more, he stopped the engines entirely, and the dead silence and suspense of "drifting" followed; when the shoalest water was struck, he cracked on the steam, carried her handsomely over, and then began to work her warily into the next system of shoal-marks; the same patient, heedful use of leads and engines followed, the boat slipped through without touching bottom, and entered upon the third and last intricacy of the crossing; imperceptibly she moved through the gloom, crept by inches into her marks, drifted tediously till the shoalest water was cried, and then, under a tremendous head of steam, went swinging over the reef and away into deep water and safety!

Ealer let his long-pent breath pour in a great relieving sigh, and said:

"That's the sweetest piece of piloting that was ever done on the Mississippi River! I wouldn't believe it could be done, if I hadn't seen it."

There was no reply, and he added:

"Just hold her five minutes longer, partner, and let me run down and get a cup of coffee."

A minute later Ealer was biting into a pie, down in the "texas," and comforting himself with coffee. Just then the night watchman happened in, and was about to happen out again, when he noticed Ealer and exclaimed:

"Who is at the wheel, sir?"

"X."

"Dart for the pilot-house, quicker than lightning!"

The next moment both men were flying up the pilot-house companionway, three steps at a jump! Nobody there! The great steamer was whistling down the middle of the river at her own sweet will! The watchman shot out of the place again; Ealer seized the wheel, set an engine back with power, and held his breath while the boat reluctantly swung away from a "towhead," which she was about to knock into the middle of the Gulf of Mexico!

By and by the watchman came back and said:

"Didn't that lunatic tell you he was asleep, when he first came up here?"

"No."

"Well, he was. I found him walking along on top of the railings, just as unconcerned as another man would walk a pavement; and I put him to bed; now just this minute there he was again, away astern, going through that sort of tight-rope deviltry the same as before."

"Well, I think I'll stay by next time he has one of those fits. But I hope he'll have them often. You just ought to have seen him take this boat through Helena crossing. *I* never saw anything so gaudy before. And if he can do such gold-leaf, kid-glove, diamond-breastpin piloting when he is sound asleep, what *couldn't* he do if he was dead!"

---

23. Roethke's Birthplace

ALLAN SEAGER

Seager (1906–1968) was a novelist and short-story writer. His books include *Equinox* (1943), *Amos Berry* (1953), *Death of Anger* (1960), and *A Frieze of Girls: Memoirs as Fiction* (1964). He studied at Michigan and Oxford and was Professor of English at the University of Michigan. Just before his death in 1968, he completed *The Glass House,* a biography of Theodore Roethke.

We came upon a river nearly as large as the Seine at Paris, the Saginaw, which the prairie grass had hidden. In the evening toward sunset we come back alone in the canoe and go down a branch of the Saginaw, such an evening as one hardly ever sees. The sky was without a cloud, the atmosphere pure and still. The river watered an immense forest and flowed so gently that we could scarcely tell the direction of the current. The wilderness was before us, just as six thousand years ago it showed itself to the father of mankind. It was a delicious, perfumed, gorgeous dwelling, a living palace made for man, though, as yet, the owner had not taken possession. The canoe glided noiselessly and without effort: all was quiet and serene. Under the softening influence of the scene, our words became fewer, our voices sank to a whisper, until at length we lapsed into a peaceful and delicious reverie.

> From entries for July, 1831,
> *Pocket Notebook, No. 2, Journey to America*
> by Alexis de Tocqueville

THIS LANDSCAPE of the Saginaw Valley * is the vision of a romantic who had grown up in the ambience of Rousseau and Chateaubriand, a vision to be supplanted a century later by that of another romantic, Roethke, and out of less facile materials. De Tocqueville, terrified but characteristically curious, had been guided through the forests from Detroit where he found Saginaw to be three log houses inhabited by fur traders. He mistakenly believed these men to have penetrated farther west than any white men on the continent and he returned to France happy in his error.

Earlier the Jesuits had probably passed through like ghosts, for there were few regions near the Great Lakes that were unknown to them, but the place must have seemed unpromising, for they left no mission.

The valley had been the home of the Sauks, one of the Algonquin tribes. They hunted the big woods and planted corn in their villages along the banks of the river, only sixteen hundred of them, tradition says, an ecologically sound distribution. They lived a soft life and they were annihilated. Their comforts excited the envy of the Chippewas to the north. The oral history of the Indians is definite about events, vague only as to the calendar. Two hundred, three hundred years before, the Chippewas scouted the Sauks' Eden and, after a council held on an island in the Straits of Mackinaw, formed an alliance with the Hurons from the east, the Pottawatamies from the south, and the Menominees from the west. They closed in, canoes coming down the shore line of Lake Huron into Saginaw Bay and up the river, other groups picking up the Sauk trails through the forests, no guns yet, tomahawks. The day they picked for the attack the Sauks were having

* In Michigan.

a harvest festival in honor of a young chief, Raven's Eye. Their enemies waited until a big yellow moon came up in the evening. They gave their yell and fell upon the hapless Sauks, killing all they could find. A few escaped but in the weeks following they were harried through the woods until all were dead. Their memorial is "Saginaw," a version of an Algonquin word that means "the place of the Sauks." Eventually all that was left of the Indians in the valley was the sibilance of their place names, Saginaw, Shiawassee, Tittabawassee.

For after the fur traders came the soldiers, only a few at first so as not to frighten with too great a show of power, then the big councils with the barrels of whisky and speeches about The Great White Father in Washington, and the treaties, an early one signed in 1819 by "Lewis Cass and one hundred and fourteen Indians" ceding most of the Chippewas' land with certain reservations to the United States Government in consideration of one thousand dollars (in silver) to be paid to the tribe annually, and a government-supported blacksmith to serve the tribe "so long as the President of the United States may think proper." (One wonders how long he stayed. It is hard to imagine the elegant Monroe thinking properly of this distant blacksmith.) The Chippewas, a hunting people, were to be ground down and thoroughly tamed for they were to be furnished with farm implements and cattle, and the government was "to employ such persons to aid them in their agriculture as the President deems expedient."

In protest a young chief, Oge-maw-ke-ke-to, wearing on his breast a superb medal presented to him by this very government, addressed the treaty commissioners, "Our people wonder what has brought you so far from your homes. Your young men have invited us to come and light the council fire. We are here to smoke the pipe of peace but not to sell our lands. Our American Father wants them, our English Father treats us better. He has never asked for them. Your people trespass upon our hunting grounds. You flock to our shores. Our waters grow warm. Our land melts away like a cake of ice. Our possessions grow smaller and smaller. The warm wave of the white man rolls in upon us and melts us away. Our women reproach us. Our children want homes. Shall we sell from under them the spot where they spread their blankets? We have not called you here. We smoke with you the pipe of peace."

Of course, it did no good. Other encroaching treaties were foisted on them, providing, among other things, for resettlement in the West until, in 1855, the Chippewas ceded all their land to the government for $220,000 and a sawmill. They lingered on in the region for years, idle and debauched. One of their last chiefs, Shop-en-a-gons, permitted himself to be photographed in civilized garb, wearing a frock coat and holding a tall silk hat. It was all dreadfully usual and pathetic.

Emigration into the Saginaw Valley was slow because the climate was unhealthy. The mosquitoes were huge. The fevers were bad, and the fur traders, unwilling to see the trees go down because they made cover for the animals, discouraged settlers. De Tocqueville has left one of the few accounts of the equipment needed to pioneer this region. The untouched land never cost more than five shillings an acre, a day's pay. When he had chosen his plot, the settler would occupy it, bringing with him an axe, a gun, a tent, a salted pig, a barrel of corn meal, some seed corn, a bushel of seed potatoes and whatever cattle he had. He lived in the tent until he had felled enough trees to make a log hut. He planted his seed potatoes among the stumps. The potatoes, the meal, the pig, and whatever game he could bring down would keep him his first winter. As soon as he had built his hut, he would girdle all the nearby trees to kill them so that their foliage would not keep the sun from his crop of corn the second year. The first two or three years were the hardest. "Afterward comes competence, and later wealth," de Tocqueville said with prophetic serenity.

The few newcomers were chiefly New England farmers who, used to wresting crops out of the fourteen or fifteen inches of dirt covering their native rock, were delighted by the bottomless alluvial soil of the Valley; a few Irish who escaped from the potato famines of the Forties; and later a few Germans, Swabians, Bavarians, reluctant to do their military service.

The pioneers were aware of the vast forests surrounding them. How could they not be? Some of the gigantic pines did not put out a branch until they had risen eighty, even ninety feet above the ground. But they saw no particular value in these trees. They built a few sawmills in the Thirties to saw boards for houses but they had no notion that there would ever be more than a local market for lumber. The Maine forests were then judged to be inexhaustible and they were closer to the big eastern centers of population. And, worse, there was no transport for Michigan lumber, only a few lake steamers plying irregularly between Detroit and Saginaw. It was not until 1847 that a cargo of Saginaw lumber reached the market at Albany, New York.

All this changed very quickly when it was discovered that there were not going to be enough trees in Maine to keep pace with the growth of the country. Lake boats were built and against prodigious difficulties rail lines were put through the woods. For a shrewd man the opportunities for the investment of capital were almost limitless and the same names recur again and again as owners of timber land and sawmills, as executives of rail and steamship companies, as proprietors of banks and wholesale and retail mercantile companies. The lumber boom began. The history of the Saginaw Valley differs little from that of the rest of the Middle West except in this. It is its unique feature.

Statistics on the number of board feet of lumber were kept from 1851 when 92,000,000 feet were cut. In 1882, the zenith of the boom, the figure had risen to over a billion feet. This meant lumber camps on the Saginaw and all its tributaries, the Shiawassee, the Tittabawassee, the Flint, the Cass. (Today there is a little concrete bridge over the Tittabawassee. The stream is barely fifteen feet wide. The water itself seems to have gone with the timber.) The cut was made in the winter when the logs could be sledded over the snow to the riverbanks, piled there until the spring thaw, then skidded into the stream to let the current take them higgledy-piggledy down to the boom where they would be sorted. Each log had been struck at one end with a special hammer and it bore in intaglio the owner's brand. The booms were enclosures that stretched halfway across the stream. Lumberjacks guided the logs into the boom. At the sorting gap at the far end, each owner claimed the logs bearing his mark, made them into rafts, and floated them further down the stream to his sawmill.

There are winter photographs of the camps, the lumberjacks standing and crouching among the pines, the ground white all around them, burly men with mustaches, wide-awake hats, wearing mackinaws and short jackets, never overcoats to get in their way, and the plumes of their breaths show in the picture—the weather was often thirty below zero. Some of these men came from the dwindling Maine woods, arrogantly bringing their skills west "to show the Michiganders how to saw logs." Many were dark French-Canadians who spoke nothing but Canuck French. After the Civil War all kinds of unemployed soldiers found work in the woods or along the streams. They called themselves the "red-sash brigade."

When the winter was over they came to town, to Saginaw, with their winter's pay intact—there was nothing to spend it on in the woods. It would only be two or three hundred dollars but, full of lust, imaginings, and fresh air, they were ready to blow it all. They would take a lustral bath at one of the hotels, buy a new outfit of clothes and a red sash, and go down to Water Street or Franklin Street where the bars and the whorehouses were. And with a terrible physical exuberance that had not been sufficiently tested against mere axe helves or saw handles, they would fight with sheer male pleasure, drunken, gouging, kicking struggles where a river man still wearing his spikes would often leave the print of them in his opponent's face. The admiring police would fill the jail with them, turn them loose when they were sober, and they would go out and do it all over again. A week, ten days of this and they would be calm and penniless. They would meekly take summer jobs in the sawmills until the weather grew cold. Then back to the woods again.

By 1900 it was all over. A few stands of virgin timber were left, islands in a sea of stumps. Roethke was born in 1908 during what seems to have been a period of stunned assessment of what was left to keep a town going on. Beans had been planted to help feed the lumberjacks; they planted more until Michigan raised more navy beans than any state in the country. They had boiled water from salt springs and wells to get pure salt; they boiled more. They discovered veins of a damp, inferior grade of coal and mined that. As they cleared out the stumps, they planted sugar beets and a sugar-industry grew up. (In my own childhood, Michigan sugar was bluish in color and the grains stuck together in lumps. This has now been corrected. The sugar is white and cannot be told from cane.) The factories that had supplied the mills and camps with hardware, boilers, and saws turned painfully to the manufacture of more suitable products or failed.

There was money there. A lot of capital had come from the East and it returned swollen with profit, but a lot of capital had been local and now with its increments it was cautiously invested in local enterprises or it went into trust funds in the vaults of Saginaw banks where it still lies, shedding beneficently its four or five per cent a year. Some of the lumber money and some of the lumber itself went into the splendid wooden houses of the rich, built in the style of the period with round towers topped by ornate finials, steeply pitched roofs, and porches running halfway around the house, set in the middle of wide lawns ornamented with beds of flowers. Many parks were laid out in what is now the center of the city and the well-to-do drove through them in landaus or victorias drawn by matched pairs of horses and later in the first Pierce-Arrows.

In 1889 the Saginaw Club was founded and, unlike many men's clubs, it had its own building where it still purveys quiet, a sound cuisine, and a sumptuous nude behind the bar for gaping at. In 1899 ten acres of farm land were purchased, turned into a nine-hole golf course, and the Saginaw Country Club was established. "An association of leading men and women" formed themselves into the Um-Zoo-Ee Club for the purpose of holding dancing parties. The Canoe Club was founded in 1904 facing the Tittabawassee River "to promote an interest in canoeing, boating, and aquatic sports among the younger element of our best citizenship." A boat landing was provided, later a stand for shooting clay pigeons, and a tennis court. The insane romantic energy of the early years was gone but certain amenities of life had arrived, and it is pleasant to think of the quiet river, once crammed with ugly logs, now supporting the svelte canoes of the lumbermen's children, filled with spooning couples and occasionally a phonograph wafting the strains of "Moonlight Bay" or "Too Much Mustard" from its fluted horn.

What was happening was a consolidation of comforts natural enough, perhaps, after the hardships of the settlement and the lumber boom. The pace of life slowed and became peaceful, and lives tended to repeat themselves without much change from one generation to the next. As they were expected to do, young men went into business, the law, a few into medicine. What had been discovered to be convenient ways of doing things crystallized into habits so rigid that any departure from them could be sustained [only] by a sense of actual guilt. The immigrants prospered, the Germans, the Italians, and later Slavs of various kinds. The lumber boom became the subject of mural paintings on the walls of the Bancroft Hotel dining room. The capitalists, being already rich, hung on to their money. Why risk it? The old civic fire burned low.

It was into this placid town that Roethke was born. What does a man take from his community; what seeps in from roundabout? The first definitions, the fruits of the primary glances, can never be supplanted, for the trees of one's childhood are the touchstones of all later trees, the grass of the back yard the measure of all greenness, and other lights fail because they are not the true sun that brightens those trees, that grass. Man is, of course, Father, and Woman, Mother. All other definitions derive from these, however tenuously. Since all take, we can assume Roethke took these. What else? As a man he had a furious energy all out of proportion to what was spent around him. How did he come by it? Is it a matter of psychology, of metabolism, or was there possibly some mysterious inheritance by rumor or example from an earlier time? It is so hard to tell that perhaps it should not even be mentioned.

A poet must take the materials of his imagery from somewhere, and it will help to describe him to see what he ignores. There is no memory of Roethke hanging around the old folks listening, like Faulkner, and his old folks were German, anyway. Their stories would have led him back to the Old Country which never interested him. He also ignores all the vivid racy tales of the lumber boom, tales that expressed courage, will, and cunning that might have engaged another man. Unlike Allen Tate or Robert Lowell, he ignores in his poetry the events of his region's history. He must have been aware of the Indians, for he collected a shoebox full of flint arrowheads in his rambles along the riverbanks. But, of course, many boys did that. There had been many Indians, many arrowheads, and they were not specially hard to find. Yet there may have been some impingement, for late in life he mentions Indians in one of his poems; and in his most recent notes, a long poem was projected based partly on the wrongs done to them. But, for the most part, he pays no attention to the history of the valley which expresses in modes of physical action an energy like his own. It is as if he had inherited the best part and did not need to acknowledge it.

Out of this prosperous region no poet, no painter or sculptor, no composer had ever emerged. When one did, a profound and innocent apathy surrounded, almost submerged him like a dune of sand on the lake shore. During his boyhood its countless, minute, unrecognized abrasions may have helped to form him both as a man and a poet and assisted unbeknown in their eventual identification.

24. Cuttings and Cuttings (Later)

THEODORE ROETHKE

Roethke (1908–1963) was born in Michigan and went to its University. He taught in various colleges across the country, including Bennington and the University of Washington, where he lived and worked during his last years. He won the Pulitzer Prize in 1954 and the National Book Award twice, in 1959 and 1965.

Cuttings

Sticks-in-a-drowse droop over sugary loam,
Their intricate stem-fur dries;
But still the delicate slips keep coaxing up water;
The small cells bulge;

One nub of growth
Nudges a sand-crumb loose,
Pokes through a musty sheath
Its pale tendrilous horn.

Cuttings (Later)

This urge, wrestle, resurrection of dry sticks,

II. Description:
Reports Through Space and Time

Cut stems struggling to put down feet,
What saint strained so much,
Rose on such lopped limbs to a new life?

I can hear, underground, that sucking and sobbing,
In my veins, in my bones I feel it,—
The small waters seeping upward,
The tight grains parting at last.
When sprouts break out,
Slippery as fish,
I quail, lean to beginnings, sheath-wet.

Suggestions for Writing

1. Write a series of sketches in the manner of Toperoff or Faulkner. Your subject, like theirs, might best be a person or place.

2. Characterize briefly a day, an hour, or an afternoon that seems special to you. If you are from the city, you might try an urban version of White's "Spring."

3. Organize an account of a place according to your actual progress through it, according, that is, to its design in space. Study the selections of Fitzgerald, Graves, and Twain. You may wish to allow yourself a digression as Graves and Twain allow themselves, but be sure that you return to the "mainstream" of your report. This would be a good moment to consider the literal meanings of "plot" and "digression" as they are used to define patterns in writing.

4. Jhabvala and Seager both characterize places. Jhabvala describes modern Delhi; Seager gives Saginaw a historical perspective. Write an account, in one of these two fashions, of your home town. If your town is large, you might write of a neighborhood instead. This paper could lead to a more extensive research project.

5. What other subjects could you treat as Bardach treats rivers and history? Mountains? Lakes? Roads? Boats? Cars? Trains? Take trains for example. If you begin with a good, brief historical account of trains, you might soon find yourself halfway into a good research project in which, as in Bardach's example, you could consider the ecological (or sociological) ramifications of your subject.

III.
Narration

The Element
of Story in Essays

"NARRATIVE" usually means fiction, but the essay can hardly do without it, especially when the writer (Twain for example) takes a passage through time. The line between essays and stories is sometimes very thin. The sketches of "Cassius" could fit in a novel. The passages from Fitzgerald and Graves have the shape of fiction, and Jhabvala actually creates brief fictions in Delhi as she moves from one typical gathering to another. The merger of essay with fiction, as we have seen, is Wolfe's explicit subject.

Narration can virtually dominate factual writing, as in the "story" of Unitas and the Baltimore Colts, of meeting Ernest Hemingway in Paris, or of Custer's Last Stand. This last encounter has become legend, but Vestal reports from a new point of view. Sexton and Feldman similarly bring fresh perspectives to familiar folk tales. They illustrate that the essential narrative drive—an urge to find out what happens next—remains strong even in the retelling of a familiar story, if that telling is good enough. They illustrate also that narratives, whether in essays or fiction, entail the teller's point of view. Sexton even begins with an argumentative thesis. How successfully do these writers bring a fresh perspective to stories you know well? How might these views have entered the formal essay, in which Snow White or the fox and gingerbread man would serve as illustration?

With McPherson's story, we move completely into fiction, if fiction can ever be said to be completely fictional. To some, the story of this young but prominent black writer may seem a fantasy; to others, actuality itself. But that is the wonder of fiction: to be true and not true simultaneously.

25. Everyone Can't Be First String

GEORGE PLIMPTON

Plimpton was a founding editor of the *Paris Review* and is well known for his personal accounts of professional athletics. *Paper Lion* appeared in 1966; his most recent book is *Mad Ducks and Bears: Football Revisited* (1973).

WHEN THE NEWS BROKE that a major convulsion had hit the Baltimore Colts on the heels of their season's miserable start (1–4)—their coach, Don McCafferty, fired, and their great quarterback, John Unitas, benched—I found myself (as a fan and erstwhile temporary last-string quarterback for four plays the year before) struck with a mounting sense of confusion and despair. It was as if the props had been knocked out from under one side of a structure as rockribbed and solid and familiar as one's own house, which one had come home to find tilted alarmingly, the piano collapsed against the downside wall in a welter of wires and keys.

What enhanced the shock was that the team's shattered state was so completely unexpected. As recently as 1970 the Colts had been the world champions, and last January missed the Super Bowl by one game. They were coached by a man, McCafferty, who had the best won-lost percentage in the National Football League, and they were led by a legend, Unitas, the best quarterback in the history of the game. Now, suddenly, this glorious, fabled team had a new coach, John Sandusky, McCafferty's close friend and former assistant, and a new quarterback, Marty Domres, a former Ivy League player. What on earth had happened?

I knew that there had been a change over the summer in ownership and management—the team exchanged by its former owner, Carroll Rosenbloom, the underwear tycoon, in a complicated trade for the Los Angeles Rams, who had been owned for a day or so by Robert Irsay, an air-conditioning magnate from Chicago. When he took over the Colts, Irsay hired as his general manager Joe Thomas, who has been widely credited for the composition of two expansion teams that in a remarkably short time became Super Bowl contenders—the Minnesota Vikings and the Miami Dolphins. Almost as soon as he was in control, Thomas had made a statement which I found very reassuring. "The team is a good balanced mixture of veterans and youth," he said, "and not an old club as some make it out to be. Unitas is as good a quarterback as there is in football. He's No. 1. The only problem is who will be No. 2?"

"Exactly," I thought at the time. "The club is in grand hands."

But then, after the fifth game, a loss to Dallas in which the offense was held scoreless, it was decided to bench Unitas, and I began to wonder what sort of hands were at the helm. When I heard the news I thought back on what I remembered of Unitas when I had been at the training camp in the summer of 1971—mainly his presence on the practice field. There, not only the rookies would glance across at him, stunned that they were in the same company, but just about everyone, veterans included, would look over at some point in the day, so that one caught oneself, jaw slightly agape, staring at the Main Man, which was football parlance for the superstar. Sometimes they called him that "damned Lithuanian," or occasionally "The Man," but usually the Main Man.

Those weeks Unitas was practicing the drop-back from the center's snap to test his recovery from an Achilles'-tendon accident the previous winter. Dozens of times a day he did it, taking those seven savage, quick, bustling steps on pipestem legs back into the protective pocket, his shoulders hunched forward under the high pads, the white helmet with the blue horseshoes turning first to one side, then the other, the pale small face within, the quick cock of the arm—an utterly familiar process to Baltimore people, as ingrained in them, presumably, as the taste of crab cakes from the Chesapeake.

Jim Brown once told me a story about superstars such as John Unitas. In 1964 the East Pro Bowl squad was coached by Allie Sherman. The coach met his players for the first time on a Los Angeles practice field and he clapped his hands and called out, "All right, let's have a first-team lineup over here." Sherman had no list to refer to; he was suggesting that the right players, out of all those stars, would amble forward. *And that is just what happened.* A team materialized with hardly a word spoken, or even a sidelong glance. The players knew where they belonged; they could evaluate themselves in some private yet universal grading system.

I thought that was extraordinary. "But suppose . . . I mean, suppose a great player was humble?" I asked.

"The others would wait for him," Brown replied. "The position would stay open until he walked in and filled it. Ballplayers know. Can you imagine any other quarterback, no matter who the guy was, shoving John Unitas aside to get into an All-Star lineup? No, man, no way."

Well, the point was now Unitas *had* been shoved aside, and when the Colts came to New York in late October with their 1–4 record to play against the Jets, I decided to go out to Shea Stadium and look at what Joe Thomas had wrought. It was announced that Marty Domres would not only start the game, but that Unitas would not play unless Domres was hurt. And, just as advertised, Domres stayed in throughout.

From time to time during the game I watched Unitas on the sidelines, hands thrust into the pockets of his blue windbreaker, standing alone, occasionally turning and restlessly stubbing at the ground with the toe of his football shoe. He was not saddled with the job of talking on the phones to the spotters on the stadium rim, which is often the duty of a back-up quarterback. The times I looked, he was alone, occasionally behind the bench, usually gazing away from where Domres huddled with the offensive coaches on the sidelines.

That last Baltimore scoring drive ended with just a minute and a half left in the game, when on fourth down Domres passed 13 yards to his flanker, Jim O'Brien, completely alone in the end zone, kneeling there to be sure of the catch. O'Brien received the pass to his midsection like a supplicant, bowing over it in gratitude. With this play the Colts went ahead 20–17. But then in his final series, Joe Namath reared back on third down and pegged an 83-yard touchdown pass to Eddie Bell that worked only because one Colt defender jumped in front of another and tipped the ball to the astonished Bell.

The locker room after a defeat of this sort is not an easy place to visit. Football players can pull themselves together after a rout, because one rationalizes that no amount of personal effort would have had any discernible effect on the outcome. But a close game—well, perhaps a block here or a tackle there, or a pass gathered in would have made the difference . . . and the players sit on the stools in front of their cubicles and think about it.

The Colt custom after a game, whatever the outcome, calls for a short prayer, invariably offered by Bob Vogel, the big offensive tackle. Vogel's prayer is a personal, very chatty address, as if God were sitting atop a ladder placed in the middle of the locker room, chin in hand, like a character in a "meaningful" Broadway play. Vogel told Him that they had messed up on various assignments and that they were going to have to knuckle down and work harder. He thanked Him for seeing to it that the Colts had gone through the game without serious injury, and he promised Him that the next time they would do better. Then the locker-room door was opened and the press was let in.

In Carroll Rosenbloom's day the Colt locker room after a game was open to anyone who took the trouble to cadge an invitation. The players had to pick their way through the crowds to get to the showers. Usually a number of youngsters stood about, in awe of where they were, holding their blue woolen Colt caps in their hands. It was very informal and friendly and it was part of the tradition of the "Colt family."

All of this Joe Thomas had changed. He had announced that the locker room was off limits to everyone except players, club officials and the press. No exceptions. Not even young Jimmy Irsay, the owner's 13-year-old son.

So for one who remembered the cocktail-party atmosphere of the Rosenbloom era, the locker room seemed almost empty. Marty Domres did have a considerable group of reporters around his cubicle. He has a lean, intelligent face, with light-hued eyes, and he bears a startling, if youthful, resemblance to Prime Minister Trudeau of Canada —the same long-shaped head, the high forehead and the hair thinning in front. He kept his voice low, the reporters leaning in on him, and it occurred to me that he was doing it out of deference to Unitas, just down the line, who, not having done anything more athletic on the sidelines than shrug his shoulders forward under his windbreaker, had taken a quick shower and was bent forward on his stool, lacing his shoes. No one was questioning him.

I continued to wander around. The players were beginning to come out of their shells. One of them pointed out Joe Thomas to me. A slight, thin figure, he was very nattily dressed in a dark pinstriped suit, moving through the locker room somewhat nervously and with an abstracted air, as if he had put an expensive pair of cuff links down and could not remember exactly where. I introduced myself and asked if I could come down to Baltimore the following week and ask him what was going on.

"Any time," he said expansively.

I stopped by Bob Vogel's cubicle. He sat with a towel around his middle. He and I share an interest in bird-watching. He has a bird-feeding station on the lawn in front of his house on the Chesapeake Bay, and he once told me that the most exciting moment of the previous year—this from a man who spends his autumn Sundays trying to remove the likes of Deacon Jones and Bob Lilly and Merlin Olsen from his path—was when a painted bunting came to feed at his station.

"Hey," he said. He did not want to talk about the football game. "Have you ever been to Hawk Mountain?"

"No," I said. "I've heard of it."

"I read somewhere that during the fall migration thousands of hawks fly past there. It's in Pennsylvania. That's what I'd like to do when I quit football—take my kids up there and look at the hawks."

"Are your kids keen on birds?" I asked.

"They'd better be," he said firmly. He looked very determined.

"Which one's Irsay?" I asked. "Is he here?"

"The new owner?" Vogel squinted. Bird watcher's eyes, I thought. "He's the one over there—beyond the towels—the florid one. Reddish plumage and beak."

I grinned at Vogel and went over to Irsay. He was staring at the floor. I introduced myself. I had heard he was painfully shy. He shook hands. He has red hair, a big friendly face, red from the cold outside, with a flat nose set upon it. He was wearing a red tie and a red-striped shirt. Vogel was right. He was florid. I told him I was sorry about the Baltimore defeat.

"Let me tell you something," he said, and he gave me a quick look.

"What's that?"

"No one gets off this world alive."

"Oh?"

"That's right."

I left the locker room knowing that it was hardly the place, especially after a Baltimore loss, to sit down with anyone and discuss aspects of the team's collapse. I knew that it was almost surely a complex matter. The mechanism that constitutes a great team is in fact a fragile balance of skills and pride and attitude, quite at variance with such easy descriptive words as "powerhouse" or "juggernaut"; the balance is sensitive enough that it does not take much jarring to throw it out of kilter.

One of the most accurate observers of a phenomenon such as the Baltimore decline would be their All-Pro center, Bill Curry. He is almost invariably referred to as the "articulate spokesman of the Colts," a description he is rueful about, wishing rather wistfully that a word more descriptive of his abilities on the field could occasionally be found: "awesome"; "superaggressive"; "animallike," etc.

I called Curry the next day, and after he had talked about the practical reasons behind the team's difficulties ("We lost our players —John Williams, Norm Bulaich, Tom Matte, Eddie Hinton, Bubba Smith"), he began to discuss the team in more general terms. "What made the Colts different," he said, "and perhaps it's the special mark of championship teams, is that we'd cultivated a genuine atmosphere of respect, even love, for our fellow players. It was a tangible thing, a *force,* and you could actually see it work in the game itself. You could spot it in the films. We'd fall behind in game after game. And yet invariably there'd be a tremendous surge: everybody'd look at each other in the huddle, and you knew that *somebody* was going to make a good play, and that somehow we'd do it in the end.

"It's a subtle quality, and I don't know how you hang onto it. But I know when it begins to slip away. It starts with doubting. You begin to doubt each other. You doubt the front office and the changes it makes in policy and procedure. You get to spending too much time discussing such things, wondering why you have a general manager and an owner who don't know your names. There are too many distractions; your concentration begins to slip away; you substitute it with complacency. You lose a game. You begin to blame others. You find that you're yelling at your teammates during a game, and they at you; and then, perhaps worst of all, you begin to realize that all the shouts of encouragement to get yourself and the others going again are phony and meaningless—'false chatter,' we call it—and that the reservoir that previously you could dip into for those qualities that had won for you . . . somehow it had dried up."

When the team began to slide, many of the veterans—Bill Curry excepted—were sanguine enough about the need for change but felt that it could have been done without players' prides being stepped on, that thoughtfulness and empathy should have been at a premium at that time. There was none of this. By all accounts, McCafferty had no warning whatsoever that if he did not conform to front-office wishes, he was going to be axed, and thus he had no opportunity to try to cope with a crisis situation. "That's just not the way you treat someone," a player said at the time. John Unitas heard about his demotion on the clubhouse phone. He picked it up and listened for 20 seconds. He hung up the receiver and gestured at the floor. "I'm benched," he said. "They hoped I wouldn't take it as a slap in the face."

The team did not accept this sort of front-office maneuvering complacently. When McCafferty was fired, Bill Curry was not only stunned, but so incensed about the blame for the team's poor showing being publicly set on the coach's shoulders that he called for a meeting of the players. Twenty-eight of them turned up in ex-Colt Ordell Braase's restaurant, the Flaming Pit, where Curry read a strong and emotional statement in which he absolved the coach of blame, criticized the team itself for its play, and the front office for its decision.

Immediately there was criticism. "Too poetic," Mike Curtis, the middle linebacker said. Others felt it was too strong. Curry was astonished. "So many of them were scared," Tom Nowatzke, the big running back, told me. "I kept comparing that meeting in my mind with the time that the Los Angeles Rams met and vowed to quit unless they got their coach, George Allen, back—and it *worked*. The stars stood up and were counted."

Finally, a somewhat watered-down statement was worked out in which the team acknowledged its share of blame for its showing, and cast its support behind John Sandusky, the new coach.

McCafferty came to see the team for the last time the next day. He spoke briefly. He said he was going to have a lot of free time now, and if anyone there wanted to make up a fourth in a golf game, why to call and let him know. In the absolute silence as he turned to walk out the door, Curry began to cry, perhaps as much for what he was watching happening around him as for his old coach.

Two days after the Colt-Jet game Joe Thomas called up from Baltimore and said that he had changed his mind and decided not to talk to me. It was a distracting matter, and what the Colt organization needed to do was forget the past and concentrate on football. "It's over and done with," he said. "I don't see any reason why that can of worms should be reopened."

"Can of worms?" I said.

"I'm not going to talk. Who the hell cares anyhow?" he went on.

"But you've made some awesome changes," I said. "Sacked McCafferty and benched Unitas. . . ."

"Who cares? I'll tell you something. People don't care. They don't care who the coach is. No one has ever paid a dollar to see a coach on the sidelines. They don't care who the quarterback is as long as he wins. They couldn't care less. They've got their own problems. Who the coach is that's walking up and down the sidelines doesn't mean a thing to them. I'm sorry. I'm not talking to you. I'm not going to reopen that can of worms."

"You sound like you're ashamed of something," I said, "that you've got something to hide."

"Ashamed?" He was outraged. "I've never been ashamed of anything I've ever done in my life. Have you?"

"Well, of course," I replied. "I mean . . . I. . . ."

"You're ashamed of what you've written? Well, what am I doing talking to a writer who's ashamed of what he writes?"

I blinked. "That's not what I meant. But now at least you've got a reason not to talk," I said lamely. "Before, it didn't seem to me you did."

We chatted a bit. I tried to dissuade him. I said I had spoken to so many of the Colts that I needed his side of things.

"I'm not going to open that can. . . ." He sounded frantic.

"Yes, yes. I know," I said.

I decided to go down to Baltimore anyway. I knew that I would not get much out of either John Unitas or Don McCafferty. Both of them have multiyear contracts; Unitas' is for "personal service" for 10 years at a reputed $50,000 a year, and as for McCafferty, he will collect a quarter of a million dollars over five years for not coaching the team. Being honored with these contracts, perhaps Unitas and McCafferty feel obligated to uphold the Colt management policies, however personally humiliating one finds them. Besides, although they both are stoical, talking to them would have been a painful business.

But there were others. I went to see Bubba Smith. Great Bubba! He moves gingerly through his new house with its purple chairs and the chandeliers and the big bed with its ceiling mirror and the rug on it with the foxtails. He is just off crutches, following his hospitalization after the most ironic of injuries: in an exhibition game in Tampa the kid holding the down marker froze as a play, with Bubba in it, moved helter-skelter toward him. Rather than backing away with the stick, which is the required procedure, he froze, wide-eyed, and Bubba hammered into the pole and drove it, by one estimate, two feet into the ground. Under the awful strain, with his legs wrapped grotesquely around the pole, the innards of his right knee were torn askew.

Bubba was delighted to learn that Joe Thomas had refused to hear me. "At least he won't try to mess with your mind," he said. That was a phrase I had heard him use so often: "messing with the mind."

"Have they been messing with yours?" I asked.

Bubba snorted. "Just today I got a letter from the front office saying that I would be fined $100 for every day I missed therapy for my knee. Well, what sort of a letter is that? I like to play football better than anyone. You think I'm going to miss therapy for my knee?" He glared at me. "Well?"

"No, Bubba," I said hastily.

"We are first class," Bubba said. "You can't treat a team that's first class like a gang of rookies. Why, when we played the Jets the first time I was fined $100 for being on the field, down by the sidelines, in my wheelchair."

"What on earth were you doing down there?" I asked. "Someone could have run into you."

"I had seen something," Bubba said. "I got myself wheeled to the bench to tell Billy Newsome [the Colt defensive end who now fills Bubba's position] that he was playing Winston Hill [the Jets' offensive tackle] all wrong. As I was talking to Billy, a policeman came running up, holding onto this walkie-talkie. He apologized and said he could scarce believe what he was supposed to tell me but that word had come down from Joe Thomas that if I didn't clear off the sidelines I was going to be fined $100. I knew what he was thinking—that I could get hurt—but what a way to ask me to leave!"

Bubba shook his head. "Crazy," he said. "I wonder if Joe Thomas noticed that Winston Hill pushed my wheelchair off the field after the game." He laughed. "A great friend. He sent flowers to me in the hospital. You've got to have friends—even if you're management. When they can't talk to their ballplayers . . ." he shrugged.

Somewhat to my surprise, Joe Thomas changed his mind, at least to the extent that he said he would see me and answer questions —although he said he would be "vague." Nonetheless, I agreed, and the day after I saw Bubba I went to talk with Thomas.

The Baltimore Colt office is in a depressed area of town; the stoop outside is often decorated by a collapsed drunk, his bottle in a paper bag beside him. Thomas was waiting for me in his office, sitting behind a desk that hemmed him in on three sides. The office was entirely functional; the desk had two gray telephones; the only attempt at décor was a fake willow bush standing in a bucket of gravel in the corner.

I began by asking Thomas about the mood of the club.

"It's hard to say," Thomas said, being "vague." But then he became more specific. "There's more wide-eyed spirit."

"Wide-eyed spirit?"

"That's my opinion. It's coming back. It's being brought back by people who really like football. There's been animosity—like there is in any family. But after a while there'll be a meeting of the minds. There'd better be," he said.

He began to talk about the anatomy of his decision-making. "What I've done has not been that difficult. I've always been involved in policy-making. After all, people who don't want to make decisions never go anyplace. From the start, I could see something was wrong. Over the past 11 games, which includes pre-season, the Colts never played good, *motivated* football. Look at last season's three final games—beaten by New England, only two touchdowns against Cleveland, none against Miami in the 21–0 loss. Well, maybe the drop-off started back then. It begins to lodge in the back of your mind—it would in the mind of any general manager—that not only is something wrong, but something's got to be done about it. A rubber band begins to stretch. First, you try to find out what's wrong—where the leaks are, so you can plug them up. If there isn't any improvement, you really have to do something about it . . . something drastic. The rubber band snaps. It can't be as drastic as firing the 47 players. You've got to blame the top man—just as the country blames the President if things aren't going right, and gets rid of him in an election."

"McCafferty. . . ."

"Out he goes. I'm not a vacillator. It's like marking a true-false test: you can't slide between one choice and another. You make your decision and you *mark* it."

"It's the old adage, isn't it?" I said. "If the bus keeps breaking down, you shoot the bus driver."

"Something like that," he said. "You can always reckon on change to stir them up."

I asked him about his methods, which most of the team found so upsetting. "What about that telephone call to Unitas?" I asked.

"There is no easy way to do that sort of thing," Thomas said. "Hell, I didn't have to call him at all. But I decided to tell him before he read it in the papers; after all, he's meant so much to the franchise. Now it's done with. It's a new slate . . . a new season. I've got to find out if this other boy can play football. If Marty can't do it, we've got to find someone else.

"I understand about sentiment," he said, looking very solemn. "But I also believe in statements like Branch Rickey's—that the greatest secret is to trade a player a year before he's through, no matter who he is. George Allen over at Washington with his retreads—well, he believes in what *he* believes in, and maybe he makes it work because he believes in it so strongly. But that's not my way."

"No, I can see," I said.

As I left Thomas' office, I remembered the players describing his first meeting with the team—that he had come to announce, quite nervous, sweating heavily: "I don't care if you guys like me or not. That's not what I'm interested in. I'm interested in winning."

Thomas' views were supported in kind by the most outspoken Colt, the brilliant middle linebacker, Mike (Mad Dog) Curtis, also called The Animal. Curtis thinks of football as an "extension of childhood" and believes that those who practice it should be treated with the authority and methods used to harness unruly children. He is the one player who will have nothing to do with the NFL Players' Association, being not only a firm believer in the benevolent patriarchy of the club owners, but that football players have never had it so good.

My own clearest memory of Mike Curtis—a vivid example of his insistence on the correctness and order of things—revolved around an incident during the Baltimore-Miami game last year. A man sitting in the front row of the stands decided suddenly to run onto the field and try to make off with the ball as a souvenir. He handed his field glasses and program to a friend sitting next to him. "Hold these, Ed," he said. "I'll be right back."

The Miami offensive huddle was just breaking when he crossed the sidelines. The 60,000 people caught sight of him almost immediately, and a vast, gusty roar of anticipation went up. Bubba Smith noticed him right away. Bubba was delighted to see him coming because the Baltimore defense had been on the field a long time and he was tired and he hoped this cat would pick up the ball and crazy-leg around the field with it, the police after him, for a good long time, permitting Bubba to thoroughly rest his bones and get his breath back. "I gave him a big smile of encouragement," Bubba told me afterward.

Smith's grin was the last thing the fan saw; just as he picked up the ball, and began scampering off between the two lines, he was hit by Curtis, darting in from his linebacker's spot with a ferocious shoulder block, and, as the ball flew off in one direction, the fan rose up into the air as if launched from a trampoline. Two policemen rushed out, and he was supported swiftly off the field. "Wha' happened?" the fan asked. "You got hit by The Animal—Mad Dog Curtis," one of the policemen answered, shaking his head in wonderment.

The general consensus was that Curtis' reaction was instinctive—that since his whole psyche is geared to removing a football from whoever is carrying it, what triggered his quick, devastating rush was a normal psychological response . . . the territorial imperative at work. (The title of Curtis' recent book is indicative: *Keep Off My Turf*.) Curtis himself, though, produced a more sophisticated reason. "It was anarchy," he told me. "That wise guy was exactly like some stranger climbing over a fence into my yard. He was interfering with the basic law that keeps people in their seats. He was like the 1% of the public that feels it can disrupt the majority with impunity. It's a weak, permissive society that lets them get away with things like that. Such people should not be allowed to disturb the tranquillity of the society," he told me firmly. "In our society there are too many malcontents and too much hogwash."

Curtis' feelings about the Colts and the changeover were more or less an extension of these views. "McCafferty set what you might call a 'lenient posture,'" he told me. "That's all right if you're winning, but it's bad if you're losing. Idealistically, ballplayers are supposed to be able to get themselves mentally prepared for a game. Realistically, someone's got to beat their tail. You don't believe that?"

"But don't some players bridle under . . . ?"

"A lot of people don't like the sort of humiliation inflicted on them by a Don Shula or a Vince Lombardi, but the point is that their system turns out better football players and stronger teams. I'm a great admirer of Shula's coaching. He just didn't permit mistakes. Mac's attitude seemed to be that mistakes were inevitable and should be kept to a minimum. Well, that's a difficult approach. It's true that Mac had two good years, but the first was a carry-over from Shula, and because we had an easy schedule, and even though that was the Super Bowl year, we didn't exactly pound anybody. It's my feeling that with a club like McCafferty's, which doesn't function under the whiplash, there's not enough intensity. You drop a ball? So what. No, give me the medieval approach."

"What about the function of management?" I asked.

"Well, at the moment the atmosphere is unsettling," Curtis admitted. "Everybody's suddenly an employee; many of them are concerned because they're not being pampered as they once were."

Certainly that was the one tremendous difference the players talked about—the change effected by the absence of Carroll Rosenbloom, the former owner, who had put together the entity of the "Colt family." He did pamper them. Gregarious, easy in public, graceful with words, he enjoyed the closest of relationships, both socially and professionally, with his players. For some of them he could also be a true inspiration at football. Bubba Smith once told me, "What used to be in the Colt locker room was a good, sweet atmosphere—and I'd sit there before a game and know that the boss was going to be coming through and that he'd lean over me and he'd say, 'Let's have a good game,' not a pep talk, nothing like that, but he said it in a way that you knew you meant something to him, that you were not just a carcass. That was something I waited for every Sunday. Not much, was it? But afterward I felt like going out and ripping up the stadium for him."

The new owner, Irsay, is the antithesis of all this. He is a shy man, uncomfortable with people, who struggles through such public events as a press conference. At his first official appearance as the owner of the Colts, he announced into a battery of microphones that the trade for the Rams had been made and that "we have transpired a deal." Against his hopes, he remains distant from his team.

He has an astonishingly difficult time with players' names; rather than embarrass them by a mispronunciation or a clean miss he calls everyone "Tiger," or occasionally "Big Fellow." It seems almost a pathological difficulty. Bubba Smith, one of the most famous players on the team, he calls "Bobo," and even his general manager, Joe Thomas, a man to whom he talks twice a day on the phone, and who possesses a foolproof name, one would think, is referred to by Irsay with the "th" pronounced . . . "Joe 'Th'omas."

Irsay has appeared once before the whole team, prior to a preseason game in Kansas City. He arrived late. In fact, McCafferty went up to the hotel lobby to look for him, and while he was gone Irsay suddenly appeared and stepped up to say a few words. He was obviously extremely shy and awkward. He talked a little about himself. He said that he was a self-made man. He had parlayed $800 into an empire. He had married a Polish girl. At this point, John Idzik, the Polish assistant coach standing in the back of the room, gave a glad cry, which caused a ripple of merriment amongst the team. But the outburst seemed to startle Irsay. He finished up quickly, wishing the team luck in the game, and rushed from the room. McCafferty reappeared, looking slightly bewildered, and said that he had looked around in the lobby and Irsay was nowhere to be found.

"Well, he's come and gone," someone told him. "He talked. You missed it."

"Oh," said McCafferty.

Irsay is evidently much more at home in the large wood-paneled office of his air-conditioning plant in Skokie, Ill. Mementos are everywhere. Behind his desk are three mounted fish—a dolphin, a barracuda and a walleyed pike, all with jaws violently ajar, ready to snap.

"Let me tell you something," he said to me there. "After watching the Colts play 10 games and looking at the players, I knew I had to make changes. We had so much talent it was not even funny. But they didn't give a damn. Everyone sulked. Nobody knew who they were playing next to. Why, they had people in the locker room talking *business* before a game. Don McCafferty is one of the greatest guys personalitywise there is. But *football-thinkingwise* . . . his method doesn't work . . . because if you lose games, something's got to be wrong with the coaching."

He got up and began pacing swiftly around his office. He was wearing red again—tie, shirt and socks. His sentences came in sharp bursts. "I talked to Mac. I guess he didn't listen too carefully. I suggested that he start Domres. Well, if he had won with Unitas, he'd have looked good. Right? But he didn't. So that was it. It's my club. I paid $19 million. It's my $19 million." He glared at me.

"I understand that," I said. "What about the methods . . . John Unitas?"

"Why couldn't they have accepted it?" he asked, almost plaintively. "Everyone can't be first string. Why can't people like Tom Matte think back when some veteran had to sit down on the bench for him to play? Why can't they accept it the way Bart Starr accepted it? [Starr, now coaching the Green Bay quarterbacks, in fact retired because of a physical ailment to his throwing arm.] We're not trying to sideline anyone. It's very hard. Why can't they be . . . well, decent about it?"

There is something truly touching about Irsay. He talks about the dream he has always had about owning a great team. Why? To win, of course. "That little win we had over Cincinnati is one of the greatest things I've ever experienced." But what actually motivates him is a child's awe of the players themselves, a blatant hero worship that tongue-ties him. "What I'd really like to do," he said, "is to invite some of them out on the *Mighty I,* my boat, after the last game this year and we could have a few beers and talk. I'd be proud to have dinner with them. I'm a Colt-lover. I saw Bobo Smith at a banquet in Cincinnati. What a guy! But maybe they won't come to the boat," he said sadly. "Some of them I guess don't like me."

I kept being reminded of what one of his players had said—that Irsay had struck them as the sort of man who wanted to be a friend, desperately, but did not have the slightest idea how to go about it.

Irsay, living in Chicago, is rarely on the scene in Baltimore. He flies in for the games. The players see him in the locker room afterward. "Hi, Tiger. Great game, Big Fellow." Joe Thomas, of course, they see much more of. He comes out to the practices. He stands quietly, often very close to the players, though rarely saying a word. The veterans, who have evolved a number of nicknames for him— "Piccolo Player" is one—refer to him at these times, seeing him come across the field, as the "Ominous Presence." "Oh-oh, look sharp, here comes the Ominous Presence." "He stands and eyeballs you," one of the players told me. "And frankly, it sort of takes the fun out of practice. He's like Poe's raven. He perches there, just a few feet away, and peers at you and you keep expecting him to cry out, 'Nevermore!'"

The routine goes on. The players work hard for John Sandusky, whom they admire. They have growing respect for Domres. With him at the quarterback position they have won four of six games since the Jet loss I saw in New York; but they speculate about what Unitas would have done in the same position, and what the younger players would have learned from his active tutelage. And the rumors continue to fly. The most persistent one is that Thomas will make a clean sweep; that he must start afresh; that subconsciously he never could have accepted a ready-made championship team. In the turmoil players find qualities in their fellows they had not appreciated before. Curry is in awe of his line coach, Red Miller, who through it all has kept his sense of determination and optimism. The humor is always there, whatever the situation; Dan Sullivan, the offensive tackle, suggests that Tom Matte, livid with fury at being sidelined and inactive, be outfitted with leather handles on the sides of his rib cage, if he really wants to contribute, so that he can be set up around the field as a tackling dummy. In the drills, Bill Curry and Mike Curtis go full at each other—almost as if they were bent on canceling their ideological differences. For Curry it is partly a therapy for getting his mind off what has been worse than a nightmare. "But, in fact, it's the best sort of practice in the world," he told me. "After a week of trying to block down on Curtis, the two of us really going at it, the linebacker you go up against on Sunday is so slow that it seems like he's running in water."

Of course, the greatest tonic for a team in the dumps is victory; in Baltimore's case, being a team of such particular tradition, a special *kind* of victory. The Colts achieved it over Cincinnati, not just "our little win," as Irsay had described it, but a triumph over adversity in which reserves of championship quality had to be tapped. After the Jet game, Baltimore had lost to Miami, beaten New England quite easily, then lost to San Francisco. This was the game in which Unitas came in for Domres, who had been knocked temporarily silly, for one awful play in which, after having received a standing ovation from the 49er crowd, he was not only thrown for a 21-yard loss on a pass attempt but fumbled the ball away to the 49ers, who quickly scored— a humiliation so appalling, considering Unitas' situation, that blessed if I, watching the game on television, didn't find myself comparing it to King Lear's on the heath. But then came the Cincinnati game—and it was the sort of donnybrook that Bill Curry had been talking about —won 20-19 as the final gun went off by a Jim O'Brien field goal. As the ball went through the uprights Curry heard a curious whooping sound behind him—Bob Vogel it turned out to be, the 10-year veteran, and he was leaping straight up and down like a klipspringer gone berserk. He shouted at Curry as they trotted off the field together that it was the best game he could remember since the Super Bowl.

"It came back right there," Curry said to me afterward. "It was like old times. I don't know whether it will stay with us. But it was there."

I had heard that Bob Vogel had decided to retire—after those 10 years at offensive tackle for the Colts. Could he have changed his mind after the Cincinnati game? I doubted it. I wondered vaguely what the true reason was, and I thought of calling him to find out. But then I remembered that in the locker room after the Jet game he had told me about Hawk Mountain, and how he had always regretted that the football season was on during the fall bird migration and interfered with going up to Pennsylvania with his children to see the hawks floating in the thermals by the hundreds above the steep stands of oak and hemlock. It would not have been worth calling to find that was not the reason.

---

26. The Man Who Killed Custer

STANLEY VESTAL

Stanley Vestal is the pseudonym of Walter S. Campbell (1887–   ). He wrote several books dealing with the American West. His subjects included the Missouri River, Kit Carson, Jim Bridger, and Sitting Bull. Under his own name, he wrote two books about the craft of writing nonfiction.

SOON AFTER the allied tribes defeated General George Crook at the Battle of the Rosebud, June 17, 1876, they pitched their camps on the prairies just west of the winding Little Big Horn River.* As White Bull related it to me, each tribe had its own camp circle, each band in its own segment, each tepee in its proper place. The Cheyenne camp circle lay farthest north, with the four Sioux circles—Sans Arc, Ogalalla, Minniconjou, Hunkpapa—upstream. Chief White Bull's tepee stood in the Sans Arc circle, since his wife of that

---

* In southeastern Montana.

115

time was a Sans Arc woman. That morning he was out with his grazing ponies about a thousand yards from the river, trying to keep them together. As usual, he carried his seventeen-shot Winchester and wore two filled cartridge belts. It was very dry and dusty with little wind, and his horses were restless, for the flies were a plague on the Little Big Horn that summer.

It was not yet time for the midday watering when White Bull heard a man yelling the alarm. Immediately he jumped on his best running horse, a fast bay, and ran his ponies back to camp. By that time he could see the column of dust to the south. First of all White Bull saw his own family mounted and sent on to safety. Then he rode as hard as he could the three miles to the camp of his uncle, Sitting Bull, the Hunkpapa circle, which Reno's troopers were approaching. By the time he reached it, the women and children had fled and nearly a thousand warriors had gathered to resist the troops. Already some Sioux had been shot down, and Major Reno's Indian scouts were running off the Sioux ponies.

Before White Bull could take any effective part in the fight, the soldiers fell back to the timber along the river, and soon after climbed into their saddles and raced away up the river looking for places to cross.

Said White Bull, "Then the Indians charged them. They used war clubs and gun barrels, shooting arrows into them, riding them down. It was like a buffalo hunt. The soldiers offered no resistance. I saw one soldier on a gray horse, aimed at him and fired, but missed. Just then I heard someone behind me yelling that soldiers were coming from the east [Custer's force] to attack the north end of the camp where I had left my ponies. We all raced downstream together. Some rode through the camps and crossed the river north of them, but I and many others crossed and rode up a gully to strike the soldiers on the flank. After a while I could see five bunches of soldiers trotting along the bluffs. I knew it would be a big fight. I stopped, unsaddled my horse, and stripped off my leggings, so that I could fight better. By the time I was near enough to shoot at the soldiers, they seemed to form four groups, heading northwest along the ridge.

"All the Indians were shooting. I saw two soldiers fall from their horses. The soldiers fired back at us from the saddle. They shot so well that some of us retreated to the south, driven out of the ravine. Soon after, the soldiers halted and some got off their horses. By that time the Indians were all around the soldiers, but most of them were between the soldiers and the river, trying to defend the camp and the ford. Several little bunches of Indians took cover where they could, and kept firing at the white men.

"When they ran me out of the ravine I rode south and worked my way over to the east of the mounted bunch of soldiers. Crazy

Horse was there with a party of warriors and I joined them. The Indians kept gathering, more and more, around this last bunch of soldiers. These mounted soldiers kept falling back along the ridge, trying to reach the rest of the soldiers who were fighting on foot.

"When I saw the soldiers retreating, I whipped up my pony, and hugging his neck, dashed across between the two troops. The soldiers shot at me but missed me. I circled back to my friends. I thought I would do it again. I yelled, 'This time I will not turn back,' and charged at a run the soldiers of the last company. Many of the Sioux joined my charge and this seemed to break the courage of those soldiers. They all ran, every man for himself, some afoot and some on horseback, to reach their comrades on the other side. All the Indians were shooting."

Such fighting, though necessary in defending the camp and killing enemies, was to the Indians "just shooting." For, to the Sioux warrior, the striking of a blow or "coup" upon an enemy's person with the hand or something held in the hand was the most glorious deed a warrior could perform, and his rating depended upon the number of such coups he could gather. Among the Sioux, four men might count a coup upon the same enemy in the same fight, and on that occasion ranked in the order of their striking him. To strike first was the greatest honor possible and the man who had done that could wear the Indian's medal of honor—an eagle's tail feather—upright in his back hair. To shoot or scalp an enemy, to capture his gun or his horse, were creditable, but none of these compared as war honors with the coup.

White Bull said, "I saw a mounted soldier waver in his saddle. I quirted my pony and raced up to strike him and count the first coup on this enemy. Before I could reach him, he fell dying from his saddle. I reined up my pony, jumped down and struck the body with my quirt. I yelled, '*Onhey!* I have overcome this one.' I took the man's revolver and cartridge belt.

"Did-Not-Go-Home struck this enemy right after me; he counted the second coup. I jumped on my horse and hurried on to join the charge through the dust and smoke drifting down the hill.

"I saw a soldier on horseback left behind; his horse had played out. I charged him, Crazy Horse following. The soldier heard me coming and tried to turn in his saddle and aim his carbine at me. But before he could shoot, I was alongside. I grabbed him by the shoulders of his blue coat and jerked hard to throw him off his horse. He fired in the air, screamed, and fell from his horse. This was another first coup for me. Crazy Horse struck this man second.

"Other soldiers were left afoot. I saw one with Indians all around him, turning from side to side, threatening them with his carbine to keep them at a distance. I rode straight at him. When I got close, he fired, but I dodged and he missed me. Then I rode him down. Bear Lice counted the second coup. The survivors of these two bunches of soldiers moved up and joined those to the north and west, about where the monument stands now. Another bunch of soldiers was down the hill nearer the river. The air was full of dust and smoke.

"Here and there through the fog you could see a wounded man left behind afoot. I saw one bleeding from a wound in his left thigh. He had a revolver in one hand and a carbine in the other. He stood all alone shooting at the Indians. They could not get at him. I rode at his back. He did not see me coming. I rode him down, counting the first coup. Brave Crow counted the second coup on this enemy. By this time, all the soldiers up the hill had let their horses go. They lay down and kept shooting.

"The horses turned loose by the soldiers—bays, sorrels and grays —were running in all directions. Lots of Indians stopped shooting to capture these horses. I tried to head some off, but other Indians were ahead of me. I caught just one sorrel.

"Now that the soldiers were all dismounted their firing was very fierce. All at once, my horse went down, and I was left afoot. For a while the Indians all took cover and kept shooting at the soldiers."

This fight, known to white men as the Battle of the Little Big Horn or Custer's Last Stand, is known to the Sioux as *Pe-hin* (Head-hair) *Hanska* (Long) *Ktepi* (Killed), for on the frontier Custer usually wore his hair long and was called "Long Hair" by the Indians. The battle, therefore, was "the fight in which Long Hair was killed."

On the day of his death Custer was considered the most dashing and successful cavalry officer in the Army. During the Civil War he had distinguished himself repeatedly, and his division had led the van in the pursuit of General Lee's forces. It was to him that the Confederates brought their white flag just before Lee's surrender. General Sheridan reported, "I know of no one whose efforts have contributed more to this happy result than those of Custer." To Custer was given the table on which Grant wrote the terms of surrender. He was celebrated as "the boy general" who had never lost a gun or color, and "Custer's luck" was a proverb in the Army.

He had been the second strongest man in his class at West Point and remained to the end a man of extraordinary vigor. Lithe, slender, with broad shoulders, he was a fine horseman and good shot, standing six feet in his boots and weighing about 165 pounds. He could ride all day, carry on his duties until midnight, then scribble long letters to his wife—one of them running to eighty pages—and still be raring to go in the morning.

At this time Custer was in disfavor with President Grant. He had been nursing a grudge against Grant's secretary of war, W. W. Belknap, and early in 1876, when Belknap was hauled before a congressional committee on charges of sharing illegally in the profits of post traders,

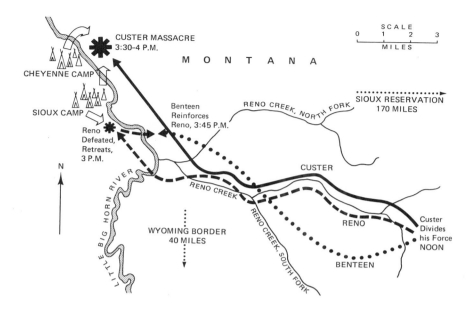

This map shows in somewhat simplified form the Battle of the Little Big Horn, June 25, 1876. Due to variations of opinion, Custer's route after he left Reno and the times given for the actions can be only approximations. But one key factor in the 7th Cavalry's defeat is clear: each of the three commands had only the faintest inkling of what was happening to the others during that hot, bloody afternoon.

Custer went to Washington to testify against him. His evidence was largely hearsay, and he defamed Belknap's character and that of Grant's younger brother—thus maligning the President himself. When Custer came to his senses, he tried to explain his position to Grant. But the President refused to see him, and to punish the hothead further, removed him from command of the crack 7th Cavalry.

Yet there was no one who could match Custer as an Indian fighter. General Terry knew this as well as anyone, and in May, Terry persuaded Grant to reinstate Custer on grounds that his services were indispensable in the campaign against the Sioux and Northern Cheyenne. But for this chance, the Battle of the Little Big Horn might never have happened.

White Bull, although only 26 years old, had already taken part in nineteen engagements. Ten of these were with white men, one with government Indian scouts, and the rest with Indian enemies. He had counted seven coups, six of them "firsts," had taken two scalps, killed three enemies, wounded one, shot three enemy horses, rescued six wounded comrades, and recovered one dead body under fire. He had captured and spared an enemy Assiniboin woman and her husband,

119

had stolen 45 enemy horses, had been hit twice in battle by bullets, and had had a horse shot from under him. Three different warrior societies had invited him to become a member, and on two occasions he had undergone the voluntary tortures of the Sun Dance. He had thrice been given a new name because of brave deeds.

Custer was stronger than White Bull, but the Indian had far more experience in hand-to-hand fighting than the officer. Such it would be now as the Indians closed in on the few remaining troopers. Here is how White Bull described it:

"I charged in. A tall, well-built soldier with yellow hair and mustache saw me coming and tried to bluff me, aiming his rifle at me. But when I rushed him, he threw his rifle at me without shooting. I dodged it. We grabbed each other and wrestled there in the dust and smoke. It was like fighting in a fog. This soldier was very strong and brave. He tried to wrench my rifle from me. I lashed him across the face with my quirt, striking the coup. He let go, then grabbed my gun with both hands until I struck him again.

"But the tall soldier fought hard. He was desperate. He hit me with his fists on the jaw and shoulders, then grabbed my long braids with both hands, pulled my face close and tried to bite my nose off. I yelled for help: 'Hey, hey, come over and help me!' I thought that soldier would kill me.

"Bear Lice and Crow Boy heard me call and came running. These friends tried to hit the soldier. But we were whirling around, back and forth, so that most of their blows hit me. They knocked me dizzy. I yelled as loud as I could to scare my enemy, but he would not let go. Finally I broke free.

"He drew his pistol. I wrenched it out of his hand and struck him with it three or four times on the head, knocked him over, shot him in the head, and fired at his heart. I took his pistol and cartridge belt. Hawk-Stays-Up struck second on his body.

"*Ho hechetu!* That was a fight, a hard fight. But it was a glorious battle, I enjoyed it. I was picking up head-feathers right and left that day.

"Now I was between the river and the soldiers on the hill. I started up the hill. Suddenly I stumbled and fell. My leg was numb, I saw that my ankle was swollen. The skin was not broken, only bruised. I must have been hit by a spent bullet. I crawled into a ditch and lay there till all the soldiers were killed. At the time I stopped fighting, only ten soldiers were on their feet. They were the last ones alive."

White Bull scoffed at the yarns about the soldiers committing mass suicide. Said he: "The soldiers looked tired, but they fought to the end. There were few cartridges left in the belts I took off the soldiers.

"I waited where I was until my friend With Horns came along

and found me. He put me on his horse and led it back across the river. The people were some distance west on the flat; they had not had time to move their tepees."

After resting, eating, and having the wound dressed, White Bull mounted his horse and forded the river to get his leggings and saddle. He then rode over the battleground to see the dead. Most of the bodies were naked. He did not see anyone mutilating the dead.

"On the hill top, I met my relative Bad Soup. He had been around Fort Abraham Lincoln and knew Long Hair by sight. When we came to the tall soldier lying on his back naked, Bad Soup pointed him out and said, 'Long Hair thought he was the greatest man in the world. Now he lies there.'

"'Well,' I said, 'if that is Long Hair, I am the man who killed him.' Nobody scalped Long Hair, because his hair was cut short."

Of course, Bad Soup was not the only Indian who had seen Custer, and others may have recognized his body. At any rate, I have never met an old-time Sioux who took part in that fight who had any doubt that White Bull killed Custer. But White Bull declared to me: "They say that I killed Long Hair, but I never saw him to know him before the battle. I do not think my cousin, Bad Soup, would have lied to me."

White Bull did not know what became of Custer's pistol, as after he was hit he could not go back to gather up his trophies. By the time he rode out to inspect the battlefield other Indians had carried them off. (According to the authority General Edward S. Godfrey, "Custer carried a Remington Sporting rifle, octagonal barrel; two Bulldog self-cocking, English white-handled pistols, with a ring in the butt for a lanyard; a hunting knife, in a beaded fringed scabbard; and a canvas cartridge belt.")

When the celebration of the fiftieth anniversary of Custer's Last Stand was held on the battlefield, White Bull and many other Indian veterans of the fight were invited to take part. Some, fearing reprisals, refused to go. But White Bull said, "I am not afraid," and attended. There General Godfrey led the 7th Cavalry over Custer's trail to the monument which was erected where he fell. Hundreds of mounted Indians in full war dress, preceded by eighty Sioux and Cheyenne survivors of the fight, followed Chief White Bull to meet the troops. They met near the monument. White Bull raised his palm, the sign for peace, and the General sheathed his sword. They shook hands, and the Chief gave the General a fine blanket; Godfrey gave the Chief a large American flag. After the ceremony, the Indians and soldiers paired off and rode back to camp. Nobody who knows Plains Indians can doubt that the man who killed Custer, if living, would be named to lead that Indian column.

Major Alson B. Ostrander, formerly of the 18th Infantry, had heard how Bad Soup had pointed out the body of Custer to Chief White

Bull on the day of the battle. The Major asked White Bull to point out the spot where he saw Custer lying naked on his back that day. White Bull immediately complied. The Major nodded and said, "That is the spot."

The Major asked White Bull, "Are you the man who killed Custer?" White Bull answered, "Maybe." He tried to find out where Custer was wounded, but none of the white officers seemed to know.

He asked me about this. "Where do the white men say Custer was wounded?"

I replied, "In the left temple and in the left side near the heart." Much gratified, he nodded. "That is right," he said.

Naturally enough, Chief White Bull was curious about Custer and why the troops came to attack the Sioux in violation of the existing treaty. He listened attentively all one afternoon while I told him all I knew of such matters, particularly all about Custer's own fame, achievements, character, and motives. But when he learned that on the night before the battle, Custer, trying to encourage his fearful Indian government scouts, had told them that if he whipped the Sioux, he would become the Grandfather—President of the United States—and would look after their people, White Bull's old eyes gleamed. The thought that he had killed Custer had warmed his heart for years. But now to think that the man he killed might have been President was a greater glory than any Sioux had ever dreamed of. Seeing him gloat, I had no doubt that he knew well enough who had killed Custer.

The Cheyenne also say that White Bull killed Long Hair, though some of them confuse the Sioux chief with a leader of their own with the same name.

Shortly after Chief White Bull's surrender to government forces in 1876, a missionary taught him to write in the Sioux language. He then obtained a ledger and in it recorded his military history, illustrating it with pictures in the old Indian style, like those originally painted on hides. At my request, he drew a set of these on separate sheets for me, signing them with his name in Sioux and English, describing the exploit briefly in Sioux, adding his age at the time of the exploit, and the date on which the picture was made. . . .

His description of the fight is in Sioux: *Kici-ecamu-Welo* (I had a fight with him), *le Wokte* (I killed him). To further identify the soldier killed and to cite a witness to attest his exploit, White Bull added *Cetan-wan-Kol-un oki-he-kte* (Hawk-Stays-Up killed him [i.e. struck him] second). This is followed by a repetition of the first Sioux phrase. Hawk-Stays-Up, of course, testified to White Bull's coup on this soldier at what one may call the Court of Honor held after the battle, at which such honors were awarded.

Because of the hostility shown towards White Bull by his white neighbors, I was unwilling to publish these facts while the Chief and his immediate connections were still alive. If those who knew him felt so strongly, I feared that if this story were published in my biography of the Chief (*Warpath, The True Story of the Fighting Sioux,* 1934) some hothead might harm the old man. Now it can be told.

27. Paris: A Little Incident in the Rue de l'Odéon

KATHERINE ANNE PORTER

Katherine Anne Porter (1894–   ) won the National Book Award in 1966 for her *Collected Stories.* Her best-known collections of stories previously were *Flowering Judas* (1935), and *Pale Horse, Pale Rider* (1939). Her novel, *Ship of Fools,* was published in 1962. Like many other writers of her generation, Miss Porter lived for some time in Paris. Subsequently, she lived for many years in Mexico.

LAST SUMMER IN PARIS I went back to the place where Sylvia Beach had lived, to the empty bookshop, Shakespeare and Company, and the flat above, where she brought together for sociable evenings the most miscellaneous lot of people I ever saw: persons you were surprised to find on the same planet together, much less under the same roof.

The bookshop at 12 Rue de l'Odéon has been closed ever since the German occupation, but her rooms have been kept piously intact by a faithful friend, more or less as she left them, except for a film-like cobweb on the objects, a grayness in the air, for Sylvia is gone, and has taken her ghost with her. All sorts of things were there, her walls of books in every room, the bushels of papers, hundreds of photographs, portraits, odd bits of funny toys, even her flimsy scraps of underwear and stockings left to dry near the kitchen window; a coffee cup and a small coffeepot as she left them on the table; in her bedroom, her looking glass, her modest entirely incidental vanities, face powder, beauty cream, lipstick. . . .

Oh, no. She was not there. And someone had taken away the tiger skin from her bed—narrow as an army cot. If it was not a tiger, then some large savage cat with good markings; real fur, I remember, spotted or streaked, a wild woodland touch shining out in the midst of the pure, spontaneous, persevering austerity of Sylvia's life: maybe a humorous hint of some hidden streak in Sylvia, this preacher's daughter of a Baltimore family, brought up in unexampled high-mindedness, gentle company and polite learning; this nervous, witty girl whose only expressed ambition in life was to have a bookshop of her own. Anywhere would do, but Paris for choice. God knows modesty could hardly take denser cover, and this she did at incredible expense of hard work and spare living and yet with the help of quiet dozens of devoted souls one after the other; the financial and personal help of her two delightful sisters and the lifetime savings of her mother, a phoenix of a mother who consumed herself to ashes time and again in aid of her wild daughter.

For she *was* wild—a wild, free spirit if ever I saw one, fearless, untamed to the last, which is not the same as being reckless or prodigal, or wicked, or suicidal. She was not really afraid of anything human, a most awe-inspiring form of courage. She trusted her own tastes and instincts and went her own way; and almost everyone who came near her trusted her too. She laid her hands gently, irresistibly on hundreds of lives, and changed them for the better: she had second sight about what each person really needed.

James Joyce, his wife, his children, his fortunes, his diet, his eye-sight, and his book *Ulysses* turned out to be the major project of her life; he was her unique darling, all his concerns were hers. One could want a rest cure after merely reading an account of her labors to get that book written in the first place, then printed and paid for and distributed even partially. Yet it was only one, if the most laborious and exhausting, of all her pastimes, concerned as she was solely with bringing artists together—writers preferred, any person with a degree of talent practicing or connected with the art of Literature, and in getting their work published and set before the eyes of the world. Painters and composers were a marginal interest. There was nothing diffused or shapeless in Sylvia's purpose: that bizarre assortment of creatures shared a common center—they were artists or were trying to be. Otherwise many of them had only Sylvia in common. She had introduced many of them to each other.

We know now from many published memoirs what Ford Madox Ford thought of Hemingway, what Hemingway thought of Ford and F. Scott Fitzgerald, how William Carlos Williams felt about Paris literary life, how Bryher felt herself a stranger to every one but Sylvia, and going back to an early book of Robert McAlmon's, *Being Geniuses Together*, what he thought of the whole lot. These recorded memories glitter with malice and hatred and jealousy, and one sees ten versions of the same incident in as many books: there are admirations and friendships and kindnesses, too, in most of them; I have not seen one that spoke meanly of Sylvia. They seemed to be agreed about her, she was a touchstone.

She was a thin, twiggy sort of woman, quick-tongued, quick-minded and light on her feet. Her nerves were as tight as a tuned-up fiddle string and she had now and then attacks of migraine that stopped her in her tracks before she spun herself to death, just in the usual run of her days.

When I first saw her, in the early spring of 1932, her hair was still the color of roasted chestnut shells, her light golden brown eyes with greenish glints in them were marvelously benign, acutely attentive, and they sparkled upon one rather than beamed, as gentle eyes are supposed to do. She was not pretty, never had been, never had tried to be: she was attractive, a center of interest, a delightful presence not accountable to any of the familiar attributes of charm. Her power was in the unconscious, natural radiation of her intense energy and concentration upon those beings and arts she loved.

Sylvia loved her hundreds of friends, and they all loved her—many of whom loved almost no one else except perhaps himself—apparently without jealousy, each one sure of his special cell in the vast honey-comb of her heart; sure of his welcome in her shop with its exhilarating air of something pretty wonderful going on at top speed. Her genius was for friendship; her besetting virtue, generosity, an all-covering charity in its true sense; and courage that reassured even Hemingway, the distrustful, the wary, the unloving, who sized people up on sight, who couldn't be easy until he had somehow got the upper hand. Half an hour after he was first in her shop, Hemingway was sitting there with a sock and shoe laid aside, showing Sylvia the still-painful scars of his war wounds got in Italy. He told her the doctors thought he would die and he was baptized there in the hospital. Sylvia wrote in her memoirs, "Baptized or not—and I am going to say this whether Hemingway shoots me or not—I have always felt he was a deeply religious man."

Hemingway tried to educate her in boxing, wrestling, any kind of manly sport, but it seemed to remain to Sylvia mere reeling and writhing and fainting in coils: but Hemingway and Hadley his wife, and Bumby the Baby, and Sylvia and Adrienne Monnier, her good friend, all together at a boxing match must have been one of the sights of Paris. Sylvia tells it with her special sense of comedy; very acute, and with tenderness. Hemingway rather turns out to be the hero of her book, helping to bootleg copies of *Ulysses* into the United States, shooting German snipers off her roof on the day the American army entered Paris: being shown in fact as the man he wished and tried to be. . . .

As I say, Sylvia's friends did not always love each other even for her sake, nor could anyone but Sylvia expect them to: yet it is plain that she did. At parties specially, or in her shop, she had a way, figuratively, of taking two of her friends, strangers to each other, by the napes of their necks and cracking their heads together, saying in effect always, and at times in so many words, "My dears, you *must* love one another!" and she could cite the best of reasons for this hope, compounding her error by describing them in turn as being of the highest rank and quality each in his own field.

Usually the strangers would give each other a straight, skeptical stare, exchange a few mumbling words under her expectant, fostering eyes; and the instant she went on to other greetings and exchanges, they faced about from each other and drifted away. There may have been some later friendships growing from this method, but I don't know of any: it never made one for me, nor, I may say, the other way about.

It was in Sylvia's shop that I saw Ernest Hemingway for the first and last time. If this sounds portentous now, it is only because of all that has happened since to make of him a tragic figure. Then he was still the *beau garçon* who loved blood sports, the black-haired, sun-burned muscle boy of American literature; the war hero with scars to show for it: the unalloyed male who had licked Style to a standstill. He had exactly the right attitude toward words like "glory" and so on. It was not particularly impressive: I preferred Joyce and Yeats and Henry James, and I had seen all the bullfights and done all the hunting I wanted in Mexico before I ever came to Paris. He seemed to me then to be the walking exemplar of the stylish literary attitudes of his time: he may have been, but I see now how very good he was; he paid heavily, as such men do, for their right to live on beyond the fashion they helped to make, to play out to the end not the role wished on them by their public but the destiny they cannot escape because there was a moment in their lives when they chose that destiny.

It was such a little incident, and so random and rather comic at the time, and Sylvia and I laughed over it again years later, the last time I saw her in New York.

I had dropped into Sylvia's shop looking for something to read, just at early dark on a cold, rainy winter evening, maybe in 1934, I am not sure. We were standing under the light at the big round table piled up with books, talking; and I was just saying good-bye when the door burst open, and Hemingway unmistakably Ernest stood before us, looking just like the snapshots of him then being everywhere published—tall, bulky, broadfaced (his season of boyish slenderness was short), cropped black moustache, watchful eyes, all reassuringly there.

He wore a streaming old raincoat and a drenched floppy rain hat pulled over his eyebrows. Sylvia ran to him calling like a bird, both arms out; they embraced in a manly sort of way (quite a feat, sizes and sexes considered), then Sylvia turned to me with that ominous apostolic sweetness in her eyes. Still holding one of Hemingway's hands, she reached at arm's length for mine. "Katherine Anne Porter," she said, pronouncing the names in full, "this is Ernest Hemingway. . . . **Ernest**, this is Katherine Anne, and I want the two best modern American writers to know each other!" Our hands were never joined.

"Modern" was a talismanic word then, but this time the magic failed. At that instant the telephone rang in the back room, Sylvia flew to answer, calling back to us merrily, merrily, "Now you two just get acquainted and I'll be right back." Hemingway and I stood and gazed unwinkingly at each other with poker faces for all of ten seconds, in silence. Hemingway then turned in one wide swing and hurled himself into the rainy darkness as he had hurled himself out of it, and that was all. I am sorry if you are disappointed. All personal lack of sympathy and attraction aside, and they were real in us both, it must have been galling to this most famous young man to have his name pronounced in the same breath as writer with someone he had never heard of, and a woman at that. I nearly felt sorry for him.

Sylvia seemed mystified that her hero had vanished. "Where did he go?" "I don't know." "What did he say?" she asked, still wondering. I had to tell her: "Nothing, not a word. Not even good-bye." She continued to think this very strange. I didn't, and don't.

TWO FAMILIAR NARRATIVES

---

28. As Fast As You Can

IRVING FELDMAN

Feldman (1928–   ) taught at Kenyon College and later at the State University of New York at Buffalo, where he now resides. His volumes of poetry to date are *Works and Days* (1961), *Pripet Marshes* (1965), *Magic Papers* (1970), and *Lost Originals* (1972), from the last of which we take this poem.

Loosed from the shaping hand, who lay
at the window, face to the open sky,

the fever of birth now cooling, cooling?
I! said the gingerbread man leaping
upright laughing; the first faint dawn
of breath roared in his lungs and toes; down
he jumped running.

       Sweet was the dream
of speed that sped the ground under, sweet
the ease of this breathing, which ran
in his body as he now ran in the wind,
leaf in the world's breathing; sweeter still
the risk he was running: of boundaries first
and then the unbounded, a murderous
roadway that ended nowhere in trees,
a cat at creamspill looking up, mysterious
schoolboys grabbing.

       (Certainly, they saw him,
a plump figure hurrying, garbed in three
white buttons, edible boots, his head a hat
in two dimensions.)

       Powerfully then
his rhythmic running overtook the dream
of his flight: he was only his breathing.
He said, entering his body, *Like this*
I can go on forever.

       Loping and leaping
the fox kept pace, hinted, feinting, over
and under wherever, licking his chops
and grinning to the hilt of his healthy gums.
Breathing to his toes the man ran faster,
free in a world that was suddenly growing
a bushy tail and a way of its own.
No less his joy for the darkening race!
Brilliant thought had dawned to his lips;
he understood it: Thrilling absolute
of original breath! and said, *The world*
desires me! Somebody wants to eat me up!
That stride transported flying him off
earth and mystic into the fox's maw
blazing. One with the world's danger
that now is nothingness and now a tooth,
he transcended the matter of bread.
His speed between the clickers was infinite.

128

Tell them this, that life is sweet!
eagerly he told the happy fox
whose pink tongue assenting glibly
assuaged the pure delirious crumbs.
(Others fable otherwise, of course:
Having outsped our sight, he dazzles
the spinning heavens, that fox our senses'
starved pretention. How else explain
the world's ubiquitous odor
of sweetness burning and the absence of ash?)

Shimmering and redolent, his spirit
tempts our subtlest appetite. There he runs!
freely on the wind. We sniff a sharp
intelligence, lunge and snap our teeth
at the breathable body of air
and murmur while it is flying by,
Life is unhappy, life is sweet!

29. Snow White and the Seven Dwarfs

ANNE SEXTON

Anne Sexton (1928–   ) teaches in a high school in
Massachusetts. A book of her poems, *Live or Die*, won the
Pulitzer Prize for 1967, and she has written several
volumes of poems since, including *Love Poems* (1969),
Transformations (1971), and *The Book of Folly* (1972). The
poem here is one of her "transformations."

No matter what life you lead
the virgin is a lovely number:
cheeks as fragile as cigarette paper,
arms and legs made of Limoges,
lips like Vin Du Rhône,

III. Narration:
The Element of Story in Essays

rolling her china-blue doll eyes
open and shut.
Open to say,
Good Day Mama,
and shut for the thrust
of the unicorn.
She is unsoiled.
She is as white as a bonefish.

Once there was a lovely virgin
called Snow White.
Say she was thirteen.
Her stepmother,
a beauty in her own right,
though eaten, of course, by age,
would hear of no beauty surpassing her own.
Beauty is a simple passion,
but, oh my friends, in the end
you will dance the fire dance in iron shoes.
The stepmother had a mirror to which she referred—
something like the weather forecast—
a mirror that proclaimed
the one beauty of the land.
She would ask,
Looking glass upon the wall,
who is fairest of us all?
And the mirror would reply,
You are fairest of us all.
Pride pumped in her like poison.

Suddenly one day the mirror replied,
Queen, you are full fair, 'tis true,
but Snow White is fairer than you.
Until that moment Snow White
had been no more important
than a dust mouse under the bed.
But now the queen saw brown spots on her hand
and four whiskers over her lip
so she condemned Snow White
to be hacked to death.
Bring me her heart, she said to the hunter,
and I will salt it and eat it.
The hunter, however, let his prisoner go
and brought a boar's heart back to the castle.
The queen chewed it up like a cube steak.

130

Now I am fairest, she said,
lapping her slim white fingers.

Snow White walked in the wildwood
for weeks and weeks.
At each turn there were twenty doorways
and at each stood a hungry wolf,
his tongue lolling out like a worm.
The birds called out lewdly,
talking like pink parrots,
and the snakes hung down in loops,
each a noose for her sweet white neck.
On the seventh week
she came to the seventh mountain
and there she found the dwarf house.
It was as droll as a honeymoon cottage
and completely equipped with
seven beds, seven chairs, seven forks
and seven chamber pots.
Snow White ate seven chicken livers
and lay down, at last, to sleep.

The dwarfs, those little hot dogs,
walked three times around Snow White,
the sleeping virgin. They were wise
and wattled like small czars.
Yes. It's a good omen,
they said, and will bring us luck.
They stood on tiptoes to watch
Snow White wake up. She told them
about the mirror and the killer-queen
and they asked her to stay and keep house.
Beware of your stepmother,
they said.
Soon she will know you are here.
While we are away in the mines
during the day, you must not
open the door.

Looking glass upon the wall . . .
The mirror told
and so the queen dressed herself in rags
and went out like a peddler to trap Snow White.
She went across seven mountains.
She came to the dwarf house

131

and Snow White opened the door
and bought a bit of lacing.
The queen fastened it tightly
around her bodice,
as tight as an Ace bandage,
so tight that Snow White swooned.
She lay on the floor, a plucked daisy.
When the dwarfs came home they undid the lace
and she revived miraculously.
She was as full of life as soda pop.
Beware of your stepmother,
they said.
She will try once more.

Looking glass upon the wall . . .
Once more the mirror told
and once more the queen dressed in rags
and once more Snow White opened the door.
This time she bought a poison comb,
a curved eight-inch scorpion,
and put it in her hair and swooned again.
The dwarfs returned and took out the comb
and she revived miraculously.
She opened her eyes as wide as Orphan Annie.
Beware, beware, they said,
but the mirror told,
the queen came,
Snow White, the dumb bunny,
opened the door
and she bit into a poison apple
and fell down for the final time.
When the dwarfs returned
they undid her bodice,
they looked for a comb,
but it did no good.
Though they washed her with wine
and rubbed her with butter
it was to no avail.
She lay as still as a gold piece.

The seven dwarfs could not bring themselves
to bury her in the black ground
so they made a glass coffin
and set it upon the seventh mountain
so that all who passed by

could peek in upon her beauty.
A prince came one June day
and would not budge.
He stayed so long his hair turned green
and still he would not leave.
The dwarfs took pity upon him
and gave him the glass Snow White—
its doll's eyes shut forever—
to keep in his far-off castle.
As the prince's men carried the coffin
they stumbled and dropped it
and the chunk of apple flew out
of her throat and she woke up miraculously.

And thus Snow White became the prince's bride.
The wicked queen was invited to the wedding feast
and when she arrived there were
red-hot iron shoes,
in the manner of red-hot roller skates,
clamped upon her feet.
First your toes will smoke
and then your heels will turn black
and you will fry upward like a frog,
she was told.
And so she danced until she was dead,
a subterranean figure,
her tongue flicking in and out
like a gas jet.
Meanwhile Snow White held court,
rolling her china-blue doll eyes open and shut
and sometimes referring to her mirror
as women do.

---

30. Of Cabbages and Kings

JAMES ALAN McPHERSON

McPherson (1943–   ) lives in the Northeast. His first
published volume of stories, *Hue and Cry* (1969), gave him

a respected place among the new generation of black writers, and among writers of fiction generally.

I

CLAUDE SHEATS had been in the Brotherhood all his life and then he had tried to get out. Some of his people and most of his friends were still in the Brotherhood and were still very good members, but Claude was no longer a good member because he had tried to get out after over twenty years. To get away from the Brotherhood and all his friends who were still active in it, he moved to Washington Square * and took to reading about being militant. But, living there, he developed a craving for whiteness the way a nicely broke-in virgin craves sex. In spite of this, he maintained a steady black girl, whom he saw at least twice a month to keep up appearances, and once he took both of us with him when he visited his uncle in Harlem who was still in the Brotherhood.

"She's a nice girl, Claude," his uncle's wife had told him that night because the girl, besides being attractive, had some very positive ideas about the Brotherhood. Her name was Marie, she worked as a secretary in my office, and it was on her suggestion that I had moved in with Claude Sheats.

"I'm glad to see you don't waste your time on hippies," the uncle had said. "All our young men are selling out these days."

The uncle was the kind of fellow who had played his cards right. He was much older than his wife, and I had the impression, that night, that he must have given her time to experience enough and to become bored enough before he overwhelmed her with his success. He wore glasses and combed his hair back and had that oily kind of composure that made me think of a waiter waiting to be tipped. He was very proud of his English, I observed, and how he always ended his words with just the right sound. He must have felt superior to people who didn't. He must have felt superior to Claude because he was still with the Brotherhood and Claude had tried to get out.

Claude did not like him and always seemed to feel guilty whenever we visited his uncle's house. "Don't mention any of my girls to him," he told me after our first visit.

"Why would I do that?" I said.

"He'll try to psych you into telling him."

"Why should he suspect you? He never comes over to the apartment."

"He just likes to know what I'm doing. I don't want him to know about my girls."

"I won't say anything," I promised.

* In the Greenwich Village section of Manhattan (New York City).

He was almost twenty-three and had no steady girls, except for Marie. He was well built, so that he had no trouble in the Village area. It was like going to the market for him. During my first days in the apartment the process had seemed like a game. And once, when he was going out, I said: "Bring back two."

Half an hour later he came back with two girls. He got their drinks and then he called me into his room to meet them.

"This is Doris," he said, pointing to the smaller one, "and I forgot your name," he said to the big blonde.

"Jane," she said.

"This is Howard," he told her.

"Hi," I said. Neither one of them smiled. The big blonde in white pants sat on the big bed and the little one sat on a chair near the window. He had given them his worst bourbon.

"Excuse me a minute," Claude said to the girls. "I want to talk to Howard for a minute." He put on a record before we went outside into the hall between our rooms. He was always extremely polite and gentle, and very soft-spoken in spite of his size.

"Listen," he said to me outside, "you can have the blonde."

"What can I do with that amazon?"

"I don't care. Just get her out of the room."

"She's dirty," I said.

"So you can give her a bath."

"It wouldn't help much."

"Well just take her out and talk to her," he told me. "Remember, you asked for her."

We went back in. "Where you from?" I said to the amazon.

"Brighton."

"What school?"

"No. I just got here."

"From where?"

"*Brighton!*"

"That's not so far," I said.

"*England,*" she said. She looked very bored. Claude Sheats looked at me.

"How did you find Washington Square so fast?"

"I got friends."

She was very superior about it all and seemed to look at us with the same slightly patient irritation of a professional theater critic waiting for a late performance to begin. The little one sat on the chair, her legs crossed, looking up at the ceiling. Her white pants were dirty too. They looked as though they would have been very relieved if we had taken off our clothes and danced for them around the room and across the bed, and made hungry sounds in our throats with our mouths slightly opened.

I said that I had to go out to the drugstore and would be back very soon; but once outside, I walked a whole hour in one direction and then I walked back. I passed them a block away from our apartment. They were walking fast and did not slow down or speak when I passed them.

Claude Sheats was drinking heavily when I came into the apartment.

"What the hell are you trying to pull?" he said.

"I couldn't find a drugstore open."

He got up from the living room table and walked toward me. "You should have asked me," he said. "I got more than enough."

"I wanted some mouthwash too," I said.

He fumed a while longer, and then told me how I had ruined his evening because the amazon would not leave the room to wait for me and the little one would not do anything with the amazon around. He suddenly thought about going down and bringing them back; and he went out for a while. But he came back without them, saying that they had been picked up again.

"When a man looks out for you, you got to look out for him," he warned me.

"I'm sorry."

"A hell of a lot of good *that* does. And that's the last time I look out for *you*, baby," he said. "From now on it's *me* all the way."

"Thanks," I said.

"If she was too much for you I could of taken the amazon."

"It didn't matter that much," I said.

"You could of had Doris if you couldn't handle the amazon."

"They were both too much," I told him.

But Claude Sheats did not answer. He just looked at me.

II

After two months of living with him I concluded that Claude hated whites as much as he loved them. And he hated himself with the very same passion. He hated the country and his place in it and he loved the country and his place in it. He loved the Brotherhood and all that being in it had taught him and he still believed in what he had been taught, even after he had left it and did not have to believe in anything.

"This Man is going *down*, Howard," he would announce with conviction.

"Why?" I would ask.

"Because it's the Black Man's time to rule again. They had five thousand years, now we get five thousand years."

"What if I don't *want* to rule?" I asked. "What happens if I don't want to take over?"

He looked at me with pity in his face. "You go down with the rest of the country."

"I guess I wouldn't mind much anyway," I said. "It would be a hell of a place with nobody to hate."

But I could never get him to smile about it the way I tried to smile about it. He was always serious. And, once, when I questioned the mysticism in the teachings of the Brotherhood, Claude almost attacked me. "Another man might kill you for saying that," he had said. "Another man might not let you get away with saying something like that." He was quite deadly and he stood over me with an air of patient superiority. And because he could afford to be generous and forgiving, being one of the saved, he sat down at the table with me under the single light bulb and began to teach me. He told me the stories about how it was in the beginning before the whites took over, and about all the little secret significances of black, and about the subtle infiltration of white superiority into everyday objects.

"You've never seen me eat white bread or white sugar, have you?"

"No," I said. He used brown bread and brown sugar.

"Or use bleached flour or white rice?"

"No."

"You know why, don't you?" He waited expectantly.

"No," I finally said. "I don't know why."

He was visibly shocked, so much so that he dropped that line of instruction and began to draw on a pad before him on the living room table. He moved his big shoulders over the yellow pad to conceal his drawings and looked across the table at me. "Now I'm going to tell you something that white men have paid thousands of dollars to learn," he said. "Men have been killed for telling this but I'm telling you for nothing. I'm warning you not to repeat it because if the whites find out you know, you could be killed too."

"You know me," I said. "I wouldn't repeat any secrets."

He gave me a long thoughtful look.

I gave him back a long, eager, honest look.

Then he leaned across the table and whispered: "Kennedy isn't buried in this country. He was the only President who never had his coffin opened during the funeral. The body was in state all that time and they never opened the coffin once. You know why?"

"No."

"Because he's not *in it!* They buried an empty coffin. Kennedy was a Thirty-third Degree Mason. His body is in Jerusalem right now."

"How do you know?" I asked.

"If I told you it would put your life in danger."

"Did his family know about it?"

"No. His lodge kept it secret."

"No one knew?"

"I'm telling you, *no!*"

"Then how did you find out?"

He sighed, more from tolerance than from boredom with my inability to comprehend the mysticism of pure reality in its most unadulterated form. Of course I could not believe him and we argued about it, back and forth; but to absolutely cap all my uncertainties he drew the thirty-three degree circle, showed me the secret signs that men had died to learn, and spoke about the time when our black ancestors chased an evil genius out of their kingdom and across a desert and onto an island somewhere in the sea; from which, hundreds of years later, this same evil genius sent forth a perfected breed of white-skinned and evil creatures who, through trickery, managed to enslave for five thousand years the one-time Black Masters of the world. He further explained the significance of the East and why all the saved must go there once during their lifetimes, and possibly be buried there, as Kennedy had been.

It was dark and late at night, and the glaring bulb cast his great shadow into the corners so that there was the sense of some outraged spirit, fuming in the halls and dark places of our closets, waiting to extract some terrible and justifiable revenge from him for disclosing to me, an unbeliever, the closest-kept of secrets. But I was aware of them only for an instant, and then I did not believe him again.

The most convincing thing about it all was that he was very intelligent and had an orderly, well regimented life-style, and yet *he* had no trouble with believing. He believed in the certainty of statistical surveys, which was his work; the nutritional value of wheat germ sprinkled on eggs; the sensuality of gin; and the dangers inherent in smoking. He was stylish in that he did not believe in God, but he was extremely moral and warm and kind; and I wanted sometimes to embrace him for his kindness and bigness and gentle manners. He lived his life so carefully that no matter what he said, I could not help but believe him sometimes. But I did not want to, because I knew that once I started I could not stop; and then there would be no purpose to my own beliefs and no real conviction or direction in my own efforts to achieve when always in the back of my regular thoughts, there would be a sense of futility and a fear of the unknown all about me. So, for the sake of necessity, I chose not to believe him.

He felt that the country was doomed and that the safe thing to do was to make enough money as soon as possible and escape to the Far East. He forecast summer riots in certain Northern cities and warned me, religiously, to avoid all implicating ties with whites so that I might have a chance to be saved when that time came. And I asked him about *his* ties, and the girls, and how it was never a movie date with coffee afterwards but always his room and the cover-all blanket of Motown sounds late into the night.

"A man has different reasons for doing certain things," he had said.

He never seemed to be comfortable with any of the girls. He never seemed to be in control. And after my third month in the apartment I had concluded that he used his virility as a tool and forged, for however long it lasted, a little area of superiority which could never, it seemed, extend itself beyond the certain confines of his room, no matter how late into the night the records played. I could see him fighting to extend the area, as if an increase in the number of girls he saw could compensate for what he had lost in duration. He saw many girls: curious students, unexpected bus-stop pickups, and assorted other one-nighters. And his rationalizations allowed him to believe that each one was an actual conquest, a physical affirmation of a psychological victory over all he hated and loved and hated in the little world of his room.

But then he seemed to have no happiness, even in this. Even here I sensed some intimations of defeat. After each girl, Claude would almost immediately come out of his room, as if there was no need for aftertalks; as if, after it was over, he felt a brooding, silent emptiness that quickly intensified into nervousness and instantaneous shyness and embarrassment so that the cold which sets in after that kind of emotional drain came in very sharp against his skin, and he could not bear to have her there any longer. And when the girl had gone, he would come into my room to talk. These were the times when he was most like a little boy; and these were the times when he really began to trust me.

"That bitch called me everything but the son of God," he would chuckle. And I would put aside my papers brought home from the office, smile at him, and listen.

He would always eat or drink afterwards and in those early days I was glad for his companionship and the return of his trust, and sometimes we drank and talked until dawn. During these times he would tell me more subtleties about the Man and would re-predict the fall of the country. Once, he warned me, in a fatherly way, about reading life from books before experiencing it; and another night he advised me on how to schedule girls so that one could run them without being run in return. These were usually good times of good-natured arguments and predictions; but as we drank more often he tended to grow more excited and quick-tempered, especially after he had just entertained. Sometimes he would seethe hate, and every drink he took gave life to increasingly bitter condemnations of the present system and our place in it. There were actually flying saucers, he told me once, piloted by things from other places in the universe which would eventually

139

destroy the country for what it had done to the black man. He had run into his room, on that occasion, and had brought out a book by a man who maintained that the government was deliberately withholding from the public overwhelming evidence of flying saucers and strange creatures from other galaxies that walked among us everyday. Claude emphasized the fact that the writer was a Ph.D. who must know what he was talking about, and insisted that the politicians withheld the information because they knew that their time was almost up and if they made it public the black man would know that he had outside friends who would help him take over the world again. Nothing I said could make him reconsider the slightest bit of his information.

"What are we going to use for weapons when we take over?" I asked him once.

"We've got atomic bombs stockpiled and waiting for the day."

"How can you believe that crap?"

He did not answer, but said instead: "You are the living example of what the Man has done to my people."

"I just try to think things out for myself," I said.

"You can't think. The handkerchief over your head is too big."

I smiled.

"I know," he continued. "I know all there is to know about whites because I've been studying them all my life."

I smiled some more.

"I ought to know," he said slowly. "I have supernatural powers."

"I'm tired," I told him. "I want to go to sleep now."

Claude started to leave the room, then he turned. "Listen," he said at the door. He pointed his finger at me to emphasize the gravity of his pronouncement. "I predict that within the next week something is going to happen to this country that will hurt it even more than Kennedy's assassination."

"Goodnight," I said as he closed the door.

He opened it again. "Remember that I predicted it when it happens," he said. For the first time I noticed that he had been deadly serious all along.

Two days later several astronauts burned to death in Florida. He raced into my room hot with the news.

"Do you believe in me *now?*" he said. "Just two days and look what happened."

I tried to explain, as much to myself as to him, that in any week of the year something unfortunate was bound to occur. But he insisted that this was only part of a divine plan to bring the country to its knees. He said that he intended to send a letter off right away to Jeane Dixon in D.C. to let her know that she was not alone because he also had the same power. Then he thought that he had better not because the FBI knew that he had been active in the Brotherhood before he got out.

At first it was good fun believing that someone important cared enough to watch us. And sometimes when the telephone was dead a long time before the dial tone sounded, I would knock on his door and together we would run through our telephone conversations for that day to see if either of us had said anything implicating or suspect, just in case they were listening. This feeling of persecution brought us closer together and soon the instruction sessions began to go on almost every night. At this point I could not help but believe him a little. And he began to trust me again, like a tolerable little brother, and even confided that the summer riots would break out simultaneously in Harlem and Watts during the second week in August. For some reason, something very difficult to put into words, I spent three hot August nights on the streets of Harlem, waiting for the riot to start.

In the seventh month of our living together, he began to introduce me to his girls again when they came in. Most of them came only once, but all of them received the same mechanical treatment. He only discriminated with liquor, the quality of which improved with the attractiveness or reluctance of the girl: gin for slow starters, bourbon for momentary strangers, and the scotch he reserved for those he hoped would come again. There was first the trek into his room, his own trip out for the ice and glasses while classical music was played within; then after a while the classical piece would be replaced by several Motowns. Finally, there was her trip to the bathroom, his calling a cab in the hall, and the sound of both their feet on the stairs as he walked her down to the cab. Then he would come to my room in his red bathrobe, glass in hand, for the aftertalk.

Then in the ninth month the trouble started. It would be very easy to pick out one incident, one day, one area of misunderstanding in that month and say: "That was where it began." It would be easy, but not accurate. It might have been one instance or a combination of many. It might have been the girl who came into the living room, when I was going over the proposed blueprints for a new settlement house, and who lingered too long outside his room in conversation because her father was a builder somewhere. Or it might have been nothing at all. But after that time he warned me about being too friendly with his company.

Another night, when I was leaving the bathroom in my shorts, he came out of his room with a girl who smiled.

"Hi," she said to me.

I nodded hello as I ducked back into the bathroom.

When he had walked her down to the door he came to my room and knocked. He did not have a drink.

"Why didn't you speak to my company?" he demanded.

"I was in my shorts."

"She felt bad about it. She asked what the hell was wrong with you. What could I tell her—'He got problems'?"

"I'm sorry," I said. "But I didn't want to stop in my shorts."

"I see through you, Howard," he said. "You're just jealous of me and try to insult my girls to get to me."

"Why should I be jealous of you?"

"Because I'm a man and you're not."

"What makes a man anyway?" I said. "Your fried eggs and wheat germ? Why should I be jealous of you *or* what you bring in?"

"Some people don't need a reason. You're a black devil and you'll get yours. I predict that you'll get yours."

"Look," I told him, "I'm sorry about the girl. Tell her I'm sorry when you see her again."

"You treated her so bad she probably won't come back."

I said nothing more and he stood there silently for a long time before he turned to leave the room. But at the door he turned again and said: "I see through you, Howard. You're a black devil."

It should have ended there and it might have with anyone else. I took great pains to speak to his girls after that, even though he tried to get them into the room as quickly as possible. But a week later he accused me of walking about in his room after he had gone out, some two weeks before.

"I swear I wasn't in your room," I protested.

"I saw your shadow on the blinds from across the street at the bus stop," he insisted.

"I've *never* been in your room when you weren't there," I told him.

"I *saw* you!"

We went into his room and I tried to explain how, even if he could see the window from the bus stop, the big lamp next to the window prevented any shadow from being cast on the blinds. But he was convinced in his mind that at every opportunity I plundered his closets and drawers. He had no respect for simple logic in these matters, no sense of the absurdity of his accusations, and the affair finally ended with my confessing that I might have done it without actually knowing; and if I had, I would not do it again.

But what had been a gesture for peace on my part became a vindication for him, proof that I *was* a black devil, capable of lying and lying until he confronted me with the inescapable truth of the situation. And so he persisted in creating situations from which, if he insisted on a point long enough and with enough self-righteousness, he could draw my inevitable confession.

And I confessed eagerly, goaded on by the necessity of maintaining peace. I confessed to mixing white sugar crystals in with his own brown crystals so that he could use it and violate the teachings of the Brotherhood; I confessed to cleaning the bathroom all the time merely because I wanted to make him feel guilty for not having ever cleaned it. I confessed to telling the faithful Marie, who brought a surprise dinner over for him, that he was working late at his office in order to implicate him with the girls who worked there. I confessed to leaving my papers about the house so that his company could ask about them and develop an interest in me. And I pleaded guilty to a record of other little infamies, which multiplied into countless others, and again subdivided into hundreds of little subtleties until my every movement was a threat to him. If I had a girlfriend to dinner, we should eat in my room instead of at the table because he had to use the bathroom a lot and, besides not wanting to seem as if he were making a pass at my girl by walking through the room so often, he was genuinely embarrassed to be seen going to the bathroom.

If I protested he would fly into a tantrum and shake his big finger at me vigorously. And so I retreated, step by step, into my room, from which I emerged only to go to the bathroom or kitchen or out of the house. I tried to stay out on nights when he had company. But he had company so often that I could not always help being in my room after he had walked her to the door. Then he would knock on my door for his talk. He might offer me a drink, and if I refused, he would go to his room for a while and then come back. He would pace about for a while, like a big little boy who wants to ask for money over his allowance. At these times my mind would move feverishly over all our contacts for as far back as I could make it reach, searching and attempting to pull out that one incident which would surely be the point of his attack. But it was never any use; it might have been anything.

"Howard, I got something on my chest and I might as well get it off."

"What is it?" I asked from my bed.

"You been acting strange lately. Haven't been talking to me. If you got something on your chest, get it off now."

"I have nothing on my chest," I said.

"Then why don't you talk?"

I did not answer.

"You hardly speak to me in the kitchen. If you have something against me, tell me now."

"I have nothing against you."

"Why don't you talk, then?" He looked directly at me. "If a man doesn't talk, you think *something's* wrong!"

"I've been nervous lately, that's all. I got problems and I don't want to talk."

"Everybody's got problems. That's no reason for going around making a man feel guilty."

"For God's sake, I don't want to talk."

"I know what's wrong with you. Your conscience is bothering you. You're so evil that your conscience is giving you trouble. You got everybody fooled but *me*. I know you're a black devil."

"I'm a black devil," I said. "Now will you let me sleep?"

He went to the door. "You dish it out but you can't take it," he said. "That's *your* trouble."

"I'm a black devil," I said.

I lay there, after he left, hating myself but thankful that he hadn't called me into his room for the fatherly talk as he had done another time. That was the worst. He had come to the door and said: "Come out of there, I want to talk to you." He had walked ahead of me into his room and had sat down in his big leather chair next to the lamp with his legs spread wide and his big hands in his lap. He had said: "Don't be afraid. I'm not going to hurt you. Sit down. I'm not going to argue. What are you so nervous about? Have a drink," in his kindest, most fatherly way, and that had been the worst of all. That was the time he had told me to eat in my room. Now I could hear him pacing about in the hall and I knew that it was not over for the night. I began to pray that I could sleep before he came and that he would not be able to wake me, no matter what he did. I did not care what he did as long as I did not have to face him. I resolved to confess to anything he accused me of if it would make him leave sooner. I was about to go out into the hall for my confession when the door was kicked open and he charged into the room.

"You black son-of-a-bitch!" he said. "I ought to *kill* you." He stood over the bed in the dark room and shook his big fist over me. And I lay there hating the overpowering cowardice in me, which kept my body still and my eyes closed, and hoping that he would kill all of it when his heavy fist landed.

"First you insult a man's company, then you ignore him. I been *good* to you. I let you live here, I let you eat my uncle's food, and I taught you things. But you're a ungrateful motherfucker. I ought to *kill* you right now!'

And I still lay there, as he went on, not hearing him, with nothing in me but a loud throbbing which pulsed through the length of my body and made the sheets move with its pounding. I lay there secure and safe in cowardice for as long as I looked up at him with my eyes big and my body twitching and my mind screaming out to him that it was all right, and I thanked him, because now I truly believed in the new five thousand years of Black Rule.

It is night again. I am in bed again, and I can hear the new blonde girl closing the bathroom door. I know that in a minute he will come out in his red robe and call a cab. His muffled voice through my closed door will seem very tired, but just as kind and patient to the dispatcher as it is to everyone, and as it was to me in those old times. I am afraid because when they came up the stairs earlier they caught me working at the living room table with my back to them. I had not expected him back so soon; but then I should have known that he would not go out. I had turned around in the chair and she smiled and said hello and I said "Hi" before he hurried her into the room. I *did* speak and I know that she heard. But I also know that I must have done something wrong; if not to her, then to him earlier today or yesterday or last week, because he glared at me before following her into the room and he almost paused to say something when he came out to get the glasses of ice. I wish that I could remember just what it was. But it does not matter. I *am* guilty and he knows it.

Now that he knows about me I am afraid. I could move away from the apartment and hide my guilt from him, but I know that he would find me. The brainwashed part of my mind tells me to call the police while he is still busy with her, but what could I charge him with when I know that he is only trying to help me. I could move the big, ragged yellow chair in front of the door, but that would not stop him, and it might make him impatient with me. Even if I pretended to be asleep and ignored him, it would not help when he comes. He has not bothered to knock for weeks.

In the black shadows over my bed and in the corners I can sense the outraged spirits who help him when they hover about his arms as he gestures with his lessons, above my bed. I am determined now to lie here and take it. It is the price I must pay for all the black secrets I have learned, and all the evil I have learned about myself. I *am* jealous of him, of his learning, of his girls. I am not the same handkerchief-head I was nine months ago. I have Marie to thank for that, and Claude, and the spirits. They know about me, and perhaps it is they who make him do it and he cannot help himself. I believe in the spirits now, just as I believe most of the time that I am a black devil.

They are going down to the cab now.

I will not ever blame him for it. He is helping me. But I blame the girls. I blame them for not staying on afterwards, and for letting all the good nice happy love talk cut off automatically after it is over. *I* need to have them there, after it is over. And he needs it; he needs it much more and much longer than they could ever need what he does for them. He should be able to teach them, as he has taught me. And he should have their appreciation, as he has mine. I blame them. I blame them for letting him try and try and never get just a little of the love there is left in the world.

I can hear him coming back from the cab.

Suggestions for Writing

1. Plimpton's study of the Colts is a feature story that relates, in its human interest and dramatic presentation, to the ideas Tom Wolfe expresses concerning a "new journalism." Can you get behind the scenes of something going on near you and report on it similarly?

2. Write a brief account of a chance meeting. Your model in this case can be Katherine Anne Porter.

3. Retell a children's story from an updated point of view. Consider the examples of Feldman and Sexton, but write your story in prose.

4. Does your acquaintance with a "brotherhood" or "sisterhood" of some kind give you a subject for a story somewhat like MacPherson's? Try writing one.

5. Select and study one of the stories presented in this chapter and try to summarize, in a straightforward manner, the ideas it expresses. Compare your account to the story. Do those ideas change when you deprive them of their fictional form?

IV.
Exposition

Comparison and Contrast

THESE SELECTIONS illustrate a fundamental principle and avoid, we hope, an equally fundamental pitfall for organizing writing. Where else does thought rise, if not in differences and identities? Thus, we compare things and contrast them. But if comparison leads only to itemized details, balancing a little of this against a little of that, where are we? What matters? Nothing is more boring than writing that declares no interest, that sustains no point of view, and indicates, in Cooley's phrase again, that no one is at home.

Comparison and contrast is a form of *exposition.* It is a way of laying out for the reader what there is to be seen. It may involve an orderly journey through time and space. But insofar as the exposition of similarities and differences may lead us to a choice, we enter again the area of argument. Arguments are implied by a sustained point of view and by interests that the whole of an essay supports.

The selections here range from Ross's essay on paired subjects of roughly equal weight to Wagner's story on one teacher contrasted with the world. Does Ross's inconclusiveness bother you? Melville, Wagner, Yeats, and Cullen contrast the savage and the civilized. Where do they stand? Where do you?

31. Football Red and Baseball Green

MURRAY ROSS

In 1971, Ross was finishing his Ph.D. in English at the
University of California (Berkeley). At this time, he was
a very partisan Los Angeles Ram fan and an admirer of the
Pittsburgh Pirates. The essay reprinted here was his first
publication.

THE 1970 SUPERBOWL, the final game of the professional football season, drew a larger television audience than either the moonwalk or Tiny Tim's wedding. This revelation is one way of indicating just how popular spectator sports are in this country. Americans, or American men anyway, seem to care about the games they watch as much as the Elizabethans cared about their plays, and I suspect for some of the same reasons. There is, in sport, some of the rudimentary drama found in popular theater: familiar plots, type characters, heroic and comic action spiced with new and unpredictable variations. And common to watching both activities is the sense of participation in a shared tradition and in shared fantasies. If it is true that sport exploits these fantasies without significantly transcending them, it seems no less satisfying for all that.

It is my guess that sport spectating involves something more than the vicarious pleasures of identifying with athletic prowess. I suspect that each sport contains a fundamental myth which it elaborates for its fans, and that our pleasure in watching such games derives in part from belonging briefly to the mythic world which the game and its players bring to life. I am especially interested in baseball and football because they are so popular and so uniquely *American;* they began here and unlike basketball they have not been widely exported. Thus whatever can be said, mythically, about these games would seem to apply directly and particularly to our own culture.

Baseball's myth may be the easier to identify since we have a greater historical perspective on the game. It was an instant success during the Industrialization, and most probably it was a reaction to the squalor, the faster pace and the dreariness of the new conditions.

Baseball was old fashioned right from the start; it seems conceived in nostalgia, in the resuscitation of the Jeffersonian dream. It established an artificial rural environment, one removed from the toil of an urban life, which spectators could be admitted to and temporarily breathe in. Baseball is a *pastoral* sport, and I think the game can be best understood as this kind of art. For baseball does what all good pastoral does—it creates an atmosphere in which everything exists in harmony.

Consider, for instance, the spatial organization of the game. A kind of controlled openness is created by having everything fan out from home plate, and the crowd sees the game through an arranged perspective that is rarely violated. Visually this means that the game is always seen as a constant, rather calm whole, and that the players and the playing field are viewed in relationship to each other. Each player has a certain position, a special area to tend, and the game often seems to be as much a dialogue between the fielders and the field as it is a contest between the players themselves: will that ball get through the hole? Can that outfielder run under that fly? As a moral genre pastoral asserts the virtue of communion with nature. As a competitive game, baseball asserts that the team which best relates to the playing field (by hitting the ball in the right places) will be the team which wins.

I suspect baseball's space has a subliminal function too, for topographically it is a sentimental mirror of older America. Most of the game is played between the pitcher and the hitter in the extreme corner of the playing area. This is the busiest, most sophisticated part of the ball park, where something is always happening, and from which all subsequent action depends. From this urban corner we move to a supporting infield, active but a little less crowded, and from there we come to the vast stretches of the outfield. As is traditional in American lore, danger increases with distance, and the outfield action is often the most spectacular in the game. The long throw, the double off the wall, the leaping catch—these plays take place in remote territory, and they belong, like most legendary feats, to the frontier.

Having established its landscape, pastoral art operates to eliminate any references to that bigger, more disturbing, more real world it has left behind. All games are to some extent insulated from the outside by having their own rules, but baseball has a circular structure as well which furthers its comfortable feeling of self-sufficiency. By this I mean that every motion of extension is also one of return—a ball hit outside is a *home* run, a full circle. Home—familiar, peaceful, secure—it is the beginning and end of everything. You must go out and you must come back, for only the completed movement is registered.

Time is a serious threat to any form of pastoral. The genre poses a timeless world of perpetual spring, and it does its best to silence the ticking of clocks which remind us that in time the green world fades into winter. One's sense of time is directly related to what happens in it, and baseball is so structured as to stretch out and ritualize whatever action it contains. Dramatic moments are few, and they are almost always isolated by the routine texture of normal play. It is certainly a game of climax and drama, but it is perhaps more a game of repeated and predictable action: the foul balls, the walks, the pitcher fussing around on the mound, the lazy fly ball to centerfield. This is, I think, as it should be, for baseball exists as an alternative to a world of too much action, struggle and change. It is a merciful release from a more grinding and insistent tempo, and its time, as William Carlos Williams suggests, makes a virtue out of idleness simply by providing it:

> The crowd at the ball game
> is moved uniformly
> by a spirit of uselessness
> which delights them . . .

Within this expanded and idle time the baseball fan is at liberty to become a ceremonial participant and a lover of style. Because the action is normalized, how something is done becomes as important as the action itself. Thus baseball's most delicate and detailed aspects are often, to the spectator, the most interesting. The pitcher's windup, the anticipatory crouch of the infielders, the quick waggle of the bat as it poises for the pitch—these subtle miniature movements are as meaningful as the homeruns and the strikeouts. It somehow matters in baseball that all the tiny rituals are observed: the shortstop must kick the dirt and the umpire must brush the plate with his pocket broom. In a sense baseball is largely a continuous series of small gestures, and I think it characteristic that the game's most treasured moment came when Babe Ruth pointed to the place where he subsequently hit a home run.

Baseball is a game where the little things mean a lot, and this, together with its clean serenity, its open space, and its ritualized action is enough to place it in a world of yesterday. Baseball evokes for us a past which may never have been ours, but which we believe was, and certainly that is enough. In the Second World War, supposedly, we fought for "Baseball, Mom and Apple Pie," and considering what baseball means that phrase is a good one. We fought then for the right to believe in a green world of tranquillity and uninterrupted contentment, where the little things would count. But now the possibilities of such a world are more remote, and it seems that while the entertainment of such a dream has an enduring appeal, it is no longer sufficient for our fantasies. I think this may be why baseball is no longer our preeminent national pastime, and why its myth is being replaced by another more appropriate to the new realities (and fantasies) of our time.

IV. Exposition:
Comparison and Contrast

Football, especially professional football, is the embodiment of a newer myth, one which in many respects is opposed to baseball's. The fundamental difference is that football is not a pastoral game; it is a heroic one. One way of seeing the difference between the two is by the juxtaposition of Babe Ruth and Jim Brown, both legendary players in their separate genres. Ruth, baseball's most powerful hitter, was a hero maternalized (his name), an epic figure destined for a second immortality as a candy bar. His image was impressive but comfortable and altogether human: round, dressed in a baggy uniform, with a schoolboy's cap and a bat which looked tiny next to him. His spindly legs supported a Santa sized torso, and this comic disproportion would increase when he was in motion. He ran delicately, with quick, very short steps, since he felt that stretching your stride slowed you down. This sort of superstition is typical of baseball players, and typical too is the way in which a personal quirk or mannerism mitigates their awesome skill and makes them poignant and vulnerable.

There was nothing funny about Jim Brown. His muscular and almost perfect physique was emphasized further by the uniform which armoured him. Babe Ruth had a tough face, but boyish and innocent; Brown was an expressionless mask under the helmet. In action he seemed invincible, the embodiment of speed and power in an inflated human shape. One can describe Brown accurately only with superlatives, for as a player he was a kind of Superman, undisguised.

Brown and Ruth are caricatures, yet they represent their games. Baseball is part of a comic tradition which insists that its participants be humans, while football, in the heroic mode, asks that its players be more than that. Football converts men into gods, and suggests that magnificence and glory are as desirable as happiness. Football is designed, therefore, to impress its audience rather differently than baseball, as I think comparison will show.

As a pastoral game, baseball attempts to close the gap between the players and the crowd. It creates the illusion, for instance, that with a lot of hard work, a little luck, and possibly some extra talent, the average spectator might well be playing; not watching. For most of us can do a few of the things the ballplayers do: catch a pop-up, field a ground ball, and maybe get a hit once in a while. Chance is allotted a good deal of play in the game. There is no guarantee, for instance, that a good pitch will be not be looped over the infield, or that a solidly batted ball will not turn into a double play. In addition to all of this, almost every fan feels he can make the manager's decision for him, and not entirely without reason. Baseball's statistics are easily calculated and rather meaningful; and the game itself, though a subtle one, is relatively lucid and comprehensible.

As a heroic game football is not concerned with a shared community of near-equals. It seeks almost the opposite relationship between its spectators and players, one which stresses the distance between them. We are not allowed to identify directly with Jim Brown any more than we are with Zeus, because to do so would undercut his stature as something more than human. The players do much of the distancing themselves by their own excesses of speed, size and strength. When Bob Brown, the giant all pro tackle says that he could "block King Kong all day," we look at him and believe. But the game itself contributes to the players' heroic isolation. As George Plimpton has graphically illustrated in *Paper Lion*, it is almost impossible to imagine yourself in a professional football game without also considering your imminent humiliation and possible injury. There is scarcely a single play that the average spectator could hope to perform adequately, and there is even a difficulty in really understanding what is going on. In baseball what happens is what meets the eye, but in football each action is the result of eleven men acting simultaneously against eleven other men, and clearly this is too much for the eye to totally comprehend. Football has become a game of staggering complexity, and coaches are now wired in to several "spotters" during the games so that they too can find out what is happening.

If football is distanced from its fans by its intricacy and its "superhuman" play, it nonetheless remains an intense spectacle. Baseball, as I have implied, dissolves time and urgency in a green expanse, thereby creating a luxurious and peaceful sense of leisure. As is appropriate to a heroic enterprise, football reverses this procedure and converts space into time. The game is ideally played in an oval stadium, not in a "park," and the difference is the elimination of perspective. This makes football a perfect television game, because even at first hand it offers a flat, perpetually moving foreground (wherever the ball is). The eye in baseball viewing opens up; in football it zeroes in. There is no democratic vista in football, and spectators are not asked to relax, but to concentrate. You are encouraged to watch the drama, not a medley of ubiquitous gestures, and you are constantly reminded that this event is taking place in time. The third element in baseball is the field; in football this element is the clock. Traditionally heroes do reckon with time, and football players are no exceptions. Time in football is wound up inexorably until it reaches the breaking point in the last minutes of a close game. More often than not it is the clock which emerges as the real enemy, and it is the sense of time running out that regularly produces a pitch of tension uncommon in baseball.

A further reason for football's intensity, surely, is that the game is played like a war. The idea is to win by going through, around or over the opposing team and the battle lines, quite literally, are drawn on every play. Violence is somewhere at the heart of the game, and the combat quality is reflected in football's army language ("blitz" "trap" "zone" "bomb" "trenches" etc.). Coaches often sound like generals when they discuss their strategy. Woody Hayes of Ohio State, for instance, explains his quarterback option play as if it had been conceived in the Pentagon: "You know," he says, "the most effective kind of warfare is siege. You have to attack on broad fronts. And that's all the option is —attacking on a broad front. You know General Sherman ran an option right through the South."

Football like war is an arena for action, and like war football leaves little room for personal style. It seems to be a game which projects "character" more than personality, and for the most part football heroes, publicly, are a rather similar lot. They tend to become personifications rather than individuals, and, with certain exceptions, they are easily read emblematically as embodiments of heroic qualities such as "strength," "confidence," "perfection," etc.—cliches really, but forceful enough when represented by the play of a Dick Butkus, a Johnny Unitas or a Bart Starr. Perhaps this simplification of personality results in part from the heroes' total identification with their mission, to the extent that they become more characterized by their work than by what they intrinsically "are." At any rate football does not make allowances for the idiosyncracies that baseball actually seems to encourage, and as a result there have been few football players as uniquely crazy or human as, say, Casey Stengel or Dizzy Dean.

A further reason for the underdeveloped qualities of football personalities, and one which gets us to the heart of the game's modernity, is that football is very much a game of modern technology. Football's action is largely interaction, and the game's complexity requires that its players mold themselves into a perfectly coordinated unit. Jerry Kramer, the veteran guard and author of *Instant Replay,* writes how Lombardi would work to develop such integration:

> He makes us execute the same plays over and over, a hundred times, two hundred times, until we do every little thing automatically. He works to make the kickoff team perfect, the punt-return team perfect, the field-goal team perfect. He ignores nothing. Technique, technique, technique, over and over and over, until we feel like we're going crazy. But we win.

Mike Garratt, the halfback, gives the player's version:

> After a while you train your mind like a computer—put the idea in, digest it, and the body acts accordingly.

As the quotations imply, pro football is insatiably preoccupied with the smoothness and precision of play execution, and most coaches believe that the team which makes the fewest mistakes will be the team that wins. Individual identity thus comes to be associated with the team or unit that one plays for to a much greater extent than in baseball. To use a reductive analogy, it is the difference between *Bonanza* and *Mission Impossible*. Ted Williams is mostly Ted Williams, but Bart Starr is mostly the Green Bay Packers. The latter metaphor is a precise one, since football heroes stand out not because of purely individual acts, but because they epitomize the action and style of the groups they are connected to. Kramer cites the obvious if somewhat self-glorifying historical precedent: "Perhaps," he writes, "we're living in Camelot." Ideally a football team should be what Camelot was supposed to have been, a group of men who function as equal parts of a larger whole, entirely dependent on each other for their total meaning.

The humanized machine as hero is something very new in sport, for in baseball anything approaching a machine has always been suspect. The famous Yankee teams of the fifties were almost flawlessly perfect and never very popular. Their admirers took pains to romanticize their precision into something more natural than plain mechanics—Joe Di-Maggio, for instance, was the "Yankee Clipper." Even so, most people hoped fervently the Brooklyn Dodgers (the "bums") would thrash them in every World Series. To take a more recent example, the victory of the Mets last year was so compelling largely because it was at the expense of a superbly homogenized team, the Baltimore Orioles, and it was accomplished by a somewhat random collection of inspired leftovers. In baseball, machinery seems tantamount to villainy, whereas in football this smooth perfection is part of the expected integration a championship team must attain.

It is not surprising, really, that we should have a game which asserts the heroic function of a mechanized group, since we have become a country where collective identity is a reality. Football as a game of groups is appealing to us as a people of groups, and for this reason football is very much an "establishment" game—since it is in the corporate business and governmental structures that group America is most highly developed. The game comments on the culture, and vice-versa:

> President Nixon, an ardent football fan, got a football team picture as an inaugural anniversary present from his cabinet . . .
> Superimposed on the faces of real gridiron players were the faces of Cabinet members. (A.P.)

This is not to say that football appeals only to a certain class, for group America is visible everywhere. A sign held high in the San Francisco Peace Moratorium last November read: "49er Fans against War, Poverty and the Baltimore Colts."

Football's collective pattern is only one aspect of the way in which it seems to echo our contemporary environment. The game, like our society, can be thought of as a cluster of people living under great tension in a state of perpetual flux. The potential for sudden disaster or triumph is as great in football as it is in our own age, and although there is something ludicrous in equating interceptions with assassinations and long passes with moonshots, there is also something valid and appealing in the analogies. It seems to me that football does successfully reflect those salient and common conditions which affect us all, and it does so with the end of making us feel better about them and our lot. For one thing, it makes us feel that something can be released and connected in all this chaos; out of the accumulated pile of bodies something can emerge—a runner breaks into the clear or a pass finds its way to a receiver. To the spectator plays such as these are human and dazzling. They suggest to the audience what it has hoped for (and been told) all along, that technology is still a tool and not a master. Fans get living proof of this every time a long pass is completed; they see at once that it is the result of careful planning, perfect integration and an effective "pattern," but they see too that it is human and that what counts as well is man, his desire, his natural skill and his "grace under pressure." Football metaphysically yokes heroic action and technology together by violence to suggest that they are mutually supportive. It's a doubtful proposition, but given how we live it has its attractions.

Football, like the space program, is a game in the grand manner, yet it is a rather sober sport and often seems to lack that positive, comic vision of which baseball's pastoral is a part. It is a winter game, as those fans who saw the Minnesota Vikings play the Detroit Lions last Thanksgiving were graphically reminded. The two teams played in a blinding snowstorm, and except for the small flags in the corners of the end zones, and a patch of mud wherever the ball was downed, the field was totally obscured. Even through the magnified television lenses the players were difficult to identify; you saw only huge shapes come out of the gloom, thump against each other and fall in a heap. The movement was repeated endlessly and silently in a muffled stadium, interrupted once or twice by a shot of a bare-legged girl who fluttered her pom-poms in the cold. The spectacle was by turns pathetic, compelling and absurd; a kind of theater of oblivion.

Games such as this are by no means unusual, and it is not difficult to see why for many football is a gladiatorial sport of pointless bludgeoning played by armoured monsters. However accurate this description may be, I still believe that even in the worst of circumstances football can be a liberating activity. In the game I have just described, for instance, there was one play, the turning point of the game, which more than compensated for the sluggishness of most of the action. Jim Marshall, the huge defensive end (who hunts on dogsleds during the off season), intercepted a pass deep in his own territory and rumbled upfield like a dinosaur through the mud, the snow, and the opposing team, lateraling at the last minute to another lineman who took the ball in for a touchdown. It was a supreme moment because Marshall's principal occupation is falling on quarterbacks, not catching the ball and running with it. His triumphant jaunt, something that went unequaled during the rest of that dark afternoon, was a hearty burlesque of the entire sport, an occasion for epic laughter in bars everywhere (though especially in Minnesota), and it was more than enough to rescue the game from the snowbound limbo it was buried in.

In the end I suppose both football and baseball could be seen as varieties of decadence. In its preoccupation with mechanization, and in its open display of violence, football is the more obvious target for social moralists, but I wonder if this is finally more "corrupt" than the seductive picture of sanctuary and tranquility that baseball has so artfully drawn for us. Almost all sport is vulnerable to such criticism because it is not strictly ethical in intent, and for this reason there will always be room for puritans like the Elizabethan John Stubbes who howled at the "wanton fruits which these cursed pastimes bring forth." As a long time dedicated fan of almost anything athletic, I confess myself out of sympathy with most of this; which is to say, I guess, that I am vulnerable to those fantasies which these games support, and that I find happiness in the company of people who feel as I do.

A final note. It is interesting that the heroic and pastoral conventions which underlie our most popular sports are almost classically opposed. The contrasts are familiar: city vs country, aspiration vs contentment, activity vs peace and so on. Judging from the rise of professional football we seem to be slowly relinquishing that unfettered rural vision of ourselves that baseball so beautifully mirrors, and we have come to cast ourselves in a genre more reflective of a nation confronted by constant and unavoidable challenges. Right now, like the Elizabethans, we seem to share both heroic and pastoral yearnings, and we reach out to both. Perhaps these divided needs account in part for the enormous attention we as a nation now give to spectator sports. For sport provides one place, at least, where we can have our football and our baseball too.

32. Residence in the Marquesas (from *Typee*)

HERMAN MELVILLE

Along with writing the largest "great American novel," *Moby Dick*, Herman Melville (1819–1891) spent some years as a sailor. His account of life during the early 1840's on the Marquesas, in the South Pacific, is firsthand.

Chapter XVII

Improvement in Health and Spirits—Felicity of the Typees—Their Enjoyments compared with those of more enlightened Communities—Comparative Wickedness of civilized and unenlightened People—A Skirmish in the Mountain with the Warriors of Happar.

DAY AFTER DAY WORE ON, and still there was no perceptible change in the conduct of the islanders towards me. Gradually I lost all knowledge of the regular occurrence of the days of the week, and sunk insensibly into that kind of apathy which ensues after some violent outbreak of despair. My limb suddenly healed, the swelling went down, the pain subsided, and I had every reason to suppose I should soon completely recover from the affliction that had so long tormented me.

As soon as I was enabled to ramble about the valley in company with the natives, troops of whom followed me whenever I sallied out of the house, I began to experience an elasticity of mind which placed me beyond the reach of those dismal forebodings to which I had so lately been a prey. Received wherever I went with the most deferential kindness; regaled perpetually with the most delightful fruits; ministered to by dark-eyed nymphs; and enjoying besides all the services of the devoted Kory-Kory, I thought that for a sojourn among cannibals, no man could have well made a more agreeable one.

To be sure there were limits set to my wanderings. Toward the sea my progress was barred by an express prohibition of the savages; and after having made two or three ineffectual attempts to reach it, as much to gratify my curiosity as anything else, I gave up the idea. It was in vain to think of reaching it by stealth, since the natives escorted me in numbers wherever I went, and not for one single moment that I can recall to mind was I ever permitted to be alone.

The green and precipitous elevations that stood ranged around the head of the vale where Marheyo's habitation was situated effectually precluded all hope of escape in that quarter, even if I could have stolen away from the thousand eyes of the savages.

But these reflections now seldom obtruded upon me; I gave myself up to the passing hour, and if ever disagreeable thoughts arose in my mind, I drove them away. When I looked around the verdant recess in which I was buried, and gazed up to the summits of the lofty eminence that hemmed me in, I was well disposed to think that I was in the "Happy Valley," and that beyond those heights there was nought but a world of care and anxiety.

As I extended my wanderings in the valley and grew more familiar with the habits of its inmates, I was fain to confess that, despite the disadvantages of his condition, the Polynesian savage, surrounded by all the luxurious provisions of nature, enjoyed an infinitely happier, though certainly a less intellectual existence, than the self-complacent European.

The naked wretch who shivers beneath the bleak skies, and starves among the inhospitable wilds of Terra-del-Fuego,* might indeed be made happier by civilization, for it would alleviate his physical wants. But the voluptuous Indian, with every desire supplied, whom Providence has bountifully provided with all the sources of pure and natural enjoyment, and from whom are removed so many of the ills and pains of life—what has he to desire at the hands of Civilization? She may "cultivate his mind,"—may "elevate his thoughts,"—these I believe are the established phrases—but will he be the happier? Let the once smiling and populous Hawaiian islands, with their now diseased, starving, and dying natives, answer the question. The missionaries may seek to disguise the matter as they will, but the facts are incontrovertible; and the devoutest Christian who visits that group with an unbiased mind, must go away mournfully asking—"Are these, alas! the fruits of twenty-five years of enlightening?"

In a primitive state of society, the enjoyments of life, though few and simple, are spread over a great extent, and are unalloyed; but Civilization, for every advantage she imparts, holds a hundred evils in reserve;—the heart burnings, the jealousies, the social rivalries, the family dissensions, and the thousand self-inflicted discomforts of refined life, which make up in units the swelling aggregate of human misery, are unknown among these unsophisticated people.

But it will be urged that these shocking unprincipled wretches are cannibals. Very true; and a rather bad trait in their character it

* The coastal areas at the southern tip of South America, near Cape Horn.

must be allowed. But they are such only when they seek to gratify the passion of revenge upon their enemies; and I ask whether the mere eating of human flesh so very far exceeds in barbarity that custom which only a few years since was practised in enlightened England:—a convicted traitor, perhaps a man found guilty of honesty, patriotism, and suchlike heinous crimes, had his head lopped off with a huge axe, his bowels dragged out and thrown into a fire; while his body, carved into four quarters, was with his head exposed upon pikes, and permitted to rot and fester among the public haunts of men!

The fiend-like skill we display in the invention of all manner of death-dealing engines, the vindictiveness with which we carry on our wars, and the misery and desolation that follow in their train, are enough of themselves to distinguish the white civilized man as the most ferocious animal on the face of the earth.

His remorseless cruelty is seen in many of the institutions of our own favoured land. There is one in particular lately adopted in one of the States of the Union, which purports to have been dictated by the most merciful considerations. To destroy our malefactors piece-meal, drying up in their veins, drop by drop, the blood we are too chicken-hearted to shed by a single blow which would at once put a period to their sufferings, is deemed to be infinitely preferable to the old-fashioned punishment of gibbeting—much less annoying to the victim, and more in accordance with the refined spirit of the age; and yet how feeble is all language to describe the horrors we inflict upon these wretches, whom we mason up in the cells of our prisons, and condemn to perpetual solitude in the very heart of our population.

But it is needless to multiply the examples of civilized barbarity; they far exceed in the amount of misery they cause the crimes which we regard with such abhorrence in our less enlightened fellow-creatures.

The term "Savage" is, I conceive, often misapplied, and indeed when I consider the vices, cruelties, and enormities of every kind that spring up in the tainted atmosphere of a feverish civilization, I am inclined to think that so far as the relative wickedness of the parties is concerned, four or five Marquesan Islanders sent to the United States as Missionaries might be quite as useful as an equal number of Americans despatched to the Islands in a similar capacity.

I once heard it given as an instance of the frightful depravity of a certain tribe in the Pacific, that they had no word in their language to express the idea of virtue. The assertion was unfounded; but were it otherwise, it might be met by stating that their language is almost entirely destitute of terms to express the delightful ideas conveyed by our endless catalogue of civilized crimes.

In the altered frame of mind to which I have referred, every object that presented itself to my notice in the valley struck me in a new light, and the opportunities I now enjoyed of observing the manners of its inmates, tended to strengthen my favourable impressions. One peculiarity that fixed my admiration was the perpetual hilarity reigning through the whole extent of the vale. There seemed to be no cares, griefs, troubles, or vexations, in all Typee. The hours tripped along as gaily as the laughing couples down a country dance.

There were none of those thousand sources of irritation that the ingenuity of civilized man has created to mar his own felicity. There were no foreclosures of mortgages, no protested notes, no bills payable, no debts of honour in Typee; no unreasonable tailors and shoe-makers, perversely bent on being paid; no duns of any description; no assault and battery attorneys, to foment discord, backing their clients up to a quarrel, and then knocking their heads together; no poor rela-tions, everlastingly occupying the spare bed-chamber, and diminishing the elbow room at the family table; no destitute widows with their children starving on the cold charities of the world; no beggars; no debtors' prisons; no proud and hard-hearted nabobs in Typee; or to sum up all in one word—no Money! "That root of all evil" was not to be found in the valley.

In this secluded abode of happiness there were no cross old women, no cruel step-dames, no withered spinsters, no love-sick maid-ens, no sour old bachelors, no inattentive husbands, no melancholy young men, no blubbering youngsters, and no squalling brats. All was mirth, fun, and high good humour. Blue devils, hypochondria, and doleful dumps, went and hid themselves among the nooks and crannies of the rocks.

Here you would see a parcel of children frolicking together the live-long day, and no quarreling, no contention, among them. The same number in our own land could not have played together for the space of an hour without biting or scratching one another. There you might have seen a throng of young females, not filled with envyings of each other's charms, nor displaying the ridiculous affectations of gentility, nor yet moving in whalebone corsets, like so many automatons, but free, inartificially happy, and unconstrained.

There were some spots in that sunny vale where they would frequently resort to decorate themselves with garlands of flowers. To have seen them reclining beneath the shadows of one of the beautiful groves; the ground about them strewn with freshly gathered buds and blossoms, employed in weaving chaplets and necklaces, one would have thought that all the train of Flora had gathered together to keep a festival in honour of their mistress.

With the young men there seemed almost always some matter of diversion or business on hand that afforded a constant variety of en-joyment. But whether fishing, or carving canoes, or polishing their ornaments, never was there exhibited the least sign of strife or con-tention among them.

As for the warriors, they maintained a tranquil dignity of demeanor, journeying occasionally from house to house, where they were always sure to be received with the attention bestowed upon distinguished guests. The old men, of whom there were many in the vale, seldom stirred from their mats, where they would recline for hours and hours, smoking and talking to one another with all the garrulity of age.

But the continual happiness, which so far as I was able to judge appeared to prevail in the valley, sprung principally from that all-pervading sensation which Rousseau has told us he at one time experienced, the mere buoyant sense of a healthful physical existence. And indeed in this particular the Typees had ample reason to felicitate themselves, for sickness was almost unknown. During the whole period of my stay I saw but one invalid among them; and on their smooth clear skins you observed no blemish or mark of disease.

The general repose, however, upon which I have just been descanting, was broken in upon about this time by an event which proved that the islanders were not entirely exempt from those occurrences which disturb the quiet of more civilized communities.

Having now been a considerable time in the valley, I began to feel surprised that the violent hostility subsisting between its inhabitants, and those of the adjoining bay of Happar, should never have manifested itself in any warlike encounter. Although the valiant Typees would often by gesticulations declare their undying hatred against their enemies, and the disgust they felt at their cannibal propensities; although they dilated upon the manifold injuries they had received at their hands, yet with a forbearance truly commendable, they appeared patiently to sit down under their grievances, and to refrain from making any reprisals. The Happars, entrenched behind their mountains, and never even showing themselves on their summits, did not appear to me to furnish adequate cause for that excess of animosity evinced towards them by the heroic tenants of our vale, and I was inclined to believe that the deeds of blood attributed to them had been greatly exaggerated.

On the other hand, as the clamours of war had not up to this period disturbed the serenity of the tribe, I began to distrust the truth of those reports which ascribed so fierce and belligerent a character to the Typee nation. Surely, thought I, all these terrible stories I have heard about the inveteracy with which they carried on the feud, their deadly intensity of hatred, and the diabolical malice with which they glutted their revenge upon the inanimate forms of the slain, are nothing more than fables, and I must confess that I experienced something like a sense of regret at having my hideous anticipations thus disappointed. I felt in some sort like a 'prentice-boy who, going to the play in the expectation of being delighted with a cut-and-thrust tragedy, is almost moved to tears of disappointment at the exhibition of a genteel comedy.

I could not avoid thinking that I had fallen in with a greatly traduced people, and I moralized not a little upon the disadvantage of having a bad name, which in this instance had given a tribe of savages, who were as pacific as so many lambkins, the reputation of a confederacy of giant-killers.

But subsequent events proved that I had been a little too premature in coming to this conclusion. One day about noon, happening to be at the Ti, I had lain down on the mats with several of the chiefs, and had gradually sunk into a most luxurious siesta, when I was awakened by a tremendous outcry, and starting up beheld the natives seizing their spears and hurrrying out, while the most puissant of the chiefs, grasping the six muskets which were ranged against the bamboos, followed after, and soon disappeared in the groves. These movements were accompanied by wild shouts, in which "Happar, Happar," greatly predominated. The islanders were now to be seen running past the Ti, and striking across the valley to the Happar side. Presently I heard the sharp report of a musket from the adjoining hills, and then a burst of voices in the same direction. At this the women, who had congregated in the groves, set up the most violent clamours, as they invariably do here as elsewhere on every occasion of excitement and alarm, with a view of tranquillizing their own minds and disturbing other people. On this particular occasion they made such an outrageous noise, and continued it with such perseverance, that for awhile, had entire volleys of musketry been fired off in the neighboring mountains, I should not have been able to have heard them.

When this female commotion had a little subsided I listened eagerly for further information. At last bang went another shot, and then a second volley of yells from the hills. Again all was quiet, and continued so for such a length of time that I began to think the contending armies had agreed upon a suspension of hostilities; when pop went a third gun, followed as before with a yell. After this, for nearly two hours nothing occurred worthy of comment, save some straggling shouts from the hill-side, sounding like the halloos of a parcel of truant boys who had lost themselves in the woods.

During this interval I had remained standing on the piazza of the "Ti," which directly fronted the Happar mountain, and with no one near me but Kory-Kory and the old superannuated savages I have before described. These latter never stirred from their mats, and seemed altogether unconscious that anything unusual was going on.

As for Kory-Kory, he appeared to think that we were in the midst of great events, and sought most zealously to impress me with a due sense of their importance. Every sound that reached us conveyed some momentous item of intelligence to him. At such times, as if he were gifted with second sight, he would go through a variety of pantomimic illustrations, showing me the precise manner in which the redoubtable

163

Typees were at that very moment chastising the insolence of the enemy. "Mehevi hanna pippee nuee Happar," he exclaimed every five minutes, giving me to understand that under that distinguished captain the warriors of his nation were performing prodigies of valour.

Having heard only four reports from the muskets, I was led to believe that they were worked by the islanders in the same manner as the Sultan Solyman's ponderous artillery at the siege of Byzantium, one of them taking an hour or two to load and train. At last, no sound whatever proceeding from the mountains, I concluded that the contest had been determined one way or the other. Such appeared, indeed, to be the case, for in a little while a courier arrived at the "Ti," almost breathless with his exertions, and communicated the news of a great victory having been achieved by his countrymen: "Happar poo arva!— Happar poo arva!" (the cowards had fled). Kory-Kory was in ecstacies, and commenced a vehement harangue, which, so far as I understood it, implied that the result exactly agreed with his expectations, and which, moreover, was intended to convince me that it would be a perfectly useless undertaking, even for an army of fire-eaters, to offer battle to the irresistible heroes of our valley. In all this I of course acquiesced, and looked forward with no little interest to the return of the conquerors, whose victory I feared might not have been purchased without cost to themselves.

But here I was again mistaken; for Mehevi, in conducting his warlike operations, rather inclined to the Fabian than to the Bonapartean tactics, husbanding his resources and exposing his troops to no unnecessary hazards. The total loss of the victors in this obstinately contested affairs was, in killed, wounded, and missing—one forefinger and part of a thumb-nail (which the late proprietor brought along with him in his hand), a severely contused arm, and a considerable effusion of blood flowing from the thigh of a chief, who had received an ugly thrust from a Happar spear. What the enemy had suffered I could not discover, but I presume they had succeeded in taking off with them the bodies of their slain.

Such was the issue of the battle, as far as its results came under my observation; and as it appeared to be considered an event of prodigious importance, I reasonably concluded that the wars of the natives were marked by no very sanguinary traits. I afterwards learned how the skirmish had originated. A number of the Happars had been discovered prowling for no good purpose on the Typee side of the mountain; the alarm was sounded, and the invaders, after a protracted resistance, had been chased over the frontier. But why had not the intrepid Mehevi carried the war into Happar? Why had he not made a descent into the hostile vale, and brought away some trophy of his victory—some materials for the cannibal entertainment which I had heard usually terminated every engagement? After all, I was much inclined to believe that such shocking festivals must occur very rarely among the islanders, if, indeed, they ever take place.

For two or three days the late event was the theme of general comment; after which the excitement gradually wore away, and the valley resumed its accustomed tranquillity.

Chapter XXXII

Apprehensions of Evil—Frightful Discovery—Some remarks on Cannibalism—Second Battle with the Happars—Savage Spectacle—Mysterious Feast—Subsequent Disclosures.

From the time of my casual encounter with Karky the artist, my life was one of absolute wretchedness. Not a day passed but I was persecuted by the solicitations of some of the natives to subject myself to the odious operation of tattooing. Their importunities drove me half wild, for I felt how easily they might work their will upon me regarding this or anything else which they took into their heads. Still, however, the behaviour of the islanders towards me was as kind as ever. Fayaway was quite as engaging; Kory-Kory as devoted: and Mehevi the king just as gracious and condescending as before. But I had now been three months in their valley, as nearly as I could estimate; I had grown familiar with the narrow limits to which my wanderings had been confined; and I began bitterly to feel the state of captivity in which I was held. There was no one with whom I could freely converse; no one to whom I could communicate my thoughts; no one who could sympathise with my sufferings. A thousand times I thought how much more endurable would have been my lot had Toby still been with me. But I was left alone, and the thought was terrible to me. Still, despite my griefs, I did all in my power to appear composed and cheerful, well knowing that by manifesting any uneasiness, or any desire to escape, I should only frustrate my object.

It was during the period I was in this unhappy frame of mind that the painful malady under which I had been labouring—after having almost completely subsided—began again to show itself, and with symptoms as violent as ever. This added calamity nearly unmanned me; the recurrence of the complaint proved that without powerful remedial applications all hope of cure was futile; and when I reflected that just beyond the elevations which bound me in, was the medical relief I needed, and that, although so near, it was impossible for me to avail myself of it, the thought was misery.

In this wretched situation, every circumstance which evinced the savage nature of the beings at whose mercy I was, augmented the fearful apprehensions that consumed me. An occurrence which happened about this time affected me most powerfully.

I have already mentioned that from the ridge-pole of Marheyo's house were suspended a number of packages enveloped in tappa. Many of these I had often seen in the hands of the natives, and their contents had been examined in my presence. But there were three packages hanging very nearly over the place where I lay, which from their remarkable appearance had often excited my curiosity. Several times I had asked Kory-Kory to show me their contents; but my servitor, who in almost every other particular had acceded to my wishes, always refused to gratify me in this.

One day, returning unexpectedly from the "Ti," my arrival seemed to throw the inmates of the house into the greatest confusion. They were seated together on the mats, and by the lines which extended from the roof to the floor I immediately perceived that the mysterious packages were for some purpose or other under inspection. The evident alarm the savages betrayed filled me with forebodings of evil, and with an uncontrollable desire to penetrate the secret so jealously guarded. Despite the efforts of Marheyo and Kory-Kory to restrain me, I forced my way into the midst of the circle, and just caught a glimpse of three human heads, which others of the party were hurriedly enveloping in the coverings from which they had been taken.

One of the three I distinctly saw. It was in a state of perfect preservation, and, from the slight glimpse I had of it, seemed to have been subjected to some smoking operation which had reduced it to the dry, hard, and mummy-like appearance it presented. The two long scalp-locks were twisted up into balls upon the crown of the head in the same way that the individual had worn them during life. The sunken cheeks were rendered yet more ghastly by the rows of glistening teeth which protruded from between the lips, while the sockets of the eyes—filled with oval bits of mother-of-pearl shell, with a black spot in the centre—heightened the hideousness of its aspect.

Two of the three were heads of the islanders; but the third, to my horror, was that of a white man. Although it had been quickly removed from my sight, still the glimpse I had of it was enough to convince me that I could not be mistaken.

Gracious God! what dreadful thoughts entered my mind! In solving this mystery perhaps I had solved another, and the fate of my lost companion might be revealed in the shocking spectacle I had just witnessed. I longed to have torn off the folds of cloth, and satisfied the awful doubts under which I laboured. But before I had recovered from the consternation into which I had been thrown, the fatal packages were hoisted aloft and once more swung over my head. The natives now gathered round me tumultuously, and laboured to convince me that what I had just seen were the heads of three Happar warriors, who had been slain in battle. This glaring falsehood added to my alarm, and it was not until I reflected that I had observed the packages swinging from their elevation before Toby's disappearance, that I could at all recover my composure.

But although this horrible apprehension had been dispelled, I had discovered enough to fill me, in my present state of mind, with the most bitter reflections. It was plain that I had seen the last relic of some unfortunate wretch, who must have been massacred on the beach by the savages, in one of those perilous trading adventures which I have before described.

It was not, however, alone the murder of the stranger that overcame me with gloom. I shuddered at the idea of the subsequent fate his inanimate body might have met with. Was the same doom reserved for me? Was I destined to perish like him—like him, perhaps, to be devoured, and my head to be preserved as a fearful memento of the event? My imagination ran riot in these horrid speculations, and I felt certain that the worst possible evils would befall me. But whatever were my misgivings, I studiously concealed them from the islanders, as well as the full extent of the discovery I had made.

Although the assurances which the Typees had often given me, that they never eat human flesh, had not convinced me that such was the case, yet, having been so long a time in the valley without witnessing anything which indicated the existence of the practice, I began to hope that it was an event of very rare occurrence, and that I should be spared the horror of witnessing it during my stay among them; but, alas! these hopes were soon destroyed.

It is a singular fact, that in all our accounts of cannibal tribes we have seldom received the testimony of an eye-witness to the revolting practice. The horrible conclusion has almost always been derived either from the second-hand evidence of Europeans, or else from the admissions of the savages themselves, after they have in some degree become civilized. The Polynesians are aware of the detestation in which Europeans hold this custom, and therefore invariably deny its existence, and, with the craft peculiar to savages, endeavour to conceal every trace of it.

The excessive unwillingness betrayed by the Sandwich Islanders, even at the present day, to allude to the unhappy fate of Cook, has been often remarked. And so well have they succeeded in covering that event with mystery, that to this very hour, despite all that has been said and written on the subject, it still remains doubtful whether they wreaked upon his murdered body the vengeance they sometimes inflicted upon their enemies.

At Karakikova, the scene of that tragedy, a strip of ship's copper nailed against an upright post in the ground used to inform the traveller that beneath reposed the "remains" of the great circumnavigator. But I am strongly inclined to believe not only that the corpse was refused Christian burial, but that the heart which was brought to Vancouver some time after the event, and which the Hawaiians stoutly maintained was that of Captain Cook, was no such thing; and that the whole affair was a piece of imposture which was sought to be palmed off upon the credulous Englishman.

A few years since there was living on the island of Mowee (one of the Sandwich group) an old chief, who, actuated by a morbid desire for notoriety, gave himself out among the foreign residents of the place as the living tomb of Captain Cook's big toe!—affirming, that at the cannibal entertainment which ensued after the lamented Briton's death, that particular portion of his body had fallen to his share. His indignant countrymen actually caused him to be prosecuted in the native courts, on a charge nearly equivalent to what we term defamation of character; but the old fellow persisting in his assertion, and no invalidating proof being adduced, the plaintiffs were cast in the suit, and the cannibal reputation of the defendant fully established. This result was the making of his fortune; ever afterwards he was in the habit of giving very profitable audiences to all curious travellers who were desirous of beholding the man who had eaten the great navigator's great toe.

About a week after my discovery of the contents of the mysterious packages, I happened to be at the Ti, when another war-alarm was sounded, and the natives rushing to their arms, sallied out to resist a second incursion of the Happar invaders. The same scene was again repeated, only that on this occasion I heard at least fifteen reports of muskets from the mountains during the time that the skirmish lasted. An hour or two after its termination, loud paeans chanted through the valley announced the approach of the victors. I stood with Kory-Kory leaning against the railing of the pi-pi awaiting their advance, when a tumultuous crowd of islanders emerged with wild clamours from the neighbouring groves. In the midst of them marched four men, one preceding the other at regular intervals of eight or ten feet, with poles of a corresponding length, extended from shoulder to shoulder, to which were lashed with thongs of bark three long narrow bundles, carefully wrapped in ample coverings of freshly plucked palm-leaves, tacked together with slivers of bamboo. Here and there upon these green winding-sheets might be seen the stains of blood, while the warriors who carried the frightful burdens displayed upon their naked limbs similar sanguinary marks. The shaven head of the foremost had a deep gash upon it, and the clotted gore which had flowed from the wound remained in dry patches around it. This savage seemed to be sinking under the weight he bore. The bright tattooing upon his body was covered with blood and dust; his inflamed eyes rolled in their sockets, and his whole appearance denoted extraordinary suffering and exertion; yet, sustained by some powerful impulse, he continued to advance, while the throng around him with wild cheers sought to encourage him.

The other three men were marked about the arms and breasts with several slight wounds, which they somewhat ostentatiously displayed.

These four individuals, having been the most active in the late encounter, claimed the honour of bearing the bodies of their slain enemies to the Ti. Such was the conclusion I drew from my own observations, and, as far as I could understand, from the explanation which Kory-Kory gave me.

The royal Mehevi walked by the side of these heroes. He carried in one hand a musket, from the barrel of which was suspended a small canvass pouch of powder, and in the other he grasped a short javelin, which he held before him and regarded with fierce exultation. This javelin he had wrested from a celebrated champion of the Happars, who had ignominiously fled, and was pursued by his foe beyond the summit of the mountain.

When within a short distance of the Ti, the warrior with the wounded head, who proved to be Narmonee, tottered forward two or three steps, and fell helplessly to the ground; but not before another had caught the end of the pole from his shoulder, and placed it upon his own.

The excited throng of islanders, who surrounded the person of the king and the dead bodies of the enemy, approached the spot where I stood, brandishing their rude implements of warfare, many of which were bruised and broken, and uttering continual shouts of triumph. When the crowd drew up opposite the Ti, I set myself to watch their proceedings most attentively; but scarcely had they halted when my servitor, who had left my side for an instant, touched my arm, and proposed our returning to Marheyo's house. To this I objected; but, to my surprise, Kory-Kory reiterated his request, and with an unusual vehemence of manner. Still, however, I refused to comply, and was retreating before him, as in his importunity he pressed upon me, when I felt a heavy hand laid upon my shoulder, and turning round, encountered the bulky form of Mow-Mow, a one-eyed chief, who had just detached himself from the crowd below, and had mounted the rear of the pi-pi upon which we stood. His cheek had been pierced by the point of a spear, and the wound imparted a still more frightful expression to his hideously tattooed face, already deformed by the loss of an eye. The warrior, without uttering a syllable, pointed fiercely in the direction of Marheyo's house, while Kory-Kory, at the same time presenting his back, desired me to mount.

I declined this offer, but intimated my willingness to withdraw, and moved slowly along the piazza, wondering what could be the cause of this unusual treatment. A few minutes' consideration convinced me that the savages were about to celebrate some hideous rite in connection with their peculiar customs, and at which they were determined I should not be present. I descended from the pi-pi, and attended by Kory-Kory, who on this occasion did not show his usual commiseration for my lameness, but seemed only anxious to hurry me on, walked away from the place. As I passed through the noisy throng, which by this time completely environed the Ti, I looked with fearful curiosity at the three packages, which now were deposited upon the ground; but although I had no doubt as to their contents, still their thick coverings prevented my actually detecting the form of a human body.

The next morning, shortly after sunrise, the same thundering sounds which had awakened me from sleep on the second day of the Feast of Calabashes, assured me that the savages were on the eve of celebrating another, and, as I fully believed, a horrible solemnity.

All the inmates of the house, with the exception of Marheyo, his son, and Tinor, after assuming their gala dresses, departed in the direction of the Taboo Groves.

Although I did not anticipate a compliance with my request, still, with a view of testing the truth of my suspicions, I proposed to Kory-Kory that, according to our usual custom in the morning, we should take a stroll to the Ti: he positively refused; and when I renewed the request, he evinced his determination to prevent my going there; and, to divert my mind from the subject, he offered to accompany me to the stream. We accordingly went, and bathed. On our coming back to the house, I was surprised to find that all its inmates had returned, and were lounging upon the mats as usual, although the drums still sounded from the groves.

The rest of the day I spent with Kory-Kory and Fayaway, wandering about a part of the valley situated in an opposite direction from the Ti; and whenever I so much as looked towards that building, although it was hidden from view by intervening trees, and at the distance of more than a mile, my attendant would exclaim, "taboo, taboo!"

At the various houses where we stopped, I found many of the inhabitants reclining at their ease, or pursuing some light occupation, as if nothing unusual were going forward; but amongst them all I did not perceive a single chief or warrior. When I asked several of the people why they were not at the "Hoolah Hoolah" (the feast), they uniformly answered the question in a manner which implied that it was not intended for them, but for Mehevi, Narmonee, Mow Mow, Kolor, Womonoo, Kalow—running over, in their desire to make me comprehend their meaning, the names of all the principal chiefs.

Everything, in short, strengthened my suspicions with regard to the nature of the festival they were now celebrating; and which amounted almost to a certainty. While in Nukuheva I had frequently been informed that the whole tribe were never present at these cannibal banquets; but the chiefs and priests only, and everything I now observed agreed with the account.

The sound of the drums continued, without intermission, the whole day, and falling continually upon my ear, caused me a sensation of horror which I am unable to describe. On the following day hearing none of those noisy indications of revelry, I concluded that the inhuman feast was terminated; and feeling a kind of morbid curiosity to discover whether the Ti might furnish any evidence of what had taken place there, I proposed to Kory-Kory to walk there. To this proposition he replied by pointing with his finger to the newly risen sun, and then up to the zenith, intimating that our visit must be deferred until noon. Shortly after that hour we accordingly proceeded to the Taboo Groves, and as soon as we entered their precincts, I looked fearfully round in quest of some memorial of the scenes which had so lately been acted there; but everything appeared as usual. On reaching the Ti, we found Mehevi and a few chiefs reclining on the mats, who gave me as friendly a reception as ever. No allusions of any kind were made by them to the recent events; and I refrained, for obvious reasons, from referring to them myself.

After staying a short time I took my leave. In passing along the piazza, previously to descending from the pi-pi, I observed a curiously carved vessel of wood, of considerable size, with a cover placed over it, of the same material, and which resembled in shape a small canoe. It was surrounded by a low railing of bamboos, the top of which was scarcely a foot from the ground. As the vessel had been placed in its present position since my last visit, I at once concluded that it must have some connection with the recent festival; and, prompted by a curiosity I could not repress, in passing it I raised one end of the cover; at the same moment the chiefs, perceiving my design, loudly ejaculated, "Taboo! taboo!" But the slight glimpse sufficed; my eyes fell upon the disordered members of a human skeleton, the bones still fresh with moisture, and with particles of flesh clinging to them here and there!

Kory-Kory, who had been a little in advance of me, attracted by the exclamations of the chiefs, turned round in time to witness the expression of horror on my countenance. He now hurried towards me, pointing at the same time to the canoe, and exclaiming rapidly, "Puarkee! puarkee!" (Pig, pig). I pretended to yield to the deception, and repeated the words after him several times, as though acquiescing in what he said. The other savages, either deceived by my conduct or unwilling to manifest their displeasure at what could not now be remedied, took no further notice of the occurrence, and I immediately left the Ti.

All that night I lay awake, revolving in my mind the fearful situation in which I was placed. The last horrid revelation had now been made, and the full sense of my condition rushed upon my mind with a force I had never before experienced.

Where, thought I, desponding, is there the slightest prospect of escape? The only person who seemed to possess the ability to assist me was the stranger Marnoo; but would he ever return to the valley? and if he did, should I be permitted to hold any communication with him? It seemed as if I were cut off from every source of hope, and that nothing remained but passively to await whatever fate was in store for me. A thousand times I endeavoured to account for the mysterious conduct of the natives. For what conceivable purpose did they thus retain me a captive? What could be their object in treating me with such apparent kindness, and did it not cover some treacherous scheme? Or, if they had no other design than to hold me a prisoner, how should I be able to pass away my days in this narrow valley, deprived of all intercourse with civilized beings, and for ever separated from friends and home?

One only hope remained to me. The French could not long defer a visit to the bay, and if they should permanently locate any of their troops in the valley, the savages could not for any length of time conceal my existence from them. But what reason had I to suppose that I should be spared until such an event occurred—an event which might be postponed by a hundred different contingencies?

---

33. Beat Down Frigid Rome

ESTHER WAGNER

Esther Wagner (1917–   ) teaches at the University of Puget Sound. Her stories have appeared in the *Atlantic Monthly*, *New Yorker*, *Harper's*, and *Ellery Queen*, among other magazines. She wrote a novel, *The Gift of Rome*, in collaboration with John Wagner, and is now working on another. Her story here won the Atlantic First prize in 1958.

T HE BELL HAD JUST RUNG for the first period, and old Latimer threw open the door with one of his long-armed, extravagant, precisely controlled gestures. He stood back to supervise with his cold ancient-looking smile the entry of his Latin I class from the Gothic marches of the corridors to the centurion atmosphere of his classroom. He had a trick of fixing his eyes on the feet of his students as they crossed the doorsill, an elaborately blank glance which stilled the last flap of every loafer, deadened the last clump of every ski boot. At the end of this morning's stream of feet came a pair of unobtrusively foreign-made, cordovan-polished brogues, and old Latimer shifted his gaze to the unlined pleasant face of his colleague, Mr. Merton, English teacher and Administrative Assistant to the Dean of Boys.

All the faculty felt rather sorry for Merton, who had to handle the college admissions correspondence and was continually writing hopeful, covertly pleading letters to the deans of admission of the great Eastern colleges. Merton had to give them the hard sell on sons of three generations of Harvard or Yale or Hurstleigh men who now found themselves doubtful candidates because they had made a couple of C's in junior year. He resented this, remembering his own easy admission to the most august of colleges during the depression years, and sometimes thinking almost savagely of their jowled fathers, survivors of the Cretaceous age of the gentleman's C. Worst of all, he couldn't even be certain that his sure-fire candidates would get just where they wanted to go.

He now brought in to old Latimer a sheaf of application papers and a student's dossier in a battered manila folder, from which a wild-eyed photograph unpromisingly slopped over at the top.

"Lang's application for the Hurstleigh scholarship, sir," he muttered, looking warily at the nearest amorphous little countenances staring apprehensively at the assignment on the blackboard or bowed in swift vocabulary review. "Here's their stuff about qualifications, and Lang's papers. The Head would like to have your letter today if it's at all possible."

"Fourth period, or end of third," said old Latimer with the effortless laconic air which marked everything he said and did. He could make long speeches or perform the most complex personal rituals without ever letting go his characteristic effects of concision, condensation, compression. No one ever analyzed these effects or dissected his techniques; the Head never sent student teachers to work under him, though they were always assigned to visit his classes in the capacity of audience. His authority was beyond formulation. The Head was the Head; the Dean was the Little Corporal or the Boss-man; the Old Man was Latimer, who had no administrative position whatever, no connection with the faculty council, was never put on committees or made Sponsor of anything. He was the Old Man of the Mountain, the Old Man of the Sea. The funny thing was that he wasn't even very old: fifty-five at the most, with thick silver-fox hair.

Merton left and the freshmen were silent. The door swung to with a click, and there rose behind it the great strange atmosphere of the Latin room, haunting to generations of students, compounded of the smell of Latimer's old beautiful tweeds, the wild fragrance of the ferns

173

in his extravagant window boxes, the stone eyes of the Roman senators in prints on the front wall, the glint of gold letters on the leather bindings ranged on the desk, the complex lines of the small, fiercely exact reproduction of a Roman trireme encased in glass.

Old Latimer's classes always began quietly enough. The students lifted their faces to him, confident, expecting something to happen. Some waited for the great gusts of temper that swept the room rhythmically, periodically, like the rise and fall of some giant breathing chest. Some hoped for a dramatic chastisement, in baritone shout or chill sibilant whisper, of some classmate; some simply wished to escape this. Old Latimer never had any trouble with discipline and never thought about it.

Now he ran rapidly over the vocabulary, asking for meanings of words, principal parts of verbs, suddenly swooping to demand a whole declension, the total conjugation of one of the hard tenses, like the future passive of the -io verbs. For good answers he gave his swift wolfish smile, baring an astonishingly long, sharp left incisor. For a slow one he waited in impassive, gentlemanly patience or in the most ill-concealed ennui, rolling up his eyes, shaking his chalk in his hand. The choice of manner depended on the personality of the student, the past performances, known ability, standing of the student after some scene of the day before, and so on.

Over kitten-like, earnest little Emily Rushmore in the front row, struggling with the forms of the infinitive in her accustomed style of mixed timidity and stubbornness, valor and misgiving, he lingered long, hinting, grinning, exhorting, correcting, suddenly thrusting his large-boned brilliant-eyed countenance within one inch of hers to hiss an ending at her, bowing with a genuine smiling courtesy when she hit happily on a correct form. The little girl's face lit and shadowed, her eyelids drooped or lifted, following this peculiar orchestration. Latimer pressed her on to the fifth declension, new for the day; her maunderings over this caused him suddenly to throw up his hands, throw out his arms, throw back his head, and shout: "Emily Rushmore! Emily Rushmore!" Out came the rush of eloquence all knew would come, this time untinged with violence, just ringing with passion, elevated, sincere. In the great hills of South Dakota, he informed her, where the Sioux thought there abided forever the spirits of the dead, there was a great slab of mountain which bore her name. He called to her mind the images of great men hewn there by tremendous effort. Even so, he told her, he had hewn into the great slabs of her blank child's mind the forms of the four great Latin declensions, "complete, Emily, with mutations and characteristic variations from the norm—the -i of the ablative of *mare, insigne, animal, exemplar.*" The low beautiful baritone rose to a deep shout as he showered on her the epithets of Slab, Granite Hillside, Erstwhile Smooth Expanse. "And now you boggle at the second

-i in *diei,*" he added, suddenly in a normal, conversational voice, and smiled.

Emily began to relax; a delicate little giggle escaped her and a deep chortle spread through the class.

"Now, the translation," said old Latimer, smothering a yawn. "It's a simplified little anecdote taken from the *Aeneid,* which you—*some* of you, I mean—will be reading late next year." He piloted them through the short story of Aeneas' landing on the coast near Carthage, Dido's reception of him, the banquet, and the beginning of the tale. He excoriated someone for making a passive active, praised someone for making the historical present a past, explained neatly and lucidly the Roman attitude toward the order of words, reminded everyone that some ablatives of manner take *cum* and some do not take *cum,* assigned a lesson dealing with the comparison of irregular adjectives, pointed out to everyone that the translation for that lesson described the love of Dido for Aeneas and incarnated the idea of romantic love which most appealed to the ancient world, "not *exactly* a valentine affair! June and moon were not its symbols, but chains and fire and destroying disease; naked force and terrible pain. Here is great Virgil telling about Dido wandering through the city, burned with it, pierced with it, sick with it . . ." and the deep beautiful voice rolled over the classroom in a tide of unintelligible sound, as strongly marked by rhythm as any music they had ever heard:

> Heu vatum ignarae mentes! quid vota furentem,
> quid delubra iuvant? Est mollis flamma medullas
> interea, et tacitum vivit sub pectore volnus.
> Uritur infelix Dido . . .

Over the faces of two or three, the incantation seekers, who would never forget this face or room, this sound, so long as they lived, came the drop-jawed, feeble-minded look of total acceptance they habitually wore at these moments. The bell rang; old Latimer seemed suddenly to forget the whole thing, smiled his briskest smile, said, "All right, now *watch those irregulars,*" and flung open his door.

IN EVERY school there is one teacher concerning whom a rumor circulates that he has a large personal fortune and teaches not for money but from some obscure disinterested motive. In Latimer's school this role fell naturally to him, and each generation increased the collection of wild stories about his personal life and background. The man's clothes, bearing, accent, all suggested some world of personal autonomy and distinction totally foreign to their own world of hard-working, commuting, cocktail-drinking, sense-talking older men, with their ordinary expensive suits, their speech full of flat *a*'s, slurred consonants, dulled vowels (*guv'munt*), and familiar well-understood words.

He seemed also a fortuitous ambassador from some world quite
different from that represented by their other teachers. All this was
augmented by the fact that nobody really did know anything much
about Latimer. The students all knew that he was an accomplished
athlete; he played an almost embarrassingly good game of tennis for
one so old, was seen with his wife on golf links and on the bridle
paths. He skated on the school pond once or twice a year, with great
competence, using a fine pair of Austrian skates. But he coached no
teams, never talked of sports or went to football games.

The faculty knew with a fair degree of certainty that he had
taught in several Eastern colleges and in at least one of the great
prep schools, and that there was some quite exciting story about his
marriage to the mother of one of his pupils. The tall dashing-looking
woman whom everybody knew only as Mrs. Latimer certainly was not
a very representative faculty wife. She was more than merely civil,
really friendly in a fast-talking, brilliantly smiling way. She gave a large
cocktail party once a year for all the faculty and served very good food
and drinks. She wore dark red or dark green or purple tweeds in the
daytime and black silk in the evening. It was thought that she had many
friends "in town"—not in the suburb where the school was located—
and that these were not suburban types. Nobody ever saw her in the
summer. She and her husband simply disappeared off the Middle
Western map, to return always just in time for the opening reception
given by the Head, coming into it as though they had never been
away, hard and precise in physical outline, clipped of speech, vague
and uninformative in conversation.

Parents and other teachers quite often felt that Latimer did not
take as much personal interest in the students as was the prevailing
mode at the school. Certainly he spent little time on his inept and
failing students. But no one dared reproach him with this, in view of the
long fanatical hours he devoted to helping the middle range of his
students, lavishing upon them his burning gaze, his infinite powers of
dramatization, his gifts of lucid explanation and varied repetition, in
an impassioned effort to bring them out of their uncertainties and into
that state of life where they could translate with confidence, decline
and conjugate with aplomb, recognize without hesitation the landmarks
of early Latin studies, indirect discourse, purpose clauses, and the like.
He never spoke to these students or to any others about their outside
life, never allowed them to speak of their family routines or their home
atmospheres. They could not feel that he was interested in them as
human beings; it seemed unlikely that he ever thought of them as such,
and probable that he did not consider them people as they had been
taught to expect that their teachers would.

Not one of them resented this. Indeed, it seemed to relieve them,
a cool, sharp, stinging astringent applied to the irritations of their ado-

lescence. And for all his lack of interest in their personal existences, when he turned that deep brilliant glance upon them to see what they knew about the passive periphrastic or whether they had studied the vocabulary, they felt *noticed* as in few other departments of their lives.

Old Latimer cared no more for himself as a human being than he did for them. His mad histrionics and Dionysian outbursts were not designed to compel their admiration nor to impose upon them a sense of his autocracy and difference. They were teaching devices. For all his personal complexities and the baroque, even rococo fabric of his individual being, he was the one person of power in their lives who wished and demanded of them something really simple and clear in outline. He wanted them to learn Latin.

HE NOW looked down at the little mess of papers on his desk. The face of his best student, Robert Lang, looked wildly up at him from the photograph, denuded of its habitual steel-rimmed glasses. He picked up the Hurstleigh folder on the classical scholarship, prepared by a man he knew well and coldly disliked, a representative at classical meetings and archaeological congresses of the billboard world of Rotarianism, adjustment, genial cooperation, and general group dynamics. Latimer narrowed his eyes and tossed the folder aside. Next he picked up the general statement of Hurstleigh's Dean of Admissions on the college's admission policies. His eye fell on the phrase "breadth of extracurricular interests" and, further on, "ability to function effectively in the group," and a savage scowl twisted the upper part of his face. It disappeared as he looked up to see Lang entering the room and quietly closing the door behind him.

The exotic airs generated in the classroom during the freshman class were dissipated in an instant as Latimer's senior student took his seat immediately opposite the master's chair and smiled his thin smile. Anything less "all-round" than the appearance and personal atmosphere of Robert Lang would be difficult to imagine. From head to foot of his physical being the general stigmata of unattractive adolescence were surcharged by the presence of an imposing array of particularities. Behind a fierce hedge of skin disorders and scattered bristle, under a layer of impermanent childish flesh, slept a finer regular profile and a nobly sculptured jawbone. But the boy's pale eyes shone with the fanaticisms of the early-blooming specialist; his encrusted shirt collar, bedraggled Fair Isle sweater, smudged shoes spoke of the sacrifice of one order of fastidiousness to another.

Latimer always sat at his desk during his conferences with Lang. He spoke in even, courteous tones, both friendly and remote, as one gentleman addressing another slightly younger. "What is it today, Bob?" he asked quietly, taking up his green Cicero and leafing through its opening pages.

177

"The peroration from the *Pro Cluentio,* sir," said Lang, and began to translate from his little student's edition. The flowery and passionate appeal for the life of an upright man unjustly charged with a low murder, the crown of the great lawyer's defense against a prosecution which had moved almost exclusively in the territories of political and class prejudice, took shape in effortless English. Here and there Lang paused for a moment to comment on a series of gerundives, to mention the names of less familiar grammatical constructions, to guess at the reason for a curious ordering of phrases.

Latimer listened in silence, inclining his head, turning the pages, catching the boy's eye from time to time over the top of his book and communicating assent. At the end he nodded gravely and said, "All right. Now read a bit of the Latin, Bob, and remember the trouble we had last time with the long *i*'s." Lang looked up from his page and did not look back at it as he recited the last section from memory, his eyes plunged deep into Latimer's. *"Orat vos Habitus, iudices, et flens obsecrat"*—his voice sank and deepened at the end of the clause, in imitation not of Latimer but of his own notion of Cicero's tones at this melodramatic moment. Latimer permitted himself a discreet smile.

"Well, Bob?" he asked, as the dying fall faded away. Lang's smile, as discreet as his own, commented restrainedly on the last measures of the speech.

"Well, sir . . . of course you can't miss the Old Silvertongue in it, the Clarence Darrow touch; naturally he had to overdo it, with that jury, and all the emotion hung over from the other trial, eight years before. But you can't help admiring his judgment. He brings it out about old Sassia being an unnatural mother and rubs it in about her coming up for the trial, such a terrible old bitch that nobody could miss it, even in the country towns. Then he pulls out the stops about Cluentius 'weeping begs you to restore him to his life, his kinsmen' and the rest of it, and then to bring up the old prejudice from the other trial when Cluentius bribed the jury—that really took nerve. Nobody else would have dared; they would have ended with the boo-hoo stuff. I think he's great. The trouble is, you can feel him thinking it, too. And you can tell he despised the jury and the court and the whole system. But it's good. You feel he knows his business. It's the thing you really can like about him in these straight law cases where he's just *being* a lawyer, the best in Rome, and forgetting the rest of it."

"The rest of it?"

"Yes, being the great philosopher and the father of his country and all that stuff that spoils him later on. The pleasures of old age part, the hysterical old woman part, all that."

"Bob," said Latimer in a soft idle voice, twirling a gold pencil, "what

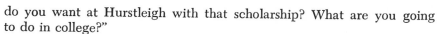

do you want at Hurstleigh with that scholarship? What are you going to do in college?"

"I don't know exactly, sir," said Lang, surprised. "Just learn Greek, I guess. Read the other Latin stuff. Try archaeology and history. Just be a classicist—learn to be one, I mean."

"Is that what you want? Just to *be* a classicist?"

"Well . . . I don't know yet what part of it I can go in for permanently. I've got to find that out."

"What, do you suppose," inquired the Old Man, a sharp, flinty note edging into his voice, "is the role of the classicist in our present society?" Bob Lang caught and held his eyes in another of those long, profoundly calm gazes. He shrugged, without impertinence. "I don't know much about it. I only know about a couple: Professor Hanley, I guess, and Ladislaw."

"Hanley! Yes, Hanley lives like a duke at what passes for a great university. He has his cigarettes and his jackets made for him in London, and he makes a large thing out of teaching the boys the names of the wines they ought to like. He does give good parties, that I'll say for him, and he keeps his invitation cards piled up on his mantel, and they *do* pile up. Everybody asks him to write introductions for their new little translation or their new little historical novel. But that, my dear Lang, is not a classicist. That is the Master of Hixon House. That is—uh, let's say, a personality."

Lang looked slightly alarmed, not so much at this novel portrait of an august figure, hitherto a name on a title page and in a catalogue, as at the sudden crackling tone in the Old Man's voice. Since he had been taken out of the regular Latin class in the middle of his second year, two years ago, he had not seen any of Latimer's famous histrionics. There was a code drawn silently between the two. It was understood that this sort of thing was not necessary.

"Ladislaw!" continued the Old Man, his voice picking up speed, though still low-pitched. "You are probably unaware, Lang, that Ladislaw reaches the age of retirement next year. Last year he had performed on himself a brain operation known as a frontal lobotomy, calculated to remove from the sufferer all traces of the anxieties and tensions which have been disordering his personality, and with them all sense of responsibility and involvement in the knottier questions of life. I understand the result has been quite striking. Both Ladislaw and his administration can envisage the next year with fortitude, if not exactly with equanimity. Equanimity is, I am afraid, quite out of the question in the Ladislaw affair. But at any rate, the enrollment in classical studies at his university has for the past decade been such that it will not be necessary to replace him."

A violent silence fell. He resumed, speaking now with great weariness, "My friend, the poet Raphael Stein, maintains a very good position at Essex Academy. His students graduate with distinction, are joyously accepted everywhere simply on his say-so, and go on to major in government, history, economics, journalism—on his advice. The knowledge of Greek and Roman letters with which he has equipped them often stays with them, as a sort of interior decoration of the mind, for quite a while before it is relegated to the mental attic where, in most of their cases, one can only admit that it belongs. But Stein is not a classicist; he is a poet, who has found an agreeable, even quite sympathetic means of support.

"Throckmorton instructs young ladies in the number of half a dozen or so annually; he retires this year, and they are replacing him with a Scotchman who will devote most of his energies to the teaching of theology. Interest in religion and anthropology grows; the classics departments are, my boy, becoming more and more interdepartmental. It may perhaps be possible for you to make use of these bodies of knowledge as stalking horses, or as ritual masks, behind which you may carry on undisturbed your classicist's freakish endeavors."

"What about the department at Hurstleigh, sir?" asked Lang in the manner of one who more or less changes the subject. There was no answer. Latimer snapped off the point of his gold pencil, looked out the window, and let the matter drop. Feeling the need to get the conference back on that impersonal level which had for years now been the scene of his most profoundly enjoyable experiences, Lang introduced another theme.

"I was reading a poem of Yeats's last night," he said cautiously, feeling his way a bit. "It goes at the end: *Whence had they come, The hand and lash that beat down frigid Rome?* I couldn't quite make it out. Why 'frigid'?"

"Oh, just to suggest something cold and resistant, not easily beaten down, I imagine," said the Old Man in the same low weary tone. "Good question, that *Whence had they come?* He has a poem about Whiggery, too: *All's Whiggery now . . .*"

"Can't get what he's trying to bring out with that 'Whiggery,' either," said Lang. "Mr. Fletcher told us what the Whigs were, and all, but it doesn't help much."

"The man himself tells you, boy! 'A levelling, rancorous, rational sort of mind.' You read a lot, don't you? Tell me what you see in Latin! What's *in* it for you?"

At it again, thought Lang. But with perfect aplomb he began to look round for something true to tell the Old Man. "Well, at first I thought it was the language itself, the constructions and all that. I like the syntax, and thinking about the forms. Take that motto, for instance, they're always using in the Renaissance: *Nec spe nec metu.* You see it in the corner of old maps all the time. Well, if it's an ablative of manner it would mean 'with neither hope nor fear,' and just bring out a kind of stoicism, a stiff-upper-lip attitude, ready to take the rough with the smooth. But it shouldn't be an ablative of manner: no *cum*, and no adjective to let them off the *cum*. Some exceptions, like *dolo* —but not many. So if it's an ablative of cause, it changes the whole thing: 'Neither because of hope nor because of fear,' and it means the man's doing whatever he's doing not because he wants to get something out of it, not because he's afraid of what will happen if he doesn't, but just because he wants to. Probably because of the thing itself. That sort of thing is interesting to think about; interesting to me, anyway. But this year, and last year with Virgil, there's a lot more to it. You start to get an idea of what it was like, with them. I guess I just *like* the Romans. They're my type, I mean." He grinned suddenly and added, "*Romani nil me alienum puto*, you could say."

Latimer grinned back at him over the pun. The bell rang. Lang snapped out of it, gathered up his books and papers, looked curiously at his folder on Latimer's desk, snuffled a bit, and lurched out of the room.

THE Old Man stared after him, then turned his glance to the pile of papers. He took up the recommendation blank, unscrewed his fine gold fountain pen, and began to write rapidly.

> Gentlemen:
>
> I am requested to write in support of the application of my student Robert Lang for admission to your freshman class as Wroxbury Scholar. As I read your statements concerning your freshman class and concerning this scholarship, I find myself rather at a loss. It seems unlikely to me that Robert Lang will satisfy your most important requirements. It is with regret that I write this, but I feel that candor is in order.
>
> The boy is the most brilliant scholar I have ever prepared. There is small doubt that his performance on the College Board will be as near perfect as the circumstances of the examination allow. His mastery of the language is complete, or nearly so; his acquaintance with Roman civilization of the late republican and early imperial period is broad and his understanding of it sensitive. He can compose sensible and elegant Latin sentences. His translations are unexceptionable both in accuracy and in grace. In short, it is difficult to imagine him as a member of your first-year Latin class under Professor Speidel.
>
> Furthermore, it would be idle to pretend that he has profited from or enjoyed his experience as manager of the basketball squad here this winter. The duties of the position demanded nothing but a little correspondence, and attendance at the games; when Lang had fulfilled these obligations, which he

found tedious but not difficult, he considered that he had done what was required. His participation in the group emotions and satisfactions made available to him through this experience was, in fact, minimal.

The truth is that Lang's extracurricular interests are not broad in the sense you intend. His grasp of three languages, Latin, French, *and* English, and his continually expanding acquaintance with the literature and histories, ancient and modern, preserved in these languages, have made it somewhat difficult for him to "function effectively in the group," if I may be forgiven for borrowing a phrase of yours. In fact, Lang's group considers him very odd indeed, and rightly so.

His complexion falls far short of the Hurstleigh ideal, and I fear his posture is inelegant. Should you wish me to supply you with any further relevant information, and should this information be in my possession, I shall of course be happy to furnish you with more details.

Very truly yours.

As the Old Man signed this letter, the door opened to admit Mr. Merton, hands full of folders and papers as usual. The young man smiled with satisfaction as he saw that the recommendation was complete and ready for the Head. Remembering with pleasure that Lang had made the highest score on record in the entire country on the junior College Board in Latin the last year, and permitting himself to hope for at least one easy admission, he stretched out his hand for the paper and let his eye run quickly over it. His expression changed rapidly as he took in the sense of the clear fine writing. Amusement and irritation gave way to a real indignation as he suddenly imagined himself showing this thing to the Head. He scowled and drew in his breath to launch his protest; then his eyes fell on Latimer, staring up at him, a muscle fluttering wildly near the temple, perspiration standing coldly at the hairline. The passion in the clawed old face was appalling.

Merton's voice stopped in his throat, and for a moment he heard nothing but the bumping, plunging of his heart. Horrified, he watched tears gather in Latimer's eyes. Silent, he left the room, clutching the sheet of paper with his others. As the bell screamed through the hall he darted on an impulse into the boys' washroom, happily empty, and leaned against the wall for a moment. He was quite young, an English teacher of the new school, fulll of ideas about communication; but he was not stupid, not unread, and above all not insensitive. He simply felt that it wasn't normal to be invaded by this kind of thing at ten thirty in the morning. He waited passively, unresentfully, for the harsh grip of pity and terror to relax, before he should plunge again into the whirling, clattering corridor of the last period before Morning Exercise.

34. Whence Had They Come?

WILLIAM BUTLER YEATS

Yeats (1865–1939) is this century's leading Irish poet, and, many would argue, the century's premier poet in English. He also wrote plays, essays, and an autobiography. Yeats was elected a senator of the Irish Free State in 1922, and was awarded the Nobel Prize for literature in 1923.

Eternity is passion, girl or boy
Cry at the onset of their sexual joy
'For ever and for ever'; then awake
Ignorant what Dramatis Personae spake;
A passion-driven exultant man sings out
Sentences that he has never thought;
The Flagellant lashes those submissive loins
Ignorant what the dramatist enjoins,
What master made the lash. Whence had they come,
The hand and lash that beat down frigid Rome?
What sacred drama through her body heaved
When world-transforming Charlemagne was conceived?

35. Heritage

COUNTEE CULLEN

(For Harold Jackman)

What is Africa to me:
Copper sun or scarlet sea,

IV. Exposition:
Comparison and Contrast

Jungle star or jungle track,
Strong bronzed men, or regal black
Women from whose loins I sprang
When the birds of Eden sang?
One three centuries removed
From the scenes his fathers loved,
Spicy grove, cinnamon tree,
What is Africa to me?

So I lie, who all day long
Want no sound except the song
Sung by wild barbaric birds
Goading massive jungle herds,
Juggernauts of flesh that pass
Trampling tall defiant grass
Where young forest lovers lie,
Plighting troth beneath the sky.
So I lie, who always hear,
Though I cram against my ear
Both my thumbs, and keep them there,
Great drums throbbing through the air.
So I lie, whose fount of pride,
Dear distress, and joy allied,
Is my somber flesh and skin,
With the dark blood dammed within
Like great pulsing tides of wine
That, I fear, must burst the fine
Channels of the chafing net
Where they surge and foam and fret.

Africa? A book one thumbs
Listlessly, till slumber comes.
Unremembered are her bats
Circling through the night, her cats
Crouching in the river reeds,
Stalking gentle flesh that feeds
By the river brink; no more
Does the bugle-throated roar
Cry that monarch claws have leapt
From the scabbards where they slept.
Silver snakes that once a year
Doff the lovely coats you wear,
Seek no covert in your fear
Lest a mortal eye should see;
What's your nakedness to me?

184

Here no leprous flowers rear
Fierce corollas in the air;
Here no bodies sleek and wet,
Dripping mingled rain and sweat,
Tread the savage measures of
Jungle boys and girls in love.
What is last year's snow to me,
Last year's anything? The tree
Budding yearly must forget
How its past arose or set—
Bough and blossom, flower, fruit,
Even what shy bird with mute
Wonder at her travail there,
Meekly labored in its hair.
One three centuries removed
From the scenes his fathers loved,
Spicy grove, cinnamon tree,
What is Africa to me?

So I lie, who find no peace
Night or day, no slight release
From the unremittant beat
Made by cruel padded feet
Walking through my body's street.
Up and down they go, and back.
Treading out a jungle track.
So I lie, who never quite
Safely sleep from rain at night—
I can never rest at all
When the rain begins to fall;
Like a soul gone mad with pain
I must match its weird refrain;
Ever must I twist and squirm,
Writhing like a baited worm,
While its primal measures drip
Through my body, crying, "Strip!
Doff this new exuberance.
Come and dance the Lover's Dance!"
In an old remembered way
Rain works on me night and day.

Quaint, outlandish heathen gods
Black men fashion out of rods,
Clay, and brittle bits of stone,
In a likeness like their own,

IV. Exposition:
Comparison and Contrast

My conversion came high-priced;
I belong to Jesus Christ,
Preacher of humility,
Heathen gods are naught to me.

Father, Son, and Holy Ghost,
So I make an idle boast;
Jesus of the twice-turned cheek,
Lamb of God, although I speak
With my mouth thus, in my heart
Do I play a double part.
Ever at Thy glowing altar
Must my heart grow sick and falter,
Wishing He I served were black,
Thinking then it would not lack
Precedent of pain to guide it,
Let who would or might deride it;
Surely then this flesh would know
Yours had borne a kindred woe.
Lord, I fashion dark gods, too,
Daring even to give You
Dark despairing features where,
Crowned with dark rebellious hair,
Patience wavers just so much as
Mortal grief compels, while touches
Quick and hot, of anger, rise
To smitten cheek and weary eyes.
Lord, forgive me if my need
Sometimes shapes a human creed.
All day long and all night through,
One thing only must I do:
Quench my pride and cool my blood,
Lest I perish in the flood,
Lest a hidden ember set
Timber that I thought was wet
Burning like the dryest flax,
Melting like the merest wax,
Lest the grave restore its dead.
Not yet has my heart or head
In the least way realized
They and I are civilized.

Suggestions for Writing

1. Use some incident from Plimpton's report on the Baltimore Colts for testing and reconsidering Ross's characterization of football. Jim Brown's anecdote about the self-selection of a first string lineup from an all-star squad is one possibility. Does that incident support Ross's understanding of football? Explain.

2. Write a similar paper about baseball, except in this case you need to cull your supporting evidence from some other source. If you write toward the end of a pennant race or during the world series, there should be plenty of material in the daily paper. But maybe your example could come as easily from spring training.

3. If the modes of football and baseball are heroic and pastoral respectively, what do you make of basketball, hockey, wrestling, tennis, or track?

4. Melville's account of residence in the Marquesas presents his understanding of the people and place before and after a crucial and telling event. Contrast your prior understanding of something with your subsequent enlightenment about it. Present both sides of the story, and try to locate and describe as precisely as you can just what happened to make you change your mind. You might, by the way, consider that last phrase. How do changes of mind occur? Do you change your mind as you change your shirt?

5. Imagine a report on your own native place by someone who considered it a savage rather than a civilized land, or by someone who first thought it innocent enough but then discovered it to be quite savage. Can you create a report that such an observer might write? Focus, of course, on the incident that caused his change of mind. Although this is a creative assignment that asks you to imagine a report from a point of view that you do not share, it is factual also in that the crucial incident might demand some research on your part before you can write it up.

6. Study Esther Wagner's story and analyze the understanding of the Latin teacher and his best student of the classical world they study. How do their understandings compare or contrast with each other?

7. Write of some person whose character and values contrast markedly with his or her surroundings. Can you get at, fictionally or otherwise, what it is that makes them different?

V.
Exposition

Cause and Effect

CAUSE AND EFFECT are the pulse of logical thought. But they often skip a beat. We often don't make connections. Studying causes and effects encourages caution. We can only estimate the probables, since causes are usually hidden and multiple, and since effects spread into the future like unsuspected dust from atomic bombs.

The writings in this section handle cause and effect differently. Wellard sees the ruins of once flourishing cities, the immediate cause of topless columns and shattered baths, and he probes for a deeper cause to explain these cities and their death. Shelley and Oppen look to effects.

Alvarez begins with a suicide and, like Wellard, tries to locate its cause. He, too, in his sphere of friendship and psychology, can only search the probable. Ellison, however, cites causes in his own life to support a probable general effect—his art—which leaps boundaries of time, place, and color. Each of these expositions is, in effect, an argument, each proposing a probable cause, or effect, for us to believe. Are you persuaded?

In the last six selections, compare the probable causes and effects the argumentative poets propose to their loves.

36. The Lost Cities

JAMES WELLARD

In addition to writing two technical books in the field of library science, James Wellard (1909–   ) wrote a biography of General Patton and two studies of Africa, from one of which we take this essay (*The Great Sahara*, 1964). His most recent book is *By the Waters of Babylon* (1972).

IT IS ALMOST IMPOSSIBLE, even when standing in the centre of a city the size of Gigthis or Leptis Magna, to visualize the order, prosperity, and, indeed, splendour of this civilization whose ruins are still scattered over tens of thousands of square miles of a continent. In comparison, subsequent invaders of North Africa have left so little behind. The Arabs left their mosques, forts, and souks, but some of their buildings wouldn't have stood up this long without the massive pillars and squared-off foundation stones pillaged from temples, amphitheatres, and public buildings. The alleys of the medinas all display their Roman columns and cornice stones helping to prop up the gimcrack buildings above; and as far down in the desert as the southern oases, Roman wells and damns and irrigation tunnels make life a little more practicable for the modern inhabitants. Arabs, Turks, Spaniards, French, and Italians have all left their imprint on this land —but it is a superficial mark compared with the civilization the Romans left behind. That civilization was smashed to pieces, of course, by subsequent invaders, but it is still visible in literally thousands of towns and villages right down into the wasteland of the central Sahara. In a sense, it is also still functioning, for Roman aqueducts, Roman wells, Roman tunnels, and cisterns are still supplying some cities and some oases with water.

A small boy named Ali takes me to see the ruins of some forgotten Roman city we think was called Uppena. Ali comes out of a hovel among the olive groves, akin architecturally to the thatched huts of the savages so despised by the Romans. We eventually find Uppena among the groves, and it is clear that this, too, was once a well-built and well-organized provincial city, with its fortress, church, theatre, and baths, and an efficient system of aqueducts and water tunnels no longer found anywhere in North Africa outside the big cities. The public buildings and private homes of Uppena also provided the museums with some of the magnificent mosaics portraying the richness and beauty of life 1,800 years ago. Yet what must life be like today to Ali and his parents? They have nothing but their hovel, a mattress, and a few cooking pots. For water they depend on a Roman well of such horrendous proportions and depth Ali, with much rolling of the eyes, tells me that it is death to approach it. One sees why. The mouth of the well is nearly twenty feet across, and its depth some eighty feet. It is beautifully constructed of fitted stones, and quite obviously Roman. The wells the Arabs made in the desert are usually only holes in the ground without proper walling, and they fill up with sand as soon as they are neglected. But when the Roman engineers went after water, they built an aqueduct or well as they built a temple or a fort.

But despite all that remains above and below ground—the hundreds of cities, the thousands of miles of roads, the frontier forts and farmhouses—we still cannot fully estimate, or even comprehend, the extent of the Roman conquest of North Africa and the desert to the south of it. At the present state of our knowledge, we can only assert that the Romans had at least 2,500,000 acres of what is now full desert colonized and under cultivation in South Algeria alone. If we assume, as the evidence suggests, that the Romans followed the same practice of building roads, forts, and irrigation networks in Morocco, Tunisia, and Libya, as in Algeria, the total area exploited under the Empire and now abandoned would be 10,000,000 acres at the lowest estimate.

Until recently this was impossible to believe in view of the almost complete desiccation of these desert zones today. How could any kind of settled communities survive in this desolation of rock and gravel, where not even a blade of grass is now growing?

Part of the answer was provided by one man who spent three years looking for the evidence. This was Colonel Jean Baradez, of the French Air Force, specialist in aerial photography and an amateur archaeologist, who spent three years, from 1946 to 1949, surveying the desert of South Algeria for traces of Roman occupation.

The results of his work is one of the most astonishing achievements of archaeology. Flying continuously for three successive years back and forth along the fringes of the desert, Colonel Baradez took hundrds of high-altitude photographs of the Roman frontier as far as it was known from the Roman road maps which give us the names of the forts along the frontier, together with the distances between them and the principal cities.[1] Baradez was not after particular or isolated ruins which could have been better studied by low- or medium-level photography; but vast expanses of country which could be examined and

[1] For instance, *The Peutinger Table,* a probable road map, and *The Antonine Itinerary,* both of the third century A.D.

192

studied to give the kind of general picture needed for a large-scale map of Roman occupation of the desert. What he found will keep the historians and archaeologists busy for the next hundred years if it were decided (or were even possible) to explore every piece of evidence that his photographs clearly and sharply reveal. In short, Colonel Baradez's survey suggests, for the first time, the full extent of the military and civil organization along the desert frontiers—an example of colonization that has no parallel for planning, efficiency, and success in all history. For the construction of ditches, roads, forts, castles, observation posts, and signalling towers along a frontier of 1,500 miles was not undertaken simply to keep the Saharan nomads from attacking the great and prosperous cities of Africa Proconsularis but to prepare and exploit the ground for a large settlement of farmers. That this policy succeeded is proved by Colonel Baradez's magnificent aerial survey which shows the remains of hundreds of villages and farming communities where today there is nothing but eroded rocks.   How wear out

Even the experts are still puzzled as to how the Romans accomplished this seemingly superhuman task of erecting so many outposts in the wasteland, let alone bringing in water without which any work of settlement was a waste of time. Arguments also continue, and will continue for a long time, as to whether the _limes_, or frontier, was a military zone intended to keep the barbarians out altogether, or, conversely, to let them come in through customs-control points. The same argument is still going on in regard to the precise function of Hadrian's Wall across Northern Britain.

In short, we know next to nothing of why, how, or when the Saharan fortifications were built, for, as in the case of the occupation of Britain, it is difficult to see why the Romans bothered with such inhospitable terrritory. Just as they got nothing except a little tin and leather out of Britain in return for their immense labours in pacifying and civilizing that province, so the produce of the Saharan settlements was negligible in terms of the great export-import trade of the North African littoral. Why did they trouble?   true

We don't really know—though the most plausible theory is that imperial Rome in the first century A.D. badly needed a new source of supply to feed the overcrowded cities. From the time of Augustus Caesar the Italian countryside was being depopulated as people flocked to the towns for free bread and circuses. The feeding of these mobs was an integral part of imperial policy. North Africa, then, was considered and looked at with a view to exploiting it as the granary of Italy. And this was what it eventually became, for once the Roman military and administrative machine had been put into motion, nothing seemed able to stop it, or change its course. The machine began its operations with the road and fortification works of the Third Augusta Legion which was sent to Africa in the reign of Augustus, and immediately set

193

about building a road from Gabes on the coast inland to their winter quarters at Haidra. For the next 200 years when the legion was not actually campaigning its engineers continued to construct a network of roads right across North Africa. At the same time they, together with the veterans of the legion, built a score of cities which were to become among the largest and most prosperous urban centres of the Empire. It was an engineer of the Third Augusta who specialized in constructing water tunnels and was constantly loaned by his commander to communities short of water. We see an example of this kind of engineering in the Roman water tunnel bored deep into the mountain from the Blue Grotto on Capri where the Emperor Tiberius took up his residence.

There were in the Roman provinces two kinds of roads, both built by the legion, one type considered civil, the other military. The civil roads were main highways, wide and well paved, used for public transport and the swift movement of the post. The military roads were narrower and more direct and usually cut straight across country from fort to fort. In their usual methodical manner the legion erected a stone signpost every mile—or, more precisely, every 1,480 metres—of the way along their vast network of main roads. Well over 2,000 of these milestones have been found and recorded. One can imagine how many more lie under the sand and rubble of North Africa.

As the legion pacified the mountains and deserts of Africa Proconsularis, they built forts at all strategic positions and linked them up by a series of turrets and towers which resembled the mile-castle system used along Hadrian's Wall in Britain. In other words, the system was designed to keep every unit of soldiers, however small, in visual touch with each other, both by night and by day. Hence the series of hundreds of castles, turrets, and observation posts along the military roads and desert frontiers. Signalling at night was done by fires; and by day either by smoke or semaphores. It was an efficient, almost foolproof system of controlling vast areas of wild country, and it explains how the Romans were able to occupy 1,500,000 square miles of North Africa for several centuries with a corps of some 12,000 men.

Once the great fertile regions south of the coast had been secured by the system of roads, forts, cities, and villages, so that oil and grain supplies by which Africa helped to feed almost the whole of Italy were assured, the army was free to push deeper into the desert. First it established camps and forts at the principal oases on the caravan routes which went down into the interior of Africa. These forts, like that at Ghadames, were built and garrisoned by detachments of the Third Augusta Legion. They were next linked together by a ditch which gradually ran right across the northern fringes of the Sahara Desert proper. Behind this ditch ran a road, or track, for the use of the army patrols. Inside, and in some cases outside, the frontier grew up in a series of fortified farmsteads designed and built under the direction of army engineers. It is probable that these farmhouses were turned over to veterans of the legion, together with the necessary slaves and servants to farm the land. From the reliefs carved on the tombs of these colonists we can get a good working picture of the activities of these frontiersmen. Horses and, later, camels are used for ploughing, and crops are harvested under the eye of the master who directs the work from his camp-chair. This frontiersman, then, can be almost directly compared to his counterpart in the Southern States of America during the eighteenth and nineteenth centuries where large plantations were hacked out of the wilderness by slave labour. And as in the case of the Romano-African colonist, the American planter belonged to an organized militia which was an integral part of a professional army. Thus new lands were developed despite the threat of the local tribesmen. The principal difference, of course, was the abundance of water in one case and the almost total absence of it in the other.

How, then, did the Romans overcome the problem of aridity in the desert?

Excavations and, in particular, Colonel Baradez's aerial survey have given us some of the answers to this key question.

The main camps and forts, of course, were always built where there were springs or wells on the theory that whoever controlled the water supply controlled the country for miles around. But the colonists who pushed farther and farther south into the actual desert—the *hammada* or *reg* as the case might be—did not always have access to springs or wells. They had to depend on the rainfall and the wadis, the nearest thing in the desert to rivers or brooks. The Arabic word *wadi*, or *oued*, is the proper word, since it implies a fissure in the earth which channels off water when there is any, and is otherwise dry, baked hard by the sun. As a source of water and irrigation, the wadis of North Africa and Tripolitania are practically useless today. Some of them which drain off the springs support life for a few inhabitants clustered nearby in huts or tents. Those which have no drainage apart from the spring rainfall are merely ravines which split up the land into cracks and fissures. But they were not so in Roman times. To the contrary, millions of acres were cultivated by means of a highly efficient system of hydraulic works and soil conservation which has never been equalled, let alone surpassed. So that one could say that of all the aspects of civilization that the Romans left us their agricultural theory and practice are the most valuable and important.

The Roman system of using the wadis, then, was simple and, as we would expect, exceedingly thorough. They harnessed the wadis by building dams and by controlling the rainfall *before* it ever reached the water-courses. This was the secret of their success. In view of this, all discussions as to whether the climate of the desert has changed within historical times are irrelevant. The matter has been summed up by an expert: 'the prosperity of Africa [in Roman times] was not a question of meteorology: it was the prize of hard work'. This hard and continuous work was directed to conserving every precious drop of water that fell from the sky, not necessarily in the water-courses (wadis) or dams, but in the soil itself and, of course, in cisterns. This is what Colonel Baradez's remarkable photographs reveal *all along the Saharan frontier*—namely a system of walls, terraces, ditches, barricades, dams, and cisterns both natural and artificial, which captured the rainfall before it could rush down the rocky escarpments and flush down the wadis to be lost in fissures in the earth. In other words, the rain was retained where it fell by means of terraces and retaining walls; that which tried to run away through gullies was directed into reservoirs for future use. The flow in the wadis themselves was controlled by barrages of stones. Particular attention was paid to the erosion of the wadis' actual channels along their whole length to prevent a heavy downpour of rain from flooding the dry ground on either side and running useless into the earth. In addition irrigation channels led off from the wadis and reservoirs to the fields which were divided up into rectangles by ditches. The water flowing along these ditches seeped gently into the soil instead of gushing away. This is a system which is still used in Southern Italy. The modern Berbers and Arabs who inhabit the wilderness where the Romans built these magnificent hydraulic works are completely ignorant of their meaning and use, but they continue to sow a little grain along the Roman ditches which retain moisture after the rest of the soil is completely arid. Apart from this, the entire irrigation system which made cultivation not only possible but profitable has now completely broken down and the desert has reclaimed its own. The similar deterioration of agriculture has occurred throughout the desert regions of the Middle East, once cultivated by Roman colonists, so that the loss of arable land and the resultant food supplies to mankind is incalculable. For those who are interested in the process of destruction by erosion, the 'dust bowls' of the United States present a modern parallel.

The question next arises, as it does to some extent in the case of Britain, as to why the administration, or Central Government of Rome, troubled to colonize and civilize the desert at all. The reasons why modern man should, and soon may be obliged to, look to land reclamation and soil conservation are obvious. The expanding population of the world demands more room and more food. Emigration to other planets is a quixotic solution to the population problem when there are 3,000,000 empty square miles in this part of Africa alone. But the Romans, while they had population and therefore food supply problems, were not humanitarians; and the opening up of the African frontiers was not undertaken out of ethical considerations. It was simply a practical solution to the overall problem of holding together a vast empire by strengthening the frontiers against the only enemy the Romans knew—the barbarians. They also knew from long experience that the first step in civilizing the savages who resided within their confines was to settle them first in agricultural communities and eventually in villages, towns, and cities, which grew naturally from such settlements. The frontier forts and farms along the limits of the Saharan Desert, then, served three main purposes: first, they were the outer defence line in the complex military system which covered the whole of North Africa; second, they were custom- and passport-control points which regulated the movements of travellers; and third, they demonstrated to the barbarian nomads to the south that Romans were stronger, richer, and more civilized than they were.

We know that to the end of the Roman Empire, and for a long time after, this system worked so efficiently that the Saharan outposts and farms which they protected were the only organized survivors of the universal destruction which followed the Vandal invasions of North Africa. In fact, these desert colonies hung on for a time even after the Arab conquest and the utter collapse of Roman-Byzantine Africa, and continued as long as the hydraulic works on which they were founded were kept in repair. But gradually the knowledge, skill, and will to work which marked the Roman period faded and disappeared altogether. To-day there remain nothing but ruins which are sinking deeper under the sand every year.

The last we hear of these frontiersmen [1] is in the letters exchanged between African bishops concerning the spiritual welfare of those colonists who were now Christians. One such letter is instructive. Writing to St. Augustine, the correspondent says that he is concerned with the way in which the guards were accepting the pagan oaths of those barbarians who crossed the frontier to work as farm labourers or porters. These nomads swore to respect all the laws and regulations of the Roman province and to report back at the end of their service at the control post. They swore by their own gods. St. Augustine replied: 'It is worse to swear falsely by the true God than to swear truly by false gods,' and he took the occasion to remind his correspondent that the safety and peace of the Afro-Roman world depended on the sincerity of these barbarian oaths.

From this we know that, as late as A.D. 400, the frontier with the actual desert was still intact, and the whole system of colonization was working well enough for the farmers to need seasonal labour from 'across the border.' The movement of these desert barbarians was still carefully controlled by military police in their forts and stations, which the archaeologists are still finding deep in the desert. The discovery in 1949 of such a fort in the Wadi Merdum, near Mselletin, tells the last phase of the story of 500 years of Roman occupation. This particular fort,

---

[1] Called in Latin *limitanei* after the *limes*, or frontier.

though it is comparatively well preserved and is still used by the local nomads, escaped the notice of earlier travellers. The interesting thing about it is that within a radius of five miles from this blockhouse over thirty Roman farmhouses have been located, though most of the region has not been explored and excavated at all. Today there is not a single farm; the wadis which were once highly cultivated are completely desiccated.

The fort at Mselletin is much bigger and stronger than would seem necessary in view of the nearby forts garrisoned by the regular army. Inside the quarters are restricted, allowing for no more than twenty men and their horses. It is axiomatic the more massive the forts and block-houses, the weaker the garrison within and the greater the danger without. Such was the lesson of the French Maginot Line in the 1939 war; and such seems to have been the fate of the desert forts and the farms they protected. The barbarians finally broke through here as they did in Britain, and that was the end for the time being of civilization. The northern Sahara was again the domain of those nomads whom the Roman legions had driven back into the mountains of the Central Desert.

Here is the conclusion of Colonel Baradez after his three years' intensive study of one section of the frontier:

> I must stress for the last time the fearful contrast between what this whole zone was like once and what it is like now. The region is terribly eroded today by ravines which are growing deeper and spreading out in all directions owing to the abandonment of the Roman soil conservation works. The impression that one now gets of the area is of a desert waste-land more stupendous than the Sahara itself: the desolation is even more depressing.
>
> In these vast expanses of desert, there are no longer any inhabitants: the only thing that moves in that landscape are the long-distance caravans. . . .

37. Ozymandias

PERCY BYSSHE SHELLEY

Shelley (1792–1822) was a famous English poet of the romantic period. He wrote an elegy for Keats and worked

closely with Byron. In 1822, he drowned off the coast of
Italy. His second wife, Mary Shelley, wrote *Frankenstein*.

I met a traveller from an antique land
Who said: Two vast and trunkless legs of stone
Stand in the desert . . . Near them, on the sand,
Half sunk, a shattered visage lies, whose frown,
And wrinkled lip, and sneer of cold command,
Tell that its sculptor well those passions read
Which yet survive, stamped on these lifeless things,
The hand that mocked them, and the heart that fed:
And on the pedestal these words appear:
'My name is Ozymandias, king of kings:
Look on my works, ye Mighty, and despair!'
Nothing beside remains. Round the decay
Of that colossal wreck, boundless and bare
The lone and level sands stretch far away.

38. Ozymandias

GEORGE OPPEN

Oppen's (1908–   ) books of poetry include *The Materials*
(1962), *This is Which* (1965), and *Of Being Numerous*
(1968). The last book mentioned won the Pulitzer Prize
in 1969.

The five
Senses gone

To the one sense,
The sense of prominence

Produce an art
De luxe.

And down town
The absurd stone trimming of the building tops

Rectangular in dawn, the shopper's
Thin morning monument.

---

39. Sylvia Plath: A Memoir

A. ALVAREZ

An English poet and critic (1929–   ), Alvarez recently
wrote *The Savage God: A Study of Suicide* (1972), in which
this study appeared. A collection of essays, *Beyond All
This Fiddle,* appeared in 1968.

AS I REMEMBER IT, I met Sylvia and her husband in London
in the spring of 1960. My first wife and I were living near Swiss
Cottage, on the unsmart edge of literary Hampstead, in a tall
Edwardian building of particularly ugly red brick; it was the color of
some old boiler that had been left out to rust for so long that even the
brightness of decay had worn off. When we moved in, the place had
just been converted by one of those grab-and-get-out property companies that did so well before the Rachman scandal. Naturally, they had
made a shoddy job of it: the fittings were cheap and the finish awful; the
window frames seemed too small for the brickwork around them, and
there were large, rough gaps at every joint. But we had sanded the floors
and painted the place out in bright colors. Then we bought bits and
pieces from the junk furniture dealers in Chalk Farm, and sanded and
painted them, too. So in the end it seemed gay enough in a fragile, skin-
deep way: just the place for the first baby, the first book, the first real
unhappiness. By the time we left, eighteen months later, there were
gaping cracks in the outer wall where the new windows had been cut.
But by that time there were gaping cracks in our lives, too, so it all
seemed to fit.

Since I was the regular poetry critic for *The Observer*, I saw few
writers. To know whom I was reviewing seemed to make too many
difficulties: nice men often write bad verse and good poets can be monsters; more often than not both the man and his work were unspeakable.

It seemed easier all round not to be able to put a face to the name, and to judge solely by the printed page. I kept to my rule even when I was told that Ted Hughes was living nearby, just across Primrose Hill, with an American wife and a small baby. Three years before he had brought out *The Hawk in the Rain,* which I admired greatly. But there was something about the poems that made me suspect that he wouldn't care what I thought. They seemed to emerge from an absorbed, physical world that was wholly his own; for all the technical skill deployed, they gave the impression that literary goings-on were no concern of the author. "Don't worry," I was told, "he never talks shop." I was also told that he had a wife called Sylvia, who also wrote poetry, "but"— and this was said reassuringly—"she's very sharp and intelligent."

In 1960 came *Lupercal.* I thought it the best book by a young poet that I had read since I began my stint on *The Observer.* When I wrote a review to say so, the paper asked for a short piece about him for one of the more gossipy pages. I phoned him and we arranged to take our kids for a walk on Primrose Hill. It seemed like a nice, neutral idea.

They were living in a tiny flat not far from the Regent's Park Zoo. Their windows faced onto a run-down square: peeling houses around a scrappy wilderness of garden. Closer to the Hill, gentility was advancing fast: smart Sunday newspaper house-agents had their boards up, the front doors were all fashionable colors—"Cantaloupe," "Tangerine," "Blueberry," "Thames Green"—and everywhere was a sense of gleaming white interiors, the old houses writ large and rich with new conversions.

Their square, however, had not yet been taken over. It was dirty, cracked, and racketty with children. The rows of houses that led off it were still occupied by the same kind of working-class families they had been built for eighty years before. No one, as yet, had made them chic and quadrupled their price—though that was to come soon enough. The Hughes' flat was one floor up a bedraggled staircase, past a pram in the hall and a bicycle. It was so small that everything seemed sideways on. You inserted yourself into a hallway so narrow and jammed that you could scarcely take off your coat. The kitchen seemed to fit one person at a time, who could span it with arms outstretched. In the living room you sat side by side, long-ways on, between a wall of books and a wall of pictures. The bedroom off it, with its flowered wallpaper, seemed to have room for nothing except a double bed. But the colors were cheerful, the bits and pieces pretty, and the whole place had a sense of liveliness about it, of things being done. A typewriter stood on a little table by the window, and they took turns at it, each working shifts while the other minded the baby. At night they cleared it away to make room for the child's cot. Later, they borrowed a room from another American poet, W. S. Merwin, where Sylvia worked the morning shift, Ted the afternoon.

THIS WAS Ted's time. He was on the edge of a considerable reputation. His first book had been well received and won all sorts of prizes in the States, which usually means that the second book will be an anticlimax. Instead, *Lupercal* effortlessly fulfilled and surpassed all the promises of *The Hawk in the Rain*. A figure had emerged on the drab scene of British poetry, powerful and undeniable. Whatever his natural hesitations and distrust of his own work, he must have had some sense of his own strength and achievement. God alone knew how far he was eventually going, but in one essential way he had already arrived. He was a tall, strong-looking man in a black corduroy jacket, black trousers, black shoes; his dark hair hung untidily forward; he had a long, witty mouth. He was in command.

In those days Sylvia seemed effaced; the poet taking a back seat to the young mother and housewife. She had a long, rather flat body, a longish face, not pretty but alert and full of feeling, with a lively mouth and fine brown eyes. Her brownish hair was scraped severely into a bun. She wore jeans and a neat shirt, briskly American: bright, clean, competent, like a young woman in a cookery advertisement, friendly and yet rather distant.

Her background, of which I knew nothing then, belied her housewifely air: she had been a child prodigy—her first poem was published when she was eight—and then a brilliant student, winning every prize to be had, first at Wellesley High School, then at Smith College: scholarships all the way, straight A's, Phi Beta Kappa, president of this and that college society, and prizes for everything. A New York glossy magazine, *Mademoiselle*, had picked her as an outstanding possibility and wined her, dined her, and photographed her all over Manhattan. Then, almost inevitably, she had won a Fulbright to Cambridge, where she met Ted Hughes. They were married in 1956, on Bloomsday. Behind Sylvia was a self-sacrificing, widowed mother, a schoolteacher who had worked herself into the ground so that her two children might flourish. Sylvia's father—ornithologist, entomologist, ichthyologist, international authority on bumblebees, and professor of biology at Boston University—had died when she was nine. Both parents were of German stock and were German-speaking, academic, and intellectual. When she and Ted went to the States after Cambridge, a glittering university career seemed both natural and assured.

On the surface it was a typical success story: the brilliant examination-passer driving forward so fast and relentlessly that nothing could ever catch up with her. And it can last a lifetime, provided nothing checks the momentum, and the vehicle of all those triumphs doesn't disintegrate into sharp fragments from sheer speed and pressure. But already her progress had twice lurched to a halt. Between her month on *Mademoiselle* and her last year in college she had had the nervous breakdown and suicide attempt which became the theme of her novel,

The Bell Jar. Then, once reestablished at Smith—"an outstanding teacher," said her colleagues—the academic prizes no longer seemed worth the effort. So in 1958 she had thrown over university life—Ted had never seriously contemplated it—and gone free-lance, trusting her luck and talent as a poet. All this I learned much later. Now Sylvia had simply slowed down; she was subdued, absorbed in her new baby daughter, and friendly only in that rather formal, shallow, transatlantic way that keeps you at your distance.

Ted went downstairs to get the pram ready while she dressed the baby. I stayed behind a minute, zipping up my son's coat. Sylvia turned to me, suddenly without gush:

"I'm so glad you picked *that* poem," she said. "It's one of my favorites but no one else seemed to like it."

For a moment I went completely blank; I didn't know what she was talking about. She noticed and helped me out.

"The one you put in *The Observer* a year ago. About the factory at night."

"For Christ's sake, Sylvia *Plath*." It was my turn to gush. "I'm sorry. It was a lovely poem."

"Lovely" wasn't the right word, but what else do you say to a bright young housewife? I had picked it from a sheaf of poems which had arrived from America, immaculately typed, with self-addressed envelope and international reply coupon efficiently supplied. All of them were stylish and talented but that in itself was not rare in those days. The late fifties was a period of particularly high style in American verse, when every campus worth its name had its own "brilliant" poetic technician in residence. But at least one of these poems had more going for it than rhetorical elegance. It had no title, though later, in *The Colossus*, she called it "Night Shift." It was one of those poems which starts by saying what it is *not* about so strongly that you don't believe the explanations that follow:

> It was not a heart, beating,
> That muted boom, that clangor
> Far off, not blood in the ears
> Drumming up any fever
>
> To impose on the evening.
> The noise came from outside:
> A metal detonating
> Native, evidently, to
>
> These stilled suburbs: nobody
> Startled at it, though the sound
> Shook the ground with its pounding.
> It took root at my coming . . .

It seemed to me more than a piece of good description, to be used and moralized upon as the fashion of that decade dictated. The note was aroused and all the details of the scene seemed continually to be turning inward. It is a poem, I suppose, about fear, and although in the course of it the fear is rationalized and explained (that pounding in the night is caused by machines turning), it ends by reasserting precisely the threatening masculine forces there were to be afraid of. It had its moments of awkwardness—for example, the prissy, pausing flourish in the manner of Wallace Stevens: "Native, evidently, to . . ." But compared with most of the stuff that thudded unsolicited through my letterbox every morning, it was that rare thing: the always unexpected, wholly genuine article.

I was embarrassed not to have known who she was. She seemed embarrassed to have reminded me, and also depressed.

AFTER THAT I saw Ted occasionally, Sylvia more rarely. He and I would meet for a beer in one of the pubs near Primrose Hill or the Heath, and sometimes we would walk our children together. We almost never talked shop; without mentioning it, we wanted to keep things unprofessional. At some point during the summer Ted and I did a broadcast together. Afterward we collected Sylvia from the flat and went across to their local. The recording had been a success and we stood outside the pub, around the baby's pram, drinking our beers and pleased with ourselves. Sylvia, too, seemed easier, wittier, less constrained than I had seen her before. For the first time I understood something of the real charm and speed of the girl.

About that time my wife and I moved from our flat near Swiss Cottage to a house higher up in Hampstead, near the Heath. A couple of days before we were due to move I broke my leg in a climbing accident, and that put out everything and everyone, since the house had to be decorated, broken leg or not. I remember sticking black and white tiles to floor after endless floor, a filthy dark brown glue coating my fingers and clothes and gumming up my hair, the great, inert plaster cast dragging behind me like a coffin as I crawled. There wasn't much time for friends. Ted occasionally dropped in and I would hobble with him briefly to the pub. But I saw Sylvia not at all. In the autumn I went to teach for a term in the States.

While I was there *The Observer* sent me her first book of poems to review. It seemed to fit the image I had of her: serious, gifted, withheld, and still partly under the massive shadow of her husband. There were poems that had been influenced by him, others which echoed Theodore Roethke or Wallace Stevens; clearly, she was still casting about for her own style. Yet the technical ability was great, and beneath most of the poems was a sense of resources and disturbances not yet tapped. "Her poems," I wrote, "rest secure in a mass of experience that is never quite brought out into the daylight. . . . It is this sense of threat, as though she were continually menaced by something she could see only out of the corners of her eyes, that gives her work its distinction."

I still stand by that judgment. In the light of her subsequent work and, more persuasively, her subsequent death, *The Colossus* has been overrated. "Anyone can see," the doctrine now runs, "that it's all there in crystalline form." There are even academic critics who prefer these elegant early poems to the more naked and brutal frontal attacks of her mature work, although when the book first appeared their reviews were cool enough. Meanwhile, hindsight can alter the historical importance but not the quality of the verse. *The Colossus* established her credentials: it contained a handful of beautiful poems, but more important was the sheer ability of the work, the precision and concentration with which she handled language, the unemphatic range of vocabulary, her ear for subtle rhythms, and her assurance in handling and subduing rhymes and half-rhymes. Obviously, she had now developed the craft to cope with anything that arrived. My mistake was to imply that at that stage she hadn't, or wouldn't, recognize the forces that shook her. It turned out that she knew them all too well: they had driven her to the thin near edge of suicide when she was nineteen, and already in the last piece in the book, the long "Poem for a Birthday," she was turning to face them. But the echoes of Roethke in the poem obscured that for me, and I couldn't see it.

When I got back from the States in February, 1961, I saw the Hugheses again, but briefly and not often. Ted had fallen out of love with London and was fretting to get away; Sylvia had been ill—first a miscarriage, then appendicitis—and I had my own problems, a divorce. I remember her thanking me for the review of *The Colossus*, adding disarmingly that she agreed with the qualifications. I also remember her enthusing about the beautiful house they had found in Devon—old, thatched, flagstoned, and with a large orchard. They moved, I moved, something was finished.

Both of them continued to send poems to *The Observer*. In May, 1961, we published Sylvia's poem about her daughter, "Morning Song"; in November of that year, "Mojave Desert," which has not yet been collected; two months later, "The Rival." The current was deepening, its flow becoming easier.

I DIDN'T SEE her again until June, 1962, when I dropped in on them on my way down to Cornwall for the long Whitsun weekend. They were living a few miles north of Exeter. By Devon standards it wasn't a pretty village: more gray stone and gloom than timber, thatch, and flowers. Where the most perfect English villages give the impression of never having been properly awakened, theirs seemed to have retired into sleep. Once it might have been a center for the surrounding countryside, a place of some presence where things happened. But not any more.

Exeter had taken over, and the life of this village had drained slowly away, like a family that has come down in the world.

The Hughes' house had once been the local manor. It was set slightly above the rest of the village, up a steep lane next to a twelfth-century church, and seemed important. It was large and thatched, the walls and passages were stone, the rooms gleamed with new paint. We sat out in the big wild garden drinking tea while little Frieda, now aged two, teetered among the flowers. There was a small army of apple and cherry trees, a vivid laburnum swaying with blossom, a vegetable patch, and, off to one side, a little hillock. It turned out to be a prehistoric burial mound. Given the Hughes' flair and tastes, it could hardly have been anything else. Flowers glowed everywhere, the grass was long and unkempt, and the whole luxuriant place seemed to be overflowing with summer.

They had had a new baby in January, a boy, and Sylvia had changed. No longer quiet and withheld, a housewifely appendage to a powerful husband, she seemed made solid and complete, her own woman again. Perhaps the birth of a son had something to do with this new confident air. But there was a sharpness and clarity about her that seemed to go beyond that. It was she who showed me round the house and the garden; the electric gadgets, the freshly painted rooms, the orchard and the burial mound—above all, the burial mound, "the wall of old corpses," she called it later in a poem—were *her* property. Ted, meanwhile, seemed content to sit back and play with little Frieda, who clung to him dependently. Since it was a strong, close marriage, he seemed unconcerned that the balance of power had shifted for the time being to her.

I understood why as I was leaving. "I'm writing again," she said. "Really writing. I'd like you to see some of the new poems." Her manner was warm and open, as though she had decided I could be trusted.

Some time before, *The Observer* had accepted a poem by her called "Finisterre." We finally published it that August. In the meantime she sent a beautiful short poem, "Crossing the Water," which is not in *Ariel*, although it is as good as many that are. It arrived with a formal note and a meticulously stamped, self-addressed envelope. She seemed to be functioning as efficiently as ever. Yet when I saw Ted sometime later in London, he was tense and preoccupied. Driving on her own, Sylvia had had an accident, hurting herself and smashing up their old Morris station wagon. It could have meant anything but I judged it was serious, if only from the way his dark presence, as he spoke, darkened an even deeper shade of gloom.

WHEN AUGUST came I went abroad for a few weeks, and by the time I got back autumn had already started. Although it was not yet mid-

September, the leaves had begun to blow about the streets and the rain came down. That first morning, when I woke up to a drowning London sky, summer seemed as far away as the Mediterranean itself. Automatically, I found myself huddling into my clothes: the London crouch. We were in for a long winter.

At the end of September *The Observer* published "Crossing the Water." One afternoon soon after, when I was working and the charlady was banging around upstairs, the bell rang. It was Sylvia, smartly dressed, determinedly bright and cheerful.

"I was just passing, so I thought I'd drop in," she said. With her formal town clothes and prim bun of hair, she had the air of an Edwardian lady performing a delicate but necessary social duty.

The little studio I rented had been converted from an old stable. It lay down a long passage, behind a garage, and was beautiful, in its crumbling way, but uncomfortable: there was nothing to lounge on—only spidery Windsor chairs and a couple of rugs on the blood-red uncarpeted lino. I poured her a drink and she settled in front of the coal stove on one of the rugs, like a student, very much at her ease, sipping whiskey and making the ice clink in her glass.

"That sound makes me homesick for the States," she said. "It's the only thing that does."

We talked about her poem in *The Observer,* then chatted about nothing in particular. Finally, I asked her why she was in town. She replied, with a kind of polished cheerfulness, that she was flat-hunting, and then added casually that she and the children were living on their own for the time being. I remembered the last time I had seen her, in that overflowing Devon garden, and it seemed impossible that anything could have disrupted the idyll. But I asked no questions and she offered no explanations. Instead, she began to talk about the new drive to write that was upon her. At least a poem a day, she said, and often more. She made it sound like demonic possession. And it occurred to me that maybe this was why she and her husband had, however temporarily, parted: it was a question not of differences but of intolerable similarities. When two genuinely original, ambitious, full-time poets join in one marriage, and both are productive, every poem one writes must feel to the other as though it had been dug out of his, or her, own skull. At a certain pitch of creative intensity it must be more unbearable for the Muse to be unfaithful to you with your partner than for him, or her, to betray you with a whole army of seducers.

"I'd like to read you some of the new poems," she said, and pulled a sheaf of typescripts from her shoulder-bag on the floor beside her.

"Gladly," I said, reaching over for them. "Let's see."

She shook her head: "No. I don't want you to read them to yourself. They've got to be read out loud. I want you to *hear* them."

V. Exposition:
Cause and Effect

So, sitting cross-legged on the uncomfortable floor, with the charlady clanking away upstairs, she read me "Berck-Plage":

> This is the sea, then, this great abeyance . . .

She read fast, in a hard, slightly nasal accent, rapping it out as though she were angry. Even now I find it a difficult poem to follow, the development indirect, the images concentrated and eliding thickly together. I had a vague impression of something injurious and faintly obscene, but I don't think I understood much. So when she finished I asked her to read it again. This time I heard it a little more clearly and could make some remarks about details. In some way, this seemed to satisfy her. We argued a bit and she read me more poems: one of them was "The Moon and the Yew Tree"; "Elm," I think, was another; there were six or eight in all. She would let me read none to myself, so I didn't get much, if anything, of their subtlety. But I did at least recognize that I was hearing something strong and new and hard to come to terms with. I suppose I picked on whatever details and slight signs of weakness I could as a kind of protection. She, in her turn, seemed happy to read, argue, and be heard sympathetically.

"She's a poet, isn't she?" asked my charlady the next day.

"Yes."

"I thought so," she said with grim satisfaction.

AFTER THAT, Sylvia dropped in fairly often on her visits to London, always with a batch of new poems to read. This way I first heard, among others, the "Bee" poems, "A Birthday Present," "The Applicant," "Getting There," "Fever 103°," "Letter in November," and "Ariel," which I thought extraordinary. I told her it was the best thing she had done, and a few days later she sent me a fair copy of it, carefully written out in her heavy, rounded script, and illuminated like a medieval manuscript with flowers and ornamental squiggles.

One day—I'm not sure when—she read me what she called "some light verse." She meant "Daddy" and "Lady Lazarus." Her voice, as she read them, was hot and full of venom. By this time I could hear the poetry fairly clearly, without too great a time-lag and sense of inadequacy. I was appalled; at first hearing, the things seemed to be not so much poetry as assault and battery. And because I now knew something about her life, there was no avoiding how much she was part of the action. But to have commented on that would have been to imply that the poems had failed as poetry, which they clearly had not. As always, my defense was to nag her about details. There was one line I picked on in particular:

> Gentlemen, ladies
>
> These are my hands
> My knees.

> I may be skin and bone,
> *I may be Japanese . . .*

"Why *Japanese?*" I niggled away at her, "Do you just need the rhyme? Or are you trying to hitch an easy lift by dragging in the atomic victims? If you're going to use this kind of violent material, you've got to play it cool . . ." She argued back sharply but later, when the poem was finally published after her death, the line had gone. And that, I think, is a pity: she did need the rhyme; the tone is quite controlled enough to support the apparently not quite relevant allusion; and I was overreacting to the initial brutality of the verse without understanding its weird elegance.

Throughout this time the evidence of the poems and the evidence of the person were utterly different. There was no trace of the poetry's despair and unforgiving destructiveness in her social manner. She remained remorselessly bright and energetic: busy with her children and her beekeeping in Devon, busy flat-hunting in London, busy seeing *The Bell Jar* through the press, busy typing and sending off her poems to largely unreceptive editors (just before she died she sent a sheaf of her best poems, most of them now classics, to one of the national British weeklies; none was accepted). She had also taken up horse-riding again, teaching herself to ride on a powerful stallion called Ariel, and was elated by this new excitement.

Cross-legged on the red floor, after reading her poems, she would talk about her riding in her twanging New England voice. And perhaps because I was also a member of the club, she talked, too, about suicide in much the same way: about her attempt ten years before which, I suppose, must have been very much on her mind as she corrected the proofs of her novel, and about her recent car crash. It had been no accident; she had gone off the road deliberately, seriously, wanting to die. But she hadn't, and all that was now in the past. For this reason I am convinced that at this time she was not contemplating suicide. On the contrary, she was able to write about the act so freely because it was already behind her. The car crash was a death she had survived, the death she sardonically felt herself fated to undergo once every decade:

> I have done it again.
> One year in every ten
> I manage it—
>
> A sort of walking miracle . . .
> I am only thirty.
> And like the cat I have nine times to die.
>
> This is Number Three . . .

In life, as in the poem, there was neither hysteria in her voice, nor any appeal for sympathy. She talked about suicide in much the same tone as she talked about any other risky, testing activity: urgently, even fiercely, but altogether without self-pity. She seemed to view death as a physical challenge she had, once again, overcome. It was an experience of much the same quality as riding Ariel or mastering a bolting horse—which she had done as a Cambridge undergraduate—or careening down a dangerous snow slope without properly knowing how to ski—an incident, also from life, which is one of the best things in *The Bell Jar.* Suicide, in short, was not a swoon into death, an attempt "to cease upon the midnight with no pain"; it was something to be felt in the nerve-ends and fought against, an initiation rite qualifying her for a *life* of her own.

God knows what wound the death of her father had inflicted on her in her childhood, but over the years this had been transformed into the conviction that to be an adult meant to be a survivor. So, for her, death was a debt to be met once every decade: in order to stay alive as a grown woman, a mother, and a poet, she had to pay—in some partial, magical way—with her life. But because this impossible payment involved also the fantasy of joining or regaining her beloved dead father, it was a passionate act, instinct as much with love as with hatred and despair. Thus in that strange, upsetting poem "The Bee Meeting," the detailed, doubtless accurate description of a gathering of local beekeepers in her Devon village gradually becomes an invocation of some deadly ritual in which she is the sacrificial virgin whose coffin, finally, waits in the sacred grove. Why this should happen becomes, perhaps, slightly less mysterious when you remember that her father was an authority on bees; so her beekeeping becomes a way of symbolically allying herself to him, and reclaiming him from the dead.

THE TONE of all these late poems is hard, factual and, despite the intensity, understated. In some strange way, I suspect she thought of herself as a realist: the deaths and resurrections of "Lady Lazarus," the nightmares of "Daddy" and the rest had all been proved on her pulses. That she brought to them an extraordinary inner wealth of imagery and associations was almost beside the point, however essential it is for the poetry itself. Because she felt she was simply describing the facts as they had happened, she was able to tap in the coolest possible way all her large reserves of skill: those subtle rhymes and half-rhymes, the flexible, echoing rhythms and offhand colloquialism by which she preserved, even in her most anguished probing, complete artistic control. Her internal horrors were as factual and precisely sensed as the barely controllable stallion on which she was learning to ride or the car she had smashed up.

So she spoke of suicide with a wry detachment, and without any mention of the suffering or drama of the act. It was obviously a matter of self-respect that her first attempt had been serious and nearly successful, instead of a mere hysterical gesture. That seemed to entitle her to speak of suicide as a subject, not as an obsession. It was an act she felt she had a right to as a grown woman and a free agent, in the same way as she felt it to be necessary to her development, given her queer conception of the adult as a survivor, an imaginary Jew from the concentration camps of the mind. Because of this there was never any question of motives: you do it because you do it, just as an artist always knows what he knows.

Perhaps this is why she scarcely mentioned her father, however clearly and deeply her fantasies of death were involved with him. The autobiographical heroine of *The Bell Jar* goes to weep at her father's grave immediately before she holes up in a cellar and swallows fifty sleeping pills. In "Daddy," describing the same episode, she hammers home her reasons with repetitions:

> At twenty I tried to die
> And get back, back, back to you.
> I thought even the bones would do.

I suspect that finding herself alone again now, however temporarily and voluntarily, all the anguish she had experienced at her father's death was reactivated: despite herself, she felt abandoned, injured, enraged, and bereaved as purely and defenselessly as she had as a child twenty years before. As a result, the pain that had built up steadily inside her all that time came flooding out. There was no need to discuss motives because the poems did that for her.

These months were an amazingly creative period, comparable, I think, to the "marvellous year" in which Keats produced nearly all the poetry on which his reputation finally rests. Earlier she had written carefully, more or less painfully, with much rewriting and, according to her husband, with constant recourse to *Roget's Thesaurus*. Now, although she abandoned none of her hard-earned skills and discipline, and still rewrote and rewrote, the poems flowed effortlessly, until, at the end, she occasionally produced as many as three a day. She also told me that she was deep into a new novel. *The Bell Jar* was finished, proofread and with her publishers; she spoke of it with some embarrassment as an autobiographical apprentice-work which she had to write in order to free herself from the past. But this new book, she implied, was the genuine article.

Considering the conditions in which she worked, her productivity was phenomenal. She was a full-time mother with a two-year-old daughter, a baby of ten months, and a house to look after. By the time the children were in bed at night she was too tired for anything more strenuous than "music and brandy and water." So she got up very early each morning and worked until the children woke. "These new poems of mine have one thing in common," she wrote in a note for a reading she prepared, but never broadcast, for the BBC, "they were all written at about four in the morning—that still blue, almost eternal hour before the baby's cry, before the glassy music of the milkman, settling his bottles." In those dead hours between night and day, she was able to gather herself into herself in silence and isolation, almost as though she were reclaiming some past innocence and freedom before life got a grip on her. Then she could write. For the rest of the day she was shared among the children, the housework, the shopping, efficient, bustling, harassed, like every other housewife.

BUT THIS DAWN SENSE of paradise temporarily regained does not explain the sudden flowering and change in her work. Technically, the clue is in her insistence that she herself should always read the poems out loud. In the early sixties this was a rare procedure. It was, after all, still a period of high formalism, of Stevensesque cadences and Empsonian ambiguities at which she herself was, as her earlier work proved, particularly adept. Essentially, this was the style of the academies, of self-imposed limitations of feeling and narrow devotion to the duties of craftsmanship which were echoed in thumping iambics and painfully analyzable imagery. But in 1958 she had made the vital decision to abandon the university career for which she had so carefully prepared herself all through her adolescence and early twenties. Only gradually over the next four years did that total commitment to her own creative life emerge in the fabric of her verse, breaking down the old, inert molds, quickening the rhythms, broadening the emotional range. The decision to abandon teaching was the first critical step toward achieving her identity as a poet, just as the birth of her children seemed, as she described it, to vindicate her as a woman. In these last poems the process was complete: the poet and the poems became one. What she wrote depended on her voice in the same way as her children depended on her love.

The other crucial element in her poetic maturity was the example of Robert Lowell's *Life Studies.* I say "example" rather than "influence" because, although Sylvia had attended Lowell's classes at Boston University in the company of Anne Sexton and George Starbuck, she never picked up his peculiarly contagious style. Instead of a style, she took from him a freedom. She told a British Council interviewer:

> I've been very excited by what I feel is the new breakthrough that came with, say, Robert Lowell's *Life Studies.* This intense breakthrough into very serious, very personal emotional experience, which I feel has been partly taboo. Robert Lowell's poems about his experiences in a mental hospital, for example, interest me very much. These peculiar private and taboo subjects I feel have been explored in recent American poetry . . .

Lowell provided her with an example of the quality she most admired outside poetry and had herself in profusion: courage. In its way, *Life Studies* was as brave and revolutionary as *The Waste Land*. After all, it appeared at the height of the tight-lipped fifties, the era of doctrinaire New Criticism, of the Intentional Fallacy, and the whole elaborate, iron dogma by which poetry was separated utterly from the man who made it. In his time, Lowell had been the darling of the school with his complex Catholic symbolism, thickly textured Eliot-Elizabethan language, and his unwavering ability to stamp every line with his own individual rhythm. Then, after nearly ten years' silence, he turned his back on it all. The symbols disappeared, the language clarified and became colloquial, the subject matter became intensely, insistently personal. He wrote as a man who had had breakdowns and was haunted at every crisis by family ghosts; and he wrote without evasions. All that was left of the former young master of Alexandrian complexity was the still unanswerable skill and originality. Even more strongly than before, it was impossible to avoid the troubled presence of Lowell himself, but now he was speaking out in a way that violated all the principles of New Criticism: there was immediacy instead of impersonality, vulnerability in place of exquisitely dandified irony.

Sylvia derived from all this, above all, a vast sense of release. It was as though Lowell had opened a door which had previously been bolted against her. At a critical moment in her development there was no longer any need to be imprisoned in her old poetic habits which despite their elegance—or maybe because of it—she now felt to be intolerably constricting. "My first book, *The Colossus*"—she told the man from the British Council—"I can't read any of the poems aloud now. I didn't write them to be read aloud. In fact, they quite privately bore me." *The Colossus* was the culmination of her apprenticeship in the craft of poetry; it completed the training she began as an eight-year-old and continued through the tensely stylist verse of her undergraduate days, when each poem seemed built up grudgingly, word by word, like a mosaic. Now all that was behind her. She had outgrown the style; more important, she had outgrown the person who had written in that oblique, reticent way. A combination of forces, some chosen deliberately, others chosen for her, had brought her to the point where she was able to write as from her true center about the forces that really moved her: destructive, volatile, demanding, a world apart from everything she had been trained to admire. "What," asked Coleridge, "is the height and ideal of mere association? Delirium." For years Sylvia had apparently agreed, pursuing formal virtues and fingertip detachment, contemptuous of the self-pity, self-advertisement, and self-indulgence of the Beatniks. Now, right on cue, came *Life Studies* to prove that the violence of the self could be written about with control, subtlety, and a dispassionate but undefended imagination.

I suspect that this is why she had first come to me with the new poems, although she knew me only glancingly. It helped that I had reviewed *The Colossus* sympathetically and had got *The Observer* to publish some of her more recent things. But more important was the introduction to my Penguin anthology, *The New Poetry*, which had been published the previous spring. In it I had attacked the British poets' nervous preference for gentility above all else, and their avoidance of the uncomfortable, destructive truths both of the inner life and of the present time. Apparently, this essay said something she wanted to hear; she spoke of it often and with approval, and was disappointed not to have been included among the poets in the book. (She was, later, since her work, more than anyone else's, vindicates my argument. But in the first edition I had stuck to British poets, with the exception of two older Americans, Lowell and Berryman, who, I felt, set the tone for the postwar, post-Eliot period.) Perhaps it made things easier for her to know that someone was making a critical case for what she was now trying to do. And perhaps it made her feel less lonely.

YET LONELY SHE WAS, touchingly and without much disguise, despite her buoyant manner. Despite, too, the energy of her poems, which are, by any standards, subtly ambiguous performances. In them she faced her private horrors steadily and without looking aside, but the effort and risk involved in doing so acted on her like a stimulant; the worse things got and the more directly she wrote about them, the more fertile her imagination became. Just as disaster, when it finally arrives, is never as bad as it seems in expectation, so she now wrote almost with relief, swiftly as though to forestall further horrors. In a way, this is what she had been waiting for all her life, and now it had come she knew she must use it. "The passion for destruction is also a creative passion," said Michael Bakunin, and for Sylvia also this was true. She turned anger, implacability, and her roused, needle-sharp sense of trouble into a kind of celebration.

I have suggested that her cool tone depends a great deal on her realism, her sense of fact. As the months went by and her poetry became progressively more extreme, this gift of transforming every detail grew steadily until, in the last weeks, each trivial event became the occasion for poetry: a cut finger, a fever, a bruise. Her drab domestic life fused with her imagination richly and without hesitation. Around this time, for example, her husband produced a strange radio play in which the hero, driving to town, runs over a hare, sells the dead animal for five shillings, and with the blood money buys two roses. Sylvia pounced on this, isolating its core, interpreting and adjusting it according to her own needs. The result was the poem "Kindness," which ends:

> The blood jet is poetry,
> There is no stopping it.
> You hand me two children, two roses.

214

There was, indeed, no stopping it. Her poetry acted as a strange, powerful lens through which her ordinary life was filtered and refigured with extraordinary intensity. Perhaps the elation that comes of writing well and often helped her to preserve that bright American façade she unfailingly presented to the world. In common with her other friends of that period, I chose to believe in this cheerfulness against all the evidence of the poems. Or rather, I believed in it, and I didn't believe. But what could one do? I felt sorry for her but she clearly didn't want that. Her jauntiness forestalled all sympathy, and, if only by her blank refusal to discuss them otherwise, she insisted that her poems were purely poems, autonomous. If attempted suicide is, as some psychiatrists believe, a cry for help, then Sylvia at this time was not suicidal. What she wanted was not help but confirmation: she needed someone to acknowledge that she was coping exceptionally well with her difficult routine life of children, nappies, shopping, and writing. She needed, even more, to know that the poems worked and were good, for although she had gone through a gate Lowell had opened, she was now far along a peculiarly solitary road on which not many would risk following her. So it was important for her to know that her messages were coming back clear and strong. Yet not even her determinedly bright self-reliance could disguise the loneliness that came from her almost palpably, like a heat haze. She asked for neither sympathy nor help but, like a bereaved widow at a wake, she simply wanted company in her mourning. I suppose it provided confirmation that, despite the odds and the internal evidence, she still existed.

ONE GLOOMY November afternoon she arrived at my studio greatly excited. As usual, she had been trudging the chill streets, house-hunting despondently and more or less aimlessly. A block away from the square near Primrose Hill where she and Ted had lived when they first came to London she saw a "To Let" notice up in front of a newly refurbished house. That in itself was something of a miracle in those impossible, overcrowded days. But more important, the house bore a blue plaque announcing that Yeats had once lived there. It was a sign, the confirmation she had been looking for. That summer she had visited Yeats' Tower at Ballylea and wrote to a friend that she thought it "the most beautiful and peaceful place in the world"; now there was a possibility of finding another Yeats tower in her favorite part of London which she could in some way share with the great poet. She hurried to the agent's and found, improbably, that she was the first to apply. Another sign. On the spot she took a five-year lease of the flat, although the rent was more than she could afford. Then she walked across dark, blowy Primrose Hill to tell me the news.

She was elated not just because she had at last found a flat but because the place and its associations seemed to her somehow preordained. In varying degrees, both she and her husband seemed to believe in the occult. As artists, I suppose, they had to, since both were intent on finding voices for their unquiet, buried selves. But there was, I think, something more to their belief than that. Ted has written that "her psychic gifts, at almost any time, were strong enough to make her frequently wish to be rid of them." That could simply have been her poet's knack of sensing the unspoken content of every situation and, later, her easy, instinctive access to her own unconscious. Yet although both of them talked often enough about astrology, dreams, and magic—enough, anyway, to imply that this was not just a casually interesting subject—I had the impression that at heart their attitudes were utterly different. Ted constantly and carefully mocked himself and deflated his pretensions, yet there was always a sense of his being in touch with some primitive area, some dark side of the self which had nothing to do with the young literary man. This, after all, was what his poems were about: an immediate, physical apprehension of the violence both of animal life and of the self—of the animality of the self. It was also part of his physical presence, a quality of threat beneath his shrewd, laconic manner. It was almost as though, despite all the reading and polish and craftsmanship, he had never properly been civilized or had, at least, never properly believed in his civilization. It was simply a shell he sardonically put up with for the sake of convenience. So all that astrology, primitive religion, and black magic he talked about, however ironically, was a kind of metaphor for the shaking but obscure creative powers he knew himself to possess. For this reason those dubious topics took on for him an immediacy which may not have implied any belief but which certainly transformed them into something beyond mere fad. Perhaps all I am describing is, quite simply, a touch of genius. But it is a genius that has little to do with the traditional Romantic concept of the word: with Shelley's canny other-worldliness or Byron's equally canny sense of his own drama. Ted, too, is canny and practical, like most Yorkshiremen, unwillingly fooled and with a fine, racing mechanic's ear for the rumblings of the literary machine. But he is also, in a curiously complete way, an original: his reactions are unpredictable, his frame of reference different. I imagine the most extreme example of this style of genius was Blake. But there are also many people of genius—perhaps the majority —who have almost nothing of that dislocating and dislocated quality: T. S. Eliot, for example, the Polish poet Zbigniew Herbert, John Donne and Keats—all men whose unusual creative intelligence and awareness seem not essentially at odds with the reality of their everyday worlds. Instead, their particular gift is to clarify and intensify the received world.

Sylvia, I think, belonged with these latter. Her intensity was of the nerves, something urban and near screaming-point. It was also, in its way, more intellectual than Ted's. It was part of the fierceness with which she had worked as a student, passing exam after exam brilliantly, easily, hungrily. With the same intensity she immersed herself in her children, her riding, her beekeeping, even her cooking; everything had to be done well and to the fullest. Since her husband was interested in the occult—for whatever clouded personal reasons—she threw herself into that, too, almost out of the desire to excel. And because her natural talents were very great, she discovered she had "psychic gifts." No doubt the results were genuine and even uncanny, but I suspect they were a triumph of mind over ectoplasm. It is the same in the poems: Ted's gain their effect by expressing his sense of menace and violence immediately, unanswerably; in Sylvia's the expression, though often more powerful, is a by-product of a compulsive need to understand.

ON CHRISTMAS EVE, 1962, Sylvia telephoned me: she and the children had finally settled into their new apartment; could I come round that evening to see the place, have a meal, and hear some new poems? As it happened, I couldn't, since I had already been invited to dinner by some friends who lived a few streets away from her. I said I'd drop in for a drink on my way.

She seemed different. Her hair, which she usually wore in a tight, schoolmistressy bun, was loose. It hung straight to her waist like a tent, giving her pale face and gaunt figure a curiously desolate, rapt air, like a priestess emptied out by the rites of her cult. When she walked in front of me down the hall passage and up the stairs to her apartment— she had the top two floors of the house—her hair gave off a strong smell, sharp as an animal's. The children were already in bed upstairs and the flat was silent. It was newly painted, white and chill. There were, as I remember, no curtains up yet, and the night pressed in coldly on the windows. She had deliberately kept the place bare: rush matting on the floor, a few books, bits of Victoriana, and cloudy blue glass on the shelves, a couple of small Leonard Baskin woodcuts. It was rather beautiful, in its chaste, stripped-down way, but cold, very cold, and the oddments of flimsy Christmas decoration made it seem doubly forlorn, each seeming to repeat that she and the children would be alone over Christmas. For the unhappy, Christmas is always a bad time: the terrible false jollity that comes at you from every side, braying about goodwill and peace and family fun, makes loneliness and depression particularly hard to bear. I had never seen her so strained.

We drank wine and, as usual, she read me some poems. One of them was "Death & Co." This time there was no escaping the meaning. When she had written about death before, it was as something survived, even surpassed: "Lady Lazarus" ends with a resurrection and a threat, and even in "Daddy" she manages finally to turn her back on the grinning, beckoning figure—"Daddy, daddy, you bastard, I'm through." Hence, perhaps, the energy of these poems, their weird jollity in the teeth of everything, their recklessness. But now, as though poetry really

were a form of black magic, the figure she had invoked so often, only to
dismiss triumphantly. had risen before her, dank, final, and not to
be denied. He appeared to her in both his usual shapes: like her father,
elderly, unforgiving, and very dead, and also younger, more seductive,
a creature of her own generation and choice.[1] This time there was no
way out for her; she could only sit still and pretend they hadn't noticed
her:

> I do not stir.
> The frost makes a flower,
> The dew makes a star,
> The dead bell,
> The dead bell.
>
> Somebody's done for.

Perhaps the bell was tolling for "somebody" other than herself; but she
didn't seem to believe so.

I didn't know what to say. The earlier poems had all insisted, in their
different ways, that she wanted nobody's help—although I suddenly
realized that maybe they had insisted in such a manner as to make you
understand that help might be acceptable, if you were willing to make
the effort. But now she was beyond the reach of anyone. In the beginning she had called up these horrors partly in the hope of exorcising
them, partly to demonstrate her omnipotence and invulnerability. Now
she was shut in with them and knew she was defenseless.

I remember arguing inanely about the phrase "The nude/Verdigris
of the condor." I said it was exaggerated, morbid. On the contrary, she
replied, that was exactly how a condor's legs looked. She was right, of
course. I was only trying, in a futile way, to reduce the tension and take
her mind momentarily off her private horrors—as though that could be
done by argument and literary criticism! She must have felt I was stupid
and insensitive. Which I was. But to have been otherwise would have
meant accepting responsibilities I didn't want and couldn't, in my own
depression, have coped with. When I left about eight o'clock to go on to
my dinner party, I knew I had let her down in some final and unfor-
givable way. And I knew she knew. I never again saw her alive.

It was an unspeakable winter, the worst, they said, in a hundred
and fifty years. The snow began just after Christmas and would not let
up. By New Year the whole country had ground to a halt. The trains
froze on the tracks, the abandoned trucks froze on the roads. The power

---

[1] In her own note on the poem, which she wrote for the BBC, Sylvia said: "This
poem—'Death & Co.'—is about the double or schizophrenic nature of death—the mar-
moreal coldness of Blake's death mask, say, hand in glove with the fearful softness of
worms, water, and other katabolists. I imagine these two aspects of death as two men,
two business friends, who have come to call."

stations, overloaded by million upon pathetic million of hopeless electric fires, broke down continually; not that the fires mattered, since the electricians were mostly out on strike. Water pipes froze solid; for a bath you had to scheme and cajole those rare friends with centrally heated houses, who became rarer and less friendly as the weeks dragged on. Doing the dishes became a major operation. The gastric rumble of water in outdated plumbing was sweeter than the sound of mandolins. Weight for weight, plumbers were as expensive as smoked salmon, and harder to find. The gas failed and Sunday joints went raw. The lights failed and candles, of course, were unobtainable. Nerves failed and marriages crumbled. Finally, the heart failed. It seemed the cold would never end. Nag, nag, nag.

In December *The Observer* had published a still uncollected poem by Sylvia called "Event"; in mid-January they published another, "Winter Trees." Sylvia wrote me a note about it, adding that maybe we should take our children to the zoo and she would show me "the nude verdigris of the condor." But she no longer dropped into my studio with poems. Later that month I met the literary editor of one of the big weeklies. He asked me if I had seen Sylvia recently.

"No. Why?"

"I was just wondering. She sent us some poems. Very strange."

"Did you like them?"

"No," he replied. "Too extreme for my taste. I sent them all back. But she sounds in a bad state. I think she needs help."

Her doctor, a sensitive, overworked man, thought the same. He prescribed sedatives and arranged for her to see a psychotherapist. Having been bitten once by American psychiatry, she hesitated for some time before writing for an appointment. But her depression did not lift, and finally the letter was sent. It did no good. Either her letter or that of the therapist arranging a consultation went astray; apparently the postman delivered it to the wrong address. The therapist's reply arrived a day or two after she died. This was one of several links in the chain of accidents, coincidences, and mistakes that ended in her death.

I AM CONVINCED by what I know of the facts that this time she did not intend to die. Her suicide attempt ten years before had been, in every sense, deadly serious. She had carefully disguised the theft of the sleeping pills, left a misleading note to cover her tracks, and hidden herself in the darkest, most unused corner of a cellar, rearranging behind her the old firelogs she had disturbed, burying herself away like a skeleton in the nethermost family closet. Then she had swallowed a bottle of fifty sleeping pills. She was found late and by accident, and survived only by a miracle. The flow of life in her was too strong even for the violence she had done it. This, anyway, is her description of the act in *The Bell Jar;* there is no reason to believe it false. So she had learned the hard way the odds against successful suicide; she had learned that despair must be counterpoised by an almost obsessional attention to detail and disguise.

By these lights she seemed, in her last attempt, to be taking care not to succeed. But this time everything conspired to destroy her. An employment agency had found her an *au pair* girl to help with the children and housework while Sylvia got on with her writing. The girl, an Australian, was due to arrive at nine o'clock on the morning of Monday, February 11th. Meanwhile, a recurrent trouble, Sylvia's sinuses were bad; the pipes in her newly converted flat froze solid; there was still no telephone, and no word from the psychotherapist; the weather continued monstrous. Illness, loneliness, depression, and cold, combined with the demands of two small children, were too much for her. So when the weekend came she went off with the babies to stay with friends in another part of London. The plan was, I think, that she would leave early enough on Monday morning to be back in time to welcome the Australian girl. Instead, she decided to go back on the Sunday. The friends were against it but she was insistent, made a great show of her old competence and seemed more cheerful than she had been for some time. So they let her go. About eleven o'clock that night she knocked on the door of the elderly painter who lived below her, asking to borrow some stamps. But she lingered in the doorway, drawing out the conversation until he told her that he got up well before nine in the morning. Then she said goodnight and went back upstairs.

God knows what kind of a sleepless night she spent or if she wrote any poetry. Certainly, within the last few days of her life she wrote one of her most beautiful poems, "Edge," which is specifically about the act she was about to perform:

> The woman is perfected.
> Her dead
>
> Body wears the smile of accomplishment,
> The illusion of a Greek necessity
>
> Flows in the scrolls of her toga,
> Her bare
>
> Feet seem to be saying:
> We have come so far, it is over.
>
> Each dead child coiled, a white serpent,
> One at each little
>
> Pitcher of milk, now empty.
> She has folded
>
> Them back into her body as petals
> Of a rose close when the garden

Stiffens and odors bleed
From the sweet, deep throats of the night flowers.

The moon has nothing to be sad about,
Staring from her hood of bone.

She is used to this sort of thing.
Her blacks crackle and drag.

It is a poem of great peace and resignation, utterly without self-pity. Even with a subject so appallingly close she remains an artist, absorbed in the practical task of letting each image develop a full, still life of its own. That she is writing about her own death is almost irrelevant. There is another poem, "Words," also very late, which is about the way language remains and echoes long after the turmoil of life has passed; like "Edge" it has the same translucent calm. If these were the last things she wrote, I think she must in the end have accepted the logic of the life she had been leading, and come to terms with its terrible necessities.

Around six A.M. she went up to the children's room and left a plate of bread and butter and two mugs of milk, in case they should wake hungry before the *au pair* girl arrived. Then she went back down to the kitchen, sealed the door and window as best she could with towels, opened the oven, laid her head in it, and turned on the gas.

The Australian girl arrived punctually at nine A.M. She rang and knocked a long time but could get no answer. So she went off to search for a telephone kiosk in order to phone the agency and make sure she had the right address. Sylvia's name, incidentally, was not on either of the doorbells. Had everything been normal, the neighbor below would have been up by then; even if he had overslept, the girl's knocking should have aroused him. But as it happened, the neighbor was very deaf and slept without his hearing aid. More important, his bedroom was immediately below Sylvia's kitchen. The gas seeped down and knocked him out cold. So he slept on through all the noise. The girl returned and tried again, still without success. Again she went off to telephone the agency and ask what to do; they told her to go back. It was now about eleven o'clock. This time she was lucky: some builders had arrived to work in the frozen-up house, and they let her in. When she knocked on Sylvia's door there was no answer and the smell of gas was overpowering. The builders forced the lock and found Sylvia sprawled in the kitchen. She was still warm. She had left a note saying, "Please call Dr.——" and giving his telephone number. But it was too late.

Had everything worked out as it should—had the gas not drugged the man downstairs, preventing him from opening the front door to the *au pair* girl—there is no doubt she would have been saved. I think she wanted to be; why else leave her doctor's telephone number? This time, unlike the occasion ten years before, there was too much holding her to life. Above all, there were the children: she was too passionate a mother to want to lose them or them to lose her. There were also the extraordinary creative powers she now unequivocally knew she possessed: the poems came daily, unbidden and unstoppable, and she was again working on a novel about which, at last, she had no reservations.

WHY, THEN, did she kill herself? In part, I suppose, it was "a cry for help" which fatally misfired. But it was also a last, desperate attempt to exorcise the death she had summoned up in her poems. I have already suggested that perhaps she had begun to write obsessively about death for two reasons. First, when she and her husband separated, however mutual the arrangement, she went through again the same piercing grief and bereavement she had felt as a child when her father, by his death, seemed to abandon her. Second, I believe she thought her car crash the previous summer had set her free; she had paid her dues, qualified as a survivor, and could now write about it. But, as I have written elsewhere, for the artist himself art is not necessarily therapeutic; he is not automatically relieved of his fantasies by expressing them. Instead, by some perverse logic of creation, the act of formal expression may simply make the dredged-up material more readily available to him. The result of handling it in his work may well be that he finds himself living it out. For the artist, in short, nature often imitates art. Or, to restate the cliché, when an artist holds a mirror up to nature he finds out who and what he is; but the knowledge may change him irredeemably so that he becomes that image.

I think Sylvia, in one way or another, sensed this. In an introductory note she wrote to "Daddy" for the BBC, she said of the poem's narrator, "she has to act out the awful little allegory once over before she is free of it." The allegory in question was, as she saw it, the struggle in her between a fantasy Nazi father and a Jewish mother. But perhaps it was also a fantasy of containing in herself her own dead father, like a woman possessed by a demon (in the poem she actually calls him a vampire). In order for her to be free of him, he has to be released like a genie from a bottle. And this is precisely what the poems did: they bodied forth the death within her. But they also did so in an intensely living and creative way. The more she wrote about death, the stronger and more fertile her imaginative world became. And this gave her everything to live for.

I suspect that in the end she wanted to have done with the theme once and for all. But the only way she could find was "to act out the awful little allegory once over." She had always been a bit of a gambler, used to taking risks. The authority of her poetry was in part due to her brave persistence in following the thread of her inspiration right down to the Minotaur's lair. And this psychic courage had its parallel in her physical arrogance and carelessness. Risks didn't frighten her; on the contrary, she found them stimulating. Freud has written, "Life loses in interest, when the highest stake in the game of living, life itself, may not be risked." Finally, Sylvia took that risk. She gambled for the last time, having worked out that the odds were in her favor, but perhaps, in her depression, not much caring whether she won or lost. Her calculations went wrong and she lost.

IT WAS A MISTAKE, then, and out of it a whole myth has grown. I don't think she would have found it much to her taste, since it is a myth of the poet as a sacrificial victim, offering herself up for the sake of her art, having been dragged by the Muses to that final altar through every kind of distress. In these terms, her suicide becomes the whole point of the story, the act which validates her poems, gives them their interest, and proves her seriousness. So people are drawn to her work in much the same spirit as *Time* featured her at length: not for the poetry but for the gossipy, extraliterary "human interest." Yet just as the suicide adds nothing at all to the poetry, so the myth of Sylvia as a passive victim is a total perversion of the woman she was. It misses altogether her liveliness, her intellectual appetite and harsh wit, her great imaginative resourcefulness and vehemence of feeling, her control. Above all, it misses the courage with which she was able to turn disaster into art. The pity is not that there is a myth of Sylvia Plath but that the myth is not simply that of an enormously gifted poet whose death came recklessly, by mistake, and too soon.

I used to think of her brightness as a façade, as though she were able, in a rather schizoid way, to turn her back on her suffering for the sake of appearances, and pretend it didn't exist. But maybe she was also able to keep her unhappiness in check because she could write about it, because she knew she was salvaging from all those horrors something rather marvelous. The end came when she felt she could stand the subject no longer. She had written it out and was ready for something new.

> The blood-jet is poetry,
> There is no stopping it.

The only method of stopping it she could see, her vision by then blinkered by depression and illness, was the last gamble. So having, as she thought, arranged to be saved, she lay down in front of the gas oven almost hopefully, almost with relief, as though she were saying, "Perhaps this will set me free."

ON FRIDAY, February 15th, there was an inquest in the drab, damp coroner's court behind Camden Town: muttered evidence, long silences, the Australian girl in tears. Earlier that morning I had gone with Ted to the undertakers in Mornington Crescent. The coffin was at the far end of a bare, draped room. She lay stiffly, a ludicrous ruff at her neck. Only her face showed. It was gray and slightly transparent, like wax. I had never before seen a dead person and I hardly recognized her; her features seemed too thin and sharp. The room smelled of apples, faint, sweet but somehow unclean, as though the apples were beginning to rot. I was glad to get out into the cold and noise of the dingy streets. It seemed impossible that she was dead.

Even now I find it hard to believe. There was too much life in her long flat, strongly boned body, and her longish face with its fine brown eyes, shrewd and full of feeling. She was practical and candid, passionate and compassionate. I believe she was a genius. I sometimes catch myself childishly thinking I'll run into her walking on Primrose Hill or the Heath, and we'll pick up the conversation where we left off. But perhaps that is because her poems still speak so distinctly in her accents: quick, sardonic, unpredictable, effortlessly inventive, a bit angry, and always utterly her own.

---

40. Hidden Name
and Complex Fate

RALPH ELLISON

Ellison (1914–   ), born in Oklahoma City, educated at Tuskegee, came to New York City, where he still lives, as a jazz trumpeter. His *Invisible Man* won the National Book Award in 1953, and two other national awards as well. He has taught and lectured widely, and published a collection of essays, *Shadow and Act,* in 1964. He serves on the Editorial Board of *The American Scholar.*

IN *Green Hills of Africa,* Ernest Hemingway reminds us that both Tolstoy and Stendhal had seen war, that Flaubert had seen a revolution and the Commune, that Dostoievsky had been sent to Siberia and that such experiences were important in shaping the art of these great masters. And he goes on to observe that "writers are forged in injustice as a sword is forged." He declined to describe the many personal forms which injustice may take in this chaotic world—who would be so mad as to try?—nor does he go into the personal wounds which each of these writers sustained. Now, however, thanks to his brother and sister, we do know something of the injustice in which he himself was forged, and this knowledge has been added to what we have long known of Hemingway's artistic temper.

In the end, however, it is the quality of his art which is primary. It is the art which allows the wars and revolutions which he knew, and the personal and social injustice which he suffered, to lay claims upon our attention; for it was through his art that they achieved their most enduring meaning. It is a matter of outrageous irony, perhaps, but in literature the great social clashes of history no less than the painful experience of the individual are secondary to the meaning which they take on through the skill, the talent, the imagination and personal vision of the writer who transforms them into art. Here they are reduced to more manageable proportions; here they are imbued with humane values; here, injustice and catastrophe become less important in themselves than what the writer makes of them. This is *not* true, however, of the writer's struggle with that recalcitrant angel called Art; and it was through *this* specific struggle that Ernest Hemingway became *Hemingway* (now refined to a total body of transcendent work, after forty years of being endlessly dismembered and resurrected, as it continues to be, in the styles, the themes, the sense of life and literature of countless other writers). And it was through this struggle with form that he became the master, the culture hero, whom we have come to know and admire.

It was suggested that it might be of interest if I discussed here this evening some of my notions of the writer's experience in the United States, hence I have evoked the name of Hemingway, not by way of inviting far-fetched comparisons but in order to establish a perspective, a set of assumptions from which I may speak, and in an attempt to avoid boring you by emphasizing those details of racial hardship which for some forty years now have been evoked whenever writers of my own cultural background have essayed their experience in public.

I do this *not* by way of denying totally the validity of these by now stylized recitals, for I have shared and still share many of their detailed injustices—what Negro can escape them?—but by way of suggesting that they are, at least in a discussion of a writer's experience, as *writer*, as artist, somewhat beside the point.

For we select neither our parents, our race nor our nation; these occur to us out of the love, the hate, the circumstances, the fate, of others. But we *do* become writers out of an act of will, out of an act of choice; a dim, confused and ofttimes regrettable choice, perhaps, but choice nevertheless. And what happens thereafter causes all those experiences which occurred before we began to function as writers to take on a special quality of uniqueness. If this does not happen then as far as writing goes, the experiences have been misused. If we do not make of them a value, if we do not transform them into forms and images of meaning which they did not possess before, then we have failed as artists.

Thus for a writer to insist that his personal suffering is of special interest in itself, or simply because he belongs to a particular racial or religious group, is to advance a claim for special privileges which members of his group who are not writers would be ashamed to demand. The kindest judgment one can make of this point of view is that it reveals a sad misunderstanding of the relationship between suffering and art. Thomas Mann and André Gide have told us much of this and there are critics, like Edmund Wilson, who have told of the connection between the wound and the bow.

As I see it, it is through the process of making artistic forms—plays, poems, novels—out of one's experience that one becomes a writer, and it is through this process, this struggle, that the writer helps give meaning to the experience of the group. And it is the process of mastering the discipline, the techniques, the fortitude, the culture, through which this is made possible that constitutes the writer's real experience as *writer*, as artist. If this sounds like an argument for the artist's withdrawal from social struggles, I would recall to you W. H. Auden's comment to the effect that:

> In our age, the mere making of a work of art is itself a political act. So long as artists exist, making what they please, and think they ought to make, even if it is not terribly good, even if it appeals to only a handful of people, they remind the Management of something managers need to be reminded of, namely, that the managed are people with faces, not anonymous members, that *Homo Laborans* is also *Homo Ludens*. . . .

Without doubt, even the most *engagé* writers—and I refer to true artists, not to artists *manqués*—begin their careers in play and puzzlement, in dreaming over the details of the world in which they become conscious of themselves.

Let Tar Baby, that enigmatic figure from Negro folklore, stand for the world. He leans, black and gleaming, against the wall of life utterly noncommittal under our scrutiny, our questioning, starkly unmoving before our naïve attempts at intimidation. Then we touch him playfully and before we can say *Sonny Liston!* we find ourselves stuck. Our playful investigations become a labor, a fearful struggle, an *agon*. Slowly we perceive that our task is to learn the proper way of freeing ourselves to develop, in other words, technique.

Sensing this, we give him our sharpest attention, we question him carefully, we struggle with more subtlety; while he, in his silent way, holds on, demanding that we perceive the necessity of calling him by his true name as the price of our freedom. It is unfortunate that he has so many, many "true names"—all spelling chaos; and in order to discover even one of these we must first come into the possession of our own names. For it is through our names that we first place ourselves in the world. Our names, being the gift of others, must be made our own.

Once while listening to the play of a two-year-old girl who did not know she was under observation, I heard her saying over and over again, at first with questioning and then with sounds of growing satisfaction, "I am Mimi Livisay? . . . *I* am Mimi Livisay. I *am* Mimi Livisay . . . I am *Mimi* Li-vi-say! I am Mimi . . ."

And in deed and in fact she was—or became so soon thereafter, by working playfully to establish the unity between herself and her name.

For many of us this is far from easy. We must learn to wear our names within all the noise and confusion of the environment in which we find ourselves; make them the center of all of our associations with the world, with man and with nature. We must charge them with all our emotions, our hopes, hates, loves, aspirations. They must become our masks and our shields and the containers of all those values and traditions which we learn and/or imagine as being the meaning of our familial past.

And when we are reminded so constantly that we bear, as Negroes, names originally possessed by those who owned our enslaved grandparents, we are apt, especially if we are potential writers, to be more than ordinarily concerned with the veiled and mysterious events, the fusions of blood, the furtive couplings, the business transactions. the violations of faith and loyalty, the assaults; yes, and the unrecognized and unrecognizable loves through which our names were handed down unto us.

So charged with emotion does this concern become for some of us, that we have, earlier, the example of the followers of Father Divine and, now, the Black Muslims, discarding their original names in rejection of the bloodstained, the brutal, the sinful images of the past. Thus they would declare new identities, would clarify a new program of intention and destroy the verbal evidence of a willed and ritualized discontinuity of blood and human intercourse.

Not all of us, actually only a few, seek to deal with our names in this manner. We take what we have and make of them what we can. And there are even those who know where the old broken connections lie, who recognize their relatives across the chasm of historical denial and the artificial barriers of society, and who see themselves as bearers of many of the qualities which were admirable in the original sources of their common line (Faulkner has made much of this); and I speak here not of mere forgiveness, nor of obsequious insensitivity to the outrages symbolized by the denial and the division, but of the conscious acceptance of the harsh realities of the human condition, of the ambiguities and hypocrisies of human history as they have played themselves out in the United States.

Perhaps, taken in aggregate, these European names (sometimes with irony, sometimes with pride, but always with personal investment) represent a certain triumph of the spirit, speaking to us of those who rallied, reassembled and transformed themselves and who under dismembering pressures refused to die. "Brothers and sisters," I once heard a Negro preacher exhort, "let us make up our faces before the world, and our names shall sound throughout the land with honor! For we ourselves are our *true* names, not their epithets! So let us, I say, Make Up Our Faces and Our Minds!"

Perhaps my preacher had read T. S. Eliot, although I doubt it. And in actuality, it was unnecessary that he do so, for a concern with names and naming was very much a part of that special area of American culture from which I come, and it is precisely for this reason that this example should come to mind in a discussion of my own experience as a writer.

Undoubtedly, writers begin their *conditioning* as manipulators of words long before they become aware of literature—certain Freudians would say at the breast. Perhaps. But if so, that is far too early to be of use at this moment. Of this, though, I am certain: that despite the misconceptions of those educators who trace the reading difficulties experienced by large numbers of Negro children in Northern schools to their Southern background, these children are, in *their* familiar South, facile manipulators of words. I know, too, that the Negro community is deadly in its ability to create nicknames and to spot all that is ludicrous in an unlikely name or that which is incongruous in conduct. Names are not qualities; nor are words, in this particular sense, actions. To assume that they are could cost one his life many times a day. Language skills depend to a large extent upon a knowledge of the details, the manners, the objects, the folkways, the psychological patterns, of a given environment. Humor and wit depend upon much the same awareness, and so does the suggestive power of names.

"A small brown bowlegged Negro with the name 'Franklin D. Roosevelt Jones' might sound like a clown to someone who looks at him from the outside," said my friend Albert Murray, "but on the other hand he just might turn out to be a hell of a fireside operator. He might just lie back in all of that comic juxtaposition of names and manipulate you deaf, dumb and blind—and you not even suspecting it, because you're thrown out of stance by his name! There you are, so dazzled by the F.D.R. image—which you *know* you can't see—and so delighted with your own superior position that you don't realize that it's *Jones* who must be confronted."

Well, as you must suspect, all of this speculation on the matter of names has a purpose, and now, because it is tied up so ironically with my own experience as a writer, I must turn to my own name.

For in the dim beginnings, before I ever thought consciously of writing, there was my own name, and there was, doubtless, a certain magic in it. From the start I was uncomfortable with it, and in my earliest years it caused me much puzzlement. Neither could I understand what a poet was, nor why, exactly, my father had chosen to name me after one. Perhaps I could have understood it perfectly well had he named me after his own father, but that name had been given to an older brother who died and thus was out of the question. But why hadn't he named me after a hero, such as Jack Johnson, or a soldier like Colonel Charles Young, or a great seaman like Admiral Dewey, or an educator like Booker T. Washington, or a great orator and abolitionist like Frederick Douglass? Or again, why hadn't he named me (as so many Negro parents had done) after President Teddy Roosevelt?

Instead, he named me after someone called Ralph Waldo Emerson, and then, when I was three, he died. It was too early for me to have understood his choice, although I'm sure he must have explained it many times, and it was also too soon for me to have made the connection between my name and my father's love for reading. Much later, after I began to write and work with words, I came to suspect that he was aware of the suggestive powers of names and of the magic involved in naming.

I recall an odd conversation with my mother during my early teens in which she mentioned their interest in, of all things, prenatal culture! But for a long time I actually knew only that my father read a lot, and that he admired this remote Mr. Emerson, who was something called a "poet and philosopher"—so much so that he named his second son after him.

I knew, also, that whatever his motives, the combination of names he'd given me caused me no end of trouble from the moment when I could talk well enough to respond to the ritualized question which grownups put to very young children. Emerson's name was quite familiar to Negroes in Oklahoma during those days when World War I was brewing, and adults, eager to show off their knowledge of literary figures, and obviously amused by the joke implicit in such a small brown nubbin of a boy carrying around such a heavy moniker, would invariably repeat my first two names and then to my great annoyance, they'd add "Emerson."

And I, in my confusion, would reply, "No, *no*, *I'm* not Emerson; he's the little boy who lives next door." Which only made them laugh all the louder. "Oh no," they'd say, "*you're* Ralph Waldo Emerson," while I had fantasies of blue murder.

For a while the presence next door of my little friend, Emerson, made it unnecessary for me to puzzle too often over this peculiar adult confusion. And since there were other Negro boys named Ralph in the city, I came to suspect that there was something about the combination of names which produced their laughter. Even today I know of only one other Ralph who had as much comedy made out of his name, a campus politician and deep-voiced orator whom I knew at Tuskegee, who was called in friendly ribbing, *Ralph Waldo Emerson Edgar Allan Poe, spelled* Powe. This must have been quite a trial for him, but I had been initiated much earlier.

During my early school years the name continued to puzzle me, for it constantly evoked in the faces of others some secret. It was as though I possessed some treasure or some defect, which was invisible to my own eyes and ears; something which I had but did not *possess,* like a piece of property in South Carolina, which was mine but which I could not have until some future time. I recall finding, about this time, while seeking adventure in back alleys—which possess for boys a superiority over playgrounds like that which kitchen utensils possess over toys designed for infants—a large photographic lens. I remember nothing of its optical qualities, of its speed or color correction, but it gleamed with crystal mystery and it was beautiful.

Mounted handsomely in a tube of shiny brass, it spoke to me of distant worlds of possibility. I played with it, looking through it with squinted eyes, holding it in shafts of sunlight, and tried to use it for a magic lantern. But most of this was as unrewarding as my attempts to make the music come from a phonograph record by holding the needle in my fingers.

I could burn holes through newspapers with it, or I could pretend that it was a telescope, the barrel of a cannon, or the third eye of a monster—*I* being the monster—but I could do nothing at all about its proper function of making images; nothing to make it yield its secret. But I could not discard it.

Older boys sought to get it away from me by offering knives or tops, agate marbles or whole zoos of grass snakes and horned toads in trade, but I held on to it. No one, not even the white boys I knew, had such a lens, and it was my own good luck to have found it. Thus I would hold on to it until such time as I could acquire the parts needed to make it function. Finally I put it aside and it remained buried in my box of treasures, dusty and dull, to be lost and forgotten as I grew older and became interested in music.

I had reached by now the grades where it was necessary to learn something about Mr. Emerson and what he had written, such as the "Concord Hymn" and the essay "Self-Reliance," and in following his advice, I reduced the "Waldo" to a simple and, I hoped, mysterious "W," and in my own reading I avoided his works like the plague. I could no more deal with my name—I shall never really master it—than I could find a creative use for my lens. Fortunately there were other problems to occupy my mind. Not that I forgot my fascination with names, but more about that later.

Negro Oklahoma City was starkly lacking in writers. In fact, there was only Roscoe Dungee, the editor of the local Negro newspaper and a very fine editorialist in that valuable tradition of personal journalism which is now rapidly disappearing; a writer who in his emphasis upon the possibilities for justice offered by the Constitution anticipated the anti-segregation struggle by decades. There were also a few reporters who drifted in and out, but these were about all. On the level of *conscious* culture the Negro community was biased in the direction of music.

These were the middle and late twenties, remember, and the state was still a new frontier state. The capital city was one of the great centers for southwestern jazz, along with Dallas and Kansas City. Orchestras which were to become famous within a few years were constantly coming and going. As were the blues singers—Ma Rainey and Ida Cox, and the old bands like that of King Oliver. But best of all, thanks to Mrs. Zelia N. Breaux, there was an active and enthusiastic school music program through which any child who had the interest and the talent could learn to play an instrument and take part in the band, the orchestra, the brass quartet. And there was a yearly operetta and a chorus and a glee club. Harmony was taught for four years and the music appreciation program was imperative. European folk dances were taught throughout the Negro school system, and we were also taught complicated patterns of military drill.

I tell you this to point out that although there were no incentives to write, there was ample opportunity to receive an artistic discipline. Indeed, once one picked up an instrument it was difficult to escape. If you chafed at the many rehearsals of the school band or orchestra and were drawn to the many small jazz groups, you were likely to discover that the jazzmen were apt to rehearse far more than the school band; it was only that they seemed to enjoy themselves better and to possess a freedom of imagination which we were denied at school. And one soon learned that the wild, transcendent moments which occurred at dances or "battles of music," moments in which memorable improvisations were ignited, depended upon a dedication to a discipline which was observed even when rehearsals had to take place in the crowded quarters of Halley Richardson's shoeshine parlor. It was not the place which counted, although a large hall with good acoustics was preferred, but what one did to perfect one's performance.

If this talk of musical discipline gives the impression that there were no forces working to nourish one who would one day blunder, after many a twist and turn, into writing, I am misleading you. And here I might give you a longish lecture on the Ironies and Uses of

Segregation. When I was a small child there was no library for Negroes in our city; and not until a Negro minister invaded the main library did we get one. For it was discovered that there was no law, only custom, which held that we could not use these public facilities. The results were the quick renting of two large rooms in a Negro office building (the recent site of a pool hall), the hiring of a young Negro librarian, the installation of shelves and a hurried stocking of the walls with any and every book possible. It was, in those first days, something of a literary chaos.

But how fortunate for a boy who loved to read! I started with the fairy tales and quickly went through the junior fiction; then through the Westerns and the detective novels, and very soon I was reading the classics—only I didn't know it. There were also the Haldeman Julius Blue Books, which seem to have floated on the air down from Girard, Kansas; the syndicated columns of O. O. McIntyre, and the copies of *Vanity Fair* and the *Literary Digest* which my mother brought home from work—how could I ever join uncritically in the heavy-handed attacks on the so-called Big Media which have become so common today?

There were also the pulp magazines and, more important, that other library which I visited when I went to help my adopted grandfather, J. D. Randolph (my parents had been living in his rooming house when I was born), at his work as custodian of the law library of the Oklahoma State Capitol. Mr. Randolph had been one of the first teachers in what became Oklahoma City; and he'd also been one of the leaders of a group who walked from Gallatin, Tennessee, to the Oklahoma Territory. He was a tall man, as brown as smoked leather, who looked like the Indians with whom he'd herded horses in the early days.

And while his status was merely the custodian of the law library, I was to see the white legislators come down on many occasions to question him on points of law, and often I was to hear him answer without recourse to the uniform rows of books on the shelves. This was a thing to marvel at in itself, and the white lawmakers did so, but even more marvelous, ironic, intriguing, haunting—call it what you will—is the fact that the Negro who knew the answers was named after Jefferson Davis. What Tennessee lost, Oklahoma was to gain, and after gaining it (a gift of courage, intelligence, fortitude and grace), used it only in concealment and, one hopes, with embarrassment.

So, let us, I say, make up our faces and our minds!

In the loosely structured community of that time, knowledge, news of other ways of living, ancient wisdom, the latest literary fads, hate literature—for years I kept a card warning Negroes away from the polls, which had been dropped by the thousands from a plane which circled over the Negro community—information of all kinds, found its level, catch-as-catch can, in the minds of those who were receptive to it. Not that there was no conscious structuring—I read my first Shaw and Maupassant, my first Harvard Classics in the home of a friend whose parents were products of that stream of New England education which had been brought to Negroes by the young and enthusiastic white teachers who staffed the schools set up for the freedmen after the Civil War. These parents were both teachers and there were others like them in our town.

But the places where a rich oral literature was truly functional were the churches, the schoolyards, the barbershops, the cotton-picking camps; places where folklore and gossip thrived. The drug store where I worked was such a place, where on days of bad weather the older men would sit with their pipes and tell tall tales, hunting yarns and homely version of the classics. It was here that I heard stories of searching for buried treasure and of headless horsemen, which I was told were my own father's versions told long before. There were even recitals of popular verse, "The Shooting of Dan McGrew," and, along with these, stories of Jesse James, of Negro outlaws and black United States marshals, of slaves who became the chiefs of Indian tribes and of the exploits of Negro cowboys. There was both truth and fantasy in this, intermingled in the mysterious fashion of literature.

Writers, in their formative period, absorb into their consciousness much that has no special value until much later, and often much which is of no special value even then—perhaps, beyond the fact that it throbs with affect and mystery and in it "time and pain and royalty in the blood" are suspended in imagery. So, long before I thought of writing, I was claimed by weather, by speech rhythms, by Negro voices and their different idioms, by husky male voices and by the high shrill singing voices of certain Negro women, by music; by tight spaces and by wide spaces in which the eyes could wander; by death, by newly born babies, by manners of various kinds, company manners and street manners; the manners of white society and those of our own high society; and by interracial manners; by street fights, circuses and minstrel shows; by vaudeville and moving pictures, by prize fights and foot races, baseball games and football matches. By spring floods and blizzards, catalpa worms and jack rabbits; honeysuckle and snapdragons (which smelled like old cigar butts); by sunflowers and hollyhocks, raw sugar cane and baked yams; pigs' feet, chili and blue haw ice cream. By parades, public dances and jam sessions, Easter sunrise ceremonies and large funerals. By contests between fire-and-brimstone preachers and by presiding elders who got "laughing-happy" when moved by the spirit of God.

I was impressed by expert players of the "dozens" and certain notorious bootleggers of corn whiskey. By jazz musicians and fortune-tellers and by men who did anything well; by strange sicknesses and by interesting brick or razor scars; by expert cursing vocabularies as well as by exalted praying and terrifying shouting, and by transcendent playing or singing of the blues. I was fascinated by old ladies, those who had seen slavery and those who were defiant of white folk and black alike; by the enticing walks of prostitutes and by the limping walks affected by Negro hustlers, especially those who wore Stetson hats, expensive shoes with well-starched overalls, usually with a diamond stickpin (when not in hock) in their tieless collars as their gambling uniforms.

And there were the blind men who preached on corners, and the blind men who sang the blues to the accompaniment of washboard and guitar; and the white junkmen who sang mountain music and the famous hucksters of fruit and vegetables.

And there was the Indian-Negro confusion. There were Negroes who were part Indian and who lived on reservations, and Indians who had children who lived in towns as Negroes, and Negroes who were Indians and traveled back and forth between the groups with no trouble. And Indians who were as wild as wild Negroes and others who were as solid and as steady as bankers. There were the teachers, too, inspiring teachers and villainous teachers who chased after the girl students, and certain female teachers who one wished would chase after young male students. And a handsome old principal of military bearing who had been blemished by his classmates at West Point when they discovered on the eve of graduation that the was a Negro. There were certain Jews, Mexicans, Chinese cooks, a German orchestra conductor and an English grocer who owned a Franklin touring car. And certain Negro mechanics —"Cadillac Slim," "Sticks" Walker, Buddy Bunn and Oscar Pitman—who had so assimilated the automobile that they seemed to be behind a steering wheel even as they walked the streets or danced with girls. And there were the whites who despised us and the others who shared our hardships and our joys.

There is much more, but this is sufficient to indicate some of what was present even in a segregated community to form the background of my work, my sense of life.

And now comes the next step. I went to Tuskegee to study music, hoping to become a composer of symphonies and there, during my second year, I read *The Waste Land* * and that, although I was then unaware of it, was the real transition to writing.

Mrs. L. C. McFarland had taught us much of Negro history in grade school and from her I'd learned of the New Negro Movement of the twenties, of Langston Hughes, Countee Cullen, Claude McKay, James Weldon Johnson and the others. They had inspired pride and had given me a closer identification with poetry (by now, oddly enough, I seldom thought of my hidden name), but with music so much on my mind it never occurred to me to try to imitate them. Still I read their work and

* By T. S. Eliot.

was excited by the glamour of the Harlem which emerged from their poems and it was good to know that there were Negro writers.—Then came *The Waste Land.*

I was much more under the spell of literature than I realized at the time. *Wuthering Heights* * had caused me an agony of unexpressible emotion and the same was true of *Jude the Obscure,* ** but the *Waste Land* seized my mind. I was intrigued by its power to move me while eluding my understanding. Somehow its rhythms were often closer to those of jazz than were those of the Negro poets, and even though I could not understand then, its range of allusion was as mixed and as varied as that of Louis Armstrong. Yet there were its discontinuities, its changes of pace and its hidden system of organization which escaped me.

There was nothing to do but look up the references in the footnotes to the poem, and thus began my conscious education in literature.

For this, the library at Tuskegee was quite adequate and I used it. Soon I was reading a whole range of subjects drawn upon by the poet, and this led, in turn, to criticism and to Pound and Ford Madox Ford, Sherwood Anderson and Gertrude Stein, Hemingway and Fitzgerald and "round about 'til I was come" back to Melville and Twain—the writers who are taught and doubtlessly overtaught today. Perhaps it was my good luck that they were not taught at Tuskegee, I wouldn't know. But at the time I was playing, having an intellectually interesting good time.

Having given so much attention to the techniques of music, the process of learning something of the craft and intention of modern poetry and fiction seemed quite familiar. Besides, it was absolutely painless because it involved no deadlines or credits. Even then, however, a process which I described earlier had begun to operate. The more I learned of literature in this conscious way, the more the details of my background became transformed. I heard undertones in remembered conversations which had escaped me before, local customs took on a more universal meaning, values which I hadn't understood were revealed; some of the people whom I had known were diminished while others were elevated in stature. More important, I began to see my own possibilities with more objective, and in some ways, more hopeful eyes.

The following summer I went to New York seeking work, which I did not find, and remained there, but the personal transformation continued. Reading had become a conscious process of growth and discovery, a method of reordering the world. And that world had widened considerably.

At Tuskegee I had handled manuscripts which Prokofiev had given to Hazel Harrison, a Negro concert pianist who taught there and who

* By Emily Bronte.
** By Thomas Hardy.

had known him in Europe, and through Miss Harrison I had become aware of Prokofiev's symphonies. I had also become aware of the radical movement in politics and art, and in New York had begun reading the work of André Malraux, not only the fiction but chapters published from his *Psychology of Art*. And in my search for an expression of modern sensibility in the works of Negro writers I discovered Richard Wright. Shortly thereafter I was to meet Wright, and it was at his suggestion that I wrote both my first book review and my first short story. These were fatal suggestions.

For although I had tried my hand at poetry while at Tuskegee, it hadn't occurred to me that I might write fiction, but once he suggested it, it seemed the most natural thing to try. Fortunately for me, Wright, then on the verge of his first success, was eager to talk with a beginner and I was able to save valuable time in searching out those works in which writing was discussed as a craft. He guided me to Henry James' prefaces, to Conrad, to Joseph Warren Beach and to the letters of Dostoievsky. There were other advisers and other books involved, of course, but what is important here is that I was consciously concerned with the art of fiction, that almost from the beginning I was grappling quite consciously with the art through which I wished to realize myself. And this was not done in isolation; the Spanish Civil War was now in progress and the Depression was still on. The world was being shaken up, and through one of those odd instances which occur to young provincials in New York, I was to hear Malraux make an appeal for the Spanish Loyalists at the same party where I first heard the folk singer Leadbelly perform. Wright and I were there seeking money for the magazine which he had come to New York to edit.

Art and politics; a great French novelist and a Negro folk singer; a young writer who was soon to publish *Uncle Tom's Children;* and I who had barely begun to study his craft. It is such accidents, such fortuitous meetings, which count for so much in our lives. I had never dreamed that I would be in the presence of Malraux, of whose work I became aware on my second day in Harlem when Langston Hughes suggested that I read *Man's Fate* and *Days of Wrath* before returning them to a friend of his. And it is this fortuitous circumstance which led to my selecting Malraux as a literary "ancestor," whom, unlike a relative, the artist is permitted to choose. There was in progress at the time all the agitation over the Scottsboro boys * and the Herndon Case, and I was aware of both. I had to be; I myself had been taken off a freight train at Decatur, Alabama, only three years before while on my way to

---

* In 1931, eight Negro boys were convicted of raping two white girls in a gondola car near Scottsboro, Alabama; all were sentenced to death. But, because of a strong Northern liberal protest, and uncertain evidence, all were spared the death penalty after a long series of appeals that reached the U.S. Supreme Court. Eventually, all except one were released or paroled from prison.

Tuskegee. But while I joined in the agitation for their release, my main energies went into learning to write.

I began to publish enough, and not too slowly, to justify my hopes for success, and as I continued, I made a most perplexing discovery; namely, that for all his conscious concern with technique, a writer did not so much create the novel as he was created *by* the novel. That is, one did not make an arbitrary gesture when one sought to write. And when I say that the novelist is created by the novel, I mean to remind you that fictional techniques are not a mere set of objective tools, but something much more intimate: a way of feeling, of seeing and of expressing one's sense of life. And the process of *acquiring* technique is a process of modifying one's responses, of learning to see and feel, to hear and observe, to evoke and evaluate the images of memory and of summoning up and directing the imagination; of learning to conceive of human values in the ways which have been established by the great writers who have developed and extended the art. And perhaps the writer's greatest freedom, as artist, lies precisely in his possession of technique; for it is through technique that he comes to possess and express the meaning of his life.

Perhaps at this point it would be useful to recapitulate the route— perhaps as mazelike as that of *Finnegan's Wake* *—which I have been trying to describe; that which leads from the writer's discovery of a sense of purpose, which is that of becoming a writer, and then the involvement in the passionate struggle required to master a bit of technique, and then, as this begins to take shape, the disconcerting discovery that it is *technique* which transforms the individual before he is able to turn to transform it. And in that personal transformation he discovers something else: he discovers that he has taken on certain obligations that he must not embarrass his chosen form, and that in order to avoid this he must develop taste. He learns—and this is most discouraging—that he is involved with values which turn in their *own* way, and not in the ways of politics, upon the central issues affecting his nation and his time. He learns that the American novel, from its first consciousness of itself as a literary form, has grappled with the meaning of the American experience; that it has been aware and has sought to define the nature of that experience by addressing itself to the specific details, the moods, the landscapes, the cityscapes, the tempo of American change. And that it has borne, at its best, the full weight of that burden of conscience and consciousness which Americans inherit as one of the results of the revolutionary circumstances of our national beginnings.

We began as a nation not through the accidents of race or religion or geography (Robert Penn Warren has dwelled on these circumstances) but when a group of men, *some* of them political philosophers, put down,

* By James Joyce.

upon what we now recognize as being quite sacred papers, their conception of the nation which they intended to establish on these shores. They described, as we know, the obligations of the state to the citizen, of the citizen to the state; they committed themselves to certain ideas of justice, just as they committed us to a system which would guarantee all of its citizens equality of opportunity.

I need not describe the problems which have arisen from these beginnings. I need only remind you that the contradiction between these noble ideals and the actualities of our conduct generated a guilt, an unease of spirit, from the very beginning, and that the American novel at its best has always been concerned with this basic moral predicament. During Melville's time and Twain's, it was an implicit aspect of their major themes; by the twentieth century and after the discouraging and traumatic effect of the Civil War and the Reconstruction it had gone underground, had become *understated*. Nevertheless it did not disappear completely and it is to be found operating in the work of Henry James as well as in that of Hemingway and Fitzgerald. And then (and as one who believes in the impelling moral function of the novel and who believes in the moral seriousness of the form) it pleases me no end that it comes into explicit statement again in the works of Richard Wright and William Faulkner, writers who lived close to moral and political problems which would not stay put underground.

I got into these details not to recapitulate the history of the American novel but to indicate the trend of thought which was set into motion when I began to discover the nature of that process with which I was actually involved. Whatever the opinions and decisions of critics, a novelist must arrive at his own conclusions as to the meaning and function of the form with which he is engaged, and these are, in all modesty, some of mine.

In order to orient myself I also began to learn that the American novel had long concerned itself with the puzzle of the one-and-the-many; the mystery of how each of us, despite his origin in diverse regions, with our diverse racial, cultural, religious backgrounds, speaking his own diverse idiom of the American in his own accent, is, nevertheless, American. And with this concern with the implicit pluralism of the country and with the composite nature of the ideal character called "the American," there goes a concern with gauging the health of the American promise, with depicting the extent to which it was being achieved, being made manifest in our daily conduct.

And with all of this there still remained the specific concerns of literature. Among these is the need to keep literary standards high, the necessity of exploring new possibilities of language which would allow it to retain that flexibility and fidelity to the common speech which has been its glory since Mark Twain. For me this meant learning to add to it the wonderful resources of Negro American speech and idiom and to bring into range as fully and eloquently as possible the complex reality of the American experience as it shaped and was shaped by the lives of my own people.

Notice that I stress as "fully" as possible, because I would no more strive to write great novels by leaving out the complexity of circumstances which go to make up the Negro experience and which alone go to make the obvious injustice bearable, than I would think of preparing myself to become President of the United States simply by studying Negro American history or confining myself to studying those laws affecting civil rights.

For it seems to me that one of the obligations I took on when I committed myself to the art and form of the novel was that of striving for the broadest range, the discovery and articulation of the most exalted values. And I must squeeze these from the life which I know best. (A highly truncated impression of that life I attempted to convey to you earlier.)

If all this sounds a bit heady, remember that I did not destroy that troublesome middle name of mine, I only suppressed it. Sometimes it reminds me of my obligations to the man who named me.

It is our fate as human beings always to give up some good things for other good things, to throw off certain bad circumstances only to create others. Thus there is a value for the writer in trying to give as thorough a report of social reality as possible. Only by doing so may we grasp and convey the cost of change. Only by considering the broadest accumulation·of data may we make choices that are based upon our own hard-earned sense of reality. Speaking from my own special area of American culture, I feel that to embrace uncritically values which are extended to us by others is to reject the validity, even the sacredness, of our own experience. It is also to forget that the small share of reality which each of our diverse groups is able to snatch from the whirling chaos of history belongs not to the group alone, but to all of us. It is a property and a witness which can be ignored only to the danger of the entire nation.

I could suppress the name of my namesake out of respect for the achievements of its original bearer but I cannot escape the obligation of attempting to achieve some of the things which he asked of the American writer. As Henry James suggested, being an American is an arduous task, and for most of us, I suspect, the difficulty begins with the name.

Address sponsored by the Gertrude Clarke Whittall Foundation, Library of Congress, January 6, 1964.

41. The Passionate Shepherd to His Love

CHRISTOPHER MARLOWE

Marlowe (1564–1593) was Shakespeare's exact contemporary but failed to live as long. Apparently he died of wounds received in a tavern brawl. He wrote poems and plays, the most famous of which is the tragedy *Dr. Faustus.*

Come live with me and be my love,
And we will all the pleasures prove
That valleys, groves, hills, and fields,
Woods, or steepy mountain yields.

And we will sit upon the rocks,
Seeing the shepherds feed their flocks,
By shallow rivers to whose falls
Melodious birds sings madrigals.

And I will make thee beds of roses
And a thousand fragrant posies,
A cap of flowers, and a kirtle
Embroidered all with leaves of myrtle.

A gown made of the finest wool
Which from our pretty lambs we pull;
Fair lined slippers for the cold,
With bucklets of the purest gold.

A belt of straw and ivy buds,
With coral clasps and amber studs;

And if these pleasures may thee move,
Come live with me, and be my love.

The shepherd swains shall dance and sing
For thy delight each May morning
If these delights thy mind may move,
Then live with me and be my love.

---

42. Answer to Marlowe

SIR WALTER RALEIGH

Raleigh (1552–1618) was a scholar, courtier, poet, and explorer. He rose to favor during the reign of Elizabeth I; he was supposed to have laid down his cloak over a muddy spot for the Queen to walk upon. He sailed to the New World, but was later arrested for treason, imprisoned, and died on the scaffold. While in prison, he wrote a world history and more verse.

If all the world and love were young,
And truth in every shepherd's tongue,
These pretty pleasures might me move
To live with thee and be thy love.

Time drives the flocks from field to fold,
When rivers rage and rocks grow cold,
And Philomel becometh dumb;
The rest complain of cares to come.

The flowers do fade, and wanton fields
To wayward winter reckoning yields;
A honey tongue, a heart of gall,
Is fancy's spring, but sorrow's fall.

Thy gowns, thy shoes, thy beds of roses,
Thy cap, thy kirtle, and thy posies

Soon break, soon wither, soon forgotten,
In folly ripe, in reason rotten.

Thy belt of straw and ivy buds,
Thy coral clasps and amber studs,
All these in me no means can move
To come to thee and be thy love.

But could you last and love still breed,
Had joys no date nor age no need,
Then these delights my mind might move
To live with thee and be thy love.

43. The Bait

JOHN DONNE

Donne (1572–1631), a churchman, was Dean of St. Paul's
in London. He was the greatest of the metaphysical poets
who wrote in the first part of the seventeenth century.
His poems, for the most part on themes of divine and
earthly love, were published posthumously in 1633.

Come live with me, and be my love,
And we will some new pleasures prove
Of golden sands, and crystal brooks:
With silken lines, and silver hooks.

There will the river whispering run
Warmed by thy eyes, more than the sun.
And there the enamored fish will stay,
Begging themselves they may betray.

When thou wilt swim in that live bath,
Each fish, which every channel hath,
Will amorously to thee swim,
Gladder to catch thee, than thou him.

If thou to be so seen be'st loath
By sun, or moon, thou dark'nest both,
And if myself have leave to see,
I need not their light, having thee.

Let others freeze with angling reeds,
And cut their legs with shells and weeds,
Or treacherously poor fish beset,
With strangling snare or windowy net:

Let coarse bold hands, from slimy nest
The bedded fish in banks out-wrest;
Or curious traitors, sleave-silk flies,
Bewitch poor fishes' wand'ring eyes.

For thee, thou need'st no such deceit,
For thou thyself art thine own bait;
That fish that is not catched thereby,
Alas, is wiser far than I.

---

44. Two Songs

C. DAY LEWIS

Cecil Day Lewis (1904–1972) was the Poet Laureate of
England when he died. His *Collected Poems* appeared in
1954. He wrote several mystery novels under the
pseudonym Nicholas Blake, and he also translated the
poetry of Vergil. During the thirties, he was considered a
Marxist poet, along with W. H. Auden and Stephen Spender,
and he was an active member of England's Communist
Party. But he quit the party later, and after World War II,
his Marxist fervor subsided.

I'VE HEARD THEM lilting at loom and belting,
Lasses lilting before dawn of day:
But now they are silent, not gamesome and gallant—
The flowers of the town are rotting away.

V. Exposition:
Cause and Effect

There was laughter and loving in the lanes at evening;
Handsome were the boys then, and girls were gay.
But lost in Flanders * by medalled commanders
The lads of the village are vanished away.

Cursed by the promise that takes our men from us—
All will be champion if you choose to obey:
They fight against hunger but still it is stronger—
The prime of our land grows cold as the clay.

The women are weary, once lilted so merry,
Waiting to marry for a year and a day:
From wooing and winning, from owning or earning
The flowers of the town are all turned away.

COME, LIVE WITH ME and be my love,
And we will all the pleasures prove
Of peace and plenty, bed and board,
That chance employment may afford.

I'll handle dainties on the docks
And thou shalt read of summer frocks:
At evening by the sour canals
We'll hope to hear some madrigals.

Care on the maiden brow shall put
A wreath of wrinkles, and thy foot
Be shod with pain: not silken dress
But toil shall tire thy loveliness.

Hunger shall make thy modest zone
And cheat fond death of all but bone—
If these delights thy mind may move,
Then live with me and be my love.

* Region in northern France and western Belgium, where many battles were fought in World War I.

45. To an Usherette

JOHN UPDIKE

Updike's (1932–   ) novels include *Rabbit, Run* (1960),
The Centaur, which won the National Book Award in 1964,
Couples (1968), *Bech, A Book* (1970), and *Rabbit Redux*
(1971). He contributes frequently to the *New Yorker,*
for which he was once a staff writer; he is also a poet and
an especially skillful writer of light verse. Born in
Pennsylvania, he went to Harvard and lives now near
Boston.

Ah come with me,
Petite chérie,
And we shall rather happy be.
I know a modest luncheonette
Where, for a little, one can get
A choplet, baby Lima beans,
And, segmented, two tangerines.

Le coup de grâce,
My petty lass,
Will be a demi-demitasse
Within a serviette conveyed
By weazened waiters, underpaid,
Who mincingly might grant us spoons
While a combo tinkles trivial tunes.

Ah with me come,
Ma faible femme,
And I shall say I love you some.

46. The Dispassionate Shepherdess

BABETTE DEUTSCH

Babette Deutsch (1895–   ) is a poet, scholar, and translator, and has also written criticism, fiction, and books for young people. A volume of her *Collected Poems* was published in 1969. Her *Poetry Handbook* is in its fourth edition. She is a member of The American Academy of Arts and Letters.

Do not live with me, do not be my love.
And yet I think we may some pleasures prove
That who enjoy each other, in the haste
Of their most inward kissing, seldom taste.

Being absent from me, you shall still delay
To come to me, and if another day,
No matter, so your greeting burn as though
The words had all the while been packed in snow.

No other gift you'll offer me but such
As I can neither wear, nor smell, nor touch—
No flowers breathing of evening, and no stones
Whose chilly fire outlasts our skeletons.

You'll give me once a thought that stings, and once
A look to make my blood doubt that it runs.
You'll give me rough and sharp perplexities,
And never, never will you give me ease.

For one another's blessing not designed,
Marked for possession only of the mind,
And soon, because such cherishing is brief,
To ask whereon was founded the belief

That there was anything at all uncommon
In what each felt for each as man and woman—
If this then be our case, if this our story,
Shall we rail at heaven? Shall we, at worst, be sorry?

Heaven's too deaf, we should grow hoarse with railing,
And sorrow never quickened what was failing.
But if you think we thus may pleasures prove,
Do not live with me, do not be my love.

Suggestions for Writing

1. Write an essay in which you consider the probable causes behind
some effect that you can see. You might write again about your home
town. Just why and how did it come to be just where and how it is?
Your university or the course of study you are following were
likewise "caused" by some complex of circumstances and ambitions
that you might examine.

2. Write an essay similar to the first, but this time examine the probable
causes of some particular circumstance in another person's life.
Why have things turned out as they have? This essay will demand
considerable tact and fairness.

3. By studying Ralph Ellison's essay, you might be encouraged to make
a similar analysis of your own life. What factors of your background
have come together to define some particular disposition or ambition
that you have? You need not envision yourself as a writer to make
an analysis comparable to his. Perhaps you can say what it is that
draws you toward science, to the social sciences, or to wish to
work with your hands.

4. Now write an essay that works in the other direction. Given some
condition as a cause, what effects will follow from it? Define the cause
as you understand it; then try to judge what its effects will be.
This is largely an exercise in prophecy. Perhaps you will want to keep
a copy of your paper in order to see how accurate your thinking
has been.

5. Write a short story based on one of the love songs in this group. Your
story might amplify one of those lyrics, following up on the
hypothetical relationship that one of the poets sets forth.

6. Write your own answer to Marlowe, or for that matter, to one of the
other poets.

VI.
Exposition

Problem
and Solution

PROBLEMS AND SOLUTIONS are as old as thought. When a man first looked at a rainbow with puzzled eyes, he set himself a problem. His early solution lasted long, as we shall see incidently in Woolley's essay, indeed until Newton analyzed the fracturing of light. A problem and its solution are simply a specific application of cause and effect, and, similarly, posing a problem and finding its solution provide a natural structure for an essay. You simply lay out for your reader the natural progress of your work. Such an essay can become a kind of narrative and move by the same compelling interest—curiosity.

The four essays in this section, widely different in subject, all move along paths of human curiosity. The authors themselves were curious. They began with a problem, tracked out a solution, and then laid before their readers the sequence of their experience. Woolley was curious about the Biblical Flood, and began to dig. Katz was perhaps more than curious. He faced the sudden problem of drugs on campus and began to dig for an answer among the students who sought his help. His solution is more speculative, more tentative; the problem is more complex. Gray, in a more leisurely way, looks into the whole problem of the white man's safari among the wildebeest and lions in the black man's new Africa. How should the new African nations govern the ecology of their unique inhabitants, man and beast? She finds her solution in a book. These writers all follow the path of *induction,* a leading into, or up to, an answer, fact by fact. It is a fundamental process of thoughtful discovery.

As you read these essays, check your curiosity, and the writer's skill in leading it on. You might try to outline the steps to solution in Woolley's work and in Gray's. See how the difference in the magnitude of the two problems affects solution and presentation. Notice too the effect of Katz's searching and his finding, at the end, the missing link to his earlier solutions. Swift's proposal is perhaps the most famous "solution" ever offered—before Hitler's horrible actuality. Swift's pattern is *deductive,* however, thus the reverse of the others, a distinction we will consider further in Section VIII. Swift's ironic exposition of his problem and solution has moved all the way to argument. And Cavafy's imaginative induction implies an equally powerful argumentative point behind "a kind of solution."

47. The Flood

SIR LEONARD WOOLLEY

Sir Charles Leonard Woolley (1880–1960), distinguished for excavating Ur and outlining Sumerian culture (which included sacrificing masses of servants), served in the British army during both World Wars, ending as lieutenant colonel. He was a Turkish prisoner (1916–1918). Among his many books is *The Wilderness of Zin* (1936), written with T. E. Lawrence ("Lawrence of Arabia").

THERE CAN BE few stories more familiar to us than that of the Flood. The word 'antediluvian' has passed into common speech, and Noah's Ark is still one of the favourite toys of the children's nursery.

The Book of Genesis tells us how the wickedness of man was such that God repented Him that He had made man upon the earth, and decided to destroy all flesh; but Noah, being the one righteous man, found grace in the eyes of the Lord. So Noah was bidden by God to build an ark, and in due time he and all his family went in, with all the beasts and the fowls of the air, going in two by two; and the doors of the ark were shut and the rain was upon the earth for forty days and forty nights, and the floods prevailed exceedingly and the earth was covered, and all flesh that moved upon the earth died, and Noah only remained alive and they that were with him in the ark. And then the floods abated. Noah sent out a raven and a dove, and at last the dove brought him back an olive leaf, proof that the dry land had appeared. And they all went forth out of the ark, and Noah built an altar and offered sacrifice, and the Lord smelt a sweet savour and promised that never again would He smite everything living, as He had done; and God set His bow in the clouds as a token of the covenant that there should not any more be a flood to destroy the earth.

For many centuries, indeed until only a few generations ago, the story of Noah was accepted as an historical fact; it was part of the Bible, it was the inspired Word of God, and therefore every word of it must be true. To deny the story was to deny the Christian faith.

Then two things happened. On the one hand scholars, examining the Hebrew text of Genesis, discovered that it was a composite narrative. There had been two versions of the Flood story which differed in certain small respects, and these two had been skilfully combined into one by the Jewish scribes four or five hundred years before the time of Christ, when they edited the sacred books of their people and gave to them the form which they have to-day. That discovery shook the faith of many old-fashioned believers, or was indignantly denied by them; they said that it was an attack on the Divine Word. Really, of course, it was nothing of the sort. Genesis is an historical book, and the writer of history does not weave the matter out of his imagination; he consults older authorities of every sort and quotes them as freely and as often as may be. The older the authorities are, and the more his account embodies theirs, the more reason we have to trust what he writes; if it be insisted that his writings are divinely inspired, the answer is that 'inspiration' consists not in dispensing with original sources but in making the right use of them. The alarm felt by the orthodox when confronted with the discoveries of scholarship was a false alarm.

The second shock came when from the ruins of the ancient cities of Mesopotamia archaeologists unearthed clay tablets on which was written another version of the Flood story—the Sumerian version. According to that, mankind had grown wicked and the gods in council decided to destroy the human race which they had made. But one of the gods happened to be a good friend of one mortal man, so he went down and warned him of what was to happen and counselled him to build an ark. And the man did so; and he took on board all his family, and his domestic animals, and shut the door, and the rain fell and the floods rose and covered all the earth. At last the storms abated and the ark ran aground, and the man sent out a dove and a swallow and a raven, and finally came forth from the ark and built an altar and did sacrifice, and the gods (who had had no food since the Flood started and were terribly hungry) 'came round the altar like flies', and the rainbow is set in the clouds as a warrant that never again will the gods destroy all men by water.

It is clear that this is the same story as we have in Genesis. But the Sumerian account was actually written before the time of Moses (whom some people had, without reason, thought to be the author of Genesis), and not only that, but before the time of Abraham. Therefore the Flood story was not by origin a Hebrew story at all but had been taken over by the Hebrews from the idolatrous folk of Babylonia; it was a pagan legend, so why should we for a moment suppose that it was true? All sorts of attempts were made to show that the Bible story was independent, or was the older of the two, but all the attempts were in vain, and to some it seemed as if the battle for the Old Testament had been lost.

Once more, it was a false alarm. Nobody had ever supposed that the Flood had affected only the Hebrew people; other people had suffered by it, and a disaster of such magnitude was bound to be remembered in their traditions; in so far as the Sumerian legend was closer in time to the event, it might be said to strengthen rather than to weaken the case for the Biblical version. But it could well be asked, 'Why should we believe a Sumerian legend which is, on the face of it, a fantastic piece of pagan mythology?' It is perfectly true that the Sumerian Flood story is a religious poem. It reflects the religious beliefs of a pagan people just as the biblical story reflects the religious beliefs of the Hebrews; and we cannot accept the Sumerian religion as true. Also, it is a poem, and everybody knows what poets are! Shakespeare certainly did:

> The poet's eye, in a fine frenzy rolling,
> Doth glance from heaven to earth, from earth to heaven,
> And, as imagination bodies forth
> The forms of things unknown, the poet's pen
> Turns them to shapes, and gives to airy nothing
> A local habitation and a name.

But the legend does not stand alone. Sober Sumerian historians wrote down a sort of skeleton of their country's history in the form of a list of its kings (like our 'William I, 1066', and all that); starting at the very beginning there is a series of perhaps fabulous rulers, and, they say, 'Then came the Flood. And after the Flood kingship again descended from heaven'; and they speak of a dynasty of kings who established themselves in the city of Kish, and next of a dynasty whose capital was Erech. Here, at least, we are upon historic ground, for archaeological excavation in modern times has recovered the material civilisation of those ancient days when Erech was indeed the chief city of Mesopotamia. The old historians were sure that not long before these days the course of their country's history had been interrupted by a great flood. If they were right, it does not, of course, mean that the Flood legend is correct in all its details, but it does at least give it a basis of fact.

In the year 1929, when we had been digging at Ur the famous 'royal graves' with their extraordinary treasures, which can be dated to something like 2800 B.C., I determined to test still lower levels so as to get an idea of what might be found by digging yet deeper. We sank a small shaft below the stratum of soil in which the graves lay, and went down through the mixed rubbish that is characteristic of an old inhabited site—a mixture of decomposed mud-brick, ashes and broken pottery, very much like what we had been finding higher up. Then suddenly it all stopped: there were no more potsherds, no ashes, only clean, water-laid mud, and the workman in the shaft told me that he had reached virgin soil; there was nothing more to be found, and he had better go elsewhere.

VI. Exposition:
Problem and Solution

I got down and looked at the evidence and agreed with him; but then I took my levels and found that 'virgin soil' was not nearly as deep down as I expected. That upset a favourite theory of mine, and I hate having my theories upset except on the very best of evidence, so I told him to get back and go on digging. Most unwillingly he did so, turning up nothing but clean soil that contained no sign of human activity; he worked down through eight feet of it and then, suddenly, flint implements appeared and sherds of painted pottery which, we were fairly sure, was the earliest pottery made in southern Mesopotamia. I was convinced of what it meant, but I wanted to see whether others would arrive at the same conclusion. I brought up two of my staff and, after pointing out the facts, asked for their conclusions. They did not know what to say. My wife came along and looked and was asked the same question, and she turned away, remarking quite casually, 'Well, of course, it's the Flood.'

So it was. But one could scarcely argue for the Deluge on the strength of a shaft a yard square; so the next season I marked out on the low ground where the graves had been a rectangle some seventy-five feet by sixty, and there dug a huge pit which went down, in the end, for sixty-four feet. The level at which we started had been the ground surface about 2600 B.C. Almost immediately we came on the ruins of houses slightly older than that; we cleared them away and found more houses below them. In the first twenty feet we dug through no fewer than eight sets of houses, each of which had been built over the ruins of the age before. Then the house ruins stopped and we were digging through a solid mass of potsherds wherein, at different levels, were the kilns in which the pots had been fired; the sherds represented those pots which went wrong in the firing and, having no commercial value, had been smashed by the potter and the bits left lying until they were so heaped up that the kilns were buried and new kilns had to be built. It was a vase factory which was running for so long a time that by the stratified sherds we could trace the course of history: near the bottom came the wares in use when Erech was the royal city, and at the very bottom was the painted ware of the land's earliest immigrants. And then came the clean, water-laid mud, eleven feet of it, mud which on analysis proved to be the silt brought down by the River Euphrates from its upper reaches hundreds of miles away; and under the silt, based on what really was virgin soil, the ruins of the houses that had been overwhelmed by the flood and buried deep beneath the mud carried by its waters.

This was the evidence we needed; a flood of a magnitude unparalleled in any later phase of Mesopotamian history; and since, as the pottery proved, it had taken place some little while before the time of the Erech dynasty, this was the Flood of the Sumerian king-lists and that of the Sumerian legend and that of Genesis.

We have proved that the Flood really happened; but that does not mean that all the details of the Flood legend are true—we did not find Noah and we did not find his ark! But take a few details. The Sumerian version says (this is not mentioned in Genesis) that antediluvian man lived in huts made of reeds; under the Flood deposit we found the wreckage of reed huts. Noah built his ark of light wood and bitumen. Just on top of the Flood deposit we found a big lump of bitumen, bearing the imprint of the basket in which it had been carried, just as I have myself seen the crude bitumen from the pits of Hit on the middle Euphrates being put in baskets for export downstream. I reckoned that to throw up an eleven-foot pile of silt against the mound on which the primitive town of Ur stood the water would have to be at least twenty-five feet deep; the account in Genesis says that the depth of the flood water was fifteen cubits, which is roughly twenty-six feet. 'Twenty-six feet?' you may say; 'that's not much of a flood!' Lower Mesopotamia is so flat and low-lying that a flood having that depth at Ur would spread over an area 300 miles long and 100 miles wide.

Noah's Flood was not a universal deluge; it was a vast flood in the valley of the Rivers Tigris and Euphrates. It drowned the whole of the habitable land between the eastern and the western deserts; for the people who lived there that was all the world. It wiped out the villages and exterminated their inhabitants, and although some of the towns set upon mounds survived, it was but a scanty and dispirited remnant of the nation that watched the waters recede at last. No wonder that they saw in this disaster the gods' punishment of a sinful generation and described it as such in a great religious poem; and if, as may well have been the case, one household managed to escape by boat from the drowned lowlands, the head of that house would naturally be made the hero of the saga.

48. The Use of Drugs in America: Toward a Better Understanding of Passivity

ALAN S. KATZ

Dr. Katz, a practicing psychiatrist, was formerly chief psychiatrist at Brown University's Student Health Service.

WHEN WE AT Boston University's Mental Health Clinic were first confronted, five years ago, with the new drug scene we knew very little about it and all pharmacology books were of little help beyond the chemical analysis which they offered. Although we were well-trained psychiatrists, drugs other than for therapeutic purposes were not part of our training. Drugs had for the most part been a ghetto problem and thus neglected and the very hard-core users were being treated in isolated government hospitals, and the results were worse than a dismal failure. But we were trained in the psychoanalytic model so we knew that we could learn, that we could see with sufficient experience how and in what way drugs affected personality, if at all.

And we talked and we listened in fine detail to a mob of new users who were as ignorant about the drugs as we were but who were demonstrating every kind of personality disturbance that we had ever seen. It was really quite frightening to us for at that time we also had very little knowledge of what pharmaceutic medications were specifically effective to combat the side effects. We did a lot of learning by trial and error. In fact our first task was to use our basic skills and to enlarge our understanding as rapidly as possible. This was incredibly difficult because of the panic that was being caused. At the same time the basic wish of the University was to deny that there was such a problem; it was a kind of philosophy which was universally typical, i.e., don't talk about it and it will go away. However, we were quickly able to show the importance of the problem to the administration of Boston University and received its full support to bring the problem out into the open and to deal with it.

Five years ago is now old hat, but for purposes of methodology it has to be reviewed. We saw kids (I call them kids for they are mostly late adolescents) who seemed little affected, but we also saw others who were overtly psychotic. It was almost impossible to distinguish between them and others who were having typical acute schizophrenic episodes. We were beginning to get the vibrations from the media and the law-enforcement agencies, which enhanced the paranoia of the users. Words like *addict, fiend, maniac, degenerate,* and *communist* were being bandied around. Finally there was the increasing panic within the university community. Wild suggestions were made by some that we ought to have them all arrested. I sarcastically replied that our enrollment could be diminished by ninety percent. We continued working intensely with drug users and we conducted a seemingly endless series of teach-ins with students to learn what they had to say and to share with them our rapidly accumulating knowledge. We also were beginning to distinguish between drug use and drug abuse.

Within a year we had a treatment model which was working effectively. The classical psychoanalytic and theoretical formulations were essentially correct but needed expansion, and this we felt was verified by the outstanding success of the treatment model. The Mental Health Unit worked closely with patients seen in private practice two to three times a week for two to three years. This provided a lot of detail to the uncompleted puzzle.

Our findings represent some 2,000 patient cases. The actual number sent was much greater than that, and it represents some 750 treated from onset to discharge. The treatment time was as short as six sessions and as long as three years. This paper is essentially about drug abuse, that is, where the pathology is manifest. This allows for drug use, which can have its proper social and in fact therapeutic value. The populations we studied were different. They were:

1) Those students seeking psychiatric help who *also* used drugs very occasionally and where the drug seemed of no significance. This has a subcategory; namely, where the drug use looked as though it might become significant.

2) Those students who were abusing drugs, that is, were using them copiously and in many forms, and where there was marked evidence of personality alteration but without signs of psychosis.

3) Those students using drugs who were prepsychotic, i.e., showing signs of confusion or the beginnings of thought disorder, or who were already psychotic, i.e., hallucinating, with gross failure in reality testing, loss of abstraction, and the other signs of psychosis.

4) The fourth group was not in treatment, but constituted over four years of about 10,000 students meeting in groups of all sizes from 15 to 600 at once to rap about drugs and all other issues which seemed relevant to late adolescence, such as sex and freedom, etc. This allowed

us to come into contact with a fairly substantial number of students who were dealing with life well or fairly well, who either did not need or had not sought professional help. This was the closest to a random population to offset the idea that we were only seeing kids who were "upset." Incidentally, there was never one meeting where I was not approached afterwards by one or more students who asked how they could get our help. We attribute this to the fact that they saw that we were on the level, that we were not working for the FBI, and above all, and I cannot emphasize this sufficiently, that our Mental Health Unit held and upheld total, absolute confidentiality as an inviolable principle. This is one of the unfortunate by-products of law enforcement: conflicted people involved in illegal activity are afraid to seek help.

What did all of this teach us? We learned that no matter what drug was used, if it was being used for other than occasional social-fun purposes (and strangely enough, this includes heroin, for heroin is used also for social purposes), it was being used to ward off or deal with tension, anxiety, and depression. And we learned what had been theoretically formulated in classical psychiatric literature: that we were dealing with a specific personality type. In psychiatry we call this the passive dependent personality. Conversely we also found that the passive dependent personality types whom we were seeing for non-drug reasons, those of the first subcategory, were tending to become more involved with drugs as their underlying anxieties started to come out in the course of therapy and sought relief by turning on in order to turn off: for us this development again was a validation.

There is to my mind, a view I share with almost every colleague I know, no greater jungle of confusion than psychiatric diagnosis, not only because of the abstractness, the differences in clinical training and skills, but also because the psychiatric label changes as the personality changes. Similarly there are few more threatening ideas than that of passivity, because passivity implies *vulnerability, helplessness,* and *dependence* on others. To tell an adolescent that he is passive is to send him up a wall. It is a major insult to his mind. But we have learned, as had others long ago, that one can protest very loudly about "give me my freedom," but if you listen closely there is frequently another little voice that is saying very firmly *"don't you dare."* This is a normal process in adolescence. But it becomes pathologic in drug abuse, I repeat, *abuse* not just *drug use.*

By "passive dependent" we were and are referring specifically to unresolved wishes to remain in a child-like dependent status despite the protestations to the contrary. This wish to remain passive ultimately has to do with anxiety about separation from the nurturing parent. It is crucial to understand the meaning of the patient's passivity.

The law of conservation of experience cannot be thwarted or surpassed by any stretch of the imagination, by therapist or patient. To treat as reality the illusion that one can discard any part of one's experience is foolishness in its most flagrant form. So the student generates anxiety within himself, assuming tacitly that growth will occur by exclusion rather than by acquisition, that one becomes an adult by putting away or discarding childish styles or ways. In reality, growth occurs from within, wherein the entire being grows but where previous ambivalent, ambiguous experiences are retained. Regression, or return to earlier styles of behavioral transactions with the world, figures so prominently in the drug abuser. When adolescents return home on vacation, they begin to bicker, argue, and squabble after a day or so of blissful reunion. This is regression. The more basic truth of passivity is its *healthy intent,* to resist *any advance* which would ignore the important, unsettled, unsatisfied blocks of experience. Passivity may be seen as a self-preserving effort. It has to be seen in terms of its usefulness of value rather than condemned wholesale. The intense threat is that passivity thrusts an individual back to or maintains a position of vulnerability linked to a sense of helplessness. The psychiatrist often becomes angry with the patient, labeling him as "passive aggressive," thereby seeing the passivity as a form of hostility, whereas more often than not in the passive dependent person it is his major defense for survival. That is, the patient in *being ill is not being bad.* The pertinence of these dynamics is crucial in giving direction towards an encompassing understanding of the patient, so that the goal becomes that of accepting the presence of the passivity rather than the rejecting of it. This allows the patient to be released from the stranglehold of his own passivity.

As I stated before, such growth ultimately has to do with the separation from the nurturing parent. The whole process begins in infancy, when the really helpless infant through the sound, smell, taste, and touch of the nurturing mother takes into himself and into his very primitive, undifferentiated psyche, or "mind," things from the outside. It is the process by which the infant learns to recognize and remember the outside. For example, when a newborn is hungry he experiences pain, which is relieved by something put into his mouth, and frequently; in the process of feeding he is touched, and fondled, and cooed to.

Some months later the newborn, who is now an infant, has learned that his mother, who is in another room, will come to him if he cries. The amazing thing that has happened is that now he has an image of mother in his head, even though she is not present in the room. Then we begin to see the smiles of recognition. The infant begins to distinguish between different people, different sounds, different smells, and different voices. Slowly all the representations of the outside world, the family, the siblings, the teachers, the society, religion are taken and stored in the unconscious, which is the total memory bank. And they are stored as they are experienced, both good and bad, happy and unhappy. Just as the child develops a sense of I, as separate from you, he must later through a whole series of tasks requiring mastery selectively learn to function independently. When the early development fosters tremendous dependency and does not allow for independent exploration, error making, and correction, when all tensions are relieved by the parent, the child holds on very intensely to the total parent, whose image he has stored in his mind. To grow, to find his own style, to achieve his own goals and destiny, he must selectively give up parts of the parental image. This is the normal process of adolescence which allows the young adult to have a profound sense of self. If this psychological separation *does not occur,* he remains dependent on his parent. The problem arises when the adolescent fights his own dependent wishes towards the parents who are so firmly entrenched in his own head, even though they may be as far away as 10,000 miles, or even dead. This concept explains the bickering in adolescence, the fighting of "I want"—"no you can't". It is shadow boxing of a kind. The problem is greatly intensified when the parents remain over-protective at a time when the child, now adolescent, should be learning to accomplish on his own. He is searching for independence but he is bound up within himself, fighting his being dependent on the image and the values of the parent in his own mind. So he is constantly expending enormous energy in a battle with those parents. He has not found his own identity, he regresses—he goes backwards under tension. He has not been given the permission to grow up and be different, nor has he utilized it when it was given. So his goal becomes to distinguish himself from his parents by being against them. He denies the meaningfulness of the values of the "straight society" but not selectively. He expresses profound disappointment in his family and this is expanded to include the large family of man. By contrast, the healthier adolescent who has not held on so tenaciously to the parental image, or who has not been held onto so tenaciously, does not feel the perpetual need for battle of dependency-independency. He finds gratification and creative goals to his own liking, to his own talents and style, and has the energy to achieve them. For him being different is not the only way of being free. The implications of this go beyond the drug scene, where origins of rebellion come, not out of ideology and idealism, but out of personal problems.

A second characteristic we found in drug abusers was a withdrawal into the self, and the greater the drug abuse, the greater the withdrawal. Withdrawal means less communication with a varied society, much time spent in reflection which does not imply productive thought but feelings of alienation, and paranoia. As there is usually an increased gap between child and family, and between the student and other peers who have not withdrawn, there is an increased need to huddle together into what we call brotherhoods, which in the last analysis are substitute families, characterized by their permissiveness, the capacity to get close physically, which is warded off in adult children towards their parents, and by the feeling of belonging without restriction and especially belonging without real commitment—commitment to another seen as an equal and not as a parent substitute. In some places these are known as communes. This is not to disparage all communes, for some have very constructive aims, but these brotherhoods can exist in the form of several people living in one room, or in a house, or in a bus, or in a reconverted hearse, or just a group that is always together.

A third characteristic found in virtually all of the patients was a state of clinical depression, with feelings of worthlessness, of loss, of sadness, and an attempt to alleviate these symptoms with various drugs. The heroin user is the extreme example. Although the patient may not recognize this state of depression, *it is always there* to the clinical eye. Some can acknowledge this feeling, for others it is an intriguing and captivating idea worth looking at. In any event, way down deep he knows that he is depressed. He describes his depression in simplistic terms of being "down on the family," "down on society," without greater elaboration. He seems to have achieved liberation from home and is eager to experience, to move, to realize, and to become. Suddenly the adolescent finds that it is lonely out there, and he comes against the unpleasant recognition that life has blockades to plans, disappointments for aspirations, a diminution of importance for aspirations, a diminution of importance and of relevance in an active crowd around him. Here the therapist is presented with the opportunity to exert his most valuable asset: his compassion, his more mature, accepting, *unalarmed* empathic attitude toward all that the human experience includes. To recognize the depression is of enormous value, for it offers the passive depressed patient an avenue of freedom towards seeing himself more realistically. The depressive crisis is not a breakdown, but rather a breakup of insufficient, antiquated ways of dealing with problems in contemporary society. It is never the aim of therapy to reduce the student to anonymity in the crowd. The abuser becomes anonymous. The student is uneradicably singular, his uniqueness is the focus of recognition. To fracture or dismantle the narcissism of the late adolescence is a cruel injustice. The promise of individualism is infinitely more potent than a substitute dependency. That is, "I will help you, but I won't do it for you." The therapy becomes the implementation of these ideas.

These were the basic ideas that we formulated to develop our treatment program. The exception to this program is the heroin user who has a particularly severe psychological deterioration and who has very special needs. But we are convinced that many of them can be helped as well, but by other techniques. The only time in our treatment program that a patient was instructed to stop using drugs was when he was prepsychotic, psychotic, or experiencing flashes. Flashing is a particular phenomenon which occurs in some individuals wherein they experience a drug trip spontaneously without having just taken the drug. There is also a cross-over phenomenon: for example, a person smoking some pot might re-experience a past LSD trip. To our minds, this is a warning sign of an impending psychotic episode if the drugs are continued.

Very briefly, the four steps to the treatment method are:

1) Make an alliance with the patient to look at the problem, don't moralize, don't probe too deeply or the patient will run from treatment.

2) Search for the underlying clinical depression and get the patient involved with this.

3) Clarify the parental relations, not with the goal of breaking up the family, but rather to help the family to grow up, to become adults with one another. This idea has to be frequently reiterated because if the dependent person hears the statement as a threat of breakup, it would mean that there will be no one to depend on.

4) Help the patient to leave the brotherhood, to get re-established with a varied society. This is the most hazardous part of the model.

Incidentally, at this point, without much or any coaxing, the drug user is in the process of voluntarily stopping. The therapist clearly sees the need to give up the drug, but the patient, though he may understand the reason, is magically bound to it. What is rational and logical is unimportant. His sense of control predominates. The passivity has its stranglehold and the patient seems not to be able to budge, for there is still something unaccomplished. With the knowledge that the patient is no longer getting the same pleasure or kind of kicks he once got from drugs, but that he is still clinging to them and their uses as an unenjoyable form of ritual, the therapist then begins to investigate the fear of no longer belonging to the peer group, which is the drug group that makes up the brotherhood. This allows the ritual to become unravelled so that the passivity loses its power. Attention is paid especially to the one, two, or three friends with whom the patient is particularly close, with whom he takes his trips. After all, they belong to the brotherhood and he can believe in the brotherhood because for him it represents the tension-free new kind of adulthood which is better than his parents' adulthood. He is terribly afraid of leaving his friends for he figures that he cannot stand on his own. He is faced with a real dilemma, for although the brotherhood no longer serves the purpose it once did, he had shared in it—in essence he had a sense of existence and meaning in it. His friends as well are threatened if he leaves them, and we see they exert a subtle and sometimes more blatant pressure on him not to believe the "shrink" so that the group will not be diminished. Separating from the brotherhood generally opens a whole vista of ideas concerning the dread of being in a neutral state, of giving up one's only friends, and one's feeling of inadequacy and fear upon entering the "straight society."

Such crises are all derivatives of the task of separation from mother and father; they are the issues of the passivity that has been unresolved but which can now be dealt with, and they are among the reasons that have led to the initial drug use. The exploration of being alone and ultimately confronting one's wishes to be dependent permit the patient to slowly take up the role required for adulthood. It is much like learning to walk. The job of the therapist is, as always, to assist in unstopping the natural growth process, so it may proceed. The new task is a big one, but it is the task which was earlier thwarted: dealing with anxiety and the achievement of goals pleasing to the self. The person is wobbly but there is a mass of energy available for *doing* rather than for just *being*.

But the matter becomes further complicated, and I hope what ensues from these ideas is an original contribution to psychiatric literature. During these years of work at the Mental Health Unit, we observed that there was a very distorted idea of what it meant to be aggressive: that competitiveness, striving, and mastery in some manner had become linked up with some destruction, that is: to compete with someone is to destroy the competitor, to achieve is to kill. In some way I came to realize that this concept was inextricably related to drug passivity. In fact, all through this work something had been missing, some factor had been overlooked which was crucial to tying things together. About two years ago it began to make sense and it was very exciting to the scientist-researcher part of me. Small but vital clues had been overlooked in a maze of accumulated data which took on significance only after my working in very intensive therapy with some patients. Obviously I had not heard all things at all times, but I began to hear material that stuck out like a sore thumb, material which I could interpret as meaning "if I take drugs I won't feel so aggressive." The therapist was having an insight. I had often wondered what was at the core of the love movement with the hippies. The hippies and the students whom I have seen and who have used LSD in the largest quantities (such as over 200 times) were in fact the most passive, nondestructive, turned-off group of all drug abusers. Their regression has the most intense infantile character: the wish to be fed, to be protected, and to be carefree. Why had I not thought of this before, because it is classic that one of the aspects of being passive is to ward off being hurt, as I've explained, but also to control the fear of hurting. So I began to review cases and there it clearly was, hundreds of times: "If my parents took drugs, they wouldn't want war." "If you took drugs, you'd understand peace." "If you took drugs, you'd see that straight people kill." "When I take drugs, I love everyone." "Man, with drugs you don't have to hassle." "Man, I don't want to hurt anyone" and so forth. The connection between taking drugs and aggressive feeling—to deal with the latter—is now blatantly clear.

I profoundly believe that aside from the social-peer purposes, aside from defying the law, aside from the fantasy of warding off depression, tension, and anxiety, the most significant unconscious, unresolved factor in passivity is to ward off the killer in oneself; that is to say, there is a tremendous rage inside, a complicated kind of rage directed at the self, at the figures on whom one is dependent, at the incapacity to bridge the gap between the age groups, a rage at the inequities in society, at the double standards of law and civil rights, against the killer instinct which is cultivated and released by war, at the frustration of not being heard, at the idea competition is war, that achievement is destructive. The drug abuser does not have the freedom to deal with these issues; he is a be-er rather than a doer. He is not a free activist, involved in a creative ideology, in idealism which demands stamina and energy. Instead I contend that he is a very dependent person who is very angry inside, who, ironically, becomes even more passive, more dependent, less aggressive, less striving, and remarkably more depressed. And whenever there is depression there is rage. So I am stating in conclusion that the use of drugs by the abuser is intended to deal with and put down his rage, over which he has poor control, the use of drugs is to do away with the killer. So he maintains and accentuates his passivity through the drugs, drugs make him more passive, and the rage is put down. Thus we have gone the full circle.

49. On Safari

FRANCINE du PLESSIX GRAY

Mrs. Gray came from Paris to the United States as a child at the start of World War II. She studied at Bryn Mawr and Barnard, earning an A.B. in philosophy and the Putnam Creative Writing Award. She has been a reporter for the United Press and several French magazines, has published stories and articles in the *New Yorker*, *Mademoiselle*, *Vogue*, and others. She has covered the New Left for the *New York Review of Books* and the *New Yorker*, from which emerged her *Divine Disobedience: Profiles in Catholic Radicalism* (1970). Her *Hawaii: The Sugar-Coated Fortress* appeared in 1972. She lives in

Warren, Connecticut, with her husband, the painter
Cleve Gray, and two young sons.

I

TEN YEARS AFTER Kenya's independence, the main bar of
Nairobi's venerable Norfolk Hotel is still called the Delamere
Room, after Kenya's legendary settler, and is decorated with the
mounted heads of His Lordship's trophies. An eager hunter thrice
mauled by lions, Lord Delamere used to ride through the streets of
Nairobi shooting out the lights of streetlamps with a pistol. He once
bought a hotel for the sole purpose of staging window-smashing contests
in it, using oranges as ammunition. What a good sport, his fellow settlers
said, he bought the hotel first.

Another settler, Major Grogan, walked all the way from Capetown
to Cairo to win his bride. Once married and settled near Nairobi, he
held a public flogging of three African rickshaw boys on the ground
that they had insulted some European ladies "by holding the vehicle's
arms up too high." Grogan was one of twenty children. Traveling
through Kenya, one repeatedly hears that its earliest English colonials,
who came before World War I, were the younger sons of small landed
gentry with large families, the kind of men who in previous years had
to settle for modest regiments and parsonages. Were their eccentricities
forged in the injustice of the nursery, by that dearth of attention which
is often a Benjamin's lot?

Lord Delamere, the largest landowner in Kenya, acquired 350,000
acres; plantations considered adequate contained thirty or forty thousand. Under Jomo Kenyatta's capitalistic, conciliatory leadership, Europeans might to this day have kept most of their land if Kenya's future
had been more predictable.

ON THE TERRACE of the Norfolk Hotel, in front of the Delamere
Room, there stands in desultory splendor a large black lacquered rickshaw. Its story was told to me the morning I arrived in Nairobi by one
of the two Big White Hunters who were about to guide us—a party
of family and friends—on a photographic safari of East African wildlife.

"In the old days in Kenya," our guide says, pronouncing it *Kee*-nya,
"there was this lovely old bloke who used to keep a sweet tame lion
on his lap when he went riding in that rickshaw. When the rickshaw
boy pulled too slowly he would tickle the lion's throat, the lion would
roar, and the boy-ee would truly hurry up. Ha ha!"

The hunter guffaws mightily, slapping his great naked thigh, ruddy
and muscled below his khaki safari shorts. He is a hulking, blond,
frenetically jovial Englishman in his middle forties, who came out with

the British army at Emergency time to quell the Mau Mau rebellion
and stayed on in Kenya to hunt big game, marrying into an old white
settler family of Major Grogan's circle. His family's land in Surrey was
bequeathed to an older brother. His father had also been an army man,
a colonel in India's Gurka regiment. We sit over Pimm's Cups alongside the rickshaw on the Norfolk Hotel terrace, going over the schedule
of our forthcoming journey.

A portrait of Kenyatta stares down at us with an inscrutable, shrewd
gaze. Our guide has driven us in from the airport past thoroughfares
named after many revolutionary African leaders: Sékou Touré,
Nkrumah, Lumumba, Nyerere. In the large colonial dining room next to
the Delamere Room is spread out a buffet more elaborate than any I
have seen in the States in some decades, comparable perhaps to Sunday
lunches at the Newport Country Club in the 1950s. Africans in red and
white livery hover over hams, turkeys, fish in aspic, innumerable salads,
and a dozen curries set alongside a battalion of puddings that includes
some ten varieties of trifle. A few blocks away, in the vicinity of Independence Avenue, more than sixty safari firms are in business to serve
the quarter of a million tourists flocking yearly to Kenya to gape at the
animals of the Pleistocene Age. Throughout Nairobi, in bars closed to
non-Caucasians until a decade ago, old-time British settlers sip their
pink gins and curse the proliferation of African bus drivers in the game
reserves. One comes here not for revolution any more, but for nostalgia.

An impulse to restore innocence on the planet we have despoiled, a
fantasy of returning to some nonviolent state of nature. All this strikes
me as pertinent to the current stampede toward East Africa, and to our
predilection for building safari parks in London, Florida, and New Jersey. The peaceable kingdom of Adam and Eve in Eden—Milton put it
this way:

> About them frisking play'd
> All Beasts of th' Earth, since wild. . . .
> Sporting the Lion ramp'd, and in his paw
> Dandl'd the Kid; Bears, Tygers, Ounces, Pards
> Gambold before them. . . .

Sweet lion out there, six yards from my minibus, we are friends
again! Few men hunt you any more save some Texans willing to pay
a thousand dollars a trophy, we have come to Kenya just to look at
you. Dear giraffe, it is your thick-lashed eyes that best answer our
longing for innocence, taking us back to that prehistoric purity we search
for. You stare back with a gaze of metaphysical surprise which seems
to ask all men: How did you reverse the clock of history? I have been
here for forty million years. Are *you* for real, or a joke?

Six A.M., WANING DARKNESS, at the Masai Mara Game Reserve where
we camp on our first day out of Nairobi. The zipper of my tent is

brusquely opened, the ripping sound tears violently through my sleep. A Kikuyu safari boy, his ear lobe elegantly looped through a hole in his upper ear, brings a kerosene lamp into my tent. "*Jambo Mensahib*," he booms cheerfully, "*chai, mensahib.*" He puts down a pot of very black tea flanked by large canisters of milk and sugar, and disappears with that faint salaaming gesture that the Arabs have bequeathed to East Africa.

Dawn is the most beautiful time in Africa, providing that glimpse into the world's morning which we have traveled to recapture. One is plunged into a euphoria of cleanliness. The grass itself smells more sweet than a tropical blossom. The trill of the palm weaver bird sounds like spring water gurgling from a narrow-necked jar. Even the dewy hyena loping under the flat-topped acacia trees looks pristinely fresh-coated. I am in an appropriately trancelike state, having slept lightly, woken repeatedly by the distant groan of a lion or the hurried panting of a leopard, and hoping always to hear the subtle sound of the elephants, creatures so soft-footed that they can walk through camp emitting no noise other than the faint rumbling of their digestive tracts.

OUR GUIDES—whom I shall call Big Hunter and Young Hunter—herd us into the Land Rover for our early morning viewing of the game. Big Hunter is perpetually in a state of exuberant cheer, and commences his voluminous commentary on the animals in the same clipped, booming tones in which he trained the Kenya Rifles. "Lovely bushbuck over there, three o'clock of where the zebra is spending a penny . . . look at that splendid ely, five legs and all that . . . we're going to circle the river bed and look for some more mating lion, the old dears put on quite a show yesterday. . . ." When he is not driving, lecturing us, or diligently organizing camp, our guide concentrates on living up to the myth of the Big White Hunter, which dictates that he be a proficient raconteur and Don Juan, besides being a great shot and an impeccable naturalist. (Hemingway, "The Short Happy Life of Francis Macomber": "Robert Wilson carried a double-sized cot on safari.")

He regales us with a repertory of hair-raising tales that all end with the phrase "And that chap *lived on* to tell the tale!" He boasts of his military expeditions against the Mau Mau, which sound curiously hedonistic and sporting. Being the British army's top star on the East African rugby team, he was picked up in the Aberdare Mountains every Friday by a patrol truck so that he could take part in the weekend games in Nairobi, then on Sunday afternoon he was returned to his command post in guerrilla country. Alternately his wife and his girlfriend accompany him throughout our trip. The women are remarkably civil to each other at their moments of encounter, as if machismo in the bush were part of the safari package, like the assurance of seeing elephants in erection.

VI. Exposition:
Problem and Solution

Young Hunter, our other guide, is a slender, blond athlete in his early twenties whose grandparents settled in the Kenya farmlands in 1911. His family still owns 27,000 acres at the foot of Mount Kenya. There is a strange bitterness about this spoiled and gifted youth who looks as if he had never endured misfortune. He expresses in an extreme form the white settlers' fears for their future after Kenyatta's death. For although our guides regard Kenyatta as "the leader of the Mau Mau" (displaying an astonishing ignorance of their own history), they also look upon him as a man totally reformed by jail, "the greatest African leader, a splendid bloke who's been frightfully decent to the Europeans."

"What will happen when Kenyatta dies and we all get thrown out?" Young Hunter murmurs to me every few days in that polite Kenya version of a public school voice which barely ever rises above a mumble. "I'll go to Rhodesia or South Africa, only decent place for a white man to live these days. How long do I have then? Ten or fifteen years at the most. But I'd rather get thrown out of Rhodesia after fifteen years of happiness than be miserable in England now. . . ."

A good part of the two guides' conversation is devoted to expressing their nostalgia for the privileges of pre-independence Kenya, to deploring the proliferation of African drivers at the wheels of tourist vehicles, and to cursing that unspeakable day when they will have to share a meal with an African. "Do you know," observes Young Hunter, "I've heard that some European women tourists actually have a drink at the end of the day with their drivers. . . ." Big Hunter shudders: "Bad show, that."

In my tent, I often reflect on the varieties of colonial behavior. The French were as bestial to the Africans as they are to each other. The French and the Portuguese were as carnally drawn to black women as were our own Southern plantation owners. Ten years after independence, the British managing Kenya's leading industry—tourism—are still rigid with fear of the black man's entering their club.

STILL, HOW BITTER it is to have found such beauty and then to lose it! Traveling through Kenya, discovering its splendor and variety, one senses the depth of the settlers' sorrow upon having to leave. Morocco, Mexico, Greece, all other landscapes pale before Kenya's. Besides the game-filled savannahs and plains of the reserves there are deserts of sublime austerity; tropical rain forests heavy with guava and mango trees; rolling upland moors thick with waterfalls, trout-filled streams, and fields of heather. There are Indian Ocean beaches rivaling the Caribbean's for their beauty, and lush riverine terrains such as Samburu, where wide streams placidly flow through groves of Doum palms, wild lilies, and eucalyptus trees.

The farmland surrounding Mount Kenya, the Olympus of East Africa where the gods legendarily bequeathed the Kikuyus their land, is a farmer's utopia: On its sumptuous loam, assured of large punctual rainfall and drained to perfection by the land's gentle slope, wheat and oats can be harvested at tenfold the yield of any English field. My favorite landscape is the ascent to Mount Kenya, reached through sumptuous stands of cedar and dense groves of high bamboo which for many years provided the Mau Maus' safest shelter. Kenya's birds are a microcosm of their land's splendor. Even the starling, the most plebeian of our species, is cloaked there in a blinding iridescence of orange, viridian, and cobalt. Sights of the Lilac-breasted Roller, the Emerald Cuckoo, the flame-red Turaco, spoil one's bird-viewing for some time to come.

ON MARCH 14 we cross the Kenya border into Tanzania to enter the Serengeti, Africa's most spectacular national park. We instantly sense an austerity that contrasts with Kenya's opulence. Within the first few hours we observe that shortage of basic staples which can afflict young socialist countries: no soda water or beer to be had in the province, there are no passport forms at the frontier post—the guard has to improvise some on blank paper—no petrol is to be found in the vicinity of our camping site. Our guides rage at these deficiencies: "Great fun, socialism, what? Ha ha!" This is their last time in Tanzania, they proclaim, they've never had anything but annoyance in this bloody Maoist country. "Chinese communist lorry," they mutter every few minutes, pointing at any vehicle on the road. "Chinese communist tractor."

We hear that several cheetah have died of heart attacks in the past months from being chased by tourist vehicles; that lion cubs are going hungry from too much close observation; and that the new African warden of the 6,000 square mile Serengeti has forbidden all vehicles to go into the plain, where the best game viewing has traditionally been had. Notwithstanding these restrictions the Serengeti animals live up to legend. In these "photographic blocks" which now make up the major part of national parks and game reserves, where no shooting has been allowed for years and where guides are not even allowed to bear weapons, the walls of our nursery come alive: which is why we are here.

Animals come close and stare, having no memory of aggression on which to base their fear. Buffalo gaze at us trustingly from below their large flat coiffure of horns, noses placidly drooling, making it hard to believe that they are the leading man-killers in Africa, and that one of their species killed Big Hunter's partner just last year during a shooting safari. Another of our guide's best friends was carried off this very year by an elephant in hunting territory. But here elephants walk closely past us in sublime and weightless serenity, allowing us to discover their surprisingly long, flirtatious eyelashes, their trunks affectionately reposing around a tusk instead of trumpeting alarm. And we observe the beauty of the smaller African antelopes—dik-diks, duikers, klipspringers, whose great expanse of liquid eye, half the size of their heads, dominates the landscapes of their bodies like enormous lakes.

Our camping site is in a flat plain filled with euphorbia and the bright yellow-barked acacia, alongside one of the beautiful tree-festooned *kopjes,* or rock outcroppings, that dot the Serengeti landscape. Our ten African safari boys have arrived a few hours before us in their truck and have already completed pitching camp. They are all Kikuyus, members of that largest and most powerful of Kenyan tribes, numbering over one tenth of the population, to which Jomo Kenyatta belongs. The kitchen fire has already been lit and alongside it the cooks are baking bread in an ingenious oven composed of a flat piece of metal, a large over-turned pan, and a strategic sprinkling of smoldering coals. The refrigerator has been plugged into its canister of gas. Each tent is flanked by a small out-house, in which portable seats are posed over a deep hole. And in the middle of the camping site stands a tented shower which functions smartly on a string-and-bucket system.

Fantasies of primitiveness: Like the camping trip of Abercrombie and Fitch executives who recently spent a week on the rooftop of their Madison Avenue office building, the classiest safaris are the most naturalistic. The cheapest mass tours go around in posh zebra-striped minibuses and confine their clients to East Africa's extraordinarily luxurious hotels. Many treat their groups to a meal at the outlandish Mount Kenya Safari Club, which matches the Westchester Biltmore for its profligate vulgarity. Whereas the more elegant tented safari outfits rumble around in shaking Land Rovers, rigidly avoiding these modern hostelries. Meanwhile we hear of Niarchos's improvisations on the new primitivism: a private plane daily flies his mail up from Nairobi when he is in the bush, and two large swimming pools are immediately dug out wherever he pitches camp, one for himself and another for his entourage.

THE KIKUYUS are notoriously gifted cooks, and a typical menu on our safari might consist of a hot fish savory, cream of avocado soup, a roast, three different vegetables, a cold passion fruit soufflé. I read that a modest safari meal in the 1950's, as described by Alan Moorehead on a fairly rough shooting trip, consisted of duck gizzards savory, wild turkey soup, nile perch, and roasted eland. It is not a question of luxury, since even a billionaire could not conjure up such fare in the disorder of French West Africa. It is rather a Kenyan safari tradition composed of the British talent for importing comfort into wilderness and the East African's prideful need to exhibit his great talents. Laundry is done daily and pressed with immense hot coal irons. One changes several times a day. It is bad form to miss tea.

I visit the cook by his fire as he is deftly whipping egg whites with an old wooden whisk. By him stands the chief steward, a powerfully built Kikuyu who has been in Big Hunter's service for some ten years. The safari boys speak little English beyond the necessities of food and laundry, and earn between one and two dollars a day. "Fair but firm," Big Hunter pronounces whenever he discusses his staff. "I've kept them from joining those blasted new safari unions by being fair but firm." Over dinner one night, our guide tells me that his chief steward is a former Mau Mau. I ask him if he is joking, and he seems offended, swiftly coming to the Mau Maus' defense. "But they're splendid old blokes actually—always were jolly good chaps—I admire them tremendously—admire anyone who's willing to fight for his country. Damn rotten lot, those who don't." Nationalism dominates all, and the former major seems to have as much respect for the Mau Mau he'd come to shoot as he has for the animals he's made a career of hunting.

Today the cook and I chat about the famous Serengeti lions. He tells me that like most of his colleagues he had never seen a wild animal until he had started on this safari job. The entire staff is so terrified of animals, he says, that although *bwana* provides tents, seven out of ten of them sleep jammed together in the lorry to be safe from marauding creatures. Wainugu also expresses great nostalgia for the hunting safaris of old which gave him so much good game to cook. The staff quickly grows despondent, he says, without the sight of freshly shot meat. He speaks longingly of gerenuk, that long-necked and most graceful gazelle of the northern plains, which makes the finest steaks, of Thompson's gazelle chops and impala roasts. Do I really like to just go out and *look* at animals? Wainugu softly laughs. He cannot imagine anything sillier and more boring.

A few days later we are startled by some unannounced rifle shooting close to camp. We discover that our guides, who nowadays do not shoot more than one or two big game animals a year, have shot an impala and a gazelle to reassure their servants of their sanity and manliness. To Africans—who look upon wild animals as enemies rampaging their crops and herds, enemies to be killed and eaten—a "looking" safari seems the maddest to date of the white man's many mad inventions.

SOME ITEMS in the *East African Standard,* Nairobi's leading paper: There are some eighty licensed hunter-guides working in Kenya, all Europeans. . . . Since independence the term "big White Hunter" has come into disfavor and they are now called "professional hunters. . . ." Notwithstanding this change of nomenclature the tradition of white hunters is so ingrained that the few Africans or Asians training for the profession will say, "I am becoming an African White Hunter" or "an Asian White Hunter . . ." Kenya's second largest safari firm bore the unfortunate name of "White Hunters, Limited," and a few years ago was forced to change its title to "Africa Tours. . . ." Among predictions that East Africa will have to accommodate one million visitors by 1980, the Kenyan government last year declared a policy of "Africanization" in its booming tourist industry. Yet as of March, 1973, the *Standard* reports, only one safari firm in Kenya (Kibo Tours) is totally African-owned.

With the new policy of Africanization, several European hunters are losing their work licenses on the grounds that they do not employ enough Africans. In an unguarded moment, one white hunter I met confided to me that in order to ensure the renewal of his license he had made his chief steward a partner in his safari firm. "We did it just on paper, actually," he remarked. "We didn't tell the poor bloke anything about it." Meanwhile, in case Africanization becomes militant and his license is revoked, one of our own white hunters has started a successful grouse shooting safari outfit in Scotland to fall back on.

THROUGHOUT THIS TRIP I suffer from claustrophobia, a curious sensation to have in the vast open plains of Africa. Severe laws dictate that the tourist on a "viewing" safari stay inside his vehicle any time he ventures out of his tiny tented camp, and forbid him to move many yards beyond his hotel room. *Homo touristicus* is continuously imprisoned behind the metal bars of his Rover, in a new kind of ambulatory zoo. The tables are turned. We parade our captivity before the disinterested eyes of the free beasts, and apprehend their whereabouts by seeing where other motorized cages have congregated on the plain. Even Africa's most famous hotel, Treetops, is a nightmarish prison in which one is incarcerated in an aerial cage, sentenced to staring for eighteen hours at an artificial pond and salt-lick frequented by obliging beasts.

Being addicted to hiking, jogging, and other forms of strenuous activity, I find my physical captivity difficult. It is even more tedious psychologically. I had suspected that the pleasure of White Hunters' company would be limited. Their racist diatribes, their disdain and ignorance of all things African besides its wildlife, are even worse than I had feared. They rush us through every village under the pretext that such places are dangerous or that we shall miss the evening game viewing. Young Hunter never passes an African farming cooperative without exclaiming, "Poor bastards, they don't know the first thing about land." Big Hunter cannot drive by an Asian family on a picnic without derisively mimicking the Kenyan Asians' lilting English, and insults African waiters with an imperiousness worthy of Major Grogan.

Young Hunter tells me that Tanzania is so Maoist-dominated that there are two million Communist Chinese living in that country. Since Tanzania's population is under twelve million, I ask how it is possible that one out of six of its residents is Chinese? He shrugs his shoulders over his breakfast kippers, and I realize that most of his clients are trophy-collecting Texans only too happy to agree with him. "Are you bringing those smelly objects into my car?" Big Hunter rages when I buy some beautiful Somali, Turkana, and Samburu dolls in a northern

Kenya village. "Don't put them on the seat, they're so frightfully filthy." It strikes me as absurd that one should travel to a country with no further purpose than to look at its wildlife, that animal-gaping trips are as narrow and atomized as culinary tours of France, ceramicists' tours of Ireland, and gay liberation tours of South America.

Yet short of renting a private plane, there is no way of leaving for a few days if I am to find my family again in Africa. Kenyan transportation is still so primitive that the only road to Ethiopia is an unpaved, blindingly dusty thoroughfare, and the road to Somaliland is akin to a mule track. Altering the schedule by a day or two is equally out of the question, for tourist accommodations are so gorged that hotel rooms and camping sites must be reserved months in advance. African wilderness these days must be booked a year ahead. This trip is remarkably similar to traveling through Russia with Intourist guides, trapped round the clock by men who command the sole means of transportation, the implacably fixed schedule, and the stupendous array of propaganda.

I acquire new respect for the mobility, the freedom, and the reality of the traditional shooting safari. The twenty or thirty miles of daily walking in order to track an animal, the reciprocity of danger, anything to escape this playhouse fantasy! Although I have been a near vegetarian and a pacifist much of my life, I entertain macabre notions of learning how to shoot and joining a hunting safari so that I can at least walk on African soil. And at night I pace the confines of the camp like one of those caged animals I have all my life wanted to liberate.

AND YET. There is an anecdote Big Hunter likes to tell which sums up that great respect and knowledge of animals which makes him such a good guide to Africa's wildlife, if to nothing else: The year before, a lioness jumped out of the bush at him, and he gambled with his life by shooting at her feet rather than killing her. "There was one chance out of four that it would frighten her—she did turn and run, actually, and I *lived on* to tell the tale." His sentiment toward animals is the essence of the white sport hunter's ethos. It is that etiquette of the sport of kings and nobles, deriving from the rich man's leisure and abundance, that is radically opposed to killing out of hunger, as the African or any poor man will do. It is a code based on the ambivalent feelings of loving and respecting what you kill, on the precept that you shoot while also safeguarding the species' young and females, that you attempt to perpetuate the species abundantly for future generations of sportsmen.

Because of the complexity of that code and their precise knowledge of it, white hunters know game as few other men do, and that is partly why they are the best guides to African wildlife. We are constantly amazed by our escorts' instinct for when and where each species can be found in the vast reserves; by their ability to identify, with their naked eyes, as buffalo or impala what to us look like a dot on the horizon; by their enormous tenderness and respect for animals, whom they manage to approach without causing the least disturbance or fear. Thanks to their skill we are twice able to observe a leopard—that most savage and solitary animal which few tourists see any more—staring down at us with its chilling green gaze from the branches of thorn trees in the Serengeti. In the same Serengeti plain—toward the end of the dry season—our guides find the site where the largest migratory herd in years is congregated: a half million zebra and wildebeest move together toward Lake Victoria in search of young grass. From a distance there is no sound but a low dull buzzing on the plain, all scale is lost in such number, one feels submerged in a plague of insects or in a myriad shoal of microscopic fish. The dun, mourning-hued mass slowly palpitates westward, occasionally enlivened by the frail prancing of the young and by a lifted head revealing dumb, muted eyes above the wildebeest's patriarchal beard.

IT IS THE SPLENDOR of lions—and our guides' skill at finding them— that dominates my memories of Africa. In the Masai Mara, Big Hunter knows from the wary stance of a vulture in a tree that a kill has been made that day. And he drives us into a thicket stiff with lion, in which a pride of some twelve animals are lying up in the shade after their feast of freshly killed young elephant. Some lift their heads and yawn, gazing at us with trusting eyes. Others continue lying on their backs, paws in the air like pups on a hot day, their white bellies grossly distended by their great repast. Meanwhile fifty yards away from the sated predators a golden-fleeced jackal commences the swift scavenging process that maintains the hygiene of the plain. His delicate ears flared out like antennae, desperately trying to decide whether the lions are sleepy enough for him to get his piece of elephant safely, he darts expectantly toward the feast and prances fearfully back a dozen times, running to and fro like a sandpiper following the turn of the surf on a beach.

Another time we come upon a pair of lions as they are about to mate on top of a huge rock of the Serengeti plain. They stand nuzzling in the sun a few yards above us, their sinews delineated as majestically as in an Assyrian bas-relief. After a particularly affectionate nuzzle the lioness lies down. The lion mounts her, gives a few raging thrusts, and then with an apocalyptic growl bites her in the back of her neck. She swiftly stands up, snarls, and gives him a resounding cuff in the jaw. He looks sheepish, and licks her tenderly. It is intimidating to think that they can repeat the performance some two hundred times that weekend, about every half an hour.

I THINK THAT people are traveling to Africa not only to bathe in nature's innocence but also to witness nature's violence. To see predators on a kill is considered to be the great moment of a safari, a new outlet for the blood lust once channeled into hunting. It is the *corrida* of the Seventies, with the animals doing all the blood-letting.

We never come upon a kill—a failure that pleases me but the one time we see predators miss their prey is grimly instructive. Driving one evening through Amboseli, at the foot of Kilimanjaro, we see twenty-one minibuses gathered near a clearing to observe three cheetah stalking. The first cheetah curtly moves through the thicket toward a small herd of impala, occasionally twitching her ears as a signal for her companions to move on. There is an exaggerated stylishness about these animals' features—extravagantly long, elegant forelegs, outlandishly small, heavily marked faces. These most endangered animals of East Africa—champion runners but unskilled at camouflage, their temperament as open as the plains they frequent—seem only too willing to be movie stars, and cock their heads photogenically toward the tourists.

After we have watched them for some twenty minutes the cheetah have approached to about 150 yards of their prey, coming close to the distance from which they make their famous sixty-mile-per-hour dash for the kill. But as they reach the critical moment minibuses start crashing about them; tourists leaning on the open rooftops of their vehicles, cameras poised, urge their drivers to get the closest possible view of the kill. Startled by the commotion, the impalas race about in circles and cough out their warning message, the baboons' terrierlike barking comes sloughing off the trees. The cheetah must know better than we that they have lost their chance for dinner but they go on stalking for a few minutes as if to finish their pose. And then, amid the clicking of some fifty cameras, the head scout abruptly turns away from the impalas. The three slink off into the plain. Their fragile rib cages seem terribly thin in the dusk, the black markings of their cheeks—like rivulets of black tears—seem to express their frustrated hunger.

We are going to kill these animals with sentiment. Having slain and trapped wild creatures for food, domesticated them for our amusement, and hunted them for sport, we are now decimating them by our fantasies of wilderness. How curious that photographic "shooting" is becoming deadlier to game than the ancient pastime of sport shooting. How regrettable that most of the intrusive drivers are Africans. The ancient code of hunting is past, a new etiquette of viewing has yet to be elaborated if the animals are to survive. I turn to Big Hunter, who, along with two other European drivers, respectfully kept his vehicle still during the cheetahs' attempted hunt. "Looking at game may become more dangerous to them than hunting," I say. "Worse than that," he remarks laconically, "it's so bloody rude to the animals."

BRIEFLY ESCAPING from the local Intourist, I visit with two young African conservationists in Tanzania. One is the newly appointed game warden of the Serengeti, David Babeu. He receives me in an office that looks like a primitive military outpost: From a line of low barracks attended by rangers dressed in austere khaki there blares the rash drone of a short-wave radio, the station's only communication with the rest of Tanzania. Babeu talks at first with diffidence—probably because of the rudeness with which my type of British guides treat him. As soon as he learns that I am an American and that I frequently write for *The New Yorker,* which has published a very fine profile of Tanzania's president, Julius Nyerere, he immediately becomes cordial. We chat morosely about the one million tourists predicted to swarm through East Africa's game reserves in 1980. And we discuss the future of his park's three most threatened species—cheetah, leopard, and ostrich—in the light of that invasion. In the past three months alone, Babeu's rangers have reported several cases of cheetah having heart attacks from being pursued by tourist vehicles, and my tale of the cheetah's missed dinner seems all too familiar to him.

"Poverty, poverty, it is always a problem of poverty and hunger," Babeu says. "The heart of the problem is the poverty of my African brothers and the terrible wealth of the tourists. African drivers are constantly being tipped by tourists to break the rules of our parks and chase its animals. What can you do, our people are poor, it is easy for them to be corrupted. And you must realize that the African has a totally different attitude toward animals from the European. For thousands of years animals have either been food to eat or a pest to kill when it destroys crops, never something to preserve for sentimental or photographic purposes."

However, Babeu is optimistic about his country's ability to preserve its animal life. Europeans like my guides, he comments slyly, had predicted the extinction of game when Tanzania became independent, claiming that socialists were bound to be indifferent to wildlife conservation. Yet Tanzania has instituted some eight new game sanctuaries in the twelve years since independence—Serengeti was its only national park previous to 1962. It is also pouring 3 percent of its annual budget into conservation: three times more per capita than the United States allotment for similar programs, and a huge sum for a young nation where priorities such as schools and hospitals are pressing. The Wildlife College at Moshi, of which Babeu is a graduate, is supported by a United Nations grant and is training hundreds of Africans to be professional wardens and conservationists. Part of the nation's wildlife budget is going into an extensive audio-visual educational program that will start at the grade school level. Its aim is to make the Tanzanians respectful of the "wild heritage" concept so difficult for most Africans to understand.

Traveling between the Serengeti and the town of Arusha, where I plan to visit with one of Babeu's colleagues, I have the impression of a country stabler and more united than Kenya. Tanzania's harmonious tribal order has not been disturbed by traditionally feuding groups such as Kenya's Kikuyu and Luo. No one I talk to disputes the great popularity of Julius Nyerere. Several people tell me that he is an austere and devout Catholic, and they seem proud that he is the only African leader whose personal life is frugal and Spartan. Some 15,000 mainland Chinese (not 2 million) are working on the 1,200 mile railroad track to Zambia under the watch of armed Chinese guards. At night, they live a secluded existence in camps where—watched by still more Chinese guards—they are denied all contact with the local population. I find that my British guides' paranoia about Maoist influence on Tanzania is vastly exaggerated. The country's pipeline to Zambia and its main highway—projects quite as crucial as its railroad—are being built, respectively, by Italy and the United States.

Half of the 85,000 Asians who lived in Tanzania in 1970 have left the country, and for them, as for many Asians in Kenya and other parts of Africa, independence has been cruel. But the Asian merchants in Dar es Salam who have Tanzanian passports now seem safe in their jobs and praise the safety of Dar's streets (Nairobi's crime rate is one of the highest in the continent). A splendid old-time British hunter who moved down from Kenya twenty years ago to open a hotel in the Serengeti says that he is totally assured of his work license being renewed, and is not even being pressured to Africanize his staff. The buffet at his lodge is almost as extravagant as in Kenyan hostelries, and has an equally formidable display of trifle. In another hotel near Arusha owned by old-time German settlers we are served dinner in candlelight by white gloved Africans outlandishly attired in red and gold livery, with white lace jabots at the throat. Tanzania has become a controversial model for many progressive young Africans who decry Kenya's Western-style capitalism, while at the same time criticizing Nyerere for allowing a good many private businesses to continue.

ONE INDEED SENSES moderation in Tanzania, a patience with slow economic progress, a latitude toward diversity that is unusual in a new socialist state. In the island of Zanzibar, part of the Tanzania Federation, which Nyerere had predicted would be "the thorn in my side," the semi-independent Afro-Shiraz Party is being allowed to pursue its own exotic, sometimes ghastly, practices. The week we are there, members of the Party's revolutionary committee kidnap three adolescent girls to be forced brides. (The girls ran to dubious safety in Addis Ababa.) The Party threatens to post guards at the airport to cut the hair of any long-haired tourist, but the guards never appear. The president of Zanzibar grants amnesty to hoarders of cloves who the previous year had been subject to jail sentences.

In Arusha, capital of the East African Community, I visit the deputy director of Tanzania's national parks, Albert Mongi. He is in his twenties, like Babeu, and has done all his university work in the United States: a BA at the University of Seattle, followed by graduate work in the wildlife of the Grand Canyon. Since many naturalists tend to be apolitical, it is curious to talk about "the problems of psychological decolonization" and "our brothers' struggle in America" in a modest office dominated by photos of giraffe, charging rhino, and wading elephants.

Mongi immediately asks me what I find to be the chief difference between Tanzania and Kenya. I tell him of the singularly narrow character of my trip, and ask him to describe the difference himself. "The Kenyans remain more colonized than we," Mongi says proudly. "They are having more trouble acting like Africans, they are more dependent on the white man and the white image. That's perhaps why Europeans feel more comfortable in Kenya, but although we welcome tourists we must *not* alter our character for the sake of tourism." And then he uses a strange word which, to the few young Tanzanians I have talked to, seems to mean the opposite of negritude, decolonization, freedom. "Kenya is more *artificial* than we are. Tanzania's leading principle is avoidance of artificiality."

BIG HUNTER AND Young Hunter took exception to my visit with African conservationists, as if I had gone slumming alone at night into dangerous bars. I hastened back to attend our scheduled departure and found that Big Hunter was engaged in searching for his briefcase, which was loaded with passports, money, and all his other indispensables. "This is where they'll steal a briefcase more easily than anywhere else," he fumed, "in Tanzania, with all these locals needing passports." My thirteen-year-old son asked how one of the locals could possibly use a British passport. "They'll take it to some Indian who'll fake it up," Young Hunter answered. "Indians can fake anything." Big Hunter found his briefcase half an hour later at the fruit market, untouched and exactly where he'd left it.

The night before I left East Africa to return to the United States I had dinner with a Kenya-born Asian acquaintance, an intellectual of notably progressive leanings who had been a friend of Tom Mboya's and other leaders of Kenyan independence. When I told him I was determined to return to Kenya to do the same trip from a radically different point of view—with African guides—he expressed great chagrin. "But that would be terrible!" he exclaimed. "You simply might not see any game! We just don't have enough properly trained men yet, except the kind of Europeans you traveled with. I assure you that your guides were more liberal than many of their colleagues!"

It would be easier, he said, to arrange the kind of trip I had in mind in Tanzania, where, as Albert Mongi remarked, the process of decolonization seemed to have proceeded at a faster pace.

II

I read some twenty books on East Africa before traveling there. Of the ones on wildlife, Norman Myers's *The Long African Day* seemed to me by far the most powerful, informative, and controversial. Its quality is equaled only by George Schaller's encyclopedic *The Serengeti Lion* (which won a National Book Award this year).

Norman Myers is a British-born, Oxford-educated, thirty-nine-year-old conservationist who has been living and working in Kenya for over a decade, and has just finished his doctorate in conservation ecology at the University of California at Berkeley. His book is certainly the most authoritative essay on the conservation problems that East Africa will face in the next few decades, and it may be the first to take into account the diverse moral, political, and sociological issues upon which the survival of wildlife ultimately depends.

Myers also offers the most vivid accounts available of the social life, the feeding and mating habits, and other principal behavior traits of over thirty African animal species. He answers a multitude of questions, such as how animals eat (lions every two or three days, when they can gorge on seventy pounds of meat at a time, while elephents need 500 pounds of grass a day). And he explains many other more obscure physical characteristics, such as the placement of eyes in animal physiognomy (herbivores' eyes are located at the sides of their heads, to maintain defensive watch on broad sweeps of environment, whereas carnivores' frontal eyesight enables them to focus intensely on a smaller field of vision. Just compare a rabbit to your pet cat). My favorite chapter of *The Long African Day* examines the social habits of wild dogs, whose unique form of participatory democracy Mr. Myers describes with the crispness, factual abundance, and immediacy that characterize his writing.

The Long African Day is a very large book. It contains over four hundred pages of closely printed text and some three hundred photographs—all taken by the author—which I found superior to Eliot Porter's material (though far less well reproduced) in *The African Experience*. My principal objection to Myers's book is the fancy time metaphor that provides some of its chronological structure and much of its rhetoric: "The slice of geologic time" in which recent African species have existed is "the merest flicker of the eye on the evolutionary time scale," etc.

It was only upon a second reading, after I had returned from Africa, that I recognized Mr. Myers's most important contribution: He has radically stripped wildlife study of the sentimentalism and fantasizing that have led Europeans to idealize animals—and their parks—as pristine havens. He refuses to consider the needs of animals without simultaneously considering the needs of the Africans sharing their terrain. He is a pragmatist who not only believes that reducing the amount of game by "cropping" is necessary to preserving the health of the animal species— a view controversial enough—he also believes in turning the surplus game into food that will improve the health of protein-starved Africans.

Mr. Myers's sympathy for the poverty of Africans is as strong as his love for animals, and his arguments for "cash cropping," as he calls his game-into-food scheme, are based upon the needs of both. The data upon which he builds his case for cash-cropping are plentiful: In 1970, for instance, enough wildebeest and zebra died of overpopulation hunger to feed 50,000 Africans as much meat as they usually eat *in one year.* Myers estimates that the scientific cropping of wildebeest alone—that prolific animal of which I saw half a million in one day—could supply 24 million pounds of canned meat yearly without in the least depriving East Africa's predator population. Myers mentions the 1970 drought that caused some 3,000 elephants to die in Kenya's Isavo Park. If they had been cropped in anticipation of this disaster, Myers estimates that their carcasses would not only have produced hundreds of thousands of pounds of edible protein, but would have averted the deaths of some 600 rhinoceros who died from the drastic foliage destruction caused by the starving elephants.

FOR THE PURIST, laissez-faire school of conservationists who maintain that nature provides animals with a built-in mechanism that eventually normalizes an overly expanded population, Mr. Myers has two principal rebuttals. However tourists and some naturalists may idealize the wilderness of parks and reserves, Mr. Myers argues, their pristineness is deceptive. For the boundaries of these rich men's zoos are by themselves a radical interference with nature which deprive the animals of their most powerful measure against overpopulation—free migration. Moreover, the animals causing the most severe damage to plant life and to the general environment are the largest and most long-lived—such as elephants and hippos. And the time-lag in whatever instinctive birth control mechanism they might have is too long for shorter-lived animals to adapt to. An entire population of gazelles and other small herbivores might starve before the larger animals' population decreased in a natural way.

To these classical arguments for controlled cropping Mr. Myers adds a few of his own, which have to do with the extremely important problems of poaching, and of Africans' aggressive, often destructive attitudes toward wildlife. He argues that cash cropping might satisfy hungry Africans' craving for meat and would at the same time protect animals from the long agony of a trapped death. It would also help to control poaching for skins. For although luxury skin animals such as leopard must be protected by astringent international agreements, the poaching of more modest species such as zebra could be minimized by filling the market with the skins of legally killed animals.

Finally, Mr. Myers maintains that cash-cropping may be the quickest and surest way of making wildlife reserves intelligible to Africans, from whose lands these parks have often been expropriated. For to the African, the tourist commerce and the preservation of animals on which tourism depends will remain an abstraction until he feels its benefits. And how is the African citizen going to grasp the meaning of high-flown phrases such as "our wild heritage" unless his family gets a slice of the tourist pie? How is he going to get that slice in a capitalistic neocolonial place like Kenya, whose president's family is the nation's wealthiest and whose most sought-after guides are Europeans stashing away as much of their income as they can in Britain or Rhodesia?

MYERS BELIEVES THAT the ecology of animals is indivisible from the sociology of the men with whom they share a nation. One part of his essay struck me with particular force after my own limited African experience: his diatribe against the traditional safari, which, however non-violent in its current form, is exclusively based on the hedonistic pastime of animal-watching and has no curiosity about the problems of the men among whom the animals live. How about safaris, Mr. Myers suggests, which include visits to self-help schools and new farming cooperatives. It is precisely the lack of this kind of experience that shocked me on my trip, the segregation of nature from men. It may be a division even more harmful than the much deplored "estrangement of man from nature" because it is more sentimental and based on false illusions of innocence which are always sure paths to brutality.

I think Mr. Myers would agree that trekking to game reserves in the company of colonials who—however knowledgeable they are about animals—are crassly hostile to the past and future of Africans is dehumanizing to anyone sympathetic to democratic principles; and that both international relations and wildlife conservation will only be harmed by these mastodon guides who deride African agriculture and predict that socialism will wipe out all game in East Africa. In my opinion, anyone with sympathy for African democracy might do well to boycott Kenya's tourist industry unless he can travel with a new breed of guides who can do well what the former generation of European colonials have done so badly: present the tourist with a view of wildlife in its total agronomic and political—therefore terrestrial—context.

Needless to say, Mr. Myers's conclusions on the threats posed by the safari business are even more pessimistic than mine, because more voluminously documented. He asserts that the close shadowing of lions by overzealous visitors leads to so many missed kills that an increasing number of cubs are starving. He cites incidents of cheetah cubs being fatally separated from their mothers by the same kind of aggressive motorized antics I witnessed at Amboseli. He believes that the wheels of tourist vehicles are doing more damage to the animals' grazing grounds than the much-maligned Masai pastoralists. In Mr. Myers's view the species of *Homo touristicus* swarming over East Africa for the exclusive purpose of swooning at the beauty and charm of its wild animals is a very great threat to the preservation of those animals, on a par with the threat of poachers.

IF ONE IS CONSISTENT about "animal liberation" (see *NYR*, April 5, 1973), it is essential to extend that liberation into the psychological sphere and protect animals' privacy, protect them from psychic domination as well as from pain. If our ambivalent and mostly selfish sentiments toward animals are extended to include respect for them, we must cease to protect them for our own sake, which is the essence of paternalism and has an inevitably brutalizing effect on any creature. We must, in Africa, liberate animals from being the victims of the affluent white man's fantasies. Otherwise, if the number of nature-greedy tourists does reach beyond its predicted one million mark in that region, there might come a day when we shall have to cease looking at its animals altogether in order to ensure their survival. We might have to close off African game parks from men as radically as the French closed off the Lascaux caves—to preserve on their walls the ideograms of animals deteriorating in human-tainted air.

50. A Modest Proposal for Preventing the Children of Ireland from Being a Burden to Their Parents or Country

JONATHAN SWIFT

Swift (1667–1745), an Anglican clergyman, author of *Gulliver's Travels,* was born in Ireland of English parents. He was prominent in London's highest political and literary circles until he became Dean of St. Patrick's Cathedral, Dublin, in 1714, aged 47. He returned to England for only two visits (1725, 1726), and became an active pamphleteer for Irish causes. He published *A Modest Proposal* in 1729.

IT IS A MELANCHOLY OBJECT to those who walk through this great town [Dublin], or travel in the country, when they see the streets, the roads, and cabin-doors, crowded with beggars of the female sex, followed by three, four, or six children, all in rags, and importuning every passenger for an alms. These mothers, instead of being able to work for their honest livelihood, are forced to employ all their time in strolling to beg sustenance for their helpless infants; who, as they grow up, either turn thieves for want of work, or leave their dear native country to fight for the Pretender in Spain, or sell themselves to the Barbadoes.

I think it is agreed by all parties, that this prodigious number of children in the arms, or on the backs, or at the heels of their mothers, and frequently of their fathers, is, in the present deplorable state of the kingdom, a very great additional grievance; and, therefore, whoever could find out a fair, cheap, and easy method of making these children sound, useful members of the commonwealth, would deserve so well of the public, as to have his statue set up for a preserver of the nation.

But my intention is very far from being confined to provide only for the children of professed beggars; it is of a much greater extent, and shall take in the whole number of infants at a certain age, who are born of parents in effect as little able to support them, as those who demand our charity in the streets.

As to my own part, having turned my thoughts for many years upon this important subject, and maturely weighed the several schemes of our projectors, I have always found them grossly mistaken in their computation. It is true, a child, just dropped from its dam, may be supported by her milk for a solar year, with little other nourishment; at most, not above the value of two shillings, which the mother may certainly get, or the value in scraps, by her lawful occupation of begging; and it is exactly at one year old that I proposed to provide for them in such a manner, as, instead of being a charge upon their parents, or the parish, or wanting food and raiment for the rest of their lives, they shall, on the contrary, contribute to the feeding and partly to the clothing, of many thousands.

There is likewise another great advantage in my scheme, that it will prevent those voluntary abortions, and that horrid practice of women murdering their bastard children, alas, too frequent among us! sacrificing the poor innocent babes, I doubt more to avoid the expense than the shame, which would move tears and pity in the most savage and inhuman breast.

The number of souls in this kingdom being usually reckoned one million and a half, of these I calculate there may be about two hundred thousand couple whose wives are breeders; from which number I subtract thirty thousand couple, who are able to maintain their own children, (although I apprehend there cannot be so many, under the present distresses of the kingdom;) but this being granted, there will remain a hundred and seventy thousand breeders. I again subtract fifty thousand, for those women who miscarry, or whose children die by accident or disease within the year. There only remain a hundred and twenty thousand children of poor parents annually born. The question therefore is, How this number shall be reared and provided for? which, as I have already said, under the present situation of affairs, is utterly impossible by all the methods hitherto proposed. For we can neither employ them in handicraft or agriculture; we neither build houses (I mean in the country,) nor cultivate land: they can very seldom pick up a livelihood by stealing, till they arrive at six years old, except where they are of towardly parts; although I confess they learn the rudiments much earlier; during which time they can, however, be properly looked upon only as probationers; as I have been informed by a principal gentleman in the county of Cavan, who protested to me, that he never knew above one or two instances under the age of six, even in a part of the kingdom so renowned for the quickest proficiency in that art.

I am assured by our merchants, that a boy or a girl before twelve years old is no saleable commodity; and even when they come to this age they will not yield above three pounds, or three pounds and half-a-crown at most, on the exchange; which cannot turn to account either to the parents or kingdom, the charge of nutriment and rags having been at least four times that value.

I shall now, therefore, humbly propose my own thoughts, which I hope will not be liable to the least objection.

I have been assured by a very knowing American of my acquaintance in London, that a young healthy child, well nursed, is, at a year old, a most delicious, nourishing, and wholesome food, whether stewed, roasted, baked, or boiled; and I make no doubt that it will equally serve in a fricassee or a ragout.

I do therefore humbly offer it to public consideration, that of the hundred and twenty thousand children already computed, twenty thousand may be reserved for breed, whereof only one-fourth part to be males; which is more than we allow to sheep, black-cattle, or swine, and my reason is, that these children are seldom the fruits of marriage, a circumstance not much regarded by our savages, therefore one male will be sufficient to serve four females. That the remaining hundred thousand may, at a year old, be offered in sale to the persons of quality and fortune through the kingdom; always advising the mother to let them suck plentifully in the last month, so as to render them plump and fat for a good table. A child will make two dishes at an entertainment for friends; and when the family dines alone, the fore or hind quarter will make a reasonable dish, and, seasoned with a little pepper or salt, will be very good boiled on the fourth day, especially in winter.

I have reckoned, upon a medium, that a child just born will weigh twelve pounds, and in a solar year, if tolerably nursed, will increase to twenty-eight pounds.

I grant this food will be somewhat dear, and therefore very proper for landlords, who, as they have already devoured most of the parents, seem to have the best title to the children.

Infant's flesh will be in season throughout the year, but more plentifully in March, and a little before and after: for we are told by a grave author, an eminent French physician, that fish being a prolific diet, there are more children born in Roman Catholic countries about nine months after Lent, than at any other season; therefore, reckoning a year after Lent, the markets will be more glutted than usual, because the number of Popish infants is at least three to one in this kingdom; and therefore it will have one other collateral advantage, by lessening the Papists among us.

I have already computed the charge of nursing a beggar's child (in

which list I reckon all cottagers, labourers, and four-fifths of the farmers)
to be about two shillings per annum, rags included; and I believe no
gentleman would repine to give ten shillings for the carcass of a good
fat child, which, as I have said, will make four dishes of excellent nutri-
tive meat, when he has only some particular friend, or his own family,
to dine with him. Thus the squire will learn to be a good landlord, and
grow popular among his tenants; the mother will have eight shillings
net profit, and be fit for work till she produces another child.

Those who are more thrifty (as I must confess the times require)
may flay the carcass; the skin of which, artificially dressed, will make
admirable gloves for ladies, and summer-boots for fine gentlemen.

As to our city of Dublin, shambles [slaughter houses] may be appointed for this purpose in the most convenient parts of it, and butchers,
we may be assured, will not be wanting; although I rather recommend
buying the children alive, then dressing them hot from the knife, as we
do roasting pigs.

A very worthy person, a true lover of his country, and whose virtues
I highly esteem, was lately pleased, in discoursing on this matter, to offer
a refinement upon my scheme. He said, that many gentlemen of this
kingdom, having of late destroyed their deer, he conceived that the want
of venison might be well supplied by the bodies of young lads and
maidens, not exceeding fourteen years of age, nor under twelve; so great
a number of both sexes in every country being now ready to starve for
want of work and service; and these to be disposed of by their parents, if
alive, or otherwise by their nearest relations. But, with due deference to
so excellent a friend, and so deserving a patriot, I cannot be altogether
in his sentiments; for as to the males, my American acquaintance assured me, from frequent experience, that their flesh was generally tough
and lean, like that of our schoolboys, by continual exercise, and their taste
disagreeable; and to fatten them would not answer the charge. Then as
to the females, it would, I think, with humble submission, be a loss to
the public, because they soon would become breeders themselves: and
besides, it is not improbable that some scrupulous people might be apt
to censure such a practice, (although indeed very unjustly,) as a little
bordering upon cruelty; which, I confess, has always been with me the
strongest objection against any project, how well soever intended.

But in order to justify my friend, he confessed that this expedient
was put into his head by the famous Psalmanazar, a native of the island
Formosa, who came from thence to London above twenty years ago;
and in conversation told my friend, that in his country, when any young
person happened to be put to death, the executioner sold the carcass
to persons of quality as a prime dainty; and that in his time the body
of a plump girl of fifteen, who was crucified for an attempt to poison
the emperor, was sold to his imperial majesty's prime minister of state,
and other great mandarins of the court, in joints from the gibbet, at four

hundred crowns. Neither indeed can I deny, that, if the same use were made of several plump young girls in this town, who, without one single groat to their fortunes, cannot stir abroad without a chair, and appear at playhouse and assemblies in foreign fineries which they never will pay for, the kingdom would not be the worse.

Some persons of a desponding spirit are in great concern about that vast number of poor people, who are aged, diseased, or maimed; and I have been desired to employ my thoughts, what course may be taken to ease the nation of so grievous an encumbrance. But I am not in the least pain upon that matter, because it is very well known, that they are every day dying, and rotting, by cold and famine, and filth and vermin, as fast as can be reasonably expected. And as to the young labourers, they are now in almost as hopeful a condition: they cannot get work, and consequently pine away for want of nourishment, to a degree, that if at any time they are accidentally hired to common labour, they have not strength to perform it; and thus the country and themselves are happily delivered from the evils to come.

I have too long digressed, and therefore shall return to my subject. I think the advantages by the proposal which I have made are obvious and many, as well as of the highest importance.

For first, as I have already observed, it would greatly lessen the number of Papists, with whom we are yearly over-run, being the principal breeders of the nation, as well as our most dangerous enemies; and who stay at home on purpose to deliver the kingdom to the Pretender, hoping to take their advantage by the absence of so many good Protestants, who have chosen rather to leave their country than stay at home and pay tithes against their conscience to an Episcopal curate.

Secondly, The poorer tenants will have something valuable of their own, which by law may be made liable to distress, and help to pay their landlord's rent; their corn and cattle being already seized, and money a thing unknown.

Thirdly, Whereas the maintenance of a hundred thousand children, from two years old and upwards, cannot be computed at less than ten shillings a piece per annum, the nation's stock will be thereby increased fifty thousand pounds per annum, beside the profit of a new dish introduced to the tables of all gentlemen of fortune in the kingdom, who have any refinement in taste. And the money will circulate among ourselves, the goods being entirely of our own growth and manufacture.

Fourthly, The constant breeders, beside the gain of eight shillings sterling per annum by the sale of their children, will be rid of the charge of maintaining them after the first year.

Fifthly, This food would likewise bring great custom to taverns; where the vintners will certainly be so prudent as to procure the best receipts for dressing it to perfection, and, consequently, have their houses frequented by all the fine gentlemen, who justly value themselves upon their knowledge in good eating: and a skilful cook, who understands how to oblige his guests, will contrive to make it as expensive as they please.

Sixthly, This would be a great inducement to marriage, which all wise nations have either encouraged by rewards, or enforced by laws and penalties. It would increase the care and tenderness of mothers toward their children, when they were sure of a settlement for life to the poor babes, provided in some sort by the public, to their annual profit or expense. We should see an honest emulation among the married women, which of them could bring the fattest child to the market. Men would become as fond of their wives during the time of their pregnancy as they are now of their mares in foal, their cows in calf, their sows when they are ready to farrow; nor offer to beat or kick them (as is too frequent a practice) for fear of a miscarriage.

Many other advantages might be enumerated. For instance, the addition of some thousand carcasses in our exportation of barrelled beef; the propagation of swine's flesh, and improvement in the art of making good bacon, so much wanted among us by the great destruction of pigs, too frequent at our table; which are no way comparable in taste or magnificence to a well-grown, fat, yearling child, which, roasted whole, will make a considerable figure at a lord mayor's feast, or any other public entertainment. But this, and many others, I omit, being studious of brevity.

Supposing that one thousand families in this city would be constant customers for infants' flesh, beside others who might have it at merry-meetings, particularly at weddings and christenings, I compute that Dublin would take off annually about twenty thousand carcasses; and the rest of the kingdom (where probably they will be sold somewhat cheaper) the remaining eighty thousand.

I can think of no one objection, that will possibly be raised against this proposal, unless it should be urged, that the number of people will be thereby much lessened in the kingdom. This I freely own, and it was indeed one principal design in offering it to the world. I desire the reader will observe, that I calculate my remedy for this one individual kingdom of Ireland, and for no other that ever was, is, or I think ever can be, upon earth. Therefore let no man talk to me of other expedients: of taxing our absentees at five shillings a pound: of using neither clothes, nor household furniture, except what is our own growth and manufacture: of utterly rejecting the materials and instruments that promote foreign luxury: of curing the expensiveness of pride, vanity, idleness, and gaming in our women: of introducing a vein of parsimony, prudence and temperance: of learning to love our country, in the want of which we differ even from LAPLANDERS, and the inhabitants of TOPINAMBOO: of quitting our animosities and factions, nor acting any longer like the Jews, who were murdering one another at the very moment their city was taken: of being a little cautious not to sell our country and conscience for nothing: of teaching landlords to have at least one degree of mercy toward their tenants: lastly, of putting a spirit of honesty, industry, and skill into our shopkeepers; who, if a resolution could now be taken to buy only our native goods, would immediately unite to cheat and exact upon us in the price, the measure, and the goodness, nor could ever yet be brought to make one fair proposal of just dealing, though often and earnestly invited to it.

Therefore I repeat, let no man talk to me of these and the like expedients, till he has at least some glimpse of hope, that there will be ever some hearty and sincere attempt to put them in practice.

But, as to myself, having been wearied out for many years with offering vain, idle, visionary thoughts, and at length utterly despairing of success, I fortunately fell upon this proposal; which, as it is wholly new, so it has something solid and real, of no expense and little trouble, full in our own power, and whereby we can incur no danger in disobliging ENGLAND. For this kind of commodity will not bear exportation, the flesh being of too tender a consistence to admit a long continuance in salt, although perhaps I could name a country, which would be glad to eat up our whole nation without it.

After all, I am not so violently bent upon my own opinion as to reject any offer proposed by wise men, which shall be found equally innocent, cheap, easy, and effectual. But before something of that kind shall be advanced in contradiction to my scheme, and offering a better, I desire the author, or authors, will be pleased maturely to consider two points. First, as things now stand, how they will be able to find food and raiment for a hundred thousand useless mouths and backs. And, secondly, there being a round million of creatures in human figure throughout this kingdom, whose whole subsistence put into a common stock would leave them in debt two millions of pounds sterling, adding those who are beggars by profession, to the bulk of farmers, cottagers, and labourers, with the wives and children who are beggars in effect; I desire those politicians who dislike my overture, and may perhaps be so bold as to attempt an answer, that they will first ask the parents of these mortals, whether they would not at this day think it a great happiness to have been sold for food at a year old, in the manner I prescribe, and thereby have avoided such a perpetual scene of misfortunes, as they have since gone through, by the oppression of landlords, the impossibility of paying rent without money or trade, the want of common sustenance, with neither house nor clothes to cover them from the inclemencies of the weather, and the most inevitable prospect of entailing the like, or greater miseries, upon their breed for ever.

I profess, in the sincerity of my heart, that I have not the least personal interest in endeavouring to promote this necessary work, having no other motive than the public good of my country, by advancing our trade, providing for infants, relieving the poor, and giving some pleasure to the rich. I have no children by which I can propose to get a single penny; the youngest being nine years old, and my wife past childbearing.

---

51. Expecting the Barbarians

C. P. CAVAFY

Cavafy (1863–1933) was born in Alexandria, Egypt, and he spent most of his life there. His language was modern Greek; and his poems, which he wrote slowly, completing only a few each year, are now respected as a major work in modern literature. For most of his adult life, Cavafy worked as a provisional clerk in the Ministry of Irrigation.

What are we waiting for, assembled in the public square?

The barbarians are to arrive today.

Why such inaction in the Senate?
Why do the Senators sit and pass no laws?

Because the barbarians are to arrive today.
What further laws can the Senators pass?
When the barbarians come they will make the laws.

Why did our emperor wake up so early,
and sits at the principal gate of the city,
on the throne, in state, wearing his crown?

Because the barbarians are to arrive today.
And the emperor waits to receive
their chief. Indeed he has prepared
to give him a scroll. Therein he engraved
many titles and names of honor.

Why have our two consuls and the praetors come out
today in their red, embroidered togas;
why do they wear amethyst-studded bracelets,
and rings with brilliant glittering emeralds;
why are they carrying costly canes today,
superbly carved with silver and gold?

Because the barbarians are to arrive today,
and such things dazzle the barbarians.

Why don't the worthy orators come as usual
to make their speeches, to have their say?

Because the barbarians are to arrive today;
and they get bored with eloquence and orations.

Why this sudden unrest and confusion?
(How solemn their faces have become.)
Why are the streets and squares clearing quickly,
and all return to their homes, so deep in thought?

Because night is here but the barbarians have not come.
Some people arrived from the frontiers,
and they said that there are no longer any barbarians.

And now what shall become of us without any barbarians?
Those people were a kind of solution.

Suggestions for Writing

1. Set up a problem you can solve—a roommate who won't sleep, a motor that won't work—and present your solution.

2. Consider a problem not neatly solvable—what shall I major in?—and write an essay working out alternatives and working toward tentative solutions.

3. Look up Woolley's *Excavations at Ur* (Ernest Benn, 1954), and write an essay on "Woolley's most important discovery." Or do the same with some other exploratory book, like Jane Goodall's *In the Shadow of Man*, Geoffrey Bibby's *Looking for Dilmun*, or Elaine Morgan's *The Descent of Woman*.

4. Write an essay "On Growing Up," "On Being Free," "On Aggression," "On Kicking a Habit," "On Leaving the Group," or some similar topic, using Katz and your own observations as evidence.

5. Write an essay on hunting, the "estrangement of man from nature,"

"animal liberation," or some similar topic suggested by Gray and your own experience.

6. Write your own modest proposal for today.

7. Write an essay explaining Cavafy's point in relation to "Beat Down Frigid Rome" (pp. 172–182) and Yeats's poem, p. 183.

VII.
Style

Tone and
Figurative Language

LISTEN AGAIN to writers' voices. See how the committed writer reaches out for an image drawn from his experience: "sand in the bottom of an hourglass"—"better mud that sticks than dust that blows away." We pause for a chapter to listen to figurative language, which seems to thrive on an individual voice. We are reminding ourselves that good writing is human.

Officialdom has no real tone of voice. It conveys no sense of personality, sees nothing concretely, takes no responsibility. Its images are all clichés: "At that point in time, it was decided that the game plan would be effectuated by those to whom authority had been fully and adequately delegated." Nothing here is specific— except the exhausted metaphor *game plan,* which can mean almost anything from advertising to murder, but which suggests, in its evasion, nothing admirable. Unlike blue jeans, language does not gain personality as it fades in use. The more we wear out a phrase, the less discriminating it becomes—no one else, on the other hand, wears our jeans—and it fades until it loses all force, with no one committed to a real picture or a real thought.

In each of the following selections, you hear the tone of voice of an individual personality, and you see the specific images that spring from one person's need to report what he sees, feels, and believes. As you read, from the toughness of Lew Archer to the wise simplicity of the old woman in New Mexico, imagine how you picture the person behind the written voice. Keep track of metaphors—something pictured as something else: an earth slide like sand in an hourglass. Are they effective? Why? And what saves Joe Hill from triteness on the last afternoon of his life? For what beliefs do these writers accept responsibility? Because we cannot be responsible for anything unless *we* know what it is, the writer knows that his images play a very large part.

52. From *Sleeping Beauty*

ROSS MACDONALD

Ross Macdonald is really Kenneth Millar (1915–   ). Born in California, raised in Canada, ripened at the University of Michigan, eventually with a Ph.D. on Coleridge, he is now famous for his novel a year on Lew Archer's cool investigations of the murderous modern scene as a private detective.

Chapter XVIII

TOPANGA COURT, where Martha Mungan lived, was a long step down from the Excalibur Arms. It was a collection of peeling stucco buildings huddled between the Pacific Coast Highway and the eroding cliff. An earth slide leaned against the cliff like sand in the bottom of an hourglass which had almost run out.

I parked in front of the central building. A sign offered family accommodations by the day or week, some with kitchen. A bell jingled over the door when I opened it.

Behind the archway which contained the desk there were television voices in a darkened room. A woman called out:

"Who is that?"

An empty registration card lay on the desk. Mentally I filled it in: Lew Archer, thief catcher, corpse finder, ear to anyone. I said:

"Do you know Joseph Sperling?"

"Joe? You bet I do. How are you, Joe?"

I didn't answer her. I stood and listened to her slow footsteps as they approached the archway. Her face was closed and blind as she came through, a middle-aged woman wearing a harsh red wig and a kimono spilling colors down her front. She blinked against the light like a nocturnal animal.

"You're not Joe Sperling. Who are you trying to kid?"

"I didn't say I was." I gave her my name. "Joe and I had a little talk this morning."

"How is Joe, anyway? I haven't seen him in years."

"He seems to be all right. But I guess he's getting older."

"Aren't we all?" Her eyes came up to mine, surprisingly bright in her drooping face. "You say you had a talk with Joe. About me?"

"About you and your husband."

A sluggish ripple of alarm moved across her face, leaving wrinkles behind it. "I don't have a husband—not any more." She took a deep sighing breath. "Is Ralph Mungan in some kind of trouble?"

"He may be."

"I've been wondering. He dropped out of sight so completely, it made me wonder if he's in jail or something."

"Something," I said, to keep her interest alive.

A loose and empty smile took over the lower half of her face. She let it talk for her while her experienced eyes studied me. "Would you be a copsie-wopsie by any chancie-wancie?"

"A private one."

"And you want some info on Ralph?"

I nodded. In the shadow world behind the archway, the daytime television voices were telling their obvious secrets. I'd love you but I have a fractured libido and nobody ever set it. I'd love you back but you resemble my father, who treated me rotten.

"Where is Ralph?"

"I don't know," I lied.

'What do you want him for?"

"Nothing very important. At least, I hope it isn't important."

She leaned across the counter, resting the burden of her breast on it. "Don't play games with me, eh? I want to know what it's all about. And what does Joe Sperling have to do with it?"

"Remember a tweed suit Joe made for Ralph's birthday one year?"

Her eyes sharpened. "That was a long time ago. What about the suit?"

"It turned up in the ocean this morning."

"So? It was just an old suit."

"Have you seen it lately, Mrs. Mungan?"

"I don't know. After Ralph left, I threw out most of his things. I've moved a lot since then."

"So you don't know who was wearing it?"

With her fingers clenched on the edge of the counter, she pushed herself upright. Something that looked like a wedding band was sunk in the flesh of the appropriate finger like a deep scar.

"Somebody was wearing it?" she said.

"A little old man with burn marks on his head and face. Do you know him, Mrs. Mungan?"

Her face went blank, as if the impact of my question had knocked all sentience from her head.

"I don't know who it could be," she said without force. "Did you say the tweed suit was in the ocean?"

"That's right. I found it myself."

"Right off here?" She gestured across the Coast Highway.

"A few miles south of here, off Pacific Point."

She was silent, while slow thought worked at her face. "What about the man?" she said finally.

"The man?"

"The little man with the burn marks. The one you were just telling me about."

"What about him?"

"Is he all right?"

"Why?" I said. "Do you know him?"

"I wouldn't say I know him. But I may have given him that suit."

"When?"

"Answer my question first," she said sharply. "Is he all right?"

"I'm afraid not. He was in the suit when I found it in the water. And he was dead."

I was watching her face for signs of shock or grief, or possibly remorse. But it seemed empty of feeling. Her eyes were the color of the low city skies under which she had moved a lot.

"How did you happen to give him the suit?" I said.

She was slow in answering. "I don't remember too well. I do quite a lot of drinking, if you want the truth, and it washes everything out, if you know what I mean. He came to the door one day when I was slightly plastered. He was just an old bum, practically in rags. I wanted to give him something to keep him warm, and that old suit of Ralph Mungan's was all I had."

I studied her face, trying to decide among three main possibilities: either she was leveling, or she was one of those natural liars who lied more convincingly than they told the truth, or her story had been carefully prepared.

"He came here, did he, Mrs. Mungan?"

"That's right. He was standing where you're standing now."

"Where did he come from?"

"He didn't say. I guess he was working his way along the beach. The last I saw of him, he was heading south."

"How long ago was this?"

"I don't even remember."

"You must have some idea, though."

"A couple of weeks, maybe longer."

"Did he have a younger man with him? A broad-shouldered man of thirty or so, about my height?"

"I didn't see any younger man." But her look was defensive, and her voice had a whine in it. "Why are you asking me all these questions? I was just being a good Samaritan to him. You can't blame a woman for being a good Samaritan."

"But you didn't remember about it at first. You thought you threw the suit out with Ralph Mungan's other things. And then you remembered that you gave it to the dead man."

"That's just the way my mind works. Anyway, he wasn't dead when I gave it to him."

"He's dead now."

"I know that."

We faced each other across the counter. Behind her in the darkened room, the shadow voices went on telling the city's parables: Daddy wasn't the only one who treated me rotten. I know that, love, and my libido wasn't my only fractured part.

The woman was long past her prime, her mind leached out by drinking, her body swollen. But I rather liked her. I didn't think she was capable of murder. No doubt she was capable of covering for it, though, if she had a guilty lover or a son.

I left, intending to pay her another visit.

53. April Twenty-Sixth

DONALD CULROSS PEATTIE

Peattie (1898–1964) graduated *cum laude* in botany from Harvard (1922), having returned to college after dropping out from Chicago and reading for a New York publisher, to gain a background for the nature-writer he had decided to become. In 1922, he also won the Witter Bynner Prize for poetry, and published his first botanical papers. In 1933, he returned to the USA after five years on the French Riviera, to live for three years on a square mile of Illinois without leaving it overnight, producing *An Almanac for Moderns* (1935), one of his more than thirty books, in which this sketch of Audubon appeared.

O N THIS DAY was born Jean Jacques Audubon, in Santo Domingo, natural son of a French captain of Nantes, who was brought up in France by the captain's forgiving wife, spoiled, petted, raised as a little fop—this man who was to give himself to the American wilderness. When first he came to Philadelphia, a young foreigner, a dilettante, a country gentleman, we see him out shooting in the woods in satin breeches, wig and pumps. We see him encounter there his English neighbor, Bakewell, who takes him home to meet a blue-eyed daughter, rising tall among the dogs by the fire—Lucy Bakewell, his wife to be.

But Nature has her eye upon the man in the elegant clothes. First she must teach him that you cannot well dream out of a window in a counting house, you cannot play the indigo market without knowledge, nor mail a thousand dollars in an open envelope, nor manage a mill while you are out hunting vireos and wrens, painting warblers and cardinals. Then, when she had broken him with misfortunes, she sent him out into the Kentucky wilderness, singing to it with his Cremona violin at his shoulder, and to his young bride.

There amidst the beeches, the passenger pigeons and the wild deer, John James Audubon let his gold hair grow long to his shoulders, learned to handle a fire and a woman and a gun. There, unknown to all the world, he painted birds, watched them, lived with them, knew them as he knew his children or his Lucy. In the cane brakes, on the Mississippi, in the Texas bayous, the palmetto islands of Florida, the sea-girt bird rocks of the Gaspé, this child of Nature, untaught in science, saw what he saw and knew what he knew.

54. A Garland for Christopher Smart

MONA VAN DUYN

Mona Van Duyn (1921–   ) was born in Waterloo, Iowa, and graduated from the University of Iowa, where she has taught in the Writer's Workshop. She was a founder of *Perspective: A Quarterly of Literature.* In 1970, Van Duyn shared the Bolligen Prize with Richard Wilbur, and in 1971, she received the National Book Award for *To See, To Take* (1970). Her other collections of poems are *Valentine to the Wide World* (1959), *A Time of Bees* (1964), and *Merciful Disguises: Published and Unpublished Poems* (1973). Christopher Smart (1722–1771), an English satirist and religious poet, wrote his greatest poem, *Song to David* (1763), while confined in an asylum for a religious mania. Smart has been favorably compared to William Blake. Van Duyn quotes Smart in the following poem.

VII. Style:
Tone and Figurative Language

I

> "For the flower glorifies God and the root parries the adversary.
> For the right names of flowers are yet in heaven. God make
> gardners better Nomenclators."

For cosmos, which has too much to live up to,
for hyacinth, which stands for all the accidents of love,
for sunflower, whose leanings we can well understand, for foxglove
and buttercup and snapdragon and candytuft and rue,

and for baby's breath, whose pre-Freudian white we value,
and for daisy, whose little sun confronts the big one
without despair, we thank good gardeners who pun
with eye and heart, who wind the great corkscrew

of naming into the cork on what we know.
While the root parries the adversary, the rest
nuzzles upward through pressure to openness,
and grows toward its name and toward its brightness and sorrow.

And we pray to be better nomenclators, at home
and in field, for the sake of the eye and heart and the claim
of all who come up without their right names,
of all that comes up without its right name.

II

> "For I bless God for the Postmaster General and
> all conveyancers of letters under his care
> especially Allen and Shelvock."

Pastor of these paper multitudes,
the white flocks of our thought that run back and forth,
preserve the coming and going of each nickel's worth
that grazed on the slope of the brain or trotted from its inroads.

And all proxies who step to the door in the stead of the upper
left hand corner, keep coming to every house,
that even the most feeble narration may find its use
when it falls into the final slot of the eye, that the mapper

of human dimension may distend that globe each day
and draw each day the connecting network of lines
that greetings and soapflake coupons and valentines
make between one heart and another. We pray

300

especially for the postman with a built-up shoe who likes dogs
and the one at the parcel post window who bears with good grace
the stupid questions of ladies, and we especially bless
the back under every pack, and the hands, and the legs.

III

> *"Let Huldah bless with the Silkworm—the ornaments of the
> Proud are from the Bowells of their Betters."*

It was a proud doorway where we saw the spider drop
and swing to drop and swing his silk, the whole
spider rose to raise it, to lower it, fell,
and dangled to make that work out of his drip.

Not speculation, but art. Likewise the honeypot
that makes a fine table, an ornament to bread.
The bees danced out its plot, and feed our pride,
and milked themselves of it, and make us sweet.

And long library shelves make proud homes.
One line, a day in Bedlam, one book, a life
sometimes, sweated onto paper. What king is half
so high as he who owns ten thousand poems?

And the world is lifted up with even more humble words,
snail-scum and limey droppings and fly-blow
and gold loops that dogs have wetted on snow—
all coming and going of beasts and bugs and birds.

IV

> *"Let Jamen rejoice with the bittern blessed be the name of
> Jesus for Denver Sluice, Ruston,
> and the draining of the fens."*

And let any system of sewage that prospers say,
"I am guide and keeper of the human mess,
signature in offal of who, over the face
of the great globe, moves, and is the great globe's glory."

And any long paving, let it utter aloud,
"I bear the coming together and the going apart
of one whose spirit-and-dirt my spirit-and-dirt
eases in passage, for the earth cherishes his load."

Let drainage ditches praise themselves, let them shout,
"I serve his needs for damp and dryness." Let mansions
cry, "We extend his name with our extensions,"
and let prefabricated houses bruit

their mounting up in a moment to preserve this creature.
Let the great globe, which rolls in the only right air,
say, "He delves me and heaps me, he shapes without fear,
he has me in his care, let him take care."

V

> *"For he purrs in thankfulness when God tells him*
> *he's a good cat.*
> *For the divine spirit comes about his body*
> *to sustain it in compleat cat.*
> *For he camels his back to bear the first notion of business."*

But let those who invest themselves in the dumb beast
go bankrupt gladly at the end of this investment,
for in answering dumb needs he is most eloquent,
but in sickness cannot ask help, and is often lost.

His smell reaches heaven, hope and faith are his fragrance.
Whether he camels his back or barks, he wears our harness,
he sits under our hearts through all his days, questionless.
His tail directs orchestras of joy at our presence.

For his nature he shivers his coat to cast off flies.
For his nature he hisses, or milks the cushion with his claws.
But he will follow our leg forever, he will give up his mouse,
he will lift up his witless face to answer our voice.

And when he burnishes our ankles or turns away from his breed
to sit beside ours, it may be that God reaches out of heaven
and pets him and tells him he's good, for love has been given.
We live a long time, and God knows it is love we need.

55. My Last Will

JOE HILL

Hill (1882–1915), born Joel Emmanuel Haaglund, a
Swedish citizen executed by firing squad for murder, in
Utah on November 19, 1915, was an organizer for the
International Workers of the World ("Wobblies"), famed for
his revolutionary lyrics. He had come to the United States
about 1901, and had emerged in a dockworkers' strike
in San Pedro, California, 1910. He arrived in Salt Lake City
in 1913, about a month before two men masked in
bandannas entered the grocery of J. B. Morrison, as he and
his two sons were closing, saying, "We've got you now!"
They killed Morrison and one of his sons, who, returning
fire, hit one assailant in the chest. Two men whom
Morrison, a former policeman, had once arrested had
recently threatened him. Two hours later, Hill (also called
Hillstrom), a severe chest wound exiting through his back,
a pistol in shoulder holster, appeared before a doctor.
He claimed a quarrel over a woman, and asked secrecy.
Throughout his arrest, he refused to say more; his known
companion disappeared; neither defense nor prosecution
could produce further evidence. The jury convicted him,
amid a political furor that eventually involved the
Swedish ambassador and President Wilson on his behalf.
As a reporter interviewed him on the afternoon before
execution, he dashed off "My Last Will," giving it to a friend
that night. After a funeral in Utah, and a huge second
funeral in Chicago, his friends put his ashes in envelopes
to be scattered to the winds "in every state of the union
and every country of the world" on May Day, 1916.
His song "The Preacher and the Slave," to the tune of
"Sweet Bye and Bye," originated the phrase "pie in the sky,"
with its refrain:

> You will eat, bye and bye,
> In that glorious land above the sky,
> Work and pray, live on hay,
> You'll get pie in the sky when you die.

My will is easy to decide,
For there is nothing to divide.

My kin don't need to fuss and moan—
"Moss does not cling to a rolling stone."

My body?—Oh!—If I could choose,
I would to ashes it reduce,
And let the merry breezes blow
My dust to where some flowers grow.

Perhaps some fading flower then
Would come to life and bloom again.
This is my last and final will.
Good luck to all of you,
                                        JOE HILL

56. Little Elegy

X. J. KENNEDY

Kennedy (1929–   ) teaches at Tufts. His poems, in
leading magazines, have won two top prizes and a Breadloaf
fellowship. His *Nude Descending a Staircase* appeared
in 1961.

FOR A CHILD WHO SKIPPED ROPE

Here lies resting, out of breath,
Out of turns, Elizabeth,
Whose quicksilver toes not quite
Cleared the whirring edge of night.

Earth, whose circles round us skim
Till they catch the lightest limb,
Shelter now Elizabeth
And for her sake trip up Death.

57. Of De Witt Williams on His Way to Lincoln Cemetary

GWENDOLYN BROOKS

He was born in Alabama.
He was bred in Illinois.
He was nothing but a
Plain black boy.

Swing low swing low sweet sweet chariot.
Nothing but a plain black boy.

Drive him past the Pool Hall.
Drive him past the Show.
Blind within his casket,
But maybe he will know.

Down through Forty-seventh Street:
Underneath the L,
And Northwest Corner, Prairie,
That he loved so well.

Don't forget the Dance Halls—
Warwick and Savoy,
Where he picked his women, where
He drank his liquid joy.

Born in Alabama.
Bred in Illinois.
He was nothing but a
Plain black boy.

Swing low swing low sweet sweet chariot.
Nothing but a plain black boy.

58. A Few Words About Breasts: Shaping Up Absurd

NORA EPHRON

Nora Ephron began in journalism at *Newsweek* and subsequently was a general-assignment reporter for the *New York Post.* Since 1968, Ephron has written on a free-lance basis. Her reports have appeared in *Esquire,* and in *New York,* where she is a contributing editor. Recently, she has collected her reports in *Wallflower at the Orgy* (1973).

I HAVE TO BEGIN with a few words about androgyny. In grammar school, in the fifth and sixth grades, we were all tyrannized by a rigid set of rules that supposedly determined whether we were boys or girls. The episode in *Huckleberry Finn* where Huck is disguised as a girl and gives himself away by the way he threads a needle and catches a ball—that kind of thing. We learned that the way you sat, crossed your legs, held a cigarette and looked at your nails, your wristwatch, the way you did these things instinctively was absolute proof of your sex. Now obviously most children did not take this literally, but I did. I thought that just one slip, just one incorrect cross of my legs or flick of an imaginary cigarette ash would turn me from whatever I was into the other thing; that would be all it took, really. Even though I was outwardly a girl and had many of the trappings generally associated with the field of girldom—a girl's name, for example, and dresses, my own telephone, an autograph book—I spent the early years of my adolescence absolutely certain that I might at any point gum it up. I did not feel at all like a girl. I was boyish. I was athletic, ambitious, outspoken, competitive, noisy, rambunctious. I had scabs on my knees and my socks slid into my loafers and I could throw a football. I wanted desperately not to be that way, not to be a mixture of both things but instead just one, a girl, a definite indisputable girl. As soft and as pink as a nursery. And nothing would do that for me, I felt, but breasts.

I was about six months younger than everyone in my class, and so for about six months after it began, for six months after my friends had begun to develop—that was the word we used, develop—I was not particularly worried. I would sit in the bathtub and look down at my breasts and know that any day now, any second now, they would start growing like everyone else's. They didn't. "I want to buy a bra," I said to my mother one night. "What for?" she said. My mother was really hateful about bras, and by the time my third sister had gotten to the point where she was ready to want one, my mother had worked the whole business into a comedy routine. "Why not use a Band-Aid instead?" she would say. It was a source of great pride to my mother that she had never even had to wear a brassiere until she had her fourth child, and then only because her gynecologist made her. It was incomprehensible to me that anyone would ever be proud of something like that. It was the 1950's, for God's sake. Jane Russell. Cashmere sweaters. Couldn't my mother see that? *"I am too old to wear an undershirt."* Screaming. Weeping. Shouting. "Then don't wear an undershirt," said my mother. "But I want to buy a bra." "What for?"

I suppose that for most girls, breasts, brassieres, that entire thing, has more trauma, more to do with the coming of adolescence, of becoming a woman, than anything else. Certainly more than getting your period, although that too was traumatic, symbolic. But you could *see* breasts; they were there; they were visible. Whereas a girl could claim to have her period for months before she actually got it and nobody would ever know the difference. Which is exactly what I did. All you had to do was make a great fuss over having enough nickels for the Kotex machine and walk around clutching your stomach and moaning for three to five days a month about The Curse and you could convince anybody. There is a school of thought somewhere in the women's lib/women's mag/gynecology establishment that claims that menstrual cramps are purely psychological, and I lean toward it. Not that I didn't have them finally. Agonizing cramps, heating-pad cramps, go-down-to-the-school-nurse-and-lie-on-the-cot cramps. But unlike any pain I had ever suffered, I adored the pain of cramps, welcomed it, wallowed in it, bragged about it. "I can't go. I have cramps." "I can't do that. I have cramps." And most of all, gigglingly, blushingly: "I can't swim. I have cramps." Nobody ever used the hard-core word. Menstruation. God, what an awful word. Never that. "I have cramps."

The morning I first got my period, I went into my mother's bedroom to tell her. And my mother, my utterly-hateful-about-bras mother, burst into tears. It was really a lovely moment, and I remember it so clearly not just because it was one of the two times I ever saw my mother cry on my account (the other was when I was caught being a six-year-old kleptomaniac), but also because the incident did not mean to me what it meant to her. Her little girl, her firstborn, had finally become a woman. That was what she was crying about. My reaction to the event, however, was that I might well be a woman in some scientific, textbook sense (and could at least stop faking every month and stop wasting all those nickels). But in another sense—in a visible sense—I was as androgynous and as liable to tip over into boyhood as ever.

I started with a 28AA bra. I don't think they made them any smaller in those days, although I gather that now you can buy bras for five year olds that don't have any cups whatsoever in them; trainer bras they are called. My first brassiere came from Robinson's Department Store in Beverly Hills. I went there alone, shaking, positive they would look me over and smile and tell me to come back next year. An actual fitter took me into the dressing room and stood over me while I took off my blouse and tried the first one on. The little puffs stood out on my chest. "Lean over," said the fitter (to this day I am not sure what fitters in bra departments do except to tell you to lean over). I leaned over, with the fleeting hope that my breasts would miraculously fall out of my body and into the puffs. Nothing.

"Don't worry about it," said my friend Libby some months later, when things had not improved. "You'll get them after you're married."

"What are you talking about?" I said.

"When you get married," Libby explained, "your husband will touch your breasts and rub them and kiss them and they'll grow."

That was the killer. Necking I could deal with. Intercourse I could deal with. But it had never crossed my mind that a man was going to touch my breasts, that breasts had something to do with all that, petting, my God they never mentioned petting in my little sex manual about the fertilization of the ovum. I became dizzy. For I knew instantly—as naïve as I had been only a moment before—that only part of what she was saying was true: the touching, rubbing, kissing part, not the growing part. And I knew that no one would ever want to marry me. I had no breasts. I would never have breasts.

My BEST FRIEND in school was Diana Raskob. She lived a block from me in a house full of wonders. English muffins, for instance. The Raskobs were the first people in Beverly Hills to have English muffins for breakfast. They also had an apricot tree in the back, and a badminton court, and a subscription to *Seventeen* magazine, and hundreds of games like Sorry and Parcheesi and Treasure Hunt and Anagrams. Diana and I spent three or four afternoons a week in their den reading and playing and eating. Diana's mother's kitchen was full of the most colossal assortment of junk food I have ever been exposed to. My house was full of apples and peaches and milk and homemade chocolate-chip cookies—which were nice, and good for you, but-not-right-before-dinner-or-you'll-spoil-your-appetite. Diana's house had nothing in it that was good for you, and what's more, you could stuff it in right up until dinner and nobody cared. Bar-B-Q potato chips (they were the first in them, too), giant bottles of ginger ale, fresh popcorn with melted butter, hot fudge sauce on Baskin-Robbins jamoca ice cream, powdered-sugar doughnuts from Van de Kamps. Diana and I had been best friends since we were seven; we were about equally popular in school (which is to say, not particularly), we had about the same success with boys (extremely intermittent) and we looked much the same. Dark. Tall. Gangly.

It is September, just before school begins. I am eleven years old, about to enter the seventh grade, and Diana and I have not seen each other all summer. I have been to camp and she has been somewhere like Banff with her parents. We are meeting, as we often do, on the street midway between our two houses and we will walk back to Diana's and eat junk and talk about what has happened to each of us that summer. I am walking down Walden Drive in my jeans and my father's shirt hanging out and my old red loafers with the socks falling into them and coming toward me is . . . I take a deep breath . . . a young woman. Diana. Her hair is curled and she has a waist and hips and a bust and she is wearing a straight skirt, an article of clothing I have been repeatedly told I will be unable to wear until I have the hips to hold it up. My jaw drops, and suddenly I am crying, crying hysterically, can't catch my breath sobbing. My best friend has betrayed me. She has gone ahead without me and done it. She has shaped up.

Here are some things I did to help:
Bought a Mark Eden Bust Developer.
Slept on my back for four years.
Splashed cold water on them every night because some French actress said in *Life* magazine that that was what *she* did for her perfect bustline.
Ultimately, I resigned myself to a bad toss and began to wear padded bras. I think about them now, think about all those years in high school I went around in them, my three padded bras, every single one of them with different sized breasts. Each time I changed bras I changed sizes: one week nice perky but not too obtrusive breasts, the next medium-sized slightly pointy ones, the next week knockers, true knockers; all the time, whatever size I was, carrying around this rubberized appendage on my chest that occasionally crashed into a wall and was poked inward and had to be poked outward—I think about all that and wonder how anyone kept a straight face through it. My parents, who normally had no restraints about needling me—why did they say nothing as they watched my chest go up and down? My friends, who would periodically inspect my breasts for signs of growth and reassure me—why didn't they at least counsel consistency?

And the bathing suits. I die when I think about the bathing suits. That was the era when you could lay an uninhabited bathing suit on the beach and someone would make a pass at it. I would put one on, an absurd swimsuit with its enormous bust built into it, the bones from the suit stabbing me in the rib cage and leaving little red welts on my body, and there I would be, my chest plunging straight downward absolutely vertically from my collarbone to the top of my suit and then suddenly, wham, out came all that padding and material and wiring absolutely horizontally.

BUSTER KLEPPER was the first boy who ever touched them. He was my boyfriend my senior year of high school. There is a picture of him in my high-school yearbook that makes him look quite attractive in a Jewish, horn-rimmed glasses sort of way, but the picture does not show the pimples, which were air-brushed out, or the dumbness. Well, that isn't really fair. He wasn't dumb. He just wasn't terriby bright. His mother refused to accept it, refused to accept the relentlessly average report cards, refused to deal with her son's inevitable destiny in some junior college or other. "He was tested," she would say to me, apropos of nothing, "and it came out 145. That's near-genius." Had the word underachiever been coined, she probably would have lobbed that one at me, too. Anyway, Buster was really very sweet—which is, I know, damning with faint praise, but there it is. I was the editor of the front page of the high-school newspaper and he was editor of the back page; we had to work together, side by side, in the print shop, and that was how it started. On our first date, we went to see *April Love* starring Pat Boone. Then we started going together. Buster had a green coupe, a 1950 Ford with an engine he had handchromed until it shone, dazzled, reflected the image of anyone who looked into it, anyone usually being Buster polishing it or the gas-station attendants he constantly asked to check the oil in order for them to be overwhelmed by the sparkle on the valves. The car also had a boot stretched over the back seat for reasons I never understood; hanging from the rearview mirror, as was the custom, was a pair of angora dice. A previous girl friend named Solange who was famous throughout Beverly Hills High School for having no pigment in her right eyebrow had knitted them for him. Buster and I would ride around town, the two of us seated to the left of the steering wheel. I would shift gears. It was nice.

There was necking. Terrific necking. First in the car, overlooking Los Angeles from what is now the Trousdale Estates. Then on the bed of his parents' cabana at Ocean House. Incredibly wonderful, frustrating necking, I loved it, really, but no further than necking, please don't, please, because there I was absolutely terrified of the general implications of going-a-step-further with a near-dummy and also terrified of his

310

finding out there was next to nothing there (which he knew, of course; he wasn't that dumb).

I broke up with him at one point. I think we were apart for about two weeks. At the end of that time I drove down to see a friend at a boarding school in Palos Verdes Estates and a disc jockey played *April Love* on the radio four times during the trip. I took it as a sign. I drove straight back to Griffith Park to a golf tournament Buster was playing in (he was the sixth-seeded teen-age golf player in Southern California) and presented myself back to him on the green of the 18th hole. It was all very dramatic. That night we went to a drive-in and I let him get his hand under my protuberances and onto my breasts. He really didn't seem to mind at all.

"Do you want to marry my son?" the woman asked me.

"Yes," I said.

I was nineteen years old, a virgin, going with this woman's son, this big strange woman who was married to a Lutheran minister in New Hampshire and pretended she was Gentile and had this son, by her first husband, this total fool of a son who ran the hero-sandwich concession at Harvard Business School and whom for one moment one December in New Hampshire I said—as much out of politeness as anything else—that I wanted to marry.

"Fine," she said. "Now, here's what you do. Always make sure you're on top of him so you won't seem so small. My bust is very large, you see, so I always lie on my back to make it look smaller, but you'll have to be on top most of the time."

I nodded. "Thank you," I said.

"I have a book for you to read," she went on. "Take it with you when you leave. Keep it." She went to the bookshelf, found it, and gave it to me. It was a book on frigidity.

"Thank you," I said.

That is a true story. Everything in this article is a true story, but I feel I have to point out that that story in particular is true. It happened on December 30, 1960. I think about it often. When it first happened, I naturally assumed that the woman's son, my boyfriend, was responsible. I invented a scenario where he had had a little heart-to-heart with his mother and had confessed that his only objection to me was that my breasts were small; his mother then took it upon herself to help out. Now I think I was wrong about the incident. The mother was acting on her own, I think: that was her way of being cruel and competitive under the guise of being helpful and maternal. You have small breasts, she was saying; therefore you will never make him as happy as I have. Or you have small breasts; therefore you will doubtless have sexual problems. Or you have small breasts; therefore you are less woman than I am. She was, as it happens, only the first of what seems

to me to be a never-ending string of women who have made competitive remarks to me about breast size. "I would love to wear a dress
like that," my friend Emily says to me, "but my bust is too big." Like
that. Why do women say these things to me? Do I attract these remarks the way other women attract married men or alcoholics or homo-
sexuals? This summer, for example. I am at a party in East Hampton
and I am introduced to a woman from Washington. She is a minor
celebrity, very pretty and Southern and blonde and outspoken and
I am flattered because she has read something I have written. We are
talking animatedly, we have been talking no more than five minutes,
when a man comes up to join us. "Look at the two of us," the woman
says to the man, indicating me and her. "The two of us together couldn't
fill an A cup." Why does she say that? It isn't even true, dammit, so
why? Is she even more addled than I am on this subject? Does she
honestly believe there is something wrong with her size breasts, which,
it seems to me, now that I look hard at them, are just right. Do I
unconsciously bring out competitiveness in women? In that form? What
did I do to deserve it?

As for men.

There were men who minded and let me know they minded.
There were men who did not mind. In any case, I always minded.

And even now, now that I have been countlessly reassured that my
figure is a good one, now that I am grown up enough to understand
that most of my feelings have very little to do with the reality of my
shape, I am nonetheless obsessed by breasts. I cannot help it. I grew
up in the terrible Fifties—with rigid stereotypical sex roles, the insistence
that men be men and dress like men and women be women and dress
like women, the intolerance of androgyny—and I cannot shake it, cannot shake my feelings of inadequacy. Well, that time is gone, right?
All those exaggerated examples of breast worship are gone, right? Those
women were freaks, right? I know all that. And yet, here I am, stuck
with the psychological remains of it all, stuck with my own peculiar
version of breast worship. You probably think I am crazy to go on like
this: here I have set out to write a confession that is meant to hit
you with the shock of recognition and instead you are sitting there
thinking I am thoroughly warped. Well, what can I tell you? If I had
had them, I would have been a completely different person. I honestly
believe that.

After I went into therapy, a process that made it possible for me
to tell total strangers at cocktail parties that breasts were the hang-up
of my life, I was often told that I was insane to have been bothered
by my condition. I was also frequently told, by close friends, that I
was extremely boring on the subject. And my girl friends, the ones with
nice big breasts, would go on endlessly about how their lives had been
far more miserable than mine. Their bra straps were snapped in class.

They couldn't sleep on their stomachs. They were stared at whenever the word "mountain" cropped up in geography. And *Evangeline,* good God what they went through every time someone had to stand up and recite the Prologue to Longfellow's *Evangeline:* "*. . . stand like druids of eld . . . / With beards that rest on their bosoms.*" It was much worse for them, they tell me. They had a terrible time of it, they assure me. I don't know how lucky I was, they say.

I have thought about their remarks, tried to put myself in their place, considered their point of view. I think they are full of shit.

---

59. The New Dress

VIRGINIA WOOLF

Mrs. Woolf (1882–1941) was educated at home in London by her illustrious literary father, Sir Leslie Stephen. After her father's death in 1904, she lived with her sister, Vanessa, and her brother, Adrian, in a house on Gordon Square, in the Bloomsbury district near the British Museum, which became the center of the vigorous aesthetic-intellectual "Bloomsbury Group." There she met and married Leonard Woolf, with whom she founded the Hogarth Press. She was an innovator in stream-of-consciousness fiction. See the article on her, on pp. 456–466.

MABEL had her first serious suspicion that something was wrong as she took her cloak off and Mrs. Barnet, while handing her the mirror and touching the brushes and thus drawing her attention, perhaps rather markedly, to all the appliances for tidying and improving hair, complexion, clothes, which existed on the dressing table, confirmed the suspicion—that it was not right, not quite right, which growing stronger as she went upstairs and springing at her, with conviction as she greeted Clarissa Dalloway, she went straight to the far end of the room, to a shaded corner where a looking-glass hung and looked. No! It was not *right*. And at once the misery which she always tried to hide, the profound dissatisfaction—the sense she had had, ever since she was a child, of being inferior to other people—set upon her, relentlessly, remorselessly, with an intensity which she could not beat off, as she would when she woke at night at home, by reading Borrow or Scott; for oh these men, oh these women, all were thinking—"What's Mabel wearing? What a fright she looks! What a hideous new dress!"— their eyelids flickering as they came up and then their lids shutting rather tight. It was her own appalling inadequacy; her cowardice; her mean, water-sprinkled blood that depressed her. And at once the whole of the room where, for ever so many hours, she had planned with the little dressmaker how it was to go, seemed sordid, repulsive; and her own drawing-room so shabby, and herself, going out, puffed up with vanity as she touched the letters on the hall table and said: "How dull!" to show off—all this now seemed unutterably silly, paltry, and provincial. All this had been absolutely destroyed, shown up, exploded, the moment she came into Mrs. Dalloway's drawing-room.

What she had thought that evening when, sitting over the teacups, Mrs. Dalloway's invitation came, was that, of course, she could not be fashionable. It was absurd to pretend it even—fashion meant cut, meant style, meant thirty guineas at least—but why not be original? Why not be herself, anyhow? And, getting up, she had taken that old fashion book of her mother's, a Paris fashion book of the time of the Empire, and had thought how much prettier, more dignified, and more womanly they were then, and so set herself—oh, it was foolish— trying to be like them, pluming herself in fact, upon being modest and old-fashioned, and very charming, giving herself up, no doubt about it, to an orgy of self-love, which deserved to be chastised, and so rigged herself out like this.

But she dared not look in the glass. She could not face the whole horror—the pale yellow, idiotically old-fashioned silk dress with its long skirt and its high sleeves and its waist and all the things that looked so charming in the fashion book, but not on her, not among all these ordinary people. She felt like a dressmaker's dummy standing there, for young people to stick pins into.

"But, my dear, it's perfectly charming!" Rose Shaw said, looking her up and down with that little satirical pucker of the lips which she expected—Rose herself being dressed in the height of the fashion, precisely like everybody else, always.

We are all like flies trying to crawl over the edge of the saucer, Mabel thought, and repeated the phrase as if she were crossing herself, as if she were trying to find some spell to annul this pain, to make this agony endurable. Tags of Shakespeare, lines from books she had read ages ago, suddenly came to her when she was in agony, and she repeated them over and over again. "Flies trying to crawl," she repeated. If she could say that over often enough and make herself see the flies, she would become numb, chill, frozen, dumb. Now she could see flies crawling slowly out of a saucer of milk with their wings stuck together;

and she strained and strained (standing in front of the looking-glass, listening to Rose Shaw) to make herself see Rose Shaw and all the other people there as flies, trying to hoist themselves out of something, or into something, meagre, insignificant, toiling flies. But she could not see them like that, not other people. She saw herself like that—she was a fly, but the others were dragonflies, butterflies, beautiful insects, dancing, fluttering, skimming, which she alone dragged herself up out of the saucer. (Envy and spite, the most detestable of the vices, were her chief faults.)

"I feel like some dowdy, decrepit, horribly dingy old fly," she said, making Robert Haydon stop just to hear her say that, just to reassure herself by furbishing up a poor weak-kneed phrase and so showing how detached she was, how witty, that she did not feel in the least out of anything. And, of course, Robert Haydon answered something, quite polite, quite insincere, which she saw through instantly, and said to herself, directly he went (again from some book), "Lies, lies, lies!" For a party makes things either much more real, or much less real, she thought; she saw in a flash to the bottom of Robert Haydon's heart; she saw through everything. She saw the truth. *This* was true, this drawing-room, this self, and the other false. Miss Milan's little workroom was really terribly hot, stuffy, sordid. It smelt of clothes and cabbage cooking; and yet, when Miss Milan put the glass in her hand, and she looked at herself with the dress on, finished, an extraordinary bliss shot through her heart. Suffused with light, she sprang into existence. Rid of cares and wrinkles, what she had dreamed of herself was there —a beautiful woman. Just for a second (she had not dared look longer, Miss Milan wanted to know about the length of the skirt), there looked at her, framed in the scrolloping mahogany, a grey-white, mysteriously smiling, charming girl, the core of herself, the soul of herself; and it was not vanity only, not only self-love that made her think it good, tender, and true. Miss Milan said that the skirt could not well be longer; if anything the skirt, said Miss Milan, puckering her forehead, considering with all her wits about her, must be shorter; and she felt, suddenly, honestly, full of love for Miss Milan, much, much fonder of Miss Milan than of any one in the whole world, and could have cried for pity that she should be crawling on the floor with her mouth full of pins, and her face red and her eyes bulging—that one human being should be doing this for another, and she saw them all as human beings merely, and herself going off to her party, and Miss Milan pulling the cover over the canary's cage, or letting him pick a hemp-seed from between her lips, and the thought of it, of this side of human nature and its patience and its endurance and its being content with such miserable, scanty, sordid, little pleasures filled her eyes with tears.

And now the whole thing had vanished. The dress, the room, the love, the pity, the scrolloping looking-glass, and the canary's cage—all had vanished, and here she was in a corner of Mrs. Dalloway's drawing-room, suffering tortures, woken wide awake to reality.

But it was all so paltry, weak-blooded, and petty-minded to care so much at her age with two children, to be still so utterly dependent on people's opinions and not have principles or convictions, not to be able to say as other people did, "There's Shakespeare! There's death! We're all weevils in a captain's biscuit"—or whatever it was that people did say.

She faced herself straight in the glass; she pecked at her left shoulder; she issued out into the room, as if spears were thrown at her yellow dress from all sides. But instead of looking fierce or tragic, as Rose Shaw would have done—Rose would have looked like Boadicea —she looked foolish and self-conscious, and simpered like a schoolgirl and slouched across the room, positively slinking, as if she were a beaten mongrel, and looked at a picture, an engraving. As if one went to a party to look at a picture! Everybody knew why she did it—it was from shame, from humiliation.

"Now the fly's in the saucer," she said to herself, "right in the middle, and can't get out, and the milk," she thought, rigidly staring at the picture, "is sticking its wings together."

"It's so old-fashioned," she said to Charles Burt, making him stop (which by itself he hated) on his way to talk to some one else.

She meant, or she tried to make herself think that she meant, that it was the picture and not her dress, that was old-fashioned. And one word of praise, one word of affection from Charles would have made all the difference to her at the moment. If he had only said, "Mabel, you're looking charming to-night!" it would have changed her life. But then she ought to have been truthful and direct. Charles said nothing of the kind, of course. He was malice itself. He always saw through one, especially if one were feeling particularly mean, paltry, or feeble-minded.

"Mabel's got a new dress!" he said, and the poor fly was absolutely shoved into the middle of the saucer. Really, he would like her to drown, she believed. He had no heart, no fundamental kindness, only a veneer of friendliness. Miss Milan was much more real, much kinder. If only one could feel that and stick to it, always. "Why," she asked herself— replying to Charles much too pertly, letting him see that she was out of temper, or "ruffled" as he called it ("Rather ruffled?" he said and went on to laugh at her with some woman over there)—"Why," she asked herself, "can't I feel one thing always, feel quite sure that Miss Milan is right, and Charles wrong and stick to it, feel sure about the canary and pity and love and not be whipped all round in a second by coming into a room full of people?" It was her odious, weak, vacillating character again, always giving at the critical moment and not being seriously interested in conchology, etymology, botany, archeology, cutting up potatoes and watching them fructify like Mary Dennis, like Violet Searle.

Then Mrs. Holman, seeing her standing there, bore down upon her. Of course a thing like a dress was beneath Mrs. Holman's notice, with her family always tumbling downstairs or having the scarlet fever. Could Mabel tell her if Elmthorpe was ever let for August and September? Oh, it was a conversation that bored her unutterably!—it made her furious to be treated like a house agent or a messenger boy, to be made use of. Not to have value, that was it, she thought, trying to grasp something hard, something real, while she tried to answer sensibly about the bathroom and the south aspect and the hot water to the top of the house; and all the time she could see little bits of her yellow dress in the round looking-glass which made them all the size of boot-buttons or tadpoles; and it was amazing to think how much humiliation and agony and self-loathing and effort and passionate ups and downs of feeling were contained in a thing the size of a threepenny bit. And what was still odder, this thing, this Mabel Waring, was separate, quite disconnected; and though Mrs. Holman (the black button) was leaning forward and telling her how her eldest boy had strained his heart running, she could see her, too, quite detached in the looking-glass, and it was impossible that the black dot, leaning forward, gesticulating, should make the yellow dot, sitting solitary, self-centered, feel what the black dot was feeling, yet they pretended.

"So impossible to keep boys quiet"—that was the kind of thing one said.

And Mrs. Holman, who could never get enough sympathy and snatched what little there was greedily, as if it were her right (but she deserved much more for there was her little girl who had come down this morning with a swollen knee-joint), took this miserable offering and looked at it suspiciously, grudgingly, as if it were a half-penny when it ought to have been a pound and put it away in her purse, must put up with it, mean and miserly though it was, times being hard, so very hard; and on she went, creaking, injured Mrs. Holman, about the girl with the swollen joints. Ah, it was tragic, this greed, this clamour of human beings, like a row of cormorants, barking and flapping their wings for sympathy—it was tragic, could one have felt it and not merely pretended to feel it!

But in her yellow dress to-night she could not wring out one drop more; she wanted it all, all for herself. She knew (she kept on looking into the glass, dipping into that dreadfully showing-up blue pool) that she was condemned, despised, left like this in a backwater, because of her being like this a feeble, vacillating creature; and it seemed to her that the yellow dress was a penance which she had deserved, and if she had been dressed like Rose Shaw, in lovely, clinging green with a ruffle of swansdown, she would have deserved that; and she thought that there was no escape for her—none whatever. But it was not her fault altogether, after all. It was being one of a family of ten; never having money enough, always skimping and paring; and her mother carrying great cans, and the linoleum worn on the stair edges, and one sordid little domestic tragedy after another—nothing catastrophic, the sheep farm failing, but not utterly; her eldest brother marrying beneath him but not very much—there was no romance, nothing extreme about them all. They petered out respectably in seaside resorts; every watering-place had one of her aunts even now asleep in some lodging with the front windows not quite facing the sea. That was so like them—they had to squint at things always. And she had done the same—she was just like her aunts. For all her dreams of living in India, married to some hero like Sir Henry Lawrence, some empire builder (still the sight of a native in a turban filled her with romance), she had failed utterly. She had married Hubert, with his safe, permanent underling's job in the Law Courts, and they managed tolerably in a smallish house, without proper maids, and hash when she was alone or just bread and butter, but now and then—Mrs. Holman was off, thinking her the most dried-up, unsympathetic twig she had ever met, absurdly dressed, too, and would tell every one about Mabel's fantastic appearance—now and then, thought Mabel Waring, left alone on the blue sofa, punching the cushion in order to look occupied, for she would not join Charles Burt and Rose Shaw, chattering like magpies and perhaps laughing at her by the fireplace—now and then, there did come to her delicious moments, reading the other night in bed, for instance, or down by the sea on the sand in the sun, at Easter—let her recall it —a great tuft of pale sand-grass standing all twisted like a shock of spears against the sky, which was blue like a smooth china egg, so firm, so hard, and then the melody of the waves—"Hush, hush," they said, and the children's shouts paddling—yes, it was a divine moment, and there she lay, she felt, in the hand of the Goddess who was the world; rather a hard-hearted, but very beautiful Goddess, a little lamb laid on the altar (one did think these silly things, and it didn't matter so long as one never said them). And also with Hubert sometimes she had quite unexpectedly—carving the mutton for Sunday lunch, for no reason, opening a letter, coming into a room—divine moments, when she said to herself (for she would never say this to anybody else), "This is it. This has happened. This is it!" And the other way about it was equally surprising—that is, when everything was arranged—music, weather, holidays, every reason for happiness was there—then nothing happened at all. One wasn't happy. It was flat, just flat, that was all.

Her wretched self again, no doubt! She had always been a fretful, weak, unsatisfactory mother, a wobbly wife, lolling about in a kind of twilight existence with nothing very clear or very bold, or more one thing than another, like all her brothers and sisters, except perhaps Herbert—they were all the same poor water-veined creatures who did nothing. Then in the midst of this creeping, crawling life, suddenly she was on the crest of a wave. That wretched fly—where had she read the story that kept coming into her mind about the fly and the saucer?—struggled out. Yes, she had those moments. But now that she was forty, they might come more and more seldom. By degrees she would cease to struggle any more. But that was deplorable! That was not to be endured! That made her feel ashamed of herself!

She would go to the London Library to-morrow. She would find some wonderful, helpful, astonishing book, quite by chance, a book by a clergyman, by an American no one had ever heard of; or she would walk down the Strand and drop, accidentally, into a hall where a miner was telling about the life in the pit, and suddenly she would become a new person. She would be absolutely transformed. She would wear a uniform; she would be called Sister Somebody; she would never give a thought to clothes again. And for ever after she would be perfectly clear about Charles Burt and Miss Milan and this room and that room; and it would be always, day after day, as if she were lying in the sun or carving the mutton. It would be it!

So she got up from the blue sofa, and the yellow button in the looking-glass got up too, and she waved her hand to Charles and Rose to show them she did not depend on them one scrap, and the yellow button moved out of the looking-glass, and all the spears were gathered into her breast as she walked towards Mrs. Dalloway and said "Good night."

"But it's too early to go," said Mrs. Dalloway, who was always so charming.

"I'm afraid I must," said Mabel Waring. "But," she added in her weak, wobbly voice which only sounded ridiculous when she tried to strengthen it, "I have enjoyed myself enormously."

"I have enjoyed myself," she said to Mr. Dalloway, whom she met on the stairs.

"Lies, lies, lies!" she said to herself, going downstairs, and "Right in the saucer!" she said to herself as she thanked Mrs. Barnet for helping her and wrapped herself, round and round and round, in the Chinese cloak she had worn these twenty years.

60. Two Languages, One Soul

ROBERT COLES

Coles (1929–   ) is one of America's leading psychiatric interpreters of children and minority peoples. His *Children in Crisis*, first published in 1967, grew to three volumes and won a Pulitzer Prize in 1973. He now lives in Albuquerque to study Chicano and Mexican families.

HERE ARE THE WORDS of a quite elderly woman who has had virtually no schooling and speaks a mixture of Spanish (which I have translated) and terse but forceful English. She lives in a small isolated mountain community well to the north of Santa Fe and enjoys talking with her visitor:

"Sometimes I have a moment to think. I look back and wonder where all the time has gone to—so many years; I cannot say I like to be reminded how many. My sister is three years older, eighty this May. She is glad to talk of her age. I don't like to mention mine. Maybe I have not her faith in God. She makes her way every day to Church. I go only on Sundays. Enough is enough; besides, I don't like the priest. He points his finger too much. He likes to accuse us—each week it is a different sin he charges us with. My mother used to read me Christ's words when I was a girl—from the old Spanish Bible her grandmother gave to her on her deathbed. I learned that Christ was a kind man: He tried to think well of people, even the lowest of the low, even those at the very bottom who are in a swamp and don't know how to get out, never mind find for themselves some high, dry land.

"But this priest of ours gives no one the benefit of a doubt. I have no right to find fault with him; I know that. Who am I to do so? I am simply an old lady, and I had better watch out: the Lord no doubt punishes those who disagree with His priests. But our old priest who died last year was so much finer, so much better to hear on a warm Sunday morning. Every once in a while he would even lead us outside to the courtyard, and talk with us there, give us a second sermon. I felt so much better for listening to him. He was not in love with the sound of his own voice, as this new priest is. He did not stop and

320

listen to the echo of his words. He did not brush away dust from his coat, or worry if the wind went through his hair. He was not always looking for a paper towel to wipe his shoes. My husband says he will buy this priest a dozen handkerchiefs and tell him they are to be used for his shoes only. Here when we get rain we are grateful, and it is not too high a price to pay, a little mud to walk through. Better mud that sticks than dust that blows away.

"Well, I should not go on so long about a vain man. We all like to catch ourselves in the mirror and find ourselves good to look at. Here I am, speaking ill of him, yet I won't let my family celebrate my birthdays any more; and when I look at myself in the mirror a feeling of sadness comes over me. I pull at my skin and try to erase the lines, but no luck. I think back: all those years when my husband and I were young, and never worried about our health, our strength, our appearance. I don't say we always do now; but there are times when we look like ghosts of ourselves. I will see my husband noticing how weak and tired I have become, how hunched over. I pretend not to see, but once the eyes have caught something, one cannot shake the picture off. And I look at him, too; he will straighten up when he feels my glance strike him, and I quickly move away. Too late, though; he has been told by me, without a word spoken, that he is old, and I am old, and that is our fate, to live through these last years.

"But it is not only pity we feel for ourselves. A few drops of rain and I feel grateful; the air is so fresh afterwards. I love to sit in the sun. We have the sun so often here, a regular visitor, a friend one can expect to see often and trust. I like to make tea for my husband and me. In mid-day we take our tea outside and sit on our bench, our backs against the wall of the house. Neither of us wants pillows; I tell my daughters and sons that they are soft—those beach chairs of theirs. Imagine beach chairs here in New Mexico, so far from any ocean! The bench feels strong to us, not uncomfortable. The tea warms us inside, the sun on the outside. I joke with my husband; I say we are part of the house: the adobe gets baked, and so do we. For the most part we say nothing, though. It is enough to sit and be part of God's world. We hear the birds talking to each other, and are grateful they come as close to us as they do; all the more reason to keep our tongues still and hold ourselves in one place. We listen to cars going by and wonder who is rushing off. A car to us is a mystery. The young understand a car. They cannot imagine themselves not driving. They have not the interest we had in horses. Who is to compare one lifetime with another, but a horse is alive and one loves a horse and is loved by a horse. Cars come and go so fast. One year they command all eyes. The next year they are a cause for shame. The third year they must be thrown away without the slightest regret. I may exaggerate, but not much!

"My moods are like the Church bell on Sunday: way up, then

down, then up again—and often just as fast. I make noises, too; my husband says he can hear me smiling and hear me turning sour. When I am sour I am really sour—sweet milk turned bad. Nothing pleases me. I am more selfish than my sister. She bends with the wind. I push my heels into the ground and won't budge. I know enough to frown at myself, but not enough to change. There was a time when I tried hard. I would talk to myself as if I was the priest. I would promise myself that tomorrow I would be different. I suppose only men and women can fool themselves that way; an animal knows better. Animals are themselves. We are always trying to be better—and often we end up even worse than we were to start with.

"But now, during the last moments of life, I think I have learned a little wisdom. I can go for days without an upset. I think I dislike our priest because he reminds me of myself. I have his long forefinger, and I can clench my fist like him and pound the table and pour vinegar on people with my remarks. It is no good to be like that. A man is lucky; it is in his nature to fight or preach. A woman should be peaceful. My mother used to say all begins the day we are born: some are born on a clear, warm day; some when it is cloudy and stormy. So, it is a consolation to find myself easy to live with these days. And I have found an answer to the few moods I still get. When I have come back from giving the horses each a cube or two of sugar, I give myself the same. I am an old horse who needs something sweet to give her more faith in life!

"The other day I thought I was going to say good-bye to this world. I was hanging up some clothes to dry. I love to do that, then stand back and watch and listen to the wind go through the socks or the pants or the dress, and see the sun warm them and make them smell fresh. I had dropped a few clothespins. and was picking them up, when suddenly I could not catch my breath, and a sharp pain seized me over my chest. I tried hard to stand up, but I couldn't. I wanted to scream but I knew there was no one nearby to hear. My husband had gone to the store. I sat down on the ground and waited. It was strong, the pain; and there was no one to tell about it. I felt as if someone had lassoed me and was pulling the rope tighter and tighter. Well here you are, an old cow, being taken in by the good Lord; that is what I thought.

"I looked at myself, sitting on the ground. For a second I was my old self again—worrying about how I must have appeared there, worrying about my dress, how dirty it would get to be. This is no place for an old lady, I thought—only for one of my little grandchildren, who love to play out here, build their castles of dirt, wetted down with water I give to them. Then more pain; I thought I had about a minute of life left. I said my prayers. I said good-bye to the house. I pictured my husband in my mind: fifty-seven years of marriage. Such a good man! I said to myself that I might not see him ever again; surely God would take him into Heaven, but as for me, I have no right to expect that outcome. Then I looked up to the sky and waited.

"My eye caught sight of a cloud. It was darker than the rest. It was alone. It was coming my way. The hand of God, I was sure of it! So that is how one dies. All my life, in the spare moments a person has, I wondered how I would go. Now I knew. Now I was ready. I thought I would soon be taken up to the cloud and across the sky I would go, and that would be that. But the cloud kept moving, and soon it was no longer above me, but beyond me; and I was still on my own land, so dear to me, so familiar after all these years. I can't be dead, I thought to myself, if I am here and the cloud is way over there, and getting further each second. Maybe the next cloud—but by then I had decided God had other things to do. Perhaps my name had come up, but He had decided to call others before me, and get around to me later. Who can ever know His reasons? Then I spotted my neighbor walking down the road, and I said to myself that I would shout for him. I did, and he heard. But you know, by the time he came I had sprung myself free. That is right, the pain was all gone.

"He helped me up, and he was ready to go find my husband and bring him back. No, I told him no; I was all right, and I did not want to risk frightening my husband. He is excitable. He might get some kind of attack himself. I went inside and put myself down on our bed and waited. For an hour—it was that long, I am sure—my eyes stared at the ceiling, held on to it for dear life. I thought of what my life had been like: a simple life, not a very important one, maybe an unnecessary one. I am sure there are better people, men and women all over the world, who have done more for their neighbors and yet not lived as long as I have. I felt ashamed for a few minutes: all the complaints I'd made to myself and to my family, when the truth has been that my fate has been to live a long and healthy life, to have a good and loyal husband, and to bring two sons and three daughters into this world. I thought of the five children we had lost, three before they had a chance to take a breath. I wondered where in the universe they were. In the evening sometimes, when I go to close loose doors that otherwise complain loudly all night, I am likely to look at the stars and feel my long-gone infants near at hand. They are far off, I know; but in my mind they have become those stars—very small, but shining there bravely, no matter how cold it is so far up. If the stars have courage, we ought have courage; that is what I was thinking, as I so often have in the past—and just then he was there, my husband, calling my name and soon looking into my eyes with his.

"I'm all right, I told him. He didn't know what had happened; our neighbor had sealed his lips, as I told him to do. But my husband knows me, so he knew I looked unusually tired; and he couldn't be easily tricked by me. The more I told him I'd just worked too hard, that is all, the more he knew I was holding back something. Finally, I pulled my ace card. I pretended to be upset by his questions and by all the attention he was giving me. I accused him: why do you make me want to cry, why do you wish me ill, with those terrible thoughts of yours, I am not ill! If you cannot let me rest without thinking I am, then God have mercy on you for having such an imagination! God have mercy! With the second plea to our Lord, he was beaten and silent. He left me alone. I was about to beg him to come back, beg his forgiveness. But I did not want him to bear the burden of knowing: he would not rest easy by day or by night. This way he can say to himself: she has always been cranky, and she will always be cranky, so thank God her black moods come only now and then—a spell followed by the bright sun again.

"I will say what I think happened: I came near going, then there was a change of heart up there in Heaven, so I have a few more days, or weeks, or months, or years—who knows? As for a doctor, I have never seen one, so why start now? Here we are so far away from a hospital. We have no money. Anglos don't like us, anyway: we are the poor ones, the lost ones. My son tells me the Anglos look down on us—old people without education and up in the hills, trying to scrape what we can from the land, and helped only by our animals. No matter; our son is proud of us. He is proud to stay here with us. He says that if he went to the city he would beg for work and be told no, no, no: eventually he might be permitted to sweep someone's floor. Better to hold on to one's land. Better to fight it out with the weather and the animals.

"Again I say it: doctors are for others. My mother and my aunt delivered my children. I once went to see a nurse; she worked for the school and she told me about my children—the diseases they get. Thank you, I said. Imagine: she thought I knew nothing about bringing up children, or about the obstacles God puts in their way to test them and make them stronger for having gone through a fever, a rash, some pain. No, I will see no nurse and no doctor. They are as far from here as the stars. Oh, that is wrong: they are much farther. The stars I know and recognize and even call by name. They are my names, of course; I don't know what others call the stars. Is it wrong to do that? Perhaps I should ask the priest. Perhaps the stars are God's to name, not ours to treat like pets—by addressing them familiarly. But it is too late; my sins have been recorded, and I will soon enough pay for each and every one of them."

True, I have pulled together remarks made over a stretch of months. And again, I have translated her Spanish into plain, understandable English, or at least I hope I have done so. I have even "cleaned up" her English to an extent: that is, I have eliminated some of the repetitive words or phrases she uses—as we all do when we talk informally to a visitor in our homes. On the other hand, I have made every effort to keep faithful to the spirit, and mostly the letter of her remarks. I have found that her Spanish is as bare, unaffected and strong as her English. I have found that in both languages she struggles not only to convey meaning, but enliven her words with her heart's burden or satisfactions. I have found that she struggles not only with her mind but her body, her whole being, to express herself. Nor is she alone, some peculiar or specially gifted person whose manner of expression is thoroughly idiosyncratic. She is one of a number of aged Spanish-speaking men and women of New Mexico I have been privileged to meet and visit in their homes. And she certainly can be saddled with negatives, however compelling her way of speaking. She is uneducated. She is superstitious. She never has attended any bilingual classes. She is poor. Maybe some doctor would find her at times forgetful, a little "senile." She and others like her are rural people; they belong to a social and economic "system" that we all know is "out-of-date," whereas the future of America is to be found in cities like Albuquerque and their suburbs. Or so we are told.

Nor is she saintly. She can be morose, and at times quite cranky and reticent. Once she asked me this: "What is the point of trying to talk to those who are deaf?" She had in mind some Anglo county officials who refused a needy cousin of hers food stamps. She had in mind an Anglo teacher or two, and yes, a Spanish-speaking teacher or two; they had said rude things to her grandchildren and to their parents, her children. So, she becomes bitter and tense, and after a while she explodes. She admits it is not in her "nature" to hold in her beliefs, her feelings. She must have her say. And when she does her hands move, her body sways a bit, and sometimes, when she is especially worked up, there is a lurch forward from the chair, so that suddenly she is standing—giving a sermon, almost like the priests she has listened to all these years. A hand goes out, then is withdrawn. The head goes up, then is lowered. A step is taken forward, then back she goes—and soon she is seated again, ready to sew and continue the conversation on a less intense level. When she searches for a word, be it in Spanish or English, she drops her needle and thread, drops a fork or spoon, drops anything she may have in her hands. She needs those old, arthritic fingers of hers. They flex and unflex; it is as if before her is a sandpile of words, and she must push and probe her way through it, until she has found what she is looking for. Then the fingers can stop, the hands can relax and go back to other business or simply be allowed a rest on her lap.

The more time I spend with this woman and her husband and their friends and neighbors and relatives, the more confused I become by much of what I read about them and their so-called "cultural disadvantage." I have no inclination to turn such people into spotless, utterly flawless human beings, yet another highly romanticized group, to be used as bludgeons against the rest of the country. They can be mean and narrow at times; the woman I have been quoting says things about "hippies," and even at times about Anglos, that I disagree with or find exaggerated, unfair, distorted. As for her own disposition, she makes clear her personal limitations. Still, she and her kind are at best pitied by many who have described their "plight." If there are grounds for pity (poverty, substantial unemployment, a degree of prejudice even in New Mexico, never mind Texas or California) there are also grounds for respect and admiration—maybe even envy. Some of us who have gone through all those schools and colleges and graduate schools, who have plenty of work and who live comfortable upper-middle-class lives, might want to stop and think about how *we* talk.

Occasionally I come home from a day spent with Chicano families or Indian families and pick up a psychiatric journal, or for that matter, the daily newspaper. Or I happen to go to a professional meeting and hear papers presented, or afterwards, people talking in lobbies or corridors or restaurants—all those words, all those ideas, spoken by men and women who have no doubt about their importance, their achievements, and certainly, their ability to "communicate." No one is proposing that jargon-filled scholars of one sort or another overcome their "cultural disadvantage." Few are examining ever so closely the rhetoric of various business and professional people, or their elected leaders— the phony, deceiving, dull, dreary, ponderous, smug, deadly words and phrases such people use and use and use. Relatively few are looking at the way such people are taught in elementary school and high school and beyond. Who is to be pitied, the old lady who can't recognize a possible coronary seizure, and instead sees the hand of God approaching her, or some of us who jabber with our clichés and don't have the slightest idea how to use a metaphor or an image in our speech?

61. I, Too

LANGSTON HUGHES

I, too, sing America.

I am the darker brother.
They send me to eat in the kitchen

When company comes,
But I laugh,
And eat well,
And grow strong.

Tomorrow,
I'll be at the table
When company comes.
Nobody'll dare
Say to me,
"Eat in the kitchen,"
Then.

Besides,
They'll see how beautiful I am
And be ashamed—

I, too, am America.

Suggestions for Writing

1. Write an extended description of a decaying building and its setting, adopting the tone and metaphorical eye of Lew Archer.

2. Take an article in the *Encyclopaedia Britannica* on someone you admire and condense it into three vivid paragraphs in the style of Donald Culross Peattie.

3. Write an essay on "The Power of Metaphor," using the poems in this section (and the prose, too, for that matter) as your evidence.

4. Write a review of Mrs. Van Duyn's poem, explaining to your readers what its weaknesses are, if any, what its strengths and qualities are, what value it has, all in all.

5. Compare the poems of Brooks, Hill, and Kennedy in a detailed analysis of tone, metaphor, and central idea.

6. Write an essay "On Feeling Inadequate," borrowing evidence and inspiration from Ephron and Woolf.

7. Write an essay on values, possessions, daily living, deriving from your responses to the woman's account of her life, in Coles.

8. Write an essay explaining the implications of Hughes's poem, in the light of Coles's "Two Languages, One Soul."

VIII. Toward Argument

Induction and Deduction

THE FLOW AND EBB OF THOUGHT. Induction: the bits and particles flow up to the full idea. Deduction: the idea spreads its details outward toward full understanding. Since these are the two major currents of thought, we can use them to organize our essays. But the way we think and the way we write are sometimes opposite. Usually, we come to our ideas *inductively,* putting details together until we suddenly grasp their meaning. Usually, we explain this same meaning *deductively,* setting forth our conviction as our thesis and then explaining the details and arguments that support it. To repeat: we usually lay out our essays deductively, first posing our thesis, then filling in the persuasive evidence and meeting the objections and ending with our thesis reaffirmed. Our exposition, therefore, directly assists an argument.

Most of the selections in this chapter, however, move inductively. They begin with bits of evidence and move up toward a central idea. Kohl starts inductively, as suits his temperament and experience, but rather early in his essay he reaches his central idea and proceeds, deductively, to illustrate it. Try to mark the point at which his direction shifts. De Angulo is beautifully and wholly inductive. His evidence flows in narrative ripples, with his central idea, still unstated at the end, still lapping the shores of our minds nevertheless. Poe is an odd case. His great synthetic spectacular, *The Raven,* is all induction. Who is that rapping? Could it be a ghost? How about the window? His dubious explanation of how he wrote the poem is deductive—"all poetic creation is rational"— even though he describes his supposedly inductive procedure. Stewart challenges Poe in almost wholly inductive steps, except for his deductive proposition at the end of his fourth paragraph: "Poe was thinking more about Barnaby's bird . . . ." Try to identify the inductive and deductive turns in his essay. Dahl's "Taste" is sheer romp on inductive-deductive reasoning. Identify these elements of the story and describe their power. Notice also how Dahl underlines the necessary facts.

62. Children Writing: The Story of an Experiment

HERBERT KOHL

Herbert Kohl has directed the Teachers and Writers Collaborative at Teachers College, Columbia University. His *The Age of Complexity* (1965), *Language and Education of the Deaf* (1966), *Stuff: A Collection . . . from Young Writers in Schools* (1967), and *36 Children* (1968) document his interest in reaching children through writing.

SHOP WITH MOM

I love to shop with mom
And talk to the friendly grocer
And help her make the list
Seems to make us closer.
    —Nellie, age 11

THE JUNKIES

When they are
in the street
they pass it
along to each
other but when
they see the
police they would
run some would
just stand still
and be beat
so pity ful
that they want
to cry
    —Mary, age 11

NELLIE'S POEM received high praise. Her teacher liked the rhyme "closer" and "grocer," and thought she said a great deal in four lines. Most of all the teacher was pleased that Nellie expressed such a pleasant and healthy thought. Nellie's poem was published in the school paper. I was moved and excited by Mary's poem and made the mistake of showing it to the teacher who edited the school newspaper. She was horrified. First of all, she informed me, Mary couldn't possibly know what junkies were, and, moreover, the other children wouldn't be interested in such a poem. There weren't any rhymes or clearly discernible meter. The word "pityful" was split up incorrectly, "be beat" wasn't proper English, and, finally, it wasn't really poetry but just the ramblings of a disturbed girl.

My initial reaction was outrage—what did she know about poetry, or about Mary? But it is too easy to be cruel about the ignorance that is so characteristic of the schools today. That teacher did believe that she knew what poetry was, and that there was a correct language in which it was expressed. Her attitude toward the correctness of language and the form of poetry was in a way identical to her attitude toward what sentiments good children's poems ought to express. Yet language is not static, nor is it possible *a priori* to establish rules governing what can or cannot be written any more than it is possible to establish rules governing what can or cannot be felt.

Not long ago when I was teaching a class of remote, resistant children in a Harlem school, as an experiment I asked these children to write. I had no great expectations. I had been told that the children were from one to three years behind in reading, that they came from "deprived" and "disadvantaged" homes and were ignorant of the language of the schools. I had also been told that their vocabulary was limited, that they couldn't make abstractions, were not introspective, oriented to physical rather than mental activity. Other teachers in the school called the children "them" and spoke of teaching as a thankless military task. I couldn't accept this mythology; I wanted my pupils to tell me about themselves. For reasons that were hardly literary I set out to explore the possibilities of teaching language, literature, and writing in ways that would enable children to speak about what they felt they were not allowed to acknowledge publicly. Much to my surprise the children wrote a great deal; and they invented their own language to do so. Only a very small number of the children had what can be called "talent," and many of them had only a single story to write and rewrite; yet almost all of them responded, and seemed to become more alive through their writing. The results of some of this exploration are presented here.

I have subsequently discovered other teachers who have explored language and literature with their pupils in this way, with results no less dramatic. The children we have taught ranged from the preschool years to high school, from lower-class ghetto children to upper-class suburban ones. There are few teaching techniques that we share in common, and no philosophy of education that binds us. Some of these teachers have tight, carefully controlled classrooms; others care less for

332

order and more for invention. There are Deweyites, traditionalists, classicists—a large range of educational philosophies and teaching styles. If there is anything common to our work it is the concern to listen to what the children have to say and the ability to respond to it as honestly as possible, no matter how painful it may be to our teacherly prides and preconceptions. We have allowed ourselves to learn from our pupils and to expect the unexpected.

Children will not write if they are afraid to talk. Initially they suspect teachers and are reluctant to be honest with them. They have had too many experiences where the loyalties of the staff and the institutional obligations of teachers have taken precedence over honesty. They have seen too much effort to maintain face, and too little respect for justifiable defiance in their school lives. I think children believe that there is a conscious collusion between all of the adults in a school to maintain the impression that the authority is *always* right, and that life is *always* pleasant and orderly. Unfortunately, the collusion is unconscious or at least unspoken. This is dramatically true in slum schools where the pressures of teaching are increased by understaffing and a vague uneasiness about race which is always in the air.

I was assigned to a school in East Harlem in September 1962 and was not sufficiently prepared for the faculty's polite lies about their success in the classroom or the resistance and defiance of the children. My sixth-grade class had thirty-six pupils, all Negro. For two months I taught in virtual isolation from my pupils. Every attempt I made to develop rapport was coldly rejected. The theme of work scheduled by the school's lesson plan for that semester was "How We Became Modern America," and my first lesson was characteristic of the dull response everything received.

It seemed natural to start by comparing a pioneer home with the modern life the children knew—or, more accurately, I thought they knew. I asked the class to think of America in the 1850s and received blank stares, although that presumably was what they had studied the previous year. I pursued the matter.

"Can anyone tell me what was happening around 1850, just before the Civil War? I mean, what do you think you'd see if you walked down Madison Avenue then?"

"Cars."

"Do you think there were cars in 1850? That was over a hundred years ago. Think of what you learned last year and try again, do you think there were cars then?"

"Yes . . . no . . . I don't know."

Someone else tried.

"Grass and trees?"

The class broke out laughing. I tried to contain my anger and frustration.

VIII. Toward Argument:
Induction and Deduction

"I don't know what you're laughing about, it's the right answer. In those days Harlem was farmland with fields and trees and a few farmhouses. There weren't any roads or houses like the ones outside, or street lights or electricity."

The class was outraged and refused to think. Bright faces took on the dull glaze that is characteristic of the Negro child who finds it less painful to be thought stupid than to be defiant. There was an uneasy drumming on desk tops. The possibility of there being a time when Harlem didn't exist had never, could never have occurred to the children. Nor did it occur to me that their experience of modern America was not what I had come to teach about. After two months, in despair, I asked the kids to write about their block.

WHAT A BLOCK!

My block is the most terrible block I've ever seen. There are at least 25 or 30 narcartic people in my block. The cops come around there and tries to act bad but I bet inside of them they are as scared as can be. They even had in the papers that this block is the worst block, not in Manhattan but in New York City. In the summer they don't do nothing except shooting, stabing, and fighting. They hang all over the stoops and when you say excuse me to them they hear you but they just don't feel like moving. Some times they make me so mad that I feel like slaping them and stuffing and bag of garbage down their throats. Theres only one policeman who can handle these people and we all call him "Sunny." When he come around in his cop car the people run around the corners, and he wont let anyone sit on the stoops. If you don't believe this story come around some time and you'll find out.

—Grace, age 11

My block is the worse block you ever saw people getting killed or stabbed men and women in buildin's taking dope . . .

—Mary, age 11

MY NEIGHBORHOOD

I live on 117 street, between Madison and 5th avenue. All the bums live around here. But the truth is they don't live here they just hang around the street. All the kids call it "Junky's Paradise."

—James, age 12

My block is a dirty crumby block!

—Clarence, age 12

The next day I threw out my notes and my lesson plans and talked to the children. What I had been assigned to teach seemed, in any case, an unreal myth about a country that never has existed. I didn't believe the tale of "progress" the curriculum had prescribed, yet had been afraid to discard it and had been willing to lie to the children. After all, I didn't want to burden them or cause them pain, and I had to teach something. I couldn't "waste their time." How scared I must have been when I started teaching in Harlem to accept those hollow rationalizations and use the "curriculum" to protect me from the children. I accepted the myth that the teacher and the book know all; that complex human questions had "right" and "wrong" answers. It was much easier than facing the world the children perceived and attempting to cope with it. I could lean on the teachers' manuals and feel justified in presenting an unambiguously "good" historical event or short story. It protected my authority as a teacher which I didn't quite believe in. It was difficult for me: pontificating during the day and knowing that I was doing so at night. Yet could I cause the class much more pain or impose greater burdens with my lies than they already had? How much time could I have "wasted" even if I let the children dance and play all day while I sought for a new approach? They had already wasted five years in school by the time they arrived in my class.

So we spoke. At first the children were suspicious and ashamed of what they'd written. But as I listened and allowed them to talk they became bolder and angrier, then finally quieter and relieved. I asked them to write down what they would do to change things, and they responded immediately.

> If I could change my block I would stand on Madison Ave and throw nothing but Teargas in it. I would have all the people I liked to get out of the block and then I would become very tall and have big hands and with my big hands I would take all of the narcartic people and pick them up with my hand and throw them in the nearest river and oceans. I would go to some of those old smart alic cops and throw them in the Ocians and Rivers too. I would let the people I like move into the projects so they could tell their friends that they live in a decent block. If I could do this you would never see 117 st again.
>
> —Grace, age 11

> If I could change my block I would put all the bums on an Island where they can work there. I would give them lots of food. But I wouldn't let no whiskey be brought to them. After a year I would ship them to new York and make them clean up junk in these back yard and make them maybe make a baseball diamond and put swings basketball courts etc.
>
> —Clarence, age 12

For several weeks after that the children wrote and wrote—what their homes were like, whom they liked, where they came from. I discovered that everything I'd been told about the children's language was irrelevant. Yes, they were hip when they spoke, inarticulate and concrete. But their writing was something else, when they felt that no white man was judging their words, threatening their confidence and pride. They faced a blank page and wrote directly and honestly. Recently I have mentioned this to teachers who have accepted the current analyses of "the language" of the "disadvantaged." They asked their children to write and have been as surprised as I was, and shocked by the obvious fact that "disadvantaged" children will not speak in class because they cannot trust their audience.

Nothing the school offered was relevant, so I read the class novels, stories, poems, brought my library to class and let them know that many people have suffered throughout history and that some were articulate enough to create literature from their lives. They didn't believe me, but they were hungry to know what had been written about and what could be written about.

It was easier for the class to forget their essays than it was for me. They were eager to go beyond their block, to move out into the broader world and into themselves. We talked of families, of brothers and sisters, of uncles, and of Kenny's favorite subject, the Tyranny of Teachers and Moms.

We spoke and read about love and madness, families, war, the birth and death of individuals and societies; and then they asked me permission to write themselves. Permission!

In the midst of one of our discussions of fathers, Sheila asked me a question that has become symbolic of my pupils' hunger for concepts. "Mr. Kohl," she said, "if you wanted to write something about your father that was true, is there a word for it?" What she meant was that if there was a word for it she would do it, but if there wasn't she would be scared. One names what is permissible, and denies names to what one fears. Sheila led us to talk about biography and autobiography, and she did get to write of her father.

A BIOGRAPHY OF MY FATHER

> My father was born in California. He wasn't a hero or anything like that to anyone but to me he was. He was a hard working man he wasn't rich but he had enough money to take care of us. He was mean in a way of his own. But I loved him and he loved me. He said to my mother when he die she would feel it. My father was a man who loved his work besides if I was a man who worked as a grocery store I would love it to. He wanted his kids to grow up to be someone and be big at name. He wanted a real life. But when he died we started a real life.

The children spoke of themselves as well. They knew what they felt and sometimes could say it. Sharon came into class angry one day and wrote about a fight.

ONE DAY THERE WAS A BIG FIGHT

One day in school a girl started getting smart with a boy. So
the boy said to the girl why don't you come outside? The girl
said alright I'll be there. The girl said you just wait. And he
said don't wait me back. And so the fight was on. One had a
swollen nose the other a black eye. And a teacher stoped the
fight. His name was Mr. Mollow. I was saying to myself I
wish they would mind their own business. It made me bad. I
had wanted to see a fight that day. So I call Mr. Mollow up.
I called him all kinds of names. I said you ugly skinney bony
man. I was red hot. And when I saw him I rolled my eyes as
if I wanted to hit him. All that afternoon I was bad at Mr.
Mollow.

I tried to talk to her about her paper, tell her that "it made me
bad" didn't make any sense. And she explained to me that "being
bad" was a way of acting and that down South a "bad nigger" was
one who was defiant of the white man's demands. She concluded by
saying that being bad was good in a way and bad in a way. I asked
the class and they agreed. In the midst of the discussion Louis asked
one of his characteristically exasperating questions: "But where do words
come from anyway?"

I stumbled over an answer as the uproar became general.

"What use are words anyway?"

"Why do people have to talk?"

"Why are there good words and bad words?"

"Why aren't you supposed to use some words in class?"

"Why can't you change words as you like?"

I felt that I was being "put on," and was tempted to pass over the
questions glibly; there were no simple answers to the children's questions, and the simplest thing to do when children ask difficult questions
is to pretend that they're not serious or they're stupid. But the children
were serious.

More and more they asked about language and would not be put
off by evasive references to the past, linguistic convention and tradition.
Children look away from adults as soon as adults say that things are
the way they are because they have always been that way. When a child
accepts such an answer it is a good indication that he has given up
and decided to be what adults would make him rather than himself.

I decided to explore language with the children, and we talked
about mythology together.

I thought of Sheila's question and Louis's question, of Sheila's desire to tell a story and her fear of doing it. The children rescued me.
Ronald told me one day that Louis was "psyching" him and asked
me to do something. I asked him what he was talking about, what he

meant by "psyching." He didn't know, and when I asked the class they couldn't quite say either, except that they all knew that Louis was "psyche," as they put it. I said that Louis couldn't be Psyche since Psyche was female. The kids laughed and asked me what I meant. I countered with the story of Cupid and Psyche and the next day followed with readings from Apuleius and C. S. Lewis. Then I talked about words that came from Psyche: psychology, psychic, psychosomatic. We even puzzled out the meaning of psyching, and one of the children asked me if there were any words from Cupid. I had never thought of cupidity in that context before, but it made sense.

From Cupid and Psyche we moved to Tantalus, the Sirens and the Odyssey. We talked of Venus and Adonis and spent a week on first Pan and panic, pan-American, then pandemonium, and finally on daemonic and demons and devils.

Some of the children wrote myths themselves and created characters named Skyview, Missile, and Morass. George used one of the words in his first novel:

> One day, in Ancient Germany, a boy was growing up. His name was Pathos. He was named after this Latin word because he had sensitive feelings.

The class began a romance with words and language that lasted all year. Slowly the children turned to writing, dissatisfied with mere passive learning. They explored their thoughts and played with the many different forms of written expression. I freed the children of the burden of spelling and grammar while they were writing. If a child asked me to comment on the substance of his work I did not talk of the sentence structure. There is no more deadly thing a teacher can do than ignore what a child is trying to express in his writing and comment merely upon the form, neatness, and heading.[1] Yet there is nothing safer if the teacher is afraid to become involved. It is not that I never taught grammar or spelling; it is rather that the teaching of grammar and spelling is not the same as the teaching of writing. Once children care about writing and see it as important to themselves they want to write well. At that moment, I found, they easily accept the discipline of learning to write correctly. Vocabulary, spelling, and grammar become the means to achieving more precise and sophisticated forms of expression and not merely empty ends in themselves.

In my class a child had permission to write whenever he felt he had to. Barbara, a taciturn girl who had never written a word,

---

[1] The habit of grading a written exercise according to form, neatness, spelling, punctuation, and heading is not surprising considering that the written part of the examination for the New York City substitute elementary school teaching license is graded that way. Content is irrelevant.

put her reader down one day and wrote for fifteen minutes. Then she handed me this:

ONE COLD AND RAINY NIGHT

It was one cold and rainy night when I was walking through the park and all was in the bed. I saw a owl up in the tree. And all you could see was his eyes. He had big white and black eyes. And it was rainy and it was very very cold that night. And I only had on one thin coat. I was cold that rainy night. I was colder than that owl. I don't know how he could sit up in that tree. It was dark in the park. And only the one who had the light was the owl. He had all the light I needed. It was rainy that stormy night. And I was all by myself. Just walking through the park on my way home. And when I got home I went to bed. And I was thinking about it all that night. And I was saying it was a cold and rainy night and all was in bed.

She explained that she had not slept and wanted to write. She only wrote occasionally after producing this paragraph. I could have encouraged her to continue writing, to build her paragraph into a story. But she didn't want to write. She wanted to exorcise an image that particular day. A teacher does not have to make everything educational, to "follow up" on all experiences and turn a meaningful moment into a "learning situation." There is no need to draw conclusions or summarize what the child said. Often teachers insult their pupils and deceive themselves by commenting and judging where no comment or judgment is called for.

Larry had been writing voluminous comic-book fantasies starring Batman, Robin, and the League of Justice. One day he got bored with these heroes and asked me if he could write about himself. I said of course, and so he produced a fragment of an autobiography, after which he returned to his fantasies. He said that the autobiography helped him to invent his own League and his adventurous novels became more personal. I asked him how it helped him, and he said he couldn't say, but he knew that it did.

THE STORY OF MY LIFE

Foreword

This story is about a boy named Larry and his life as it is and how it will be. Larry is in the six grade now but this story will tell about his past, present, and future. It will tell you how he lived and how he liked it or disliked it. It will tell you how important he was and happy or said he was in this world it will tell you all his thoughts. It may be pleasant and it may be horrible in place but what ever it is it will be good and exciting but! their will be horrible parts. This story will be made simple and easy but in places hard to understand. This is a nonfiction book.

Where I Was Born

In all story they beat around the bush before they tell you the story well I am not this story takes place in the Metropolitan Hospitale.

When I was born I couldn't see at first, but like all families my father was waiting outside after a hour or so I could see shadows. The hospital was very large and their were millions of beds and plenty of people. And their were people in chairs rolling around, people in beds, and people walking around with trays with food or medicine on it. Their was people rolling people in bed and there were people bleeding crying yelling or praying I was put at a window with other babies so my father could see me their was a big glass and lots of people around me so I could see a lot of black shapes. And since I was a baby I tried to go through the glass but I didn't succeed. All the people kept looking I got scared and cryed soon the nurse came and took all the babies back to their mothers. . . .

George was shy and quiet and invented his own characters from the beginning. He was the class artist and drew pictures for everybody. He wrote for himself.

A JOURNEY THROUGH TIME AND SPACE

Chapter III Just a Tramp

George had been in jail for so long, that he lost everything he had. He didn't even have a cent. "Well," he thought, "I guess I'll have to get a job." He went by a restaurant and got a job as a waiter. One day, a drunky came into the restaurant and ordered some wine. George brought him his wine then after he got through drinking it out of the bottle the drunky said, "How's 'bout yous an' me goin' to a bar t'night?" George was afraid he would lose his job if he had been caught drinking. So he said, "Get out of this restaurant, or I'll call the manager!" With that, the drunken man hit George in the jaw with his fist and knocked him down. George couldn't take being pushed around any longer, so he got up and knocked the drunky down. The drunky got up and pulled out a knife. George grabbed at the knife and tried to make him drop it. They both fought for the knife knocking chairs and taking the worst beatings.

The manager was so afraid that he ran to get the police. Two policemen came in, and the minute George saw them, he knew he would have to spend another month in jail. So he jumped out the restaurant door and ran down the street. The policemen pursued George around the corner where George hid in a hallway and the police passed him. "Whew," he panted quietly, "I'm glad they're gone! But now, I guess, I'm just a tramp. If I leave town, it won't do no good." So he decided to hide in his basement ex-laboratory. He had been in jail for so long he had forgtten where it was. He strolled along the streets day and night. His clothes were getting raggety and people laughed at him. His mother taught him not to beg, even if he didn't have a penny. And George never did beg. And kids made up a song for him:

We know a bum who walks down the street,
In rain, or snow, or slush or sleet
He can't afford to do anything right;
'cause if you see him you'll pop like dynamite!

They made lots more of him like this:

We know a tramp who walks in the damp,
Like a dirty, stinkin' phoney ol' scamp.
He can't afford no money at all,
Or have a great big party or ball
'cause he's just a big fat slob.
And never has he gotten a job.

The kids sounded on him every day, and he never did get a decent job. But he still had his mind on being a scientist. To invent things and modernize his country.

There is no limit to the forms of writing that children will experiment with. They will readily become involved in provocative open assignments if they are convinced that the teacher does not want a correct answer to an unambiguous question, but rather to hear what they have to say. Themes such as "On Playing Around" and "Walls" do not prejudge how a child must respond. "On How Nice the Summer Is" does. The same is true for open forms of writing such as the fable or the parable. The teacher can provide the framework for many written exercises, but the substance of the children's responses must be drawn from their life and imagination.

This is only part of the story, however, the part which can be attempted with a whole class. It is much more difficult to encourage each child to seek his own voice, and to accept the fact that not everyone will have a literary one. It is a mistake to assume that all children have the energy and devotion necessary to write novels or poems. Children select the forms they are most comfortable with, and therefore it is not easy to teach writing. One cannot teach a sixth-grade class to write novels. The best that can be done is to reveal novels to them and be ready to teach those who want to do more than read. I never made "creative writing" compulsory because it cannot be made compulsory. Writing must be taught qualitatively—how can one best express oneself, in what way? I found that the children understood these most complex questions, and took great pleasure in listening to the various voices of their classmates.

For example, after I read Aesop's fables to my class and we had talked about them, they wrote fables of their own.

> Once upon a time there was a pig and a cat. The cat kept saying old dirty pig who want to eat you. And the pig replied when I die I'll be made use of, but when you die you'll just rot. The cat always thought he was better than the pig. When the pig died he was used as food for the people to eat. When the cat died he was buried in old dirt.
> Moral: Live dirty die clean.
>
> —Barbara, age 11

> Once a boy was standing on a huge metal flattening machine. The flattener was coming down slowly. Now this boy was a boy who love insects and bugs. The boy could have stopped the machine from coming down but there were two ladie bugs on the button and in order to push the button he would kill the two ladie bugs. The flattener was about a half inch over his head now he made a decision he would have to kill the ladie bugs he quickly pressed the button. The machine stoped he was saved and the ladie bugs were dead.
> Moral: smash or be smashed
>
> —Kenneth, age 11

In writings of this sort we can sense the exhilaration felt by children in saying things that might have been out of bounds in the atmosphere of the conventional classroom. In fact the conventional classroom itself sometimes becomes the subject of their essays.[2]

> WHY DO RUSSIANS PLANT TREES?
>
> Children sit in classroom waiting for teacher to come. Teacher walks in. Writes on the board. Question is, Why do Russians plant trees?
> Some answers are, They plant trees to hide their artillery; To hide their cruelty to the people; So we can't see their secret weapons.
> Teacher writes wrong on all. Real answer is Russians plant trees because trees are pretty.
>
> —William Barbour

> WE CAN TEACH EACH OTHER
>
> Inside I feel like I am a nice person; but I have to act like one too: I have to know what kind of person I am. Sometimes, I forget that other people have feelings. Teachers for example; sometimes I hurt them without knowing it. I can say or do something that is so hurtful that they can't say any-

[2] These essays appeared in a magazine *What's Happening,* run by teenagers and sponsored by Elaine Avidon.

thing but, "Get up and get out." They say this so they can go on and teach the rest of us a lesson. But Teachers can hurt you too and they do it just to teach you a lesson.

You are a child of learning in some ways, but in other ways children teach teachers. I don't know what a teacher is like or how she feels, just like a teacher doesn't really know what I'm like or how I feel. So I can teach her what and how I think and feel. Teachers have been children before, but they seem to forget what it's like because the time changes in the way that the weather changes. So they can't say, well it's like when I was a child.

No, it's not like that, because people are changing and our minds are changing too. So children teach teachers a new lesson, about children today.

—Patricia Williams

With some children it is more difficult to see the potential. I once had a young Puerto Rican boy in a sixth-grade class. He was shy, and according to the record had an IQ of 79 and was illiterate. He listened intensely in class when I taught reading, otherwise he seemed to be somewhere else. He never spoke in class; yet after the Christmas holiday he came to me and told me that I had taught him how to read. It seemed that the idea that words were divided into syllables excited him, and so over the Christmas vacation he divided all the names under "A" in the phone book into syllables and learned how to read. I was astonished at his excitement over a fact of grammar that seemed dull and matter-of-fact to me. I encouraged Carlos to write, and for all his struggle with the English language a beautiful, sad world emerged:

One cold rainy day I was going to school and I had to go 1,000 miles to get there and there wasn't no cars and no buses and train so I had to walk. I got soke a wet. I still had 500 more miles to go at last I almost got there and went I got there the school was close and I thought for a minute and then I remember it was a haliday and then I droped deid.

It rains too much and my flowers vegetable and gardens they get too much water. I got to think of something fast because if it keeps on like this my plants can't grow. So one day I was walking in the street when I saw this store selling rain supplies so I went in and got some then I went back home and I had one that will just rite rain so I planted in the ground and the next day I couldn't believe my eyes all the plants were just growing up. So I live haplly ever after.

I just don't like to think because every time I think I get a headache because one time I was thinking about the world fair and I build a mental picture in my mind I was enjoying myself then I stop thinking. I was going home went suddenly I felt something in my mind and I got a headache and I was criing because my mind hurt. From that day on I can't think.

> It happens every time I go to bed I forget to brush your teeth. Then the second time I forgot the third time I forgot too so I had to do something, so one day I was very sleepy I was going to my bed then sudently I open my eyes then I remember and I ran back to bath tob and I brush my teeth you didn't got me this time so I went back to bed and then every single day I brush my teeth live happly ever after.
>
> —Carlos, age 12

I gave Carlos books to read and encouraged him to listen to the people around him and record their speech and manner, and try to understand and capture their style. Trying to help Carlos I found there were kinds of heightened perception that supposedly "limited" children can develop as enthusiastically as they evolve their own styles of life. I feel that there are many unexplored possibilities of developing writing and perception, perhaps for the not so sensitive as well as for the hypersensitive.

Carlos still tries to write in a halfhearted manner, but he receives no encouragement. It seems that writing is not a subject given high priority at the junior high school he attends. It is more concerned to teach mathematics and science to those few children who will make it.

Up to this point I have been primarily concerned with the writing that can be taught all children. Any significant program must also provide for those few children who not only write but write with a seriousness and intensity that are not usual. These children, even at the age of twelve, would like to become writers, and in a few cases there are children whose work shows such a stamp of individuality and such unmistakable perception and love of language that there is hope that if they are taken seriously they could become writers.

Such children pose special problems for the schools because they may not conform to the usual measure of academic success. They are not likely to be excellent scientists or mathematicians and are more than likely individualistic, somewhat withdrawn and self-sufficient. Most teachers do not know what to do with these children and are usually content to let them sit silently in their classes. If their talents are discovered they are not made much of since they are not so likely to fit into the rigid categories that the teacher judges as excellent.

The story of the last child I would like to introduce here is a sad and continuing tragic waste of human talent. Louis, a boy of eleven, passionately loved language, and whenever he was not overburdened with his personal problems he played with language with unusual mastery. I never had a pupil who absorbed words more quickly and intuitively than Louis. Nor have I had one who was so discontent with static, colorless style, or so articulate in criticizing the banal readers that are provided in the schools.

When I took Louis to see Cacoyannis's *Elektra* he said, "You mean that a myth is a way of saying something about yourself, something that you can communicate to other people by telling them a story that represents what they feel, what they see as important? That means I could write my Electra, the story of me and my mother and sister only not us, but something that other people could understand and would be better than us, more beautiful, it wouldn't hurt me so much to tell it that way."

> Foreword
> This story called Elektra is of the deepest passion and the deepest hope of avengence of her father's death. Her father was called Aggememnon. Aggememnon was the rightful ruler of Argos . . . He had been cruely slaughtered by his wife Clytemnestra and her lover Aegisthus.

Louis never finished *Electra.* Nor did he finish *The Boy in the Slums,* still one of his family's prized possessions.

> THE BOY IN THE SLUMS
>
> Foreword
> This story is about a boy namely me, who live in an apartment in and around the slum area. I feel that other people should be interested in what I have to say and just like me, *TRY* to do something about it, either by literal or diatribe means. This book is only to be read by men and women boys and girls who feel deeply about segregation and feel that this is no joke. Especially when you are younger you have a better opportunity to speak about and be willing to work for these problems of the slums.
>
> 1–Do you live in the slums?
> 2–How do you think you would feel if you did?
> 3–Would you rather be rich have maids and servants to take care of you while your mother is away to dinners, nightclubs, and business trips? Or would you rather be poor and your mother'd be home to *Love* and take care of you?
>
> Before I wrote the last question down I made sure that at least *I* knew the answer. I had a decision to make also because my mother asked me that same question just a few days ago and take it from me its not easy to answer a question like that. But if just by mere curiosity you would like to know my answer to this question just open the pages of this book and read to your hearts content and do me a favor (just as a friend) tell other people about this book and *maybe* they may be encouraged to read this Book. (Oh, by the way all through this book a word will be underlined and if by any chance you want to know what this word means just look it up in the back of this Book it is called "Louis' Slang Dictionary")

I–An Introduction to My Mother

I am dreaming and crying in my sleep.

I am dreaming because I have nothing better to do and crying because I am dreaming about a problem I had in school, you see I promise myself I'll be good and try to learn more, but everytime I come into the classroom (in my dream) my teacher right then and there starts to pick on me Louis this or Louis that. So I say to myself "Enough is too much, everyday the same old problem" why that's enough even to make a laughing hyena cry (wouldn't you if you were in my situation?)

Just as I was about to cry in my sleep for the second time unexpectedly a hand hit me right on my rear end (I knew it was a hand because I had felt this more than once) Of course I woke up and immediately knew that it was time for my brothers and my sisters and me to get ready to go to school. My youngest sisters name is Rene she is 3 years next comes Pamela she is 8 years old, my next sister's name is Alice. She is 9 years old, then comes my Brother who's name is Robert he is 10, then comes me Louis I am 11 then comes my next sister Diane she is 12 years going on 13, and last but not least My Oldest Sister who's name is Barbara she is 14. I know you're not interested in my private life but I'll fill you in a little way just to have something interesting to say. The first thing I have to do is head straight for the Bathe-room (PS By the way the word Bathe is just a fancy word I picked up from my teacher "Mr. Herbert Kohl". You know I'll let you in on a little secret. Mr. Kohl is kind of fancy himself. The reason why I'm telling you this is because my teacher told me to express myself to the *fullest extent* (that's another fancy word I learned from my teacher)

And the first thing I do in the Bathe room is to wash my face and comb my hair while my mother is ironing my shirt and pants. Oh by the way my mother's name is Mrs. Helen Frost (you can call her *ma* or Mrs. Helen cause that what I always call her and she doesn't get mad either). The next thing I do is eat my breakfast which consists of two or three jelly sandwiches and a glass of water or if I'm lucky I'll have a bowl of cereal with *can milk*. At this time it should be 8:30 time to go to school. P.S. 79 here I come I say as I start out of the door to my building. As I walk to the school which is within walking distance from my house I begin to think of things that could but then again couldn't happen. For example: (Maybe someday I'll be a scientist or a big business man or maybe even an engineer or then again the President of the United States or maybe even the mayor. As long as it is somebody important. You see! some people are lucky enough to be born important but not me I'll have to work my way up to what I want to be (my personal opinion of the situation!) if I'm even lucky enough to get that far up as a matter of

fact Ill even be lucky if I get past the sixth grade the way
things are going now. If you ever get into a situation similar
to mine take my advise don't give up you have to work for
your goal, don't worry you'll never be alone in your problems
other people just like you are sharing your same problems.

I feel I have to close this chapter now for I'm digging
into my long buried problems which you probably wouldn't
be interested in anyhow. But do me a favor, read on to the
next chapter.

At present Louis is nowhere. His interest in writing is useless in
school and his sensitivity to words useless on the streets. He believes
in himself and refuses to yield his pride, even if it drives him out of
school. The guidance counselor of his junior high school insisted he take
a vocational course in high school, but Louis persisted and is now in
an academic course in high school. His teachers feel it is a mistake.
He laughs and has taken an Arabic name, an "original" name, a name
that is his strength. His Muslim commitment is not out of hatred—it
is a melancholy sign of the pride and self-love he has been able to
preserve in an unbelieving and hating world.

It is hard to believe that this is necessary or inevitable. Teachers
must be taught to look for sensibility and feeling in their pupils, as well
as the abilities to perform intellectual tasks. Children's literature involves experiment and play. Teachers usually try too hard to interpret
their pupil's work. If a child writes about violence he is looked upon
as expressing violent impulses that are "really" within him. If he writes
about loneliness his teacher tries to provide him with companionship.
This usual view of writing condescendingly implies that the child is
incapable of literary exploration. Worse, it implies he is as humorless
as the adults who assume responsibility for his education. I have laughed,
cried, been duped, outraged, and sometimes bored by what my pupils
have written—and I have told them this. Their effort to understand
themselves and the things around them demands no less.

63. *From* "Indians in Overalls"

JAIME DE ANGULO

The work of Jaime De Angulo (1887–1950), largely
uncollected and unpublished, and unknown since his death,
will soon begin to appear in nine or more volumes under
the auspices of the Jaime De Angulo Library, San Francisco.
Ezra Pound called him "the American Ovid"; Marianne
Moore, E. E. Cummings, Henry Miller, and William Carlos
Williams shared Pound's enthusiasm for his poetry and
prose. He was a Spaniard by birth and was educated in
Paris before graduating in medicine from Johns Hopkins in
1912. He practiced medicine, and served in the Army
Medical Corps in World War I. He became interested in
Indian medicine, and then in Indian magic and languages,
maintaining an intimate study for forty years with an
Indian shaman in Modoc County, northeastern California.
De Angulo made lasting contributions in both Indian
linguistics and folk lore.

I

A STREET IN A LITTLE TOWN on the high desert plateau of
northeastern California. Clear air, blue sky, smell of sagebrush,
smell of burning juniper wood. I was looking for Jack Folsom, an
Indian of the Pit River tribe.

I saw some Paiutes loafing on a corner. I crossed over and asked
them if Jack Folsom was in town. They did not answer me.

I strolled along with my hands in my pockets. Then I saw him, standing in front of a store. Same old Jack; squat, broad figure; very dark
skin, gray hair; battered hat and brand-new overalls; and the same
humorous, quizzical, gray eyes.

"Hallo, Jack."

"Why . . . Doc! Where you been all this time? What you doing
here now? Looking for another cattle ranch?"

"No. No more cattle ranches for me. I came back here to study the
Indian language."

"What you mean, Doc? You mean you want to learn our talk, Pit
River talk? You can't do that, Doc, no use you trying. No white man can

348

learn our words. There ain't a white man in this whole country can talk Pit River. Some fellows, some cowboys think they do but all they know is a couple dirty words. Now, Modoc, or Paiute, that's easy talk. Why don't you try them? There is quite a few white men around here speak pretty good Paiute. I can talk Paiute, too. But Pit River, that's hard talk, Doc."

"Well, I can try, anyhow. Will you teach me?"

"Sure I will. Where you staying at, Doc?"

"Nowhere. I just got in on the train last night. Where are you living now, Jack?"

"Same old place. That little piece Indian land I got from the Government. I got a shack on it. Good water, I got a well. You been there before, Doc, you remember."

"Oh yes, I remember. Have you still got the same woman?"

"Yes, Lena. Big and fat. She still talks about you. She never knew a white man who was willing to sit down and eat with Indians!"

"Say, Jack, may I stay with you?"

"What you mean, Doc? You can't live with Indians!"

"Why not?"

"What would the white men say? They wouldn't allow you. They wouldn't talk to you. They would think you were a dog like us."

"To hell with the white men. I don't like them either. Will you let me stay with you?"

"Why sure I will! I have known you a long time, Doc. But I ain't got blankets enough . . . unless you want to get in bed with Lena and me, but that woman is too big. Ain't hardly room for me alone."

"That's all right, Jack. I'll go and buy some blankets."

"All right, Doc. Throw them in my wagon. That's my wagon there. I'll go and buy some grub. . . ."

All afternoon we drove through the sagebrush. Strong and pungent smell. Jackrabbits. Sometimes a clump of juniper trees, rough bark, gnarled branches. Wide, wide valley almost like a sea. Barely notice the mountains. Canyons with perpendicular sides and rim-rocks frowning. Jog, jog, jogging team of horses, a bay and a roan, raising the dust. There jumps another jackrabbit. Afternoon changing into sunset. A turn of the road around a hill. A crazy fence. Open the gate and almost fall with it. "Indian gate!" laughs Jack. Another turn around the hill in the gathering dusk, and there is the shack. Big fat Lena comes to the door. She sees me. She smiles: "Hallo, Doc!" just as if she had known I was coming, just as if I had left only last week. That was Lena. Always took life like that, as it came.

I had bought a tent and I put it up in the moonlight. It was September and already there was a chill to the night. Jack brought a rabbit-skin blanket and spread it on my bed. "Bet you'll need it before morning, Doc. You don't see many of these any more. Indians too lazy now. Takes hundred and fifty, maybe two hundred rabbits. Well, good night."

I scooped a hollow in the ground for my hips and got in under the blankets. I smoked a cigarette and listened to the coyotes howling and yapping out there in the moonlight. After a while the pack moved away into the distance and their bark was very faintly heard. Silence and moonlight through the tent door. I could not sleep. I smoked cigarette after cigarette. . . .

There was not much in that shack, except a few blankets on a pile of tule stalks in a corner. A good deal of the sky could be seen through the roof. There was a cooking stove, but it had no legs and reposed directly on the floor. Lena had removed the legs so that she could squat on the ground while cooking. She felt that was the proper way to cook, just like a campfire. Many Indian women are quite fat, but Lena was a very mountain of flesh, and getting to her feet was a strenuous operation. It surprised me to see how much she could do without raising her fundament from the floor. She could roll over and reach a frying pan six feet away. But "rolling over" does not describe adequately that peculiar motion, besides imparting to it something of the undignified. Have you ever observed in an aquarium an octopus creeping over a rock? It was a little like that. The rolls of flesh seemed to creep over the floor in advancing waves of cotton print, a brown arm uncoiled itself, the frying pan was reached inexorably.

Lena was not always cooking, although she always squatted on the floor. She also did beadwork, stringing beads of different colors in Indian designs, for belts, for hatbands, for tobacco pouches. The mind of a weaver must be a strange sort of mind, building a picture level after level. From side to side, from left to right, from right to left, it rises all along the line bit by bit. The whole composition has been visualized from the first and no retouching is possible. I used to wonder what went on in her head when her fat fingers got tired and she sat looking through the open door at the hills beyond. In the afternoons the sun came through the door, an autumn sun already, and the air was clear and bright. Lena spoke very little, and when she did it was in a very low voice, almost a whisper.

Big, placid, silent Lena, and her occasional chuckle. She and Jack got along very well. She was his fourth wife. . . .

In the old days the Pit River Indians did not live in individual houses. In summertime they camped around in the hills and the valleys, here and there, moving about in small groups somewhat like our own families, fishing, hunting, gathering crops of roots and seeds, and practicing conscientiously a lot of good healthy loafing. In the fall, when the nights were getting sharp and the mule-deer were turning red, all these wandering small families returned home, converging from the hills, from the higher valleys and swales, down the canyons, through the juniper, through the forests of tall pine, down to the sagebrush flats, all trekking home to some wintering ground, at Astaghiwa where there is a spring of hot water, at Tapaslu where the valley ends in a cul-de-sac, at Dalmo'ma where there are lots of wild turnips, to all the wintering grounds, there to dig themselves in for the coming winter and snow and blizzards and days of calm with the sun shining bright and the air cracking with frost.

You can imagine them, straggling home, the men usually stark naked, or some with a loin-cloth or a G-string; the women wore a kind of apron or hula-skirt of reeds; they carried their burdens on their backs from tump-lines from the forehead or from above the breast, both men and women, for there was not much division of labor among these Indians, except that the men did all the hunting with bow and arrows; they all wore their hair long and often coiled it in a chignon and stuck a long wooden pin to hold it in place. There they come down the trail in single file, grunting under their packs, squat bodies with broad shoulders, skins of chocolate—although many are tall and lithe, like the Paiutes of the Nevada desert with whom they intermarried much. There are not many children because only the most sturdy and the most lucky can survive.

And now, from everywhere around they arrive at the winter grounds, one family today, another the next, and another, and another. Here's old Red Tracks and his people: that young woman there she is related to me, and who is that young felllow, seems to me I have seen him somewhere. I don't think he is a relation of mine, oh! and look at the woman of Stalks-in-the-reeds, she is packing a new baby. . . . "Is kaadzi! Is kaakaadzi! Man, you are living! Man, you are living! We got here five days ago. . . . Where is Standing-alone?" "Oh, he left us, said he was going to winter at Hanti'u, he has relations there. Has the old Blind Chief arrived?" "No, but there are four, five chiefs here already. . . ."

There would be forty, fifty, sixty people, wintering at one place, all of them living together, living on top of each other, in one big communal house, a kind of underground cave. That was the *astsuy*, no, I mean the *astsūy*.*

I should have given a great deal to be able to spend some time in one of those old-time winter houses, and see just exactly how did life go on, get a real feeling of their social organization, their family life, their kinship system. All these are just words. I had read them in books on anthropology, but they were just labels, dried specimens, lifeless.

I had always wanted to live with really primitive people, real Stone Age men, and see how they thought, and felt. I had read books on primitive psychology, some of them excellent books like Lévy-Brühl's (who, by the way, never left Paris, or so I have been told), but I wasn't convinced. All that was too theoretical.

* The marks indicate a rise in pitch as opposed to level pitch on the second syllable.

VIII. Toward Argument:
Induction and Deduction

Really primitive people, not like the already cultured Indians of the Southwest with their sun-worship, their secret societies, their esoteric ceremonials. But real Stone Age men. . . . Well, these had been it, until a very short time ago. Here was Jack Folsom who was a little boy when the first white men arrived. Was there anything left? How much had they changed? My God, think of it, to pass in one lifetime from the stone axe to wireless telegraphy! Indians in overalls; no, there was nothing picturesque about these Indians, no feather headdresses or beaded moccasins, nothing to delight the tourists about these "digger Indians" in their battered hats and cheap calicos, picking the offal of the whites on the garbage dumps at the edge of town. My Indians in overalls! . . .

I followed the Pit River downstream. . . . It was getting dark and I was looking for a place to camp. Then, not far from the road, I saw a fire burning and some people camping under a big tall pine. I went over, and that's how I made the acquaintance of Sukmit, alias Frank Martin, also known as Bieber Frank, also as "that crazy hunchback Indian doctor," who later became my inseparable companion—(how many ditches have we shared for a bed with a bottle of fire-water?!). Crazy as they come, long powerful arms, one eye gone, the other malicious, an enormous leering mouth with a few teeth here and there. He was a young man in his thirties.

"Hallo, can I camp here?"

"Sure! Why not? This is my land, Indian land, I am not like white man, I let everybody stay on me. Everybody welcome. I am Indian doctor. Where you come from? Where you going? Sit down here with us. I bet you never eat acorn-mush before. Taste better with salt. Old-time Indians didn't have salt. You eat salt and it give you sore eyes." . . .

Sukmit was a better informant than Jack, linguistically. By this time I had discovered that there were six modes in the Pit River verb: indicative, subjunctive, interrogative, volitional present or future, and optative (Oh, those so-simple languages of the primitive peoples!); but it was impossible to make Jack stick to one mode. In giving me a paradigm (I eat, you eat, he eats . . . etc.), he would jump from one mode to another. Not so with Sukmit; once started on one mode he followed it rigidly. The old lady was a different type again; she wasn't going to follow any paradigms. She changed from one verb to another if she thought it was more interesting—on the other hand, she was excellent at dissecting a long periphrastic form into its component parts. I would exclaim "Oh . . . I see . . ." and she would chuckle: "Ha . . . ha . . . ha . . . you white man!" When she chuckled, her belly also chuckled.

Sukmit and his mother were forever quarreling, usually in Pit River, but sometimes in English for my edification. At first it worried me but after a while I paid no more attention to it than to the breeze. The old lady had been born in an old-time Indian house. She described it to me in detail, and even made me a little model of it one day with sticks and bits of mud. She was very keen at explaining to me many apparently meaningless details, which become quite important when you consider the realities of life, and the necessities of a materially primitive culture. She had been born and reared in such a culture and had an artist's eye for the significant differences. For instance she was explaining to me that there was no door in the communal winter house (which was really a sort of cave or cellar dug out of the ground and roofed over with sod)—people went in or out through the smokehole by climbing a step-ladder set up against the center-post. But at one end of the house there was a tunnel that led out to the outside ground, like a rabbit warren. This was for purposes of ventilation, of establishing a draft of air into and through the crowded house and out through the smoke-hole. The chiefs, the important men, usually sat or lay there on their backs, smoking their stone-pipes and enjoying the fresh air (forty or fifty humans including babies can make a thick atmosphere!). Now, mothers and fathers climbed the ladder with small children in their arms, or on the hip, or strapped to the cradle-board; but bigger youngsters crawled out through the rabbit warren; and the chiefs would grab them, and hug them, and tease them, as grownups do the world over. Such a description put the whole picture in focus for me. And again the old lady (who had a pornographic mind) would say: ". . . the smoke-hole pretty big— have to step across, grab pole—young girl take time step across show everything. . . . Ha, ha, ha! . . . you white man, ha, ha, ha! . . ."

The old lady Gordon, she of the gray hair and fiery eyes, was a very different type. As we were sitting by the campfire she told me of the wars they had with the Paiutes and the Modocs. It seems that the Indians liked to meet in two enemy lines facing each other and shoot with bow and arrow. Each woman stood behind her man, holding onto his belt, and passed the arrows to his hand. After the fight they danced to placate the shadows of the dead. They strung the ears on an arrow shaft and held them to the fire and chanted. Old Gordon took a stick and held it to the fire and chanted in a deep contralto. It was weird and made me shiver. For once, Sukmit was silent but old Mary had to break the silence and chuckle: ". . . Ha, ha, ha . . . you white man . . ."

I only stayed a few days with Sukmit and his people, that time. One morning he started to move camp, piling things into his decrepit automobile, and I saddled my horse. But his departure was in the grand manner. I must explain that Indians' cars, in those days, were of the "tin lizzie" type, held together with bale-wire. This was before the days of the self-starter—and cranking the engine was a back-breaking and discouraging task. Indians had discovered a very good way to start the engine: prop up the hind end of the car with a jack, then start the engine by spinning the rear wheels, then kick off the jack, run after the car as it zigzagged through the sagebrush, climb in at the back, and grab the steering wheel. Very good, but hard for Sukmit the hunchback. That morning, there was a heated discussion between him and the old lady. He wanted her to sit at the wheel and steer the car while he started it Indian fashion. But she would have none of it. He argued and argued that it was easy, very easy. But she was obdurate. Finally he yelled: "Get in, Christ Almighty, do you want to live forever?"

I started back along the Pit River toward the Hot Springs. I saw a dilapidated shack and went in. . . . I had gone into that house looking for an old fellow named Blind Hall, or Johnny Hall (his name, I found out later, was Tahteumi, meaning "red trail," or "red track," or "sunset trail"). They had told me he was one of the most powerful medicine-men around. But the tattooing girl said he wasn't there; this was his house, but he had gone to another camp. She said he was sick. "He was going to town the other day with his old woman; they were driving along in their old buggy; automobile come from behind; upset buggy; old Hall didn't know he was hurt, but he must have dropped his shadow; he went on to Hantiyu, but he got pretty sick; he is coming back today; he is going to doctor himself tonight."

That sounded interesting. I thought I would hang around. Maybe I would learn something. So I wandered around. About noon Blind Hall arrived in the old rattling creaking swaying buggy with his old woman and the old old decrepit horse. I knew right away I had seen him before somewhere, sometime; that massive face, the sightless eyes, the very thick lips and quite a lot of white beard for an Indian. "Hallo, white man, I remember you, you stop once, we camp side road, you give me can beans, bacon, you eat with us, you treat me good, you all right, I remember you. I remember your voice—I am pretty sick now, dropped my shadow on the road, can't live without my shadow, maybe I die, dunno. . . . I doctor myself tonight. You stay, you help sing tonight."

Blind Hall called his medicine "my poison." The Indian word is *damaagome.* Some Indians translate it in English as "medicine," or "power," sometimes "dog" (in the sense of pet dog, or trained dog). Blind Hall was not boastful like Sukmit; he was full of quiet dignity; as to his age, goodness knows, he said he and Jack Folsom were young men together, and once they got mad at each other: "I called him by his name and he called me by my name" (you are not supposed to call an Indian by his personal name; that's too personal, too private; you call him by his term of relationship to you—uncle, grandfather, brother-in-law, or whatever—or by his nickname).

Blind Hall was groaning and bellyaching about the pain in his ribs. We were sitting in the sun. "Give me a cigarette, white man. Mebbe I die. I dunno. That autocar he knock my shadow out of me; shadow he stay on the road now can't find me; can't live without my shadow! . . . It's too bad, mebbe I die . . . tonight I doctor myself, I ask my poisons . . . I got several poisons . . . I got Raven, he live on top mountain Wadaqtsuudzi, he know everything, watch everything. . . . I got Bullsnake, he pretty good too. . . . I got Louse, Crablouse, live with people, much friends, he tell me lots things. . . . I got Jim Lizard, he sit on rock all day, he pretty clever but not serious, he dam liar. . . . Sometime I doctor sick man, call my poisons come over my head, they fight. Raven he says that man poisoned, Bullsnake say no he not poisoned, he broke rule hunting . . . and then this here Jim Lizard he say, Oh! let's go home that man going to die anyhow! . . . Then Raven he shake his finger at him he say: Who ask you what you think? Why don't you help our father?" (The poisons call the medicine-man "my father," *ittu ai*—the medicine-man calls his poison *ittu damaagome* "my *damaagome*," or whatever you want to translate that word by: medicine, poison, power. . . .) "You can go home if you want to, we will stay here and help our father. Then Jim Lizard mebbe he stay and help and mebbe he tell me lie. I can't depend on him. . . . Ohh . . . it hurt me inside here. Maybe I die. Everybody die sometime. . . . I ask my poison tonight. You white man, you help, you sing too. More people sing more good. Sometime my poison very far away, not hear. Lots people sing, he hear better."

At this place of Astaghiwa (meaning "hot being," because there is a hot spring) there also lived Robert Spring (he took the name from the spring—but his brother was Jim Bailey, and why?? but Jim Bailey was the son of Blind Hall's woman, but Blind Hall was not his father. . . . Indian relationships are very complex, and the adoption of white men's names does not simplify things). This Robert Spring was a very quiet individual, very shy, about thirty or thirty-five years old, well set up, spoke English fairly well. He asked me to show him how he could write his own language: "I been to school at Fort Bidwell; I can write English; I try write our language but can't do it. Yet you do it. Will you show me?" It was interesting to see that he was aware of the differences due to tones, but of course he had no idea of arranging tones in a sequence or scale. And *my* conception of a tone as "low" and another as "high" was extremely puzzling to him. "Why don't you say that one is to the right and the other to the left?" he asked. I had no answer, of course.

We were sitting on a log. He said: "Goddammit! an Indian camp is always dirty. . . . Look at that!" In truth it was pretty messy: broken wagon-wheels askew against a juniper trunk. A couple of shacks made of boards and flattened tin cans for roof. A tent. Piles of ashes, old campfires. Tin cans, tin cans, tin cans. A broken coffee-pot—but a beautiful panoramic view. Undulations of sagebrush and the distant mountains all around. This is a country of vast distances. That does not look like such a big hill over there . . . but it rises three thousand feet and it is about fifteen miles from here. Very fooling, this clear atmosphere.

A buggy rattled in. There were two old Indians in it, a man and a woman. "That's Hantiyu Bill. You wouldn't think so but that fellow is pretty old. He got that woman as a present. They used to do that in the old days sometimes. Her father and Bill were great friends and he gave the woman to him."

I asked him about that "shadow" that Blind Hall had lost. "That's what we call the *de'lamdzi*," he said. "Does that mean 'shadow,' like the shadow of a tree? Or does it mean shadow like what the white people call the 'soul'?" "I dunno about that last word, how you pronounce it? I have heard the white people talk about it but I don't understand what it means. But the shadow from a tree, that's different. That's *dalilamdzi*. Yes, they sound very much the same, don't they? I never noticed that before, *de'lamdzi, dalilamdzi. . . .*" [1]

His mother, old Hall's woman, passes by. She is going to dig for roots, on the flats. Little old woman, all wrinkles, bent over under her conical pack-basket, tottering away with the help of her digging stick. She is eternally mumbling something. Once in a while she pokes into the ground, bends over, pulls a wild turnip and throws it over her shoulder into the pack-basket on her back. She looks very small in all that vastness of landscape. Robert Spring watches her and smiles: "See, she thinks she is helping. Old people are like that."

Robert Spring had a good ear; he would have been an excellent phonetician. He made me notice the difference between *dihoomi* "to run," and *dihommi* "the wind." A question of length: in one the vowel is long; in the other it is the consonant which is long. Quantity is as important in this language as it is in Latin prosody.

That evening we all gathered at sundown. Jack Steel, an Indian from Hantiyu who usually acted as Blind Hall's "interpreter," had arrived. He went out a little way into the sagebrush and called the poisons. "Raven, you, my poison, COME! (*qaq, mi', ittu damaagome, tunnoo*). . . . Bull-snake, my poison, come. . . . Crablouse, my poison, cooome. . . . You all, my poisons, COOOME!!" It was kind of weird, this man out in the sagebrush calling and calling for the poisons, just like a farmer calling his cows home.

We all gathered around the fire; some were sitting on the ground, some were lying on their side. Blind Hall began singing one of his medicine-songs. Two or three who knew that song well joined him. Others hummed for a while before catching on. Robert Spring said to me: "Come on, sing. Don't be afraid. Everybody must help." At that time

---

[1] I found out later that *de'lamdzi* is a noun, while *dalilamdzi* is a verb. Thus:
    salilamdzi—I make a shadow (on the ground)
    ittu dalilamdzi—my shadow (on the ground)
    ittu de'lamdzi—my shadow (in the sense of soul)
Compare Latin *"anima,"* a current of air, wind, breath, vital principle.
The etymology of Anglo-Saxon "soul" is unknown.

I had not yet learned to sing Indian fashion. The melody puzzled me. But I joined in, bashfully at first, then when I realized that nobody was paying any attention to me, with gusto.

Blind Hall had soon stopped singing, himself. He had dropped into a sort of brown study, or as if he were listening to something inside his belly. Suddenly he clapped his hands, the singing stopped abruptly. In the silence he shouted something which the "interpreter," Jack Steel, repeated. And before Jack Steel was through, Blind Hall was shouting again, which the interpreter also repeated, and so on, five or six times. It was not an exchange between Blind Hall and Jack Steel. Jack Steel was simply repeating word for word what Blind Hall was shouting. It was an exchange between Hall and his poison, Raven. First, Hall would shout a query which the interpreter repeated; then Hall would listen to what Raven (hovering unseen above our heads) was answering—and he would repeat that answer of Raven which he, Hall, had heard in his mind—and the interpreter would repeat the repetition. Then Hall emitted a sort of grunted "Aaaah . . . ," and relapsed into a brown study. Everybody else, Jack Steel included, relaxed. Some lit cigarettes; others gossiped. A woman said to me: "You did pretty good; you help; that's good!" Robert Spring said: "Sure, everybody must help. Sometimes the poisons are far away. They don't hear. Everybody must sing together to wake them up."

The woman who had praised me for singing said for my benefit: "He ask his Raven if he going to die. Raven say he don't know; ask the others." Blind Hall started humming another medicine-song, and everything went on like before. That way four or five times. At one time he got pretty excited and started to jump and dance, and fell down. It must be hell to be blind.

The whole performance lasted about a couple of hours. Then everybody dispersed.

The next morning Blind Hall felt much better. . . .

It was Robert Spring who first made me understand about the *dinihowi*. "That's what we Indians call *luck*. A man has got to have luck, no matter for what, whether it's for gambling, or for hunting, for making love, for anything, unless he wants to be just a common Indian . . . like me."

We were lying flat on our backs under a juniper. After a silence he started again: "When a fellow is young, everybody is after him to go to the mountains and get himself a *dinihowi*. The old men say: 'You'll never amount to anything if you don't go and catch a *dinihowi*.' And then you hear other fellows brag about their luck at gambling, or how they got a good *dinihowi* for hunting. Well, there come a time when a young fellow starts to feel uneasy, kind of sad, kind of worried, that's just about the time he's getting to be a man grown up. Then he start to 'wander,' that's what we call it, wandering. They say: Leave him alone, he is wandering. That's the time you go to the hills, you don't come home, you stay out all night, you get scared, you cry: two, three days you go hungry. Sometime your people get worried, come after you, but you throw rocks at them: Go away, I don't want you, leave me alone. You get pretty hungry, you get dizzy, you are afraid of grizzly bears. Maybe you fall asleep and someone come wake you up, maybe a wolf, push your head with his foot, maybe bluejay peck at your face, maybe little fly get in your ear, he say: Hey! Wake up! What you doing here? Your people worrying about you! You better go home! I see you wandering here, crying, hungry, I pity you, I like you. I help you. Listen, this is my song. Remember that song. When you want me, you come here and sing my song. I'll hear you. I'll come. . . ."

I said to Robert Spring: "But then, I don't see what is the difference between the *dinihowi* and the *damaagome*. . . ." "There is no difference. It's all the same. Only the *damaagome* that's for doctors." "How does the doctor get his *damaagomes*?" "Just like you and me get a *dinihowi*. He goes to the mountain. He cries. Then someone comes and says, this is my song, I'll help you." "Well then, I don't see any difference." "I am telling you there is no difference. Only the *dinihowi* that's for plain Indians like you and me, and the *damaagome* that's for doctors. . . . Well, I'll tell you, there is maybe some difference. The *damaagome* is kind of mean, quarrelsome, always fighting. The *dinihowi* is more peaceful." . . .

I found Jack Folsom and Lena at their place. He told me that the Pit Rivers have a word for "year" and one for "month." The word for money is the same as that for moon, of course. What surprised me was that they use the same word (*tsulh*) for sun and moon; if they want to specify, they was "night *tsulh*" or "day *tsulh*." They named the months: month of the groundhog; month of the squirrel; month of the wild turnips; month of the deer running, etc. They had twelve such months, and every fourth year they repeated the midwinter month (they were aware of the solstices). This was the occasion for a lot of quarreling. As Jack Folsom put it: "It used to get pretty stinky in the winter house, especially after Indians got dogs. After two or three months of winter the litter of tules was lousy with vermin and fleas and bugs. People scratch all the time, want to get out go to the hills. Mebbe next moon is groundhog moon, and then next is squirrel moon, and then wild-turnip moon, that's the time people get out and go to the hills. They were in a hurry for the winter to end. And they argued and argued about it, the old men, the chiefs, did. This is the year we have to repeat the mid-winter moon. No, it's next year. No, we did it three years ago. Ah, you don't know, you are too old, you are mixed up. We young fellows, we used to laugh listening to the old men argue. . . . Yes, Doc, the winters used to drag in the old-time *astsūy*. That's the time when you tell long stories, stories of long ago, *dilasini'qi* we call it. About Coyote, and Silver Fox, and Lizard, them all they used to be people, long long ago." . . .

From there I went back with Jack and Lena to their shack tucked away in the sagebrush, behind a hill not far from Alturas. We took up the study of language again, and went out in the brush with his rifle to shoot jackrabbits (hares) for the cooking pot. There were hundreds and hundreds of them, darting from every bush. In a minute or two we would bag one, which was enough for the three of us. Then we would sit down and talk and talk. . . . "Jack, have you got a *dinihowi?*" Jack looked at me, squinting a smile: "Where did you learn that word, Doc?"—"Oh, here and there, Blind Hall. . . ." Jack snorted. "That old bastard hasn't got any *dinihowis*. They wouldn't live with his poisons. You want to know what that old man does with *dinihowis?* He steals them, just like he steals other doctors' *damaagomes*. He steals honest Indians' *dinihowis* but he can't keep them. They won't live with his poisons. When he wants to get a woman he goes into the brush and he calls for a lice from her. . . ." "For a what?" "For a lice. Them things crawl around between your legs." "Oh, a louse." "I dunno. I always heard white people call them lice. We say *a'mits*. Lots of Indians got them. So this Hall goes into the bush, and he has got an *a'mits* himself for one of his poisons. And he gets his *a'mits* to call for her *a'mits*. And pretty soon the woman get up from her campfire, she don't know why but she go wandering into the sagebrush and old Hall is there waiting for her."

"But Jack, that lice is not her *damaagome!*" "How the hell do I know it ain't her *damaagome*. It might be her *dinihowi*. I didn't say it was her *damaagome*."

"No, that's right, I made a mistake. I meant her *dinihowi*."

"I didn't say it was her *dinihowi*. Lots of us got them lice between our legs."

I shut up. Jack was a very kind man, but whenever I seemed stupid he would sort of lose his temper and get cross and squint across the hills. I had learned the weather signals. So I shut up.

We were still sitting in the same spot. Jack says, out of the blue: "Yes, I got a *dinihowi*. Must be a damn poor Indian without a *dinihowi*. When I was a young fellow, old people always get after us. You go get luck for yourself. You can't live without luck. Go and run up the mountain in the afternoon. Try to beat the sun, the red light, to the top, get there first. Keep your breath. Run steady. . . . You know, Doc, I used to be a good runner. We used to have foot-races in the old-time days. All the young Indians we used to try beat each other going from one place to another, maybe five mile, maybe ten mile. Run through the sagebrush, keep your breath in, don't slow down, don't sit down and sleep, don't get scared, keep running through the brush, sometimes awful high brush, higher than your head. . . . I was pretty good runner in them days. Now I make my race-horses run. . . . Well, the old people kept after me. You beat the sun to the top of the mountain, then you'll be a man. I tried, and I tried. Then one day a big frog was standing in the road, right in the dust of the trail. He says: You'll never get to the top without me helping you. I been watching you. It's awful how hard you try. I'll help you. . . ."

"Did you get to the top that day?"

"Yes, I got to the top. There ain't nothing there."

"Then what?"

"Then I came down."

"Oh. . . ."

"What do you mean, oh? I got my *dinihowi*, didn't I? I am always trying to tell you things, Doc, but you are worse than a young Indian." . . .

II

I was up again, the next year. This time I had a jalopy, myself. Progress. You can't defend yourself against progress. So this time I came up following the Pit River from Redding up. I was meeting more and more Indians after Montgomery Creek. I had never been through that territory before, only once, years before with a drove of horses, through a snowstorm. I didn't even recognize the country.

I got into the upper land. It was getting dark. I had a wolfish-looking bitch swaying on the back, on top of my camping stuff. I was getting tired driving that damned car. I hate them. When I got to Big Valley I couldn't stand the driving over the rough road any more. I saw a campfire a little south of the road. I was awfully tired. I thought: They must be Indians.

I got out and walked over, being careful to make a noise. There was no need for care. There comes Sukmit: "I have been watching for you. I got lonesome for you. I sent my poison after you. The old lady is there, in the camp. Old lady Gordon died. The other woman, my uncle, she is dead. We are all going to die. We can't help it. What have you got there? Is that a coyote? Looks a coyote. Don't growl at me, you son-of-a-bitch. I am Indian doctor. I ain't afraid of you. Want to be my poison? Say, Jaime, did you get my message? I got lonesome for you. You want to be a doctor? I teach you. I am Indian doctor. I teach you, pretty bad, get scared, I teach you, you no white man. . . ."

Under this avalanche I was being dragged across some wasteland toward the campfire I had seen. There were no introductions of any kind whatever. Nobody paid any attention to me at all. I sat in a corner. I said nothing. Then a little boy brought me a basket full of some kind of mush, and it had salt in it, too. I was reserved and very careful, keeping out of the way, in the outer light of the fire. Then Mary's chuckle came out of the darkness (I hadn't seen her until that moment, sitting there beyond the firelight): "Ha-ha, you white man."

I followed that bunch for several weeks. I never saw such a goddam lot of improbable people. Sukmit was the only acknowledged shaman, but he wasn't a leader. He was no chief, no *weheelu,* among them. We went around the brush. We would stop anywhere, evidently by common consent. We would stop in the brush. Always there was a spring near by. I never knew where we were going. We were going somewhere. I didn't care at all. We were going somewhere, maybe. And if we were not going somewhere, we were not going, that's all. In the evening we would make a fire, several fires (there were several families of us). In the morning we moved again. I don't know where we were going. I don't think the Indians knew. We made quite a procession through the sagebrush, about six or seven of us, my car usually tagging at the end. I didn't know where we were going, nobody seemed to know where we were going, and then the night would settle on us, the fires would die down. The coyotes would begin barking from out in the brush. The Indians' dogs would howl back. Then everything would smolder back into the darkness.

Then one morning I was made to realize that there was something wrong about the white man's conception of the "taciturn" Indian. That happened the next day. We were going along the sagebrush, no road, just sagebrush, wind left, wind right, avoid this big clump, here's bad one, bump into the ditch . . . but there is no road at all anywhere, you are going through the brush, bumpety bump, all of us, six, seven, maybe eight cars, eight tin lizzies rattling through the sagebrush. Then, one morning, we had to stop. One of the tin lizzies was on the blink, and everybody got out to help. Then I witnessed something that amazed me. I had made up my mind that these men were straight out of the old Stone Age. I myself am not a mechanic; I hate machines; I am all thumbs; I don't understand machines; horses, yes; machines, no. And here I was watching these Stone Age men unscrew and re-screw and take things apart or out of the engine and spread them on a piece of canvas on the ground . . . but the amazing thing to me was their argumentation. It was perfectly logical. ". . . Can't be the ignition, look, I get a spark . . . I tell you, it's in the transmission . . . Now pull that lever . . ." Maybe I was overimpressed because the simplest machine smells of magic to me. Maybe I missed a lot of their argument because off and on they would lapse into Pit River. They called the battery *hadatsi* "heart"; a wheel is *pi'nine* (a hoop used in the old days for target practice); and so on and so forth. But certainly they made use of logic just as any white man would. Finally the engine, or whatever was wrong, was repaired. Then I overheard one young fellow say to another: "You know why this happened? Because he has been sleeping with his woman while she was menstruating! That's against the rules."

At last everything was fixed: the engine put together again, everything rescrewed . . . but the trek of the tin lizzies was not resumed. We just stayed there.

I don't know why we stayed there. We just stayed there, in the middle of nowhere, in the middle of the sagebrush. After that car which had broken down had been repaired, I naturally expected that everybody would get back into their cars, and the procession be resumed. But no, nobody got back into the cars; everybody was drifting around, sitting here, sitting there, gossiping, yawning.

I asked a man: "Are we going on, or do we camp here?" He answered: "I dunno. I am not the chief. Ask that old man over there." I went to the old man over there. He said he was not the chief. Ask that fellow over there. That fellow over there was a middle-aged man. He said: "Hell, I am not the one to say, I am not a chief!" "Well, who is a chief here?" "I dunno. That old man over there, I guess. He is old enough to have the say. Go and ask him." That old man over there was the same old man over there, and he gave me the same treatment. He was no chief. Who said he was a chief? They could start when they liked, when they jolly well liked, he didn't care, he didn't even know where they were going, where the hell were they going, did they know where they were going, did I know where they were going?? . . . He sat on the foot-board of one of the cars. He was squinting into the afternoon sun; it was late afternoon, by then. He was chewing tobacco and spitting the brown juice. He paid no more attention to me and went back to his reverie, squinting into the sun.

I noticed a woman had started a campfire. Very soon another one did likewise. So I went to my car and drove it next to Sukmit's. Old Mary was sitting on the ground in the shade of the car, weaving a rough basket of willow twigs. "Where is Sukmit?" "*Tsesuwi diimas'adi*, I don't know, went off in the brush some place, that boy is crazy, *yalu'tuusi*, always looking for *damaagomes*; you bring me firewood, white man, I cook." "All right."

The sun was going down. I heard two or three shots, off in the sagebrush. I made our fire. There were four or five other campfires. A man came by; he had several hares by the ears; he tossed one over to us. Mary drew it, threw the guts to my bitch, hacked it in four pieces, and stuck these on sticks to broil over the fire. No sight of Sukmit. We ate. Then Mary told me an old-time story. I spread my blankets on the ground. I rolled a cigarette and watched the stars. Some coyotes started a howling, not far off. My bitch stood up, all bristles, and she howled back (in answering coyotes, most dogs howl instead of barking). I went to sleep with my head full of old-time stories, tin lizzies, *damaagomes* mixed up with engines, coyotes and sagebrush.

I was awakened by the usual quarrel between Sukmit and his

mother. The smell of coffee was in the air. We ate. I observed the camp. There were no preparations for starting. Everybody lolling around. Mary took up her basket and kept on weaving. Another woman went to the spring with a bucket (there was a spring, nearby; of course they must have known). A man was tinkering with his car. Another one went off into the brush with his gun. That old man, the supposed "chief," was going around poking at things with a stick. He was almost blind. The morning was drawing on. I took out my notebook and started working on linguistics.

The days went by. Not so many days, but four, five days, maybe. I don't remember exactly. I was not taking notes. I was living. Sage-brush. Old-time stories, hares cooking over the fire, slow gossip, So-and-So is poisoning So-and-So, I don't believe it, yes he is, how do you know, well his paternal aunt belongs to the *hammaawi*, and they poi-soned his *apau*. "That doesn't make him related!" "Who said related? I didn't say related. I said they poisoned him." . . . The days went by, four, five, six days.

Then it happened. It was midday, or near. I heard a man say, way off: "*S.huptsiidzima.*" If he had said *lhuptiidza toolol*, "Let's all go," it would have been different. But no, it was not in the imperative mode, it was in the indicative: "We are going, all of us, *toolol*, we are going, *s.huptsiidzima*, we are all going." He didn't say: LET'S ALL GO! No, he merely stated a fact: WE ARE ALL GOING.

It was like a whirlwind. I turned around. Women were throwing baskets into the tin lizzies. Then without any further warning or con-sultation one of the tin lizzies started off in a cloud of dust. Another was right on its heels. Then a third one, but this one had hardly started when someone yelled, "Hey! you are forgetting your baby!!" The car backed, a young woman jumped out and ran to a juniper tree where the baby was sleeping in the cradle-board swinging under a branch; she slung the cradle-board over her shoulder and ran back to the car, laughing and laughing; everybody was laughing; then the car started again.

Sukmit yelled at me: "*Lhupta*, let's go! For Christ's sake, are you going to stay here forever?!" I picked up my papers and ran for my own car. . . . We go, we go, we wind in and out, all afternoon, all the cars more or less following each other, we skirted the town of Alturas, never stopped, we were going north, the sun went down, there was a moon, we kept going, somehow or other no car broke down, not even a flat tire, we had luck with us, and toward morning we stopped on those flats by Davis Creek. . . .

I was going back to Berkeley. . . .

. . . I said to him: "Sukmit, let's record one of your own medicine-songs." The old lady had heard me, and she cried from where she was

sitting at the campfire. "Don't do it, Sukmit, don't do it, *tse-dutsee,
tse-dutsee!!*" He seemed dubious, torn two ways by his vanity and his
fear of possible consequences. "See, suppose I put my song in the
machine; now you go to Berkeley; sometime you play my song; my
damaagome he hear it, he say: Ha! my father is calling me, I'd better
go and find him, maybe he needs me. . . . So he come here to Berkeley,
strange place, maybe he get lost, maybe somebody steal him . . . then
I get sick, maybe I die. . . ." "Aw! he couldn't hear that phonograph
all the way from Alturas!" "Sure he can! Just like 'lectricity, it goes underground, but it don't need no wires." [5] "What do you know about electricity?! Electricity doesn't work that way!" "Hell, what do you know
about *damaagomes?* You are nothing but a white man, a goddam
tramp." [6] "No, I am not a white man!" "Yes, you are a white man, you
are a white man forever!!"

Old Mary chuckled from over the campfire. "You two always quarreling like two old men. You Indian, you white man, ha-ha-ha! You
both crazy!"

So I took them down to Berkeley in my auto, Sukmit and old Mary
(she once told me her Indian name; it had something to do with tule
reeds at dawn; but I never heard any one call her by it; Sukmit called
her *niini,* baby-talk for *nen* "mother"; and I also called her that after a
while; other Indians called her "aunt," or "sister-in-law on the brother's
side," which is *wattulaawi,* or whatever the relationship term if they
were related; if not related to her they just called her *wiya'tsaale,* which
is equivalent to "old lady").

The city was a great disappointment to Sukmit. Didn't interest
him at all. "Too many people crawling around just like ants—makes me
crazy. . . ." He spent most of his time wandering in the hills back of
the University campus. He looked sad and dejected. He didn't quarrel
any more.

One day I said to him: "Sukmit, I know what's troubling you. . . .
You have been wandering in the hills and calling your *damaagomes,*
and they don't hear you!" He looked at me and I thought he was going
to burst into tears. "Yes," he said, "you and *niini,* you were right; they
don't hear me; they don't come! I am going to die if I stay here."

So I sent them back on the train. Funny-looking pair they made
at the station, bewildered, he with his long hair and his black som-
brero, his long arms and his hump; she clutching a bundle; and her
gray hair under a bright silk handkerchief we had just bought for her.

[5] This was before the days of wireless (at least before wireless became common
knowledge)—an interesting example of so-called "primitive mentality."

[6] The Pit Rivers call the whites *enellaaduwi,* literally "wanderer," from the verbal
root —*llaa*— "to wander," plus the adverbial suffix —*duw*— "around." What struck the
Pit Rivers most about the first whites (prospectors, trappers, etc.) was that they appeared to be homeless.

I spoke a word to the conductor for them. He smiled broadly: "Sure I'll take care of them. I know Indians. I was raised in Oklahoma."

As the train pulled out, old Mary gave me the Pit River goodby: *Is tus'i taakaadzee,* Man, live well! *Ittu toolol hakaadzigudzuma,* We also will live.

III

I went up north again the next summer. I found Jack Folsom and Lena at their place behind the little hill in the sagebrush. I noticed that Lena seemed apathetic, ill. Jack was as usual, with his quizzical smile, his quiet ways, his practical sense. . . .

. . . Lena's own father arrived from Hat Creek country. His name was Jack Wilson. He drove in in a horse-wagon, and with him was an "elder brother" (or cousin) of his, who must have been close to ninety or a hundred; Jack Folsom (who didn't know his own age by years) said of Bob-Chief, or Tom-Chief (like all Indians he had a variety of American names): "When I was a young fellow that old man had already buried three wives." He was still erect, but walked slowly; his skin was the color of chocolate; a few long white whiskers made him look like a walrus.

Jack Wilson was a "sort of doctor," according to Jack Folsom. He would doctor his own daughter, that night. Old Tom-Chief would interpret. Jack Wilson was a tall man, very silent. During the day Tom-Chief, who usually sat on a log, would totter into the sagebrush and make a sort of speech. "What is he doing?" I asked Jack. "Oh, he is telling old-time stories, what the people used to do long ago." "But there is nobody there. To whom is he talking?" Jack shrugged his shoulders: "To the sagebrush, I guess."

When evening came, old Tom-Chief went out and called the *dama-agomes.* Three young Indians had arrrived; but they were slightly drunk. They sang a *contre-temps* and laughed. Jack had to reprimand them. Old Tom was very deaf; he didn't hear what the doctor said; so everybody had to shout at him what the shaman had said so he could repeat it; the whole thing was a failure. After about an hour Jack Wilson gave up in despair. "No use! My poison don't hear. Mountain lion, wolf, too far away, don't hear!"

In the morning he said to me: "I lost all my children. This the last one. I lose her too."

It was in the afternoon. Autumn and warm. The door of the cabin stood open. Away to the west I could see the hills of sagebrush, silent, and the mountains beyond. One of those days that do not move. There were half a dozen of us in the cabin, and the sick woman breathing heavily on her pile of blankets. I don't know how we all knew it, but we all felt that she was dying just then. At last, Jack

Folsom broke down. He buried his face in his hands and started to cry. He cried like a little child, with convulsive sobs. Then that awful sound of the rattle. And even before that had died away Jessie began the wail. Oh, that weird, wild, atrocious thing that goes mounting like the shriek of a wounded beast, that infernal yell drawn away until it falls in a series of exhausted sobs. And again, and again. I was to hear that wail all night through the sagebrush until it drove me mad.

The old man, her father, was kneeling at her head. His face twitched uncontrollably. He closed her eyes, and laid a handkerchief over her face. Then he, too, broke down. He took the head of his child in his lap, he raised it to his breast, and he sobbed and sobbed.

All night long Jessie wandered through the brush, wailing, wailing. And all through the night Indians kept arriving. The men sat against the wall. The women went out into the night and wailed.

One Indian is dead.

Then Jack took his wife's body away to bury it in Hat Creek, her home. He said to me: "I'll be back here in about two weeks, and then we will burn her. Will you stay here for me, Doc?"

I was sort of puzzled about this business of burying first, and burning her after, but I didn't ask him any questions. I said I would stay until he got back. He said: "You sure won't be scared?" "No, . . . why should I?" "Account of the woman who died." "But why?" "She might come and kill you by mistake." "Hell no!" I said.

The very night after they had left, Wild Bill arrived. He was a horse-breaker by trade and I had known him in the days of my venture in ranching. A delightful fellow, always full of fun and jokes, and a superb rider; in fact he was a crazy daredevil. We had always been friends. . . .

Wild Bill said he would stay here and wait for Jack Folsom and the rest of the party to come back from the *atsuge* country. That evening he told me a lot about Coyote and the Coyote saga. The Coyote stories form a regular cycle, a saga. This is true of all of California; and it extends eastward even as far as the Pueblos of Arizona and New Mexico. Coyote has a double personality. He is at once the Creator, and the Fool. This antinomy is very important. Unless you understand it you will miss the Indian psychology completely—at least you will miss the significance of their literature (because I call their tales, their "old-time stories," literature).

The wise man and the buffoon: the two aspects of Coyote, Coyote Old Man. Note that I don't call them the good and the evil, because that conception of morality does not seem to play much part in the Pit River attitude to life. Their mores are not much concerned with good and evil. You have a definite attitude toward moral right and moral wrong. I don't think the Pit River has. At least, if he has, he does not try to coerce. I have heard Indians say: "That's not right what he is doing, that fellow. . . ." "What d'you mean it's not right?" ". . . Well . . . you ain't supposed to do things that way . . . it never was done that way . . . there'll be trouble." "Then why don't you stop him?" "Stop him? How can I stop him? It's his way."

The Pit Rivers (except the younger ones who have gone to the Government School at Fort Bidwell) don't ever seem to get a very clear conception of what you mean by the term God. This is true even of those who speak American fluently, like Wild Bill. He said to me: "What is this thing that the white people call God? They are always talking about it. It's goddam this and goddam that, and in the name of the god, and the god made the world. Who is that god, Doc! They say that Coyote is the Indian God, but if I say to them that God is Coyote, they get mad at me. Why?"

"Listen, Bill, tell me. . . . Do the Indians think, really think that Coyote made the world? I mean, do they really think so? Do you really think so?"

"Why of course I do. . . . Why not? . . . Anyway . . . that's what the old people always said . . . only they don't all tell the same story. Here is one way I heard it: it seems like there was nothing everywhere but a kind of fog. Fog and water mixed, they say, no land anywhere, and this here Silver Fox. . . ."

"You mean Coyote?"

"No, no, I mean Silver Fox. Coyote comes later. You'll see, but right now, somewhere in the fog, they say, Silver Fox was wandering and feeling lonely. *Tsikuellaaduwi maandza tsikualaasa.*[10] He was feeling lonely, the Silver Fox. I wish I would meet someone, he said to himself, the Silver Fox did. He was walking along in the fog. He met Coyote. 'I thought I was going to meet someone,' he said. The Coyote looked at him, but he didn't say anything. 'Where are you traveling?' says Fox. 'But where are YOU traveling? Why do you travel like that?' 'Because I am worried.'[11] 'I also am wandering,' said the Coyote, 'I also am worrying and traveling.' 'I thought I would meet someone, I thought I would meet someone. Let's you and I travel together. It's better for two people to be traveling together, that's what they always say. . . .' "

"Wait a minute, Bill. . . . Who said that?"

"The Fox said that. I don't know who he meant when he said: *that's*

[10] When you tell old-time stories of long ago, every verb must begin with *tsik–*, which then is more or less blended with the pronominal prefix.

[11] To be worried,—*insimallauw*—(conjugation II). When an Indian is worried, he goes wandering,—*inilladuw*—. When he is "wandering" he goes around the mountains, cries, breaks pieces of wood, hurls stones. Some of his relatives may be watching him from afar, but they never come near.

what they always say. It's funny, isn't it? How could he talk about *other* people since there had never been anybody before? I don't know. . . . I wonder about that sometimes, myself. I have asked some of the old people and they say: That's what I have been wondering myself, but that's the way we have always heard it told. And then you hear the Paiutes tell it different! And our own people down the river, they also tell it a little bit different from us. Doc, maybe the whole thing just never happened. . . . And maybe it did happen but everybody tells it different. People often do that, you know. . . ."

"Well, go on with the story. You said that Fox had met Coyote. . . ."

"Oh, yah. . . . Well, this Coyote he says: 'What are we going to do now?' 'What do you think?' says Fox. 'I don't know,' says Coyote. 'Well then,' says Fox, 'I'll tell you: LET'S MAKE THE WORLD.' 'And how are we going to do that?' 'WE WILL SING,' says the Fox.

"So, there they were singing up there in the sky. They were singing and stomping [12] and dancing around each other in a circle. Then the Fox he thought in his mind: CLUMP OF SOD, come!! That's the way he made it come: *by thinking.*[13] Pretty soon he had it in his hands. And he was singing, all the while he had it in his hands. They were both singing and stomping. All of a sudden the Fox threw that clump of sod, that *tsapettia,*[14] he threw it down into the clouds. 'Don't look down!' he said to the Coyote. 'Keep on singing! Shut your eyes, and keep them shut until I tell you.' So they kept on singing and stomping around each other in a circle for quite a while. Then the Fox said to the Coyote: 'Now, look down there. What do you see?' 'I see something . . . I see something . . . but I don't know what it is.' 'All right. Shut your eyes again!' Now they started singing and stomping again, and the Fox thought and wished: 'Stretch! Stretch! 'Now look down again. What do you see?' 'Oh! it's getting biggger!' 'Shut your eyes again and don't look down!' And they went on singing and stomping up there in the sky. 'Now look down again!' 'Oooh! Now it's big enough!' said the Coyote.

"That's the way they made the world, Doc. Then they both jumped down on it and they stretched it some more. Then they made moun-

---

[12] Indian dancing is not like the European, by lifting the heels and balancing the body on the toes; on the contrary, one foot is raised *flat* from the ground while the other foot is pressed into the ground (by flexing the knee); then a very slight pause with one foot in the air; then the other foot is stamped flat into the ground while the first one is lifted. That is the fundamental idea; there are many variations; besides, the shoulders and head are made to synchronize or syncopate.

[13] I am not romancing, nor translating loosely; *hay-dutsi-la* means literally "by thinking." The radical *hay—* means "thought"; *dutsi* is the verb "to be" used here as an auxiliary in participial form (i.e. "being"); *—la* is the suffix representing the instrumental case (i.e. "by").

[14] Those big clumps of coarse grass and sod which gradually rise above the level of the water on the marshes are called *tsapettia.*

tains and valleys; they made trees and rocks and everything. It took them a long time to do all that!"

"Didn't they make people, too?"

"No. Not people. Not Indians.[15] The Indians came much later, after the world was spoiled by a crazy woman, Loon. But that's a long story. . . . I'll tell you some day."

"All right. Bill, but tell me just one thing now: there was a world now; then there were a lot of animals living on it, but there were no people then. . . ."

"Whad'you mean there were no people? Ain't animals people?"

"Yes, they are . . . but . . ."

"They are not Indians, but they are people, they are alive . . . Whad'you mean animal?"

"Well . . . how do you say 'animal' in Pit River?"

". . . I dunno. . . ."

"But suppose you wanted to say it?"

"Well . . . I guess I would say something like *teeqaade-wade toolol aakaadzi* (world-over, all living) . . . I guess that means animals, Doc."

"I don't see how, Bill. That means people, also. People are living, aren't they?"

"Sure they are! that's what I am telling you. Everything is living, even the rocks, even that bench you are sitting on. Somebody *made that bench for a purpose*, didn't he? Well then *it's alive*, isn't it? Everything is alive. That's what we Indians believe. White people think everything is dead. . . ."

"Listen, Bill. How do you say 'people'?"

"I don't know . . . just *is*, I guess."

"I thought that meant 'Indian.' "

"Say . . . Ain't we *people?!*"

"So are the whites!"

"Like hell they are!! We call them *inillaaduwi*, 'tramps,' nothing but tramps. They don't believe anything is alive. They are dead themselves. I don't call that 'people.' They are smart, but they don't know anything. . . . Say, it's getting late, Doc, I am getting sleepy. I guess I'll go out and sleep on top of the haystack. . . ."

Finally, one day about noon, Jack and all the relatives returned; five or six wagons full of them, and immediately everything was confusion and pandemonium in this quiet corner of the sagebrush behind the little hill. . . .

Jack Folsom himself didn't seem to be doing anything except going around, wailing, crying, grunting. He came into my tent and sat on my cot and sobbed like a little child. "She was very good, that

---

[15] The word for "people" is *is*. Nowadays it is applied especially to Indians, in contradistinction to the term applied to the whites: *enellaaduwi*.

woman, Doc. She never quarreled. I have had four, no, five, before her. We have been together a long time now. You know my daughter Jessie, well she raised her. Jessie has got grandchildren now."

"But, Jack, I thought Jessie was this woman's daughter. . . ."

"No, another woman's. I have had three women already, no, four. No, two only, according to Indian way. This woman I paid for her and she paid for me. That's according to Indian law. I gave Jack Wilson, you know . . . the old fellow who was singing that night, I gave him a white mare, she was awful fast, she had won several races for me, and her people gave me the right to fish on Hat Creek. . . . But you noticed that woman that's come in with them? She is ordering everything around, she is bossing everybody. . . ."

"Yes, I noticed her. Who is she?"

"She is younger sister of the woman who died, what we call *enun,* same as what you call 'cousin.' So, she has come to claim me."

"What do you mean, claim you?"

"It's this way, Doc: according to Indian law, *the dead people have got the say;* the relations of the dead person have got the right. If I had died, then my people, my relations, they are the ones who have the right to bring another man in my place. It don't matter he is an old man good for nothing. They say: We bought that woman, she belongs to us now; here's a man for her; she take him, or give us back our present; we gave you a horse for her; where is that horse? Now, this woman who died I married her according to Indian law. So, her people, her relations, they come here with this other woman, and they say to me: You lost one, here's another, you got no claim against us."

"Well, then, it's all right, isn't it?"

"No, it ain't all right, Doc. I don't want that woman. She is all right. She is young, I know. She is clean; she is a good worker . . . but she is bossy as hell! She'll boss me . . . I am too old to be bossed!"

Afterwards I took Jack down to my little ranch in the mountains south of Monterey. We had to go fifty miles by horse-stage, then fifteen miles more by trail over the ridges. When we were on top of the highest ridge the sun was dipping into the ocean, and we stopped to eat some sandwiches and make a little coffee. But before he ate, Jack chewed a piece and spat some to the east, and to the north, and to the south, and to the west. "See, Doc, I am doing that because I am in a new country. Them people you don't see, them coyotes and foxes and all kinds of *dinihowis* and *damaagomes* that live around here, they don't know me, because I am a stranger. They might hurt me. So I am telling them: I am all right, I don't mean no harm to you people, see, I am feeding you; and you people don't hurt me neither, because I am a stranger but I want to be friends with you. That's the way to do, Doc, that's the good way."

Night overtook us, and we went down the steep trail in the dark. Jack was stumbling. "Say, Doc, you sure picked you a darn steep country for your homestead." We reached the cabin at last, and I lit a fire in the hearth. There was an old rock mortar, of the kind the Indians use to pound acorns with a stone pestle. They still use them in Central California, but, for some reason which I don't understand, they don't use them any more in the Pit River country. Indeed, the Pit River Indians are afraid to touch them. "Them things are dangerous, Doc, them things are full of power. You come across one lying on the ground, some place; and next day you'll find him mebbe a mile further away! He moved during the night!" Whether it was only the ones that were lying abandoned "some place," or whether it was *all* mortars, I never found out. Anyway, I never saw any in use among the Pit Rivers. And now, Jack was very much shocked because I had one of these mortars lying near the hearth! "You shouldn't do that, Doc! He is getting too hot there, near the fire . . . make him mad . . . he is liable to hurt you, bring you bad luck, maybe make your children sick. . . ."

But Jack did not stay very long at my little ranch. He was having bad dreams. "I been dreaming of blood, Doc. It's those people working against me, my wife's people, the one who died. They have got some powerful doctors on their side. I should have married that sister of hers when she came to claim me. That's Indian law. I can't get out of it!"

So I put him on the stage and he went back to Modoc and the joys of matrimony.

When I saw him the next summer he looked subdued. He greeted me with his usual warmth, but when I asked him how he was getting along with his quondam sister-in-law, he said: "Oh, it's hell, Doc, just hell. I don't draw a free breath of my own."

I saw him again the next summer. He was radiant. "I got rid of her, Doc. I was camped at Davis Creek, and her brother he come and see me, and he says: Jack, I wouldn't stay with that woman, if I were you. She is too damn bossy! . . . Well, Doc, that's all I wanted to hear. He was her elder brother, so he had the say. So I called my own boy, Millard, you know him, and I said: I am going—when that woman comes back to the camp, don't tell her where I am gone—you don't know nothing about it, *sabe?*"

A few years later I found her married to Sukmit, of all people! But she had found her mate. They were yelling at each other, while old Mary smiled on complacently. Old Mary had earned her rest. . . .

64. The Raven

EDGAR ALLAN POE

Poe (1809–1849), an orphan at two, was educated in
Scotland, England, and Richmond, Virginia, by his god-
father, John Allan. Poe made his mark in 1845 with "The
Raven," after bouts with the army, West Point, alcohol,
gambling, and journalism. Although he did not
receive significant public attention until he wrote
"The Raven," Poe had already made his major
contributions to fiction of the macabre and mysterious.

Once upon a midnight dreary, while I pondered, weak and weary,
Over many a quaint and curious volume of forgotten lore—
While I nodded, nearly napping, suddenly there came a tapping,
As of some one gently rapping, rapping at my chamber door.
" 'Tis some visiter," I muttered, "tapping at my chamber door—
      Only this and nothing more."

Ah, distinctly I remember it was in the bleak December;
And each separate dying ember wrought its ghost upon the floor.
Eagerly I wished the morrow;—vainly I had sought to borrow
From my books surcease of sorrow—sorrow for the lost Lenore—
For the rare and radiant maiden whom the angels name Lenore—
      Nameless *here* for evermore.

And the silken, sad, uncertain rustling of each purple curtain
Thrilled me—filled me with fantastic terrors never felt before;
So that now, to still the beating of my heart, I stood repeating
" 'Tis some visiter entreating entrance at my chamber door—
Some late visiter entreating entrance at my chamber door;—
      This it is and nothing more."

Presently my soul grew stronger; hesitating then no longer,
"Sir," said I, "or Madam, truly your forgiveness I implore;
But the fact is I was napping, and so gently you came rapping,
And so faintly you came tapping, tapping at my chamber door,
That I scarce was sure I heard you"—here I opened wide the door;——
       Darkness there and nothing more.

Deep into that darkness peering, long I stood there wondering, fearing,
Doubting, dreaming dreams no mortal ever dared to dream before;
But the silence was unbroken, and the stillness gave no token,
And the only word there spoken was the whispered word, "Lenore?"
This I whispered, and an echo murmured back the word, "Lenore!"
       Merely this and nothing more.

Back into the chamber turning, all my soul within me burning,
Soon again I heard a tapping somewhat louder than before.
"Surely," said I, "surely that is something at my window lattice;
Let me see, then, what thereat is, and this mystery explore—
Let my heart be still a moment and this mystery explore;—
       'Tis the wind and nothing more!"

Open here I flung the shutter, when, with many a flirt and flutter,
In there stepped a stately Raven of the saintly days of yore;
Not the least obeisance made he; not a moment stopped or stayed he;
But, with mien of lord or lady, perched above my chamber door—
Perched upon a bust of Pallas just above my chamber door—
       Perched, and sat, and nothing more.

Then this ebony bird beguiling my sad fancy into smiling,
By the grave and stern decorum of the countenance it wore,
"Though thy crest be shorn and shaven, thou," I said, "art sure no craven,
Ghastly grim and ancient Raven wandering from the Nightly shore—
Tell me what thy lordly name is on the Night's Plutonian shore!"
       Quoth the Raven "Nevermore."

Much I marvelled this ungainly fowl to hear discourse so plainly,
Though its answer little meaning—little relevancy bore;
For we cannot help agreeing that no living human being
Ever yet was blessed with seeing bird above his chamber door—
Bird or beast upon the sculptured bust above his chamber door,
       With such name as "Nevermore."

But the Raven, sitting lonely on the placid bust, spoke only
That one word, as if his soul in that one word he did outpour.

VIII. Toward Argument:
Induction and Deduction

Nothing farther then he uttered—not a feather then he fluttered—
Till I scarcely more than muttered "Other friends have flown before—
On the morrow *he* will leave me, as my Hopes have flown before."
            Then the bird said "Nevermore."

Startled at the stillness broken by reply so aptly spoken,
"Doubtless," said I, "what it utters is its only stock and store
Caught from some unhappy master whom unmerciful Disaster
Followed fast and followed faster till his songs one burden bore—
Till the dirges of his Hope that melancholy burden bore
            Of 'Never—nevermore.' "

But the Raven still beguiling all my fancy into smiling,
Straight I wheeled a cushioned seat in front of bird, and bust and door;
Then, upon the velvet sinking, I betook myself to linking
Fancy unto fancy, thinking what this ominous bird of yore—
What this grim, ungainly, ghastly, gaunt, and ominous bird of yore
            Meant in croaking "Nevermore."

This I sat engaged in guessing, but no syllable expressing
To the fowl whose fiery eyes now burned into my bosom's core;
This and more I sat divining, with my head at ease reclining
On the cushion's velvet lining that the lamp-light gloated o'er,
But whose velvet-violet lining with the lamp-light gloating o'er,
            She shall press, ah, nevermore!

Then, methought, the air grew denser, perfumed from an unseen censer
Swung by Seraphim whose foot-falls tinkled on the tufted floor.
"Wretch," I cried, "thy God hath lent thee—by these angels he hath
        sent thee
Respite—respite and nepenthe from thy memories of Lenore;
Quaff, oh quaff this kind nepenthe and forget this lost Lenore!"
            Quoth the Raven "Nevermore."

"Prophet!" said I, "thing of evil!—prophet still, if bird or devil!—
Whether Tempter sent, or whether tempest tossed thee here ashore,
Desolate yet all undaunted, on this desert land enchanted—
On this home by Horror haunted—tell me truly, I implore—
Is there—*is* there balm in Gilead?—tell me—tell me, I implore!"
            Quoth the Raven "Nevermore."

"Prophet!" said I, "thing of evil!—prophet still, if bird or devil!
By that Heaven that bends above us—by that God we both adore—
Tell this soul with sorrow laden if, within the distant Aidenn,

It shall clasp a sainted maiden whom the angels name Lenore—
Clasp a rare and radiant maiden whom the angels name Lenore."
Quoth the Raven "Nevermore."

"Be that word our sign of parting, bird or fiend!" I shrieked, upstarting—
"Get thee back into the tempest and the Night's Plutonian shore!
Leave no black plume as a token of that lie thy soul hath spoken!
Leave my loneliness unbroken!—quit the bust above my door!
Take thy beak from out my heart, and take thy form from off my door!"
Quoth the Raven "Nevermore."

And the Raven, never flitting, still is sitting, *still* is sitting
On the pallid bust of Pallas just above my chamber door;
And his eyes have all the seeming of a demon's that is dreaming,
And the lamp-light o'er him streaming throws his shadow on the floor;
And my soul from out that shadow that lies floating on the floor
Shall be lifted—nevermore!

---

65. The Philosophy of Composition

EDGAR ALLAN POE

Charles Dickens, in a note now lying before me, alluding to an examination I once made of the mechanism of "Barnaby Rudge," says— "By the way, are you aware that Godwin wrote his 'Caleb Williams' backwards?[1] He first involved his hero in a web of difficulties, forming the second volume, and then, for the first, cast about him for some mode of accounting for what had been done."

I cannot think this the *precise* mode of procedure on the part of Godwin—and indeed what he himself acknowledges, is not altogether in accordance with Mr. Dickens' idea—but the author of "Caleb Williams" was too good an artist not to perceive the advantage derivable from at least a somewhat similar process. Nothing is more clear than

[1] *Caleb Williams,* a novel by the English writer and reformer William Godwin (1759–1836), appeared in 1794.

that every plot, worth the name, must be elaborated to its *dénoue-ment* before anything be attempted with the pen. It is only with the *dénouement* constantly in view that we can give a plot its indispensable air of consequence, or causation, by making the incidents, and especially the tone at all points, tend to the development of the intention.

There is a radical error, I think, in the usual mode of constructing a story. Either history affords a thesis—or one is suggested by an incident of the day—or, at best, the author sets himself to work in the combination of striking events to form merely the basis of his narrative—designing, generally, to fill in with description, dialogue, or autorial comment, whatever crevices of fact, or action, may, from page to page, render themselves apparent.

I prefer commencing with the consideration of an *effect*. Keeping originality *always* in view—for he is false to himself who ventures to dispense with so obvious and so easily attainable a source of interest—I say to myself, in the first place, "Of the innumerable effects, or impressions, of which the heart, the intellect, or (more generally) the soul is susceptible, what one shall I, on the present occasion, select?" Having chosen a novel, first, and secondly a vivid effect, I consider whether it can be best wrought by incident or tone—whether by ordinary incidents and peculiar tone, or the converse, or by peculiarity both of incident and tone—afterward looking about me (or rather within) for such combinations of event, or tone, as shall best aid me in the construction of the effect.

I have often thought how interesting a magazine paper might be written by any author who would—that is to say who could—detail, step by step, the processes by which any one of his compositions attained its ultimate point of completion. Why such a paper has never been given to the world, I am much at a loss to say—but, perhaps, the autorial vanity has had more to do with the omission than any one other cause. Most writers—poets in especial—prefer having it understood that they compose by a species of fine frenzy—an ecstatic intuition—and would positively shudder at letting the public take a peep behind the scenes, at the elaborate and vacillating crudities of thought —at the true purposes seized only at the last moment—at the innumerable glimpses of idea that arrived not at the maturity of full view—at the fully matured fancies discarded in despair as unmanageable—at the cautious selections and rejections—at the painful erasures and interpolations—in a word, at the wheels and pinions—the tackle for scene-shifting—the step-ladders and demon-traps—the cock's feathers, the red paint and the black patches, which, in ninety-nine cases out of the hundred, constitute the properties of the literary *histrio*.

I am aware, on the other hand, that the case is by no means common, in which an author is at all in condition to retrace the steps by which his conclusions have been attained. In general, suggestions, having arisen pell-mell, are pursued and forgotten in a similar manner.

For my own part, I have neither sympathy with the repugnance alluded to, nor, at any time the least difficulty in recalling to mind the progressive steps of any of my compositions; and, since the interest of an analysis, or reconstruction, such as I have considered a *desideratum,* is quite independent of any real or fancied interest in the thing analyzed, it will not be regarded as a breach of decorum on my part to show the *modus operandi* by which some one of my own works was put together. I select "The Raven," as most generally known. It is my design to render it manifest that no one point in its composition is referable either to accident or intuition—that the work proceeded, step by step, to its completion with the precision and rigid consequence of a mathematical problem.

Let us dismiss, as irrelevant to the poem, *per se,* the circumstance —or say the necessity—which, in the first place, gave rise to the intention of composing *a* poem that should suit at once the popular and the critical taste.

We commence, then, with this intention.

The initial consideration was that of extent. If any literary work is too long to be read at one sitting, we must be content to dispense with the immensely important effect derivable from unity of impression—for, if two sittings be required, the affairs of the world interfere, and every thing like totality is at once destroyed. But since, *ceteris paribus* [other things being equal], no poet can afford to dispense with *any thing* that may advance his design, it but remains to be seen whether there is, in extent, any advantage to counterbalance the loss of unity which attends it. Here I say no, at once. What we term a long poem is, in fact, merely a succession of brief ones—that is to say, of brief poetical effects. It is needless to demonstrate that a poem is such, only inasmuch as it intensely excites, by elevating, the soul; and all intense excitements are, through a psychal necessity, brief. For this reason, at least one half of the "Paradise Lost" is essentially prose—a succession of poetical excitements interspersed, *inevitably,* with corresponding depressions—the whole being deprived, through the extremeness of its length, of the vastly important artistic element, totality, or unity, of effect.

It appears evident, then, that there is a distinct limit, as regards length, to all works of literary art—the limit of a single sitting—and that, although in certain classes of prose composition, such as "Robinson Crusoe," (demanding no unity) this limit may be advantageously overpassed, it can never properly be overpassed in a poem. Within this limit, the extent of a poem may be made to bear mathematical relation to its merit—in other words, to the excitement or elevation—again in other words, to the degree of the true poetical effect which it is capable of inducing; for it is clear that the brevity must be in direct ratio of the intensity of the intended effect:—this, with one proviso—that a certain degree of duration is absolutely requisite for the production of any effect at all.

Holding in view these considerations, as well as that degree of excitement which I deemed not above the popular, while not below the critical, taste, I reached at once what I conceived the proper *length* for my intended poem—a length of about one hundred lines. It is, in fact, a hundred and eight.

My next thought concerned the choice of an impression, or effect, to be conveyed: and here I may as well observe that, throughout the construction, I kept steadily in view the design of rendering the work *universally* appreciable. I should be carried too far out of my immediate topic were I to demonstrate a point upon which I have repeatedly insisted, and which, with the poetical, stands not in the slightest need of demonstration—the point, I mean, that Beauty is the sole legitimate province of the poem. A few words, however, in elucidation of my real meaning, which some of my friends have evinced a disposition to misrepresent. That pleasure which is at once the most intense, the most elevating, and the most pure, is, I believe, found in the contemplation of the beautiful. When, indeed, men speak of Beauty, they mean, precisely, not a quality, as is supposed, but an effect—they refer, in short, just to that intense and pure elevation of *soul—not* of intellect, or of heart—upon which I have commented, and which is experienced in consequence of contemplating "the beautiful." Now I designate Beauty as the province of the poem, merely because it is an obvious rule of Art that effects should be made to spring from direct causes—that objects should be attained through means best adapted for their attainment—no one as yet having been weak enough to deny that the peculiar elevation alluded to is *most readily* attained in this poem. Now the object, Truth, or the satisfaction of the intellect, and the object Passion, or the excitement of the heart, are, although attainable, to a certain extent, in poetry, far more readily attainable in prose. Truth, in fact, demands a precision, and Passion a *homeliness* (the truly passionate will comprehend me) which are absolutely antagonistic to that Beauty which, I maintain, is the excitement, or pleasurable elevation, of the soul. It by no means follows from any thing here said, that passion, or even truth, may not be introduced, and even profitably introduced, into a poem—for they may serve in elucidation, or aid the general effect, as do discords in music, by contrast—but the true artist will always contrive, first, to tone them into proper subservience to the predominant aim, and secondly, to enveil them, as far as possible, in that Beauty which is the atmosphere and the essence of the poem.

Regarding, then, Beauty as my province, my next question referred to the *tone* of its highest manifestation—and all experience has shown that this tone is one of *sadness.* Beauty of whatever kind, in its supreme development, invariably excites the sensitive soul to tears. Melancholy is thus the most legitimate of all the poetical tones.

The length, the province, and the tone, being thus determined, I betook myself to ordinary induction, with the view of obtaining some artistic piquancy which might serve me as a keynote in the construction of the poem—some pivot upon which the whole structure might turn. In carefully thinking over all the usual artistic effects—or more properly *points,* in the theatrical sense—I did not fail to perceive immediately that no one had been so universally employed as that of the *refrain.* The universality of its employment sufficed to assure me of its intrinsic value, and spared me the necessity of submitting it to analysis. I considered it, however, with regard to its susceptibility of improvement, and soon saw it to be in a primitive condition. As commonly used, the *refrain,* or burden, not only is limited to lyric verse, but depends for its impression upon the force of monotone—both in sound and thought. The pleasure is deduced solely from the sense of identity —of repetition. I resolved to diversify, and so heighten, the effect, by adhering, in general, to the monotone of sound, while I continually varied that of thought: that is to say, I determined to produce continuously novel effects, by the variation of *the application* of the *refrain*—the *refrain* itself remaining, for the most part, unvaried.

These points being settled, I next bethought me of the *nature* of my *refrain.* Since its application was to be repeatedly varied, it was clear that the *refrain* itself must be brief, for there would have been an insurmountable difficulty in frequent variations of application in any sentence of length. In proportion to the brevity of the sentence, would, of course, be the facility of the variation. This led me at once to a single word as the best *refrain.*

The question now arose as to the character of the word. Having made up my mind to a *refrain,* the division of the poem into stanzas was, of course, a corollary: the *refrain* forming the close of each stanza. That such a close, to have force, must be sonorous and susceptible of protracted emphasis, admitted no doubt: and these considerations inevitably led me to the long *o* as the most sonorous vowel, in connection with *r* as the most producible consonant.

The sound of the *refrain* being thus determined, it became necessary to select a word embodying this sound, and at the same time in the fullest possible keeping with that melancholy which I had predetermined as the tone of the poem. In such a search it would have been absolutely impossible to overlook the word "Nevermore." In fact, it was the very first which presented itself.

The next *desideratum* was a pretext for the continuous use of the one word "Nevermore." In observing the difficulty which I at once found in inventing a sufficiently plausible reason for its continuous repetition, I did not fail to perceive that this difficulty arose solely from the pre-assumption that the word was to be so continuously or monotonously spoken by a *human* being—I did not fail to perceive, in short, that the difficulty lay in the reconciliation of this monotony with the exercise of reason on the part of the creature repeating the word. Here, then, immediately arose the idea of a *non*-reasoning creature capable of speech; and, very naturally, a parrot, in the first instance, suggested itself, but was superseded forthwith by a Raven, as equally capable of speech, and infinitely more in keeping with the intended *tone*.

I had now gone so far as the conception of a Raven—the bird of ill omen—monotonously repeating the one word, "Nevermore," at the conclusion of each stanza, in a poem of melancholy tone, and in length about one hundred lines. Now, never losing sight of the object *supremeness*, or perfection, at all points, I asked myself—"Of all melancholy topics, what, according to the *universal* understanding of mankind, is the *most* melancholy?" Death—was the obvious reply. "And when," I said, "is this most melancholy of topics most poetical?" From what I have already explained at some length, the answer, here also, is obvious—"When it most closely allies itself to *Beauty*: the death, then, of a beautiful woman is, unquestionably, the most poetical topic in the world—and equally is it beyond doubt that the lips best suited for such topic are those of a bereaved lover."

I had now to combine the two ideas, of a lover lamenting his deceased mistress and a Raven continuously repeating the word "Nevermore"—I had to combine these, bearing in mind my design of varying, at every turn, the *application* of the word repeated; but the only intelligible mode of such combination is that of imagining the Raven employing the word in answer to the queries of the lover. And here it was that I saw at once the opportunity afforded for the effect on which I had been depending—that is to say, the effect of the *variation of application*. I saw that I could make the first query propounded by the lover—the first query to which the Raven should reply "Nevermore"—that I could make this first query a commonplace one—the second less so—the third still less, and so on—until at length the lover, startled from his original *nonchalance* by the melancholy character of the word itself—by its frequent repetition—and by a consideration of the ominous reputation of the fowl that uttered it—is at length excited to superstition, and wildly propounds queries of a far different character—queries whose solution he has passionately at heart—propounds them half in superstition and half in that species of despair which delights in self-torture—propounds them not altogether because he believes in the prophetic or demoniac character of the bird (which, reason assures him, is merely repeating a lesson learned by rote) but because he experiences a phrenzied pleasure in so modeling his questions as to receive from the *expected* "Nevermore" the most delicious because the most intolerable of sorrow. Perceiving the opportunity thus afforded me—or, more strictly, thus forced upon me in the progress of the construction—I first established in mind the climax, or concluding query—that query to which "Nevermore" should be in the last place an answer—that in reply to which this word "Nevermore" should involve the utmost conceivable amount of sorrow and despair.

Here then the poem may be said to have its beginning—at the end, where all works of art should begin—for it was here, at this point of my preconsiderations, that I first put pen to paper in the composition of the stanza:

> "Prophet," said I, "thing of evil! prophet still if bird or
> devil!
> By that heaven that bends above us—by that God we both
> adore,
> Tell this soul with sorrow laden, if within the distant Aidenn,
> It shall clasp a sainted maiden whom the angels name
> Lenore—
> Clasp a rare and radiant maiden whom the angels name
> Lenore."
>
> Quoth the Raven "Nevermore."

I composed this stanza, at this point, first that, by establishing the climax, I might the better vary and graduate, as regards seriousness and importance, the preceding queries of the lover—and, secondly, that I might definitely settle the rhythm, the metre, and the length and general arrangement of the stanza—as well as graduate the stanzas which were to precede, so that none of them might surpass this in rhythmical effect. Had I been able, in the subsequent composition, to construct more vigorous stanzas, I should, without scruple, have purposely enfeebled them, so as not to interfere with the climacteric effect.

And here I may as well say a few words of the versification. My first object (as usual) was originality. The extent to which this has been neglected, in versification, is one of the most unaccountable things in the world. Admitting that there is little possibility of variety in mere *rhythm*, it is still clear that the possible varieties of metre and stanza are absolutely infinite—and yet, *for centuries, no man, in verse, has ever done, or ever seemed to think of doing, an original thing.* The fact is, that originality (unless in minds of very unusual force) is by no means a matter, as some suppose, of impulse or intuition. In general, to be found, it must be elaborately sought, and although a positive merit of the highest class, demands in its attainment less of invention than negation.

Of course, I pretend to no originality in either the rhythm or metre of the "Raven." The former is trochaic—the latter is octameter acatalectic, alternating with heptameter catalectic repeated in the *refrain* of the fifth verse, and terminating with tetrameter catalectic. Less pedantically

—the feet employed throughout (trochees) consist of a long syllable followed by a short: the first line of the stanza consists of eight of these feet—the second of seven and a half (in effect two-thirds)—the third of eight—the fourth of seven and a half—the fifth the same—the sixth three and a half. Now, each of these lines, taken individually, has been employed before, and what originality the "Raven" has, is in their *combination into stanza;* nothing even remotely approaching this combination has ever been attempted. The effect of this originality of combination is aided by other unusual, and some altogether novel effects, arising from an extension of the application of the principles of rhyme and alliteration.

The next point to be considered was the mode of bringing together the lover and the Raven—and the first branch of this consideration was the *locale.* For this the most natural suggestion might seem to be a forest, or the fields—but it has always appeared to me that a close *circumscription of space* is absolutely necessary to the effect of insulated incident:—it has the force of a frame to a picture. It has an indisputable moral power in keeping concentrated the attention, and, of course, must not be confounded with mere unity of place.

I determined, then, to place the lover in his chamber—in a chamber rendered sacred to him by memories of her who had frequented it. The room is represented as richly furnished—this in mere pursuance of the ideas I have already explained on the subject of Beauty, as the sole true poetical thesis.

The *locale* being thus determined, I had now to introduce the bird —and the thought of introducing him through the window, was inevitable. The idea of making the lover suppose, in the first instance, that the flapping of the wings of the bird against the shutter, is a "tapping" at the door, originated in a wish to increase, by prolonging the reader's curiosity, and in a desire to admit the incidental effect arising from the lover's throwing open the door, finding all dark, and thence adopting the half-fancy that it was the spirit of his mistress that knocked.

I made the night tempestuous, first, to account for the Raven's seeking admission, and secondly, for the effect of contrast with the (physical) serenity within the chamber.

I made the bird alight on the bust of Pallas, also for the effect of contrast between the marble and the plumage—it being understood that the bust was absolutely *suggested* by the bird—the bust of *Pallas* being chosen, first, as most in keeping with the scholarship of the lover, and secondly, for the sonorousness of the word, Pallas, itself.

About the middle of the poem, also, I have availed myself of the force of contrast, with a view of deepening the ultimate impression. For example, an air of the fantastic—approaching as nearly to the ludicrous as was admissible—is given to the Raven's entrance. He comes in "with many a flirt and flutter."

> *Not the least obeisance made he*—not a moment stopped or
>   stayed he,
> *But with mien of lord or lady*, perched above my chamber
>   door.

In the two stanzas which follow, the design is more obviously carried out:—

> Then this ebony bird beguiling my sad fancy into smiling
> By the *grave and stern decorum of the countenance it wore*,
> "Though thy *crest be shorn and shaven* thou," I said, "art
>   sure no craven,
> Ghastly grim and ancient Raven wandering from the nightly
>   shore—
> Tell me what thy lordly name is on the Night's Plutonian
>   shore?"
>   Quoth the Raven "Nevermore."
> Much I marvelled *this ungainly fowl* to hear discourse so
>   plainly
> Though its answer little meaning—little relevancy bore;
> For we cannot help agreeing that no living human being
> *Ever yet was blessed with seeing bird above his chamber
>   door—*
> *Bird or beast upon the sculptured bust above his chamber
>   door,*
>   With such name as "Nevermore."

The effect of the *dénouement* being thus provided for, I immediately drop the fantastic for a tone of the most profound seriousness:— this tone commencing in the stanza directly following the one last quoted, with the line,

> But the Raven, sitting lonely on that placid bust, spoke only,
>   etc.

From this epoch the lover no longer jests—no longer sees any thing even of the fantastic in the Raven's demeanor. He speaks of him as a "grim, ungainly, ghastly, gaunt, and ominous bird of yore," and feels the "fiery eyes" burning into his "bosom's core." This revolution of thought, or fancy, on the lover's part, is intended to induce a similar one on the part of the reader—to bring the mind into a proper frame for the *dénouement*—which is now brought about as rapidly and as *directly* as possible.

With the *dénouement* proper—with the Raven's reply, "Nevermore," to the lover's final demand if he shall meet his mistress in another world—the poem, in its obvious phase, that of a simple narrative, may be said to have its completion. So far, every thing is within the limits of the accountable—of the real. A raven, having learned by rote the single word "Nevermore," and having escaped from the custody of its owner, is driven at midnight, through the violence of a storm, to seek admission at a window from which a light still gleams—the chamber-window of a student, occupied half in poring over a volume, half in dreaming of a beloved mistress deceased. The casement being thrown open at the fluttering of the bird's wings, the bird itself perches on the most convenient seat out of the immediate reach of the student, who, amused by the incident and the oddity of the visitor's demeanor, demands of it, in jest and without looking for a reply, its name. The raven addressed, answers with its customary word, "Nevermore"—a word which finds immediate echo in the melancholy heart of the student, who, giving utterance aloud to certain thoughts suggested by the occasion, is again startled by the fowl's repetition of "Nevermore." The student now guesses the state of the case, but is impelled, as I have before explained, by the human thirst for self-torture, and in part by superstition, to propound such queries to the bird as will bring him, the lover, the most of the luxury of sorrow, through the anticipated answer "Nevermore." With the indulgence, to the extreme, of this self-torture, the narration, in what I have termed its first or obvious phase, has a natural termination, and so far there has been no overstepping of the limits of the real.

But in subjects so handled, however skilfully, or with however vivid an array of incident, there is always a certain hardness or nakedness, which repels the artistical eye. Two things are invariably required—first, some amount of complexity, or more properly, adaptation; and, secondly, some amount of suggestiveness—some under-current, however indefinite, of meaning. It is this latter, in especial, which imparts to a work of art so much of that *richness* (to borrow from colloquy a forcible term) which we are too fond of confounding with *the ideal*. It is the *excess* of the suggested meaning—it is the rendering this the upper instead of the under-current of the theme—which turns into prose (and that of the very flattest kind) the so called poetry of the so called transcendentalists.

Holding these opinions, I added the two concluding stanzas of the poem—their suggestiveness being thus made to pervade all the narrative which has preceded them. The under-current of meaning is rendered first apparent in the lines—

> "Take thy beak from out *my heart*, and take thy form from off my door."
>
> Quoth the Raven "Nevermore!"

It will be observed that the words, "from out my heart," involve the first metaphorical expression in the poem. They, with the answer,

"Nevermore," dispose the mind to seek a moral in all that has been previously narrated. The reader begins now to regard the Raven as emblematical—but it is not until the very last line of the very last stanza, that the intention of making him emblematical of *Mournful and Never-ending Remembrance* is permitted distinctly to be seen:

> And the Raven, never flitting, still is sitting, still is sitting,
> On the pallid bust of Pallas, just above my chamber door;
> And his eyes have all the seeming of a demon's that is
>   dreaming,
> And the lamplight o'er him streaming throws his shadow on
>   the floor;
> And my soul *from out that shadow* that lies floating on the
>   floor
>
>   Shall be lifted—nevermore.

66. A Pilfering by Poe

CHARLES D. STEWART

Charles David Stewart, born in Zanesville, Ohio, in 1868, began his career as novelist in 1905, living and writing for the rest of his life in Wisconsin, the source of his articles on natural history ("The Bee's Knees," "The Breath of Life"), which he contributed regularly to the *Atlantic Monthly*, along with poems and stories. He also published *Some Textual Difficulties in Shakespeare* (1914).

If you have read Charles Dickens' interesting novel *Barnaby Rudge*, you will recall that poor Barnaby had a pet raven named Grip. The raven was almost a part of Barnaby because Barnaby carried the bird in a cage on his back. Thus Grip went along when Barnaby was thrown into Newgate prison at the time of the Gordon riots. The bird, having a somewhat limited vocabulary, was constantly repeating himself, and one of his favorite statements was, "I'm a devil, I'm a devil." As Dickens tells it, Grip would sometimes combine the phrase with another, saying, "Polly put the kettle on—I'm a devil, I'm a devil."

This reminds us of what Poe says to his own bird in his poem "The Raven." Beginning with the fifteenth stanza he says, " 'Prophet!'

said I, 'thing of evil!—prophet still, if bird or devil!'" and at the beginning of the next stanza, as if for emphasis, he repeats the line.

Dickens calls attention to the bright red shining in Grip's eye as boy and bird sit in their prison cell, looking out at the light from the burning buildings. "As if," Dickens says, "it were a spark from the fires of the Gordon riots."

Poe, sitting in his dreary chamber at midnight, had little illumination. The fire in the fireplace had almost gone out. "And each separate dying ember wrought its ghost upon the floor." There was a lamp above the bust of Pallas upon which the raven sat—such a meager flame as lamps gave before the days of kerosene. There was not much light there—hardly anything "fiery"—and yet Poe pictures himself as sitting in the lonesome chamber looking up at the visiting fowl "whose fiery eyes now burned into my bosom's core." From what source of fire or conflagration would these fiery eyes get such notable reflection? It would seem here that Poe was thinking more about Barnaby's bird than the one he was writing about.

Poe said that the fascinating quality of his visiting raven was due to its prophetic nature—a brainless bird giving an answer that fit right in with the question asked, and especially an answer with such a doleful future as "Nevermore."

Barnaby's mother sat with him during much of the time that he spent behind the bars. She expressed the hope that they would soon be given their freedom. "You hope," said Barnaby. "Ay, but your hoping will not undo these chains. I hope, but they do not mind that. Grip hopes, but who cares for Grip?" The raven gave a short melancholy croak. It said "Nobody" as plainly as a croak could speak. Later on, Barnaby asked the question, "But who cares for Grip?" Again the raven answered "Nobody." "Nobody" and "Never" were among his favorite words.

Here then we have that same prophetic quality and the same doleful meaning coming from a brainless bird which Poe, in his essay on "The Raven," said was so necessary to the success of his poem.

How are we going to account for these coincidences between Dickens' novel, published in 1841, and Poe's "The Raven," which came out on January 29, 1845? Coincidences are just chance, and they hardly occur so often in such short space. As yet we shall not accuse Poe of plagiarism. He himself accused too many of plagiarism. He was noted for finding literary thieves and liars to right and left of him, and he made many enemies thereby. He summed up his activity in that line by speaking of "Longfellow and other plagiarists." And New England retaliated by calling him "the jingle man."

Let us now consider what likelihood there might be that Poe would take ideas from Dickens, and especially from *Barnaby Rudge*. Poe knew more about the novel than anyone else living, so it was said. The

Encyclopædia Britannica, eleventh edition, under the heading "Charles Dickens," tells us: "The plot [of *Barnaby Rudge*] is of the utmost complexity; and Edgar Allan Poe, who predicted the conclusion, must be one of the few persons who ever really mastered it."

As the novel came out serially in an American publication, Poe attracted much attention when he successfully predicted, from early numbers, the course and outcome of the story. He was therefore deeply familiar with every detail of the passages about Grip, Barnaby's raven.

When the book came out, Poe reviewed it. In the review he shows evidence of being much impressed by the raven. He said, "The raven, too, intensely amusing as it is, might have been made, more than we now see it, a portion of the conception of the fantastic Barnaby. Its croakings might have been *prophetically* heard in the course of the drama." (The italics are Poe's.)

So now what have we? We have Poe, sometime before he wrote the poem, beginning to have ideas. The two vital and fundamental ideas of the poem are here quite explicitly expressed—the ideas of having a brainless bird who could give answers that would happen to fit in with the question asked and that would strike the imagination as being prophetic. And then a word of a doleful nature. Dickens provided such words. Grip's favorite words were "Never" and "Nobody." Poe made his raven's "Nevermore." They were both prophetic in their use. Shall we accuse Poe of plagiarism?

To be sure of our work we must look into it a little more deeply. In 1845 "The Raven" made its appearance in the New York *Evening Mirror*. It soon became the best-known poem in America. When "The Raven" was an established success, Poe wrote a review of it himself. In the review he undertook to explain to the public that every idea, every line of the poem, seemingly inspired, was a work of pure reason. Each step was thought out. It was shrewdly devised. It was an achievement of intellect. He had calculated the effect of each word and sound and image. The poem was not the result of mysterious inward promptings or suggestion from without; this he is careful to have you understand. And this, it would seem, is his reason for writing a review of the poem himself. It is a sort of confession to the public of how such things are done.

His thoroughness in implanting this point of view is interestingly exhibited in the so-called review. He starts with the word "Nevermore" and the effect to be worked by its reiteration. And so problem number one is to choose a speaker. First he thought of using a human being, but decided that it would not do to use a reasoning creature. The effect of brainless reiteration would be hard to contrive. Then he took up the parrot and thought that over. It would not do; he said it was "unnatural." Then he hit upon the idea of using the raven; he said it was "equally capable of speech with the parrot" and "infinitely in keeping with the intended tone." Thus he goes on with his review, or confession, and never once mentions the raven with which he became so familiar in reviewing *Barnaby Rudge*.

Now, must we force ourselves to believe that never at any moment while he was writing "The Raven," and then writing his review of "The Raven," did he recall that other raven named Grip? Did he forget what he had observed so carefully in Barnaby's bird: the effect of prophecy that could be achieved by the reiterated word? Did he never think of Grip's words "Never" and "Nobody" and compare them with his own "Nevermore"? Would it be possible for a man with any memory at all to have had so much to do with Grip as Poe had and then forget all about it? Did Poe forget that Barnaby's bird was repeatedly calling himself a devil, and that he, Poe, made his own bird a visitor from the nether regions? Was all this so far gone from Poe's mind that when it came to choosing a mouthpiece for "Nevermore" he had to think it all out—first a human being, then a parrot, and finally, at last, a raven?

Poe had made quite a reputation by attacking other writers as plagiarists. Now that his own poem was a great success he would naturally begin to feel uneasy. He would want nothing that might be called plagiarism attached to that. And so what would he do? He would head it all off by writing a so-called review of his own poem. He would be careful not to say a word about *Barnaby Rudge*.

Poe was a detective in the sense that he was the originator of the detective story. He would now use his craft in throwing literary detectives off the trail. But he overdid it. When a detective has a culprit in hand, the wrongdoer will keep away as far as possible from the object of the search. A detective is often able to tell by little moves of the culprit's hand or arm, little opposed pressures which the detective can feel, just where the object is.

That is just what Poe is doing in this so-called review. He is keeping the public mind as far as possible from Barnaby Rudge's raven.

Mr. Poe accuses himself of plagiarism.

67. Taste

ROALD DAHL

Dahl (1916–   ), born in South Wales, married actress Patricia Neal in 1953. He won the Edgar Allan Poe Award of the Mystery Writers of America in 1954 and again in 1959. He has written a number of books for children, and two collections of stories, *Someone Like You* (1953—which reprinted "Taste" from the *New Yorker*) and *Kiss Kiss* (1960). He lives in Gypsy House, Great Misenden, Buckinghamshire, England, with his wife and some of his five daughters.

THERE WERE SIX OF US to dinner that night at Mike Schofield's house in London: Mike and his wife and daughter, my wife and I, and a man called Richard Pratt.

Richard Pratt was a famous gourmet. He was president of a small society known as the Epicures, and each month he circulated privately to its members a pamphlet on food and wines. He organized dinners where sumptuous dishes and rare wines were served. He refused to smoke for fear of harming his palate, and when discussing a wine, he had a curious, rather droll habit of referring to it as though it were a living being. "A prudent wine," he would say, "rather diffident and evasive, but quite prudent." Or, "a good-humored wine, benevolent and cheerful—slightly obscene, perhaps, but nonetheless good-humored."

I had been to dinner at Mike's twice before when Richard Pratt was there, and on each occasion Mike and his wife had gone out of their way to produce a special meal for the famous gourmet. And this one, clearly, was to be no exception. The moment we entered the dining room, I could see that the table was laid for a feast. The tall candles, the yellow roses, the quantity of shining silver, the three wineglasses to each person, and above all, the faint scent of roasting meat from the kitchen brought the first warm oozings of saliva to my mouth.

As we sat down, I remembered that on both Richard Pratt's previous visits Mike had played a little betting game with him over the claret, challenging him to name its breed and its vintage. Pratt had replied that that should not be too difficult provided it was one of the great years. Mike had then bet him a case of the wine in question that he could not do it. Pratt had accepted, and had won both times. Tonight I felt sure that the little game would be played over again, for Mike was quite willing to lose the bet in order to prove that his wine was good enough to be recognized, and Pratt, for his part, seemed to take a grave, restrained pleasure in displaying his knowledge.

The meal began with a plate of whitebait, fried very crisp in butter, and to go with it there was a Moselle. Mike got up and poured the wine himself, and when he sat down again, I could see that he was watching Richard Pratt. He had set the bottle in front of me so that I could read the label. It said, "Geierslay Ohligsberg, 1945." He leaned over and whispered to me that Geierslay was a tiny village in the Moselle, almost unknown outside Germany. He said that this wine we were drinking was something unusual, that the output of the vineyard was so small that it was almost impossible for a stranger to get any of it. He had visited Geierslay personally the previous summer in order to obtain a few dozen bottles that they had finally allowed him to have.

"I doubt anyone else in the country has any of it at the moment," he said. I saw him glance again at Richard Pratt. "Great thing about Moselle," he continued, raising his voice, "it's the perfect wine to serve before a claret. A lot of people serve a Rhine wine instead, but that's because they don't know any better. A Rhine wine will kill a delicate claret, you know that? It's barbaric to serve a Rhine before a claret. But a Moselle—ah!—a Moselle is exactly right."

Mike Schofield was an amiable, middle-aged man. But he was a stock-broker. To be precise, he was a jobber in the stock market, and like a number of his kind, he seemed to be somewhat embarrassed, almost ashamed to find that he had made so much money with so slight a talent. In his heart he knew that he was not really much more than a bookmaker—an unctuous, infinitely respectable, secretly unscrupulous bookmaker—and he knew that his friends knew it, too. So he was seeking now to become a man of culture, to cultivate a literary and aesthetic taste, to collect paintings, music, books, and all the rest of it. His little sermon about Rhine wine and Moselle was a part of this thing, this culture that he sought.

"A charming little wine, don't you think?" he said. He was still watching Richard Pratt. I could see him give a rapid furtive glance down the table each time he dropped his head to take a mouthful of whitebait. I could almost *feel* him waiting for the moment when Pratt would take his first sip, and look up from his glass with a smile of pleasure, of astonishment, perhaps even of wonder, and then there would be a discussion and Mike would tell him about the village of Geierslay.

But Richard Pratt did not taste his wine. He was completely engrossed in conversation with Mike's eighteen-year-old daughter, Louise. He was half turned toward her, smiling at her, telling her, so far as I could gather, some story about a chef in a Paris restaurant. As he spoke, he leaned closer and closer to her, seeming in his eagerness almost to impinge upon her, and the poor girl leaned as far as she could away from him, nodding politely, rather desperately, and looking not at his face but at the topmost button of his dinner jacket.

We finished our fish, and the maid came around removing the plates. When she came to Pratt, she saw that he had not yet touched his food, so she hesitated, and Pratt noticed her. He waved her away, broke off his conversation, and quickly began to eat, popping the little crisp brown fish quickly into his mouth with rapid jabbing movements of his fork. Then, when he had finished, he reached for his glass, and in two short swallows he tipped the wine down his throat and turned immediately to resume his conversation with Louise Schofield.

Mike saw it all. I was conscious of him sitting there, very still, containing himself, looking at his guest. His round jovial face seemed to loosen slightly and to sag, but he contained himself and was still and said nothing.

Soon the maid came forward with the second course. This was a large roast of beef. She placed it on the table in front of Mike who stood up and carved it, cutting the slices very thin, laying them gently on the plates for the maid to take around. When he had served everyone, including himself, he put down the carving knife and leaned forward with both hands on the edge of the table.

"Now," he said, speaking to all of us but looking at Richard Pratt. "Now for the claret. I must go and fetch the claret, if you'll excuse me."

"You go and fetch it, Mike?" I said. "Where is it?"

"In my study, with the cork out—breathing."

"Why the study?"

"Acquiring room temperature, of course. It's been there twenty-four hours."

"But why the study?"

"It's the best place in the house. Richard helped me choose it last time he was here."

At the sound of his name, Pratt looked around.

"That's right, isn't it?" Mike said.

"Yes," Pratt answered, nodding gravely. "That's right."

"On top of the green filing cabinet in my study," Mike said. "That's the place we chose. A good draft-free spot in a room with an even temperature. Excuse me now, will you, while I fetch it."

The thought of another wine to play with had restored his humor, and he hurried out the door, to return a minute later more slowly, walking softly, holding in both hands a wine basket in which a dark bottle lay. The label was out of sight, facing downward. "Now!" he cried as he came toward the table. "What about this one, Richard? You'll never name this one!"

Richard Pratt turned slowly and looked up at Mike; then his eyes travelled down to the bottle nestling in its small wicker basket, and he raised his eyebrows, a slight, supercilious arching of the brows, and with it a pushing outward of the wet lower lip, suddenly imperious and ugly.

"You'll never get it," Mike said. "Not in a hundred years."

"A claret?" Richard Pratt asked, condescending.

"Of course."

"I assume, then, that it's from one of the smaller vineyards?"

"Maybe it is, Richard. And then again, maybe it isn't."

"But it's a good year? One of the great years?"

"Yes, I guarantee that."

"Then it shouldn't be too difficult," Richard Pratt said, drawling his words, looking exceedingly bored. Except that, to me, there was something strange about his drawling and his boredom: between the eyes a shadow of something evil, and in his bearing an intentness that gave me a faint sense of uneasiness as I watched him.

"This one is really rather difficult," Mike said, "I won't force you to bet on this one."

"Indeed. And why not?" Again the slow arching of the brows, the cool, intent look.

"Because it's difficult."

"That's not very complimentary to me, you know."

"My dear man," Mike said, "I'll bet you with pleasure, if that's what you wish."

"It shouldn't be too hard to name it."

"You mean you want to bet?"

"I'm perfectly willing to bet," Richard Pratt said.

"All right, then, we'll have the usual. A case of the wine itself."

"You don't think I'll be able to name it, do you?"

"As a matter of fact, and with all due respect, I don't," Mike said. He was making some effort to remain polite, but Pratt was not bothering overmuch to conceal his contempt for the whole proceeding. And yet, curiously, his next question seemed to betray a certain interest.

"You like to increase the bet?"

"No, Richard. A case is plenty."

"Would you like to bet fifty cases?"

"That would be silly."

Mike stood very still behind his chair at the head of the table, carefully holding the bottle in its ridiculous wicker basket. There was a trace of whiteness around his nostrils now, and his mouth was shut very tight.

Pratt was lolling back in his chair, looking up at him, the eyebrows raised, the eyes half closed, a little smile touching the corners of his lips. And again I saw, or thought I saw, something distinctly disturbing about the man's face, that shadow of intentness between the eyes, and in the eyes themselves, right in their centers where it was black, a small slow spark of shrewdness, hiding.

"So you don't want to increase the bet?"

"As far as I'm concerned, old man, I don't give a damn," Mike said. "I'll bet you anything you like."

The three women and I sat quietly, watching the two men. Mike's wife was becoming annoyed; her mouth had gone sour and I felt that at any moment she was going to interrupt. Our roast beef lay before us on our plates, slowly steaming.

"So you'll bet me anything I like?"

"That's what I told you. I'll bet you anything you damn well please, if you want to make an issue out of it."

"Even ten thousand pounds?"

"Certainly I will, if that's the way you want it." Mike was more confident now. He knew quite well that he could call any sum Pratt cared to mention.

"So you say I can name the bet?" Pratt asked again.

"That's what I said."

There was a pause while Pratt looked slowly around the table, first at me, then at the three women, each in turn. He appeared to be reminding us that we were witness to the offer.

"Mike!" Mrs. Schofield said. "Mike, why don't we stop this nonsense and eat our food. It's getting cold."

"But it isn't nonsense," Pratt told her evenly. "We're making a little bet."

I noticed the maid standing in the background holding a dish of vegetables, wondering whether to come forward with them or not.

"All right, then," Pratt said. "I'll tell you what I want you to bet."

"Come on, then," Mike said, rather reckless. "I don't give a damn what it is—you're on."

Pratt nodded, and again the little smile moved the corners of his lips, and then, quite slowly, looking at Mike all the time, he said, "I want you to bet me the hand of your daughter in marriage."

Louise Schofield gave a jump. "Hey!" she cried. "No! That's not funny! Look here, Daddy, that's not funny at all."

"No, dear," her mother said. "They're only joking."

"I'm not joking," Richard Pratt said.

"It's ridiculous," Mike said. He was off balance again now.

"You said you'd bet anything I liked."

"I meant money."

"You didn't *say* money."

"That's what I meant."

"Then it's a pity you didn't say it. But anyway, if you wish to go back on your offer, that's quite all right with me."

"It's not a question of going back on my offer, old man. It's a no-bet anyway, because you can't match the stake. You yourself don't happen to have a daughter to put up against mine in case you lose. And if you had, I wouldn't want to marry her."

"I'm glad of that, dear," his wife said.

"I'll put up anything you like," Pratt announced. "My house, for example. How about my house?"

"Which one?" Mike asked, joking now.

"The country one."

"Why not the other one as well?"

"All right then, if you wish it. Both my houses."

At that point I saw Mike pause. He took a step forward and placed the bottle in its basket gently down on the table. He moved the saltcellar to one side, then the pepper, and then he picked up his knife, studied the blade thoughtfully for a moment, and put it down again. His daughter, too, had seen him pause.

"Now, Daddy!" she cried. "Don't be *absurd!* It's *too* silly for words. I refuse to be betted on like this."

"Quite right, dear," her mother said. "Stop it at once, Mike, and sit down and eat your food."

Mike ignored her. He looked over at his daughter and he smiled, a slow, fatherly, protective smile. But in his eyes, suddenly, there glimmered a little triumph. "You know," he said, smiling as he spoke. "You know, Louise, we ought to think about this a bit."

"Now, stop it, Daddy! I refuse even to listen to you! Why, I've never heard anything so ridiculous in my life!"

"No, seriously, my dear. Just wait a moment and hear what I have to say."

"But I don't *want* to hear it."

"Louise! Please! It's like this. Richard, here, has offered us a serious bet. He is the one who wants to make it, not me. And if he loses, he will have to hand over a considerable amount of property. Now, wait a minute, my dear, don't interrupt. The point is this. *He cannot possibly win.*"

"He seems to think he can."

"Now listen to me, because I know what I'm talking about. The expert, when tasting a claret—so long as it is not one of the famous great wines like Lafite or Latour—can only get a certain way toward naming the vineyard. He can, of course, tell you the Bordeaux district from which the wine comes, whether it is from St. Emilion, Pomerol, Graves, or Médoc. But then each district has several communes, little counties, and each county has many, many small vineyards. It is impossible for a man to differentiate between them all by taste and smell alone. I don't mind telling you that this one I've got here is a wine from a small vineyard that is surrounded by many other small vineyards, and he'll never get it. It's impossible."

"You can't be sure of that," his daughter said.

"I'm telling you I can. Though I say it myself, I understand quite a bit about this wine business, you know. And anyway, heavens alive, girl, I'm your father and you don't think I'd let you in for—for something you didn't want, do you? I'm trying to make you some money."

"Mike!" his wife said sharply. "Stop it now, Mike, please!"

Again he ignored her. "If you will take this bet," he said to his daughter, "in ten mintues you will be the owner of two large houses."

"But I don't want two large houses, Daddy."

"Then sell them. Sell them back to him on the spot. I'll arrange all that for you. And then, just think of it, my dear, you'll be rich! You'll be independent for the rest of your life!"

"Oh, Daddy, I don't like it. I think it's silly."

"So do I," the mother said. She jerked her head briskly up and down as she spoke, like a hen. "You ought to be ashamed of yourself, Michael, ever suggesting such a thing! Your own daughter, too!"

Mike didn't even look at her. "Take it!" he said eagerly, staring hard at the girl. "Take it, quick! I'll guarantee you won't lose."

"But I don't like it, Daddy."

"Come on, girl. Take it!"

Mike was pushing her hard. He was leaning toward her, fixing her with two hard bright eyes, and it was not easy for the daughter to resist him.

"But what if I lose?"

"I keep telling you, you can't lose. I'll guarantee it."

"Oh, Daddy, must I?"

"I'm making you a fortune. So come on now. What do you say, Louise? All right?"

For the last time, she hesitated. Then she gave a helpless little shrug of the shoulders and said, "Oh, all right, then. Just so long as you swear there's no danger of losing."

"Good!" Mike cried. "That's fine! Then it's a bet!"

"Yes," Richard Pratt said, looking at the girl. "It's a bet."

Immediately, Mike picked up the wine, tipped the first thimbleful into his own glass, then skipped excitedly around the table filling up the others. Now everyone was watching Richard Pratt, watching his face as he reached slowly for his glass with his right hand and lifted it to his nose. The man was about fifty years old and he did not have a pleasant face. Somehow, it was all mouth—mouth and lips—the full, wet lips of the professional gourmet, the lower lip hanging downward in the center, a pendulous, permanently open taster's lip, shaped open to receive the rim of a glass or a morsel of food. Like a keyhole, I thought, watching it; his mouth is like a large wet keyhole.

Slowly he lifted the glass to his nose. The point of the nose entered the glass and moved over the surface of the wine, delicately sniffing. He swirled the wine gently around in the glass to receive the bouquet. His concentration was intense. He had closed his eyes, and now the whole top half of his body, the head and neck and chest, seemed to become a kind of huge sensitive smelling-machine, receiving, filtering, analyzing the message from the sniffing nose.

Mike, I noticed, was lounging in his chair, apparently unconcerned, but he was watching every move. Mrs. Schofield, the wife, sat prim and upright at the other end of the table, looking straight ahead, her face tight with disapproval. The daughter, Louise, had shifted her chair away a little, and sidewise, facing the gourmet, and she, like her father, was watching closely.

For at least a minute, the smelling process continued; then, without opening his eyes or moving his head, Pratt lowered the glass to his mouth and tipped in almost half the contents. He paused, his mouth full of wine, getting the first taste; then he permitted some of it to trickle down his throat and I saw his Adam's apple move as it passed by. But most of it he retained in his mouth. And now, without swallowing again, he drew in through his lips a thin breath of air which mingled with the fumes of the wine in the mouth and passed on down into his lungs. He held the breath, blew it out through his nose, and finally began to roll the wine around under the tongue, and chewed it, actually chewed it with his teeth as though it were bread.

It was a solemn, impressive performance, and I must say he did it well.

"Um," he said, putting down the glass, running a pink tongue over his lips. "Um—yes. A very interesting little wine—gentle and gracious, almost feminine in the aftertaste."

There was an excess of saliva in his mouth, and as he spoke he spat an occasional bright speck of it onto the table.

"Now we can start to eliminate," he said. "You will pardon me for doing this carefully, but there is much at stake. Normally I would perhaps take a bit of a chance, leaping forward quickly and landing right in the middle of the vineyard of my choice. But this time—I must move cautiously this time, must I not?" He looked up at Mike and he smiled, a thick-lipped, wet-lipped smile. Mike did not smile back.

"First, then, which district in Bordeaux does this wine come from? That is not too difficult to guess. It is far too light in the body to be from either St. Emilion or Graves. It is obviously a Médoc. There's no doubt about *that*.

"Now—from which commune in Médoc does it come? That also, by elimination, should not be too difficult to decide. Margaux? No. It

cannot be Margaux. It has not the violent bouquet of a Margaux.
Pauillac? It cannot be Pauillac, either. It is too tender, too gentle and
wistful for a Pauillac. The wine of Pauillac has a character that is almost
imperious in its taste. And also, to me, a Pauillac contains just a little
pith, a curious, dusty, pithy flavor that the grape acquires from the soil
of the district. No, no. This—this is a very gentle wine, demure and
bashful in the first taste, emerging shyly but quite graciously in the
second. A little arch, perhaps, in the second taste, and a little naughty
also, teasing the tongue with a trace, just a trace, of tannin. Then, in
the aftertaste, delightful—consoling and feminine, with a certain
blithely generous quality that one associates only with the wines of the
commune of St. Julien. Unmistakably this is a St. Julien."

He leaned back in his chair, held his hands up level with his chest,
and placed the fingertips carefully together. He was becoming ridicu-
lously pompous, but I thought that some of it was deliberate, simply
to mock his host. I found myself waiting rather tensely for him to go on.
The girl Louise was lighting a cigarette. Pratt heard the match strike
and he turned on her, flaring suddenly with real anger. "Please!" he
said. "Please don't do that! It's a disgusting habit, to smoke at table!"

She looked up at him, still holding the burning match in one hand,
the big slow eyes settling on his face, resting there a moment, moving
away again, slow and contemptuous. She bent her head and blew out
the match. but continued to hold the unlighted cigarette in her fingers.

"I'm sorry, my dear," Pratt said, "but I simply cannot have smoking
at table."

She didn't look at him again.

"Now, let me see—where were we?" he said. "Ah, yes. This wine is
from Bordeaux, from the commune of St. Julien, in the district of
Médoc. So far, so good. But now we come to the more difficult part—the
name of the vineyard itself. For in St. Julien there are many vineyards,
and as our host so rightly remarked earlier on, there is often not much
difference between the wine of one and the wine of another. But we
shall see."

He paused again, closing his eyes. "I am trying to establish the
'growth,'" he said. "If I can do that, it will be half the battle. Now,
let me see. This wine is obviously not from a first-growth vineyard—
nor even a second. It is not a great wine. The quality, the—the—what
do you call it?—the radiance, the power, is lacking. But a third growth—
that it could be. And yet I doubt it. We know it is a good year—our
host has said so—and this is probably flattering it a little bit. I must be
careful. I must be very careful here."

He picked up his glass and took another small sip.

"Yes," he said, sucking his lips, "I was right. It is a fourth growth.
Now I am sure of it. A fourth growth from a very good year—from a great
year, in fact. And that's what made it taste for a moment like a third—or

even a second-growth wine. Good! That's better! Now we are closing in! What are the fourth-growth vineyards in the commune of St. Julien?"

Again he paused, took up his glass, and held the rim against that sagging, pendulous lower lip of his. Then I saw the tongue shoot out, pink and narrow, the tip of it dipping into the wine, withdrawing swiftly again—a repulsive sight. When he lowered the glass, his eyes remained closed, the face concentrated, only the lips moving, sliding over each other like two pieces of wet, spongy rubber.

"There it is again!" he cried. "Tannin in the middle taste, and the quick astringent squeeze upon the tongue. Yes, yes, of course! Now I have it! This wine comes from one of those small vineyards around Beychevelle. I remember now. The Beychevelle district, and the river and the little harbor that has silted up so the wine ships can no longer use it. Beychevelle . . . could it actually be a Beychevelle itself? No, I don't think so. Not quite. But it is somewhere very close. Château Talbot? Could it be Talbot? Yes, it could. Wait one moment."

He sipped the wine again, and out of the side of my eye I noticed Mike Schofield and how he was leaning farther and farther forward over the table, his mouth slightly open, his small eyes fixed upon Richard Pratt.

"No. I was wrong. It was not a Talbot. A Talbot comes forward to you just a little quicker than this one; the fruit is nearer to the surface. If it is a '34, which I believe it is, then it couldn't be Talbot. Well, well. Let me think. It is not a Beychevelle and it is not a Talbot, and yet—yet it is so close to both of them, so close, that the vineyard must be almost in between. Now, which could that be?"

He hesitated, and we waited, watching his face. Everyone, even Mike's wife, was watching him now. I heard the maid put down the dish of vegetables on the sideboard behind me, gently, so as not to disturb the silence.

"Ah!" he cried. "I have it! Yes, I think I have it!"

For the last time, he sipped the wine. Then, still holding the glass up near his mouth, he turned to Mike and he smiled, a slow, silky smile, and he said, "You know what this is? This is the little Château Branaire-Ducru."

Mike sat tight, not moving.

"And the year, 1934."

We all looked at Mike, waiting for him to turn the bottle around in its basket and show the label.

"Is that your final answer?" Mike said.

"Yes, I think so."

"Well, is it or isn't it?"

"Yes, it is."

"What was the name again?"

"Château Branaire-Ducru. Pretty little vineyard. Lovely old

château. Know it quite well. Can't thank why I didn't recognize it at once."

"Come on, Daddy," the girl said. "Turn it round and let's have a peek. I want my two houses."

"Just a minute," Mike said. "Wait just a minute." He was sitting very quiet, bewildered-looking, and his face was becoming puffy and pale, as though all the force was draining slowly out of him.

"Michael!" his wife called sharply from the other end of the table. "What's the matter?"

"Keep out of this, Margaret, will you please."

Richard Pratt was looking at Mike, smiling with his mouth, his eyes small and bright. Mike was not looking at anyone.

"Daddy!" the daughter cried, agonized. "But, Daddy, you don't mean to say he's guessed it right!"

"Now, stop worrying, my dear," Mike said. "There's nothing to worry about."

I think it was more to get away from his family than anything else that Mike then turned to Richard Pratt and said, "I'll tell you what, Richard. I think you and I better slip off into the next room and have a little chat?"

"I don't want a little chat," Pratt said. "All I want is to see the label on that bottle." He knew he was a winner now; he had the bearing, the quiet arrogance of a winner, and I could see that he was prepared to become thoroughly nasty if there was any trouble. "What are you waiting for?" he said to Mike. "Go on and turn it round."

Then this happened: The maid, the tiny, erect figure of the maid in her white-and-black uniform, was standing beside Richard Pratt, holding something out in her hand. "I believe these are yours, sir," she said.

Pratt glanced around, saw the pair of thin horn-rimmed spectacles that she held out to him, and for a moment he hesitated. "Are they? Perhaps they are. I don't know."

"Yes sir, they're yours." The maid was an elderly woman—nearer seventy than sixty—a faithful family retainer of many years standing. She put the spectacles down on the table beside him.

Without thanking her, Pratt took them up and slipped them into his top pocket, behind the white handkerchief.

But the maid didn't go away. She remained standing beside and slightly behind Richard Pratt, and there was something so unusual in her manner and in the way she stood there, small, motionless, and erect, that I for one found myself watching her with a sudden apprehension. Her old gray face had a frosty, determined look, the lips were compressed, the little chin was out, and the hands were clasped together tight before her. The curious cap on her head and the flash of white down the front of her uniform made her seem like some tiny, ruffled, white-breasted bird.

"You left them in Mr. Schofield's study," she said. Her voice was unnaturally, deliberately polite. "On top of the green filing cabinet in his study, sir, when you happened to go in there by yourself before dinner."

It took a few moments for the full meaning of her words to penetrate, and in the silence that followed I became aware of Mike and how he was slowly drawing himself up in his chair, and the color coming to his face, and the eyes opening wide, and the curl of the mouth, and the dangerous little patch of whiteness beginning to spread around the area of the nostrils.

"Now, Michael!" his wife said. "Keep calm now, Michael, dear! Keep calm!"

Suggestions for Writing

1. Write an essay on untutored language, using examples from Kohl, De Angulo, and your own observation.

2. Write an inductive essay on any question you have puzzled through to an answer, raising possibilities and eliminating them, somewhat as the gourmet does in Dahl's story.

3. Write an essay on the three "Raven" pieces, defending Poe against Stewart or expanding Stewart's argument (he misses at least one obvious point), analyzing the poem itself for points to support your position.

4. Write a thorough analysis of Dahl's story, pointing out his effects and how he achieves them. He names and places the fourth-growth vineyards of St. Julien accurately, incidentally, which suggests that the rest of his wine lore is accurate, too.

IX. Growing Argumentative

Definitions, or Pinning Distinctions Down

DEFINITION is drawing limits, between earth and sky, between night and day. But drawing the line through the intervening twilights is difficult. And an even deeper difficulty remains. Once we have separated night from day, we still must say what "day" is and what "night" is. Thus, defining challenges our deepest intellectual and expository powers. What is life? What is the world? What is God? And because we assert our definitions as both new and accurate, for our readers to believe as we believe, our definitions are very close to arguments. Indeed, definition is the basis for argumentation.

You begin by setting one thing against another, drawing the line between. Then you seek to pin down the attributes and essences of the thing you would define. All this you must do in language, which, as Coles, De Angulo, and Kohl imply, as Barthes suggests in this section and Steiner in the next, is itself a mystery that defies ultimate definition. You must simply pin your distinctions down as firmly as you can. Four steps will help to check the possibilities: (1) saying what it is, (2) saying what it is not, (3) saying what it is like, (4) saying what it is not like. You might consider also what it can and can not do.

In the end, definitions remain tentative. However positively we, or the dictionary, assert our definition, we secretly know that another mind will challenge it, change it, move the defining line left or right, bring forward some detail we slighted or missed. Hence the excitement of definition. A mind stretches itself to bring limits and essences into new clarity, yet knows how unfixed its solutions are. The excitement of definition is in its daring; the satisfaction is in seeing things clearly, as we silently add, in renewed humility, "I think this is it, but I know it is not all."

You can examine this process in the selections that follow. Hofstadter's definition is an early part of his much larger argumentative essay, "Democracy and Anti-Intellectualism in America." He sets it immediately after he has established his thesis that American democracy is now seriously threatened by an anti-intellectualism as deep as our roots. Barthes, in defining an author, discovers virtually the same distinction that Hofstadter makes. Both writers illustrate how drawing the line between this thing and that is the essence of definition. Observe which half

402

of Hofstadter's distinction matches which half of Barthes's, and note how their emphases differ. Orwell's strategy is different. As he argues for good language over bad, he gives us examples, and we gather the defining distinction. Bigelow follows a somewhat different process, deploying the elements of definition, piece by piece, to make the whole of a defining essay. After establishing his thesis (that we need to know what existentialism is to understand modern literature and modern thought), he constructs a comprehensive definition of existentialism by dividing and describing its parts and sub-parts. We leave all these essays with a sense of having found, at last, some distinctions made clear, of seeing something pinned down, of discovering a line put confidently through the middle of twilight.

You will notice also how these essays define by comparison and contrast, with Bigelow concentrating more steadily on distinctions of parts within a whole. Keats takes us further into the thing itself, as he delineates "autumn" with only one contrasting glance at spring to underline his concentration.

68. Intellectualism and Democracy

RICHARD HOFSTADTER

Hofstadter (1916–1970), born in Buffalo, educated at the University of Buffalo and at Columbia, returned to Columbia permanently in 1946 as professor of American history after teaching at Maryland, Brooklyn, and City College, New York. Among his thirteen books and many awards, his tenth book, *Anti-Intellectualism in American Life* (1963), won both the Pulitzer Prize and the Emerson Award.

BUT WHAT IS AN INTELLECTUAL, really? This is a problem of definition that I found, when I came to it, far more elusive than I had anticipated. A great deal of what might be called the journeyman's work of our culture—the work of engineers, physicians, newspapermen, and indeed of most professors—does not strike me as distinctively intellectual, although it is certainly work based in an important sense on ideas. The distinction that we must recognize, then, is one originally made by Max Weber between living *for* ideas and living *off* ideas. The intellectual lives for ideas; the journeyman lives off them. The engineer or the physician—I don't mean here to be invidious—needs to have a pretty considerable capital stock in frozen ideas to do his work; but they serve for him a purely instrumental purpose: he lives off them, not for them. Of course he may also be, in his private role and his personal ways of thought, an intellectual, but it is not necessary for him to be one in order to work at his profession. There is in fact no profession which demands that one be an intellectual. There do seem to be vocations, however, which almost demand that one be an anti-intellectual, in which those who live off ideas seem to have an implacable hatred for those who live for them. The marginal intellectual workers and the unfrocked intellectuals who work in journalism, advertising, and mass communication are the bitterest and most powerful among those who work at such vocations.

It will help, too, to make the further distinction between living for ideas and living for *an idea*. History is full of cases of great men with good minds, a capacity to deal with abstractions, and a desire to make systems of them—all qualities we associate with the intellectual. But when, as it has in many of them, this concern with ideas, no matter how dedicated and sincere, reduces in the end to the ingenious use of them for a central preconception, however grand, then I think we have very little intellectualism and a great deal of something else. A good historical illustration is that of Lenin, who, as his more theoretical works show, had in him a powerful element of intellectuality; but this intellectuality was rendered thin by his all-absorbing concern with certain very limiting political values. His book on philosophy, *Materialism and Empirio-Criticism,* a shrill work and an extremely depressing one to read, makes it altogether clear that the politician in him swallowed up the intellectual. I choose the illustration of Lenin because it helps me to make another point that seems unfortunately necessary because of the present tendency to identify intellectuals with subversives. That point is that the idea of a party line and political messianism is inherently inconsistent with intellectualism, and those few intellectuals who have in some way survived that tension are few, pitiable, and on the whole sterile.

The journeyman of ideas, and the janizary who makes a somewhat complicated but highly instrumental use of ideas, provide us with two illustrations of people who work with ideas but are not precisely intellectuals, as I understand the term. What, then, are the differences between the men who work with ideas but are *not* intellectuals and the men who work with ideas and *are* intellectuals?

Two things, that seem in fact to be mutually at odds, mark off the intellectual from the journeyman of ideas; one is playfulness, the other is piety.

Certainly the intellectual, if he is nothing else, is one who relishes *the play of the mind* for its own sake, for whom it is one of the major ends of life. The intellectual has a full quotient of what Veblen called "idle curiosity." His mind, instead of falling to rest when it has provided him with his girl and his automobile and his dinner, becomes even more active. Indeed if we had to define him in physiological terms, we might define him as the creature whose mind is *most* likely to be active after dinner.

I speak of playfulness too because of the peculiar nature of the relationship, in the intellectual's mind, between ideas and practicality. To the journeyman of ideas the be-all and end-all of ideas lies in their practical efficacy. Now the intellectual, by contrast, is not necessarily impractical; I can think of some intellectuals like Thomas Jefferson and Robert Owen and John Maynard Keynes who have been eminently practical, and I consider the notion that the intellectual is inherently impractical to be one of the most contemptible of the delusions with which the anti-intellectual quiets his envy—the intellectual is not impractical but primarily concerned with a quality of ideas that does not depend upon their practicality. He neither reveres nor disdains practical consequences; for him they are either marginal or irrelevant. And when he does talk about the practicality or the "relevance" of ideas, the kind of practicality that he is concerned with is itself somewhat different from the practicality of building a bridge, curing a disease, or making a profit—it is practical relevance to spiritual values themselves.

The best illustration of the intellectual's view of the purely practical that has recently come to my attention is the reaction of Clerk Maxwell, the great nineteenth-century mathematician and theoretical physicist, to the invention of the telephone. Maxwell was asked to give a lecture on the workings of this wonderful new instrument, which he began by saying how difficult it was to believe, when the word first came from America, that such a thing had actually been devised. But then, he said, "when at last this little instrument appeared, consisting, as it does, of parts, every one of which is familiar to us, and capable of being put together by an amateur, the disappointment arising from its humble appearance was only partially relieved on finding that it was really able to talk." Perhaps, then, this regrettable appearance of simplicity might be redeemed by the presence somewhere of "recondite physical principles, the study of which might worthily occupy an hour's time of an academic audience." But no; Maxwell had not met a single person who could not understand the physical processes involved, and even the science reporters for the daily press had almost got it right! The thing was a disappointing bore; it was not recondite, it was not profound, it was not complex, it was not *intellectually* new.

To be sure, what this illustration suggests is not merely that the telephone disappointed Maxwell as a pure scientist and an intellectual, but that the strain of intellectuality in him was not as broadly developed as it might have been. The telephone might well excite not merely the commercial imagination but the historical imagination. But my point is, after all, not that Maxwell was a universal intellectual, but that he was displaying the attitude of the intellectual in his particular sphere of interest.

The second element in intellectualism is its religious strain, the note of piety. What I mean by this is simply that for the intellectual the whole world of moral values becomes attached to ideas and to the life dedicated to ideas. The life given over to the search for truth takes on for him a primary moral significance. Intellectualism, although hardly confined to doubters, is often the sole piety of the skeptic. A few years ago a distinguished sociologist asked me to read a brief manuscript which he had written primarily for students planning to go on to advanced work in his field, the purpose of which was to illustrate various ways in which the life of the mind might be cultivated. The essay had about it a little too much of the how-to-do books, and my friend abandoned it. But the nub of the matter from the standpoint of our present problem was that I found myself to be reading a piece of devotional literature, comparable perhaps to Cotton Mather's *Essays to do Good* or Richard Steele's *The Tradesman's Calling*. My friend was trying to communicate his sense of dedication to the life of ideas, which he conceived much in the fashion of the old Protestant writers as a *calling*. To work is to pray. Yes, and for this kind of man, to think —really to think—is to pray. What he knows best, when he is at his best, is the pursuit of truth; but *easy* truths bore him. What he is certain of becomes unsatisfactory always; the meaning of his intellectual life lies in the quest for new uncertainties.

In a bygone day when men lived even more by dogma than they do now, there were two kinds of men whose special office it was to seek for and utter the truth; and they symbolize these two sides of the intellectual's nature. One was the angelic doctor, the learned school-man, the conserver of old orthodoxies but also the maker of the new, and the prodder at the outer limits of received truths. The other was the jester, the professional fool, who had license to say on occasion for the purposes of amusement and release those things that bordered on lèse majesté and could not be uttered by others who were accounted serious men.

The fool and the schoolman are very far apart. No doubt you will ask whether there is not a contradiction between these two qualities of the intellectual, piety and playfulness. Certainly there is great tension between them; human beings are tissues of contradictions, and the life even of the intellectual is not logic, to borrow from Holmes, but experience. If you will think of the intellectuals you know, some will occur to you in whom the note of playfulness seems stronger, others who are predominantly pious. But I believe that in all intellectuals who have any stability as intellectuals—and that includes the angelic doctors of the middle ages—each of these characteristics is at some point qualified by the other. Perhaps the tensile strength of the intellectual can be gauged by his ability to maintain a fair equipoise between these aspects of himself. At one end of the scale, an excess of playfulness leads to triviality, to dilettantism, to cynicism, to the failure of all sustained creative effort. At the other, an excess of piety leads to fanaticism, to messianism, to ways of life that may be morally magnificent or morally mean, but in either case are not quite the ways of intellectualism. It is of the essence of the intellectual that he strikes a balance.

69. Authors and Writers

ROLAND BARTHES

Barthes (1915–   ), a leading French intellectual and
writer, lives in Paris. He was Professor of Letters and Fellow
at the National Center for Scientific Research in Paris
(1952–1961) and Director of Studies at *L'École des Hautes
Études,* the Sorbonne (1962). He was Visiting Professor
at Johns Hopkins University in 1967.

WHO SPEAKS? WHO WRITES? We still lack a sociology of
language. What we know is that language is a power, and that,
from public body to social class, a group of men is sufficiently
defined if it possesses, to various degrees, the national language. Now
for a very long time—probably for the entire classical capitalist period
—i.e., from the sixteenth to the nineteenth century, in France—the un-
contested owners of the language were authors and they alone. If, with
the exception of preachers and jurists (enclosed moreover in functional languages), no one else spoke, and this "monopoly" of the
language produced a rigid order, an order less of producers than of
production: it was not the literary *profession* which was stratified (it
has developed greatly in three hundred years, from the domestic poet
to the businessman-writer), but the very *substance* of this literary discourse which was subjected to rules of use, genre, and composition more
or less immutable from Marot to Verlaine, from Montaigne to Gide.
Contrary to so-called primitive societies, in which there is witchcraft
only through the agency of a witch-doctor, as Marcel Mauss has shown,
the literary *institution* transcended the literary *functions,* and within
this institution what presides is its essential substance, language. In-
stitutionally, the literature of France is its language, a half-linguistic,
half-aesthetic system which has not lacked a mythic dimension as well,
that of its *clarity.*

When, in France, did the author cease being the only one to speak?
Doubtless at the time of the Revolution, when there first appear men
who appropriate the authors' language for political ends. The institution
remains in place: it is still a matter of that great French language,
whose lexicon and euphony are respectfully preserved throughout the
greatest paroxysm of French history; but the functions change, the

personnel is increased for the next hundred years; the authors themselves, from Chateaubriand or Maistre to Hugo or Zola, help broaden the literary function, transform this institutionalized language of which they are still the acknowledged owners into the instrument of a new action; and alongside these *authors*, in the strict sense of the word, a new group is constituted and develops, a new custodian of the public language. Intellectuals? The word has a complex resonance; [1] I prefer calling them here *writers*. And since the present may be that fragile moment in history when the two functions coexist, I should like to sketch a comparative typology of the author and the writer with reference to the substance they share: language.

The author performs a function, the writer an activity. Not that the author is a pure essence: he acts, but his action is immanent in its object, it is performed paradoxically on its own instrument: language. The author is the man who *labors*, who *works up* his utterance (even if he is inspired) and functionally absorbs himself in this labor, this work. His activity involves two kinds of norm: of technique (composition, genre, style) and of craft (patience, correctness, perfection). The paradox is that the substance becoming in a sense its own end, literature is at bottom a tautological activity, like that of those cybernetic machines constructed *for themselves* (Ashby's homeostat): the author is a man who radically absorbs the world's *why* in a *how-to-write*. And the miracle, so to speak, is that this narcissistic activity has always provoked an interrogation of the world: by enclosing himself in the *how-to-write*, the author ultimately discovers the open question par excellence: why the world? What is the meaning of things? In short, it is precisely when the author's work becomes its own end that it regains a mediating character: the author conceives of literature as an end, the world restores it to him as a means: and it is in this perpetual *inconclusiveness* that the author rediscovers the world, an alien world moreover, since literature represents it as a question—never, finally, as an answer.

Language is neither an instrument nor a vehicle: it is a structure, as we increasingly suspect; but the author is the only man, by definition, to lose his own structure and that of the world in the structure of language. Yet this language is an (infinitely) labored substance; it is a little like a super-language. Reality is never anything but a pretext for it (for the author, *to write* is an intransitive verb); hence it can never explain the world, or at least, when it claims to explain the world, it does so only the better to conceal the world's ambiguity: once the explanation is fixed in a *work*, it immediately becomes an ambiguous product of the real, to which it is linked by perspective.

---

[1] Apparently the word *intellectual*, in the sense we give it today, was born at the time of the Dreyfus Affair, obviously applied by the anti-Dreyfusards to the Dreyfusards.

In short, literature is always unrealistic, but its very unreality permits it to question the world—though these questions can never be direct: starting from a theocratic explanation of the world, Balzac finally does nothing but interrogate. Thus the author existentially forbids himself two kinds of language, whatever the intelligence or the sincerity of his enterprise: first, *doctrine,* since he converts despite himself, by his very project, every explanation into a spectacle: he is always an agent of ambiguity;[2] second, *evidence:* since he has consigned himself to language, the author cannot have a naïve consciousness, cannot "work up" an outcry without his message bearing finally much more on the working-up than on the outcry. By identifying himself with language, the author loses all claim to truth, for language is precisely that structure whose very goal (at least historically, since the Sophists), once it is no longer rigorously transitive, is to neutralize the true and the false.[3] But what he obviously gains is the power to disturb the world, to afford it the dizzying spectacle of *praxis* without sanction. This is why it is absurd to ask an author for "commitment": a "committed" author claims simultaneous participation in two structures, inevitably a source of deception. What we can ask of an author is that he be responsible. Again, let there be no mistake: whether or not an author is responsible for his *opinions* is unimportant; whether or not an author assumes, more or less intelligently, the ideological implications of his work is also secondary; an author's true responsibility is to support literature as *a failed commitment,* as a Mosaic glance at the Promised Land of the real (this is Kafka's kind of responsibility, for example).

Naturally, literature is not a grace, it is the body of the projects and decisions which lead a man to fulfill himself (that is, in a sense, to essentialize himself) in language alone: an author is a man who wants to be an author. Naturally too, society, which consumes the author, transforms project into vocation, labor into talent, and technique into art. Thus is born the myth of *fine writing:* the author is a salaried priest, he is the half-respectable, half-ridiculous guardian of the sanctuary of the great French Language, a kind of national treasure, a sacred merchandise, produced, taught, consumed, and exported in the context of a sublime economy of values. This sacralization of the author's labor on his form has great consequences, and not merely formal ones: it permits society to distance the work's content when it risks becoming an embarrassment, to convert it into pure spectacle to which

---

[2] An author can produce a system, but it will never be consumed as such.

[3] Structure of reality and structure of language: no better indication of the difficulty of a coincidence between the two than the constant failure of dialectic, once it becomes discourse; for language is not dialectic, it can only say *"we must be dialectical,"* but it cannot be so itself: language is a representation without perspective, except precisely for the author's; but the author dialecticizes himself, he does not dialecticize the world.

it is entitled to apply a liberal (i.e., an indifferent) judgment, to neutralize the revolt of passion, the subversion of criticism (which forces the "committed" author into an incessant and impotent provocation) —in short, to assimilate the author: every author is eventually digested by the literary institution, unless he scuttles himself, i.e., unless he ceases to identify his being with that of language. This is why so few authors renounce writing, for that is literally to kill themselves, to die to the being they have chosen; and if there are such authors, their silence echoes like an inexplicable conversion (Rimbaud).[4]

The *writer*, on the other hand, is a "transitive" man: he posits a goal (to give evidence, to explain, to instruct) of which language is merely a means; for him language supports a *praxis*, it does not constitute one. Thus language is restored to the nature of an instrument of communication, a vehicle of "thought." Even if the writer pays some attention to style, this concern is never ontological. The writer performs no essential technical action upon language; he employs an utterance common to all writers, a *koine* in which we can of course distinguish certain dialects (Marxist, for example, or Christian, or existentialist), but very rarely styles. For what defines the writer is the fact that his project of communication is *naïve:* he does not admit that his message is reflexive, that it closes over itself, and that we can read in it, diagnostically, anything else but what he means: what writer would tolerate a psychoanalysis of his language? He believes that his work resolves an ambiguity, institutes an irreversible explanation (even if he regards himself as a modest instructor); whereas for the author, as we have seen, it is just the other way around: he knows that his language, intransitive by choice and by labor, inaugurates an ambiguity, even if it appears to be peremptory, that it offers itself, paradoxically, as a monumental silence to be deciphered, that it can have no other motto but Jacques Rigaut's profound remark: *and even when I affirm, I am still questioning.*

The author participates in the priest's role, the writer in the clerk's; the author's language is an intransitive act (hence, in a sense, a gesture), the writer's an activity. The paradox is that society consumes a transitive language with many more reservations than an intransitive one: the writer's status, even today when writers abound, is much more problematic than the author's. This is primarily the consequence of a material circumstance: the author's language is a merchandise offered through traditional channels, it is the unique object of an institution created only for literature; the writer's language, on the contrary, can be produced and consumed only in the shadow of institutions which have, originally, an entirely different function

---

[4] These are the modern elements of the problem. We know that on the contrary Racine's contemporaries were not at all surprised when he suddenly stopped writing tragedies and became a royal functionary.

than to focus on language: the university, scientific and scholarly re-search, politics, etc. Then, too, the writer's language is dependent in another way: from the fact that it is (or considers itself) no more than a simple vehicle, its nature as merchandise is transferred to the project of which it is the instrument: we are presumed to sell "thought" ex-clusive of any art. Now the chief mythic attribute of "pure" thought (it would be better to say "unapplied" thought) is precisely that it is produced outside the channel of money: contrary to form (which costs a lot, as Valéry said), thought costs nothing, but it also does not sell itself, it gives itself—generously. This points up at least two new differ-ences between author and writer. First, the writer's production always has a free but also a somewhat "insistent" character: the writer offers society what society does not always ask of him: situated on the margin of institutions and transactions, his language appears para-doxically more individual, at least in its motifs, than the author's lan-guage: *the writer's function is to say at once and on every occasion what he thinks;* [5] and this function suffices, he thinks, to justify him; whence the critical, urgent aspect of the writer's language: it always seems to indicate a conflict between thought's irrepressible character and the inertia of a society reluctant to consume a merchandise which no specific institution normalizes. Thus we see *a contrario*—and this is the second difference—that the social function of literary language (that of the author) is precisely *to transform thought* (or consciousness, or outcry) *into merchandise;* society wages a kind of vital warfare to appropriate, to acclimatize, to institutionalize the risk of thought, and it is language, that model institution, which affords it the means to do so. The paradox here is that "provocative" *language* is readily ac-commodated by the literary institution: the scandals of language, from Rimbaud to Ionesco, are rapidly and perfectly integrated; whereas "provocative" *thought,* insofar as it is to be immediate (without media-tion), can only exhaust itself in the no-man's-land of form: the scandal is never total.

I am describing here a contradiction which, in fact, is rarely pure: everyone today moves more or less openly between the two positions, the author's and the writer's; it is doubtless the responsibility of history which has brought us into the world too late to be complacent authors and too soon to be heeded writers. Today, each member of the intelligentsia harbors both roles in himself, one or the other of which he "retracts" more or less well: authors occasionally have the impulses, the impatiences of writers; writers sometimes gain access to the theater of language. We want *to write something,* and at the

---

[5] This function of *immediate manifestation* is the very opposite of the author's: 1) the author hoards, he publishes at a rhythm which is not that of his consciousness; 2) he mediatizes what he thinks by a laborious and "regular" form; 3) he permits a free interrogation of his work, he is anything but dogmatic.

same time *we write* (intransitively). In short, our age produces a bastard type: the author-writer. His function is inevitably paradoxical: he provokes and exorcises at the same time; formally, his language is free, screened from the institution of literary language, and yet, enclosed in this very freedom, it secretes its own rules in the form of a common style; having emerged from the club of men-of-letters, the author-writer finds another club, that of the intelligentsia. On the scale of society as a whole, this new group has a *complementary* function: the intellectual's style functions as the paradoxical sign of a non-language, it permits society to experience the dream of a communication without system (without institution): to write without "style," to communicate "pure thought" without such communication developing any parasitical message—that is the model which the author-writer creates for society. It is a model at once distant and necessary, with which society plays something of a cat-and-mouse game: it acknowledges the author-writer by buying his books (however few), recognizing their public character; and at the same time it keeps him at a distance, obliging him to support himself by means of the subsidiary institutions it controls (the university, for instance), constantly accusing him of intellectualism, i.e., sterility (a reproach the author never incurs). In short, from an anthropological viewpoint, the author-writer is an excluded figure integrated by his very exclusion, a remote descendant of the Accursed: his function in society as a whole is perhaps related to the one Lévi-Strauss attributes to the witch-doctor: a function of complementarity, both witch-doctor and intellectual in a sense stabilizing a disease which is necessary to the collective economy of health. And naturally it is not surprising that such a conflict (or such a contract, if you prefer) should be joined on the level of language; for language is this paradox: the institutionalization of subjectivity.

(Translated from the French by Richard Howard)

70. Politics and the English Language

GEORGE ORWELL

Orwell (1903–1950), whose real name was Eric Arthur Blair, was born in Motihari, Bengal, of British parents. He won a scholarship to Eton, and, at nineteen, joined the Indian Imperial Police in Burma (1922–1927). He returned to Europe and lived in poverty and sickness, by odd jobs, producing his first book, *Down and Out in Paris and London* (1933). He had joined the communist movement, and had taught in private schools and worked in a London bookshop and store from 1933 to 1935, when he went to fight on the communist side in the Spanish Civil War, which added the communists to the imperialists in his aversion to authoritarian governments. His *Animal Farm* (1945) is anti-Stalinist, and his *Nineteen Eighty-Four* (written 1948, published 1949) is against all politics and what he sees as the modern drift of all governments toward totalitarian control. Rejected as physically unfit when he volunteered for the British army in World War II, he entered the British Broadcasting Corporation's Indian service. He died in London.

MOST PEOPLE who bother with the matter at all would admit that the English language is in a bad way, but it is generally assumed that we cannot by conscious action do anything about it. Our civilization is decadent and our language—so the argument runs —must inevitably share in the general collapse. It follows that any struggle against the abuse of language is a sentimental archaism, like preferring candles to electric light or hansom cabs to aeroplanes. Underneath this lies the half-conscious belief that language is a natural growth and not an instrument which we shape for our own purposes.

Now, it is clear that the decline of a language must ultimately have political and economic causes: it is not due simply to the bad influence of this or that individual writer. But an effect can become a cause, reinforcing the original cause and producing the same effect

414

in an intensified form, and so on indefinitely. A man may take to drink because he feels himself to be a failure, and then fail all the more completely because he drinks. It is rather the same thing that is happening to the English language. It becomes ugly and inaccurate because our thoughts are foolish, but the slovenliness of our language makes it easier for us to have foolish thoughts. The point is that the process is reversible. Modern English, especially written English, is full of bad habits which spread by imitation and which can be avoided if one is willing to take the necessary trouble. If one gets rid of these habits one can think more clearly, and to think clearly is a necessary first step towards political regeneration: so that the fight against bad English is not frivolous and is not the exclusive concern of professional writers. I will come back to this presently, and I hope that by that time the meaning of what I have said here will have become clearer. Meanwhile, here are five specimens of the English language as it is now habitually written.

These five passages have not been picked out because they are especially bad—I could have quoted far worse if I had chosen—but because they illustrate various of the mental vices from which we now suffer. They are a little below the average, but are fairly representative samples. I number them so that I can refer back to them when necessary:

(1) I am not, indeed, sure whether it is not true to say that the Milton who once seemed not unlike a seventeenth-century Shelley had not become, out of an experience ever more bitter in each year, more alien [*sic*] to the founder of that Jesuit sect which nothing could induce him to tolerate.

PROFESSOR HAROLD LASKI
(ESSAY IN *Freedom of Expression*).

(2) Above all, we cannot play ducks and drakes with a native battery of idioms which prescribes such egregious collocations of vocables as the Basic *put up with* for *tolerate* or *put at a loss* for *bewilder*.

PROFESSOR LANCELOT HOGBEN
(*Interglossa*).

(3) On the one side we have the free personality: by definition it is not neurotic, for it has neither conflict nor dream. Its desires, such as they are, are transparent, for they are just what institutional approval keeps in the forefront of consciousness; another institutional pattern would alter their number and intensity; there is little in them that is natural, irreducible, or culturally dangerous. But *on the other side,* the social bond itself is nothing but the mutual reflection of these self-secure integrities. Recall the definition of love. Is not this the very

picture of a small academic? Where is there a place in this hall of mirrors for either personality or fraternity?

ESSAY ON PSYCHOLOGY IN Politics (NEW YORK).

(4) All the "best people" from the gentlemen's clubs, and all the frantic fascist captains, united in common hatred of Socialism and bestial horror of the rising tide of the mass revolutionary movement, have turned to acts of provocation, to foul incendiarism, to medieval legends of poisoned wells, to legalize their own destruction of proletarian organizations, and rouse the agitated petty-bourgeoisie to chauvinistic fervor on behalf of the fight against the revolutionary way out of the crisis.

COMMUNIST PAMPHLET.

(5) If a new spirit *is* to be infused into this old country, there is one thorny and contentious reform which must be tackled, and that is the humanization and galvanization of the B.B.C.* Timidity here will bespeak canker and atrophy of the soul. The heart of Britain may be sound and of strong beat, for instance, but the British lion's roar at present is like that of Bottom in Shakespeare's *Midsummer Night's Dream*—as gentle as any sucking dove. A virile new Britain cannot continue indefinitely to be traduced in the eyes or rather ears, of the world by the effete languors of Langham Place, brazenly masquerading as "standard English." When the voice of Britain is heard at nine o'clock, better far and infinitely less ludicrous to hear aitches honestly dropped than the present priggish, inflated, inhibited, school-ma'amish arch braying of blameless bashful mewing maidens!

LETTER IN Tribune.

Each of these passages has faults of its own, but, quite apart from avoidable ugliness, two qualities are common to all of them. The first is staleness of imagery; the other is lack of precision. The writer either has a meaning and cannot express it, or he inadvertently says something else, or he is almost indifferent as to whether his words mean anything or not. This mixture of vagueness and sheer incompetence is the most marked characteristic of modern English prose, and especially of any kind of political writing. As soon as certain topics are raised, the concrete melts into the abstract and no one seems able to think of turns of speech that are not hackneyed: prose consists less and less of *words* chosen for the sake of their meaning, and more and more of *phrases* tacked together like the sections of a prefabricated hen-house. I list below, with notes and examples, various of the tricks by means of which the work of prose-construction is habitually dodged:

Dying metaphors. A newly invented metaphor assists thought by evoking a visual image, while on the other hand a metaphor which is

* British Broadcasting Corporation.

technically "dead" (e.g. *iron resolution*) has in effect reverted to being an ordinary word and can generally be used without loss of vividness. But in between these two classes there is a huge dump of worn-out metaphors which have lost all evocative power and are merely used because they save people the trouble of inventing phrases for themselves. Examples are: *Ring the changes on, take up the cudgels for, toe the line, ride roughshod over, stand shoulder to shoulder with, play into the hands of, no axe to grind, grist to the mill, fishing in troubled waters, on the order of the day, Achilles' heel, swan song, hotbed.* Many of these are used without knowledge of their meaning (what is a "rift," for instance?), and incompatible metaphors are frequently mixed, a sure sign that the writer is not interested in what he is saying. Some metaphors now current have been twisted out of their original meaning without those who use them even being aware of the fact. For example, *toe the line* is sometimes written *tow the line.* Another example is *the hammer and the anvil,* now always used with the implication that the anvil gets the worst of it. In real life it is always the anvil that breaks the hammer, never the other way about: a writer who stopped to think what he was saying would be aware of this, and would avoid perverting the original phrase.

Operators or *verbal false limbs.* These save the trouble of picking out appropriate verbs and nouns, and at the same time pad each sentence with extra syllables which give it an appearance of symmetry. Characteristic phrases are *render inoperative, militate against, make contact with, be subjected to, give rise to, give grounds for, have the effect of, play a leading part (role) in, make itself felt, take effect, exhibit a tendency to, serve the purpose of, etc., etc.* The keynote is the elimination of simple verbs. Instead of being a single word, such as *break, stop, spoil, mend, kill,* a verb becomes a *phrase,* made up of a noun or adjective tacked on to some general-purpose verb such as *prove, serve, form, play, render.* In addition, the passive voice is wherever possible used in preference to the active, and noun constructions are used instead of gerunds (*by examination of* instead of *by examining*). The range of verbs is further cut down by means of the *-ize* and *de-* formations, and the banal statements are given an appearance of profundity by means of the *not un-* formation. Simple conjunctions and prepositions are replaced by such phrases as *with respect to, having regard to, the fact that, by dint of, in view of, in the interests of, on the hypothesis that;* and the ends of sentences are saved from anticlimax by such resounding commonplaces as *greatly to be desired, cannot be left out of account, a development to be expected in the near future, deserving of serious consideration, brought to a satisfactory conclusion,* and so on and so forth.

Pretentious diction. Words like *phenomenon, element, individual* (as noun), *objective, categorical, effective, virtual, basic, primary, pro-*

mote, constitute, exhibit, exploit, utilize, eliminate, liquidate, are used
to dress up simple statements and give an air of scientific impartiality
to biased judgments. Adjectives like *epoch-making, epic, historic, un-*
forgettable, triumphant, age-old, inevitable, inexorable, veritable, are
used to dignify the sordid processes of international politics, while writing that aims at glorifying war usually takes on an archaic color, its
characteristic words being: *realm, throne, chariot, mailed, fist, trident,*
sword, shield, buckler, banner, jackboot, clarion. Foreign words and
expressions such as *cul de sac, ancien régime, deus ex machina, mu-*
tatis mutandis, status quo, gleichschaltung, weltanschauung, are used
to give an air of culture and elegance. Except for the useful abbrevia-
tions *i.e., e.g.,* and *etc.,* there is no real need for any of the hundreds
of foreign phrases now current in English. Bad writers, and especially
scientific, political and sociological writers, are nearly always haunted
by the notion that Latin or Greek words are grander than Saxon ones,
and unnecessary words like *expedite, ameliorate, predict, extraneous,*
deracinated, clandestine, subaqueous and hundreds of others constantly
gain ground from their Anglo-Saxon opposite numbers.[1] The jargon
peculiar to Marxist writing (*hyena, hangman, cannibal, petty bourgeois,*
these gentry, lacquey, flunkey, mad dog, White Guard, etc.) consists
largely of words and phrases translated from Russian, German or
French; but the normal way of coining a new word is to use a Latin
or Greek root with the appropriate affix and, where necessary, the *-ize*
formation. It is often easier to make up words of this kind (*deregion-*
alize, impermissible, extramarital, non-fragmentary and so forth) than
to think up the English words that will cover one's meaning. The result, in general, is an increase in slovenliness and vagueness.

Meaningless words. In certain kinds of writing, particularly in art
criticism and literary criticism, it is normal to come across long passages which are almost completely lacking in meaning.[2] Words like
romantic, plastic, values, human, dead, sentimental, natural, vitality, as
used in art criticism, are strictly meaningless, in the sense that they
not only do not point to any discoverable object, but are hardly ever expected to do so by the reader. When one critic writes, "The outstanding feature of Mr. X's work is its living quality," while another writes,

[1] An interesting illustration of this is the way in which the English flower names
which were in use till very recently are being ousted by Greek ones, *snapdragon* becoming *antirrhinum, forget-me-not* becoming *myosotis,* etc. It is hard to see any
practical reason for this change of fashion: it is probably due to an instinctive turning-
away from the more homely word and a vague feeling that the Greek word is scientific.

[2] Example: "Comfort's catholicity of perception and image, strangely Whit-
manesque in range, almost the exact opposite in aesthetic compulsion, continues to
evoke that trembling atmospheric accumulative hinting at a cruel, an inexorably serene
timelessness. . . . Wrey Gardiner scores by aiming at simple bull's-eyes with precision.
Only they are not so simple, and through this contented sadness runs more than the
surface bittersweet of resignation." (*Poetry Quarterly.*)

418

"The immediately striking thing about Mr. X's work is its peculiar deadness," the reader accepts this as a simple difference of opinion. If words like *black* and *white* were involved, instead of the jargon words *dead* and *living*, he would see at once that language was being used in an improper way. Many political words are similarly abused. The word *Fascism* has now no meaning except in so far as it signifies "something not desirable." The words *democracy, socialism, freedom, patriotic, realistic, justice*, have each of them several different meanings which cannot be reconciled with one another. In the case of a word like *democracy*, not only is there no agreed definition, but the attempt to make one is resisted from all sides. It is almost universally felt that when we call a country democratic we are praising it: consequently the defenders of every kind of régime claim that it is a democracy, and fear that they might have to stop using the word if it were tied down to any one meaning. Words of this kind are often used in a consciously dishonest way. That is, the person who uses them has his own private definition, but allows his hearer to think he means something quite different. Statements like *Marshal Pétain was a true patriot, The Soviet Press is the freest in the world, The Catholic Church is opposed to persecution*, are almost always made with intent to deceive. Other words used in variable meanings, in most cases more or less dishonestly, are: *class, totalitarian, science, progressive, reactionary, bourgeois, equality.*

Now that I have made this catalogue of swindles and perversions, let me give another example of the kind of writing that they lead to. This time it must of its nature be an imaginary one. I am going to translate a passage of good English into modern English of the worst sort. Here is a well-known verse from *Ecclesiastes*:

"I returned and saw under the sun, that the race is not to the swift, nor the battle to the strong, neither yet bread to the wise, nor yet riches to men of understanding, nor yet favour to men of skill; but time and chance happeneth to them all."

Here it is in modern English:

"Objective consideration of contemporary phenomena compels the conclusion that success or failure in competitive activities exhibits no tendency to be commensurate with innate capacity, but that a considerable element of the unpredictable must invariably be taken into account."

This is a parody, but not a very gross one. Exhibit (3), above, for instance, contains several patches of the same kind of English. It will be seen that I have not made a full translation. The beginning and ending of the sentence follow the original meaning fairly closely, but in the middle the concrete illustrations—race, battle, bread—dissolve into the vague phrase "success or failure in competitive activities." This had to be so, because no modern writer of the kind I am discussing—

no one capable of using phrases like "objective consideration of contemporary phenomena"—would ever tabulate his thoughts in that precise and detailed way. The whole tendency of modern prose is away from concreteness. Now analyse these two sentences a little more closely. The first contains forty-nine words but only sixty syllables, and all its words are those of everyday life. The second contains thirty-eight words of ninety syllables: eighteen of its words are from Latin roots, and one from Greek. The first sentence contains six vivid images, and only one phrase ("time and chance") that could be called vague. The second contains not a single fresh, arresting phrase, and in spite of its ninety syllables it gives only a shortened version of the meaning contained in the first. Yet without a doubt it is the second kind of sentence that is gaining ground in modern English. I do not want to exaggerate. This kind of writing is not yet universal, and outcrops of simplicity will occur here and there in the worst-written page. Still, if you or I were told to write a few lines on the uncertainty of human fortunes, we should probably come much nearer to my imaginary sentence than to the one from *Ecclesiastes.*

As I have tried to show, modern writing at its worst does not consist in picking out words for the sake of their meaning and inventing images in order to make the meaning clearer. It consists in gumming together long strips of words which have already been set in order by someone else, and making the results presentable by sheer humbug. The attraction of this way of writing is that it is easy. It is easier—even quicker, once you have the habit—to say *In my opinion it is not an unjustifiable assumption that* than to say *I think.* If you use ready-made phrases, you not only don't have to hunt about for words; you also don't have to bother with the rhythms of your sentences, since these phrases are generally so arranged as to be more or less euphonious. When you are composing in a hurry—when you are dictating to a stenographer, for instance, or making a public speech—it is natural to fall into a pretentious, Latinized style. Tags like *a consideration which we should do well to bear in mind* or *a conclusion to which all of us would readily assent* will save many a sentence from coming down with a bump. By using stale metaphors, similes and idioms, you save much mental effort, at the cost of leaving your meaning vague, not only for your reader but for yourself. This is the significance of mixed metaphors. The sole aim of a metaphor is to call up a visual image. When these images clash—as in *The Fascist octopus has sung its swan song, the jackboot is thrown into the melting pot*—it can be taken as certain that the writer is not seeing a mental image of the objects he is naming; in other words he is not really thinking. Look again at the examples I gave at the beginning of this essay. Professor Laski (1) uses five negatives in fifty-three words. One of these is superfluous, making nonsense of the whole passage, and in addition there is the slip *alien* for akin, making further nonsense, and several avoidable pieces of clumsiness which increase the general vagueness. Professor Hogben (2) plays ducks and drakes with a battery which is able to write prescriptions, and, while disapproving of the everyday phrase *put up with,* is unwilling to look *egregious* up in the dictionary and see what it means; (3), if one takes an uncharitable attitude towards it, is simply meaningless: probably one could work out its intended meaning by reading the whole of the article in which it occurs. In (4), the writer knows more or less what he wants to say, but an accumulation of stale phrases chokes him like tea leaves blocking a sink. In (5), words and meaning have almost parted company. People who write in this manner usually have a general emotional meaning —they dislike one thing and want to express solidarity with another— but they are not interested in the detail of what they are saying. A scrupulous writer, in every sentence that he writes, will ask himself at least four questions, thus: What am I trying to say? What words will express it? What image or idiom will make it clearer? Is this image fresh enough to have an effect? And he will probably ask himself two more: Could I put it more shortly? Have I said anything that is avoidably ugly? But you are not obliged to go to all this trouble. You can shirk it by simply throwing your mind open and letting the ready-made phrases come crowding in. They will construct your sentences for you— even think your thoughts for you, to a certain extent—and at need they will perform the important service of partially concealing your meaning even from yourself. It is at this point that the special connection between politics and the debasement of language becomes clear.

In our time it is broadly true that political writing is bad writing. Where it is not true, it will generally be found that the writer is some kind of rebel, expressing his private opinions and not a "party line." Orthodoxy, of whatever color, seems to demand a lifeless, imitative style. The political dialects to be found in pamphlets, leading articles, manifestos, White Papers and the speeches of under-secretaries do, of course, vary from party to party, but they are all alike in that one almost never finds in them a fresh, vivid, home-made turn of speech. When one watches some tired hack on the platform mechanically repeating the familiar phrases—*bestial atrocities, iron heel, bloodstained tyranny, free peoples of the world, stand shoulder to shoulder*—one often has a curious feeling that one is not watching a live human being but some kind of dummy: a feeling which suddenly becomes stronger at moments when the light catches the speaker's spectacles and turns them into blank discs which seem to have no eyes behind them. And this is not altogether fanciful. A speaker who uses that kind of phraseology has gone some distance towards turning himself into a machine. The appropriate noises are coming out of his larynx, but his brain is not involved as it would be if he were choosing his words for himself. If the speech he is making is one that he is accustomed to make over and over again, he may be almost unconscious of what he is saying, as one is when one utters the responses in church. And this reduced state of consciousness, if not indispensable, is at any rate favorable to political conformity.

In our time, political speech and writing are largely the defence of the indefensible. Things like the continuance of British rule in India, the Russian purges and deportations, the dropping of the atom bombs on Japan, can indeed be defended, but only by arguments which are too brutal for most people to face, and which do not square with the professed aims of political parties. Thus political language has to consist largely of euphemism, question-begging and sheer cloudy vagueness. Defenceless villages are bombarded from the air, the inhabitants driven out into the countryside, the cattle machine-gunned, the huts set on fire with incendiary bullets: this is called *pacification*. Millions of peasants are robbed of their farms and sent trudging along the roads with no more than they can carry: this is called *transfer of population* or *rectification of frontiers*. People are imprisoned for years without trial, or shot in the back of the neck or sent to die of scurvy in Arctic lumber camps: this is called *elimination of unreliable elements*. Such phraseology is needed if one wants to name things without calling up mental pictures of them. Consider for instance some comfortable English professor defending Russian totalitarianism. He cannot say outright, "I believe in killing off your opponents when you can get good results by doing so." Probably, therefore, he will say something like this:

"While freely conceding that the Soviet régime exhibits certain features which the humanitarian may be inclined to deplore, we must, I think, agree that a certain curtailment of the right to political opposition is an unavoidable concomitant of transitional periods, and that the rigors which the Russian people have been called upon to undergo have been amply justified in the sphere of concrete achievement."

The inflated style is itself a kind of euphemism. A mass of Latin words falls upon the facts like soft snow, blurring the outlines and covering up all the details. The great enemy of clear language is insincerity. When there is a gap between one's real and one's declared aims, one turns as it were instinctively to long words and exhausted idioms, like a cuttlefish squirting out ink. In our age there is no such thing as "keeping out of politics." All issues are political issues, and politics itself is a mass of lies, evasions, folly, hatred and schizophrenia. When the general atmosphere is bad, language must suffer. I should expect to find—this is a guess which I have not sufficient knowledge to verify—that the German, Russian and Italian languages have all deteriorated in the last ten or fifteen years, as a result of dictatorship.

But if thought corrupts language, language can also corrupt thought. A bad usage can spread by tradition and imitation, even among people who should and do know better. The debased language that I have been discussing is in some ways very convenient. Phrases like *a not unjustifiable assumption, leaves much to be desired, would serve no good purpose, a consideration which we should do well to bear in mind,* are a continuous temptation, a packet of aspirins always at one's elbow. Look back through this essay, and for certain you will find that I have again and again committed the very faults I am protesting against. By this morning's post I have received a pamphlet dealing with conditions in Germany. The author tells me that he "felt impelled" to write it. I open it at random, and here is almost the first sentence that I see: "[The Allies] have an opportunity not only of achieving a radical transformation of Germany's social and political structure in such a way as to avoid a nationalistic reaction in Germany itself, but at the same time of laying the foundations of a cooperative and uni- fied Europe." You see, he "feels impelled" to write—feels, presumably, that he has something new to say—and yet his words, like cavalry horses answering the bugle, group themselves automatically into the familiar dreary pattern. This invasion of one's mind by ready-made phrases (*lay the foundations, achieve a radical transformation*) can only be prevented if one is constantly on guard against them, and every such phrase anaesthetizes a portion of one's brain.

I said earlier that the decadence of our language is probably curable. Those who deny this would argue, if they produced an argu- ment at all, that language merely reflects existing social conditions, and that we cannot influence its development by any direct tinkering with words and constructions. So far as the general tone or spirit of a language goes, this may be true, but it is not true in detail. Silly words and expressions have often disappeared, not through any evolu- tionary process but owing to the conscious action of a minority. Two recent examples were *explore every avenue* and *leave no stone un- turned,* which were killed by the jeers of a few journalists. There is a long list of flyblown metaphors which could similarly be got rid of if enough people would interest themselves in the job; and it should also be possible to laugh the *not un-* formation out of existence,[3] to reduce the amount of Latin and Greek in the average sentence, to drive out foreign phrases and strayed scientific words, and, in general, to make pretentiousness unfashionable. But all these are minor points. The defence of the English language implies more than this, and perhaps it is best to start by saying what it does *not* imply.

To begin with it has nothing to do with archaism, with the sal- vaging of obsolete words and turns of speech, or with the setting up of a "standard English" which must never be departed from. On the con- trary, it is especially concerned with the scrapping of every word or

---

[3] One can cure oneself of the *not un-* formation by memorizing this sentence: *A not unblack dog was chasing a not unsmall rabbit across a not ungreen field.*

idiom which has outworn its usefulness. It has nothing to do with correct grammar and syntax, which are of no importance so long as one makes one's meaning clear, or with the avoidance of Americanisms, or with having what is called a "good prose style." On the other hand it is not concerned with fake simplicity and the attempt to make written English colloquial. Nor does it even imply in every case preferring the Saxon word to the Latin one, though it does imply using the fewest and shortest words that will cover one's meaning. What is above all needed is to let the meaning choose the word, and not the other way about. In prose, the worst thing one can do with words is to surrender to them. When you think of a concrete object, you think wordlessly, and then, if you want to describe the thing you have been visualizing you probably hunt about till you find the exact words that seem to fit it. When you think of something abstract you are more inclined to use words from the start, and unless you make a conscious effort to prevent it, the existing dialect will come rushing in and do the job for you, at the expense of blurring or even changing your meaning. Probably it is better to put off using words as long as possible and get one's meaning as clear as one can through pictures or sensations. Afterwards one can choose—not simply *accept*—the phrases that will best cover the meaning, and then switch round and decide what impression one's words are likely to make on another person. This last effort of the mind cuts out all stale or mixed images, all prefabricated phrases, needless repetitions, and humbug and vagueness generally. But one can often be in doubt about the effect of a word or a phrase, and one needs rules that one can rely on when instinct fails. I think the following rules will cover most cases:

(i)   Never use a metaphor, simile or other figure of speech which you are used to seeing in print.

(ii)   Never use a long word where a short one will do.

(iii)   If it is possible to cut a word out, always cut it out.

(iv)   Never use the passive where you can use the active.

(v)   Never use a foreign phrase, a scientific word or a jargon word if you can think of an everyday English equivalent.

(vi)   Break any of these rules sooner than say anything outright barbarous.

These rules sound elementary, and so they are, but they demand a deep change of attitude in anyone who has grown used to writing in the style now fashionable. One could keep all of them and still write bad English, but one could not write the kind of stuff that I quoted in those five specimens at the beginning of this article.

I have not here been considering the literary use of language, but merely language as an instrument for expressing and not for concealing or preventing thought. Stuart Chase and others have come near to

424

claiming that all abstract words are meaningless, and have used this as a pretext for advocating a kind of political quietism. Since you don't know what Fascism is, how can you struggle against Fascism? One need not swallow such absurdities as this, but one ought to recognize that the present political chaos is connected with the decay of language, and that one can probably bring about some improvement by starting at the verbal end. If you simplify your English, you are freed from the worst follies of orthodoxy. You cannot speak any of the necessary dialects, and when you make a stupid remark its stupidity will be obvious, even to yourself. Political language—and with variations this is true of all political parties, from Conservatives to Anarchists—is designed to make lies sound truthful and murder respectable, and to give an appearance of solidity to pure wind. One cannot change this all in a moment, but one can at least change one's own habits, and from time to time one can even, if one jeers loudly enough, send some worn-out and useless phrase—some *jackboot, Achilles heel, hotbed, melting pot, acid test, veritable inferno* or other lump of verbal refuse—into the dustbin where it belongs.

71. A Primer of Existentialism

GORDON E. BIGELOW

Bigelow (1919–   ), born in Springfield, Massachusetts, earned his doctorate at Johns Hopkins in 1959, after serving with the Army Air Force (1941–1945). He has taught American literature at the University of Florida since 1951. He has published widely, including two books: *Rhetoric and American Poetry of the Early National Period* (1960), *Frontier Eden: The Literary Career of Marjorie Kinnan Rawlings* (1966).

FOR SOME YEARS I FOUGHT the word by irritably looking the other way whenever I stumbled across it, hoping that like dadaism and some of the other "isms" of the French *avant garde* it would go away if I ignored it. But existentialism was apparently more than the picture it evoked of uncombed beards, smoky basement cafes, and

French beatniks regaling one another between sips of absinthe with brilliant variations on the theme of despair. It turned out to be of major importance to literature and the arts, to philosophy and theology, and of increasing importance to the social sciences. To learn more about it, I read several of the self-styled introductions to the subject, with the baffled sensation of a man who reads a critical introduction to a novel only to find that he must read the novel before he can understand the introduction. Therefore, I should like to provide here something most discussions of existentialism take for granted, a simple statement of its basic characteristics. This is a reckless thing to do because there are several kinds of existentialism and what one says of one kind may not be true of another, but there is an area of agreement, and it is this common ground that I should like to set forth here. We should not run into trouble so long as we understand from the outset that the six major themes outlined below will apply in varying degrees to particular existentialists. A reader should be able to go from here to the existentialists themselves, to the more specialized critiques of them, or be able to recognize an existentialist theme or coloration in literature when he sees it.

A word first about the kinds of existentialism. Like transcendentalism of the last century, there are almost as many varieties of this *ism* as there are individual writers to whom the word is applied (not all of them claim it). But without being facetious we might group them into two main kinds, the *ungodly* and the *godly*. To take the ungodly or atheistic first, we would list as the chief spokesmen among many others Jean-Paul Sartre, Albert Camus, and Simone de Beauvoir. Several of this important group of French writers had rigorous and significant experience in the Resistance during the Nazi occupation of France in World War II. Out of the despair which came with the collapse of their nation during those terrible years they found unexpected strength in the single indomitable human spirit, which even under severe torture could maintain the spirit of resistance, the unextinguishable ability to say "No." From this irreducible core in the human spirit, they erected after the war a philosophy which was a twentieth-century variation of the philosophy of Descartes. But instead of saying "I think, therefore I am," they said "I can say No, therefore I exist." As we shall presently see, the use of the word "exist" is of prime significance. This group is chiefly responsible for giving existentialism its status in the popular mind as a literary-philosophical cult.

Of the godly or theistic existentialists we should mention first a mid-nineteenth-century Danish writer, Søren Kierkegaard; two contemporary French Roman Catholics, Gabriel Marcel and Jacques Maritain; two Protestant theologians, Paul Tillich and Nicholas Berdyaev; and Martin Buber, an important contemporary Jewish theologian. Taken together, their writings constitute one of the most significant developments in modern theology. Behind both groups of existentialists stand other important figures, chiefly philosophers, who exert powerful influence upon the movement—Blaise Pascal, Friedrich Nietzsche, Henri Bergson, Martin Heidegger, Karl Jaspers, among others. Several literary figures, notably Tolstoy and Dostoievsky, are frequently cited because existentialist attitudes and themes are prominent in their writings. The eclectic nature of this movement should already be sufficiently clear and the danger of applying too rigidly to any particular figure the general characteristics of the movement which I now make bold to describe:

1. Existence before essence. Existentialism gets its name from an insistence that human life is understandable only in terms of an individual man's existence, his particular experience of life. It says that a man *lives* (has existence) rather than *is* (has being or essence), and that every man's experience of life is unique, radically different from everyone else's and can be understood truly only in terms of his involvement in life or commitment to it. It strenuously shuns that view which assumes an ideal of Man or Mankind, a universal of human nature of which each man is only one example. It eschews the question of Greek philosophy, *"What is mankind?"* which suggests that man can be defined if he is ranged in his proper place in the order of nature; it asks instead the question of Job and St. Augustine, *"Who am I?"* with its suggestion of the uniqueness and mystery of each human life and its emphasis upon the subjective or personal rather than the objective or impersonal. From the outside a man appears to be just another natural creature; from the inside he is an entire universe, the center of infinity. The existentialist insists upon this latter radically subjective view, and from this grows much of the rest of existentialism.

2. Reason is impotent to deal with the depths of human life. There are two parts to this proposition—first, that human reason is relatively weak and imperfect, and second, that there are dark places in human life which are "nonreason" and to which reason scarcely penetrates. Since Plato, Western civilization has usually assumed a separation of reason from the rest of the human psyche, and has glorified reason as suited to command the nonrational part. The classic statement of this separation appears in the *Phaedrus,* where Plato describes the psyche in the myth of the chariot which is drawn by the white steeds of the emotions and the black unruly steeds of the appetites. The driver of the chariot is Reason who holds the reins which control the horses and the whip to subdue the surging black steeds of passion. Only the driver, the rational nature, is given human form; the rest of the psyche, the nonrational part, is given a lower, animal form. This separation and exaltation of reason is carried further in the allegory of the cave in the *Republic.* You recall the sombre picture of human life with which the story begins: men are chained in the dark in a cave, with their backs to a flickering firelight, able to see only uncertain shadows moving on the wall before them, able to hear only confused echoes of sounds. One of the men, breaking free from his chains, is able to turn and look upon the objects themselves and the light which casts the shadows; even, at last, he is able to work his way entirely out of the cave into the sunlight beyond. All this he is able to do through his reason; he escapes from the bondage of error, from time and change, from death itself, into the realm of changeless eternal ideas or Truth, and the lower nature which had chained him in darkness is left behind.

Existentialism in our time, and this is one of its most important characteristics, insists upon reuniting the "lower" or irrational parts of the psyche with the "higher." It insists that man must be taken in his wholeness and not in some divided state, that whole man contains not only intellect but also anxiety, guilt, and the will to power—which modify and sometimes overwhelm the reason. A man seen in this light is fundamentally ambiguous, if not mysterious, full of contradictions and tensions which cannot be dissolved simply by taking thought. "Human life," said Berdyaev, "is permeated by underground streams." One is reminded of D. H. Lawrence's outburst against Franklin and his rational attempt to achieve moral perfection: "The Perfectability of Man! . . . The perfectability of which man? I am many men. Which of them are you going to perfect? I am not a mechanical contrivance. . . . It's a queer thing is a man's soul. It is the whole of him. Which means it is the unknown as well as the known. . . . The soul of man is a dark vast forest, with wild life in it." The emphasis in existentialism is not on idea but upon the thinker who has the idea. It accepts not only his power of thought, but his contingency and fallibility, his fraility, his body, blood, and bones, and above all his death. Kierkegaard emphasized the distinction between *subjective* truth (what a person *is*) and *objective* truth (what the person *knows*), and said that we encounter the true self not in the detachment of thought but in the involvement and agony of choice and in the pathos of commitment to our choice. This distrust of rational systems helps to explain why many existential writers in their own expression are paradoxical or prophetic or gnomic, why their works often belong more to literature than to philosophy.

3. Alienation or estrangement. One major result of the dissociation of reason from the rest of the psyche has been the growth of science, which has become one of the hallmarks of Western civilization and an ever-increasing rational ordering of men in society. As the existentialists view them, the main forces of history since the Renaissance have progressively separated man from concrete earthy existence, have forced him to live at ever higher levels of abstraction, have collectivized individual man out of existence, have driven God from the heavens, or what is the same thing, from the hearts of men. They are convinced that modern man lives in a fourfold condition of alienation: from God, from nature, from other men, from his own true self.

The estrangement from God is most shockingly expressed by Nietzsche's anguished cry, "God is dead," a cry which has continuously echoed through the writings of the existentialists, particularly the French. This theme of spiritual barrenness is a commonplace in literature of this century, from Eliot's "Hollow Man" to the novels of Dos Passos, Hemingway, and Faulkner. It often appears in writers not commonly associated with the existentialists as in this remarkable passage from *A Story-Teller's Story,* where Sherwood Anderson describes his own awakening to his spiritual emptiness. He tells of walking alone late at night along a moonlit road when,

> I had suddenly an odd, and to my own seeming, a ridiculous desire to abase myself before something not human and so stepping into the moonlit road, I knelt in the dust. Having no God, the gods having been taken from me by the life about me, as a personal God has been taken from all modern men by the force within that man himself does not understand but that is called the intellect, I kept smiling at the figure I cut in my own eyes as I knelt in the road. . . .
>
> There was no God in the sky, no God in myself, no conviction in myself that I had the power to believe in a God, and so I merely knelt in the dust in silence and no words came to my lips.

In another passage Anderson wondered if the giving of itself by an entire generation to mechanical things was not really making all men impotent, if the desire for a greater navy, a greater army, taller public buildings, was not a sign of growing impotence. He felt that Puritanism and the industrialism which was its offspring had sterilized modern life, and proposed that men return to a healthful animal vigor by renewed contact with simple things of the earth, among them untrammeled sexual expression. One is reminded of the unkempt and delectable raffishness of Steinbeck's *Cannery Row* or of D. H. Lawrence's quasi-religious doctrine of sex, "blood consciousness" and the "divine otherness" of animal existence.

Man's estrangement from nature has been a major theme in literature at least since Rousseau and the Romantic movement, and can hardly be said to be the property of existentialists. But this group nevertheless adds its own insistence that one of modern man's most urgent dangers is that he builds ever higher the brick and steel walls of technology which shut him away from a health-giving life according to "nature." Their treatment of this theme is most commonly expressed as part of a broader insistence that modern man needs to shun abstraction and return to "concreteness" or "wholeness."

A third estrangement has occurred at the social level and its sign is growing dismay at man's helplessness before the great machine-like colossus of industrialized society. This is another major theme of Western literature, and here again, though they hardly discovered the danger or began the protest, the existentialists in our time renew the protest against any pattern or force which would stifle the unique and spontaneous in individual life. The crowding of men into cities, the subdivision of labor which submerges the man in his economic function, the burgeoning of centralized government, the growth of advertising, propaganda, and mass media of entertainment and communication—all the things which force men into Riesman's "Lonely Crowd"—these same things drive men asunder by destroying their individuality and making them live on the surface of life, content to deal with things rather than people. "Exteriorization," says Berdyaev, "is the source of slavery, whereas freedom is interiorization. Slavery always indicates alienation, the ejection of human nature into the external." This kind of alienation is exemplified by Zero, in Elmer Rice's play "The Adding Machine." Zero's twenty-five years as a bookkeeper in a department store have dried up his humanity, making him incapable of love, of friendship, of any deeply felt, freely expressed emotion. Such estrangement is often given as the reason for man's inhumanity to man, the explanation of injustice in modern society. In Camus' short novel, aptly called *The Stranger*, a young man is convicted by a court of murder. This is a homicide which he has actually committed under extenuating circumstances. But the court never listens to any of the relevant evidence, seems never to hear anything that pertains to the crime itself; it convicts the young man on wholly irrelevant grounds—because he had behaved in an unconventional way at his mother's funeral the day before the homicide. In this book one feels the same dream-like distortion of reality as in the trial scene in *Alice in Wonderland,* a suffocating sense of being enclosed by events which are irrational or absurd but also inexorable. Most disturbing of all is the young man's aloneness, the impermeable membrane of estrangement which surrounds him and prevents anyone else from penetrating to his experience of life or sympathizing with it.

The fourth kind of alienation, man's estrangement from his own true self, especially as his nature is distorted by an exaltation of reason, is another theme having an extensive history as a major part of the Romantic revolt. Of the many writers who treat the theme, Hawthorne comes particularly close to the emphasis of contemporary existentialists. His Ethan Brand, Dr. Rappaccini, and Roger Chillingworth are a recurrent figure who represents the dislocation in human nature which results when an overdeveloped or misapplied intellect severs "the magnetic chain of human sympathy." Hawthorne is thoroughly existential in his concern for the sanctity of the individual human soul, as well

430

as in his preoccupation with sin and the dark side of human nature, which must be seen in part as his attempt to build back some fullness to the flattened image of man bequeathed to him by the Enlightenment. Whitman was trying to do this when he added flesh and bone and a sexual nature to the spiritualized image of man he inherited from Emerson, though his image remains diffused and attenuated by the same cosmic optimism. Many of the nineteenth-century depictions of man represent him as a figure of power or of potential power, sometimes as daimonic, like Melville's Ahab, but after World War I the power is gone; man is not merely distorted or truncated, he is hollow, powerless, faceless. At the time when his command over natural forces seems to be unlimited, man is pictured as weak, ridden with nameless dread. And this brings us to another of the major themes of existentialism.

4. "Fear and trembling," anxiety. At Stockholm when he accepted the Nobel Prize, William Faulkner said that "Our tragedy today is a general and universal physical fear so long sustained by now that we can even bear it. There are no longer problems of the spirit. There is only one question: When will I be blown up?" The optimistic vision of the Enlightenment which saw man, through reason and its extensions in science, conquering all nature and solving all social and political problems in a continuous upward spiral of Progress, cracked open like a melon on the rock of World War I. The theories which held such high hopes died in that sickening and unimaginable butchery. Here was a concrete fact of human nature and society which the theories could not contain. The Great Depression and World War II deepened the sense of dismay which the loss of these ideals brought, but only with the atomic bomb did this become an unbearable terror, a threat of instant annihilation which confronted all men, even those most insulated by the thick crust of material goods and services. Now the most unthinking person could sense that each advance in mechanical technique carried not only a chromium and plush promise of comfort but a threat as well.

Sartre, following Kierkegaard, speaks of another kind of anxiety which oppresses modern man—"the anguish of Abraham"—the necessity which is laid upon him to make moral choices on his own responsibility. A military officer in wartime knows the agony of choice which forces him to sacrifice part of his army to preserve the rest, as does a man in high political office, who must make decisions affecting the lives of millions. The existentialists claim that each of us must make moral decisions in our own lives which involve the same anguish. Kierkegaard finds that this necessity is one thing which makes each life unique, which makes it impossible to speculate or generalize about human life, because each man's case is irretrievably his own, something in which he is personally and passionately involved. His book *Fear and*

Trembling is an elaborate and fascinating commentary on the Old Testament story of Abraham, who was commanded by God to sacrifice his beloved son Isaac. Abraham thus becomes the emblem of man who must make a harrowing choice, in this case between love for his son and love for God, between the universal moral law which says categorically, "thou shalt not kill," and the unique inner demand of his religious faith. Abraham's decision, which is to violate the abstract and collective moral law, has to be made not in arrogance but in fear and trembling, one of the inferences being that sometimes one must make an exception to the general law because he is (existentially) an exception, a concrete being whose existence can never be completely subsumed under any universal.

5. *The encounter with nothingness.* For the man alienated from God, from nature, from his fellow man and from himself, what is left at last but Nothingness? The testimony of the existentialists is that this is where modern man now finds himself, not on the highway of upward Progress toward a radiant Utopia but on the brink of a catastrophic precipice, below which yawns the absolute void, an uncompromised black Nothingness. In one sense this is Eliot's Wasteland inhabited by his Hollow Man, who is

> Shape without form, shade without color
> Paralyzed force, gesture without motion.

That is what moves E. A. Robinson's Richard Cory, the man who is everything that might make us wish that we were in his place, to go home one calm summer night and put a bullet through his head.

One of the most convincing statements of the encounter with Nothingness is made by Leo Tolstoy in "My Confession." He tells how in good health, in the prime of life, when he had everything that a man could desire—wealth, fame, aristocratic social position, a beautiful wife and children, a brilliant mind and great artistic talent in the height of their powers, he nevertheless was seized with a growing uneasiness, a nameless discontent which he could not shake or alleviate. His experience was like that of a man who falls sick, with symptoms which he disregards as insignificant; but the symptoms return again and again until they merge into a continuous suffering. And the patient suddenly is confronted with the overwhelming fact that what he took for mere indisposition is more important to him than anything else on earth, that it is death! "I felt the ground on which I stood was crumbling, that there was nothing for me to stand on, that what I had been living for was nothing, that I had no reason for living. . . . To stop was impossible, to go back was impossible; and it was impossible to shut my eyes so as to see that there was nothing before me but suffering and actual death, absolute annihilation." This is the "Sickness Unto Death" of Kierkegaard, the despair in which one wishes to die but cannot. Hemingway's short story, "A Clean, Well-Lighted Place," gives an unforgettable expression of this theme. At the end of the story, the old waiter climbs into bed late at night saying to himself, "What did he fear? It was not fear or dread. It was a nothing which he knew too well. It was all a nothing and a man was nothing too. . . . Nada y pues nada, y nada y pues nada." And then because he has experienced the death of God he goes on to recite the Lord's Prayer in blasphemous despair: "Our Nothing who are in Nothing, nothing be thy nothing. . . ." And then the Ave Maria, "Hail nothing, full of nothing. . . ." This is stark, even for Hemingway, but the old waiter does no more than name the void felt by most people in the early Hemingway novels, a hunger they seek to assuage with alcohol, sex, and violence in an aimless progress from bar to bed to bull-ring. It goes without saying that much of the despair and pessimism in other contemporary authors springs from a similar sense of the void in modern life.

6. Freedom. Sooner or later, as a theme that includes all the others, the existentialist writings bear upon freedom. The themes we have outlined above describe either some loss of man's freedom or some threat to it, and all existentialists of whatever sort are concerned to enlarge the range of human freedom.

For the avowed atheists like Sartre freedom means human autonomy. In a purposeless universe man is *condemned* to freedom because he is the only creature who is "self-surpassing," who can become something other than he is. Precisely because there is no God to give purpose to the universe, each man must accept individual responsibility for his own becoming, a burden made heavier by the fact that in choosing for himself he chooses for all men "the image of man as he ought to be." A man *is* the sum total of the acts that make up his life—no more, no less—and though the coward has made himself cowardly, it is always possible for him to change and make himself heroic. In Sartre's novel, *The Age of Reason,* one of the least likable of the characters, almost overwhelmed by despair and self-disgust at his homosexual tendencies, is on the point of solving his problem by mutilating himself with a razor, when in an effort of will he throws the instrument down, and we are given to understand that from this moment he will have mastery over his aberrant drive. Thus in the daily course of ordinary life must men shape their becoming in Sartre's world.

The religious existentialists interpret man's freedom differently. They use much the same language as Sartre, develop the same themes concerning the predicament of man, but always include God as a radical factor. They stress the man of faith rather than the man of will. They interpret man's existential condition as a state of alienation from his essential nature which is God-like, the problem of his life being to heal the chasm between the two, that is, to find salvation. The mystery and ambiguity of man's existence they attribute to his being the intersection of two realms. "Man bears within himself," writes Berdyaev, "the image which is both the image of man and the image of God, and is the image of man as far as the image of God is actualized." Tillich describes salvation as "the act in which the cleavage between the essential being and the existential situation is overcome." Freedom here, as for Sartre, involves an acceptance of responsibility for choice and a *commitment* to one's choice. This is the meaning of faith, a faith like Abraham's, the commitment which is an agonizing sacrifice of one's own desire and will and dearest treasure to God's will.

A final word. Just as one should not expect to find in a particular writer all of the characteristics of existentialism as we have described them, he should also be aware that some of the most striking expressions of existentialism in literature and the arts come to us by indirection, often through symbols or through innovations in conventional form. Take the preoccupation of contemporary writers with time. In *The Sound and the Fury,* Faulkner both collapses and expands normal clock time, or by juxtapositions of past and present blurs time into a single amorphous pool. He does this by using various forms of "stream of consciousness" or other techniques which see life in terms of unique, subjective experience—that is, existentially. The conventional view of externalized life, a rational orderly progression cut into uniform segments by the hands of a clock, he rejects in favor of a view which sees life as opaque, ambiguous, and irrational—that is, as the existentialist sees it. Graham Greene does something like this in *The Power and the Glory.* He creates a scene isolated in time and cut off from the rest of the world, steamy and suffocating as if a bell jar had been placed over it. Through this atmosphere fetid with impending death and human suffering, stumbles the whiskey priest, lonely and confused, pursued by a police lieutenant who has experienced the void and the death of God.

Such expressions in literature do not mean necessarily that the authors are conscious existentialist theorizers, or even that they know the writings of such theorizers. Faulkner may never have read Heidegger —or St. Augustine—both of whom attempt to demonstrate that time is more within a man and subject to his unique experience of it than it is outside him. But it is legitimate to call Faulkner's views of time and life "existential" in this novel because in recent years existentialist theorizers have given such views a local habitation and a name. One of the attractions, and one of the dangers, of existential themes is that they become like Sir Thomas Browne's quincunx: once one begins to look for them, he sees them everywhere. But if one applies restraint and discrimination, he will find that they illuminate much of contemporary literature and sometimes the literature of the past as well.

72. To Autumn

JOHN KEATS

Keats (1795–1821), whose father had run a livery stable
in London until his death (when Keats was nine), began
studying medicine at sixteen as a surgeon's apprentice. He
had passed his surgeon's examination before poetry began
to absorb all his energies six years later. In the summer
of 1818, exhausted from a hiking tour through northern
England and Scotland, he suffered the first symptoms of
tuberculosis. In the autumn of that year, he nursed his
brother Tom, ill from tuberculosis for several years, through
his last illness and death. In the following year, 1819,
already severely ill himself at the age of twenty-four, he
wrote his greatest poems, including "To Autumn." In
September, 1820, he sailed for Rome to preserve his
health, and died there a year later at twenty-six.

Season of mists and mellow fruitfulness,
 Close bosom-friend of the maturing sun;
Conspiring with him how to load and bless
 With fruit the vines that round the thatch-eaves run;
To bend with apples the moss'd cottage-trees,
 And fill all fruit with ripeness to the core;
  To swell the gourd, and plump the hazel shells
With a sweet kernel; to set budding more,
 And still more, later flowers for the bees,
 Until they think warm days will never cease,
  For Summer has o'er-brimm'd their clammy cells.

Who hath not seen thee oft amid thy store?
 Sometimes whoever seeks abroad may find
Thee sitting careless on a granary floor,
 Thy hair soft-lifted by the winnowing wind;
Or on a half-reap'd furrow sound asleep,
 Drows'd with the fume of poppies, while thy hook
  Spares the next swath and all its twined flowers:
And sometimes like a gleaner thou dost keep
 Steady thy laden head across a brook;

Or by a cider-press, with patient look,
  Thou watchest the last oozings hours by hours.

Where are the songs of Spring? Ay, where are they?
  Think not of them, thou hast thy music too,—
While barred clouds bloom the soft-dying day,
  And touch the stubble-plains with rosy hue;
Then in a wailful choir the small gnats mourn
  Among the river sallows, borne aloft
    Or sinking as the light wind lives or dies;
And full-grown lambs loud bleat from hilly bourn;
  Hedge-crickets sing; and now with treble soft
The redbreast whistles from a garden-croft;
  And gathering swallows twitter in the skies.

Suggestions for Writing

1. Write a paragraph defining some common concept—love, friendship, happiness, honesty, sportsmanship—by saying (1) what it is, (2) what it is not, (3) what it is like, (4) what it is not like. Perhaps the best order is in reverse, leading up to *is:* "Love is not like an onion, with a slippery skin and scalding center; it is more like a peach, smooth, fragrant, and sweet to the taste. It is not a . . ."

2. Write an essay based on a definition like that of Hofstadter or Barthes: a student, an education, a vacation, fun, recreation, sports, a baseball team. The idea is to distinguish a real education from that which also passes under the name, a real ball club from the general run, and so forth (some evidence from Plimpton, pp. 101–115, would help with the second suggestion).

3. Take a dull textbook or other clinker and write an essay analyzing it with reference to Orwell.

4. With quotations from newspapers and other sources of official prose (that of university officials, for example), write an essay showing whether or not Orwell's comments on political prose still apply.

5. Analyze some *-ism—communism, structuralism, nihilism, positivism—* along the lines of Bigelow's essay. This will take a bit of research.

6. Write an analysis of Keats's "To Autumn" explaining his central point, his implied thesis, and showing how the details of his definition bear it out.

X. Growing Argumentative

Analysis and Responsible Speculation

LIKE ALL OTHER MODES OF EXPOSITION, analysis leads toward argument. And it leads as naturally to speculation. An informed mind considers and reconsiders the facts until an inescapable hypothesis emerges. As a writer presents his hypo-thesis and the evidence for it, speculations extend onward from the information he holds. More than forty years ago, Cooley, considering students around him, advanced an analysis of the "youth movement." Insofar as he sought his readers' agreement, his analysis was in effect an argument. It was highly speculative also, and insofar as it now seems prophetic, we might agree that his thought was responsible and sound.

The four essays in this section all follow this process. Cooley's is brief, almost epigrammatic, with facts distilled into crystalline speculation. Steiner selects his data, curious, illustrative, amusing, and odd, as he speculates on the shifting epicenter of English. Diana Trilling and William Maxwell both consider enigmatic women. They sift through facts and theories concerning Marilyn Monroe and Virginia Woolf respectively, but their ultimate understanding is an informed speculation, not susceptible to exacting proof, but exciting in its intelligent energy and probable truth. You may wish to compare Alvarez's study of Sylvia Plath (Section V) as to thoroughness of analysis and responsibility of speculation. And then ask of Roethke's poem, "Did he know a woman?"

73. Strategy of the Youth Movement

CHARLES HORTON COOLEY

ALTHOUGH THE YOUTH of our day are not so different from those of the past as they think they are, there is a distinct and perhaps lasting change in their situation. They have a new base and line of supplies. We have encouraged them to form social organizations of their own in connection with schools and amusements. Aided by telephones, motor cars and all the new appliance of intercourse, they have done this so effectively that they no longer depend for their patterns and mores upon adult groups and traditions, but have a continuous system of their own in which such things may grow and be perpetuated. They no longer get their contacts with the world and the past through a parent-ruled family, but in their own way and with their own kind, existing in a distinct milieu and a social heritage not sifted and censored by the mature. In the old novels you may see that the young rebelled indeed but that they saw it as rebellion, did not question that the elders were in authority, had no thought of a separate state. Now the channel of prestige is shifted, they flow in their own current, have their own orthodoxy, and in case of conflict it is the elders who appear ridiculous nonconformers to what youth regards as a matter of course. What can be done except to leave them to work out their own salvation by the aid of any advice they are inclined to take?

While formerly whatever organization there was of the young was of either sex by itself, the new system includes both, associating in all possible intimacy. They discuss freely and apparently have the power to decide not only matters of religion and education but of sex conduct. The elders may still amuse themselves with property and politics.

74. A Supplement to the Oxford English Dictionary

GEORGE STEINER

George Steiner (1929–   ), born in Paris, came to the United States at 11 and was naturalized at 15. He took a bachelor's degree in literature and philosophy at the University of Paris, another A.B. at Chicago in 1948, and an M.A., with the Bell Prize in American Literature, at Harvard in 1950. He became a Rhodes Scholar to Oxford (1950–1952), staying to take a D.Phil. in 1955. He was on the staff of the London *Economist* (1952–1956), and a member of the Institute for Advanced Study, Princeton University (1956–1958). He has been a Fellow of Churchill College, Cambridge University, since 1961. He has published a number of books and articles on literature and language, and won the O'Henry Short Story Prize in 1959.

P UBLISHED IN 1933, the first Supplement to the Oxford English Dictionary was intended to cover accessions to the language over the years 1884–1928, in which the original OED had been produced. The new Supplement, of which A-G is now published, will run to three volumes. It is far more ambitious than its predecessor. It will incorporate and thus supersede all the material assembled in 1933. It will include words in current use excluded from the original OED on grounds of technicality or decorum. It will attempt to cover and record the mutations in the language from 1884 to the present.

There are many levels on which this project is an important, fascinating enterprise. Statistically, this volume comprises some 18,000 entries. Since 1957, when compilation began, readers for the Oxford University Press have extracted about a million and a half quotations from literature, scientific texts, journals, periodicals of high and low brow, compendia of slang and newspapers of every description. One hundred and thirty-thousand illustrative citations have been reproduced. Their authors range from Dylan Thomas to Germaine Greer and Charlie Chaplin, from The Cheyenne Daily Leader to the Cahiers de Lexicologie. If Eisenhower makes no contribution—a surprising fact in view of the mournful molasses of his prose—Cole Porter does (see *beguine*).

But the interest of the project is more central. Roughly speaking, the 40 years which divide the completion of the OED and the first Supplement from the present, mark a crucial turn in the condition of English or "British" English. The center of linguistic gravity, the energy core, has passed away from England. It is no longer in the British Isles that the English language is being spoken and written at the highest levels of inventive intensity. It is no longer "British English" (as the editors of the new Supplement call it) which sets the pace of invention, of assimilative suppleness and resilient informing of experience.

With the dramatic decline in English political and economic power, with the slowing of social reflexes and hardening of political arteries in a community worn by two world wars and the weight of almost 1,000 years of conscious history, linguistic force too has drained away. Given our present, rudimentary techniques of socio-linguistics and comparative semantics, this sort of general proposition is extremely difficult to prove. It is too generalized to allow satisfactory tabulation. It infers a suspect metaphor of languages as organic wholes, which they are not, or certainly not in any simple "biological" sense. But anyone who tries to register honestly the state of the language in England today and who compares it with the evolution of English elsewhere will know what I mean.

The literary evidence is unmistakable. There has not been a major "English English" voice since that of D. H. Lawrence. From Ezra Pound, T. S. Eliot and Wallace Stevens down to Robert Lowell and John Berryman, the masters of poetry have been Americans. Yeats, of course, was Irish. As were Shaw, Joyce and O'Casey. Though it reaches fully into this century, the achievement of John Cowper Powys is radically a 19th-century phenomenon. Today, in the prose of the imagined, it is Updike, Roth, Malamud, Bellow who matter. Linguistically the most inventive of prose writers is Nabokov, an extraterritorialist. Much of current writing in England is either frankly imitative of the American model or reductive in a revealing way. It retrenches, it deals parsimoniously with diminishing resources. The talent of Pinter is that of a minimalist, making do with old, fragile counters from a reduced stock. In a betraying, inherently puerile maneuver, Ted Hughes, probably the most gifted of younger English poets, experiments with a made-up, purely musicalized idiom.

Literature is only the surface. The decrease in articulate energy, in the pressure of language on the imagination, pervades many aspects of English social and political existence. Whatever its inspiring function during war, Churchillian rhetoric left a suspect taste. The new note was gray and corner of the mouth. High eloquence has suffered a universal decline. But in England this alteration mattered more. For better or worse, an explicit sonority and elevation of syntactic forms, rooted ultimately in the Authorized Version and Shakespeare, had served as the code of political order at home and of imperial confidence abroad. Its swift recession from English public modes and education marks a more general crisis of nerve.

The economic disasters of the 1930's and the end of World War II led to the revolution of caste and of social relations in which England is today painfully enmeshed. There are many ways of thinking about this revolution: one would be in terms of controlling, normative images and dreams. What Disraeli had called "the two nations" was really the coexistence of a highly articulate élite and of a largely underprivileged majority. The unique feature of the arrangement (looking back it seems little short of uncanny) lay in the fact that the large mass of the working class acquiesced in, often actively adhered to, the myths and images of national destiny and moral end articulated by the ruling minority.

After 1945 this was no longer the case. Those who had so long borne the brunt of economic stress and war now pressed for the fulfillment of *their* dreams, for the realization of *their* images of the good life. But here is the key point: there was no ready idiom from within English literacy itself in which to articulate this new populist, mass-consumer vision. Like the desired objects themselves—elegant but inexpensive dress, warm housing at moderate cost, a more varied, attractive diet, travel abroad, better cars and roads, television, social advancement for one's children, iceboxes, a permanent for the working-girl—the language of new hopes came largely from America. Hence the enormous impact of American movies, television shows, magazines and comics on the English mass consciousness in the years following the war. American lyrics and American pulp, American humor and American slang encoded the intoxicating promise of a better, more zestful life for the very common man. This was precisely what "British English," with its cruel emphasis on accentual propriety, on grammatical correctness, on range of implicit reference, had refused to do. The Beatles have constituted a brilliant counterattack, a sudden export drive of English fantasies and dynamism; but they represent an isolated case.

Today the dynamics of English are centrifugal. The powers of rapid assimilation from foreign sources—Yiddish, Hispanic, Negro—which similarly characterized the open genius of Elizabethan speech, are most evident in America. At its best (which is most certainly not that of politics, advertisement or genteel pap), American speech has a raw precision of imagery, a musical wealth, a vulnerability to the uprush of argotic and neological experiments, a sheer onrush—the proposition seeking out the listener with a palpable directness—which recall the explosive enhancement of Tudor and Elizabethan English. Contrast Mailer's pamphleteering with the best of English social polemics; set the idiom of "Malcolm X" beside any English social memoir since Orwell. The contrast in vitality, in linguistic invention and aggression (a great style *is* an act of aggression) springs to view.

No novelist working in England is even distantly of a stature with Patrick White in Australia. Canadian English, the English of South Africa, of India, of the West Indies, with their creative admixture of alien elements, are providing new cores of imaginative strength and assay. For "British" or home-ground English the situation is one of extreme ambiguity. Inevitably the new modes stream in from outside, via the mass media, via immigration. But simultaneously instincts of nostalgic purity run strong. At a moment when it is being dragged with sullen distaste into the Common Market, England is more than ever on the psychological defensive, more than ever obsessed with a resplendent past. The Victorian age, the sedate calamities of the Boer War, the heroics of 1914 and 1940 cover the bookstall and the television screen, the museum galas and the movies. There is in current English sensibility an inebriation with the past, an attempt, almost desperate, to keep the present at arm's length. John Osborne's "Entertainer" is the classic statement of hurt atavism.

This is why the launching of a new OED Supplement is such a problematic, intriguing venture. This is why the editor's statement, "we have made bold forays into the written English of regions outside the British Isles particularly into that of North America, Australia, New Zealand, South Africa, India and Pakistan. . . . Readers will discover by constant use of the Supplement that the written English of regions like Australia, South Africa and India has been accorded the kind of treatment that lexicographers of a former generation might have reserved for the English of Britain alone," is at once so important and inadequate.

Rightly, the Supplement heralds its inclusion of the "central and enduring vocabulary" of such new disciplines as computer science, sociology, mathematical linguistics and the new branches of psychology. Rightly again, it underlines its treatment of the language of "drugs, beatniks, hippies, sit-ins, protest, space, go-kart, and drag-car racing, surfing . . . the frisbee, and the frug." But how deep is the irony. It is not from the realities and language-worlds of Oxford English that either these new intellectual disciplines or phenomena of politics and play have derived. It is from Cape Kennedy and Detroit, from the pads of San Francisco and the research laboratories of M.I.T. In short, this is not so much a "supplement" to that sovereign monument of English English confidence and authority, the original OED, as it is an interim report, an attempt to inventory the English language at a moment when much of its life-force can be found registered (though messily and incompletely) in Webster's Third New International or in Eugene Landy's invaluable "Underground Dictionary."

To a non-lexicographer the results look at once immensely impressive and uneven. With what is, one hopes, mock-solemnity, Mr. R. W.

Burchfield, the editor, has announced to the world that the sexual taboos observed by all Oxford lexicography hitherto are now abolished. The two ultimate unmentionables, "once considered too gross and vulgar to be given countenance in the decent environment of a dictionary, now appear with full supporting evidence along with a wide range of colloquial and coarse expressions referring to sexual and excretory functions." The claim that "by 1957 neither word had appeared in any general dictionary of English, large or small" happens to be inaccurate (see Bailey's "Universal Etymological English Dictionary" of 1735). And although *cunnilingus, fellatio* and *frigging* are boldly included, *bun,* in its erotic usage, is not.

But it is less the libertarian motion in itself which is interesting. It is the fact that so many of these terms were in widespread and very probably trivial currency among the English agricultural and industrial classes for at least the past three centuries. Their exclusion from the great OED and its 1933 auxiliary points once more to the social insulation and self-conscious moralism of the speech of the governing caste. The new OED Supplement is a political, social even more than a linguistic statement. It seeks to close the ancient, strategically effective gap between "British English" and the uncouth, vaguely menacing babel of the semiliterate or largely oral world.

If *grass,* meaning marijuana, is included (does the term really not antedate 1943?), *acid* and *acid-head* are not an astounding omission from a dictionary which claims an explicit regard to the idiom of narcotics and hippies. *Bio-feedback,* one of the key terms in current thinking about consciousness and the regulatory mechanisms of the mind-body relations is left out. The phonographic aspects of *disc* are thoroughly covered, but not the uses of *disc* and associated terms in regard to computers. Instructively, this oversight somewhat distorts the range of illustrative example in the rubric on *data.* A good many archaic oddities gain entry, where current locutions are missed. Too much Tolkien; too little Leo Rosten.

But it is a facile sport to pick holes in so large and intricate an edifice. There is God's plenty of solid information and of the kind of stray nugget to set one dreaming in a lexicon whose sources range from the New Zealand Journal of Agriculture to The Village Voice. How fascinating it is to learn that H. G. Wells was probably the first to see a plane as a *bird,* that George Orwell thought of young women as *birds* back in 1935 and that Time magazine, in 1951, was the first to spot the use of *birds* in the lingo of missilemen. Or to be told that the French *demi-vierges* modulates into American English via a splendid sentence in Raymond Chandler's "Long Good-Bye": "A couple of streamlined demi-virgins went by."

Or to be informed (though not necessarily persuaded) that *girlie,* in the sense of a *girlie show* does not antedate an American usage of

1942. Indeed, this problem of precedence is always difficult. "Gizmo" is cited as appearing for the first time in Time for July, 1943, but in the very passage, Time describes the word as "of universal significance." Where had it come from, how had it gained general currency? In exchange, how much of the history of feeling lies in the simple fact that the first citation for *ecology* derives from Thoreau, or that one of the earliest uses of *economic war* should be in Pound's *"Pisan Cantos."* In short, this Supplement is a piece of vital history, a register of consciousness even more than of philological and grammatical fact.

As Hans Aarsleff of Princeton has demonstrated, the historical genius of the OED, the plan to let each word "set forth its own life-history," goes back to the principles of a German classicist Franz Passow, put forward in 1812. This ideal was transmitted to the original editors of the OED via the great Greek dictionary of Liddell and Scott (1843). In the OED itself it achieved an unrivaled fulfillment. What is hoped for now is a revision of the OED along guidelines partly tested in the Supplement. Marghanita Laski, one of the most omnivorous word-hunters in the Oxford team, has set out a blueprint for a complete overhaul. Ante- and postdatings in the OED are, in very numerous instances, hopelessly obsolete or inaccurate. Not only the literary giants but writers of ephemera, of letters and diaries should be drawn into the network of quotation. Many "rare" words have either become common or lapsed altogether. Spellings need thorough revision in view of the American imports and of the general erosion of "difficult" or opaque phonetic traditions.

Just because English English is now under extreme pressure, the OED, like England itself, can play a unique, formidably important role in making visible a new equipoise, a new interaction between genuine civilization and the energies of colloquial change. "I put forward the suggestion," writes Miss Laski, "of a publicly supported perpetual Trust, charged with the task of continually revising the Oxford English Dictionary. . . . We could hardly hope for a revised first fascicle of A by 1984, the centenary year: but once this had appeared, we might hope that century by century a revised OED could, despite the enormous enlargement it would need, be completed." The year 1984 rings a bell. Whether it will truly be the centenary of the greatest dictionary in our language or the year of Orwell's *Newspeak* is a question which involves far more than lexicography.

75. The Death of Marilyn Monroe

DIANA TRILLING

Born Diana Rubin in New York City, where she now lives with her husband, Professor Lionel Trilling of Columbia University, Mrs. Trilling has continued an active essayist and critic in the nation's liveliest magazines. She won a Guggenheim Award in 1950. Her *Claremont Essays,* in which this present essay appears, was published in 1964.

O N A SUNDAY MORNING in August 1962, Marilyn Monroe, aged thirty-six, was found dead in the bedroom of her home in Los Angeles, her hand on the telephone as if she had just received or, far more likely, been about to make a call. On the night table next to her bed stood a formidable array of medicines, among them a bottle that had held twenty-five Nembutal pills, now empty. Two weeks later a team of psychiatrists, appointed by the state in conformity with California law, brought in its report on the background and circumstances of her death, declaring it a suicide. There had of course never been any suggestion of foul play. The death was clearly self-inflicted, a climax of extended mental suffering. In fact, it was soon revealed that on Saturday evening Marilyn Monroe had made an emergency call to the psychoanalyst who had been treating her for her acute sleeplessness, her anxieties and depression, and that he had paid her a visit. But the formal psychiatric verdict had to do with the highly technical question of whether the overdose of barbiturates was purposeful or accidental: had Marilyn Monroe *intended* to kill herself when she took the twenty-five sleeping pills? The jury of experts now ruled it was purposeful: she had wanted to die.

It is an opinion, or at least a formulation, that can bear, I believe, a certain amount of modification. Obviously, I'm not proposing that Marilyn Monroe's death was accidental in the sense that she took so large a dose of pills with no knowledge of their lethal properties. But I think it would be more precise to call this kind of death incidental rather than purposeful—incidental to the desire to escape the pain of living. I am not a psychiatrist and I never knew Marilyn Monroe, but it seems to me that a person can want to be released from consciousness without seeking actual death; that someone can want to stop living without wishing to die. And this is my feeling about Marilyn Monroe, that even when she had spoken of "wanting to die" she really meant that she wanted to end her suffering, not her life. She wanted to destroy consciousness rather than herself. Then, having taken the pills, she realized she might never return from the sleep she craved so passionately and reached for the phone for help.

But this is of course only speculation, and more appropriately engaged in by the medical profession than by the layman. For the rest of us, the motives surrounding Marilyn Monroe's suicide fade in importance before the all-encompassing reality of the act itself: Marilyn Monroe terminated her life. While the medical experts pondered the delicate difference between accident and suicide, the public recognized that the inevitable had at last occurred: Marilyn Monroe had killed herself. Shocked and grieved as everyone was, no one was at all surprised that she had died by her own hand, because for some years now the world had been prepared for just some such tragic outcome to one of the extraordinary careers of our time.

The potentiality of suicide or, at any rate, the threat of extreme mental breakdown had been, after all, conveyed to us by virtually every news story about Marilyn Monroe of recent years. I don't mean that it had been spelled out that she would one day take her life or otherwise go off the deep psychic end. But no one seemed able to write about her without reassuring us that despite her instability and the graveness of her emotional problems, she was still vital and eager, still, however precariously, a going concern. Marilyn Monroe was an earnest, ambitious actress, determined to improve her skill; Marilyn Monroe had failed in several marriages but she was still in pursuit of fulfillment in love; Marilyn Monroe had several times miscarried but she still looked forward to having children; Marilyn Monroe was seriously engaged in psychoanalysis; Marilyn Monroe's figure was better than ever; she was learning to be prompter; she was coping, or was struggling to cope, with whatever it was that had intervened in the making of her last picture —so, on the well-worn track, ran all the news stories. Even what may have been her last interview to appear in print (by the time it came out, she was already dead) sounded the same dominant chord of hopefulness, telling us of a Marilyn Monroe full of confidence that she would improve her acting and find her roles, and that between the two therapies, hard work and psychoanalysis, she would achieve the peace of mind that had for so long eluded her.

Where there is this much need for optimism, surely there is great peril, and the public got the message. But what is striking is the fact that throughout this period of her mounting difficulties, with which we were made so familiar, the popular image remained intact. Whatever we were told of her weak hold on life, we retained our image of Marilyn Monroe as the very embodiment of life energy. I think my response to her death was the common one: it came to me with the impact of a personal deprivation but I also felt it as I might a catastrophe in history or in nature; there was less in life, there was less of life, because she had ceased to exist. In her loss life itself had been injured.

In my own instance, it happens that she was already an established star before I knew her as anything except the latest pin-up girl. There is always this shield of irony some of us raise between ourselves and any object of popular adulation, and I had made my dull point of snubbing her pictures. Then one evening I chanced on a television trailer for *Bus Stop,* and there she was. I'm not even sure I knew whom I was seeing on the screen, but a light had gone on in the room. Where everything had been gray there was all at once an illumination, a glow of something beyond the ordinarily human. It was a remarkable moment, of a kind I don't recall having had with any other actress, and it has its place with certain rare, cherished experiences of art such as my youthful remembrance of Pavlova, the most perfect of performing artists, whose control of her body was like a radiance, or even the quite recent experience of seeing some photographs of Nijinsky in motion. Marilyn Monroe was in motion, too, which is important, since no still picture could quite catch her electric quality; in posed pictures the redundancy of flesh was what first imposed itself, dimming one's perception of its peculiar aliveness, of the translucence that infused body with spirit. In a moment's flash of light, the ironies with which I had resisted this sex idol, this object of an undifferentiating public taste, dropped from me never to be restored.

But mine was a minority problem; the world had long since recognized Marilyn Monroe's unique gift of physical being and responded to it as any such gift of life demands. From the start of her public career it had acknowledged the genius of biology or chemistry or whatever it was that set this young woman apart from the general kind. And once it had admitted her magic, nothing it was to learn of her "morbidity" could weigh against the conviction that she was alive in a way not granted the rest of us, or, more accurately, that she communicated such a charge of vitality as altered our imagination of life, which is of course the whole job and wonder of art.

Since her death it has occurred to me that perhaps the reason we were able to keep these two aspects in which we knew Marilyn Monroe —her life affirmation and her impulse to death—in such discreet balance was that they never presented themselves to us as mutually exclusive but, on the contrary, as two intimately related, even expectable, facets of her extraordinary endowment. It is as if the world that loved Marilyn Monroe understood that her superabundant biology had necessarily to provoke its own restraint, that this is the cruel law by which nature, or at least nature within civilization, punishes those of us who ask too much of life or bring too much to life. We are told that when one of the senses is defective, nature frequently provides a compensation in another of the senses; the blind often hear better than the seeing, or have a sharper sense of touch. What we are not told but perhaps understand nonetheless is the working of nature's system of negative compensation—the price we pay for gift, the revenge that life seems so regularly to take upon distinction. Certainly our awareness of the more, the plus, in Marilyn Monroe prepared us for some sort of minus. The fact that this young woman whose biological gift was so out of the ordinary was in mental pain seemed to balance the ledger. And one can speculate that had we not known of her emotional suffering, we would have been prepared for some other awful fate for her—an airplane disaster, maybe, or a deforming illness. So superstition may be thought of as an accurate reading of the harder rules of life.

And yet it is difficult to suppose the gods could be all that jealous. Had Marilyn Monroe not been enough punished in childhood to ensure her against further misfortune? Once this poor forlorn girl had been so magically brought into her own, the most superstitious of us had the right to ask happiness for her ever after. It was impossible to think of Marilyn Monroe except as Cinderella. The strange power of her physical being seemed best explained and justified by the extreme circumstances of her early life—the illegitimate birth, the mad mother, the orphanage and near-mad foster homes, the rape by one of her early guardians. If there was no good fairy in Marilyn Monroe's life and no Prince Charming, unless Hollywood, this didn't rob her story of its fairybook miraculousness; it merely assimilated to the old tale our newer legend of the self-made hero or heroine. Grace Kelly had had her good Philadelphia family to pave her path and validate her right to a crown. But Marilyn Monroe reigned only by virtue of her beauty and her determination to be raised out of the squalor and darkness, and to shine in the full, the fullest, light. It is scarcely a surprise that the brighter her radiance, the more we listened for the stroke of midnight that would put a limit on such transcendence.

But it was not only the distance Marilyn Monroe had traveled from her unhappy beginnings that represented for us a challenge of reality, to be punished by reality. If her gift is to be regarded not as that of the stage or screen, which I think it primarily was not, but as the gift of biology, she was among those who are greatly touched with power; she was of the true company of artists. And her talent was so out of the range of the usual that we were bound to feel of it that it was not to be contained in society as we know it; therefore it proposed its own dissolution. Like any great artistic gift, Marilyn Monroe's power of biology was explosive, a primitive and savage force. It had, therefore and inevitably, to be a danger both to herself and to the world in which it did its work. All art is fierce in the measure that it matters, finally, and in its savagery it chooses either to push against society, against the restrictions that hedge it in, or against the artist himself. And no doubt it is the incapacity of most human beings to sustain this inordinate pressure that accounts for the fact that the artist is an exception in any civilized population. To mediate between the assault upon oneself and upon society, to keep alive in the battle and come out more or less intact, is a giant undertaking in which the native endowment of what we call talent is probably but a small element.

Among the very few weapons available to the artist in this monstrous struggle, naïveté can be the most useful. But it is not at all my impression that Marilyn Monroe was a naïve person. I think she was innocent, which is very different. To be naïve is to be simple or stupid on the basis of experience, and Marilyn Monroe was far from stupid; no one who was stupid could have been so quick to turn her wit against herself, or to manage the ruefulness with which she habitually replied to awkward questioning. To be innocent is to suffer one's experience without being able to learn self-protection from it; as if willessly, innocence is at the mercy of experience, unable to mobilize counterforces to fortune.

Of Ernest Hemingway, for example, I feel much as I do of Marilyn Monroe, that he was unable to marshal any adequate defense against the painful events of his childhood, and this despite his famous toughness and the courage he could call upon in war, in hunting, in all the dangerous enterprises that seduced him. He was an innocent man, not a naïve man, though not always intelligent. Marilyn Monroe offers us a similar paradox. Even while she symbolized an extreme of experience, of sexual knowingness, she took each new circumstance of life, as it came to her or as she sought it, like a newborn babe. And yet this was what made her luminous—her innocence. The glow was not rubbed off her by her experience of the ugliness of life because finally, in some vital depth, she had been untouched by it.

From the psychiatrist's point of view, too much innocence, a radical disproportion between what has happened to a person and what he has absorbed from his experience, is a symptom, and alarming. It can indicate a rude break in his connection with himself, and if he is in treatment, it suggests a difficult cure, since, in emotional logic, he will probably be as impervious to the therapy as to the events through which he has passed, and yet without any mitigation of suffering. In the creative spheres, an excess of innocence unquestionably exercises an enormous fascination on us; it produces the purity of expression which leads us to say of an artistic creation or performance that it is "out of this world." But the pyschiatric judgment has to pick its way on tiptoe between the gift and the pathology. What constitutes a person's art may eventually spell his emotional undoing.

450

I can suppose of Marilyn Monroe that she was peculiarly elusive to the psychiatrists or analysts who tried to help her, that emotionally speaking she presented herself to them as a kind of blank page on which nothing had been written, failing to make the connection between herself and them even as she pleaded for it. And yet disconnection was at the heart of her gift, it defined her charm for the world, much as Hemingway's dissociation from his own experience was determinative of his gift.

For several decades, scores of writers have tried to imitate Hemingway's style: the flexibility and purity of his prose, the bright, cogent distance he was able to put between himself and the object under examination. But none has succeeded. And I believe this is because his prose was, among many other things, a direct report of the unbridgeable distance between external reality and his emotions. Just so, Marilyn Monroe was inimitable. Hollywood, Broadway, the night clubs: they all regularly produce their quota of sex queens, but the public takes them and leaves them, or doesn't really take them; the world is not enslaved as it was by Marilyn Monroe because none but Marilyn Monroe could suggest such a purity of sexual delight. The boldness with which she could parade herself and yet never be gross, her sexual flamboyance and bravado which yet breathed an air of mystery and even reticence, her voice which carried such ripe overtones of erotic excitement and yet was the voice of a shy child—these complications were integral to her gift. And they described a young woman trapped in some never-never land of unawareness.

What I imply here, of course, is a considerable factitiousness in Marilyn Monroe as a sexual figure. Certainly the two or three men I've known who met her in "real life" were agreed on her lack of direct sexual impact; she was sweet and beautiful and lovely, yes, but somehow not at all the arousing woman they had expected. The nature of true sexuality is most difficult to define, so much of what we find sexually compelling has its source in phantasies that have little to do with the primary sexual instinct. Especially in the case of a movie star we enter a realm where dream and biology make their easiest merger. The art of acting is the art of *performing as if,* and the success of this feat of suggestion depends upon the degree to which it speaks to some phantasy of the onlookers.

Marilyn Monroe spoke to our dreams as much as to our animal nature, but in a most unusual way. For what she appealed to was our determination to be rid of phantasy and to get down to the rock-bottom actuality. She gratified our wish to confront our erotic desires without romance, without diversion. And working within a civilization like ours, in which sexuality is so surrounded with restraints and fears and prohibitions, she perhaps came as close as possible to giving us the real thing. But she didn't give us the real thing; she merely acted as if she were giving it to us. She glamorized sexuality to the point at which it lost its terrors for us; and maybe it was this veil that she raised to sexual reality that permitted women, no less than men, to respond to her so generously. Instinctively, I think, women understood that this seemingly most sexual of female creatures was no threat to them.

The myth of Marilyn Monroe was thus even more of a myth than we realized, for this girl who was supposed to release us from our dreams into sexual actuality was in all probability not actual even to herself. Least of all could she have been sexually actual to herself and at the same time such a marvelous public performer of sex, such a conscious artist of sex. And we can conjecture that it was this deep alienation from her own feelings, including her sexual feeling, that enabled her to sustain the disorder of her early years even as long and as well as she did, and to speak of her awful childhood so simply and publicly. For most of us, the smallest "shame" in our past must be kept locked from others. We prefer that the least menacing of skeletons remain in the closet lest our current image of ourselves be violated by its emergence into the open. But Marilyn Monroe had no need for such reserves. She told the public the most gruesome facts of her personal history, for all the world as if we on the outside were worthy of such confidences—except that in some odd, generous response to her innocence, we exceeded ourselves in her instance and didn't take the advantage of her that we might have. Judged from the point of view of what we require of the artist, that he have the will and fearlessness to rise above the conventions which bind those of us with less gift, Marilyn Monroe's candor about her early life was something to be celebrated. But from another point of view her frankness was a warning that the normal barriers of self-protection were down or non-existent, leaving her grievously exposed to the winds of circumstance.

And indeed the very word "exposed" is a key word in the pattern of her life. She was an actress and she exposed her person and her personality to the public gaze. She was an exposed human being who told the truth about herself too readily, too publicly. And more than most actresses, she exposed her body, with but inadequate understanding of what this involved. We recall, for instance, the awkward little scandal about her having once posed naked for a calendar and the bewildered poise, the really untoward innocence and failure of comprehension, with which she met the dismay of her studio, as if to say, "But that was me yesterday when I needed money. That isn't me today; today I have money." Just as today and yesterday were discontinuous with each other, she was discontinuous with herself, held together, one feels, only and all too temporarily by her success.

And this success was perhaps more intimately connected with her awareness of her physical appeal than we always understood. It may well have been the fact that she was so much and so admiringly in the public eye that gave Marilyn Monroe the largest part of her sense of a personal identity. Not long before her death, we now discover, she had herself photographed in the nude, carefully editing the many pictures as if to be certain she left the best possible record for posterity. The photographs leave, however, a record only of wasted beauty, at least of the famous body—while Marilyn Monroe's face is lovely as ever, apparently unscarred by her intense suffering, her body looked ravaged and ill, already drained of life. Recently the pictures have been published in an expensive magazine devoted to erotica. If their high price, prohibitive to the general buyer, could be interpreted as a precaution against their being too easily available to a sensation-seeking audience, the restraint was not really necessary. At the last, the nude Marilyn Monroe could excite no decent viewer to anything but the gentlest pity, and much fear.

But even before this ultimate moment the public success had been threatened. The great career was already failing. There had not been a Marilyn Monroe movie for a long time, and the last film she had worked on had had to be halted because she was unable to appear. And there was no private life to fall back upon, not even the formal structure of one: no marriage, no family, apparently not even friends. One had come, indeed, to think of her as the loneliest of people, so that it was not without bitterness that, on her death, one discovered that it was not only oneself who had wished to help her but many other strangers, especially women to whose protectiveness her extreme vulnerability spoke so directly. But we were the friends of whom she knew nothing, and among the people she knew it would seem that real relationships were out of reach across the desert emptiness that barricades whoever is out of touch with his feelings. One thinks of her that last evening of her life, alone and distraught, groping for human comfort and finding nothing but those endless bottles of medicine, and one confronts a pathos worse than tragedy.

Certainly it strains justice as well as imagination that the world's most glamorous woman should have been alone, with no date, on a Saturday night—for it was, in fact, a Saturday night when she killed herself. On other nights but Saturday, we are allowed our own company. Saturday night is when all American boys and girls must prove themselves sexually. This is when we must be "out," out in the world where we can be seen among the sexually chosen. Yet the American girl who symbolized sexual success for all of us spent her last Saturday night alone in despair. Every man in the country would have wanted to date Marilyn Monroe, or so he would say, but no man who knew her did.

Or, contemplating her loneliness, we think of her funeral, which, contrived to give her the peace and privacy that had so strenuously eluded her throughout her life, yet by its very restraint and limited attendance reminded us of the limitations of her actual connection with the world. Joe DiMaggio, who had been her husband for a few brief months earlier in her career, was the chief mourner. It was DiMaggio to whom, she had told us, it was impossible to be married because he had no conversation; at meals, instead of talking to her, he read the papers or looked at television. The more recent husband, *with* conversation, was not present, no doubt for his own inviolable reasons, but it was saddening. I do not know what, if anything, was read at the service, but I'd like to think it was of an elevated and literary kind, such as might be read at the funeral of a person of the first intellectual rank.

For of the cruelties directed at this young woman even by the public that loved her, it seems to me that the most biting, and unworthy of the supposedly enlightened people who were particularly guilty of it, was the mockery of her wish to be educated, or thought educated. Granting our right to be a bit confused when our sex idol protests a taste for Dostoevsky, surely the source of our discomfort must yet be located in our suspicions of Dostoevsky's worth for us and in our own sexual unease rather than in Marilyn Monroe. For what our mockery signifies is our disbelief that anyone who has enough sexuality needs to read Dostoevsky. The notion that someone with Marilyn Monroe's sexual advantages could have wanted anything except to make love robbed us of a prized illusion, that enough sexual possibility is enough everything.

I doubt that sex was enough anything for Marilyn Monroe, except the means for advancing herself in the world. One of the touching revelations of her early life was her description of how she discovered that somehow she was sexually different from other girls her age: the boys all whistled at her and crowded to her like bears to honey, so she came to realize that she must have something special about her, which she could use to rise above her poor circumstances. Her sexual awareness, that is, came to her from outside herself. It would be my guess that it remained outside her always, leaving a great emptiness, where a true sexuality would have supplied her with a sense of herself as a person with connection and content.

This void she tried to fill in every way available, with worldly goods, with fame and public attention and marriage, and also in ways that turned out to be unavailable, like children and domesticity—nothing could be more moving than the eagerness with which she seized upon a Jewish mother-in-law, even upon Jewish ceremonials and cooking, as if in the home life of her last husband's people she would find the secret of emotional plenitude. She also tried to fill her emptiness with books and learning. How mean-spirited can we be, to have denied her whatever might have added to her confidence that she was really a solid person and not just an uninhabited body?

And that she had the intellectual capacity for education there can be no question, had it but been matched with emotional capacity. No one without a sharp native intelligence could have spoofed herself as gracefully as she did or parried reporters with such finesse. If we are to judge by her interviews, she was as singularly lacking in the endemic off-stage dullness of actors and actresses, the trained courtesy and charm that is only another boring statement of their self-love, as she was deficient in the established defenses of her profession: one recalls no instance of even implied jealousy of her colleagues or of censure of others—directors, script-writers, husbands—for her own failures. Her generosity of spirit, indeed, was part of the shine that was on her. But unfortunately it spared everyone but herself; she had never studied self-justification. To herself she was not kind. She made fun of herself and of all that she had to go on in life: her biology. Certainly this added to her lovableness but it cut from under her the little ground that she could call her own. When she exhibited her sexual abundance with that wonderful, gay exaggeration of hers, or looked wide-eyed upon the havoc she wrought, it was her way of saying, "Don't be afraid. I don't take myself seriously so you don't have to take me seriously either." Her talent for comedy, in other words, was a public beneficence but a personal depredation, for, far more than most people, she precisely needed the assurance that she weighed in the scheme of human life, that she had substance and reality, that she had all the qualifications that make for a person we take seriously. Her self a supplicant, she gave us comfort. Herself a beggar, she distributed alms.

At her death, several writers of good will who undertook to deal with the tragedy of her suicide blamed it on Hollywood. In the industry that had made millions from her and in the methods by which Hollywood had exploited her, they found the explanation of her failed life; they wrote about her as the sacrificial lamb on the altar of American vulgarity and greed. I share their disgust with Hollywood and I honor their need to isolate Marilyn Monroe from the nastiness that fed on her, but I find it impossible to believe that this girl would have been an iota better off were Hollywood to have been other than what we all know it to be, a madness in our culture.

The self-destructiveness that Marilyn Monroe carried within her had not been put there by the "system," however overbearing in its ugliness. Just as her sweetness was her own, and immune to the influences of Hollywood, her terrors were also her own. They were not implanted in her, though undoubtedly they were increased, by the grandiosity of being a star. Neither for better nor worse, I feel, was she essentially falsified or distorted by her public role, though she must often have suffered cruelly from the inescapability of the public glare. In fact, it would be my conjecture that had she never gone into the movies and become rich and world-famous, her troubled spirit would long since have had its way with her. She would have been equally undone, and sooner, and with none of the many alleviations and compensations that she must have known in these years of success.

This doesn't mean that I don't think she was a "victim." But she was not primarily a victim of Hollywood commercialism, or exploitation, or of the inhumanity of the press. She was not even primarily a victim of the narcissistic inflation that so regularly attends the grim business of being a great screen personality. Primarily she was a victim of her gift, a biological victim, a victim of life itself. It is one of the excesses of contemporary thought that we like to blame our very faulty culture for tragedies that are inherent in human existence—at least, inherent in human existence in civilization. I think Marilyn Monroe was a tragedy of civilization, but this is something quite else again from, and even more poignant than, being a specifically American tragedy.

---

76. Virginia Stephen/ Virginia Woolf

WILLIAM MAXWELL

Maxwell (1908–   ), a staff writer and editor for the *New Yorker* since 1936, studied at the University of Illinois and Harvard, but took no degree. He has written seven novels and many short stories, and has served as President of the National Institute of Arts and Letters.

I T IS NOW THIRTY-TWO YEARS since Virginia Woolf placed a letter to her husband on the mantelpiece of the upstairs sitting room of their house in Sussex, and another to her sister, and, without his seeing her, made her way through the water meadows to the river. Her suicide by drowning has not receded into the past but continues to trouble the imagination.

Mrs. Woolf's literary reputation has stayed pretty much what it was during her lifetime. A great deal has been written about her novels and not very much about her. She has figured in the memoirs of her contemporaries, as one would expect, and Leonard Woolf's five-volume autobiography is inevitably (since he devoted a good part of his adult life to holding her back when the pit of insanity opened) as much about her as it is about him, but what he wrote about her is in the context of their marriage—heartbreaking and essentially a private matter.

In 1953, there was a biography, or what passed for it—"The Moth and the Star," by Aileen Pippett, who met Mrs. Woolf once, at a small party in the middle nineteen-thirties. It is noticeably short on facts —the chief sources being "A Writer's Diary," which she was allowed to see before its publication, and Mrs. Woolf's letters to V. Sackville West. It is also written in a wide-eyed, girlish style that is a continual inducement to throw the book out of the window. Miss Pippett was neither hindered nor greatly helped by Leonard Woolf, who eventually—it is one more instance of his unfailing good sense—persuaded Mrs. Woolf's nephew, Quentin Bell, to undertake a full-scale life. "Virginia Woolf" (Harcourt Brace Jovanovich) is so well done that it is possible to complain, and even then not very seriously, only about what is left out.

In the foreword, Mr. Bell remarks, "The purpose of the present volume is purely historical; and although I hope that I may assist those who attempt to explain and to assess the writing of Virginia Woolf, I can do so only by presenting facts which hitherto have not been generally known and by providing what will, I hope, be a clear and truthful account of the character and personal development of my subject. In no other way can I contribute to literary criticism. Even if I had the equipment for such a task I should not have the inclination; I have found the work of the biographer sufficiently difficult without adventuring in other directions."

No doubt this will be held against him, but the fact remains that there have been at least two dozen books and more than a hundred and fifty articles about the lyrical and narrative devices, the internal organization and pattern, etc., of Virginia Woolf's novels, and surely, for the time being, that is enough. It isn't at all difficult to distinguish her successes from her failures, nor do her novels require elucidation. When on the last page of "Jacob's Room," Betty Flanders asks "What am I to do with these, Mr. Bonamy?" and holds out a pair of Jacob's old shoes, the reader feels what he is meant to feel. What is interesting at this point, what one wants to know about and has always wanted to know about, is Sir Leslie Stephen's high-strung, overimaginative youngest daughter.

Mr. Bell had access to a large quantity of unpublished material: the twenty-seven manuscript volumes of Mrs. Woolf's diaries, the early notebook diaries, and the letters now in the Berg Collection of the New York Public Library; the letters and papers of his father and mother, Clive and Vanessa Bell, and of the painter Duncan Grant; Adrian Stephen's diary; a memoir written by Leslie Stephen after the death of his wife, in 1895; and old family letters to and from Mrs. Stephen and her children. In the middle fifties, Leonard Woolf began to assemble copies of Virginia Woolf's letters, intending to publish them. Mr. Bell says that the intention was abandoned—why? And is one never to be allowed to read them or the full text of the diaries?—but the copies were retained, and so he was familiar with letters whose whereabouts he did not always know. There were also the letters and manuscripts made available to him by Leonard Woolf for the purpose of this biography, and the papers and "laconic but trustworthy" diaries that formed part of Mr. Woolf's estate. In short, Mr. Bell had material that nobody before him had had, and more than enough for an important biography, which his book certainly is, but also for an ample one. Not counting the supplementary material, the two volumes (which were printed separately in England, with Virginia Stephen's marriage to Leonard Woolf as the dividing point, but over here are bound as one) add up to a little more than four hundred pages. If not quite laconic, Mr. Bell is relentlessly concise.

The run-of-the-mill novel is written by a person who is not a novelist. The run-of-the-mill biography is written by a person who has never even learned how to write. This cannot be said of Mr. Bell, who, in the course of publishing several books of art criticism and a sensible little treatise on who and what the term "Bloomsbury" can properly be said to stand for, has acquired a steady, well-shaped, readable prose style. Through it one begins to sense gradually his personality—truth-loving, ironic, masculine, sensitive, an aesthete, amused at confusion in others while not permitting it in himself, and with a horror of long-windedness and of any other kind of sprawl. His sentences are packed with information, and the information has already been scrutinized as to its value and implications, so the reader is continually drawn along on a strong thread of meaning. His thought is at all times clear and his construction careful, but occasionally he gives way to impatience and proceeds at too fast a clip. In speaking of Virginia Woolf's Stephen forebears, he remarks that a pamphlet written by her great-grandfather James Stephen "resulted in the Orders in Council, the Continental Blockade and, much to Stephen's chagrin and astonishment, the War of 1812." How, one wants to know. There is always the encyclopedia, of course, but either Mr. Bell is assuming a greater knowledge of history than the ordinary reader possesses or he just did not feel like going into it. Not even the chagrin. Again, he is very interesting about the character of her grandfather Sir James Stephen, and of her uncle Sir James Fitzjames Stephen, but doesn't do justice to their position and accomplishments, which were considerable. And Laura Stephen, Leslie Stephen's daughter by his first wife, and the granddaughter of Thackeray, is shoved right off the page into a nursing home and then an asylum in York before the reader has quite got over his astonishment at learning that Virginia Woolf had a half-sister who was mad.

In his role of biographer, Mr. Bell is continually required to make judgments. About his father and mother, as about other people who were close to him, and about Mrs. Woolf herself, he manages to write sympathetically and still not depart from or soften the truth. If her behavior was reprehensible, as it sometimes was, he says so, but without ever seeming to set himself either morally above or psychologically apart from her. The truth is, Mr. Bell is half a novelist. Consider this vignette of a young woman who had been taken on as helper at the Hogarth Press: "She set to work with more enthusiasm than competence, so that often enough Leonard had to take down and reset the formes after she had gone home. She chattered, she was lively and decorative and never grumbled—as well she might have, for her wages amounted to only a meat meal on the days when she worked, an assurance of shelter in case of air raids, and a proportion of the profits, which proportion she received after two months' work, when Leonard pressed half a crown into her hand. The real wages, one imagines, were Virginia's company and the opportunity of talking about her rather agitated life to a sympathetic listener." The judgment of the angels could hardly be more fair, or more dispassionate.

Mr. Bell also has a gift for running narrative: "There was bound to be a reckoning. It came at Charleston on 19 August, when in those years there was always a birthday party. This anniversary fell so fortunately—all the family being there, the grouse being just high enough for eating, the weather usually propitious—that it was for some years celebrated with considerable brio. Brio, or at least noise—noise induced by good food and drink, by Clive's social volubility, by Virginia's sallies—describes the tone of the evening, until the clamour in that hot candle-lit room was suddenly stilled by Virginia, who rose, staggered, turned exactly the colour of a duck's egg and tried blindly and inefficiently to make her way out of the room. At that juncture, when most of the company sat in stupid amazement, two persons acted promptly: Leonard and Vanessa moved swiftly and decisively, with the efficiency of long training, to do what was necessary—to take Virginia away from the room to fresh air, to a bed, and to administer whatever medicines experience had shown to be useful."

The phrase "the colour of a duck's egg" could not have been written by someone who was not present. I am even tempted to think that it couldn't have been written by someone who was not going to grow up to be an art critic. But anyway, what we are being given, though he doesn't say so, is the testimony of an eyewitness. A glance into *Who's Who* has revealed that the birthday they were celebrating was his.

More than anything else, what gives the book its special quality is the fact that it is written from a special position— that it is by Virginia Woolf's nephew, who is himself, through his mother, a Stephen. His father was half in love with Mrs. Woolf, and her very close friend and literary confidant. His mother was one of the two people she loved with her whole heart. The devotion was mutual. And both fathers and mothers have a way of passing their affections down, by means that are largely unspoken, to their children. Though it was no doubt tremendously helpful to have access to all those letters and diaries, a mountain of such documentary evidence would not have produced anything like the knowledge, conscious and half-conscious, that Mr. Bell started with. In that relaxed, free-thinking painter's household there were no hypocritical attitudes at the dinner table and no mysteries about what went on behind the closed bedroom door. The candor of the conversation of Clive and Vanessa Bell and their friends was even by present-day standards extraordinary. Add to this the fact that the knowledge went all the way back to Quentin Bell's childhood—to a time when "The announcement: 'Virginia is coming to tea' was like a warm capricious breeze blowing in from the south-west and bringing with it a kind of amazed joy. Of the miseries of her life, they [his brother and sister and he] were allowed to know nothing, nor did it seem, in their company, that she could be unhappy." He was thirty at the time of her death—old enough to have learned that she could be very unhappy indeed, and the various forms her unhappiness took. And to appreciate—rather than, as a child, merely to accept—the marvellous spontaneity of her fantasizing.

The one thing never fully understood within a family that has a distinguished member is his position in the eyes of the world. It is a problem in perspective. Mr. Bell treats Virginia Woolf very seriously as a writer. And for the rest she is presented as a woman whose health required that she lead a secluded life and who found sociability— having friends to tea, dining out, concerts, the ballet, the theatre— irresistible. Shortly after her death, T. S. Eliot, who was not given to making careless statements, said something that should have been conveyed in this book and isn't: "Virginia Woolf was the centre, not merely of an esoteric group, but of the literary life of London. Her position was due to a concurrence of qualities and circumstances which never happened before, and which I do not think will ever happen again. It maintained the dignified and admirable tradition of Victorian upper-middle-class culture—a situation in which the artist was neither the servant of the exalted patron, the parasite of the plutocrat, nor the entertainer of the mob—a situation in which the producer and the consumer of art were on an equal footing, and that neither the highest nor the lowest. With the death of Virginia Woolf, a whole pattern of culture is broken: she may be, from one point of view, only the symbol of it; but she would not be the symbol if she had not been, more than anyone in her time, the maintainer of it. Her work will remain; something of her personality will be recorded: but how can her position in the life of her own time be understood by those to whom her time will be so remote that they will not even know how far they fail to understand it?"

ON THE FOURTH OF SEPTEMBER, 1927, Mrs. Woolf wrote in her diary, "A cold grey blowy day, made memorable by the sight of a kingfisher and by my sense, waking early, of being again visited by 'the spirit of delight.' 'Rarely, rarely, comest thou, spirit of delight.' That was I singing this time last year; and sang so poignantly that I have never forgotten it, or my vision of a fin rising on a wide blank sea. No biographer could possibly guess this important fact about my life in the late summer of 1926. Yet biographers pretend they know people."

"They don't," Mr. Bell goes on to say, after quoting this passage, "or at least they ought not to. All that they can claim is that they know a little more than does the public at large and that, by catching at a few indications given here and there in recollections and writings, they can correct some misconceptions and trace, if they are very skilful or very lucky, an outline that is consistent and convincing, but which, like all outlines, is but tenuously connected with the actual form of the sitter in all lights, poses, moods, and disguises."

The "little more" that he knew and that there was no way for an outsider to know included two things that do not easily pass from the reader's mind. The first concerns George Duckworth, the elder of Mrs. Stephen's two sons by her first marriage. After her death (at which time he was twenty-seven), he was endlessly kind and generous to his adolescent half-sisters; "his shoulder was there for them to weep on; his arms were open for their relief." At what point this developed into something *not* kind and comforting Mr. Bell is unable to say. "Vanessa came to believe that . . . what had started with pure sympathy ended by becoming a nasty erotic skirmish. There were fondlings and fumblings in public when Virginia was at her lessons [she and her sister were tutored at home] and these were carried to greater lengths—indeed I know not to what lengths—when, with the easy assurance of a fond and privileged brother, George carried his affections from the schoolroom into the night nursery. To the sisters it simply appeared that their loving brother was transformed before their eyes

461

into a monster . . . against whom they had no defence"—his character
in the eyes of the family being such that no one would have believed
them. "Virginia felt that George had spoilt her life before it had fairly
begun. Naturally shy in sexual matters, she was from this time terrified back into a posture of frozen and defensive panic."

The second concerns Leonard Woolf: "Neither Vanessa nor Adrian
gave him a detailed and explicit account of Virginia's illnesses or told
him how deadly serious they might be, until this greatest and worst
crisis occurred. [She had found the case in which her husband kept
drugs unlocked and taken a hundred grains of veronal and had nearly
died.] Her insanity was clothed, like some other painful things in that
family, in a jest. 'Oh you know very well the Goat's mad.' This was
easily said and easily disregarded. Virginia herself, then and later
on, would cheerfully allude to the times when she was 'off her head.'
Thus, in effect if not in intention, Leonard was allowed to think of
Virginia's illnesses as something not desperately serious, and he was
allowed to marry her without knowing how fearful a care such a union
might be. In fairness to all parties it must be said that, even if Virginia's brother and sister had been as explicit and circumstantial as
they ought to have been, Leonard certainly would not have been de-
flected from his purpose of marrying Virginia; but his subsequent
treatment of one who was, in fact, already dangerously ill might
well have been different. As it was, he learnt the hard way and one
can only wonder, seeing how hard it was, and that he had for so long
to endure the constant threat of her suicide, to exert continual vigilance,
to exercise endless persuasive tact at mealtimes and to suffer the
perpetual alternations of hope and disappointment, that he too did not
go mad."

It has always bothered me that in "A Writer's Diary" Mrs. Woolf
revealed herself as endlessly and on the whole tiresomely concerned
about the public reception of her work, and I am grateful to Mr. Bell
for correcting this misconception: it was not vanity and competitiveness
but something immediately forgivable—or, rather, something that doesn't
even require forgiveness: "Her novels were very close to her own private
imaginings; she was always conscious that, to the outside world, they
might simply appear to be mad, or, worse still, that they really were
mad. Her dread of the ruthless mockery of the world contained within
it the deeper fear that her art, and therefore her self, was a kind of
sham, an idiot's dream of no value to anyone. For her, therefore, a
favourable notice was more valuable than mere praise; it was a kind
of certificate of sanity."

As for the outline—but he is much too modest. It is not a figure in
outline that he has drawn but a carefully and delicately shaded portrait
(in what follows the language is mostly his, but I have dispensed with

462

quotation marks) of a woman who with the passing of the years grew more angular, more bony, more austere, lost whatever prettiness she once had, and continued to be very beautiful; who hated buying clothes and was made utterly miserable for twenty-four hours because her brother-in-law didn't like her hat; whose conversation was full of surprises, of unpredictable questions, of fantasy and laughter; who could not be trusted with secrets, not so much because she was a mischief-maker as because of an alarming tendency to say whatever came into her mind; who was sometimes irritable and in later life rather enjoyed being socially terrifying; who was both a snob and able to understand the subtle corruption of values implicit in snobbery; whose attempts to follow her husband into political activity were bewildering both to herself and to those who had to collaborate with her; who was subject to violent alternations of feeling concerning the value of her work and also concerning her friends and acquaintances; who was not insensible of physical perfections but who got no pleasure from making love, disliked the sexual passion in men, and even the quality of masculinity; who found it excessively hard to be doing nothing, and so worked in the morning, walked in the afternoon, and read at night; who liked setting type and was good at it, and who also liked driving off to Rodmell on a hot Friday evening and having cold ham and sitting on the terrace, smoking a cigar and listening to the owls; who wrote a good part of those highly formal novels on a lapboard, seated before a gas fire, in an old armchair with the stuffing coming out of it, in a disorderly storeroom, surrounded by an accumulation of empty ink bottles and unemptied ashtrays, used envelopes and galley proofs, old pen nibs, paper clips, buttons, and fluff; who as a kind of game invented characters for people that were bewilderingly far from the truth; who was capable of saying to herself, "Never pretend that the things you haven't got are not worth having"; who suffered from a perennial and incurable regret that she had no children; who during her good periods thought nothing of walking seven or eight miles, leaping over stiles, climbing hills, parting barbed wire and brambles, and during her bad periods suffered from headaches, sleeplessness, depression, a sense of guilt, and an aversion to food and thought people were laughing at her and that she was the cause of everyone's troubles; whose speaking voice was beautiful; who neither courted sorrow nor wallowed in grief; who went mad four times and, in that unfortunate state, suffered from hallucinations, was violent, and heard voices—heard the birds singing in Greek, and Edward VII, in the azaleas, using the foulest possible language; who wrote in her diary, on the sixteenth of November, 1931, "But Oh the happiness of this life," and, on the first of March, 1937, "I know that I must go on doing this dance on hot bricks till I die." And in that letter to her husband that she left on the mantelpiece, "If anybody could have saved me it would have been you. Everything has gone from me but the certainty of your goodness. I can't go on spoiling your life any longer. . . ."

"RECOLLECTIONS OF VIRGINIA WOOLF *by Her Contemporaries,*" edited by Joan Russell Noble (Morrow), is, taken as a whole, disappointing, as such compilations tend to be. Impressions superimposed result in a blur. With one exception, the best essays—by Rose Macaulay, William Plomer, and T. S. Eliot (which I have already quoted from) —all appeared in the May, 1941, issue of *Horizon.*

Mr. Plomer has added some new material, but he doesn't say, and has perhaps forgotten, that, shortly after he made the acquaintance of the Woolfs, he was invited down to Rodmell and at some point Virginia Woolf took him to call on her sister. "Mr. Plomer," she said, "has been telling me all about himself. He is descended from Shakespeare and also from William Blake." He had, of course, said nothing of the kind, and the result, Mr. Bell observes, "was to make it appear that he, who was the quietest and most modest of men, had been outrageously self-important and vainglorious."

Miss Macaulay's essay conveys nicely Mrs. Woolf's pleasure in scandal ("Go on; this is enthralling. People keep telling me different bits of this story; I feel as if a buried statue were being dug up piece by piece") but does not mention a dinner party that she gave on the night of Wednesday, March 24, 1926: "The Woolfs were very late. [Again, I am quoting from Mr. Bell's biography.] They had been machining and they hurried from Tavistock Square without changing the clothes or removing all the printer's ink that they had on. Virginia had assumed that they would dine at what she called a 'pothouse'; but this was no Bloomsbury dinner. Miss Macaulay received her guests in a very superior establishment. There were a dozen guests, all ladies and gentlemen of letters, all in pearls and white waistcoats; there was a platoon of waiters to serve them. Leonard and Virginia were utterly unprepared for such a party; it was not the kind of party that they themselves would ever have given; they were conscious of being late, of having kept everyone waiting, of making a very bad impression. When Leonard was unnerved, the habitual trembling of his hands became wild and ungovernable. He now made conversation impossible by beating violently upon his soup plate."

The other contributions are for the most part repetitious in their attempts to describe Mrs. Woolf's appearance and her conversational flights, and to determine whether she was or was not malicious, and so on. There is so little that is freshly said or deeply felt, and they are all—even Eliot and Rose Macaulay and William Plomer—put to shame by Louie Mayer, the Woolfs' cook. Like Quentin Bell, she is writing from a special position: "The floors in Monk's House were very thin, the bathroom was directly above the kitchen and when Mrs. Woolf was having her bath before breakfast I could hear her talking to herself. On and on she went, talk, talk, talk: asking questions and giving herself the answers. I thought there must be two or three people up there with her."

Virginia Woolf was given to exclaiming "Life! Life!" in her novels and essays. Well, here it is—how Mrs. Woolf's relatives who lived nearby came to see her all the time, particularly her sister and her niece; how Mr. Woolf came into the kitchen every morning at eight o'clock to make the coffee; how her cigarettes were made from a special tobacco called My Mixture ("Mr. Woolf bought it for her in London and, in the evenings, they used to sit by the fire and make these cigarettes themselves"); how her bedroom was always outside the house in the garden ("I used to think how inconvenient it must be to have to go out in the rain to go to bed"); how there were pencils and paper beside her bed, and in the morning there would be pieces of paper, some of them containing the same sentence written over and over again, in heaps about the room; how a cow came one night and put its head through the window ("It amused Mrs. Woolf very much, but in case it happened again Mr. Woolf bought the field and added part of it to the garden. Then, because the writing-room was small, he had a larger one built for her at the end of the garden against the church wall. When it was finished, Mrs. Woolf had a beautiful view eastwards across the meadows to Mount Caburn, and that is where she used to sit every day and work"); how, if she began to develop bad headaches, he stopped all visitors from coming to the house and insisted that she have complete rest. ("I knew when Mrs. Woolf's health was reaching this stage because she used to come into the kitchen and sit down and wonder what it was she had come to tell me. Then she would go out into the garden and walk about very slowly as though trying to remember. I have seen her bump into trees while she walked, not really knowing what she was doing. There were times, too, when she looked exhausted after they had driven down from London. I think this was usually in the winter when it was very cold. She hated to feel cold at any time: it seemed to affect her in a strange way—almost to frighten her. They used to sit by a log fire and drink coffee until she was warm and felt better.")

Mrs. Mayer alone saw Virginia Woolf returning to the house from her garden room, with the letters that were found on the mantelpiece, and we are indebted to her for the only published description of all that happened afterward:

"When I rang the bell at 1 o'clock to tell Mr. Woolf that lunch was ready, he said he was going upstairs to hear the news on the radio and would only be a few minutes. The next moment he came running down the stairs to the kitchen calling me, 'Louie!' he said, 'I think

something has happened to Mrs. Woolf! I think she might have tried
to kill herself! Which way did she go—did you see her leave the house?'
'She went through the top gate a little while ago,' I said. It was suddenly a terrible nightmare. We ran out into the garden and I went to
find the gardener, in case he had seen Mrs. Woolf return. Mr. Woolf
went to the top gate and ran down towards the river. The gardener
had not seen Mrs. Woolf, so he went as fast as he could to find the
policeman on duty in the village. They both went down to the river
to see if they could help Mr. Woolf. He had found her walking-stick
stuck in the mud by the bank, but there was no sign of Mrs. Woolf.
They looked for her for a long time but there was nothing to tell
them where she was. Mr. Woolf wondered if she had left her stick there
to mislead them and had perhaps gone up to Shepherd's Cottage.
This was one of her favourite walks and it was possible she had gone
that way so that she could be alone, not knowing really what she was
doing. I went with him to Shepherd's Cottage, but she was not there.
We went back and looked for her along the water meadows, and the
river bank, and the brooks, until it was night-time and we had to
give up. There was nothing more that any of us could do."

77. I Knew a Woman

THEODORE ROETHKE

I knew a woman, lovely in her bones,
When small birds sighed, she would sigh back at them;
Ah, when she moved, she moved more ways than one:
The shapes a bright container can contain!
Of her choice virtues only gods should speak,
Or English poets who grew up on Greek
(I'd have them sing in chorus, cheek to cheek).

How well her wishes went! She stroked my chin,
She taught me Turn, and Counter-turn, and Stand;
She taught me Touch, that undulant white skin;
I nibbled meekly from her proffered hand;
She was the sickle; I, poor I, the rake,
Coming behind her for her pretty sake
(But what prodigious mowing we did make).

Love likes a gander, and adores a goose:
Her full lips pursed, the errant note to seize;
She played it quick, she played it light and loose;
My eyes, they dazzled at her flowing knees;
Her several parts could keep a pure repose,
Or one hip quiver with a mobile nose
(She moved in circles, and those circles moved).

Let seed be grass, and grass turn into hay:
I'm martyr to a motion not my own;
What's freedom for? To know eternity.
I swear she cast a shadow white as stone.
But who would count eternity in days?
These old bones live to learn her wanton ways:
(I measure time by how a body sways).

Suggestions for Writing

1. Defend, attack, or qualify what Cooley says about youth from your own experience, observation, and reading, using evidence also from Katz (pp. 256–264).

2. Using evidence from Coles, Kohl, De Angulo, and any other bursts of colloquial zest you may have observed among your friends or in this volume, write an essay concerning Steiner's statement about the raw precision of imagery, musical wealth, and absorptiveness of American speech (p. 442).

3. Look through Melville (pp. 158–172) and Cooley (pp. 3–5 and 439) for words and phrases that seem old-fashioned, and, on the other hand, for words and phrases that seem perfectly fresh. See what you can do with an essay considering what Steiner calls an equipoise "between genuine civilization and the energies of colloquial change," or on any aspect of change and permanence in language.

4. Write an essay on "The Sex Object," drawing some of your points from the attitudes and facts of Germaine Greer, White (and others in Section I), Nora Ephron, Diana Trilling, and Roethke.

5. Write an essay comparing the lives and personalities of Sylvia Plath (pp. 200–224), Marilyn Monroe, and Virginia Woolf.

XI.
Argument

The Shape of Thesis and Evidence

ARGUMENT is an intensified form of exposition; it uses whatever descriptive, narrative, and expository means it needs for its persuasive end. All other kinds of writing, as we have seen, lead toward argumentative propositions that may be openly stated or submerged. Indeed, any central idea is a kind of argumentative thesis for which the writer seeks your agreement and support. The presentation of thesis and evidence must have a shape. Since it flows through time, it must start somewhere, then arch through some middle fulfillment, and end with a sense of completion. It needs to coordinate a beginning, middle, and end.

Authors may exploit or mute this inescapable form in many ways. But we gain both as readers and writers if we can chart the essential patterns. Each of the authors in this section has a firm sense of form, setting forth a clear beginning, building his middle arch in smoothly fitted segments, and leaving us satisfied with a completed end. Young opens with an inductive thesis—what are the facts about Pocahontas, what does her story mean?—and proceeds through orderly sections to conclude with his most important finding, the grand meaning of it all. Making a brief outline of Young's major sections will strengthen your perception of form, as will doing the same for Foster.

Foster is also a master of paragraphing. Glance at the shape of his paragraphs, all more or less of a size. Then notice how each has its clear topic sentence (its beginning), each its smoothly fitted middle, each its firm concluding sentence or phrase. Nelson, a more casual writer, submerges his structural edges, though his sense of form is no less firm. Try to formulate a terse thesis-statement for him; then decide where you might place it to mark off an unmistakable beginning section. How does his paragraphing compare with Foster's? Einstein (with whom Nelson has some fun) shapes his essay with lucid simplicity, setting his thesis clearly at the end of his first paragraph. He then brings us to admire Kepler by explaining in simple language, and without diagrams, the essence of Kepler's difficult astronomical discovery. One also admires Einstein for the clarity of his prose. Einstein's ability here to lead our minds out to planetary space, and to help us picture an astronomical concept with a simple lantern and orderly steps, using words instead of diagrams, is remarkable.

78. The Mother of Us All: Pocahontas Reconsidered

PHILIP YOUNG

Young (1918–   ) is Research Professor of English at Pennsylvania State University. His *Ernest Hemingway* (1952), published only with Hemingway's reluctant permission, after extended efforts to block it, put forth the autobiographical nature of Hemingway's fiction, especially its common psychological basis in the shock of Hemingway's severe wounding, by mortar shell and machine-gun fire, agent to Italian soldiers in World War I. Young has been while distributing chocolate bars as Red Cross canteen appointed by Mrs. Mary Hemingway to assess and put into print Hemingway's unpublished manuscripts. His *The Adventures of Nick Adams* (1973) deals with several stories found among these papers.

"Were there two sides to Pocahontas?
Did she have a fourth dimension?"
　　　　　　—Ernest Hemingway

. . . having feasted him after their best barbarous manner they could, a long consultation was held, but the conclusion was, two great stones were brought before *Powhatan:* then as many as could layd hands on him, dragged him to them, and thereon laid his head, and being ready with their clubs, to beate out his braines, *Pocahontas* the Kings dearest daughter, when no intreaty could prevail, got his head in her armes, and laid her owne upon his to save him from death: whereat the Emperour was contented he should live to make him hatchets, and her bells, beads, and copper. . . .

OF COURSE IT MAY NEVER have happened at all and even if it did we think we may be a little tired of it. Yet three and a half centuries have elapsed, and this interminable sentence about an incident from the travels of Captain John Smith still lives. Americans, their literature swarming with its offspring, still without revulsion can summon up the old image: Smith pinned down by savages, his head on

471

a rock, all those clubs about to smash it; and the lovely Indian princess, curiously moved out from the crowd and across all the allegiances of her family, home and land, her religion and her race, lowering her head to his. Why can this commonplace, even banal, picture absorb us yet?

Shopworn by sentimentality, Pocahontas endures and stands with the most appealing of our saints. She has passed subtly into our folklore, where she lives as a popular fable—a parable taught children who carry some vague memory of her through their lives. She is an American legend, a woman whose actual story has blended with imaginary elements in time become traditional. Finally, she is one of our few, true native myths, for with our poets she has successfully attained the status of goddess, has been beatified, made holy, and offered as a magical and moving explanation of our national origins. What has happened to her story, why did it happen—and in fact what really was her story? It may be that our very familiarity with Pocahontas has kept us from looking at her closely enough to see what is there.

I

Even in the sketchiest of outlines, the story from which all the folklore and legends take off is a good one. As every schoolboy knows, the English arrived in Jamestown in 1607. During December of that year, while exploring the Chickahominy River, Smith—who had worked his way up from prisoner to leader of the expedition—was captured by men of chief Powhatan, and two of his companions were killed. It was at this time that he reputedly was rescued from death by the chief's favorite child, a young girl—no more than twelve or thirteen—called Pocahontas. Then, after what struck him as some very odd behavior on the part of the Indians, he was allowed to return to Jamestown, a place where—the great majority of its members dying within a year of their arrival—one of the most appalling casualty rates in history was being established. By placating Indians and planting corn, and with the help again of Pocahontas, who is said often to have brought supplies, and once to have come through the forest on a dark night to warn of an attack by her father, Smith is usually credited with having temporarily saved the colony. He gave the credit to her, however, as having done most, "next under God," to preserve the settlers.

The Captain returned to England in 1609, and in that year ships under Sir Thomas Gates brought relief to a group of people so desperate that one man had eaten his wife. The *Sea Venture,* flagship of the fleet, was wrecked in Bermuda, but its survivors somehow built a new vessel, and with it made Jamestown. One of its passengers was an Englishman named John Rolfe. Some time elapsed before he saw Pocahontas, because for a while she had no connection with the vicissitudes of the colonists. But in 1613, while visiting the chief of the Potomacs, she was tricked into captivity by an Indian bribed with a copper kettle, and taken as security for English men and equipment held by Powhatan. Now she met Rolfe, whose first wife had died in Virginia, and soon they expressed a desire to marry. Powhatan gave his approval but Rolfe had to get permission from his own superiors, and wrote Sir Thomas Dale a passionate, tedious letter protesting that he wished to marry Pocahontas despite, as he put it, her "rude education, manners barbarous and cursed generation," for the good of the plantation, the honor of England, the glory of God, and his own salvation—not "to gorge myself with incontinency" but, according to God's wish, to convert the girl. Even Smith had said that conversion was the first duty of the settlers; permission was granted. Dale gave the girl a good deal of religious instruction, christened her Rebecca—it was the first such conversion by the colonists—and in April of 1614 she and Rolfe were married.

Rolfe, it is generally believed, was primarily responsible for the production of the tobacco—detested by both King James and Smith—which made the colony permanent, and in 1616 he and his wife and their son Thomas were taken abroad by Dale to publicize the success of Jamestown. Thus it was that Pocahontas, less than six weeks after the death of William Shakespeare, arrived in England. In the party too was an Indian named Tomocomo, whom a thoughtful Powhatan had sent as a scout. He had a sheaf of sticks in which he was to place a notch for each white person he encountered, and some equally troublesome instruction to see this "God" about whom the English talked so much.

Pocahontas fared better, for a time. She was honored by the church and feted by the King and Queen, to whom Smith in glowing terms had commended her as his savior. James Stuart demanded to know if her commoner husband had not committed a treasonable act in marrying a princess. The Lady Rebecca became the toast of London, where alert pubs changed their names to "La Belle Sauvage." But not everything went well. She saw Smith again and was mysteriously displeased. Then while preparing for her return to Jamestown she was taken sick, very likely with smallpox, and died. She made a godly end, according to Smith, at the age of perhaps twenty-two, and was buried on the 21st of March, 1617, at Gravesend, on the banks of the Thames.

Her father survived her by only a year. Her husband returned to Virginia alone, married once again, and was killed four years later by Indians led by her uncle. Her son Thomas grew up in England, and then came back to this country to start the line of proud Virginians—of Jeffersons and Lees, of Randolphs, Marshalls, and an estimated two million other people—who to this day trace their ancestry back to the Indian girl. Smith transferred his affections to New England, which he named, but was never able to get the colonial job he wanted and died in bed in 1631. As for Pocahontas, the exact place of her burial is unknown, and the only tangible remains of her are a pair of earrings and a portrait, done in 1616, showing a dark and handsome if uncomfortable young lady, incongruously overdressed in English clothes.

There are other details of a more or less factual nature that have been added to this story by people who knew Pocahontas, or who wrote of her during her lifetime. Smith himself supplies some of them. It is he who describes that day in England when he somehow so upset her, and she "turned about, obscured her face," on seeing him—an event which, since Smith either could not explain it or did not wish to, has tantalized generations of romantics.

There is also the testimony of Samuel Purchas, who was present when Pocahontas was received by the Lord-Bishop of London with even more pomp than was accorded other great ladies of the time, and who records in *Hakluytus Posthumus* or *Purchas his Pilgrimes* (1625) the impressive dignity with which the young lady received her honors. And in his *True Discourse of the Present Estate of Virginia* (1615) Ralph Hamor put down the pious details of her conversion and marriage.

But not all these additions conform to the somewhat stuffy reputation that has been built for her. Smith, for instance, coldly comments that he might have married the girl himself—or "done what he listed" with her. He also supplies a colorful but usually neglected incident relating how she and "her women" came one day "naked out of the woods, onely covered behind and before with a few green leaves . . . singing and dauncing with most excellent ill varietie, oft falling into their infernall passions"; and also tells how, later, "all these Nymphes more tormented him than ever, with crowding, pressing and hanging about him, most tediously crying, Love you not me?"

In addition, William Strachey, in his *Historie of Travaile into Virginia Britannia,* written about 1615, supplies information which does not appear in Sunday School versions of the story. The first secretary of America's oldest colony and the friend of great poets, including Donne, Jonson, and probably Shakespeare, Strachey disturbs the tender-hearted by noting that Rolfe's future bride is already married, to a "private captaine, called Kocoum." Even worse is his description of Pocahontas in earlier days as a "well-featured but wanton yong girle" who used to come to the fort and "get the boyes forth with her into the markett place, and make them wheele, falling on their hands, turning their heels upwards, whome she would followe and wheele so herselfe, naked as she was, all the fort over."

These are all the important sources of the Pocahontas story. Strachey's intelligence was not published until some 234 years after he wrote. Smith's swashbuckling accounts of his own adventures were taken as gospel for even longer, though for quite a while the story of Pocahontas had very little circulation, and was seldom repeated outside a couple of books on Virginia. But when about the start of the nineteenth century

Americans began to search intensely for their history the romance was resurrected, and Pocahontas began to loom large as the guardian angel of our oldest colony. Exaggerating even Smith's accounts of her, historians entered into a quaint struggle to outdo each other with praise, concentrating of course on the rescue story. Considering the flimsiness of the evidence, it is odd that for a long time no one seems to have entertained the slightest doubt of its authenticity. On all sides, instead, sprung up the most assiduous and vigilant defense of the lady. Here the case of the Honorable Waddy Thompson is instructive. Poor Thompson, who had been our minister to Mexico, published in 1846 his "Recollections" of that place, and in his desire to praise a girl named Marina, "the *chère amie* and interpreter of Cortez," he let slip a remark he must have regretted the rest of his days. He said that Pocahontas was "thrown into the shade" by her.

The response to these imprudent words was dreadful; an anonymous Kentuckian rushed into print a whole pamphlet Vindicating her Memory. He appealed to all Virginians, to all Americans, and finally "to the admirers of virtue, humanity, and nobleness of soul, wherever to be found," against this Erroneous Judgment. Pocahontas had every gift Marina possessed, and—no *chère amie*—she had also, he added, her "good name." Indeed, it is not possible to improve on her, and to demonstrate either this or his scholarship the gentleman from Kentucky appended long accounts of her from the work of twenty-six historians, including French, German, and Italian representatives. Her character is "not surpassed by any in the whole range of history" is one estimate.

The author of this pamphlet also spoke of "proof" that Pocahontas rescued Smith, which he called "one of the most incontestable facts in history": "The proof is, the account of it given by Captain Smith, a man incapable of falsehood or exaggeration . . . hundreds of eye-witnesses . . . and to this may be added tradition." Here the gentleman defends, somewhat ineptly, what no man is known to have attacked, despite the fact that there have always been excellent reasons for contesting the rescue. For one thing, the Captain had a real inclination toward this sort of tale. His *Generall Historie* of 1624, which tells the full story for the first time, reveals a peculiar talent for being "offered rescue and protection in my greatest dangers" by various "honorable and vertuous Ladies." Most striking of these is the Lady Tragabigzanda, who fell in love with him when he was in bondage, not this time to her father but to her husband, the powerful Bashaw Bogall of Constantinople. She delivered him from this slavery, and sent him to her brother, "till time made her Master of her selfe"—before which, however, Smith made a fantastic escape.

Then, much worse and apparent from the beginning, there is the well-known fact that Smith's *True Relation* of 1608, which tells of his capture by Powhatan, and speaks also of the chief's kindness and assurances of early release, contains no mention at all of any rescue. He had plenty of other opportunities to tell the story, too, but neither he nor anyone else who wrote on Jamestown is known to have referred to the event until 1622, when he remarked in his *New England Trials,* which includes his third version of his capture: "God made Pocahontas the King's daughter the means to deliver me." Then in 1624 when his *Generall Historie* was published he told the story as we know it, and also printed for the first time his letter of eight years before to Queen Anne.

The obvious inference here is that if the rescue was actually performed Smith would have said so in the first place or, if he had not, would have told the story to others who would have repeated it. His *Historie* is boastful; it is hard to know how much of it he may have made up or borrowed from other travelers of the period. And there was a historical precedent for the Pocahontas tale: the story of a soldier, Juan Ortiz, who was lost on an expedition to Florida in 1528 and was found there by De Soto about twelve years later. Ortiz said he had been captured by Indians, and saved at the last second from burning at the stake by the chief's daughter, who later came at night in peril of her life to warn him of her father's plot to kill him. This story had appeared in London, in an English translation by Richard Hakluyt, in 1609, the year of Smith's return to that city.

Despite all grounds for suspicion, however, Smith's tale went unchallenged for well over two centuries—until about 1860, that is, when two historians, Edward D. Neill (who became known as the scavenger of Virginia history) and Charles Deane, began to make what now seem the obvious objections. These men were quickly joined by others, and in order to publicize Deane's case there entered the cause no less an intellect than that of Henry Adams. Writing anonymously in the *North American Review* in 1867, Adams lowered his biggest guns and patiently blasted what he called "the most romantic episode" in our history into what must have seemed to him and his crushed readers total oblivion. Henry Cabot Lodge concurred that the rescue belongs to fiction. Many other great men expressed themselves on the question, and quickly it became the custom to speak of the Pocahontas "legend."

Other historians, however, rushed to the defense. Chief among these were John Fiske, the philosopher and historian, and William Wirt Henry. Fiske in 1879 flatly dismissed the dismissals, and went on to champion the story. Why is it not in the *True Relation* of 1608? Because the editor of that work had obeyed an injunction against printing anything that might discourage potential colonists, and in a preface had explained that Smith had written "somewhat more" than was being published. Certainly the Captain was not allowed simply to go free, after having killed two Indians. The rescue by Pocahontas was quite in accordance with Indian custom. Any member of a tribe had a right to claim a prisoner as son or lover—but how could Smith have known enough about this to invent the tale? That scene in which he describes the weird behavior of his captors following his rescue was clearly a ceremony of adoption into the tribe, the natural consequence of Pocahontas' act. Why didn't Smith tell the story to his compatriots? Because he feared that if they knew the favor of an Indian woman was possible they would desert.

And so the battle, which continues to the present day, was on. There is a rebuttal. Why for example censor from Smith's first book a charming rescue story (which might cause desertions) and include as the editor did an excessively discouraging description of one of Smith's companions, "John Robbinson slaine, with 20 or 30. arrowes" in him? There is no easy answer to that. But, after the short period of the story's disrepute (conveniently passed in time for the Jamestown Tercentenary of 1907), wide acceptance ruled again—especially with proudly celebrating Virginians, who appeared to have forgotten that by their rules the girl was colored. Credence in the story, however, is of course not limited to the South. Indeed by 1957, when the 350th anniversary of the founding was elaborately solemnized, most Americans, including a majority of the published authorities, seemed to subscribe to the tale as fact. For the celebrations Paul Green wrote a "Symphonic Outdoor Drama" called *The Founders,* in which the key events of the young lady's life took on the force of ritual observance in performances at Williamsburg. Since the evidence is not decisive, perhaps everybody has a right to believe as he wishes.

II

Exactly what happened would not seem to make any enormous difference anyway. What counts more is the truly extraordinary way in which the story—despite the profound awkwardness of a climax that comes in the very opening scene—pervades our culture. Pocahontas is represented in countless paintings and monuments; she gives her name to ships, motels, coal mines, towns, counties, and pseudonymous writers, to secret orders and business firms. There are histories of her and Smith by everyone from poet (John Gould Fletcher) to politician ("Alfalfa Bill" Murray, a descendant). But all other signs of her fade before the plays, poems, novels, and children's books which for the last 150 years have flooded our literature. Dramatizing the story from the alleged facts, and filling gaps or inadequacies with invented material usually presented as fact, there are so many different treatments, ranging from the serious to the absurd, that they begin to look numberless.

But they fall into patterns. The first person to make literary use of Pocahontas was no less a writer than the rare Ben Jonson, who included an obscure reference to her in his *Staple of News* of 1625. Then, much later, she was treated at length in a little novel called *The Female American* (1767). Here the story as we know it is, however, simply a rehearsal for far greater events, and the really memorable thing about the book is that its author was an English lady known as Unca Eliza Winkfield, who changed Pocahontas' name to Unca, and Smith's to Winkfield, and gave her a daughter called, once more, Unca.

The writer who really started things, by first romanticizing the story in a proper way, was still another Englishman—an adventuresome fellow named John Davis, a sailor who came to this country in 1798 and spent nearly five years traveling about on foot. Very young and romantic, hyperthyroid, chronically tumescent and rather charming, Davis wrote a book about his journey called *Travels of Four Years and a Half in the United States of America*. As a part of this work he "delivered to the world" the history of Pocahontas which, he announced, was reserved for his pen. Possessed of a lively and libidinous imagination, which he seemed unable to distinguish from his written sources, Davis tore into the story with hearty masculine appetite.

He begins with Smith in the hands of Powhatan, who keeps offering his prisoner a woman. The squaws fight fiercely for the honor, but to Pocahontas' "unspeakable joy" Smith is stern and turns them all down. After she has rescued him she comes to Jamestown, weeping "in all the tumultuous extasy of love." In order to cure her Smith slips off to England, instructing his compatriots to tell the girl he has died. She prostrates herself on his empty grave, beats her bosom, and utters piercing cries. One night while she is strewing flowers about his resting place she is come upon by Rolfe, secretly in love with her and of late much given to taking moonlight walks while composing love poems. ("Of these effusions I have three in my possession," says Davis, and he prints them.) Surprised by Rolfe's appearance, Pocahontas inadvertently falls in his arms, whereupon he seizes his opportunity and drinks from her lips "the poison of delight." A woman is "never more susceptible of a new passion than when agitated by the remains of a former one," is Davis' dark but profitable explanation, and thus it is that hours later, come dawn, Rolfe "still rioted in the draught of intoxication from her lips." Eventually they marrry ("nor did satiety necessarily follow from fruition," the author adds anxiously). They go to England, and Pocahontas dies there.

Davis made it clear that he wrote as a historian: "I have adhered inviolably to facts; rejecting every circumstance that had not evidence to support it," he insisted, speaking of "recourse to records and original papers." The man was too modest, for of course these were, like Rolfe's poems, original enough but with him. And he should be given credit too for having seen the possibilities of uniting richly embroidered history with a mammary fixation (habitually the bosoms of his Indian women are either "throbbing" or "in convulsive throes"). That he did see the promise of this combination, and in advance of his time, is indicated by the fact that he himself soon wrote what he called a "historical novel" on "Pokahontas." The book is formally titled *First Settlers of Virginia* (1806), but it simply pads the previous account of the girl's adventures to novel length. Dropping Rolfe's claim to the poetry, Davis managed to add a couple of mildly pornographic native scenes, to use Smith's story of the enamored Indian girls ("Love you not me?") twice, and to present Pochahontas as "unrobed" in her first scene with Rolfe. He also prefaced a second edition with a letter from Thomas Jefferson to the effect that the President of the United States "subscribed with pleasure" to this Indian Tale.

After Davis, the deluge. This began with a vast number of plays now mostly lost, but including four prominent and commercially successful ones which are preserved. To James Nelson Barker, ex-mayor of Philadelphia and future first controller of the Treasury in Van Buren's cabinet, goes a series of firsts: his *Indian Princess* of 1808 (although anticipated in 1784 by the little-known German *Pocahontas* of Johann Wilhelm Rose) was the first important Pocahontas play and the first to be produced of the Indian plays which soon threatened to take over our stage completely; it is generally cited also as the first American play to appear in London after opening in this country. Hugely popular, and rather deservedly so, Barker's success was followed by that of George Washington Parke Curtis, step-grandson of our first president, with his *Pocahontas* of 1830, and by Robert Dale Owen. The latter, son of the more famous Robert Owen, founder of the radical Owenite communities, and himself a very early advocate of birth control, the free discussion of sex, and the rights of women, made his Pocahontas (1837) an anachronistic feminist. His play, though over-long, is not incompetent and reads very well beside *The Forest Princess* (1844) of Charlotte Barnes Conner. Mrs. Conner, an actress, stuck close to the worst nineteenth-century concepts of theatre and produced a series of unlikely postures which are epitomized in her final scene, where a pious Rebecca dying in England, hand stretched heavenward, speaks her last iambics:

> I hear my father—Husband, fare thee well.
> We part—but we shall meet—above!

after which the hand drops with the curtain.

John Brougham's *Pocahontas* (1855) was honorably designed to stop this sort of thing, and his travesty did stop the production of "serious" Pocahontas plays for quite a time, greatly diminishing the popularity of the Indian drama to boot. But today his play is, to speak politely, "dated," for the humor depends mainly on puns ("What *iron* fortune *led* you to our shores?" "To now ill-use us would be base *illusion!*") (italics his), line after line for two long acts.

Brougham's burlesque was extremely well-received, however, and it performed a service for our drama that nothing has adequately performed for our poetry. Pocahontas poems, produced in the nineteenth century by the carload, are almost uniformly dull, tasteless, and interminable. The efforts of Lydia Huntly Sigourney and William Makepeace Thackeray stand out only a little from the average. Most nineteenth century Pocahontas poems seem to begin either with some silly sylvan scene or with "Descend O Muse, and this poor pen . . ." Smith always arrives as expected, but the Muse invariably has other things to do.

Equally forbidding are the Pocahontas poems written in the manner of Henry Wadsworth Longfellow. Longfellow neglected to produce any Pocahontas items himself, but there are a great many poems, and several plays in verse, which have sought to rectify his oversight. These pieces are all distinguished by lines of unrimed trochaic tetrameter ("By the shore of Gitche Gumee / By the shining Big-Sea-Water") which produce a stultifying effect the poets seem to equate with an Indian atmosphere; they suffer from what might properly be known as the Curse of Hiawatha. Of course Longfellow got his famous Hiawatha line from a German translation of a national epic of the Finns, but this is not known to have stopped anyone, and on they go:

> Then the maiden Pocahontas
> Rushes forward, none can stop her,
> Throws her arms about the captive,
> Cries,—"oh spare him! Spare the Paleface!"

What burlesque and abuse cannot destroy will just have to wear itself out. Although the machinery that mass-produces low-quality Pocahontas literature has long shown signs of collapse, the end is not yet. As recently as 1958 a Pocahontas novel by one Noel B. Gerson, with nothing to recommend it but the story, was smiled on by a very large book club. And so still they come with the story, juggling the climax or devising a new one, and trying to make up somehow for the fact that Smith never married the girl. Both problems can of course be solved at once by ending with the scene from Smith in which he and Pocahontas meet in London. Here Rebecca is overcome at the sight of her lost Captain and dies in his arms, usually of a broken heart; indeed it has become a convention to do it that way. But that has not helped, and it is the plays, particularly, which indicate that an industry really is exhausted. The best written and most interesting parts of their scripts are those that deal with such matters as the construction of campfires with electric fans, logs, and strips of red cloth.

One last sign of the popular Pocahontas drama's waning was the appearance (once Brougham was well-forgotten) of an Everything but the Kitchen Sink School. There exists, for instance, an operetta in which Smith has a "regulation negro" servant, comically named Mahogany, who plays a banjo. A better sample is the *Pocahontas* (1906) of Edwin O. Ropp. Mr. Ropp named three of his Indians Hiawatha, Minnehaha, and Geronimo; and there is a rough spot in the action when a man named simply Roger (Williams?), insisting on the freedom of religious thought, disappears for good in the Virginia forest. As for Pocahontas, she is taken through her marriage with Rolfe, to England and back again to Virginia, where she lives out her days in the wilderness with her husband, two children, and their Christian grandpapa, Powhatan, singing the praises of home sweet home, as the play ends with lines lifted from the poem of that name. Mr. Ropp dedicated his play, it should be recorded, to a Moral Purpose, to the Jamestown Exposition of 1907, and to Those Who Construct the Panama Canal. The world was ready for another burlesque when, in 1918, Philip Moeller published his *Beautiful Legend of the Amorous Indian.* In this play only one character, the senile mother of Powhatan, speaks Hiawathan, and there is a heart-warming moment in the dialogue when Powhatan's wife says of her aging mother-in-law: "When she talks in that old manner it nearly drives me crazy."

III

It is not hard to find reasons for the low quality of a large part of our Pocahontas literature: the writers had no talent, for instance. A less obvious difficulty has been that most of the poets and playwrights have prided themselves that their works were founded firmly on "historical sources." This impeded the imaginations of most of them, who tried to romanticize history instead of letting the facts act as a stimulus to fiction. As a result of sentimentality and inaccuracy, there is little or no historical value in their products. And because the works are based so solidly on "history," often footnoted, they seldom have any value as fiction, for invariably events are related not because they are dramatic but because they happened—which is aesthetically irrelevant. If the story is to satisfy a modern audience, it must be treated imaginatively.

Properly told it could be a truly epic story. This is indicated by the fact that elements in the relationships of the characters are so like those in other epics of other countries—the *Aeneid*, for instance. Aeneas, we recall, was an adventurer who also sought a westward land and finally anchored at the mouth of a river. The country there was ruled by a king, Latinus, who had a beautiful daughter, Lavinia. Latinus had dreamed that his daughter's husband would come from a foreign land, and that from this union would spring a race destined to rule the world, so he received Aeneas and feasted him. Later tradition goes on to record the marriage, the birth of a son, and the founding of the city in which Romulus and Remus were born. Other parallels—with the stories of Odysseus and Nausicaa, and of Jason and Medea—likewise suggest the epic possibilities of the American tale.

To be sure, a few writers, usually in a far more modest fashion, have tried to make something of Pocahontas. Fewer still have succeeded, but even some of the failures are interesting. Working from the probability that a letter by Strachey, who was on the wrecked *Sea Venture* with Rolfe, provided Shakespeare with material for *The Tempest,* John Esten Cooke wrote a polite novel called *My Lady Pocahontas* (1885) in which he made Shakespeare dependent on the lady and Smith for his characters Miranda and Ferdinand. At the climax, Pocahontas recognizes herself on the stage of the Globe.

Much of this invention has been blithely repeated as history, but such an attempt at legend fails anyway for being too literary. Other attempts have failed for not being literary enough. Mary Virginia Wall in 1908 wrote a book on Pocahontas as *The Daughter of Virginia Dare—* the child, that is, of this first native-born "American," who mysteriously disappeared, and Powhatan. Thus it is the spirit of Virginia Dare which accounts for the Indian girl's compassion. Now this could be a fruitful merger, uniting two of our best stories and giving Americans a kind of spiritual genealogy. The fact that to have been Pocahontas' mother Virginia would have had to bear a child at eight does not really matter much. But such scenes as the one in which the daughter comes to her end matter a good deal. On her deathbed, a place that has proved scarcely less fatal for authors than for their heroine, Pocahontas stoutly carols "Hark the Herald Angel Sings" (the Amen "begun on earth and ending in heaven"), and what started with some small promise has backed all the way out of it.

Another, but much better, novel which tries to do something with the story is the *Pocahontas* (1933) of David Garnett. This is a good historical novel with a thesis. In scenes of hideous but authentic brutality, Garnett shows the Indian women torturing their naked prisoners to death in orgies of obscene cruelty. These lead directly to orgies of sexual passion which act as a purge. To this sequence he contrasts the cruelty of the whites, which they sanction with self-righteousness and piety and follow with guilt. Garnett's book is a romantic and primitivistic performance after the manner of D. H. Lawrence which uses Pocahontas, more tender than her compatriots, as a vehicle for a lesson on the superiority of uncivilized peoples. Doctrinaire, and intellectually a little sentimental, this is still probably the best Pocahontas novel.[1]

---

[1] It is not nearly so good as John Barth's *The Sot-Weed Factor* (1960), but this unprecedented novel is only incidentally about Pocahontas. Included in it, however, are John Smith's *Secret Historie,* parallel—but far superior—to John Davis' discovery of John Rolfe's poems, and the *Privie Journall* of a rival character. In the course of these extended tours-de-force a tribal custom is revealed that requires a prospective suitor to take the maidenhead of his bride before marrying her. In the case of Pocahontas no man has been successful in fracturing this membrane (indeed "most had done them selves hurt withal, in there efforts"). But with the aid of a fantastically invigorating vegetable device Smith publicly accomplishes the feat. In its review of the book, entitled "Novelist Libels Pocahontas Story," the *Richmond News-Leader* demanded to know if, in view of the respectability of the lady's descendants, all this was not "actionable."

Equally good, or maybe better, are two twentieth-century plays, Margaret Ullman's *Pocahontas* (1912) and Virgil Geddes' *Pocahontas and the Elders* (1933). More interesting than the plays themselves, however, are prefatory remarks their authors made about their material. In an introductory quotation Miss Ullman speaks of her heroine as a "Sweet-smelling sacrifice to the good of Western Planting." Geddes writes that his play is a "folkpiece" and his characters "part of the soul's inheritance." Both writers, in other words, were pointing to some pregnant quality of the story which goes beyond its facts. This was a direction which an informal group of modern poets was taking too. The result was the elevation of Pocahontas to myth.

It is Vachel Lindsay who was primarily responsible for this development. In his "Cool Tombs" Carl Sandburg had asked a question:

> Pocahontas' body, lovely as a poplar, sweet
> as a red haw in November or a pawpaw in May—
> did she wonder? does she remember—in the
> dust—in the cool tombs?

About 1918 Lindsay quoted this passage, answered yes, she remembers, and went on to explain in a poem which transforms the savior of Jamestown into a symbol of the American spirit. He supplies a magical genealogy whereby the girl becomes, as in his title, "Our Mother Pocahontas." Powhatan is the son of lightning and an oak; his daughter is the lover and bride of the forest. Thus

> John Rolfe is not our ancestor.
> We rise from out the soul of her
> Held in native wonderland,
> While the sun's rays kissed her hand,
> In the springtime,
> In Virginia,
> Our mother, Pocahontas.

Though she died in England, Lindsay acknowledges, she returned to Virginia and walked the continent, "Waking, / Thrilling, / The midnight land," and blending with it. We in turn are born not of Europe but of her, like a crop, and we are sustained by our inheritance.

One statement does not make a myth, but this concept was passed to other poets, notably to Hart Crane. First, though, came William Carlos Williams. A part of his prose study of the national past, called *In the American Grain* (1925), was devoted to an excoriation of the Puritans, after the fashion of the '20s, and to praise for the sensual joy of the Indians, who are again taken over as an element of our spiritual ancestry. Williams gave only brief notice to Pocahontas, but he quoted Strachey's description of a naked, wheeling Indian girl.

These are the materials from which Crane, in *The Bridge* (1930), raised Pocahontas to full mythic stature. In some notes he made for the poem, Crane saw her as "the natural body of American fertility," the land that lay before Columbus "like a woman, ripe, waiting to be taken." He followed his notes, and the part of his long poem called "Powhatan's Daughter" develops them. Starting with the quotation from Strachey (which he took from a *transition* review of Williams by Kay Boyle) the poet in a waking dream at the harbor dawn finds someone with him ("Your cool arms murmurously about me lay . . . *a forest shudders in your hair!*"). She disappears, then, from his semiconsciousness to reappear later as the American continent, most familiar to hoboes who "know a body under the wide rain," as the poet himself is familiar with trains that "Wail into distances I knew were hers." The land blooms with her, she becomes a bride (but "virgin to the last of men"), passes herself then to a pioneer mother, a living symbol of the fertility of the land, and makes her last appearance as the earth again—"our native clay . . . red, eternal flesh of Pocahontas. . . ."

Like these four poets, Archibald MacLeish in his *Frescoes for Mr. Rockefeller's City* (1933) was discovering his own land and his faith in its future. Dedicating his book to Sandburg, and deriving a symbol from Crane, MacLeish describes a "Landscape as a Nude"—the American continent as a beautiful naked Indian girl, inviting lovers. With this repetition the concept has taken hold. Thus we have a sort of American Ceres, or Demeter, or Gaea, developed from Pocahontas—a fertility-goddess, the mother of us all. We, by our descent from her, become a new race, innocent of both European and all human origins—a race from the earth, as in ancient mythologies of other lands, but an earth that is made of her. We take on a brave, free, mythical past as our alternative to the more prosaic, sordid explanation of history. And the thing is alive, as an image of the beautiful Indian girl is set in perpetual motion, and comes cartwheeling through our veins and down our generations.

IV

For all our concern with Pocahontas, one of the most interesting facts about her seems to have escaped everyone: the story John Smith told, which we have embraced so long, is one of the oldest stories known to man—not just roughly speaking, as in the Odysseus and Aeneas myths, but precisely in all essential parts. The tale of an adventurer, that is, who becomes the captive of the king of another country and another faith, and is rescued by his beautiful daughter, a princess who then gives up her land and her religion for his, is a story known to the popular literatures of many peoples for many centuries. The theme was so common in the Middle Ages that medieval scholars have a name for it: "The Enamoured Moslem Princess." This figure is a woman who characteristically offers herself to a captive Christian knight, the prisoner of her father, rescues him, is converted to Christianity, and goes to his native land—these events usually being followed by combat between his compatriots and hers.[2]

This is, for instance, the substance of a fifteenth-century French story about *un seigneur de Jagov* who went with a German army to Turkey, was imprisoned and sold as a slave to a *grand seigneur Turk,* whose daughter intervenes in the usual fashion and is converted to Christianity. There is also a medieval story, with roots in the legends of Charlemagne, called *The Sowdone of Babylone*—of Laban, the Sultan, and his daughter Floripas.[3] In the tenth book of Ordericus Vitalis' *Historia Ecclesiastica,* whose origins are in the twelfth century, the story is the same—this time about a Frenchman, Bohemond, his Turkish captor, Daliman, and his daughter Melaz. It is the same in a romance in which Elie de Saint Gille, a Frank, is carried from Brittany, captive of the amil (prince) Macabré, to the land of the Saracens, where Rosamonde, the amil's daughter, betrays her father, saves Elie, is converted and baptized. There are many other similar old stories: one called "The Turkish Lady and the English Slave"; another, a Balkan ballad, called "Marko Kraljević and the Arab King's Daughter"; still another involving *two* Magyars who are shut in a dungeon by a sultan, then freed by his daughter. The popularity of the tale is further indicated by its inclusion in the *Arabian Nights,* whose origins fade into ancient folklore. Here it appears as an interlude in the longer "Tale of Kamar al-Zaman." Bostán, the beautiful Magian daughter of Bahram, rescues As'ad from her father and is converted to Mohammedanism. Another version, once popular, is in the *Gesta Romanorum,* a collection of "Entertaining Moral Stories" compiled about 1300 from much older but obscure sources. These Latin anecdotes, which contain the germs of plots used by Chaucer and Shakespeare, were widely read in translation in late sixteenth-century England (hence Smith may have known them). Tale V, called "Of Fidelity," is about a youth wasting away as a prisoner of pirates. Their chief has a lovely

---

[2] See, for instance, F. M. Warren, "The Enamoured Moslem Princess in Orderic Vital and the French Epic," *PMLA,* XXIX (1914), 341–58. It is a mistake, however, to speak of this theme as if it where wholly a matter of the distant past. For instance, the Enamoured Moslem Princess figures prominently in the Fourth Canto (1821) of Byron's *Don Juan.* Here she is Haidée, whose mother was a Moor; her father is Lambro, a pirate leader who holds the Christian Juan captive. The chieftain is about to kill his prisoner "When Haidée threw herself her boy before; / . . . 'On me,' she cried, 'let death descend. . . .' " Juan is saved, but is taken off, and Haidée withers away and dies.

[3] The same story, dramatized, is still performed once a year in Portugal, and has its own historical parallel in Brazilian history. See Vianna Moog, *Bandeirantes e Pioneiros, Parelelo entre Duas Culturas,* Pôrto Alegre, Globo, 1955, pp. 97–103. For that matter, there is an Oriental historical analogue: during the seventeenth century Hindu-Muslim wars around Delhi, the Muslim princess Zebunnisha saved, in 1664, the rebel Hindu prince Shivaji from her father, Alamgir. They never married. Like the Pocahontas rescue, this incident is frequently used in historical romances of India.

and virtuous daughter who frees the young man and, being promised marriage, goes to his country. The origins of this version may be in Seneca the Elder, who at the beginning of the Christian era formulated precisely the same situation in his *Controversia* as an imaginary legal case for debate. It is possible that he in turn got the story from the Greek Sophists, who had a lively interest in literature and disputation. There is no telling where they may have learned it, but something very like it is in the ancient Greek myth of Ariadne, the daughter of Minos, king of Crete, who rescued an Athenian named Theseus from a labyrinth where her father had imprisoned him to be eaten by the Minotaur, and then went away with him.

It has always been an uncomfortable fact of the Pocahontas story, and an apparently formidable obstacle to its survival, that after appearing to offer herself to Smith the heroine never married the hero. It is a startling fact, and bewildering, that this curiosity has been an element of the story from the beginning. Though Ariadne had deserted her parents and motherland for Theseus, he for some unknown reason abandoned her by the shore of the sea and sailed away; she later married Dionysus. Orderic's Melaz did not marry Bohemond, but his younger friend Roger. In the tale of Kamar al-Zaman, Bostán marries not As'ad but his brother. Floripas, the Sowdone's daughter, also marries someone other than the man for whom she betrayed her father. Elie de Saint Gille never married Rosamonde; since Szilágyi Niklas says he has a love at home that Sultan's daughter has to settle for the other Magyar, his companion; though he was later remorseful, Marko neglected the Arab king's daughter after his escape. In a few versions one is left to supply his own denouement, and may presume if he wishes that the hero and heroine marry and live happily ever after. But it is extremely curious that there appear to be no accounts in which we are told specifically that what we might expect invariably to happen actually happens.[4]

The presence of a disturbing element in a popular story is hard to explain. The notion that melodies unheard are sweetest and cannot fade, that the lover who has not his bliss then can love forever and she be fair

---

[4] The widely known and excellent ballad called "Young Beichan" seems an exception, but only because a new element, the motif of promised marriage, has been grafted on. Beichan is London-born, and longs strange lands for to see, but is taken by a savage Moor whose daughter, Susan Pye, steals her father's keys and releases him from a prison, after which he goes back to England, having promised to marry the girl in seven years. Later she abandons her country for England, is converted to Christianity, and gets a new name. She arrives in England to discover that Young Beichan has just married. But the ceremony is not yet consummated ("of her body I am free") and Susie Pye, now Lady Jane, is able to marry him after all. F. J. Child prints fourteen versions of this ballad in his *English and Scottish Popular Ballads,* while mentioning many related items in Norse, Spanish, Italian, and German. In its various forms it may have been affected by a fairly well-known legend on more or less the same theme, originating in the thirteenth century and concerning Gilbert Becket, father of St. Thomas à Becket. This also has the happy ending.

does not seem to account for this peculiarity; it was never that way at all. Yet there must be something obscurely "right" about an apparently unsatisfactory ending, or over the many centuries we should have succeeded in changing it. And the durable popularity of the story also urges the presence of some appeal that is not on the surface, some force that has given an advantage in the struggle for survival which we should make out if we can. The notion that the story is symbolic of something is not new. The monks who used it for religious instruction hundreds of years ago sensed this and had their own reading: the young man, they said, represents the human race. Led irresistibly by the force of original sin into the prison of the devil, he is redeemed by Christ, in the form of the girl. But this interpretation incongruously makes Jesus the daughter of Satan, and seems also a little arbitrary. It is too utilitarian—but in that it offers one clue to the story's longevity.

Nothing survives indefinitely without filling some function, and the usefulness of this story is clear: the tale approves and propagates the beliefs of anyone who cares to tell it. An informal survey of the children's sections of two small Midwestern libraries disclosed twenty-six different books on Pocahontas—and no wonder. Quite apart from the opportunity she presents to give children some notion of self-sacrifice, she is, in addition to all her other appeals, perfectly ideal propaganda for both church and state. The story has long been, among other things, a tale of religious conversion, and in its American form is so eloquent a tribute to accepted institutions that there is no need to deflate its power by so much as even mentioning the obvious lesson it teaches. Of course the thing is a little chauvinistic. It is always either indifferent to the attitudes of the betrayed or unconscious of them. Indeed it is a tribute to the high regard we have for ourselves that Pocahontas has never once been cast as a villainess, for she would make an excellent one. From the point of view of her own people her crimes—repeated acts of treason, and cultural and religious apostasy—were serious. But one does not resent a betrayal to his own side, and we can always bear reassuring: love exists, love matters, and we are very eligible, Pocahontas tells us.

The story will work for any culture, informing us, whoever we are, that we are chosen, or preferred. Our own ways, race, religion must be better—so much better that even an Indian (Magian, Moor, Turk), albeit an unusually fine one (witness her recognition of our superiority), perceived our rectitude. But it nicely eases the guilt we have felt since the start of its popularity over the way we had already begun, by 1608, to treat the Indians. Pocahontas is a female Quanto, a "good" Indian, and by taking her to our national bosom we experience a partial absolution. In the lowering of her head we feel a benediction. We are so wonderful she loved us anyway.

And yet the story has an appeal which easily transcends such crude and frequently imperialistic functions—especially in the rescue scene, which implies all the new allegiances that follow from it. There is a picture there, at least in the American rendering, which has compelled us for so long that it must certainly contain meanings that go beyond the illustrations of it in the children's books. It is characteristic of all hallowed images that they cannot adequately be put into words, and no single rendering would articulate all that might be stated anyway. But these are feeble excuses for total silence, and it does not take any great sensitivity to perceive that Pocahontas' gesture—accomplished not by any subterfuge, but by the frank placing of her own body between Smith's and death—is fairly ringing with overtones. This is because we see her act as a rite, a ceremonial sign which bestows life. A surface part of that symbolism has always been clear. The Indians understood it as we do, and immediately Smith was alive and free. But what we have not been conscious of, though the modern poets sensed something like it, is that her candor was that of a bride. That is one thing, buried beneath awareness, that has dimly stirred us. Unable to put it into words, we have let the girl keep her secret, but the ritual that we feel in her action is itself an unorthodox and dramatic ceremony of marriage, and we are touched. We see Pocahontas at the moment of womanhood, coming voluntarily from the assembly to the altar, where she pledges the sacrifice of her own integrity for the giving of life. This is an offering up of innocence to experience, a thing that is always—in our recognition of its necessity— oddly moving. It is an act which bespeaks total renunciation, the giving up of home, land, faith, self, and perhaps even life, that life may go on.

Perhaps this helps to explain why it is that what, in its flattery of him, is at first glance so much a man's story should also be greatly promoted by women. Apparently it is a very pleasant vicarious experience for us all. Yet in the depths of our response to the heart of the story, the rescue, there is something more profoundly wishful than a simple identification with persons in a touching adventure. All myths have an element of wish somewhere in them. But there is something about this one that is also wistful, as though it expressed a wish that did not really expect to be gratified. It is as though something in us says "if only it were true. . . ."

We surely ought to know what it is we wish for. In our fondness for Pocahontas can we make out a longing that is buried somewhere below even the affection we bear for our fair selves and white causes? This yearning might be for another kind of love entirely, a love that has forever been hidden under the differences that set countries, creeds, and colors against each other. From the freedom and noble impracticality of childhood, we as a people have taken this Indian girl to heart. Could we be hinting at a wish for a love that would really cross the barriers of race? When the beautiful brown head comes down, does a whole nation dream this dream?

But it is still only a dream. And that fact helps to explain why it is that from the very beginning the story has had what looks like the wrong ending, why the wedding of the protagonists remains a symbol that was never realized. To be sure the girl eventually married, and the groom was usually the hero's compatriot, but by then the event has lost its joy and its force—seems a substitute for the real thing, and not at all satisfactory. But the story might have died centuries before us, and we would have made much less of Pocahontas, if the substitution were not in some way fit and right. We sense that the adventure has to end the way it does partly because we know the difference between what we dream and what we get. We are not particularly happy with the denouement, but we feel its correctness, and with it we acknowledge that this is all just make-believe.

To understand the rest of our dim and reluctant perception of the propriety of the story's outcome, Americans must see the Indian girl in one last way: as progenitress of all the "Dark Ladies" of our culture—all the erotic and joyous temptresses, the sensual, brunette heroines, whom our civilization (particularly our literature: Hawthorne, Cooper, Melville, and many others) has summoned up only to repress. John Smith is the first man on this continent known to have made this rejection; his refusal to embrace "the wild spirit" embodied in the girl was epic, and a precedent for centuries of denial. Prototypes too, and just as important, were the arrogantly hypocritical Rolfe and the rest of the colonists, who baptized, christened, commercialized, and ruined the young lady. With censorship and piety as tools, American writers—a few poets, far too late, aside—completed the job, until Pocahontas was domesticated for the whole of our society, where from the very start any healthy, dark happiness in the flesh is supposed to be hidden, or disapproved. Pocahontas is the archetypal sacrifice to respectability in America—a victim of what has been from the beginning our overwhelming anxiety to housebreak all things in nature, until wilderness and wildness be reduced to a few state parks and a few wild oats. Our affection for Pocahontas is the sign of our temptation, and our feeling that her misfortunes in love have a final, awkward fitness comes from our knowing that all that madness is not for us.

79. On Translating Hieroglyphic Love Songs

JOHN L. FOSTER

Foster (1930–) is Professor of English and Speech at Roosevelt University, Chicago, and former Chairman of the Department. After a doctorate in American literature (Michigan, 1961) and teaching in Connecticut and Wisconsin, his awakening interest in ancient Egyptian poetry moved him to the neighborhood of the Oriental Institute, University of Chicago, and won him two fellowships for study in Egypt. His *Love Songs of the New Kingdom* appeared in 1974.

"The clarity of Egyptian is much aided by a strict word-order . . ."

—Sir Alan Gardiner, *Egyptian Grammar*

"since feeling is first
who pays any attention
to the syntax of things
will never wholly kiss you . . ."

—e e cummings

I

EVERY TRANSLATOR OF POETRY walks a tightrope across an abyss, trying to keep his balance on a thread of meaning until he can arrive at the far side of his text intact. For the translator is a sort of acrobat, an aerialist; and each step must be faultless. And his performance seldom satisfies all his audience, which divides into two groups of partisans, the philologist and the poet, each calling upon him to lean a little more to the right or the left. If he leans too far in either direction, of course, the act suddenly ends. Nevertheless, his is the necessary and proper audience; the callings of philologist and poet are honorable each in itself, both deal with verbal communication, and each of the partisans can sit in legitimate judgment upon at least part of the translator's performance. The poet—limited only by the scope of his own imagination, his skill with words, and the richness of his feelings, and working with his native language—can ask: Is the performance a poem? The philologist—expert in and respecting the vocabulary, grammatical structures, idioms, and the whole means of communication of the language in which the original was expressed—can ask: Is the performance accurate? Does the performer do justice to the native style of acting?

The translator must respect and satisfactorily answer both kinds of question; for otherwise there is no translation. If he has an ear only for the philologists in the audience, he comes up with a literal translation —one which will surely satisfy only the philologist, and one which should have been left to that expert in the first place. If he listens only to the poets, he comes up (if he is good enough) with a poem—an original poem of his own, but not one that catches the texture or meaning (and, perhaps, the strangeness) of the original. Which is all very fine, and literary, but is not a literary translation. So, for the translator-acrobat it really does come down to a matter of balance: he must exhibit enough of both the philologist and the poet to move ahead upright and astride the meaning, enough of both knowledge and intuition to sense when a shift of balance to the left or the right is needed to keep his feet.

Balancing the claims of philology and poetry is of course a commonplace in the theory of verse translation; but, when one comes to think of it, masterly performances are few. There is Fitzgerald's *Rubaiyat*, or Pound's *Cathay*, or the other Fitzgerald's *Odyssey* in the Anglo-American tradition (I accept opinion here; for I do not know any of the originals); but definitive literary translations seem not to be common. Why? I suspect that without too much oversimplification one can argue that the bent, the basic urge, the attitudes toward the job exhibited by the philologist and poet are different, conflicting, and even antithetical. The philologist insists upon respect for the facts of his chosen language; he gathers data—occurrences, instances, parallels, contexts of words, usages, and grammatical forms. And he builds what he finds into sets of rules and a system which describes the way meaning in that language is communicated according to the best evidence he has. But, respecting his facts, he is cautious: "There is as yet no occurrence of that word with that particular shade of meaning." "The grammatical structure of the language does not allow for that particular interpretation of the passage." "Our evidence suggests the image or the idiom you use is not native to the language." Translating too "imaginatively" is dangerous; it is not scholarly; it goes beyond the facts. The poet, of course, functions quite another way. For him, imagination is everything. Confronted by rules, or even the current linguistic description of his native language, he is a lawbreaker and a nonconformist, always looking for new ways to speak, to express thought and feeling. He has faith in the resilience of his language; and he seeks what is fresh and novel to convey what he has to say. He tries to force fallen words back toward image and metaphor, back to their prelapsarian state. And he is a gambler with language, always hoping to snatch the grace beyond the reach of art; he takes chances with words, knowing that so often it is catching the main chance that makes the poem.

If these two portraits are at all accurate, they perhaps explain why the good literary translation is relatively rare. The translator *is* a tight-rope walker; and the concept of balance *is* of profound importance to his art. For somewhere down at the very wellspring of his urge to write he must strike the balance between conflicting claims—the scholar's right-ful caution and the poet's right to gamble, rights which inherently tend to cancel each other out, or which lead at the very least to an unpleas-ant wavering along the rope. The translator is such, then, by virtue of his double calling: he somehow has the talent to integrate his respect for the uniqueness of his original with an equal respect for the uniqueness of the living language of his own time. The art and the role are in the balance, which he must preserve at all costs—keeping an ear out for the claims and cautions of both sides but never, despite all cries of the ex-perts seated there (and in this he finds his proper use), leaning too far to the left or to the right.

II

Keeping one's balance is a particularly formidable task with a language like ancient Egyptian hieroglyphic, which is both exotic and dead. It is, after all, only during the past century and a half that a language whose history and development spanned more than three millennia has begun to be recovered. For most of the Christian era (and for some cen-turies before that) the hieroglyphs on the monuments of ancient Egypt have been only pretty little pictures for tourists to goggle at and scrawl their graffiti beside in Greek, Latin, Arabic, French, and English. Deci-pherment of hieroglyphic only began around 1800 when Napoleon's soldiers, digging a fort, found the Rosetta stone, a trilingual inscription in Greek, demotic, and hieroglyphic. Since then, enough progress has been made for scholars to compile dictionaries and grammars and com-pose what seem to be accurate literal translations of most of the surviv-ing texts. But there is much still to be learned; and discussion still goes on about the exact meaning of words, the implications of grammatical structures, and the relationship of sentences.

The translator who would render the ancient hieroglyphic into modern English faces many problems; and for him who is interested primarily in the literature, and most particularly in the verse, the prob-lems are compounded. First of all, the ancient Egyptian did not draw the vowels when writing his words; he knew what sounds to expect and how to pronounce the words, so that showing them in the writing was unnecessary. But since knowledge of hieroglyphic died out, the sounds of the words were lost. All we have now are their consonantal skeletons; and the language is unpronounceable. Since the Egyptian philologist must speak the words somehow, he simply fakes the pronunciation by adding the sound of short *e* between consonants; but the claim is never made that this convention approximates the actual sounds of the ancient language. Thus, the hieroglyph of the wave of water (the alphabetic sign for the consonant *n*) is pronounced "en"; the chessboard (designating the biliteral *mn*) is pronounced "men"; and the heart and windpipe sign (for the triliteral *nfr*) is sounded "nefer." This makeshift at least enables one to "speak" a hieroglyphic sentence or line of verse after a fashion; and thus one can, for instance, approximate the number of syllables in the total length of a line. This, fortunately, is sufficient evidence to demonstrate that the lines of verse in an ancient poem were of unequal length—a point of importance to the translator, as we shall see later.

But ignorance of the sound system of hieroglyphic is still a profound loss to the translator aiming at a version of literary caliber: he cannot know the rhythm of the original piece. Though he can roughly tell the line lengths of a poem, he cannot know exactly how the words were accented, whether a slow, heavy rhythm or a light, skipping rhythm was employed, where stressed words were clustered for emphasis, or where patterns of dark or light vowels were used to color the meaning of a passage. The verse translator is in the rather ridiculous situation of knowing whether or not a passage alliterates but unable to tell if assonance was employed in the same passage. He simply must live with the fact that he cannot at present approximate either the sound or rhythmic system of the original. That part is almost pure guesswork.

Another kind of problem for the translator centers on uncertainties about the tense and mood of the Egyptian verb. Though the problem is too complicated to detail here, it seems that the ancient Egyptians thought of an action not so much in terms of when it occurred (past, present, or future—our tenses) but rather according to its duration—how long it took or whether it was a distinct, completed act or one which was continuous, repeated, or habitual. Durative acts tended to employ a tense analogous to our present tense, since they were not finished yet and hence not yet in the past; completed acts were over and hence tended to use a tense analogous to our past tense. The philologist is all too often forced back to the context of a passage in order to determine the tense of specific verbs. The translator of course faces the same problems; and although at times it does not particularly matter whether a passage is translated as present or past, at other times (say, in an historical document) the very basis of interpretation rests on the time of the action. Similar uncertainties of interpretation also occur with regard to the moods of the verb—whether a statement is made or a question asked, whether the verb includes a notion of wishing, commanding, or stating a condition to be fulfilled, or whether some special part of the sentence, other than the verb, is meant to be emphasized. It can be demonstrated from those verbs whose stems are mutable that indicators for such moods occurred in the language; but with most verbs such knowledge is masked by the absence of the vowels.

Understanding hieroglyphic is not all a darkness, however. The grammar is known, after all, and the language can be translated, even if many of its nuances are uncertain. Even though Sir Alan Gardiner in his *Egyptian Grammar* can begin one chapter by listing eighteen different ways in which the phrase, "His majesty went forth," can be written in hieroglyphs (each way originally having some special nuance of meaning or emphasis), the situation for the translator is not that hopeless. The bedrock of translation from this language is syntax—the word order of the individual sentence: verb, subject, indirect object, object, abverb or prepositional phrase. Often an indicator (a "particle") occurs at the beginning of the sentence to signal the special way in which the entire sentence is to be read (question, condition, new paragraph, dependency on previous sentence, and in some cases, tense). And if the syntax of the sentence varies from the basic pattern, one understands that some part of the sentence is being awarded special emphasis. The language itself provides some means for dispelling the ignorance generated by the loss of the vowel system.

Another major problem for the translator of the hieroglyphs lies with the ancient Egyptian vocabulary, the meanings of the individual words themselves. For anyone desiring a literary translation, especially of verse texts, the situation is critical; for so often in looking up the meaning of an unfamiliar word in even the monumental *Wörterbuch der Ägyptische Sprache,* one finds only citations of the texts where the word occurs (usually not one's own text) and a question mark. Even the brute denotations of many of the less familiar words are unknown, as indeed are the secondary meanings and connotations of a good many fairly common ones, particularly those words dealing with private and personal life or with human moods and feelings—the very stuff of literature. The student of ancient Egyptian is reduced to compiling his own dictionary as he goes, accumulating file-drawers full of 3×5 cards, each bearing a hieroglyphic word, the text where it occurred, and all too often another question mark for its translation.

The Egyptian language is constituted from picture signs, some of which represent ideas of concrete things (ideograms) and some of which represent sounds (phonograms). The latter consist primarily of alphabetic, biliteral, and triliteral signs (representing one, two, and three consonants respectively). The situation is somewhat complicated by the fact that the language is not merely alphabetic and that some of the signs can be used either for their ideogrammic or phonetic values. In addition, there is a third very significant category of signs called determinatives, which indicate the general area of meaning of a word; they might be thought of as determining the broader "genus" of the "species" of word spelled out by phonograms preceding the determinative. Thus, one may not be able to tell if an unknown word signifies berries or pomegranates, but from the determinative he can at least be sure it is some kind of fruit. Since the meanings of almost all determinatives are known, they are a great help to the translator slogging through unfamiliar terrain. As with much of the grammar, the nuances may be elusive, but the general outlines are known.

Although Egyptian hieroglyphic employs picture signs, it is not really picture writing (ideogrammic), since the language had advanced to a proto-alphabet and words in most cases were spelled out. One unfamiliar with the language sees only the appeal of the things depicted by the signs; but to the philologist an owl, no matter how beautifully drawn, is after all simply the letter *m*. And he would argue that to an ancient Egyptian this sign no more meant "owl" than our letter *A* means "head of a bull."

And yet, for us today, the hieroglyphs do have an important appeal as pictures—there is an aesthetic dimension in simply seeing a well-drawn hieroglyphic text. Additionally, I think one can argue that ancient Egyptain is at least residually ideogrammic, enough of the signs still *can* mean the object depicted for one to say that the idea meant to be conveyed is also often *seen*. Three wavy horizontal lines, one under the other, *do* mean "water"; one does *see* the female silhouette in the sign for "woman"; one can distinguish between a certain kind of tree and its fruit by looking at the determinatives of the words. This ideogrammic dimension to the language—of seeing the idea mentioned—has a special importance for anyone interested in the aesthetic values and the literature of the language. One has only to recall Ezra Pound's interest in Chinese as an ideogrammic language and the rather elaborate theory of poetry his artist's imagination developed from the insight: an ideogrammic language is automatically the language of poetry par excellence because it is inherently so concrete and imagistic. One of the cornerstones of modernist poetic theory has been an insistence upon concrete language and a direct presentation of the subject matter—the poet must not merely describe his subject, he must show it, dramatize it, present it concretely before his reader's imagination. The mind's eye must *see* the subject of the poem in action. Pound argued that any pictorial language was inherently more poetic than one like English because one can see something going on, in no matter how rudimentary a manner, at the same time he is thinking and feeling about the meaning conveyed. Egyptian hieroglyphic is this kind of language.

In addition to its ideogrammic value as a poetic language, ancient Egyptian exhibits a vocabulary rich in sensory appeal, in concrete words and phrases. At least some students of ancient Egypt argue that the consciousness of an ancient Egyptian was "pre-logical" or "mythopoeic," innocent of or not interested in the processes of abstraction and generalization developed by the Greeks. However accurate that might be historically, it does seem that the surviving texts concerned with such problems are not "philosophic" in our sense but rather "wisdom" texts: instead of the generalization or principle we have the observation; instead of the syllogism we have the maxim. In the Egyptian texts the emphasis is more limited to the individual instance or situation, the practical, the actual, the moral—the accumulations of experience gained over a career and passed on to a son. Such writings seem more limited to the concrete and particular.

And the Egyptian vocabulary in general seems to reflect this situation. It is especially rich in concrete words, words for objects, words for the natural world to which the ancient Egyptian was so closely tied, epithets concretely describing the qualities and powers of the invisible gods. And unless it is our ignorance of an entire level of the ancient language speaking, we can say that Egyptian was grudging in its employment of abstract, general words. So far as we know, there was a single word ("maat") to express what to us would be the differing concepts of "justice," "truth," and "order." The Egyptian would tend to speak, not of the concept of "love" (though a noun for "love" does exist), but the activity of "loving," the condition of "being in love," or the person "beloved." The difference, I think, is fundamental to the translator of the literature because it shifts emphasis from the general or the abstract to the particular and concrete, to the more personal and sensory. And (again) of such stuff is literature made.

A similar kind of example, perhaps more clearly demonstrating the concrete, "poetic" emphasis in the language, concerns the circumlocutions often used to describe personal qualities, moods and feelings, and aspects of human character. Thus one who is joyful is described as "long of heart"; one who is generous is called "long of hand." A presumptuous person is "high of back," while the alert man is called "sharp of face." There is a whole vocabulary of such phrases, most dealing with human attributes; and in them, where the philologist may see only a clumsy periphrasis, the translator, if he has the wit to catch it, perceives the very concreteness of image and vigor of phrase so necessary to modern literary idiom. As with the residual ideograms, these phrases demonstrate that certain highly literary qualities are inherent in the language—it is wonderfully rich in sensory appeal. Both characteristics are a kind of compensation to the translator for the loss of the sounds and rhythms of ancient Egyptian.

But there are other problems to be faced from an entirely different quarter, especially for one working with literary texts. Almost all the latter appear either on papyri or on ostraca (pieces of pottery or stone smoothed and used for writing). Such texts are not written in hiero-glyphic at all but in hieratic, the cursive form of ancient Egyptian adapted to the use of brush on either of these two surfaces (whereas the hieroglyphs proper resulted from use of chisel on stone). The two kinds of writing are merely variants of the same language; but the understanding of hieratic does require additional study, and it displays conventions of its own. There is the added problem (sometimes insur-mountable) of trying to decipher the handwriting of someone who lived and wrote three or four thousand years ago. So, as well as knowing what the cursive form of the hieroglyphic signs are, the translator must know his scribe—the idiosyncrasies of his handwriting, his flourishes and ab-breviations, the method at his period of forming given signs. And often (though not so much with literary texts), the translator is faced with the work of a writer who is hurried, careless, or even semi-illiterate. Or just plain hungry: one man from the New Kingdom village where workers on the royal tombs were housed scrawled, "Go get me one fat goose—quick, quick, quick!"

Many of the texts, both on papyri and ostraca, are schoolboy exer-cises, copied out as the young student was learning his profession of scribe; and some still exhibit in the margins the instructor's corrections of badly formed hieratic signs. Such texts are sometimes horribly garbled, full of misspellings, undecipherable tracks, and obviously wrong words; but we are forced to be thankful for them, since some of the most important and charming literary productions of ancient Egypt survive only because of the sweat of these fledgling professionals. And if one is lucky, enough fragmentary "duplicates" of the more renowned works sur-vive for the modern philologist to piece together a fairly respectable synthetic version of what the original must have been like.

But completely apart from the intricacies of hieratic and the whims of student compositions, the translator is faced with the brute facts of the condition of his texts. The first fact is that the texts are between three and four thousand years old; and the second, that things deteriorate: papyrus tatters, stone and pottery flake and crumble. Perhaps the mira-cle is that any texts survive at all. Anyway, one can say without too much exaggeration that there is scarcely a text from ancient Egypt fully in-tact; the Egyptologist is at home with lacunae. Most of the surviving "classics" of ancient Egypt are fragmentary: the beginning or end of a papyrus lost or its entirety so threadbare with age that it is full of holes and its writing faded into the remaining fibers, or an ostracon broken in half, chipped at the corners and around the edges, or its surface flaking —or worse: only the broken corner surviving. These things, unfortunately, are the rule rather than the exception. Some papyri (obviously untrans-lated) are only heaps of crumbs in a box. Shorter pieces, by their very brevity, fare better: individual lyrics and letters have often survived almost intact. The philologist does what he can with the remains; and enough has endured for the scholar to reconstruct the general outlines of ancient Egyptian literature, filling it in here and there with specific pieces, and now and then a masterwork.

And there is a compensation here too. Though faced with fragments, the translator can hope for, and even expect, the appearance of new texts with some regularity. They are always emerging from the sand or appearing from tomb excavations. When I was in Luxor not long ago, news came to Chicago House that the French expedition had just the day before unearthed a new cache of ostraca in the ancient workmen's village across the River in Western Thebes. There is probably more of the literature still in the sand than has come to light during the past two centuries. At another point during my trip to Egypt, as my guide was driving us out into the desert to look at Zoser's Step Pyramid, and as we approached it on a "road" consisting of a double rut through the sand, he said, "You realize, of course, that we are driving over the tops of tombs." So, the translator of hieroglyphic, despite having largely to view only remains of texts, is a sort of eternal optimist: there is so much sand—so much unexcavated—that something will turn up to keep him busy, to fill in a passage of a text, to clarify the working of an inscription or a point of grammar or clinch the meaning of a word.

III

As for the love songs of ancient Egypt, those known to date survive in four main collections, none of them very extensive by our standards: Papyrus Chester Beatty I and P. Harris 500 (both in the British Museum), P. Turin 1966 (in the Egyptian Museum of Turin, Italy), and Cairo Ostracon 25218 (in the Cairo Museum). Beatty I is in fine condition, well written, with few lacunae, and with only the first part of the roll missing—a philologist's delight. Harris 500, like Beatty I a literary "anthology," is currently on display in an Egyptian gallery of the British Museum; it is fragmentary, threadbare, and full of lacunae, but contains the single most extensive group of the surviving love songs. The Turin Love Papyrus consists of four pieces originally constituting two full columns (pages) from a more extensive roll; what survives here (the last three of a group of love songs) is in good condition, but translation originally was thwarted by the fact that the pieces were mounted in the wrong sequence and no one could make any sense of them. The Cairo Ostracon is a piece of broken pottery, with a good deal of the original text apparently missing and with the remaining surface fading and flaking. Scholars date all four of these collections to the later New Kingdom of ancient Egypt, Dynasties XIX and XX, or about 1300–1100 B.C. The total of the love songs amounts to only about sixty pieces—and some of these too fragmentary to recover as poems. There are hints of a few other such songs appearing on ostraca scattered here and there in various museum collections in Europe and America; but most present texts, too fragmentary to translate meaningfully, are identified as love songs only by a characteristic word or phrase or by some small clue as to situation or setting.

It is from such material the translator interested in the love lyrics (and in ancient Egyptian verse generally) tries to recreate poems in English. What can be said concerning the style of these lyrics? Not much is known with any certainty about ancient Egyptian poetry; scholarly study of the verse has only begun; and the few initial attempts (that I know of) seem to limit the subject in a manner no longer current among students of literature to a study of "prosody" or "metrics," which after all is merely one branch of "stylistics" or "poetics." Because the subject is in its early stages, and because of the uncertainties which persist concerning many of the finer points of ancient hieroglyphic, it behooves the translator to be diffident in his description of the ancient verse. What follows, then, is tentative, leaning as much toward impression as firm description, and based primarily upon the corpus of love songs.

Most ancient Egyptian verse can be physically identified (leaving aside for the moment the more important criteria of diction, imagery, figurative language, etc.) by the presence of "verse points." These are simply dots, usually in red ink as opposed to the black of the writing itself, appearing above the signs after each phrase or "line" of the poem. They are the stylistic units of Egyptian verse; and almost all contain one major verbal form (active or passive verb, infinitive, or participle), while some contain two. More than two such verbal forms per line seems to be as rare as no verb at all. The entire verse line then consists of either a complete short sentence or a grammatical clause in terms of Egyptian syntax. The two exceptions that I am aware of are (1) the line consisting of two distinct epithets plus their modifiers (and often one of these will have some notion of action) and (2) the line identifying one thing with another (the metaphorical equation, with the copula, *is*, understood).

From the verse point structure one can affirm that the lines of any given poem vary in length: although we cannot count the exact number of syllables or discover the accents, we can say some lines are shorter and some longer. And they vary according to no hitherto demonstrated pattern other than the number of words and syllables required to complete the sentence, phrase, pair of epithets, or equation. Such knowledge, meagre as it is, has important implications for the verse translator desiring to approximate the varying line lengths of the ancient poem; for apparently that verse is strophic, not metered. Thus one perhaps ought not to use any of the metered lines common in English (blank verse, heroic couplet, tetrameter, etc.) but catch the swing of the original through the cadenced line employing the rhythms of the spoken phrase as unit: that means 20th century American free verse.

The poems in the ancient collections occur in short series, though not usually with any narrative or structural connection; and they are separated by a hieroglyph (an arm with hand, palm down) signifying a pause or separation. In one case in P. Beatty I, each of a series of seven poems is introduced by the designation "house" or "compartment" (= section) the first, the second, etc. The love songs are relatively short, varying from as few as four lines up to twenty or thirty. Most range from a dozen to sixteen. And they exhibit a genuine lyric structure; that is, the meaning of the poem centers upon a mood or emotion, or the working out in a speaker's mind of an observation, insight, or perception, or the speaker's immediate inner reaction to some external event. The experience reflected in these poems is eminently human and usually personal and private—unlike much of ancient Egyptian literature, which so often is public, serious in tone, and rhetorical.

In addition, and most significantly for the translator, the Egyptian verse lines seem to occur in pairs. The pairs do not rhyme, however—a fact which can be determined from the surviving consonantal skeletons of the words—so the translator should not think in terms of, say, the heroic couplet. The pairing occurs in terms of the thought expressed, not the sound heard, and might as a stylistic device aptly be termed "thought rhyme" or "thought couplets." It can be illustrated by four such lines (two couplets) translated literally from the "Hymn" to the Inundation, the Nile flood which fertilized the banks of the River each year and which was deified as the god, Hapy,

> Who brings food, who is magnanimous of provisions,
> Who produces every variety of his good things.
> Lord of awe, who is sweet of aromas,
> Who makes peace at his returning.

The halves of the couplet do not merely repeat each other but employ the device known as incremental repetition, whereby the second line can offer a second expression of the same idea using a different image, figure, or description. Nor are thought couplets limited to such repetition; sometimes the second line provides a conclusion to a question or condition posed by the first, or it can make a statement in contrast to the first. Over the length of a strophe or poem such pairings build up a rhetorical and structural pattern which includes all the permutations of the stylistic devices of identity, parallelism, series, variation, balance, and antithethis.

The Egyptian thought couplet is a very flexible vehicle; and one seeking parallels in our own literary tradition thinks of the "half-lines" of the old Anglo-Saxon alliterative verse (minus the alliteration) or of the rhetorical and structural flavor of 18th century British poetry (minus the meter and rhyme). Among Egyptian philologists the phrase "parallelism of members" has been used to describe the thought couplet; but in the references I have seen the concept is described too narrowly, not doing justice to the wide flexibility of the device in Egyptian poetry, and the discussions lean too heavily on analogues to ancient Hebrew poetry (familiar to us in the King James version of the Old Testament). One eminent Egyptian philologist (Adolf Erman) went so far as to denigrate this structural usage because it impeded the narrative flow of the verse (it wasn't swift enough, repetitiously saying the same thing over and over when one should get on with it). He evidently never compehended that a major way for "poetry" to become such is through rich and intricate interweaving of a tapestry of sound, image, and meaning. With poetry the delight is not merely in arriving; one likes to enjoy the trip! One also diffidently mentions the name of Milton, or Pope, or Hopkins, or Thomas. At any rate, the texture of ancient Egyptian poetry is of the latter kind—more intricate and densely harmonious in the hymns and eulogies while clearer, simpler, more graceful in the love lyrics—but usually developing within the structure of the thought couplet.

Another striking characteristic of the love songs is the use of concrete language. Whether this is the natural result of the concrete, mythopoeic consciousness attributed to the ancient Egyptians, or whether it is more a trait stemming from the residually ideogrammic nature of the language, the poetry is highly imagistic. Here too one senses an analogy with 20th century poetry in English—in this case, the Imagists. While the Egyptian poem does not seem to "speak" primarily through a development of images, as does the ideal Imagist poem, it nevertheless presents a relatively high density of sensory experience. Hieroglyphic imagery, however, is simple and clear; there seems not to be any analogy with the intellectual complexity or the yoking of dissimilar categories characteristic of 17th century or modern "metaphysical" poetry.

The love songs also employ figurative language regularly. Not only does one find the implied identities of metaphor, there is also a pervasive use of simile (indicated by the Egyptian word, *mi*, for "like" or "as") and the kind of comparison signifying that one thing is like another but "better than" or "more so" (indicated by a special usage of the preposition *r*). But whether conveyed in word, image, or figure, the sensory experience referred to would be (for the ancient Egyptian) simple, common and everyday, neither exotic nor "metaphysical" but easily understood and "universal."

The songs flash with a kaleidoscope of images of life along the Nile: the River itself, without which the civilization could not have existed; the irrigation canals; the bankside thickets, the marshes, and trees; the fields under cultivation, rescued from the desert by the yearly inundation and human effort; the flowers and gardens; and the hot and sterile deserts hemming in the River and its culture on either side. The references are equally rich to the creatures carrying on their activities

501

in these habitats, as well as to the various human occupations—hunting, fowling, fishing, agriculture, and the various domestic pursuits. And pervading all such images, even in the love songs, a sense of deity in all things, emanations of the hidden gods, and signs of their influence at work guiding and thwarting human beings at work or in love.

But the apparent simplicity of syntax, diction, image, and figure is not the full picture of ancient Egyptian poetry; for the poets enjoyed playing with words. It can be demonstrated, even in the love songs, that the poets employed the devices of alliteration (and so, presumably, assonance), punning, and irony, and made extensive use of humor; and they would sometimes play the variations upon the root meaning of a word, discovering how many ways it could be used in its various grammatical forms and parts of speech in a single passage. So, the simplicity of the verse is deceptive; and to that characteristic must be added the qualities of wit and cleverness. One thinks of Pope's "what oft was thought but ne'er so well expressed"; and here too there seems to be a parallel to 18th century neoclassic verse, or—for the love songs—to the amatory verse of 17th century Cavalier poets like Suckling and Lovelace.

Indeed, any attempt to characterize the style of ancient Egyptian poetry must result in the conclusion that such verse was composed by highly sophisticated poets. Though their names do not survive (with the possible exception of Akhtoy, who may have composed the "Hymn to the Inundation"), these poets were craftsmen with words working within the conventions of a complex and flexible poetic which bears some resemblance to both 18th century British and 20th century modernist American verse. What these ancient poets did not do was spontaneously warble native Nile-notes wild.

IV

One pleasure of translating these lyrics comes with the knowledge that, amid the turbulence of history, love endures; for, fused with the portrait of a life and civilization so different from our own occur characters—lovers and other speakers—and a spectrum of moods, feelings, and tones quite like those known from our own experience. The whole range is there, all the varieties of loving. The themes, despite the exotic setting, are perennial. There is the set description of the beloved—for the speaker she is "one and only," and he catalogues her beauties head to toe. There are the standard situations of lovelonging, unrequited love, wish-fulfillment, dreams of mastery, even prayers to deity to aid in conquest. There are the devices of enticement, deception, duplicity—clever moves on the chessboard of love. There are the moments of absence and separation; invitations, sports, activities, and the games people play; the conversations of lovers; union and the act of love; its loss and the aftermath of love.

And we see all the characters of lovers, usually young, and both sexes speaking. There is the featherheaded neophyte, off for a chat with her girlfriend, who suddenly sights her secret love on the road and, all brashness gone, is paralyzed with uncertainty. There is the girl out walking at night for a glimpse of her beloved (and he is found conveniently standing in the doorway of his house). Or, there is the couple sitting in the twilight in their garden to catch the evening breeze after a hot day. Or, the young sophisticate kneeling for an ironic prayer to Hathor, goddess of love, to retrieve his wandering girlfriend. Or the girl coaxing her friend to go bathing with her by promising to wear her new swimsuit (which, as she carefully explains to him, goes sheer in the water). One young man takes to his bed, feigning violent illness and hoping his love will come to visit him out of pity and another, in the single case where character and theme overlap in different lyrics, imagines a similar ploy as his lucidity begins to falter under the pressure of his girlfriend's week-long absence. Still others spur themselves with erotic daydreams of the cornering and conquest of maidens not yet brought to bed. And there are young lady speakers with parallel thoughts and dreams.

In one instance from P. Harris 500 there is an entire cycle of eight poems linked by a narrative thread. Telling a story by concentrating only on the "poetic" lyric peaks of emotion and drama while omitting the "prosaic" connecting events—an idea developed by modernist poets like Pound, Eliot, and Williams—is not so new after all. In the Egyptian analogue the story is a simple one of unrequited love. The speaker of all eight lyrics is a virginal young girl swept away by her feelings, perhaps a first love; and we watch the progress of the affair from her initial stratagems, through her hopes and fears concerning her success, to the physical culmination, her discovery of her lover's duplicity, and her final loneliness. The ancient poet has given us an appealing persona and presented her deepest feelings in a unified sequence of lyric moments as the experience works to its inevitable conclusion. After three millennia the modern reader can still be moved by her disappointment and emptiness.

One other "character" deserves mention. She is Hathor, the Egyptian goddess of love; and her function in these lyrics is much like that of the Greek Aphrodite. Lovers regularly appeal to her for aid, usually to provide the elusive beloved for them; they are always aware of her invisible presence and power; and at least one attributes the imminent conquest of his latest lady to long and faithful service in her behalf. Though there is no machinery of Cupid and his amorous darts in the Egyptian conception, the capriciousness of love is simply and obviously Hathor at work manipulating Egyptian heartstrings.

The variety of tone in these lyrics thus is seen to express most of the moods of love. The speakers can, on the one hand, be innocent and pure of heart, hesitant, or self-sacrificing in love's duties; but on the other hand, they can be intensely passionate, patently physical in their desire, or even given to sexual innuendo, bawdry, and lust. The tones in which they express these attitudes and conditions thus range the entire gamut from the romantic and idyllic, through the simple and naive, to the humorously realistic and even satirical, and on to the openly sexual and erotic.

The most prevalent tone gives an impression of grace, liveliness, and charm—of a kind observed over and over again in the scenes of daily life depicted on the tomb walls of Western Thebes (paintings for which these songs must be the verbal equivalent): the noble ladies in their finest party dresses, the riot of food and drink, the female singers, musicians, and dancers, the naked servant girls and entertainers, and the harpers (often, like Homer, blind) plucking out dinner music. It is as if life and eternity alike were an unending banquet. Sometimes, written in hieroglyphs beside their portraits, we even have snatches of the songs being sung and played by the performers. And mural and song alike attest that these ancient people, far from being in love with death, as misinformation has it, were so delighted with life in the Nile valley that they took great pains to preserve those bodies which had served them so well in this world in order to use them with equal happiness forever.

The liveliness and the grace are certainly there; but in the Egyptian songs there is almost always an element of physical attraction and delight which will often become an expression of erotic longing. I return to this aspect because it seems to have been passed over too lightly by students of Egyptology. Perhaps it is because earlier phases of Egyptology were an outgrowth of Biblical studies, where all too often emphasis was placed not on daily life but upon another world and transcendence of the urges and mundane loves of the flesh. One philologist, footnoting a lyric he had translated, excused the ancient Egyptian delight in the body as due to the hot blood of the Mediterranean temperament. But the broadening of subject matter which has occurred in modern poetry makes possible what I think is a more genuine response to the presence of the erotic in the ancient poetry. This is another parallel to modernist poetry; and one can cite the love poems of Cummings and Williams or the more "classic" early love songs of Pound.

But graceful and charming or erotic and physical, the Egyptian lyrics sometimes plumb deeper than the surfaces of human experience. The young girl who falls in and out of love is appealing, and the intricacies of the game of love are pleasant and often amusing; but now and then, there is more. The woman who tries to persuade her lover not to leave her bed begins with the teasing speeches of love combat; but by the end of the poem her light words seem to mask a more enduring feeling, a strength of attachment that will be genuinely injured by the looming separation. Elsewhere, a young man breaks his daily routine, gives in to his wanderlust, and heads for the big city—taking a boat trip downriver to Memphis, capital of the Old Kingdom.* A girl is one of his goals, to be sure; but the poem is based fundamentally on the human urge to wander, to seek adventure, to answer the call of the city lights. On board the ferry, as he watches the Nile go by in the twilight, he experiences an almost mystical communion with the triad of gods who watch over Memphis, sensing their presence around him and projecting their influence over his future activities in the city of his dreams. Such expressions of deeper experiences are the exception rather than the rule in the love songs; but they do occur, showing that at times the ancient authors could and would probe beyond the conventions of the genre to profounder experience.

Examination of theme, character, and tone in the love songs suggests certain conclusions regarding the literary traditions to which they can be assigned. First, they belong to the tradition of pastoral verse—not all of them, but enough to support the generalization. In the linked sequence from P. Harris 500 mentioned above, for instance, the speaker is the daughter of a birdcatcher, her experience is that of the outdoors, and her allusions refer to the locales and creatures connected with fowling. In other poems the setting is a garden or orchard where lovers can enjoy the shade of trees (which were not all that common, and provided welcome relief from a scorching sun), look at the wide variety of flowers always in bloom, take a leisurely walk about garden paths, or sit by the pool. The modern reader must realize how idyllic such a setting must have been to the ancient Egyptian; for always on either side of the River, and not too far beyond the narrow limits of cultivation, rose the cliffs of the Eastern and Western deserts. These lyrics fit the pastoral tradition because they represent a retreat or escape from the routines of daily life for characters who are at leisure to do so and who seem to be persons attached to the nobility rather than "swains" bound to the soil. Pastoralism is also apparent in the "rural" setting, in the pervasive emphasis upon love themes, and in the sophistication of convention and style displayed by poets. All these elements are part of the usual definition. One is reminded of the pastoral verse of the Elizabethan Age, with here, instead of shepherds, milkmaids, sheep, and farms, a panorama of fowlers, birdcatcher's daughters, marshes and fields, gardens and orchards.

The second tradition to which the songs can be assigned is that of courtly love. If the later conventions connected with feudalism and chivalry are not present in the Egyptian poems, they nevertheless express the experience of love as it was developed into an elaborate system by skilled poets. We have seen that most of the conditions and

---

* A discussion of this poem begins on page 510.

activities open to a lover are there—the symptoms and psychology of love are as well-developed as in later stages of the tradition. Love usually is a witty and intricate game, with a major emphasis on the sensuous (or sensual) and on conquest; and so far as I can determine, as in the later tradition, marriage is not necessarily the goal. The love here *can* be described as illicit, though such considerations do not seem to function in the Egyptian poem, which conveys rather the joy of living life to the full and a delight in sensory experience—in nature, with one's love, of the world in general.

V

The would-be translator of such songs must try never to forget that it was not a printing press or a photoduplicating machine but the living hand of some now forgotten Egyptian that once carefully (or sometimes not so carefully) formed the hieratic characters on a clean, untattered papyrus or an unchipped, unflaked ostracon. He was probably not the author of the song, and he may have been only a scribe copying out the text for his master (for we today have only copies); but someone thought enough of these lyrics to have them written down for his own library. For himself, not for us; but we have them, and they are ours now too.

If some Egyptian then could be moved and delighted by these songs, the modern translator, keeping faith with that dead hand from the past, must honor them as poems, making them new for his own time. These ancient verses must sing as poetry to our modern ear, and they must be as faithful as our knowledge of the ancient Egyptian language allows to the texture and idiom—the feel—of the original. We want to know the exact words of these speakers; but we also want to know the implications of their words, how they felt—about to love, in love, or the far side of love. The speakers must come alive again for us, after their millennia of frozen silence in the limbo of a forgotten language. Only in this way, in this kind of a translation, can the continuity of human imagination and feeling over the centuries be perceived.

How does the translator go about attaining the ideal? How does he walk the tightrope, balancing the legitimate claims of philologist and poet, and survive with a poem that keeps its ancient integrity? Here, of course, there is room for a variety of defensible translations depending upon which (or how many) qualities of the original the translator can retain, emphasize, or enhance in the current idiom of his native language and upon what parallels and analogues to ancient practice he can find in the conventions and styles of the poets of his own time. What follows, then, is merely a description of the choices I would make in trying to recreate the ancient Egyptian love songs as modern American poems.

To clarify my assumption that the translation must be a poem, I would add (and here my choice probably diverges most widely from that of the philologist) that the goal is a *tonal equivalent* of the original —defining "tone" as a combination both of the attitudes of speaker and author toward the subject matter of the poem *and* of the mood, emotion, or feeling expressed. After working for some time with this kind of goal, I came across an observation by Robert Lowell in his Introduction to *Imitations* which puts this aim succinctly:

> Boris Pasternak has said that the usual reliable translator gets the literal meaning but misses the tone, and that in poetry tone is of course everything. I have been reckless with literal meaning, and labored hard to get the tone. Most often this has been *a* tone, for *the* tone is something that will always more or less escape transference to another language and cultural moment. I have tried to write alive English and to do what my authors might have done if they were writing their poems now and in America.

Except for the second half of the final sentence (where I would want to try to capture more of the flavor and strangeness of the original), I think this passage should stand as a kind of credo for the verse translator. More literal-minded translators, who usually employ the old metrical forms as if modern poetry had never occurred, though their work is honestly done (Lowell again speaking) "are taxidermists, not poets, and their poems are likely to be stuffed birds." Their translations lack the one essential of any poem, life.

How does one accomplish the resurrection? For the Egyptian love lyric, the first step is transcribing the hieratic of the original text into its corresponding hieroglyphic signs, simply because the latter is easier to read and work with (a convention approved by Egyptologists). This process is the most tedious of all and involves a good deal of staring and mulling as one tries to decipher the handwriting. Then, there is the transliteration of the hieroglyphs into their equivalents in our alphabet (an owl becomes *m*). Next, the text is rearranged into lines of verse, an easy process when verse points exist but more difficult and chancy otherwise. And then comes the more involved process of attempting to determine the meaning of the piece by composing a literal translation—here confronting the text with all the knowledge of the ancient Egyptian language one can muster, checking grammatical structures, and looking up words in the dictionaries. Such steps are all necessary before one can begin to dream that the text might one day be a poem in English. Indeed, the literal translation, as anyone who has struggled with the first stages of any foreign language knows, is pretty wooden; and usually no meaning flows clear and uninterrupted from the first line to the last. The student of ancient Egyptian usually finds his first translation reads like bad King-James-ese.

But assuming all the important preliminary steps have been taken, how does one breathe in the life, transmuting the literal into the poetic? The thing not to do is proceed line by line from the beginning. My own experience with the love songs suggests that this is the second staring and mulling phase, where little should be committed to paper. For the translator here is seeking the *gestalt* of the poem (if that is not too pretentious a word)—he wants to discover that trait of character in the speaker, that bit of situation, that image or comparison, or that turn of phrase in the original which seems to give energy and life to the poem as a whole, unifying it into a single, complete, vital experience. And he always hopes (though of course he can never be sure) that, once he does discover the germ or seed of the poem, it is the very factor which inspired the original poem in the imagination of its now anonymous maker. So, this phase is more a matter of checking the range of meaning of a word, determining which of several homonyms is required, finding how a phrase at the opening of the text can harmonize with one toward the end, and so on. What one does, in effect, is ask those questions familiar to every beginning student of poetry from his freshman or sophomore handbook: Who, and what sort of person, is the speaker of the poem? What is the occasion? When and where is the poem set? What is the experience portrayed? What is the speaker's reaction to that experience in terms of thought, feeling, and physical movement? What is the tone of the poem? Commonplace as such questions are, they are absolutely essential to reading any poetry with understanding, English or Egyptian; and for the ancient love lyrics they really work, providing that basic knowledge of character, situation, and tone which, with luck, enables the translator to come up with a poem.

I recall one poem from the Cairo Ostracon, whose speaker was a young lover standing on the near bank of the Nile. He was wondering how he could get across and bemoaning the fact that his ladylove lived on the other side. The text itself had simply "the far side." As I was thinking over the phrase, it occurred to me that the other side, for the speaker, was really "the too far side"; and the addition of the one word not in the text—and the rhythm it brought provided the clue and the impetus for translation of the entire piece. For I felt I had penetrated beyond what he literally had said to what he meant by what he said, how he felt about it, and how much he felt. One might take that as an instance, in brief, of the difference between a literal translation and a tonal equivalent.

With a language imperfectly recovered, like Egyptian hieroglyphic, seeking a tonal equivalent is a risky business, of course; but the alternative, it seems to me, results in Lowell's stuffed bird. At any rate, once the translator feels he has discovered the gestalt or germ of the poem—and one assumes he is honest enough with himself to base it upon sufficient literal evidence—he can then return to the foggier words, phrases, and allusions. Usually, most of these become clearer (or the range of variant meanings narrows), and the details fall into place. When the primary experience or dramatic situation of the poem is understood by the translator, it begins to crystallize into a unified whole.

But for almost every poem the text exhibits unknown words and, worse yet, lacunae. Since even a stuffed bird needs all its feathers, my choice, consciously taken, has been simply and unashamedly to fill in, supply, fake what is unknown or missing according to the best guess possible based upon whatever evidence I can muster from dictionary or context. The principle at stake here is the integrity of the poem as a whole; for few "poems" can exist as such with series of dots scarring the body of the text.

Once the translator catches the central idea and feels he has at least the outlines of the original experience, based upon evidence of character, situation, and mood, he then turns to matters of rhythm, diction, imagery, figurative language, and structure. And for the techniques to express them he turns to the parallels he has discovered between ancient and modern stylistic practice. The actual process is obviously not this neat. Sometimes a precise word or phrase, or an image, or a rhythm with the proper amount of weight to it will appear early in the process of translation—even at the literal stage—and endure unchanged to the final version of the poem. But the usual state of affairs is a battle with banality, and the issue in doubt: wooden phrases, stilted words, gaps in continuity, lines too long or too short, mummified images, and so on. On such material the translator now brings to bear all his knowledge of poetry and instinct for verse technique, gambling on the rightness of meanings, polishing words and images, truing the joints of clauses—shaping the material into a poem and instilling it with life.

Here it remains only to summarize the techniques mentioned earlier in the description of ancient Egyptian poetic style. Thus, because the ancient verse line varies in length, is unrhymed, and seems not to employ meter, the modern tonal equivalent should use the rhythms and prose accents of the cadenced line. Because the speeches and situations of the lovers are personal and private, and because, to the slight extent one can determine levels of diction in ancient Egyptian, the lovers speak familiarly, the translation would employ a contemporary diction which is simple and unpretentiously colloquial except when elevated by the power of strong feeling or when slipping over into the sometimes slangy verbal patterns of irony or humor. The language of the translation would be conversational, quiet, the usages of personal and private speech (for these are the kinds of words for lovers). Because of the residually ideogrammic nature of the hieroglyphs and the high density of imagery in the original, the modern poem would take pains to be imagistic, to preserve the flavor of the original sensory experience—though imagery is not a major problem in translation: once the object or referent is known, it can, unlike a rhythm or the aura of meaning about a word, be transferred to the new language almost intact. The same process applies for figures of speech, instances of irony, and rhetorical structures in the original—one tries to preserve them when one finds them. Here, the only caution would be to try to retain the strangeness of experience, milieu, and allusion in the original wherever it occurs, thus keeping the modern reader aware that, although he is reading a "poem," it is the distillation of experience in an alien time and culture. As noted earlier, the texture of the love songs emphasizes the similarities of the love experience with our own time rather than the strangeness; with the more formal and public Egyptian poems, however, the latter predominates.

One last note should be added. He who aims at a tonal equivalent does well at some stage of his translating to check his emerging version with the literal translations that do exist through the efforts of Egyptian philologists. There are only a few, but they can point out an exit from a blind alley; wrong as often as right at the cruxes, they can still improve the final version. The best procedure here is to make the comparison only after one feels he has discovered the germ of the poem and partly developed the tonal equivalent; otherwise he runs the risk of being overwhelmed by the literalness or erudition of the scholarly translation— and that is death to a poem. The songs of the philologist-poet must not go forth naked, but they must wear the mantle of scholarship lightly. Most of all they must be alive, and sing with real voices.

[The first part of Foster's two-part essay ends here. The following passages and illustrations are derived from the second part of his essay (see footnote below)]

* * * * *

There are four steps in the literary translation of an ancient Egyptian poem, illustrated here by the fifth lyric of the first cycle of love songs in Papyrus Harris 500, "The Memphis Ferry." * The first step is simply obtaining a photographic copy of the text. It is written in hieratic, the cursive form of hieroglyphic adapted for the use of brush (i.e., pen) on papyrus. The characters are written continuously and without punctuation from right to left. An approximation of the hieratic appears in Fig-

* Professor Foster has written these two introductory paragraphs for *The Crowell College Reader*. In addition, he has made for the *Reader* a few minor modifications in the figures and the translations of "The Memphis Ferry." The figures and the translations first appeared in the second part of his essay, which dealt with several translations and which was published in the *Chicago Review* (Vol. 23, No. 3.) The last two paragraphs on page 514 conclude Foster's essay.

ure I. As the hieratic is deciphered, it is rewritten in the corresponding hieroglyphs. These are usually written from right to left and, for verse texts, divided into lines of poetry (Figure II). From his hieroglyphic text, the translator develops a line-by-line literal translation, at this stage attempting to be accurate rather than poetic. The last stage, of course, is the poem in the new language (text of "The Memphis Ferry").

The shaded portions in my approximation of the hieratic original indicate gaps, or holes, in the papyrus manuscript. I have also indicated these gaps with shading in my hieroglyphic transcription. The literal translation contains my restorations, most of which are based on the surrounding context. A few words and phrases were inserted because of the similarity of the surrounding passages with those in other hieratic love poems, in terms of structure and poetic conventions.

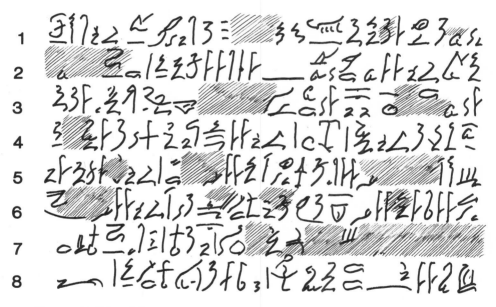

FIGURE I. "THE MEMPHIS FERRY."
APPROXIMATION OF THE HIERATIC ORIGINAL

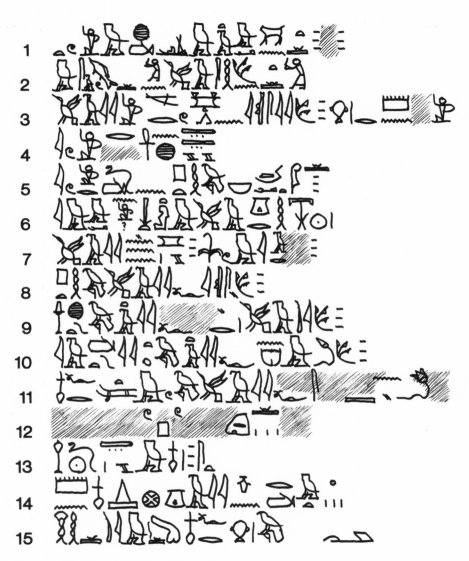

FIGURE II. "THE MEMPHIS FERRY"
HIEROGLYPHIC TRANSCRIPTION

"The Memphis Ferry"
Literal Translation from Hieroglyphic Transcription

1   I am going downstream in the ferryboat
2   Like (?) one who strains (?) against the command
3   My bundle of old clothes (?) upon my shoulder
4   I shall go to "The Life-of-the-Two-Lands"
5   I shall say to [Ptah,] Lord of Justice
6   Give to me a sister in the night
7   The sea—it is among rushes (?)
8   Ptah is its reeds
9   Sakhmet is its lotus pads
10   She-who-is-the-Dew (?) is its lotus buds
11   Nefertem is its lotus blossoms
12   . . . . [joy?]
13   When dawn comes with her beauties
14   "The Enduring-of-Beauty" is a bowl of love-apples (?)
15   Set in the presence of the "Beautiful-of-Face"

"The Memphis Ferry"
Poetic Translation

Oh I'm bound downstream on the Memphis ferry,
            like a runaway, snapping all ties,
With my bundle of old clothes over my shoulder.

I'm going down there where the living is,
            going down there to that big city,
And there I'll tell Ptah (Lord who loves justice):
            "Give me a girl tonight!"

Look at the River! eddying,
            in love with the young vegetation.
Ptah himself is the life of those reedshoots,
            Lady Sakhmet of the lilies—
Yes, Our Lady of Dew dwells among lilypads—
            and their son, Nefertem, sweet boy,
Blossoms newborn in the blue lotus.
            Twilight is heavy with gods. . . .

XI. Argument:
The Shape of Thesis and Evidence

And the quiet joy of tomorrow,
              dawn whitening over her loveliness:
Oh Memphis my city, beauty forever!—
              you are a bowl of love's own berries,
Dish set for Ptah your god,
              god of the handsome face.

The translator's aim is a poem, of course, but more specifically (and more accurately) it is a feeling that the final version catches not what the original said but what its author must have meant by employing the words he did. With a language as long dead as Egyptian hieroglyphic, that goal is a gamble against rather long odds. All too often there is, perhaps, *a* poem, but without the inner conviction that it recreates *the* poem; and the translator sadly recalls the clever observation that a poem is never finished, it is only abandoned. No matter how convincing the tonal equivalent seems to be when freshly finished, it should always be set aside for several weeks or months and then examined again to see if any cracks have developed in its construction. Often what one thought was a fine phrase or a lively image dries and deadens with time, needing change. So, one tries to revise, checking, teasing, and polishing.

And once in a while, with a new word or phrase the poem is finally and really there; the translator feels he can do no more with it. Nor does he wish to, for it now is as right as he can make it. He feels he has caught the life of the ancient text and time in words and rhythms that are alive now: he has really been back there, and returned. It is a good feeling; for it is a victory, no matter how small or momentary, over death and decay and time—the death of lovers, of papyri, of authors and civilizations, of emotions and consciousness. And I hope that it is not too pretentious a way of putting it; for that, it seems to me, it the way it is—the ultimate motive for translation: keeping traditions of civilization alive, recreating people of flesh and blood out of the distant past.

80. Science and the Irresponsible Imagination

NORMAN E. NELSON

Nelson (1899–   ), born in Minnesota, educated at Illinois and Harvard, is Professor Emeritus of English at the University of Michigan, where for years his course in critical theory was an essential feature of the doctoral program. His central book is *Peter Ramus and the Confusion of Logic, Rhetoric, and Poetry* (1947).

THE LITERARY GENERATION I grew up with sustained the first impact, in America at least, of Nietzsche, Freud, Marx, and Einstein. Young ones throughout the land caught whiffs of air that seemed fresher and winier than any we had breathed before; we lifted our faces to the East and took heady gulps of the new doctrines. Encouraged by the scolding of our elders, we read what we could get hold of and moved as near to the Eastern seaboard as we could to get the full benefit. Even so we did not imbibe an undiluted air. Being Americans, we depended on translations, often on popularizations, and more often still on what we heard at parties from authoritative young people who had read neither. I am disposed to be indulgent towards the follies of our youth: we had no guide but Mencken.* The physics professor refused to suspend his demonstrations to tell us about Einstein's new theories, and the new doctrines seemed to sanction our resistance to stuffy taboos and pieties and offered us a new world in which there were no fixities. We sniffed the promise of the full life.

But now those of us who have not died are getting old, and, what is more significant, these ideas of our flaming youth are getting on in years and ought to settle down and act their age. This they are not, in my opinion, doing. Freud is not quite so wildly misrepresented as in the 'twenties, Marx's light is for the moment at least under a bushel, and Thomas Mann has sorted out the good from the bad in Nietzsche; yet the popularizers still ride the magazine circuit, and in one field especially I have noticed that the wiseacres are almost never challenged or

* H. L. Mencken (1880–1956), American journalist.

heckled. In the space-time continuum that Professor Einstein rules as his domain there are few indeed who dare to raise their heads and look inquiringly about them.

When I read the popularized physics of our present decade I am compelled to recall the 'twenties and my own uneasy bemusement which culminated when I read "The Nature of the Physical World." Therein Eddington * said, or seemed to say, that an iron bar is at one and the same time of different lengths according to the way its atoms are distributed by the magnetic field surrounding it, that magnetic field being determined not by where the bar is but by where it is observed from—the lonely platforms circling in space, each with a scientist peering through his telescope and jotting down his calculations. Since Eddington was acknowledged even by his grim fellow scientists to be the Lord Bishop of the physical universe, and since I was worn down by the effort to comprehend him, I succumbed to his style. I was therefore off balance when he struck boldly with the thought that the world spread round us in space and time is revealed to us by only one facet depending on our own stance in space-time, and would reveal itself to us in quite another and wondrous wise if we could only whip around fast enough to catch it unaware in another dimension. In all fairness I must acknowledge Eddington's warning that such fourth-dimensional acrobatics were simply not feasible; nevertheless I tried. Of course, like everyone else, I was overwhelmed by his proof of the freedom of our wills and spirit from the unaccountable behavior of subatomic particles.

Eddington was no mere popularizer and I do not visualize myself as reducing him to confusion in debate. My quarrel is with myself for believing what I did not understand, and, as time goes on, with semi-scientific popularizers who disseminate what they clearly do not understand. Time should have brought a sifting of the first extravagant conjectures and reassertion of the human right to examine what we are asked to believe. Time has brought no such thing. Because some awesome speculations have exploded convincingly in the mid-Pacific, few of us are rash enough to quibble about anything bearing the label of the new physics.

When Zeno * first pointed out the rift in the universe, life and thought were less complex. According to his teaching, a tortoise with a head start on Achilles would always maintain a light or at least an infinitesimal lead, since he would always be covering *some* distance while Achilles was catching up to where he had just been. It took mathematicians almost two thousand years to catch up with Zeno and solve the problem by the differential calculus. But in the simple ancient days it was always comfortingly possible for anyone to pass a tortoise if there was one about. Today the man in the street must set out at fantastic speeds

* Sir Arthur Stanley Eddington (1882–1944), English astronomer.
* (c.336–c.264 B.C.) Greek philosopher who founded stoicism.

over unimaginable distances in several directions at once in order to detect whether there is or is not a discrepancy so slight that even a tax collector would disregard it. In such circumstances the man in the street prudently keeps his mouth shut and waits for the experts to give him the answer.

But when scientific authority is invoked for social and cultural views and attitudes, the right to challenge is as inalienable as the right to utter. Otherwise there is the possibility of a new dogmatism spread by the camp followers of science on the march. The propagation of highly conjectural speculations as if they had been verified by adequate scientific procedures, the casual misrepresentation of scientific statements, and the gaping inferences drawn by the magic of analogy from the world of verifiable facts to the world of human values and judgments: these may present us with a new authoritarianism disguised as freedom from authority, a new obscurantism to stifle our critical intelligence. Scientists, of course, should be left alone to settle among themselves the scientific validity of speculations by their more imaginative colleagues, though I could wish that they would occasionally disclaim in public some of the rasher extrascientific inferences made by enthusiasts in the name of science. But they give only a random glance, amused or exasperated according to temperament, at the popular transmogrifications of their professional mysteries. If the scientists themselves will not turn aside to liberate us from the spellbinders of metascience the amateurs must make the try. Since Thurber did such a magnificent job on pseudo-psychological gabble in "Let Your Mind Alone," I have wished for some time that we could turn him loose on the astrophysical plane. Much might be done, or, better still, undone.

Being neither a scientist nor a Thurber, I do not expect much success or even gratitude for my efforts to police the cosmos, particularly since my own approach is a somewhat limited one: I am a reader of contemporary literature with a puzzled interest in the theorizing that goes on to explain it. There is, however, no more eager market for new and unsettling ideas than among creative artists, especially those who use words as their medium. The poet's imagination must be free and has progressively thrown off the trammels of respectability, tradition, and more recently the established conventions of communication by language. Writers, therefore, rejoiced greatly when the solid mechanism of nineteenth-century science fell apart and began to dissolve into a fluid and, later, a somewhat gaseous state. The poet-critics, not at all inclined to be silent, were revising cosmographies and gloating over the death of truisms without listening carefully to what the scientist with the armed vision was saying. The criterion was not the validity of the new idea but its power to confound the Philistine. If I had to choose between these mad-hatters and the brash simpletons who find the universe not surprising at all but quite what one would expect, I would certainly choose to be mad: the universe is doubtless stranger and more wonderful than men will ever be able to realize. But it is possible to recognize the mysterious without presuming to promulgate its secrets, and the hollow incantations of the literary witch doctors do the universe more harm than good, particularly if, as Rimbaud ruefully admitted, they project the private disorder of their minds upon the world around them.

Dostoievski was, I believe, the first to announce with calm effrontery that whereas two plus two equals four is an interesting proposition, the proposition two plus two equals five is equally or even more so. This blast of inspired insolence must have shaken the rugged Scottish hills on which Dr. Johnson was treading heavily when he cited the immutability of the old count to enforce one of his prejudices on the complaisant Boswell.* Except for Housman, who concedes the point with sullen heart, most literary calculators in recent years have been making the sum out to be five or three, or at least not four. Proust in "Sodome et Gomorrhe" makes it out five, and André Breton quotes Dostoievski's proposition as one of the ten commandments of Surrealism. Our own Cummings enforced the point in the title of an early book of poems, and most recently Saroyan, of the wistful vistas, has proclaimed the new arithmetic over a nation-wide television hook-up. Of course none of these gentlemen would permit any such nonsense from the waiter adding up their checks.

They have, however, received some apparent support from philosophers. Whitehead * stuns the reader with this problem: One plus one equals two, but suppose they are drops of water. What then? The reader's sanity, reeling from this blow, may recover itself by reflecting on Whitehead's valuable distinction between the world of experience and the system of abstract symbols convenient for scientists. Of course two plus two makes four, though that does not explain fusion or fission any more than the multiplication table accounts for the propagation of the species. To turn the philosopher's doubt of the adequacy of symbols into a sanction for the misuse of them is to make symbols still less useful and to encourage an addlepated tendency already sufficiently evident in ourselves.

But the fun that the literary mystagogue has with arithmetic is nothing to what is possible when he begins taking liberties with the laws of physics. Perhaps the clearest illustration of this is the almost universal misunderstanding of the Heisenberg principle of indeterminacy. Like many great scientific discoveries, including Galileo's epochal account of falling bodies and of missile trajectories, this principle is popularly mistaken to be the direct expression of experimental observation, but in fact it is a rational inference from an unobserved universal

* James Boswell (1740–1795), author of *The Life of Samuel Johnson*. Johnson (1709–1784), critic and essayist, published *A Dictionary of the English Language* in 1755.
* Alfred North Whitehead (1861–1947), British philosopher and mathematician.

assumption to an unobservable universal conclusion. Heisenberg * wanted to trace the path and note the speed of electrons moving within the atom. He found that the only way one can pin-point an electron for observation is by catching it in a beam of light of the very shortest wave length, therefore of the very highest frequency, therefore, alas, of such violent force as to joggle the very electron one is trying to observe, altering both its speed and its direction. His conclusion, the Heisenberg principle, is that we shall never be able experimentally to find out precisely what the electrons are doing and will have to be content with a statistical estimate of probability as to their carryings-on.

It seems incredible that any moderately intelligent person could confuse our own uncertainty about the electron's behavior with capricious or chaotic behavior on the part of the electrons. If mere caprice or chaos obtained we couldn't even achieve statistical estimates, for some regularity is necessary to provide for the probability and for the constancy of Planck's constant.* The principle is not that the electron is undertermined in its behavior but that we cannot determine what its behavior is. The presumption is unavoidable if unacknowledged that there is regularity if we could only detect it. Scientists have learned to operate with statistical probability since that is all they can get, but there is no reason why the universe has to conform to the limits of scientific information. Yet popular expositions of Einstein's universe and even articles in the "Scientific Monthly" explicitly assert the capricious irregularity of the universe on the authority of Heisenberg.

It is no wonder then that the literary world reacted extravagantly to the disturbing news. Leo Stein's "Journey Into the Self" provides an amusing sample of the tendency to react with vast emotional concern to something we are not willing to take pains to understand. Stein immediately concocted a portentous image of mankind doomed henceforth to dwell on a thin crust of scenery concealing a chaotic and presumably treacherous reality. But Stein's gloomy masochist joy was nothing to the exultation of the literary mystics who received the wayward electron as proof positive of man's free will in an exciting new universe, preferable in every way to the mechanical model of the nineteenth century. Eddington, presiding in full scientific regalia over the rebirth of freedom, was received as a latter-day prophet, and the Heisenberg principle enshrined in Franz Werfel's preface to "Goat Song."

The uncritical transfer of scientific proof and authority from the limited sphere of physics to the intangible problems of human life and culture is habitual in literary circles. When the atom was discovered to be not a homogeneous lump of irreducible matter but a bundle of

---

* Werner Heisenberg (1901–   ), German physicist.
* Max Planck (1858–1947), German physicist mainly noted for the initial development of the Quantum Theory, which ultimately breaks light and energy down into discrete units. *Planck's constant* is a part of the mathematics of Quantum Mechanics.

energies held together by inner tension rather than by an outer skin, the critics hailed the new dynamism not merely as a persuasive analogy or fresh illustration of the ancient literary principle of organic unity but as a revolutionary development. The principle of artistic unity could now be founded not on the waning authority of Aristotle or Coleridge but on the bedrock of scientific demonstration. Of course the argument "as an atom is so must a poem be," no matter what scientific airs it gives itself, has even less cogency than Horace's dictum about poetry and painting. The poem need not aspire to the condition of the atom; if organic is better than mechanical unity in a poem it is so because human needs and wishes are better served, not because the poem is put together just like something else that is not a poem. Without insisting on Byzantine artificiality as poetry's chief merit, one might nevertheless say that it is a characteristic which sometimes appeals to us more than the naturalness of life—of which, in case we prefer the organic, there is no noticeable shortage.

But the impact of atomic physics on the literary mind was as nothing to that of relativity which opened up a new realm of faërie to the poets and still more to their critical camp followers. In the "Letters of Ezra Pound" there is a comical and significant exchange between the young and ardent Blackmur, who wants to know how the master has metabolized the new concepts of space and time, and Pound, who replies testily that of course he realized Dante's journey through the center of the earth would have brought him out not on the Isle of Purgatory but somewhere near Australia. Further than Copernicus he refused to be drawn, professing not only ignorance but indifference. Pound, of course, was not nearly so much interested in contemplating the turbulent vortices that produce our space-time continuum as he was in projecting the Vorticism created by his own turbulence and calculated to produce a pleasing chaos in literary circles. Hart Crane seems at times to have thought that relativity in some unspecified way had validated his own intuitions, but he had no time to spare for such ideologies from the fascinated exploration of the springs of song within him—though he does adorn his Pocahontas with

> Time like a serpent down her shoulder, dark
> And space an eaglet's wing laid on her hair.

Poets of our century have as much right to take cosmic, or cosmetic, liberties with Einstein as Milton had to conjure up Lucretius' pagan atoms in his Christian Hell or play fast and loose with Copernicus; the critic, too, has a right to expatiate in as spooky a universe as he chooses. But if the critic asks me in the name of science to accept these imaginative décors as sober accounts of the reality I live in, I have the usual right to self-protection and may sift the poetic statements for truth on my own responsibility.

When, for example, I am assured by my aesthetic acquaintances that a straight line is no longer, under Einstein, the shortest distance between two points, I have a right to ask them to point me out a shorter. The shortest distance between points on a spherical surface is the straight line through the circle, whatever the surface distance may be. The Riemann surface often used to clinch their argument turns out to be a mathematician's construct with a strictly theoretical barrier between the points. Still more frequently cited is the fact that light-rays, like everything else in a gravitational field, travel in a curve. But, however sorry one may be for the light having to go round, it is difficult to see how that alters the distance between the points. Of course, if our literary minds confuse the unqualified with the negotiable distance they can make the universe out to be as queer as they like—and they do like.

On the other hand, we cannot dismiss as mere bogey the disquieting results of the Michelson-Morley experiment, which proved that a beam of light travels just as fast with as it does against or across the earth's motion through space. This constancy of the speed of light is the firm foundation of all relativity theory, but it is a very upsetting constancy. If the speed of light is unaffected by the speed of the object it takes off from and by the speed of its recipient, then light is very constant indeed but everything else is bewilderingly inconstant. Although physicists do not attempt to explain why this is so, and have not yet shown how light defies the ground rules, nevertheless they have been able to obtain greater verifiable accuracy in their calculations by using this theory than by rejecting it. Without pretending to resolve these perplexities I should like to reassure the man in the street and to mitigate the delicious vertigo of the literary relativist by remarking that neither the light-beam nor the earth is traveling at more than one speed whatever speed that may be. If they were, all bets and calculations would be off. The relativity is not in the speeds themselves but in the relationship between them—somehow.

Einstein very reasonably holds that no one inside the time-space continuum can have an absolute point of observation from which to determine the absolute motion of anything. To know the absolute motion of our automobile we would have to add to the speedometer reading the rotation of the earth on its axis and around the sun, any drift of our solar system in our galaxy, or, dizzying thought, any drift of our galaxy in space. If it is argued that, from different platforms in space, observers would clock the car at different speeds, even then the relativity would be in the observations and not in the motion of the car: the car is going at such a speed as to measure so much from one platform and so much from another. The literary relativist, having confused our limited observation of the fact with the fact itself, ascribes the perplexities of our observation to the fact, but the fact is not perplexed and the universe is not nearly so crazy as some of the people in it. If scientists find it convenient to accept the wave theory and the quantum theory of light on alternate days, light does not change its nature to conform to their theories but continues to be whatever it is throughout the week.

The same confusion leads us to deny simultaneity because we cannot know *now* what is going on *now* on Arcturus * but must wait till the light-ray gets here with the news in 1990. Einstein's own proof that we cannot apply simultaneity to the universe at large proceeds from the explicit assumption of a simultaneous instant to the reasonable conclusion that the observation of the event by different observers will occur at different times. Whether we are able or not to calculate all of the speeds involved and so tag the identical light-ray does not affect the fact that we must accept objective simultaneity in order to realize the relativity of our experience.

But our imaginative friends are not content to be earth bound and let the light-rays do the moving about. They long to launch themselves in rockets whizzing so fast that their clocks and hearts will imperceptibly slow down, thus extending their youth and lives. Since the fright and physiological strain of crowding the light barrier would more than offset the effect of relativity on their metabolisms, it is just as well that they remain chair-borne. I have no wish to dispute Einstein's theory on this point; I do, however, protest the careless rapture with which it is ex-ploited in literary circles and not merely in limericks about the young lady who set out one day in a relative way and returned the previous night. A poet-critic speaking to a university audience in defense of modern poetry argued that reality has turned out to be as irrational as any poet's dream. On the authority of Harvard scientists (unnamed), he assured us that two men, leaving the earth at the same instant in different rockets might return either one before the other, or (trium-phantly) *each* before the other. Since the physicist sitting next me made no protest beyond a subdued groan, the argument went unchallenged to support poetry about corners striving to get round themselves. How could anyone be certified insane, or sane for that matter, in such a uni-verse? We academics are so conscious of our historic role as enemies of new talent and new insights that we dare not challenge any folly that comes to us in the name of novelty. The irresponsibles have us buffaloed.

If ever I am lured, quaking, aboard a space ship, it will be on the promise to take me, not just for a spin and back, but to that well-known point where parallel lines meet. I have grown so skeptical of that Ultima Thule that I should insist on reaching out from the porthole to touch the exact spot. But by the time I get there I expect it will have moved on. Indeed, in my present unreconstructed state, I believe it to be a quibble calculated to give us just the kind of metascientific thrill we can't resist. Mathematicians have a way of talking about infinity as a limit—as a straight line is the limit of circularity—just because such limits are

* A star about 37 "light-years" from the earth.

like the square root of minus one, convenient in their work. The mathematician as such doesn't care two pins whether actual lines actually meet or not. But my Einsteinian friends appeal to the principle of the finite universe, the space-time continuum which terminates all lines and parallels and beyond which there is nothing—nothing at all. Within this universe, they say, no lines are straight but all are curved, since the very light-beams by which we sight a line are themselves curved. I should think in that case it would be more accurate as well as more comprehensible to say in the first place that no truly parallel lines can be observed; but then I don't suppose that would be a mystifying paradox.

One may even doubt if space and time have really been reduced to a finite space-time continuum. For if the universe is a finite system it is also an expanding system, and one is bound to ask: What space is it expanding into? Moreover, it will one day, we are assured, revert to an unorganized homogeneity. One is bound to ask: When the space-time continuum is thus dissolved, what becomes of time? The answer given by the popularizers is that as the universe runs down its matter-energy will be dissipated into empty space, or as one writer puts it, the insatiable void. Thus when all system and order has vanished from the universe, there will be no direction of time: time must have a stop, and there will be nothing but perpetual stagnation.

The plain reader is apt to feel that there is an equivocation somewhere here. If there is no longer either space or time, but only space-time curved about the stars, where do we put this insatiable void? And where does all this perpetuity come in? If, as Jeans * put it, our space-time bubble is made of empty space welded onto empty time, when the bubble gets unwelded the original parts are not thereby destroyed. So there we are again with space as well as time on our hands.

The application of this space-time continuum to aesthetic and literary theory always seems to be dubious. Thus Picasso, by cramming the usual three dimensions into a two-dimensional arrangement and making the spectator supply the multiple perspectives, gets the credit for anticipating the fourth dimension. My objection to this kind of arithmetic does not in the least imply a distaste for the new art: there is nothing wrong with a busted guitar if you don't have to play it. Similarly Joyce and Proust, severely restricting their time span in order to reproduce the full richness of psychological experience, are given dubious credit for reducing time to space. If they really did spatialize time they would be completely at odds with the new physics, which has been busy temporalizing space for the last fifty years. Fortunately the praise is undeserved. The experience presented to the reader is not static: granted it is slow motion; nevertheless, as Galileo may have said, it moves.

The temporalizing of space does offer some suggestive analogies in aesthetics: it helps us to the dynamic view of a painting not as a merely

* Sir James Jeans (1877–1946), English physicist and astronomer.

static disposition in space but as an organization of our energies activated by the artist. But even here there is the danger that the analogy will be pressed with blind logic. It does not follow, as Dewey thought, that the poem or picture has to be justified as an engine to bring about social or cultural change. One may even grant Whitehead his continuum in which every object or "event" is conditioned by every other unto the farthest speck of atomic dust drifting in outer space, and yet maintain that one of the greatest opportunities of art is to exclude and so achieve a limited wholeness. Empson has sufficiently exhibited the ingenious folly of pumping up a poem till it means everything. In like manner, one may accept without prejudice the inevitability of novelty in a world of "process," and yet resist the fashionable assumption that newness is itself a value. Our literary folk are so obsessed with this notion that they are trying to hustle history along at an unseemly gait, but there is no visible need for literary folk to go in for experimental writing in vain rivalry with science. Whitehead's sanguine faith in creativity prevented him from seeing the need for some tests of value amid all the novelty.

One service that Whitehead has rendered along with Ortega y Gasset * is to insist that relativity means relatedness and not mere chaos or anarchy. Perhaps the vulgarest of all uses of the doctrine is to appeal to it to sanction the individual's interpretation or evaluation of a work of art, no matter how idiosyncratic. To Whitehead, relatedness is characteristic of our apprehension. And Ortega rightly asserts that in an important sense Einstein's theory replaces with a new absolute the real relativism of the nineteenth century. Certainly Einstein condemns our provincial tendency to impose our particular perspective on the rest of the universe; yet no other observation platform is any better than ours and we ought to make full and accurate use of it. Einstein would have small patience with anyone asserting his right to see things as he chooses or to differ at will in his calculations. If we are to draw analogies in cultural matters from the field of physics we must recognize the assumption of uniformity in observers, the presumption of ultimate agreement in theory, and the feasibility of calculating the perspectives of other observation platforms and so of arriving at a unified theory which embraces the relativities.

Another potent influence on literary relativism is the subjective idealism which developed to the point of solipsism in the last century. Infinitely wise philosophers sat in their studies in the suburbs of London and Paris between 1870 and 1910 convincing themselves that space and time are not real and objective around us but subjective and created from within. Space and time, naturally, are hospitable enough to contain any number of solipsists and their private universes too. And quite understandably, the private universe has an irresistible appeal to the creative artist: Flaubert finds it more possible to achieve aesthetic order

* José Ortega y Gasset (1883–1955), Spanish philosopher and statesman.

in his study than to achieve moral or social integration in a shared and common world; and Joyce and Gertrude Stein find it more convenient to create Ireland or America in a foreign city where there are few compatriots to distract them. And in his padded cell, Proust engulfs his past life in his morbid imagination and reissues it to the reader in the time sequence not of the events recalled but of his warped memory and his artistic purpose. As Gide protested that no matter how many characters populate the novel, Proust is always talking about himself, so it should be remarked that Proust's time is an interior time private to himself. Granted that he was able to render his perverse world almost as fascinating to the reader as to himself, the reader should know that he is looking at an internal landscape. Relativity has nothing to say, one way or the other, about such private continuums. Einstein brooding over the vast abyss may have inadvertently troubled the waters and made good fishing.

The same critics who invoke the space-time continuum to justify the flood-sweep of *Finnegan's Wake* or *Remembrance of Things Past* are equally ready to appeal to the great principle of discontinuity in quantum theory in order to justify the elliptical style and arbitrary juxtapositions in the symbolist poetry of Mallarmé, Yeats, or Eliot. Anyone who cares to make the effort can work out the puzzles in such writing and discover great poetry without thereby committing himself to the quantum theory any more than to a belief in drowned Phoenician sailors or Rosicrucian gyres and gimbles. If a poet can create an imaginary order out of the real disorder in his mind, he has at least a Nietzschean justification: One must first have chaos within to give birth to a dancing star. But the artistic validity does not carry with it any guarantee of validity in the real world, natural or human.

The real source of literary discontinuity is Coleridge's theory of the creative imagination dissolving the observed world in order to recombine the parts in a new order. The French Romantics developed this doctrine until it appears in Remy de Gourmont as the doctrine of *dissociations*. The chief function of the poet, according to this theory, is to disrupt all the connections in the observed world in order to make the most startling and violently unlikely combinations that the poet's imagination can concoct. De Gourmont particularly admired Hugo's bold comparison of the bight of a ship's rope to the bend of an actress's leg in a posture of tragic despair. One of Eliot's greatest critical coups was his clever inversion of de Gourmont's term: according to Eliot the difference between an ordinary person and a poet is that the ordinary person has a dissociated sensibility and is unable to see the connections between things whereas the poet has unified sensibility and, in Eliot's famous illustration, can unite such apparently disparate items as the sound of his typewriter, being in love, the smell of cooking, and reading Spinoza. Being an ordinary person, I am utterly unable to see any connection, but

XI. Argument:
The Shape of Thesis and Evidence

I have read enough of Eliot to know that the feat is well within his powers. What I admire especially is Eliot's strategy in making dissociation or disorder characteristic of the lay mind and order and integration the distinguishing quality of poetry. It should be permissible, however, to point out that the poet's strenuous fancy can have no effect on the presumed indifference of the typewriter to kitchen smells, or whatever reciprocity there may be between reading Spinoza and being in love. The real order of things is such that if we really unified such disparates we would have to be confined in an upstairs room. I can see no harm in imagining such a unity, with Eliot's help of course, but I do not see how the physical principle of discontinuity makes it necessary for the poet to confront the reader with an artificial chaos. Critics who quote Whitehead in support of symbolist poetry discreetly ignore his tacit disapproval of such poetry: he preferred his romanticism straight, in Shelley or even Swinburne.

Another nineteenth-century notion, fostered by the impressionist painters and Bergson's * earlier philosophy, does seem at first to bear a close analogy to Einstein's later conception of our relative point of view in space-time: that is the notion of the poem or picture as fixing the transitory moment of the artist's experience, a haystack in a certain light, or Wallace Stevens' jar in Tennessee; but the uniqueness of the concrete experience is to Einstin not an end in itself. It is no more than the starting point of calculations leading to an inclusive comprehension expressible only in abstract terms.

It seems more fruitful to accept Ortega's analogy of a cultural relativity in which it is impossible for any of us really to have anyone else's point of view, but happily possible to extend one's own limited perspective by sharing imaginatively in the response to the world of as many others as can express their points of view. To the extent that all works of art inevitably express variations in space and time, no doubt the discipline of sympathetic recreation of the poem's experience would have a broadening as well as a chastening effect upon the widely-read man of the world. The development of this more inclusive view seems to me one of the greatest justifications of literature and the teaching of literature, and for our effort to understand the difficult moderns.

Unfortunately, this sound theory is used most often to encourage the exclusive reading of such highly eccentric geniuses as Mallarmé, Rilke, Lorca, or Wallace Stevens. By the time the reader has been drawn into this international cult of special pleaders, of men who are expressing in various idioms a resentment toward the world and a pharisaical disdain for the people who are not as they are, the reader has cut himself off from more human experience than he has gained. His cultivated ear

* Henri Bergson (1859–1941), French philosopher. Proponent of dynamic *élan vital* (life force) as contrasted with resistant matter, Bergson emphasized the rôle of intuition in human thought.

for the oblique, elliptical, and symbolic expression of maladive poetry has become deaf to the voice that is the voice of many men.

Eliot has another Bergsonian conception of a time continuum in which each new major poet continues the tradition of past great poetry, at the same time altering that tradition retroactively by the contribution of his new talent. Homer will never be the same since Eliot wrote "Sweeney among the Nightingales." I am convinced that in a certain sense this is true, but if so it is a pity. The noble voice of European poetry that tried to speak for all and to all and in such a way that all could understand has dwindled to a querulous quaver. Baudelaire chewing bitterly at his own entrails began the process of self-destruction, and now the poets are pitifully echoing Apollinaire's charge that the poet, a divine simpleton, is being assassinated by coarse Philistines. Granted that the youthful poet ought to be much better cared for, he must share with his money-making father the blame for his own unhappy place in the human family. Certainly Einstein would not support a relativism that arrogantly excludes so many nonpoetical points of view as the theory of the contemporary poet-critic does.

But far and away the most appealing notion to the creative genius is in direct opposition to relativity, the notion that he can, actually and literally, transcend space and time in moments of mystic vision. Since the whole point of relativity is that we have to derive our knowledge of the universe from the data observable from our particular point of view within the space-time sequence, Einstein can hardly be responsible for the diabolical sublimities of Joyce or Gertrude's Sibylline small talk. As a matter of fact this notion is as old as the romantic hills, and can be traced all the way from Shelley to his ungrateful heir, T. S. Eliot.

There can be, I admit, no demonstration, scientific or otherwise, that poets do not enjoy the inexpressible bliss of a brief sojourn out of space and time before they return to face their typewriters. I am inclined to think they must have been somewhere special. But they cannot honestly say that the new physics provided the transportation. Science does not validate or invalidate poetry or poetic theory in any substantive way. After all, whatever validity there is to Eliot's theory of the impersonality of the poet does not depend on his impressive analogy of the poet with platinum as catalytic acting upon oxygen and sulphur dioxide to produce sulphurous acid without entering into the product itself. It would be all over with his theory if it did so depend, for four chemists have assured me that platinum would have no such effect. Significantly, the authority of Mr. Eliot's style has carried his point unchallenged for more than thirty years. When critics and poets appeal to the authority and prestige of science to support their critical principles and poetic practice they not only distort and misrepresent science but actually endanger the poetic values by providing such insecure support. Anyway the scientists have enough to worry about. Overwhelmed like the sorcerer's apprentice by their sudden and excessive powers, and dismayed by the goals set for them by the prophetic revelations of science fiction, they are in as perilous a plight from the adulation of uncritical enthusiasts as are the poets from the misapprehensions of metascientific critics. The freedom of the poet's imagination cannot but be imperiled by making him responsible for the nature of the physical world.

81. Johannes Kepler

ALBERT EINSTEIN

Einstein (1879–1955) was born at Ulm, Germany, and grew up in Munich, where his father started a small factory. He finished his schooling in Switzerland when his family moved to Italy, eventually earning a teacher's certificate in mathematics and physics in 1900 and becoming a Swiss citizen. Finding no opening for teachers, he went to work for the Swiss patent office in Berne, screening patent applications and finding time to evolve four major papers, published 1905, each containing a major discovery in physics and establishing his major contributions, his theories of relativity, motion, light, and the equivalence of mass and energy. He won the Nobel Prize in 1921. After a visit to California in 1932, and seeing the growing shadow of Hitler, he moved permanently to the Institute for Advanced Study, Princeton University, where he stayed until his death. He became a U.S. citizen in 1940, and urged Franklin D. Roosevelt to start the Manhattan Project to meet the wartime threat of German physicists who had discovered how to split the uranium atom in 1939.

IN ANXIOUS AND UNCERTAIN TIMES like ours, when it is difficult to find pleasure in humanity and the course of human affairs, it is particularly consoling to think of the serene greatness of a Kepler.* Kepler lived in an age in which the reign of law in nature was by no means an accepted certainty. How great must his faith in a uniform law have been, to have given him the strength to devote ten years

* Johannes Kepler (1571–1630), German astronomer.

of hard and patient work to the empirical investigation of the movement of the planets and the mathematical laws of that movement, entirely on his own, supported by no one and understood by very few! If we would honor his memory worthily, we must get as clear a picture as we can of his problem and the stages of its solution.

Copernicus * had opened the eyes of the most intelligent to the fact that the best way to get a clear grasp of the apparent movements of the planets in the heavens was by regarding them as movements around the sun conceived as stationary. If the planets moved uniformly in a circle around the sun, it would have been comparatively easy to discover how these movements must look from the earth. Since, however, the phenomena to be dealt with were much more complicated than that, the task was a far harder one. The first thing to be done was to determine these movements empirically from the observations of Tycho Brahe. Only then did it become possible to think about discovering the general laws which these movements satisfy.

To grasp how difficult a business it was even to find out about the actual rotating movements, one has to realize the following. One can never see where a planet really is at any given moment, but only in what direction it can be seen just then from the earth, which is itself moving in an unknown manner around the sun. The difficulties thus seemed practically unsurmountable.

Kepler had to discover a way of bringing order into this chaos. To start with, he saw that it was necessary first to try and find out about the motion of the earth itself. This would simply have been impossible if there had existed only the sun, the earth and the fixed stars, but no other planets. For in that case one could ascertain nothing empirically except how the direction of the straight sun-earth line changes in the course of the year (apparent movement of the sun with reference to the fixed stars). In this way it was possible to discover that these sun-earth directions all lay in a plane stationary with reference to the fixed stars, at least according to the accuracy of observation achieved in those days, when there were no telescopes. By this means it could also be ascertained in what manner the sun-earth revolves round the sun. It turned out that the angular velocity of this motion went through regular change in the course of the year. But this was not of much use, as it was still not known how the distance from the earth to the sun alters in the course of the year. It was only when they found out about these changes that the real shape of the earth's orbit and the manner in which it is described were discovered.

Kepler found a marvelous way out of this dilemma. To begin with it was apparent from observations of the sun that the apparent path of the sun against the background of the fixed stars differed in speed at

* Nicolaus Copernicus (1473–1543), Polish astronomer, regarded as the founder of modern astronomy.

different times of the year, but that the angular velocity of this movement was always the same at the same point in the astronomical year, and therefore that the speed of rotation of the straight line earth-sun was always the same when it pointed to the same region of the fixed stars. It was thus legitimate to suppose that the earth's orbit was a self-enclosed one, described by the earth in the same way every year—which was by no means obvious *a priori*. For the adherent of the Copernican system it was thus as good as certain that this must also apply to the orbits of the rest of the planets.

This certainty made things easier. But how to ascertain the real shape of the earth's orbit? Imagine a brightly shining lantern M somewhere in the plane of the orbit. We know that this lantern remains permanently in its place and thus forms a kind of fixed triangulation point for determining the earth's orbit, a point which the inhabitants of the earth can take a sight on at any time of year. Let this lantern M be further away from the sun than the earth. With the help of such a lantern it was possible to determine the earth's orbit, in the following way:—

First of all, in every year there comes a moment when the earth E lies exactly on the line joining the sun S and the lantern M. If at this moment we look from the earth E at the lantern M, our line of sight will coincide with the line SM (sun-lantern). Suppose the latter to be marked in the heavens. Now imagine the earth in a different position and at a different time. Since the sun S and the lantern M can both be seen from the Earth, the angle at E in the triangle SEM is known. But we also know the direction of SE in relation to the fixed stars through direct solar observations, while the direction of the line SM in relation to the fixed stars was finally ascertained previously. But in the triangle SEM we also know the angle at S. Therefore, with the base SM arbitrarily laid down on a sheet of paper, we can, in virtue of our knowledge of the angles at E and S, construct the triangle SEM. We might do this at frequent intervals during the year; each time we should get on our piece of paper a position of the earth E with a date attached to it and a certain position in relation to the permanently fixed base SM. The earth's orbit would thereby be empirically determined, apart from its absolute size, of course.

But, you will say, where did Kepler get his lantern M? His genius and Nature, benevolent in this case, gave it to him. There was, for example, the planet Mars; and the length of the Martian year—i.e., one rotation of Mars around the sun—was known. It might happen one fine day that the sun, the earth and Mars lie absolutely in the same straight line. This position of Mars regularly recurs after one, two, etc., Martian years, as Mars has a self-enclosed orbit. At these known moments, therefore, SM always presents the same base, while the earth is always at a different point in its orbit. The observations of the sun and Mars at these moments thus constitute a means of determining the true orbit of the earth, as Mars then plays the part of our imaginary lantern. Thus it was that Kepler discovered the true shape of the earth's orbit and the way in which the earth describes it, and we who come after—Europeans, Germans, or even Swabians—may well admire and honor him for it.

Now that the earth's orbit had been empirically determined, the true position and length of the line SE at any moment was known, and it was not so terribly difficult for Kepler to calculate the orbits and motions of the rest of the planets too from observations—at least in principle. It was nevertheless an immense work, especially considering the state of mathematics at the time.

Now came the second and no less arduous part of Kepler's life work. The orbits were empirically known, but their laws had to be deduced from the empirical data. First he had to make a guess at the mathematical nature of the curve described by the orbit, and then try it out on a vast assemblage of figures. If it did not fit, another hypothesis had to be devised and again tested. After tremendous search, the conjecture that the orbit was an ellipse with the sun at one of its foci was found to fit the facts. Kepler also discovered the law governing the variation in speed during rotation, which is that the line sun-planet sweeps out equal areas in equal periods of time. Finally he also discovered that the square of the period of circulation around the sun varies as the cube of the major axes of the ellipse.

Our admiration for this splendid man is accompanied by another feeling of admiration and reverence, the object of which is no man but the mysterious harmony of nature into which we are born. As far back as ancient times people devised the lines exhibiting the simplest conceivable form of regularity. Among these, next to the straight line and the circle, the most important were the ellipse and the hyperbola. We see the last two embodied—at least very nearly so—in the orbits of the heavenly bodies.

It seems that the human mind has first to construct forms independently before we can find them in things. Kepler's marvelous achievement is a particularly fine example of the truth that knowledge cannot spring from experience alone but only from the comparison of the inventions of the intellect with observed fact.

Suggestions for Writing

1. Take some familiar fairy tales (*Beauty and the Beast, Jack and the Bean Stalk*), or some myth like those Kohl discussed with his class ("Cupid and Psyche," "Odysseus and the Sirens"), and write an essay analyzing it for its psychological and social meanings, along the lines Young follows in the last section of his "Pocahontas."

2. Write a research paper on some similar piece of popular history—Plymouth Rock, Thanksgiving turkey, the naming of your home town—again following Young's procedure.

3. Write an essay comparing translations of a poem, or a paragraph in prose, with the original in some language you can handle, keeping in mind Foster's tightrope walker.

4. Write an essay on the thesis: "John Foster's essay on translating Egyptian poetry dispells a number of our ordinary assumptions about the Egyptians"—and perhaps about poetry as well. Or, in some other way, write an essay getting at the essential attractiveness and interest of Foster's treatment of this out-of-the-way subject. How much does his own ability as a writer contribute?

5. Compare Foster and Nelson as essayists, and stylists, considering their metaphors and such phrases as "keeping one's balance," "emerging from the sand," "some awesome speculations have exploded convincingly in the mid-Pacific," "efforts to police the cosmos," "carryings-on," "light defies the ground rules," and so forth.

6. Write an essay on some common assumption like "everything is relative," "time is an illusion" or "man imposes order on a chaotic reality," using evidence from Nelson, Einstein, and your own observations as to how the sun seems to keep getting up on time every morning.

7. Write an essay on one of the literary works, or writers, Nelson mentions, or on some piece of science fiction—H. G. Wells, Vonnegut, Buck Rogers, and so forth.

8. Write an essay explaining some scientific concept, or some practical operation like that of a pump, a gasoline engine (the Wankel, for instance), a dressmaker, or a carpenter, trying to attain the lucidity of Einstein on Kepler.

XII. Varieties of Argument

ARGUMENT culminates the expository drive, absorbing all modes of prose into its persuasive purpose. It energizes the more passive, or neutral, spirit of description and exposition, and it gives direction to the self-absorption of stories. At its best, it is reason at its best, exposing and overcoming all hidden assumptions and all logical objections. The good argument must take in and defeat the other side, usually before moving on to its positive evidence, the advantages of the information it holds.

You can see much of this process in each of the following selections. Marvell's famous seventeenth-century poem, probably the best in English on the famous classical theme of seizing the day while one can, contains all the elements of argument: his concession to the opposite side, his own argumentative thesis, his answer to the other side, his persuasive evidence. Halpern argues Marvell's case in a modern mode, and Kemp amusingly puts the case for the opposition, exposing Marvell's hidden assumption. About forty years before Marvell, Donne had bumptiously based the same argument on a flea, inadvertently disclosing that our hygienic assumptions have changed, even if love has not.

The four essays argue with differing intensities. In Ogden and Chomsky, you can find again the major components of argumentation. Outline the *pro's* and *con's* of Ogden's argument; mark the turns he makes from his own position to bring in and answer the other. Do the same with Chomsky's more intense argument. How fairly does he handle his opposition? (We print only the first part of a long article.)

With Faulkner and Solzhenitsyn, we see argument refined to a distillation. Here the convictions run so deep that the opposition is only a shadow, brushed aside as not worth time or notice. These writers assert their convictions as truths, to stand on their own and persuade us. Can you raise objections to support any shadowy opposition they dismiss? Notice now that argument has come full circle, as it becomes the description, narration, and exposition of the author's deepest beliefs, and proof of his voice.

82. To His Coy Mistress

ANDREW MARVELL

Marvell (1621–1678) grew up in Hull, a seaport in northern England on the banks of the Humber River, mentioned in his poem. He entered Cambridge at thirteen, took an A.B. at eighteen, traveled in Europe as a tutor, missing the English civil war, then became tutor to William Dutton, the ward of Oliver Cromwell, now ruler of England after deposing and beheading Charles I. Marvell became Foreign Secretary in 1657, and in 1659 was elected Member of Parliament for Hull, a seat he held for the rest of his life. He remained a bachelor. He was a friend of Milton's. His housekeeper found and published his poems, most of them probably written in the 1640's and early '50's, after his death.

Had we but world enough, and time,
This coyness, Lady, were no crime.
We would sit down, and think which way
To walk, and pass our long love's day.
Thou by the Indian Ganges' side
Shouldst rubies find; I by the tide
Of Humber would complain. I would
Love you ten years before the Flood,
And you should, if you please, refuse
Till the Conversion of the Jews.
My vegetable love should grow
Vaster than empires and more slow;
An hundred years should go to praise
Thine eyes, and on thy forehead gaze;
Two hundred to adore each breast,
But thirty thousand to the rest;

An age at least to every part,
And the last age should show your heart.
For, Lady, you deserve this state,
Nor would I love at lower rate.
    But at my back I always hear
Time's wingèd chariot hurrying near;
And yonder all before us lie
Deserts of vast eternity.
Thy beauty shall no more be found,
Nor, in thy marble vault, shall sound
My echoing song; then worms shall try
That long-preserved virginity,
And your quaint honour turn to dust,
And into ashes all my lust:
The grave's a fine and private place,
But none, I think, do there embrace.
    Now therefore, while the youthful hue
Sits on thy skin like morning dew,
And while thy willing soul transpires
At every pore with instant fires,
Now let us sport us while we may,
And now, like amorous birds of prey,
Rather at once our time devour
Than languish in his slow-chapt power.
Let us roll all our strength and all
Our sweetness up into one ball,
And tear our pleasures with rough strife
Thorough the iron gates of life;
Thus, though we cannot make our sun
Stand still, yet we will make him run.

---

83. To His Coy Mistress

MARTIN HALPERN

Halpern (1929–   ), with degrees from Rochester and
Harvard, has taught in the Theater Arts Department of
Brandeis University since 1965. His poems have appeared
in many magazines and in his book, *Two Sides of an*

Island and Other Poems (1963). He has written a critical
volume on William Vaughn Moody (1964). His plays have
been produced in university and experimental theaters
in New York, Cambridge (Massachusetts), San Francisco,
and Berkeley.

Well since we are not built for despair,
Our parts being so obsoletely
Elastic, and since there's a fair
Chance that we'll never grow completely

Accustomed to the notion that dying
Might really be dying, and that hell
Might really be hell; and since in trying
As hard as we know how to tell

Ourselves that there is nothing wrong
With us a little love won't cure,
We have a way to make the long
Postponement easier to endure;

And since your eyes are very blue
As eyes go, and your lips as lips
Go, of a warmth and redness to
My taste; since furthermore your hips

And thighs are neither too large nor lean
And rather shapely as it were,
Whereas your breasts—or what I've seen
Of them—are even shapelier;

It seems a reasonable thing,
My sweet, for me to kiss your eyes
And then your lips, then lingering
Before your breasts and hips and thighs

Just long enough to make quite sure
No thoughts of despair or dying or hell
Will interfere, proceed to cure
My ills, and some of yours as well.

84. The Coy Mistress Replies

LYSANDER KEMP

Kemp (1920–   ), born in Randolph, Vermont, educated at Bates College (A.B.) and Boston University (M.A.), taught English at the University of Buffalo for seven years, before free-lancing in Mexico for thirteen years. He has published two books of poems, *The Northern Stranger* (1946), *The Conquest* (1970), and a number of translations from the Spanish, among them *The Labyrinth of Solitude* by Octavio Paz, *The Broken Spears: The Aztec Account of the Conquest of Mexico,* and *The Selected Poems of Ruben Dario.* He has been Editor of the University of Texas Press since 1966.

If Time, whose gentle Trot was right,
Hath learnt to gallop over-night;
If this capacious World so soon
Is shrunk, and shrivell'd like a prune;
If heav'nly Virtue's now a crime,
Concupiscence instead sublime:
Then these are Marvell's marvels, known
To his gross wit, and his alone:
Such fables cannot frighten mee
Out of my pretious Chastity.
    Yet, if hee'll quit his prattling talk
Of flesh to dust, of bones to chalk,
Of wintry Toombes, and am'rous worms,
And seek my love with fairer terms;
I'll melt, I'll be no longer coy,
Welcoming honourable Joy:
Then we'll turn pale, and lose our breath,
And find a livelier kind of Death:
For, if today he'll wed me right,
Why then, I'll die with him tonight.
    If not, then Fie to his rough strife,
He wants a bawd, and not a Wife.

85. The Flea

JOHN DONNE

Mark but this flea, and mark in this
How little that which thou deny'st me is;
It sucked me first, and now sucks thee,
And in this flea our two bloods mingled be;
Thou know'st that this cannot be said
A sin, nor shame, nor loss of maidenhead,
   Yet this enjoys before it woo,
     And pampered swells with one blood made of two,
     And this, alas, is more than we would do.

Oh stay, three lives in one flea spare,
Where we almost, yea more than married are.
This flea is you and I, and this
Our marriage bed, and marriage temple is;
Though parents grudge, and you, we're met
And cloistered in these living walls of jet.
   Though use make you apt to kill me,
     Let not to that, self-murder added be,
     And sacrilege, three sins in killing three.

Cruel and sudden, hast thou since
Purpled thy nail in blood of innocence?
Wherein could this flea guilty be,
Except in that drop which it sucked from thee?
Yet thou triumph'st, and say'st that thou
Find'st not thyself, nor me, the weaker now;
   'Tis true; then learn how false, fears be;
     Just so much honor, when thou yield'st to me,
     Will waste, as this flea's death took life from thee.

86. The Uses of History

H. V. S. OGDEN

Ogden (1905–   ), born in Milwaukee, holds an A.B. from Harvard and advanced degrees from Chicago, has taught at the University of Michigan for nearly forty years. He has written major articles on the history of ideas, pedagogical theory, Milton, Henry James, and others. His translation from the Latin of More's *Utopia* is widely used. His *English Taste in Landscape in the Seventeenth Century* (with his wife, Margaret S. Ogden, a medical scholar), copiously illustrated from the landscape painters, is definitive.

W E ALL ASSUME that history is a social science. Our catalogues so list it. Indeed, historian E. H. Carr has recently asserted its dual function as a social science: "to enable man to understand the society of the past and to increase his mastery over the society of the present" (*What is History,* New York, 1963, pp. 109–110). Carr clearly regards the understanding as subservient to the mastery, with which social architects, statesmen, and even voters, can determine the shape of things to come (pp. 84–112). This is an exciting claim, and I do not see how anyone could wholly deny its validity.

But I believe that we have put history in the wrong category. I believe that history is properly one of the humanities, and that its claims are other and deeper than those Carr makes for it. History *is* a humanity, not a science. The humanities are *studies,* and though studies may contribute new knowledge in any field, they are primarily carried on by students, whose goal is self-understanding and personal development. The image of a student studying history and other humanities is not so dramatic as that of the social scientist designing futures and guiding destinies. But in the long run, the student may prove more significant—as he develops himself, and contributes that self to society. History then is primarily a humane study.

We should not confuse history with the technical knowledge historians use. History is not bibliography, diplomatics, palaeography, or the like. Nor is it miscellaneous knowledge about the past. Ten predicates about ten subjects do not constitute history, even if the ten subjects are events in the term of one American president. No one doubts the distinction between annals and history.

More insidious is the notion that history is a complete knowledge of the past, and that any particular history is a "slice of the past," as though the past somehow existed somewhere as a sliceable totality. This notion is attractive, of course. It offers the historian an ideal completeness and (by implication) objectivity. It implies that the past is like a field of nature, objectively existent and present, and that history is a field of knowledge similar to a natural science.

But the past is not a field of nature, and the ideal is a mare's nest. We can think of the past as a totality, but, as soon as we probe that concept, we find it useless. Does it include all past events? No, only the significant ones. As soon as we appeal to significance, we face concepts of what is important, of what is valuable, and of what constitutes satisfactory explanation—and we see that our ideal of the past as a totality is useless. Total inclusiveness is impossible, and our ideal objectivity ignores completely the concepts of *significance* and *value*.

What is significant? The beginning and the end of the historian's task—but not the middle—is to answer this question. Initially he derives his concepts of significance from his culture (culture in the anthropologist's sense) and from his reading and reflection (culture in the humanist's sense). In particular, he has at his disposal all the concepts his fellow historians have developed. Let us call these concepts the historian's *values*. If he is a good historian, he has self-consciously analyzed his values and appraised them critically. His values tell him what is worth writing about, what questions are worth asking, and what kinds of answers are adequate. They enable him to formulate his guiding purposes, and these in turn dominate his interpretation of data and his organization of data into his narrative. The historian creates history by marrying his values (i.e., his concepts of what is significant) to his data, so as to beget interpretive narratives, and these are history. The knowledge history offers is knowledge in history books, and the word *history* really means "historical narratives." Apart from the books, there is no history. There are only memories of the past, and surviving artifacts, inscriptions, documents, annals, and earlier historical narratives. The past itself no longer exists.

Since historians do not often make fully explicit the values behind their choices, we usually must infer these from the purpose and the organization of the books themselves. What are some of the common purposes? One is to write textbooks to introduce the young to their own culture, and to inculcate loyalty to its institutions. Such books usually contain some special pleading or plain fraud. Their dominant values are the public values of their society, but those values accepted uncritically to select the data or to distort it wilfully. The greater the insecurity of the society, the greater the distortion. Presumably a society pays a penalty for accepting false views of its history, often in internal or external strife. In what ways, and to what extent, would we be better off if we had all been brought up on histories of America in which the values and data alike were criticized by philosophical historians committed to scrutinizing their values?

Good histories are written by scholars who recognize certain aspects of their society as important and valuable, and who construct narratives to *test* the value of these aspects and to explain their nature—for example the many histories of Great Britain trace the development of political freedom, and stress the rule of law, the winning of legal rights, and the constitutional balances. Such books approve certain aspects of a society as final causes toward which the genetic process has worked. The authors are usually conservatives. Their opposites are the historians who recognize various deficiencies in society, and who trace the evolution of these evils, partly to define them, partly to recommend changes. Histories of the Industrial Revolution in Great Britain are often of this kind.

To conclude that every historian is born "either a little liberal or else a little conservative" is to miss the point. Historians need not, and should not, manipulate their narratives to support a *parti pris*. No doubt historians rarely achieve complete detachment and impartiality, but the attempt to do so assures some degree of disinterestedness. Even Professor Carr somewhat grudgingly admits that historians may "transcend" their "own situation," though he is happier in pointing to their failures (especially that of Friedrich Meinecke, pp. 43–54). The historian's impartiality depends on his persistence in testing his initial values. His choosing, ordering, and interpreting the historical data are constantly putting these values to the test.

As his values interplay with his data, the historian must keep asking himself such questions as these: How can my values be tested by more data and especially by data relevant to my narrative but of a different kind? Do my values lead to an adequate interpretation of all the data now available to me? Are my values corroborated by the coherence and adequacy of the narrative they have patterned? What alternative or additional values might lead to a better interpretation of my data?

In testing his values, the historian will usually modify them somewhat. A critical mind cannot work on a body of historical data for any length of time without qualifying or even rejecting some of its previous assumptions, beliefs, and loyalties. For the historian himself, his labor will modify and sharpen the public, professional, and personal values with which he began. His readers may gain a similar modification of their own values, and sometimes, perhaps, a whole culture may gain some true adjustment in its current public values partly as a result of the historian's labors.

Values, then, dominate histories—as we can see in one of our best-known histories. The values that brought Gibbon * to write *The Decline*

---

* Edward Gibbon (1737–1794), English historian.

and Fall of the Roman Empire, and that led him to handle his subject as he did, are not far to seek. They are dominant values of the Enlightenment, and Gibbon may be said to have derived them from his culture, although he assuredly made them his "own" by reflection, substantiation, and commitment. They are, broadly, the political values of *civilization,* and they are apparent in his very first paragraph. The Romans of the second century, he says, were "the most civilized portion of mankind." They defended their boundaries with "disciplined valour." "The gentle but powerful influence of laws and manners had gradually cemented the union of the provinces." He evinces a Virgilian preoccupation with peace; Rome was great because of the *pax romana.* "They [the five "good" emperors] preserved peace by a constant preparation for war; and while justice regulated their conduct, they announced to the nations on their confines that they were as little disposed to endure as to offer injury."

"Domestic peace and union were the natural consequences of the moderate and comprehensive policy embraced by the Romans" (Mod.Lib.,I.ii.38). The description of the Roman state in the first three chapters shows that, in spite of Rome's shortcomings and latent weaknesses, Gibbon felt that its decline and fall were worth the telling because the Roman state had achieved a higher degree of civilization and on a larger scale than any other polity known to him.

Gibbon clearly holds two other values related to the values of civilization. These are the values of a "rational" understanding of human motives and of a "rational" attitude toward religion. Like most eighteenth-century writers, Gibbon accepted the egoistic theory of the passions inherited from Hobbes and La Rochefoucauld. Consequently, he is careful to explain the actual motives of men and to exhibit their illusions, and pretences. Diocletian's abilities, he tells us, included "above all the great art of submitting his own passions, as well as those of others, to the interest of his ambition, and of colouring his ambition with the most specious pretences of justice and public utility" (I.ii.304). Or with characteristic irony: "Since the eunuch Amantius had been defrauded of his money, it became necessary to deprive him of his life" (II.xl.130). Gibbon's "rational" attitude toward religion included a complete scepticism toward the supernatural, an imputation of all religious and ecclesiastical behavior to self-seeking motives, a recognition that religion may be used beneficially by enlightened statesmen in governing the masses, and finally a high regard for religious toleration:

> But how shall we excuse the supine inattention of the Pagan and philosophic world to those evidences which were presented by the hand of Omnipotence, not to their reason, but to their senses? During the age of Christ, of his apostles, and of their first disciples, the doctrine which they preached was confirmed by innumerable prodigies. The lame walked,

the blind saw, the sick were healed, and dead were raised, daemons were expelled, and the laws of Nature were frequently suspended for the benefit of the church. But the sages of Greece and Rome turned aside from the awful spectacle, and, pursuing the ordinary occupations of life and study, appeared unconscious of any alterations in the moral or physical government of the world. (I.xv. 443–444)

The satisfactory experience that the relics of saints were more valuable than gold or precious stones stimulated the clergy to multiply the treasures of the church. (I.xxviii. 1024)

The policy of the emperors and the senate, as far as it concerned religion, was happily seconded by the reflections of the enlightened, and by the habits of the superstitious, part of their subjects. The various modes of worship, which prevailed in the Roman world, were all considered by the people, as equally true; by the philosopher, as equally false; and by the magistrate, as equally useful. And thus toleration produced not only mutual indulgence, but even religious concord. (I.ii. 25–26)

Gibbon's pervasive irony is nowhere more apparent than when he can heighten his perception of the discrepancy between real and professed motives by pointing to the further discrepancy between Christian belief and self-seeking behavior.

Such are not the main values underlying Gibbon's great work and controlling his narrative. Roughly speaking, he devotes space to each emperor proportionate to his importance as gauged by these values. He treats extensively those who did much either to defend Roman civilization or to hasten its decline, viewing the defenders sympathetically and the weaklings with aversion, though always with various qualifications stemming from the values of "rationality." Thus Julian the Apostate is prominent through most of four chapters (xix,xxii–xxiv), both because of his efforts to maintain the Roman state and because of his religious toleration. Gibbon's critics have been eager to point to omissions or misinterpretations of data; but notwithstanding the attacks of Christian apologists and others, the values that control his narrative successfully survive the testing implicit in their use. *The Decline and Fall of the Roman Empire* is an exploration of these values, a definition and expression of them, and a large though by no means definitive display of their validity. The reader understands them the better for the exploration and definition, and although he may not accept them wholly for himself, he must acknowledge that they are such as a civilized man may accept.

In constantly testing its values, history reveals itself as a "humanity," differing considerably from the typical social science. For one thing, it differs in the concept of a "field." The social scientist, like the natural scientist, stakes out a field that contains recurring and repeatable regularities. He abstracts his field from the rest of experience to analyse its regularities without interference. The historian, in constructing an interpretive narrative of the past, does not set up a field in this sense. He is concerned with unique sequences of events. To be sure, he views these events in the light of general concepts and values. (Professor Carr's handling of this matter seems to me very sound—pp. 79–80.) He will often point to similarities between events, but he will not reduce events to uniform cases or to units in a class. Instead of analysing regular recurrences, he will point out differences between similar events.

The historian and the social scientist also differ conspicuously in their views of causation. The social scientist strives to define causes sharply. His success depends on finding the causes of uniform and invariable effects within his defined field. The historian offers causal explanations, but the causes he cites are rarely the necessary and sufficient causes of the scientist. Consider, for example, the two principal causes Thucydides * uses in his *History of the Peloponnesian War* to explain both the war and the subsequent behavior of the belligerents: the drive to dominate and the fear of domination. Thucydides explores their operation and defines their effects more explicitly than historians usually do. But, even in the context of the *History*, no scientist would regard them as the kind of causes essential to scientific explanation. For any event, they may explain too much or too little. They may operate universally or sporadically. And they usually seem to combine with other unspecified causes. Furthermore, other historians, not to mention social scientists, might define these causes differently or subordinate them to other causes in explaining the same events. No historian can test the validity of cause-effect claims by observing repeated and identical examples, notwithstanding Thucydides's twice-asserted claim that his two causes will lead men to act in the future as they have in the past. Not that Thucydides's prediction is wrong; it is most probably right. But it is not based on the precise, isolated, and invariable causes that yield the certain predictions of scientists.

Consequently conclusions of social scientists have, in theory at least, a general validity that has no counterpart in the writings of historians. If two social scientists disagree, the conclusions of one or the other must be modified. But histories offering unlike interpretations of the same events may be accepted as complementary, and even if they are contradictory, they may be regarded as having some validity. We can easily imagine the conclusions of social scientists as constituting a corpus of knowledge, existing objectively and publicly accepted. But history books do not add up to a coherent and consistent body of

* Athenian statesman and historian (c.471–c.400 B.C.).

knowledge. Each one offers knowledge embodying the values of its author.

Lastly, the historian and the social scientist stand in a different relationship to their values. Like the historian, the social scientist starts with values derived from his culture, from his fellow scientists, and from his personal reading and reflection. In the light of these, he chooses his problem. But once he applies the scientific method, he excludes all his values except the values implicit in his method. He is using and testing only these. For the time being, he lays aside all his other values, and they will neither be tested nor modified by his activities as a social scientist. If the historian seems more humane than the social scientist, he seems so because the writing of history necessarily engages a wide range of his lesser values. Alternatively, he may choose to exclude large sectors of human experience; Thucydides ignores women, the gods, and economics. But whatever the exclusions, the historian's involvement in his history is human and personal, and his interpretation of events will be shot through with his value judgments.

Consequently, the student of history encounters the historian's values in his narrative of past events. History functions as one of the humanities by contributing to the development of individual minds. We must think of the young student in two lights, as a product being formed by his society and as an individual developing his mental potentialities. As an individual, he begins by taking the concepts, values, and expectations his society offers him, accepting them automatically and uncritically as long as he lacks the capacity for scrutinizing and judging them. Unless he develops this capacity, he will entertain a set of crude simplifications about his society's past, and he will see his own past and future in terms of ready-made concepts. He may become a well-adjusted member of his society as a stock product of his culture, but he will lack self-awareness and a consciously held set of values.

Contrariwise, if he encounters the stimulus and the opportunity to reflect on the past and on his relationship to his society, he may begin to make himself into a different and differentiated person. The stimulus may come from other persons or from books, especially from imaginative literature, history, and philosophy. The opportunity lies mainly in the combination of leisure and books. The process begins in contemplating the alternatives to his society's current concepts and values. From historical narratives, he will get a fuller and more meaningful account of his society's past, as well as pictures of alternative societies, for comparison. As he reflects on his reading, he will test the values offered by historians against his own acquired values and against his own limited experience and observation. He will learn to examine his own ideas with detachment. He will evaluate his society's way of life, and accept or modify or possibly reject some of its values. Those he accepts, he will hold with a significant difference; he will have made them his *own,* holding them now with a self-conscious understanding and a willing commitment, to be gained only by a critical examination.

In some such fashion as this, history helps to develop the individual's mind. Which is more important, history's direct contribution to society as a social science, or its contribution to the individual minds as a humanity? The question of progress raises this issue concretely. Professor Carr sees the chief function of history, as a social science, in contributing to progress. History, he says, increases "man's understanding of, and mastery over, his environment" (p.111). That is, he goes on to explain, history enables man to achieve those goals which history itself reveals as desirable, and, in the future, history will continue to help man achieve whatever goals history uncovers (pp.155–158). This, if I understand him rightly, is what Carr means by progress. He slides away from specifying what these future goals may be, so his confession of faith in progress seems sufficiently cautious. But he mentions, among other things, the diminishing of "inequalities of race and wealth" and the better ordering of society, both national and international. He clearly conceives of progress as essentially social and political, and external to the individual, affecting man's inner life only secondarily. Like most twentieth-century liberals, he seems to believe that if external social and political arrangements are improved, the individual's well-being will take care of itself.

Certainly the individual is likely to benefit, but this is only part of the truth, the easiest part to comprehend and hence the easiest to apply in action. But proponents of social progress tend to ignore that, although human excellence may *arise* from external society, it *consists* of inner mental states. They forget how easily we imagine brave new worlds where technology makes us wealthy and social organization reduces our tension and strife, but where rulers and the ruled are respectively well-informed and well-indoctrinated barbarians.

Where is the genuine progress in reducing inequalities of race or of wealth, if the equalizing is only external arrangement? Those "equalized up" will have a grudging satisfaction; those "equalized down" a grudging resentment. If the inner states of mind which caused the old inequalities persist, perhaps with exacerbated intensity, the gain is hardly secure. Only the achievement of more ultimate inner values (involving, ironically, new inequalities) would fully justify egalitarian programs, and their claims to progress.

True progress consists of increasing the number of persons who have human excellences, thus increasing society's corporate stock of excellence. These human excellences are of the mind, and come, in part, from studying the humanities, history along with the others. Let me label some of them; a self-conscious awareness of one's inner life and of one's relationship to society; a consciously scrutinized set of social and personal values: a commitment to the value of developing mental potentialities for oneself and for others; and a commitment to the value which implies all these, the value of understanding. These are the values that give meaning to any proximate public goals of political adjustment and social planning.

If we admit that the quality of the inner life of individuals, as gauged by these values, really defines civilization and the goals of social progress, we immediately see that conscious and purposeful progress can be made only by a society that already accepts these "humanistic" values. Fortunately, we do not have to ask how we became aware of these values. We have inherited a humanist tradition, and, though we comprehend it and affirm it weakly, we may at least consider how to go about using it. The practical question is: how can we best use our various kinds of knowledge, including historical knowledge, to achieve progress toward a genuinely higher civilization?

We may turn first to the historian, since he can survey the records of more than five thousand years during which the civilizing process has been intermittently at work. The historian's answer may well follow the paradigm first set forth in Plato's *Republic*, though strengthened and refined by cultural anthropology, social psychology, and the other social sciences. Once begun, no matter how, the humanizing process is an interaction between society and individuals, a good society producing excellent men and such men functioning so as to maintain and strengthen the good society. In this reciprocal process, the intellectual and moral development of the individual mind is crucial, since this development is simultaneously the means by which the civilizing process is carried on and the goal toward which civilization is directed. Our answer to the practical question, then, is this: progress can be attained only by producing excellent men through an education based on humanistic values.

The image of the student studying history now takes on a more dramatic significance. Unless social planners, statesmen, and indeed ordinary voters, have become imbued with humanist values, they will seek external, often futile, and sometimes wholly destructive, goals. There can be no security for civilization and little probability of real progress, if men strive for goals which, as Professor Carr puts it, "can be defined only as we advance towards them, and the validity of which can be verified only in a process of attaining them" (p. 158). How verified, and at what cost? Unless men are in some degree philosophers as well as kings, they will have no criteria for judging the validity of goals which come into fashion, no means for discerning and rejecting illusions. What they need is the inner order of humanistic values, the inner light of an understanding developed by the study of history, literature, and philosophy, the intellectual creations through which men have explored and formulated their living values since the dawn of civilization.

548

87. From "The Case Against B. F. Skinner"

NOAM CHOMSKY

Chomsky (1928–   ) was born in Philadelphia and educated at the University of Pennsylvania, where he earned his Ph.D. in 1955, after four years as a Junior Fellow, Harvard Society of Fellows. He went directly to the faculty of Massachusetts Institute of Technology, where he remains today. But he has visited numerous universities for professorships and fellowships, here and abroad, including a year at the Institute for Advanced Studies at Princeton. He is one of the world's leading linguists, the propounder of generative grammar and of Cartesian linguistics, both of which hypothesize deep seminal ideas from which our various sentences and languages spring. He vigorously criticized America's involvement in Viet Nam.

I

A CENTURY AGO, a voice of British liberalism described the "Chinaman" as "an inferior race of malleable orientals." [1] During the same years, anthropology became professionalized as a discipline, "intimately associated with the rise of raciology." [2] Presented with the claims of nineteenth-century racist anthropology, a rational person will ask two sorts of questions: What is the scientific status of the claims? What social or ideological needs do they serve? The questions are logically independent, but the second type of question naturally comes to the fore as scientific pretensions are undermined. The question of the scientific status of nineteenth-century racist anthropology is no longer seriously at issue, and its social function is not difficult to perceive.

---

[1] *Economist*, October 31, 1862. Cited by Frederick F. Clairmonte, review of R. Segal, *The Race War, Journal of Modern African Studies*, forthcoming.

[2] Marvin Harris, *The Rise of Anthropological Theory* (Crowell: 1968), pp. 100–1. By the 1860s, he writes, "anthropology and racial determinism had become almost synonyms."

549

If the "Chinaman" is malleable by nature, then what objection can there be to controls exercised by a superior race?

Consider now a generalized version of the pseudo-science of the nineteenth century: it is not merely the heathen Chinese who are malleable by nature, but rather all people. Science has revealed that it is an illusion to speak of "freedom" and "dignity." What a person does is fully determined by his genetic endowment and history of "reinforcement." Therefore we should make use of the best behavioral technology to shape and control behavior in the common interest.

Again, we may inquire into the exact meaning and scientific status of the claim, and the social functions it serves. Again, if the scientific status is slight, then it is particularly interesting to consider the climate of opinion within which the claim is taken seriously.

In his speculations on human behavior, which are to be clearly distinguished from his experimental investigations of conditioning behavior, B. F. Skinner offers a particular version of the theory of human malleability. The public reception of his work is a matter of some interest. Skinner has been condemned as a proponent of totalitarian thinking and lauded for his advocacy of a tightly managed social environment. He is accused of immorality and praised as a spokesman for science and rationality in human affairs. He appears to be attacking fundamental human values, demanding control in place of the defense of freedom and dignity. There seems something scandalous in this, and since Skinner invokes the authority of science, some critics condemn science itself, or "the scientific view of man," for supporting such conclusions, while others assure us that science will "win out" over mysticism and irrational belief.

A close analysis shows that the appearance is misleading. Skinner is saying nothing about freedom and dignity, though he uses the words "freedom" and "dignity" in several odd and idiosyncratic senses. His speculations are devoid of scientific content and do not even hint at general outlines of a possible science of human behavior. Furthermore, Skinner imposes certain arbitrary limitations on scientific research which virtually guarantee continued failure.

As to its social implications, Skinner's science of human behavior, being quite vacuous, is as congenial to the libertarian as to the fascist. If certain of his remarks suggest one or another interpretation, these, it must be stressed, do not follow from his "science" any more than their opposites do. I think it would be more accurate to regard Skinner's *Beyond Freedom and Dignity* as a kind of Rorschach test.* The fact that it is widely regarded as pointing the way to 1984 is, perhaps, a suggestive indication of certain tendencies in modern industrial society. There is little doubt that a theory of human malleability might be put

* The "inkblot" association tests, devised by Hermann Rorschach.

to the service of totalitarian doctrine. If, indeed, freedom and dignity are merely the relics of outdated mystical beliefs, then what objection can there be to narrow and effective controls instituted to ensure "the survival of a culture"?

In view of the prestige of science and the tendencies toward centralized authoritarian control which can easily be detected in modern industrial society, it is important to investigate seriously the claim that the science of behavior and a related technology provide the rationale and the means for control of behavior. What, in fact, has been demonstrated, or even plausibly suggested in this regard?

Skinner assures us repeatedly that his science of behavior is advancing mightily and that there exists an effective technology of control. It is, he claims, a "fact that all control is exacted by the environment" (p. 82). Consequently, "When we seem to turn control over to a person himself, we simply shift from one mode of control to another" (p. 97). The only serious task, then, is to design less "aversive" and more effective controls, an engineering problem. "The outlines of a technology are already clear" (p. 149). "We have the physical, biological, and behavioral technologies needed 'to save ourselves'; the problem is how to get people to use them" (p. 158).

It is a fact, Skinner maintains, that "behavior is shaped and maintained by its consequences" and that as the consequences contingent on behavior are investigated, more and more "they are taking over the explanatory functions previously assigned to personalities, states of mind, feelings, traits of character, purposes, and intentions" (p. 18).

> As a *science of behavior* adopts the strategy of physics and biology, the autonomous agent to which behavior has traditionally been attributed is replaced by the environment—the environment in which the species evolved and in which the behavior of the individual is shaped and maintained. (p. 184.)

A "behavioral analysis" is thus replacing the "traditional appeal to states of mind, feelings, and other aspects of the autonomous man," and "is in fact much further advanced than its critics usually realize" (p. 160). Human behavior is a function of "conditions, environmental or genetic," and people should not object "when a scientific analysis traces their behavior to external conditions" (p. 75), or when a behavioral technology improves the system of control.

Not only has all of this been demonstrated, according to Skinner, but as the science of behavior progresses, it will, *inevitably*, more fully establish these facts. "It is in the nature of scientific progress that the functions of autonomous man be taken over one by one as the role of the environment is better understood" (p. 58). This is the "scientific view," and "it is in the nature of scientific inquiry" that the evidence should shift in its favor (p. 101). "It is in the nature of an experimental analysis of human behavior that it should strip away the functions previously assigned to autonomous man and transfer them one by one to the controlling environment" (p. 198). Furthermore, physiology some day "will explain why behavior is indeed related to the antecedent events of which it can be shown to be a function" (p. 195).

These claims fall into two categories. In the first are claims about what has been discovered: in the second, assertions about what science must discover in its inexorable progress. It is likely that the hope or fear or resignation induced by Skinner's proclamations results, in part, from his assertions that scientific progress will inevitably demonstrate both that all control is exerted by the environment and that the ability of "autonomous man" to choose is an illusion.

Claims of the first sort must be evaluated according to the evidence presented for them. In the present instance, this is a simple task, since no evidence is presented, as will become clear when we turn to more specific examples. In fact, the question of evidence is beside the point, since the claims dissolve into triviality or incoherence under analysis. Claims with regard to the inevitability of future discoveries are more ambiguous. Is Skinner saying that, as a matter of necessity, science will show that behavior is completely determined by the environment? If so, his claim can be dismissed as pure dogmatism, foreign to the "nature of scientific inquiry." It is quite conceivable that as scientific understanding advances, it will reveal that even with full details about genetic endowment and personal history, a Laplacean * omniscience could predict very little about what an organism will do. It is even possible that science may some day provide principled reasons for this conclusion (if indeed it is true).

But perhaps Skinner is suggesting merely that the term "scientific understanding" be restricted to the prediction of behavior from environmental conditions. If so, then science may reveal, as it progresses, that "scientific understanding of human behavior," in this sense, is inherently limited. At the moment we have virtually no scientific evidence and not even the germs of an interesting hypothesis about how human behavior is determined. Consequently, we can only express our hopes and guesses about what some future science may demonstrate. In any event, the claims that Skinner puts forth in this category are either dogmatic or uninteresting, depending on which interpretation we give to them.

* Pierre Simon de Laplace (1749–1827), French astronomer and mathematician, made major advances in the development of probability theory, including the prediction of events based on the pattern of past, similar events.

The dogmatic element in Skinner's thinking is further revealed when he states that "the task of a scientific analysis is to explain how the behavior of a person as a physical system is related to the conditions under which the human species evolved and the conditions under which the individual lives" (p. 14). Surely the task of a scientific analysis is to discover the facts and explain them. Suppose that in fact the human brain operates by physical principles (perhaps now unknown) that provide for free choice, appropriate to situations but only marginally affected by environmental contingencies. The task of scientific analysis is not as Skinner believes—to demonstrate that the conditions to which he restricts his attention fully determine human behavior, but rather to discover whether in fact they do (or whether they are at all significant), a very different matter. If they do not, as seems plausible, the "task of a scientific analysis" will be to clarify the issues and discover an intelligible explanatory theory that will deal with the actual facts. Surely no scientist would follow Skinner in insisting on the a priori necessity that scientific investigation will lead to a particular conclusion, specified in advance.

In support of his belief that science will demonstrate that behavior is entirely a function of antecedent events, Skinner notes that physics advanced only when it "stopped personifying things" and attributing to them "wills, impulses, feelings, purposes," and so on (p. 8). Therefore, he concludes, the science of behavior will progress only when it stops personifying people and avoids reference to "internal states." No doubt physics advanced by rejecting the view that a rock's wish to fall is a factor in its "behavior," because in fact a rock has no such wish. For Skinner's argument to have any force, he must show that people have wills, impulses, feelings, purposes, and the like no more than rocks do. If people do differ from rocks in this respect, then a sense of human behavior will have to take account of this fact.

Similarly, Skinner is correct in asserting that "modern physics or most of biology" does not discuss such matters as "a crisis of belief" or "loss of confidence" (p. 10). Evidently, from this correct observation nothing follows about the science of human behavior. Physics and biology, Skinner observes, "did not advance by looking more closely at the jubilance of a falling body, or . . . the nature of vital spirits, and we do not need to try to discover what personalities, states of mind, feelings, traits of character, plans, purposes, intentions, or the other perquisites of autonomous man really are in order to get on with a scientific analysis of behavior"; and we must neglect "supposed mediating states of mind" (p. 15).

This is true enough, if indeed there are no mediating states that can be characterized by an abstract theory of mind, and if personalities, etc., are no more real than the jubilance of a falling body. But if the factual assumptions are false, then we certainly do need to try to discover what the "perquisites of autonomous man" really are. Skinner might argue, more rationally, that his "science" does not overlook these "perquisites," but rather accounts in other ways for the phenomena discussed in these terms. We shall see directly what substance there is to such a claim.

It is hardly possible to argue that science has advanced only by repudiating hypotheses concerning "internal states." By rejecting the study of postulated inner states Skinner reveals his hostility not only to "the nature of scientific inquiry" but even to common engineering practice. For example, Skinner believes that "information theory" ran into a "problem when an inner 'processor' had to be invented to convert input into output" (p. 18).

This is a strange way of describing the matter. Suppose that an engineer is presented with a device whose functioning he does not understand, and suppose that through experiment he can obtain information about input-output relations of this device. He would not hesitate, if rational, to construct a theory of the internal states of the device and to test it against further evidence. He might also go on to try to determine the mechanisms that function in the ways described by his theory of internal states, and the physical principles at work—leaving open the possibility that new and unknown physical principles might be involved, a particularly important matter in the study of behavior of organisms. His theory of internal states might well be the only useful guide to further research. By objecting, a priori, to this research strategy, Skinner merely condemns his strange variety of "behavioral science" to continued ineptitude.

We cannot specify, a priori, what postulates and hypotheses are legitimate. Skinner's a priorism in this regard is no more legitimate than the claim that classical physics is not "science" because it appeals to the "occult force of gravity." If a concept or principle finds its place in an explanatory theory, it cannot be excluded on methodological grounds, as Skinner continually insists. In general, Skinner's conception of science is very odd. Not only do his a priori methodological assumptions rule out all but the most trivial scientific theories: he is, furthermore, given to strange pronouncements such as the assertion that "the laws of science are descriptions of contingencies of reinforcement" (p. 189)—which I happily leave to others to decode.

It is important to bear in mind that Skinner's strictures do not define the practice of behavioral science. In fact, those who call themselves "behavioral scientists" or even "behaviorists" vary widely in the kinds of theoretical constructions that they are willing to admit. W. V. O. Quine, who on other occasions has attempted to work within Skinner's framework, goes so far as to define "behaviorism" simply as the insistence that conjectures and conclusions must eventually be verified by observations.[3] As he points out, any reasonable person is a "behaviorist" in this sense. Quine's proposal signifies the demise of behaviorism as a substantive point of view, which is just as well. Whatever function "behaviorism" may have served in the past, it has become nothing more than a set of arbitrary restrictions on "legitimate" theory construction, and there is no reason why someone who investigates man and society should accept the kind of intellectual shackles that physical scientists would surely not tolerate and that condemn any intellectual pursuit to insignificance.

[3] "Linguistics and philosophy," in S. Hook (ed.), *Language and Philosophy* (New York University, 1969), p. 97.

---

88. Nobel Prize Acceptance Speech

WILLIAM FAULKNER

I FEEL THAT THIS AWARD was not made to me as a man, but to my work—a life's work in the agony and sweat of the human spirit, not for glory and least of all for profit, but to create out of the materials of the human spirit something which did not exist before. So this award is only mine in trust. It will not be difficult to find a dedication for the money part of it commensurate with the purpose and significance of its origin. But I would like to do the same with the acclaim too, by using this moment as a pinnacle from which I might be listened to by the young men and women already dedicated to the same anguish and travail, among whom is already that one who will some day stand here where I am standing.

Our tragedy today is a general and universal physical fear so long sustained by now that we can even bear it. There are no longer problems of the spirit. There is only the question: When will I be blown up? Because of this, the young man or woman writing today has forgotten the problems of the human heart in conflict with itself which alone can make good writing because only this is worth writing about, worth the agony and the sweat.

He must learn them again. He must teach himself that the basest of all things is to be afraid; and, teaching himself that, forget it forever, leaving no room in his workshop for anything but the old verities and truths of the heart, the old universal truths lacking which any story is ephemeral and doomed—love and honor and pity and pride and compassion and sacrifice. Until he does so, he labors under a curse. He writes not of love but of lust, of defeats in which nobody loses anything of value, of victories without hope and, worst of all, without pity or compassion. His griefs grieve on no universal bones, leaving no scars. He writes not of the heart but of the glands.

Until he relearns these things, he will write as though he stood among and watched the end of man. I decline to accept the end of man. It is easy enough to say that man is immortal simply because he will endure: that when the last ding-dong of doom has clanged and faded from the last worthless rock hanging tideless in the last red and dying evening, that even then there will still be one more sound: that of his puny inexhaustible voice, still talking. I refuse to accept this. I believe that man will not merely endure: he will prevail. He is immortal, not because he alone among creatures has an inexhaustible voice, but because he has a soul, a spirit capable of compassion and sacrifice and endurance. The poet's, the writer's, duty is to write about these things. It is his privilege to help man endure by lifting his heart, by reminding him of the courage and honor and hope and pride and compassion and pity and sacrifice which have been the glory of his past. The poet's voice need not merely be the record of man, it can be one of the props, the pillars to help him endure and prevail.

[*The text printed here has been taken from Faulkner's original typescript of the version which was first printed in the* New York Herald Tribune Book Review, *January 14, 1951. This version was slightly revised from that which he delivered in Stockholm, and which was published in American newspapers at the time.*]

---

89. Nobel Lecture

ALEXANDER SOLZHENITSYN

Solzhenitsyn (1918–   ), wounded and twice decorated for bravery in World War II, served a sentence of eight years in Siberia at forced labor, beginning 1945, for "slurring Stalin in a personal letter." He was officially rehabilitated after Stalin's death when his prison-camp novel, *One Day in* the *Life of Ivan Denisovich* (1962), happened to suit Khrushchev's anti-Stalinization campaign. But the government banned it after Khrushchev's fall, and his *The First Circle* and *Cancer Ward* were smuggled out of Russia to be published in the West in 1968. He did not go to Stockholm to receive his 1970 Nobel Prize, fearing permanent exile if he left his country.

1

AS THE SAVAGE, WHO in bewilderment has picked up a strange sea-leaving, a thing hidden in the sand, or an incomprehensible something fallen out of the sky—something intricately curved, sometimes shimmering dully, sometimes shining in a bright ray of light —turns it this way and that, turns it looking for a way to use it, for some ordinary use to which he can put it, without suspecting an extraordinary one . . .

So we, holding Art in our hands, self-confidently consider ourselves its owners, brashly give it aim, renovate it, re-form it, make manifestoes of it, sell it for cash, play up to the powerful with it, and turn it around at times for entertainment, even in vaudeville songs and in nightclubs, and at times—using stopper or stick, whichever comes first—for transitory political or limited social needs. But Art is not profaned by our attempts, does not because of them lose touch with its source. Each time and by each use it yields us a part of its mysterious inner light.

But will we comprehend *all* that light? Who will dare say that he has DEFINED art? That he has tabulated all its facets? Perhaps someone in ages past did understand and named them for us, but we could not hold still; we listened; we were scornful; we discarded them at once, always in a hurry to replace even the best with anything new! And when the old truth is told us again, we do not remember that we once possessed it.

One kind of artist imagines himself the creator of an independent spiritual world and shoulders the act of creating that world and the people in it, assuming total responsibility for it—but he collapses, for no mortal genius is able to hold up under such a load. Just as man, who once declared himself the center of existence, has not been able to create a stable spiritual system. When failure overwhelms him, he blames it on the age-old discord of the world, on the complexity of the fragmented and torn modern soul, or on the public's lack of understanding.

Another artist acknowledges a higher power above him and joyfully works as a common apprentice under God's heaven, although his responsibility for all that he writes down or depicts, and for those who understand him, is all the greater. On the other hand, he did not create the world, it is not given direction by him, it is a world about whose foundations he has no doubt. The task of the artist is to sense more keenly than others the harmony of the world, the beauty and the outrage of what man has done to it, and poignantly to let people know. In failure as well as in the lower depths—in poverty, in prison, in illness—the consciousness of a stable harmony will never leave him.

All the irrationality of art, however, its blinding sudden turns, its unpredictable discoveries, its profound impact on people, are too magical to be exhausted by the artist's view of the world, by his overall design, or by the work of his unworthy hands.

Archaeologists have uncovered no early stages of human existence so primitive that they were without art. Even before the dawn of civilization we had received this gift from Hands we were not quick enough to discern. And we were not quick enough to ask: WHAT is this gift FOR? What are we to do with it?

All who predict that art is disintegrating, that it has outgrown its forms, and that it is dying are wrong and will be wrong. We will die, but art will remain. Will we, before we go under, ever understand all its facets and all its ends?

Not everything has a name. Some things lead us into a realm beyond words. Art warms even an icy and depressed heart, opening it to lofty spiritual experience. By means of art we are sometimes sent —dimly, briefly—revelations unattainable by reason.

Like that little mirror in the fairy tales—look into it, and you will see not yourself but, for a moment, that which passeth understanding, a realm to which no man can ride or fly. And for which the soul begins to ache . . .

2

Dostoevsky once enigmatically let drop the phrase: "Beauty will save the world." What does this mean? For a long time I thought it merely a phrase. Was such a thing possible? When in our bloodthirsty history did beauty ever save anyone from anything? Ennobled, elevated, yes; but whom has it saved?

There is, however, something special in the essence of beauty, a special quality in art: the conviction carried by a genuine work of art is absolute and subdues even a resistant heart. A political speech, hasty newspaper comment, a social program, a philosophical system can, as far as appearances are concerned, be built smoothly and consistently on an error or a lie; and what is concealed and distorted will not be immediately clear. But then to counteract it comes a contradictory speech, commentary, program, or differently constructed philosophy—and again everything seems smooth and graceful, and again hangs together. That is why they inspire trust—and distrust.

There is no point asserting and reasserting what the heart cannot believe.

A work of art contains its verification in itself: artificial, strained concepts do not withstand the test of being turned into images; they fall to pieces, turn out to be sickly and pale, convince no one. Works which draw on truth and present it to us in live and concentrated form grip us, compellingly involve us, and no one ever, not even ages hence, will come forth to refute them.

Perhaps then the old trinity of Truth, Goodness, and Beauty is not simply the dressed-up, worn-out formula we thought it in our presumptuous, materialistic youth? If the crowns of these three trees meet, as scholars have asserted, and if the too obvious, too straight sprouts of Truth and Goodness have been knocked down, cut off, not let grow, perhaps the whimsical, unpredictable, unexpected branches of Beauty will work their way through, rise up TO THAT VERY PLACE, and thus complete the work of all three?

Then what Dostoevsky wrote—"Beauty will save the world"—is not a slip of the tongue but a prophecy. After all, *he* had the gift of seeing much, a man wondrously filled with light.

And in that case could not art and literature, in fact, help the modern world?

What little I have managed to learn about this over the years I will try to set forth here today.

3

To reach this chair from which the Nobel Lecture is delivered—a chair by no means offered to every writer and offered only once in a lifetime —I have mounted not three or four temporary steps but hundreds or even thousands, fixed, steep, covered with ice, out of the dark and the cold where I was fated to survive, but others, perhaps more talented, stronger than I, perished. I myself met but few of them in the Gulag Archipelago,* a multitude of scattered island fragments. Indeed, under the millstone of surveillance and mistrust, I did not talk to just any man; of some I only heard; and of others I only guessed. Those with a name in literature who vanished into that abyss are, at least, known; but how many were unrecognized, never once publicly mentioned? And so very few, almost no one ever managed to return. A whole national literature is there, buried without a coffin, without even underwear, naked, a number tagged on its toe. Not for a moment did Russian literature cease, yet from outside it seemed a wasteland. Where a harmonious forest

* Gulag is the state prison-camp administration.

could have grown, there were left, after all the cutting, two or three trees accidentally overlooked.

And today how am I, accompanied by the shades of the fallen, my head bowed to let pass forward to this platform others worthy long before me, today how am I to guess and to express what *they* would have wished to say?

This obligation has long lain on us, and we have understood it. In Vladimir Solovyov's words:

> But even chained, we must ourselves complete
> That circle which the gods have preordained.

In agonizing moments in camp, in columns of prisoners at night in the freezing darkness through which the little chains of lanterns shone, there often rose in our throats something we wanted to shout out to the whole world, if only the world could have heard one of us. Then it seemed very clear what our lucky messenger would say and how immediately and positively the whole world would respond. Our field of vision was filled with physical objects and spiritual forces, and in that clearly focused world nothing seemed to outbalance them. Such ideas came not from books and were not borrowed for the sake of harmony or coherence; they were formulated in prison cells and around forest campfires, in conversations with persons now dead, were hardened by *that* life, developed *out of there.*

When the outside pressures were reduced, my outlook and our outlook widened, and gradually, although through a tiny crack, that "whole world" outside came in sight and was recognized. Startlingly for us, the "whole world" turned out to be not at all what we had hoped: it was a world leading "not up there" but exclaiming at the sight of a dismal swamp, "What an enchanting meadow!" or at a set of prisoner's concrete stocks, "What an exquisite necklace!"—a world in which, while flowing tears rolled down the cheeks of some, others danced to the carefree tunes of a musical.

How did this come about? Why did such an abyss open? Were we unfeeling, or was the world? Or was it because of a difference in language? Why are people not capable of grasping each other's every clear and distinct speech? Words die away and flow off like water— leaving no taste, no color, no smell. Not a trace.

Insofar as I understand it, the structure, import, and tone of speech possible for me—of my speech here today—have changed with the years.

It now scarcely resembles the speech which I first conceived on those freezing nights in prison camp.

4

For ages, such has been man's nature that his view of the world (when not induced by hypnosis), his motivation and scale of values, his actions and his intentions have been determined by his own personal and group experiences of life. As the Russian proverb puts it, "Don't trust your brother, trust your own bad eye." This is the soundest basis for understanding one's environment and one's behavior in it. During the long eras when our world was obscurely and bewilderingly fragmented, before a unified communications system had transformed it and it had turned into a single, convulsively beating lump, men were unerringly guided by practical experience in their own local area, then in their own community, in their own society, and finally in their own national territory. The possibility then existed for an individual to see with his own eyes and to accept a common scale of values—what was considered average, what improbable; what was cruel, what beyond all bounds of evil; what was honesty, what deceit. Even though widely scattered peoples lived differently and their scales of social values might be strikingly dissimilar, like their systems of weights and measures, these differences surprised none but the occasional tourist, were written up as heathen wonders, and in no way threatened the rest of not yet united mankind.

In recent decades, however, mankind has imperceptibly, suddenly, become one, united in a way which offers both hope and danger, for shock and infection in one part are almost instantaneously transmitted to others, which often have no immunity. Mankind has become one, but not in the way the community or even the nation used to be stably united, not through accumulated practical experience, not through its own, good-naturedly so-called bad *eye*, not even through its own well-understood, native tongue, but, leaping over all barriers, through the international press and radio. A wave of events washes over us and, in a moment, half the world hears the splash, but the standards for measuring these things and for evaluating them, according to the laws of those parts of the world about which we know nothing, are not and cannot be broadcast through the ether or reduced to newsprint. These standards have too long and too specifically been accepted by and incorporated in too special a way into the lives of various lands and societies to be communicated in thin air. In various parts of the world, men apply to events a scale of values achieved by their own long suffering, and they uncompromisingly, self-reliantly judge only by their own scale, and by no one else's.

If there are not a multitude of such scales in the world, nevertheless there are at least several: a scale for local events, a scale for things far away; for old societies, and for new; for the prosperous, and for the disadvantaged. The points and markings on the scale glaringly do not coincide; they confuse us, hurt our eyes, and so, to avoid pain, we brush aside all scales not our own, as if they were follies or delusions, and confidently judge the whole world according to our own domestic values. Therefore, what seems to us more important, more painful, and more unendurable is really not what is more important, more painful, and more unendurable but merely that which is closer to home. Everything distant which, for all its moans and muffled cries, its ruined lives and, even, millions of victims, does not threaten to come rolling up to our threshold today we consider, in general, endurable and of tolerable dimensions.

On one side, persecuted no less than under the old Romans, hundreds of thousands of mute Christians give up their lives for their belief in God. On the other side of the world, a madman (and probably he is not the only one) roars across the ocean in order to FREE us from religion with a blow of steel at the Pontiff! Using his own personal scale, he has decided things for everyone.

What on one scale seems, from far off, to be enviable and prosperous freedom, on another, close up, is felt to be irritating coercion calling for the overturning of buses. What in one country seems a dream of improbable prosperity in another arouses indignation as savage exploitation calling for an immediate strike. Scales of values differ even for natural calamities: a flood with two hundred thousand victims matters less than a local traffic accident. Scales differ for personal insults: at times, merely a sardonic smile or a dismissive gesture is humiliating, whereas, at others, cruel beatings are regarded as a bad joke. Scales differ for punishments and for wrongdoing. On one scale, a month's arrest, or exile to the country, or "solitary confinement" on white bread and milk rocks the imagination and fills the newspaper columns with outrage. On another, both accepted and excused are prison terms of twenty-five years, solitary confinement in cells with ice covered walls and prisoners stripped to their underclothing, insane asylums for healthy men, and border shootings of countless foolish people who, for some reason, keep trying to escape. The heart is especially at ease with regard to that exotic land about which nothing is known, from which no events ever reach us except the belated and trivial conjectures of a few correspondents.

For such ambivalence, for such thickheaded lack of understanding of someone else's far-off grief, however, mankind is not at fault: that is how man is made. But for mankind as a whole, squeezed into one lump, such mutual lack of understanding carries the threat of imminent and violent destruction. Given six, four, or even two scales of values, there cannot be one world, one single humanity: the difference in rhythms, in oscillations, will tear mankind asunder. We will not survive together on one Earth, just as a man with two hearts is not meant for this world.

5

Who will coordinate these scales of values, and how? Who will give mankind one single system for reading its instruments, both for wrongdoing and for doing good, for the intolerable and the tolerable as they are distinguished from each other today? Who will make clear for mankind what is really oppressive and unbearable and what, for being so near, rubs us raw—and thus direct our anger against what is in fact terrible and not merely near at hand? Who is capable of extending such an understanding across the boundaries of his own personal experience? Who has the skill to make a narrow, obstinate human being aware of others' far-off grief and joy, to make him understand dimensions and delusions he himself has never lived through? Propaganda, coercion, and scientific proofs are all powerless. But, happily, in our world there is a way. It is art, and it is literature.

There is a miracle which they can work: they can overcome man's unfortunate trait of learning only through his own experience, unaffected by that of others. From man to man, compensating for his brief time on earth, art communicates whole the burden of another's long life experience with all its hardships, colors, and vitality, recreating in the flesh what another has experienced, and allowing it to be acquired as one's own.

More important, much more important: countries and whole continents belatedly repeat each other's mistakes, sometimes after centuries when, it would seem, everything should be so clear! No: what some nations have gone through, thought through, and rejected, suddenly seems to be the latest word in other nations. Here too the only substitute for what we ourselves have not experienced is art and literature. They have the marvelous capacity of transmitting from one nation to another—despite differences in language, customs, and social structure—practical experience, the harsh national experience of many decades never tasted by the other nation. Sometimes this may save a whole nation from what is a dangerous or mistaken or plainly disastrous path, thus lessening the twists and turns of human history.

Today, from this Nobel lecture platform, I should like to emphasize this great, beneficent attribute of art.

Literature transmits condensed and irrefutable human experience in still another priceless way: from generation to generation. It thus becomes the living memory of a nation. What has faded into history it thus keeps warm and preserves in a form that defies distortion and falsehood. Thus literature, together with language, preserves and protects a nation's soul.

(It has become fashionable in recent times to talk of the leveling of nations, and of various peoples disappearing into the melting pot of contemporary civilization. I disagree with this, but that is another matter; all that should be said here is that the disappearance of whole nations would impoverish us no less than if all people were to become identical, with the same character and the same face. Nations are the wealth of humanity, its generalized personalities. The least among them has its own special colors, and harbors within itself a special aspect of God's design.)

But woe to the nation whose literature is cut off by the interposition of force. That is not simply a violation of "freedom of the press"; it is stopping up the nation's heart, carving out the nation's memory. The nation loses its memory; it loses its spiritual unity—and, despite their supposedly common language, fellow countrymen suddenly cease understanding each other. Speechless generations are born and die, having recounted nothing of themselves either to their own times or to their descendants. That such masters as Akhmatova and Zamyatin were buried behind four walls for their whole lives and condemned even to the grave to create in silence, without hearing one reverberation of what they wrote, is not only their own personal misfortune but tragedy for the whole nation—and, too, a real threat to all nationalities.

In certain cases, it is a danger for all mankind as well: when HISTORY as a whole ceases to be understood because of that silence.

6

At various times in various places people have argued hotly, angrily, and elegantly about whether art and the artist should have a life of their own or whether they should always keep in mind their duty to society and serve it, even though in an unbiased way. For me there is no problem here, but I will not again go into this argument. One of the most brilliant speeches on this subject was Albert Camus's Nobel lecture, the conclusions of which I happily support. Indeed, for decades Russian literature has leaned in that direction—not spending too much time in self-admiration, not flitting about too frivolously—and I am not ashamed to continue in that tradition as best I can. From way back, ingrained in Russian literature has been the notion that a writer can do much among his own people—and that he must.

We will not trample on the artist's RIGHT to express exclusively personal experiences and observations, ignoring everything that happens in the rest of the world. We will not DEMAND anything of the artist, but we will be permitted to reproach him, to make requests, to appeal to him and to coax him. After all, he himself only partially develops his talent, the greater portion of which is breathed into him, ready-made, at birth and, along with it, responsibility for his free will. Even granting that the artist DOES NOT OWE anybody anything, it is painful to see how, retreating into a world of his own creation or into the vast spaces of subjective fancies, he CAN deliver the real world into the hands of self-seeking, insignificant, or even insane people.

Our twentieth century has turned out to be more cruel than those preceding it, and all that is terrible in it did not come to an end with the first half. The same old caveman feelings—greed, envy, violence,

and mutual hate, which along the way assumed respectable pseu-
donyms like class struggle, racial struggle, mass struggle, labor-union
struggle—are tearing our world to pieces. The caveman refusal to
accept compromise has been turned into a theoretical principle and
is considered to be a virtue of orthodoxy. It demands millions of victims
in endless civil wars; it packs our hearts with the notion that there are
no fixed universal human concepts called good and justice, that they
are fluid, changing, and that therefore one must always do what will
benefit one's party. Any and every professional group, as soon as it finds
a convenient moment TO RIP OFF A PIECE, unearned or not, extra or
not, immediately rips it off, let all of society come crashing down if it
will. As seen from outside, the mass of waste in Western society is approaching the limit beyond which the system will become metastable
and must collapse. Violence, less and less restricted by the framework
of age-old legality, brazenly and victoriously strides throughout the
world, unconcerned that its futility has been demonstrated and exposed
by history many times. It is not simply naked force that triumphs but
its trumpeted justification: the whole world overflows with the brazen
conviction that force can do everything and justice nothing. Dostoevsky's DEMONS,* a provincial nightmare of the last century, one
would have thought, are, before our very eyes, crawling over the whole
world into countries where they were unimaginable, and by the hijack-
ing of planes, by seizing HOSTAGES, by the bomb explosions, and by
the fires of recent years signal their determination to shake civilization
apart and to annihilate it! And they may very well succeed. Young
people, being at an age when they have no experience except sexual,
when they have as yet no years of personal suffering and personal wisdom behind them, enthusiastically repeat our discredited Russian lessons of the nineteenth century and think that they are discovering
something new. They take as a splendid example the Chinese Red
Guard's degradation of people into nonentities. A superficial lack of understanding of the timeless essence of humanity, a naïve smugness on the
part of their inexperienced hearts—We'll kick out *those* fierce, greedy op-
pressors, those governors, and the rest (we!), we'll then lay down our
grenades and machine guns, and become just and compassionate. Oh,
of course! Of those who have lived their lives and have come to understand, who could refute the young, many DO NOT DARE argue against
them; on the contrary, they flatter them in order not to seem "conservative," again a Russian phenomenon of the nineteenth century,
something which Dostoevsky called SLAVERY TO HALF-COCKED PROGRES-
SIVE IDEAS.

The spirit of Munich has by no means retreated into the past; it
was not a brief episode. I even venture to say that the spirit of Munich

* A reference to the novel known as *The Possessed* and *The Devils*, but which
in Russian is literally *The Demons*.

is dominant in the twentieth century. The intimidated civilized world has found nothing to oppose the onslaught of a suddenly resurgent fang-baring barbarism, except concessions and smiles. The spirit of Munich is a disease of the will of prosperous people; it is the daily state of those who have given themselves over to a craving for prosperity in every way, to material well-being as the chief goal of life on earth. Such people—and there are many of them in the world today —choose passivity and retreat, anything if only the life to which they are accustomed might go on, anything so as not to have to cross over to rough terrain today, because tomorrow, see, everything will be all right. (But it never will! The reckoning for cowardice will only be more cruel. Courage and the power to overcome will be ours only when we dare to make sacrifices.)

We are also threatened by the catastrophe that the physically squeezed, constrained world is not allowed to become one spiritually; molecules of knowledge and compassion are not allowed to move across from one half of the world to the other. This is a grave danger: THE STOPPAGE OF INFORMATION between the parts of the planet. Contemporary science knows that such stoppage is the way of entropy, of universal destruction. Stoppage of information makes international signatures and treaties unreal: within the zone of STUNNED SILENCE any treaty can easily be reinterpreted at will or, more simply, covered up, as if it had never existed (Orwell understood this beautifully). Within the zone of stunned silence lives—seemingly not Earth's inhabitants at all—a Martian expeditionary force, knowing nothing whatever about the rest of the Earth and ready to trample it flat in the holy conviction that they are "liberating" it.

A quarter of a century ago, with the great hopes of mankind, the United Nations were born. Alas, in the immoral world it, too, became immoral. It is not a United Nations but a United Governments, in which those freely elected and those imposed by force and those which seized power by arms are all on a par. Through the mercenary bias of the majority, the UN jealously worries about the freedom of some peoples and pays no attention to the freedom of others. By an officious vote it rejected the review of PRIVATE COMPLAINTS—the groans, shouts, and pleadings of individual, common PLAIN PEOPLE—insects too small for such a great organization. The UN never tried to make BINDING on governments, a CONDITION of their membership, the Declaration of Human Rights, the outstanding document of its twenty-five years—and thus the UN betrayed the common people to the will of governments they had not chosen.

One might think that the shape of the modern world is entirely in the hands of scientists, that they determine mankind's technological steps. One might think that what will happen to the world depends not on politicians but specifically on the international cooperation of scientists. Especially because the example of individuals shows how much could be accomplished by moving together. But no; scientists have made no clear effort to become an important, independently active force of mankind. Whole congresses at a time, they back away from the suffering of others; it is more comfortable to stay within the bounds of science. That same spirit of Munich has spread its debilitating wings over them.

In this cruel, dynamic, explosive world on the edge of its ten destructions, what is the place and role of the writer? We send off no rockets, do not even push the lowliest handcart, are scorned by those who respect only material power. Would it not be natural for us, too, to retreat, to lose our faith in the steadfastness of good, in the indivisibility of truth, and merely to let the world have our bitter observations, as of a bystander, about how hopelessly corrupted mankind is, how petty men have become, and how difficult it is for lonely, sensitive, beautiful souls today?

We do not have even this way out. Once pledged to the WORD, there is no getting away from it: a writer is no sideline judge of his fellow countrymen and contemporaries; he is equally guilty of all the evil done in his country or by his people. If his country's tanks spill blood on the streets of some alien capital, the brown stains are splashed forever on the writer's face. If, some fatal night, his trusting friend is choked to death while sleeping, the bruises from the rope are on the writer's hands. If his young fellow citizens in their easygoing way declare the superiority of debauchery over frugal labor, abandon themselves to drugs or seize HOSTAGES, the stink of it mixes with the writer's breathing.

Will we have the impudence to announce that we are not responsible for the sores of the world today?

7

I am, however, encouraged by a keen sense of WORLD LITERATURE as the one great heart that beats for the cares and misfortunes of our world, even though each corner sees and experiences them in a different way.

In past times, also, besides age-old national literatures there existed a concept of world literature as the link between the summits of national literatures and as the aggregate of reciprocal literary influences. But there was a time lag: readers and writers came to know foreign writers only belatedly, sometimes centuries later, so that mutual influences were delayed and the network of national literary high points was visible not to contemporaries but to later generations.

Today, between writers of one country and the readers and writers of another, there is an almost instantaneous reciprocity, as I myself know. My books, unpublished, alas, **in my own country, despite hasty** and often bad translations have quickly found a responsive world readership. Critical analysis of them has been undertaken by such leading Western writers as Heinrich Böll. During all these recent years, when both my work and my freedom did not collapse, when against the laws of gravity they held on seemingly in thin air, seemingly ON NOTHING, on the invisible, mute surface tension of sympathetic people, with warm gratitude I learned, to my complete surprise, of the support of the world's writing fraternity. On my fiftieth birthday I was astounded to receive greetings from well-known European writers. No pressure put on me now passed unnoticed. During the dangerous weeks when I was being expelled from the Writers' Union, THE PROTECTIVE WALL put forward by prominent writers of the world saved me from worse persecution, and Norwegian writers and artists hospitably prepared shelter for me in the event that I was exiled from my country. Finally, my being nominated for a Nobel Prize was originated not in the land where I live and write but by François Mauriac and his colleagues. Afterward, national writers' organizations expressed unanimous support for me.

As I have understood it and experienced it myself, world literature is no longer an abstraction or a generalized concept invented by literary critics, but a common body and common spirit, a living, heartfelt unity reflecting the growing spiritual unity of mankind. State borders still turn crimson, heated red-hot by electric fences and machine-gun fire; some ministries of internal affairs still suppose that literature is "an internal affair" of the countries under their jurisdiction; and newspaper headlines still herald, "They have no right to interfere in our internal affairs!" Meanwhile, no such thing as INTERNAL AFFAIRS remains on our crowded Earth. Mankind's salvation lies exclusively in everyone's making everything his business, in the people of the East being anything but indifferent to what is thought in the West, and in the people of the West being anything but indifferent to what happens in the East. Literature, one of the most sensitive and responsive tools of human existence, has been the first to pick up, adopt, and assimilate this sense of the growing unity of mankind. I therefore confidently turn to the world literature of the present, to hundreds of friends whom I have not met face to face and perhaps never will see.

My friends! Let us try to be helpful, if we are worth anything. In our own countries, torn by differences among parties, movements, castes, and groups, who for ages past has been not the dividing but the uniting force? This, essentially, is the position of writers, spokesmen of a national language, of the chief tie binding the nation, the very soil which the people inhabit, and, in fortunate circumstances, the nation's spirit too.

I think that world literature has the power in these frightening times to help mankind see itself accurately despite what is advocated by partisans and by parties. It has the power to transmit the condensed experience of one region to another, so that   different scales of values are combined, and so that one people accurately and concisely knows the true history of another with a power of recognition and acute awareness as if it had lived through that history itself—and could thus be spared repeating old mistakes. At the same time, perhaps we ourselves may succeed in developing our own WORLD-WIDE VIEW, like any man, with the center of the eye seeing what is nearby but the periphery of vision taking in what is happening in the rest of the world. We will make correlations and maintain world-wide standards.

Who, if not writers, are to condemn their own unsuccessful governments (in some states this is the easiest way to make a living; every one who is not too lazy does it) as well as society itself, whether for its cowardly humiliation or for its self-satisfied weakness, or the light-headed escapades of the young, or the youthful pirates brandishing knives?

We will be told: What can literature do against the pitiless onslaught of naked violence? Let us not forget that violence does not and cannot flourish by itself; it is inevitably intertwined with LYING. Between them there is the closest, the most profound and natural bond: nothing screens violence except lies, and the only way lies can hold out is by violence. Whoever has once announced violence as his METHOD must inexorably choose lying as his PRINCIPLE. At birth, violence behaves openly and even proudly. But as soon as it becomes stronger and firmly established, it senses the thinning of the air around it and cannot go on without befogging itself in lies, coating itself with lying's sugary oratory. It does not always or necessarily go straight for the gullet; usually it demands of its victims only allegiance to the lie, only complicity in the lie.

The simple act of an ordinary courageous man is not to take part, not to support lies! Let *that* come into the world and even reign over it, but not through me. Writers and artists can do more: they can VANQUISH LIES! In the struggle against lies, art has always won and always will. Conspicuously, incontestably for everyone. Lies can stand up against much in the world, but not against art.

Once lies have been dispelled, the repulsive nakedness of violence will be exposed—and hollow violence will collapse.

That, my friends, is why I think we can help the world in its red-hot hour: not by the nay-saying of having no armaments, not by abandoning oneself to the carefree life, but by going into battle!

In Russian, proverbs about TRUTH are favorites. They persistently express the considerable, bitter, grim experience of the people, often astonishingly:

ONE WORD OF TRUTH OUTWEIGHS THE WORLD.

On such a seemingly fantastic violation of the law of the conservation of mass and energy are based both my own activities and my appeal to the writers of the whole world.

Suggestions for Writing

1. Write a close explication of Marvell's poem on the thesis "Marvell's apparently effortless poem is really intricate in its organization of phrasing, imagery, and thought."

2. Write an essay arguing that Halpern's poem is an example of the modern in poetry and attitude, by comparing it with Marvell's.

3. Pick either "To His Coy Mistress" or "The Flea," and write an essay arguing that the poem of your choice is better than the other, bringing in everything to be said for the other side, and supporting your points with close comparison and analysis. You might try a thesis built on the pattern "————— is a better poem than ————— because it —————————."

4. Write an essay "On Values," explaining, supplementing, or disputing, from your own experience in reading and growing up, Ogden's discussion beginning with the paragraph on p. 546 that opens "Consequently, the student of history encounters the historian's values . . . ."

5. Write an essay "On Freedom and Control," explaining how Ogden and Chomsky disagree with Skinner and Carr (whom Ogden quotes), and bringing in examples of freedom and control in home, classroom, university, and state, or other books you have read—*1984, Catch 22, Brave New World, Dr. Strangelove, Walden*—perhaps drawing also from Germaine Greer and Nora Ephron.

6. Write an essay arguing that Faulkner's remarks about "the old universal truths" do or do not apply to some recent book or movie you have read or seen.

7. Write an essay supporting or disputing one of Solzhenitsyn's points.

Thematic Table of Contents

For readers who want to work with thematic as well as rhetorical groupings of selections, we are suggesting broad groupings of selections by theme. Some of the selections, of course, treat more than one major theme; we have listed them under two, or even more, headings. But we are sure the reader will find that a number of selections fit into groups other than those in which we have listed them. And we are equally sure that the serious reader will discover important thematic groupings not listed in this contents.

XII. Science, Evidence, and Logic

XIII. Varieties of Education

XIV. Perceiving the Past

XV. Language, Words, and Writing

XVI. The Travail of the Artist

Author and Title Index